PHILIP'S

STREET

C000178416

Dorset
Bournemouth and Poole
Christchurch, Dorchester, Weymouth

www.philips-maps.co.uk
First published in 2002 by Philip's,
Philip's, a division of
Octopus Publishing Group Ltd
www.octopusbooks.co.uk
Endeavour House
189 Shaftesbury Avenue
London WC2H 8JY
An Hachette UK Company
www.hachette.co.uk
Third edition 2010
Second impression 2013

DORCA

ISBN 978-1-84907-095-9 (spiral)

© Philip's 2010

Contents

Digital Data

The exceptionally high-quality mapping found in this atlas is available as digital data in TIFF format, which is easily convertible to other bitmapped (raster) image formats.

The index is also available in digital form as a standard database table. It contains all the details found in the printed index together with the National Grid reference for the map square in which each entry is named.

For further information and to discuss your requirements, please contact philips@mapsinternational.co.uk

Mobile safety cameras

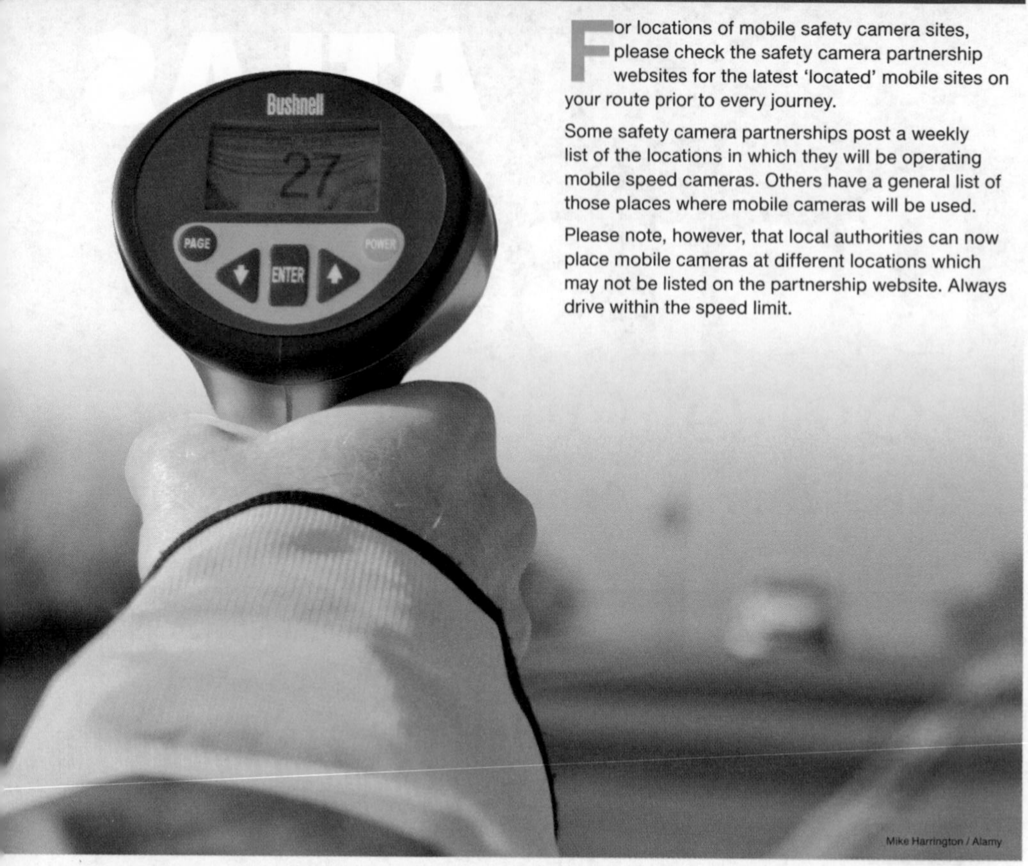

Mike Harrington / Alamy

For locations of mobile safety camera sites, please check the safety camera partnership websites for the latest 'located' mobile sites on your route prior to every journey.

Some safety camera partnerships post a weekly list of the locations in which they will be operating mobile speed cameras. Others have a general list of those places where mobile cameras will be used.

Please note, however, that local authorities can now place mobile cameras at different locations which may not be listed on the partnership website. Always drive within the speed limit.

Useful websites

Dorset Road Safe
www.dorsetsafetycameras.org.uk/

Devon and Cornwall Safety Camera Partnership
http://www.dcsafetycameras.org/

Hampshire Constabulary Safer Roads Unit
www.saferroadspartnership.co.uk

Avon and Somerset Police Speed Enforcement Unit
http://www.avonandsomerset.police.uk/units_and_departments/
criminal_justice_department/speed-enforcement-unit/

Somerset Road Safety Partnership
www.roadsafetysomerset.org.uk

Further information
www.dvla.gov.uk
www.thinkroadsafety.gov.uk
www.dft.gov.uk
www.road-safe.org

Key to map symbols

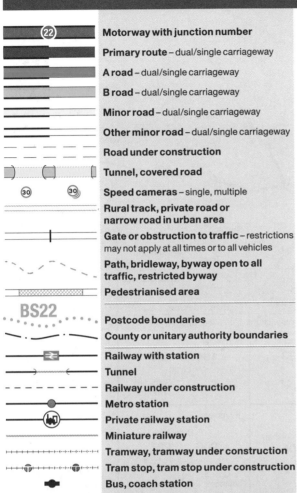

Motorway with junction number	
Primary route – dual/single carriageway	
A road – dual/single carriageway	
B road – dual/single carriageway	
Minor road – dual/single carriageway	
Other minor road – dual/single carriageway	
Road under construction	
Tunnel, covered road	
Speed cameras – single, multiple	
Rural track, private road or narrow road in urban area	
Gate or obstruction to traffic – restrictions may not apply at all times or to all vehicles	
Path, bridleway, byway open to all traffic, restricted byway	
Pedestrianised area	
BS22 Postcode boundaries	
County or unitary authority boundaries	
Railway with station	
Tunnel	
Railway under construction	
Metro station	
Private railway station	
Miniature railway	
Tramway, tramway under construction	
Tram stop, tram stop under construction	
Bus, coach station	

Ambulance station	
Coastguard station	
Fire station	
Police station	
Accident and Emergency entrance to hospital	
Hospital	
Place of worship	
Information centre – open all year	
Shopping centre, parking	
Park and Ride, Post Office	
Camping site, caravan site	
Golf course, picnic site	
Church ROMAN FORT Non-Roman antiquity, Roman antiquity	
Univ Important buildings, schools, colleges, universities and hospitals	
Woods, built-up area	
River Medway Water name	
River, weir	
Stream	
Canal, lock, tunnel	
Water	
Tidal water	

Adjoining page indicators and overlap bands – the colour of the arrow and band indicates the scale of the adjoining or overlapping page (see scales below)

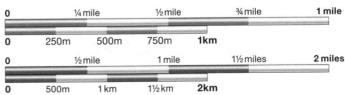

The dark grey border on the inside edge of some pages indicates that the mapping does not continue onto the adjacent page

The small numbers around the edges of the maps identify the 1-kilometre National Grid lines

Abbreviations

Acad	Academy	Meml	Memorial
Allot Gdns	Allotments	Mon	Monument
Cemy	Cemetery	Mus	Museum
C Ctr	Civic centre	Obsy	Observatory
CH	Club house	Pal	Royal palace
Coll	College	PH	Public house
Crem	Crematorium	Recn Gd	Recreation ground
Ent	Enterprise		
Ex H	Exhibition hall	Resr	Reservoir
Ind Est	Industrial Estate	Ret Pk	Retail park
IRB Sta	Inshore rescue boat station	Sch	School
		Sh Ctr	Shopping centre
Inst	Institute	TH	Town hall / house
Ct	Law court	Trad Est	Trading estate
L Ctr	Leisure centre	Univ	University
LC	Level crossing	W Twr	Water tower
Liby	Library	Wks	Works
Mkt	Market	YH	Youth hostel

The map scale on the pages numbered in blue is 3½ inches to 1 mile
5.52 cm to 1 km • 1:18 103

0	¼ mile	½ mile	¾ mile	1 mile
0	250m	500m	750m	1km

The map scale on the pages numbered in green is 1¾ inches to 1 mile
2.76 cm to 1 km • 1:36 206

0	½ mile	1 mile	1½ miles	2 miles
0	500m	1 km	1½ km	2km

IV

Wedmore

Frome

Wells A371

Shepton Mallet

Evercreech

Bruton

Castle Cary

Penselwood **1** **2** Zeals

Bourton

Somerton

Wincanton Milton on Stour **4** **5**

Cucklington

Rodgrove

8 **9** West **10** Stour

Kington Magna

Taunton

Somerset STREET ATLAS

South Petherton

Rimpton **14** **15** **16** **17** Yenston **18** **19** Stour Provost **20** **21**

Mudford Poyntington Henstridge Pillwell

Trent Milborne Port

Over Compton **28** A30 **29** Sherborne **30** **31** Stalbridge **32** **33** Hinton St Mary **34** **35**

Brympton D'Evercy **26** **27** Yeovil Bradford Abbas Alweston Stourton Caundle Sturminster Newton

Ilminster

Dinnington Merriott Hardington Mandeville Barwick Longburton Bishop's Caundle **196** Okeford Fitzpaine **197**

Chard **191** **192** **193** Yetminster **194** **195**

Crewkerne North Perrott Leigh Pulham Ibberton

Clapton Halstock Chetnole Glanvilles Wootton

Devon STREET ATLAS

Drimpton Mosterton Evershot Buckland Newton Hilton

Thorncombe Broadwindsor **202** **203** **204** **205** Rampisham **206** **207** Batcombe **208** **209**

Hawkchurch Beaminster Cerne Abbas Piddletrenthide Cheselbourne

Axminster Netherbury Hooke Cattistock Sydling St Nicholas Dewlish

Toller Porcorum

Seaton Wootton Fitzpaine **64** **65** Broadoak **66** **67** Salwayash **68** **69** Powerstock **70** **71** Maiden Newton **72** **73** Godmanstone **74** **75** Piddlehinton **76** **77** Milborne St Andrew **78** **79**

Morcombelake Bradpole West Compton Frampton Charlton Down Puddletown

Charmouth Chideock Bridport Askerswell Compton Valence Stratton Affpuddle

Lyme Regis **96** **97** **98** **99** **100** **101** **102** **103** **104** **105** **106** **107** **108** **109** **110** **111**

Lower Eype Shipton Gorge Litton Cheney Winterborne Abbas Dorchester Stinsford Woodsford

Burton Bradstock Littlebredy Martinstown **134** **135** Crossways Moreton

128 **129** Punknowle **132** **133** Winterborne Monkton **136** **137** **138**

130 **131** Portesham West Knighton

Abbotsbury **148** **149** **150** **151** Upwey Owermoigne A352

Langton Herring Preston **152** **153** **154** **155** **156**

Chickerell Osmington Osmington Mills Chaldon Herring

165 **166** **167** **168** **169** **170** **171**

Weymouth

Wyke Regis **180** **181**

Fortuneswell **186** **187**

Easton

Southwell

Scale
0 | 5 | 10 | 15 | 20 km
0 | 5 | 10 miles

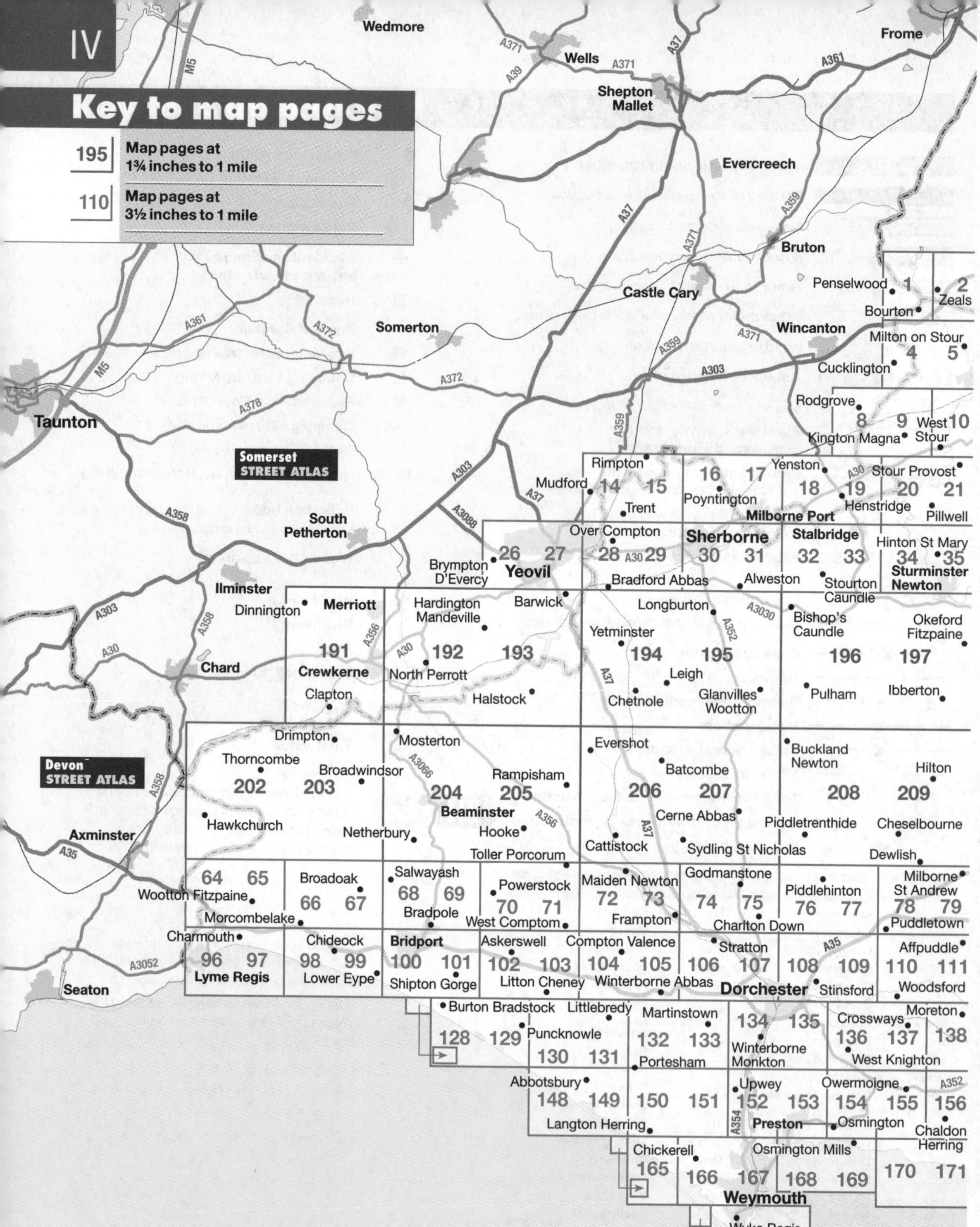

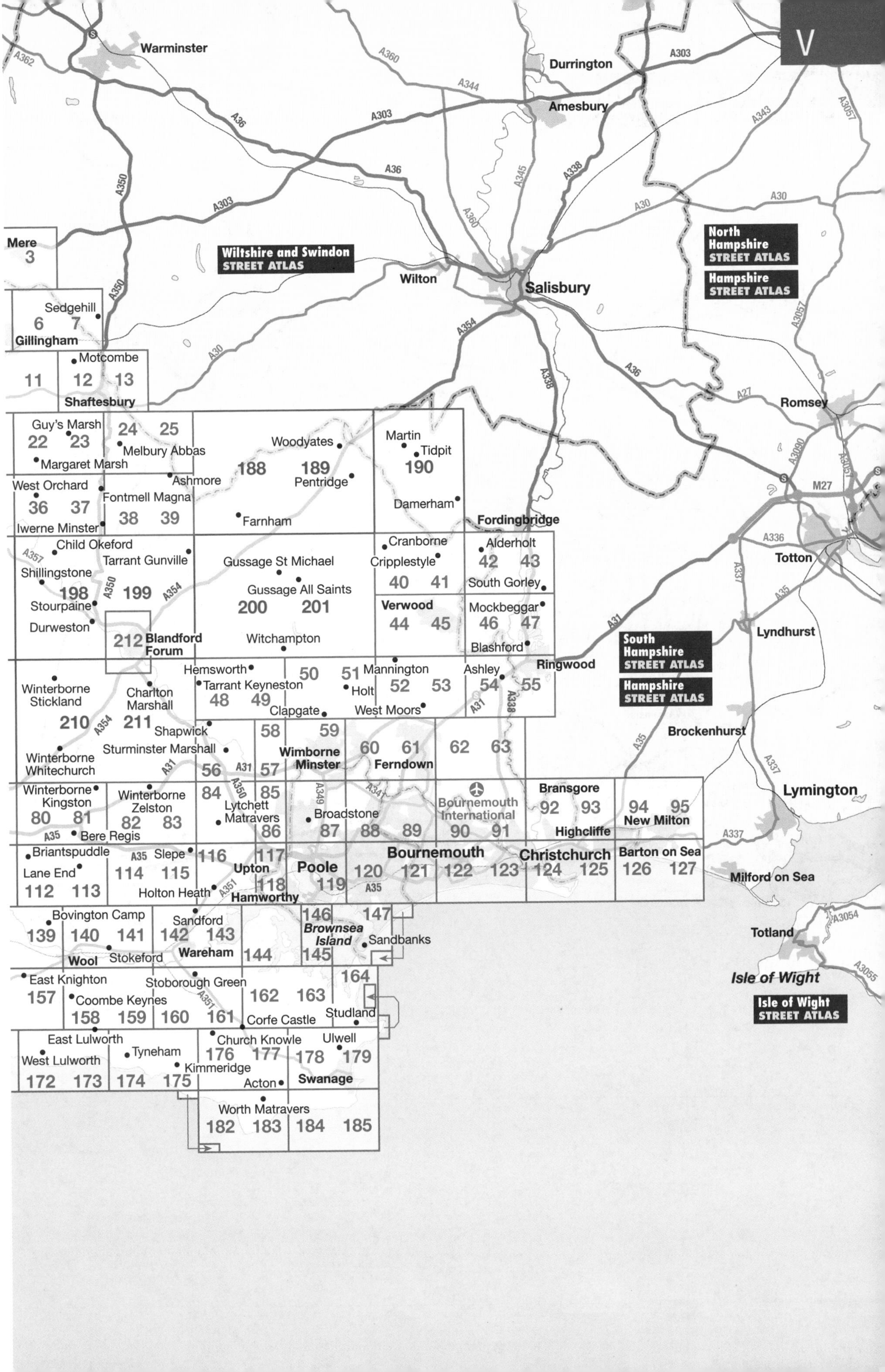

V

Warminster

Durrington

Amesbury

A362

A36

A303

A360

A344

A303

A343

A345

A338

A303

A30

A30

A3057

North
Hampshire
STREET ATLAS

Hampshire
STREET ATLAS

A350

A303

Wiltshire and Swindon
STREET ATLAS

Wilton

Salisbury

A354

A36

Romsey

A3090

A3057

A36

M27

Mere
3

A350

Sedgehill
6 7
Gillingham

Motcombe
11 12 13
Shaftesbury

A30

A338

Totton

A336

A3035

Guy's Marsh
22 23
Margaret Marsh

24 25
Melbury Abbas

Woodyates
188 189
Pentridge

Martin
Tidpit
190

Damerham

Fordingbridge

A35

A337

West Orchard
36 37
Iwerne Minster

Fontmell Magna
38 39
Ashmore

Farnham

Cranborne
Cripplestyle
40 41

Alderholt
42 43
South Gorley

A31

South
Hampshire
STREET ATLAS

Hampshire
STREET ATLAS

Lyndhurst

Child Okeford
Shillingstone
198
Stourpaine
Durweston

A357

A350

Tarrant Gunville
199

A354

Gussage St Michael
Gussage All Saints
200 201
Witchampton

Verwood
44 45

Mockbeggar
46 47
Blashford

Ringwood

A35

Brockenhurst

A337

Lymington

212 Blandford
Forum

Hemsworth
Tarrant Keyneston
48 49
Clapgate

50 51
Mannington
Holt
52 53
West Moors

Ashley
54 55

A31

A338

Winterborne
Stickland
210
Winterborne
Whitechurch

A354

Charlton
Marshall
211
Shapwick
Sturminster Marshall

A31

58
Wimborne
Minster
56 57

A31

A350

59
60 61
Ferndown

A349

A31

62 63

Winterborne
Kingston
80 81

A35

Winterborne
Zelston
82 83
Bere Regis

Lytchett
Matravers
84 85
86

A350

Broadstone
87

A349

88 89

A341

Bournemouth
International
90 91

Bransgore
92 93
Highcliffe

94 95
New Milton

A337

Briantspuddle
Lane End
112 113

A35

Slepe
114 115
Holton Heath

116
Upton
117
118
Hamworthy

A351

Poole
119

120 121

A35

122 123

Bournemouth

Christchurch
124 125

Barton on Sea
126 127

Milford on Sea

Bovington Camp
139 140 141
Wool
Stokeford

Sandford
142 143
Wareham
144

146 147
Brownsea
Island
145
Sandbanks

Totland

Isle of Wight

East Knighton
157
Coombe Keynes
158 159 160 161

A351

Stoborough Green
162 163
Corfe Castle

164
Studland

A3054

Isle of Wight
STREET ATLAS

A3055

East Lulworth
West Lulworth
172 173
Tyneham
174 175
Kimmeridge
Acton

Church Knowle
176 177
178 179
Ulwell
Swanage

Worth Matravers
182 183 184 185

Route planning

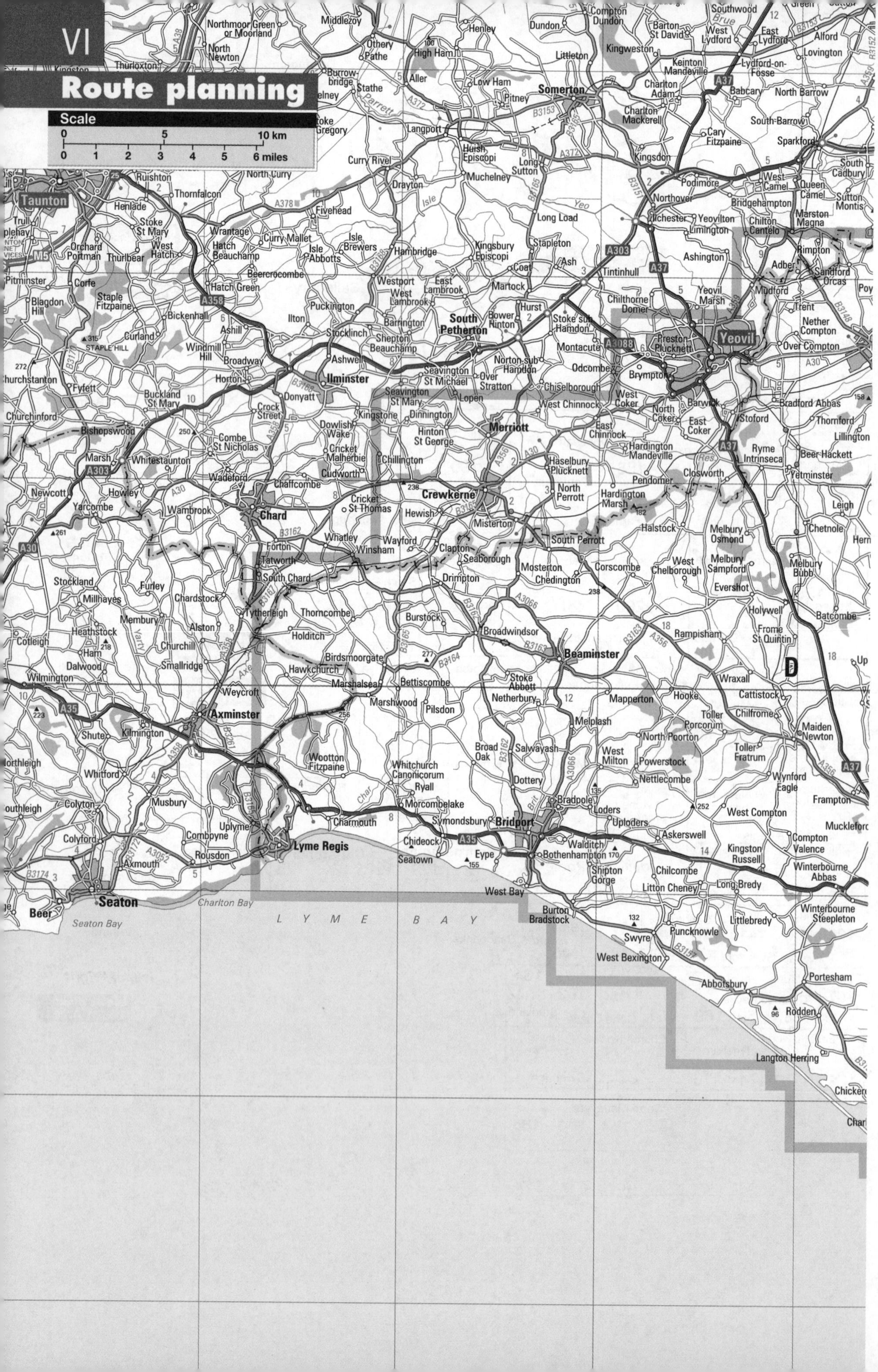
Scale
0 5 10 km
0 1 2 3 4 5 6 miles
Taunton
Northmoor Green or Moorland
North Newton
Thurloxton
Middlezoy
Othery
Pathe
Burrowbridge
Stathe
High Ham
Aller
Low Ham
Henley
Pitney
Dundon
Compton Dundon
Somerton
Littleton
Kingweston
Barton St David
Southwood
West Lydford
East Lydford
Alford
Lovington
Keinton Mandeville
Lydford-on-Fosse
Charlton Adam
Babcary
North Barrow
Charlton Mackerell
South Barrow
Cary Fitzpaine
Sparkford
Kingsdon
Langport
Huish Episcopi
Long Sutton
Curry Rivel
Muchelney
Drayton
Podimore
West Camel
Queen Camel
South Cadbury
Northover
Bridgehampton
Sutton Montis
Ilchester
Yeovilton
Limington
Chilton Cantelo
Marston Magna
Long Load
Ashington
Rimpton
Adber
Sandford Orcas
Mudford
Trent
Nether Compton
Over Compton
Yeovil
Preston Plucknett
Brympton
Ruishton
Thornfalcon
North Curry
Henlade
Stoke St Mary
West Hatch
Orchard Portman
Thurlbear
Hatch Beauchamp
Wrantage
Curry Mallet
Fivehead
Isle Brewers
Isle Abbotts
Hambridge
Kingsbury Episcopi
Stapleton
Beercrocombe
Hatch Green
Pitminster
Corfe
Blagdon Hill
Staple Fitzpaine
Bickenhall
Curland
Staple Hill
Westport
West Lambrook
East Lambrook
Martock
Coat
Ash
Tintinhull
Chilthorne Domer
Yeovil Marsh
Puckington
Ilton
Barrington
Stocklinch
Shepton Beauchamp
South Petherton
Bower Hinton
Hurst
Stoke sub Hamdon
Montacute
Ashill
Windmill Hill
Broadway
Horton
Ashwell
Ilminster
Seavington St Michael
Seavington St Mary
Over Stratton
Norton sub Hamdon
Chiselborough
Odcombe
Lopen
West Chinnock
West Coker
North Coker
East Coker
Barwick
Stoford
Bradford Abbas
Thornford
Churchstanton
Fyfett
Buckland St Mary
Donyatt
Crock Street
Kingstone
Dinnington
Hinton St George
Merriott
East Chinnock
Hardington Mandeville
Churchinford
Bishopswood
Combe St Nicholas
Dowlish Wake
Cricket Malherbie
Chillington
Haselbury Plucknett
Closworth
Ryme Intrinseca
Lillington
Beer Hackett
Marsh
Whitestaunton
Wadeford
Cudworth
Yetminster
Pendomer
Newcott
Howley
Chaffcombe
Cricket St Thomas
Crewkerne
North Perrott
Hardington Marsh
Yarcombe
Wambrook
Chard
Hewish
Misterton
Leigh
Chetnole
Whatley
Winsham
Wayford
Clapton
Seaborough
South Perrott
Halstock
Melbury Osmond
Forton
Tatworth
South Chard
Mosterton
Chedington
Corscombe
West Chelborough
Melbury Sampford
Melbury Bubb
Stockland
Furley
Drimpton
Evershot
Millhayes
Chardstock
Burstock
Holywell
Membury
Tytherleigh
Thorncombe
Broadwindsor
Rampisham
Frome St Quintin
Batcombe
Heathstock
Alston
Holditch
Beaminster
Cotleigh
Churchill
Birdsmoorgate
Ham
Smallridge
Hawkchurch
Stoke Abbott
Wraxall
Dalwood
Marshalsea
Bettiscombe
Netherbury
Mapperton
Hooke
Cattistock
Wilmington
Weycroft
Marshwood
Pilsdon
Toller Porcorum
Chilfrome
Axminster
Melplash
Maiden Newton
Shute
Kilmington
North Poorton
Broad Oak
Salwayash
West Milton
Toller Fratrum
Wootton Fitzpaine
Whitchurch Canonicorum
Powerstock
Whitford
Ryall
Dottery
Nettlecombe
Wynford Eagle
Musbury
Morcombelake
Bradpole
Loders
West Compton
Frampton
Colyton
Charmouth
Symondsbury
Bridport
Uploders
Uplyme
Combpyne
Askerswell
Colyford
Lyme Regis
Chideock
Walditch
Compton Valence
Rousdon
Eype
Bothenhampton
Kingston Russell
Axmouth
Seatown
Shipton Gorge
Chilcombe
Winterbourne Abbas
Seaton
Charlton Bay
West Bay
Litton Cheney
Long Bredy
Beer
Seaton Bay
LYME BAY
Burton Bradstock
Littlebredy
Winterbourne Steepleton
Swyre
Puncknowle
West Bexington
Abbotsbury
Portesham
Rodden
Langton Herring
A30
A35
A37
A303
A358
A356
A3066
A378
A372
A3088
B3165
B3162
B3163
B3153
B3151
B3157
M5
Parrett
Isle
Yeo
Axe
Yarty
Char
Brit
D

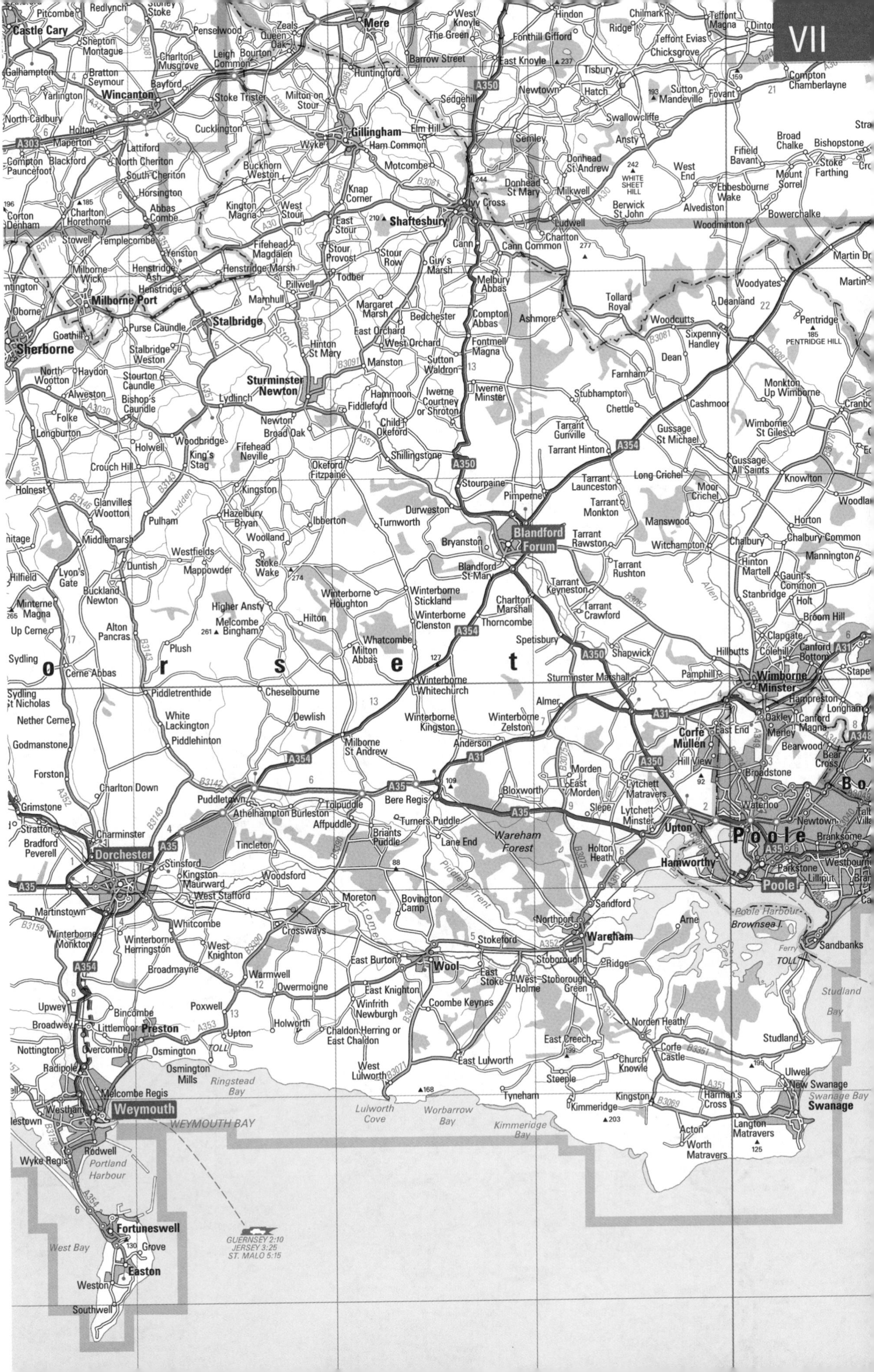
Pitcombe
Redlynch
Stoke
Castle Cary
Shepton Montague
Penselwood
Zeals
Queen Oak
Mere
West Knoyle
The Green
Hindon
Fonthill Gifford
Chilmark
Ridge
Teffont Magna
Dinton
Teffont Evias
Chicksgrove
Charlton Musgrove
Leigh Common
Bourton
Barrow Street
East Knoyle
237
Tisbury
Galhampton
Bratton Seymour
Bayford
Huntingford
Compton Chamberlayne
159
Yarlington
Wincanton
Stoke Trister
Milton on Stour
Sedgehill
Newtown
Hatch
193
Sutton Mandeville
Fovant
North Cadbury
Holton
Cucklington
Gillingham
Elm Hill
Swallowcliffe
Maperton
Wyke
Ham Common
Semley
Ansty
Fifield Bavant
Broad Chalke
Bishopstone
Lattiford
North Cheriton
Compton Pauncefoot
Blackford
Buckhorn Weston
Motcombe
Donhead St Andrew
242
WHITE SHEET HILL
West End
Stoke Farthing
South Cheriton
244
Donhead St Mary
Milkwell
Ebbesbourne Wake
Mount Sorrel
185
Horsington
Knap Corner
Berwick St John
Alvediston
Corton Denham
Charlton Horethorne
Abbas Combe
Kington Magna
West Stour
Ivy Cross
210
Shaftesbury
Ludwell
Woodminton
Bowerchalke
East Stour
Charlton
Stowell
Templecombe
Fifehead Magdalen
Stour Provost
Cann
Cann Common
277
Yenston
Stour Row
Guy's Marsh
Martin Dr
Henstridge Ash
Henstridge Marsh
Melbury Abbas
Milborne Wick
Todber
Martin
Woodyates
Henstridge
Pillwell
Tollard Royal
Milborne Port
Marnhull
Margaret Marsh
Ashmore
Deanland
22
Oborne
Bedchester
Compton Abbas
Woodcutts
Pentridge
Purse Caundle
Stalbridge
East Orchard
Sixpenny Handley
185
PENTRIDGE HILL
Goathill
Hinton St Mary
West Orchard
Fontmell Magna
Sherborne
Stalbridge Weston
Manston
Sutton Waldron
Dean
Farnham
North Wootton
Haydon
Stourton Caundle
Sturminster Newton
Monkton Up Wimborne
Alweston
Bishop's Caundle
Lydlinch
Hammoon
Iwerne Courtney or Shroton
Iwerne Minster
Stubhampton
Cashmoor
Folke
Fiddleford
Chettle
Wimborne St Giles
Longburton
Newton
Broad Oak
Child Okeford
Tarrant Gunville
Gussage St Michael
Holwell
Woodbridge
King's Stag
Fifehead Neville
Shillingstone
Tarrant Hinton
Gussage All Saints
Crouch Hill
Okeford Fitzpaine
Long Crichel
Knowlton
Holnest
Kingston
Stourpaine
Tarrant Launceston
Moor Crichel
Glanvilles Wootton
Pimperne
Tarrant Monkton
Pulham
Hazelbury Bryan
Ibberton
Turnworth
Durweston
Blandford Forum
Manswood
Horton
Middlemarsh
Woolland
Bryanston
Tarrant Rawston
Witchampton
Chalbury
Chalbury Common
Westfields
Tarrant Rushton
Hinton Martell
Mannington
Duntish
Mappowder
Stoke Wake
274
Blandford St Mary
Tarrant Keyneston
Gaunt's Common
Hilfield
Lyon's Gate
Buckland Newton
Winterborne Houghton
Winterborne Stickland
Charlton Marshall
Stanbridge
Holt
Minterne Magna
265
Higher Ansty
Tarrant Crawford
Allen
Broom Hill
Hilton
Winterborne Clenston
Thorncombe
Up Cerne
Alton Pancras
Melcombe Bingham
261
Whatcombe
Spetisbury
Clapgate
Milton Abbas
Colehill
Canford Bottom
Sydling
Plush
127
Shapwick
Hillbutts
Cerne Abbas
o r s e t
Winterborne Whitechurch
Pamphill
Wimborne Minster
Stapehill
Sydling St Nicholas
Piddletrenthide
Cheselbourne
Sturminster Marshall
Hampreston
Longham
Nether Cerne
White Lackington
Dewlish
Almer
Winterborne Kingston
Winterborne Zelston
Corfe Mullen
East End
Oakley
Merley
Canford Magna
Godmanstone
Piddlehinton
Milborne St Andrew
Anderson
Bearwood
Bear Cross
Forston
Morden
Hill View
Broadstone
92
Charlton Down
Bloxworth
East Morden
Lytchett Matravers
Grimstone
Puddletown
Tolpuddle
Bere Regis
109
Slepe
Lytchett Minster
Waterloo
Stratton
Athelhampton
Burleston
Affpuddle
Turners Puddle
Upton
Poole
Newtown
Bradford Peverell
Charminster
Briants Puddle
Lane End
Wareham Forest
Branksome
Dorchester
Tincleton
Holton Heath
Hamworthy
Parkstone
Westbourne
Stinsford
Kingston Maurward
Woodsford
88
Lilliput
West Stafford
Moreton
Bovington Camp
Piddle or Trent
Sandford
Martinstown
Whitcombe
Frome
Northport
Poole Harbour
Brownsea I.
Winterborne Monkton
Winterborne Herrington
West Knighton
Crossways
Stokeford
Wareham
Arne
Sandbanks
East Burton
Wool
Stoborough
Ridge
Ferry
TOLL
Broadmayne
Warmwell
Owermoigne
East Stoke
West Holme
Stoborough Green
East Knighton
Studland Bay
Upwey
Bincombe
Poxwell
Winfrith Newburgh
Coombe Keynes
Broadwey
Littlemoor
Preston
Upton
Holworth
Chaldon Herring or East Chaldon
Norden Heath
Studland
Nottington
Overcombe
Osmington
TOLL
East Creech
199
Corfe Castle
Radipole
Osmington Mills
Ringstead Bay
West Lulworth
East Lulworth
Church Knowle
199
Ulwell
Melcombe Regis
168
Steeple
New Swanage
Westham
Weymouth
Tyneham
Kingston
Harman's Cross
Swanage Bay
Swanage
Lulworth Cove
Worbarrow Bay
Kimmeridge
203
WEYMOUTH BAY
Kimmeridge Bay
Langton Matravers
Acton
Worth Matravers
125
Rodwell
Wyke Regis
Portland Harbour
Fortuneswell
West Bay
130
Grove
GUERNSEY 2:10
JERSEY 3:25
ST. MALO 5:15
Easton
Weston
Southwell
A303
A30
A350
A354
A35
A31
A352
A357
A353
A351
B3081
B3092
B3091
B3143
B3142
B3390
B3071
B3070
B3075
B3082
B3078
B3069
B3351
B3159
B3156

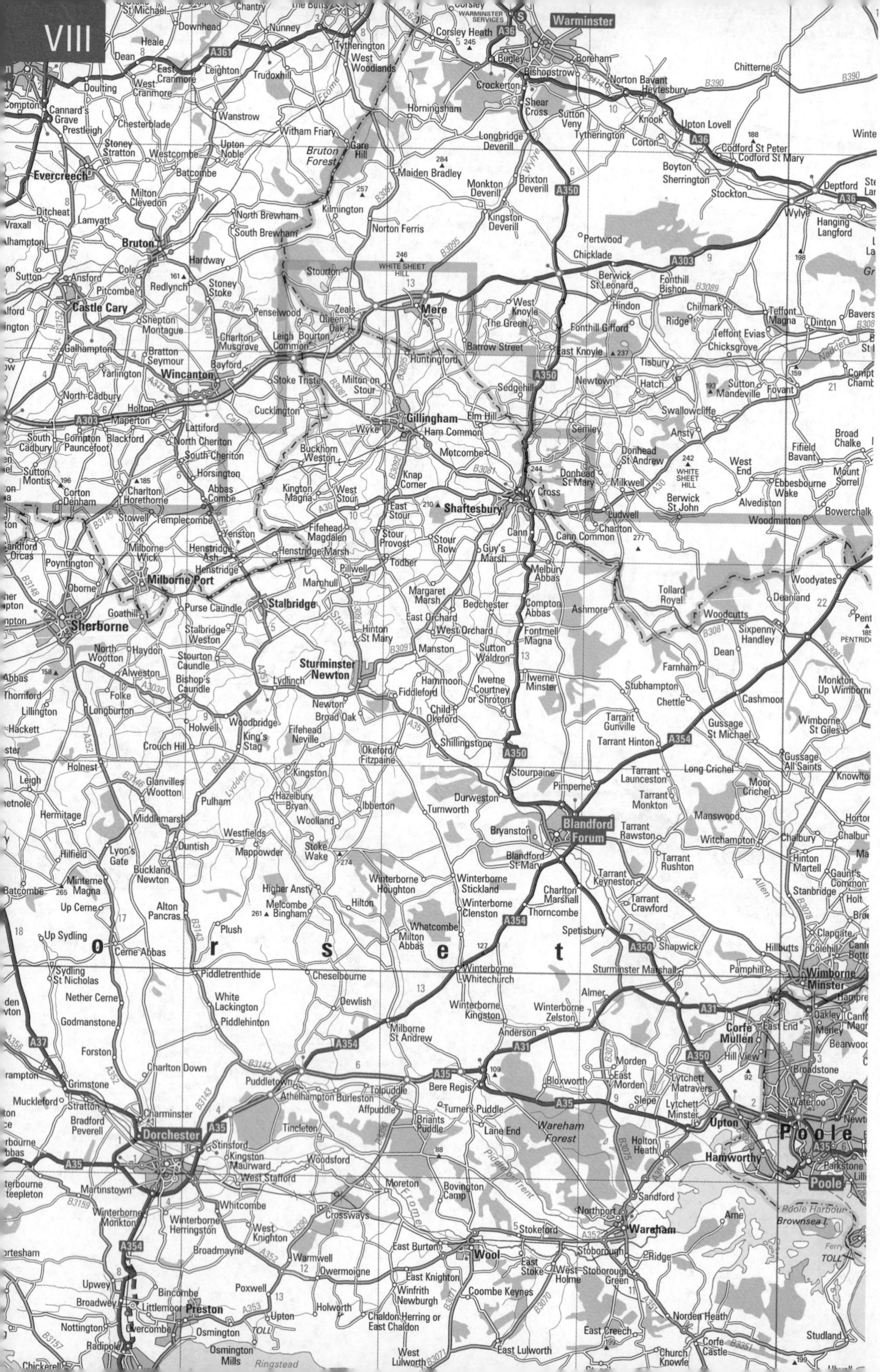
Warminster
Stoke St Michael
Downhead
Heale
Dean
Nunney
Tytherington
West Woodlands
Corsley Heath
Bugley
Boreham
Chitterne
Leighton
Trudoxhill
East Cranmore
West Cranmore
Doulting
Bishopstrow
Crockerton
Shear Cross
Norton Bavant
Heytesbury
Compton
Cannard's Grave
Prestleigh
Chesterblade
Wanstrow
Horningsham
Sutton Veny
Knook
Upton Lovell
Tytherington
Corton
Witham Friary
Gare Hill
Bruton Forest
Longbridge Deverill
Codford St Peter
Codford St Mary
Stoney Stratton
Westcombe
Upton Noble
Batcombe
Evercreech
Maiden Bradley
Monkton Deverill
Brixton Deverill
Boyton
Sherrington
Stockton
Deptford
Milton Clevedon
Kilmington
Wylye
Hanging Langford
Ditcheat
Lamyatt
North Brewham
South Brewham
Norton Ferris
Kingston Deverill
Vraxall
Bruton
Pertwood
Chicklade
Hardway
Stourton
White Sheet Hill
Sutton
Ansford
Cole
Redlynch
Stoney Stoke
Pitcombe
Berwick St Leonard
Fonthill Bishop
Castle Cary
Mere
West Knoyle
The Green
Hindon
Chilmark
Teffont Magna
Dinton
Zeals
Queen Oak
Penselwood
Shepton Montague
Ridge
Teffont Evias
Chicksgrove
Galhampton
Charlton Musgrove
Leigh Common
Bourton
Fonthill Gifford
Barrow Street
East Knoyle
Bratton Seymour
Huntingford
Tisbury
Yarlington
Wincanton
Bayford
Stoke Trister
Milton on Stour
Newtown
Hatch
Sutton Mandeville
Fovant
North Cadbury
Sedgehill
Holton
Maperton
Cucklington
Gillingham
Elm Hill
Swallowcliffe
Lattiford
Wyke
Ham Common
Semley
South Cadbury
Compton Pauncefoot
Blackford
North Cheriton
South Cheriton
Buckhorn Weston
Motcombe
Ansty
Donhead St Andrew
Fifield Bavant
Broad Chalke
Sutton Montis
Corton Denham
Charlton Horethorne
Horsington
Abbas Combe
Kington Magna
West Stour
Knap Corner
Ivy Cross
Donhead St Mary
Milkwell
West End
Ebbesbourne Wake
Mount Sorrel
Berwick St John
Alvediston
Shaftesbury
East Stour
Stowell
Templecombe
Ludwell
Charlton
Woodminton
Bowerchalke
Sandford Orcas
Fifehead Magdalen
Stour Provost
Stour Row
Cann
Cann Common
Yenston
Poyntington
Milborne Wick
Henstridge Ash
Henstridge Marsh
Todber
Guy's Marsh
Henstridge
Oborne
Milborne Port
Pillwell
Marnhull
Margaret Marsh
Melbury Abbas
Tollard Royal
Woodyates
Deanland
Purse Caundle
Stalbridge
Bedchester
Compton Abbas
Ashmore
Goathill
Sherborne
Stalbridge Weston
Hinton St Mary
East Orchard
West Orchard
Fontmell Magna
Woodcutts
Sixpenny Handley
Pentridge
North Wootton
Haydon
Stourton Caundle
Manston
Sutton Waldron
Dean
Alweston
Bishop's Caundle
Sturminster Newton
Lydlinch
Hammoon
Iwerne Courtney or Shroton
Iwerne Minster
Farnham
Stubhampton
Monkton Up Wimborne
Thornford
Folke
Fiddleford
Chettle
Cashmoor
Lillington
Longburton
Newton
Broad Oak
Child Okeford
Tarrant Gunville
Gussage St Michael
Wimborne St Giles
Hackett
Holwell
Woodbridge
King's Stag
Fifehead Neville
Shillingstone
Tarrant Hinton
Crouch Hill
Holnest
Okeford Fitzpaine
Gussage All Saints
Knowlton
Kingston
Tarrant Launceston
Long Crichel
Leigh
Glanvilles Wootton
Hazelbury Bryan
Stourpaine
Pimperne
Moor Crichel
Pulham
Ibberton
Durweston
Tarrant Monkton
Turnworth
Hermitage
Middlemarsh
Woolland
Manswood
Horton
Blandford Forum
Bryanston
Tarrant Rawston
Witchampton
Chalbury
Westfields
Hilfield
Lyon's Gate
Dunt
Mappowder
Stoke Wake
Blandford St Mary
Tarrant Rushton
Hinton Martell
Gaunt's Common
Buckland Newton
Minterne Magna
Batcombe
Winterborne Houghton
Winterborne Stickland
Tarrant Keyneston
Higher Ansty
Charlton Marshall
Stanbridge
Holt
Up Cerne
Alton Pancras
Melcombe Bingham
Hilton
Winterborne Clenston
Thorncombe
Tarrant Crawford
Whatcombe
Milton Abbas
Spetisbury
Up Sydling
Plush
Shapwick
Clapgate
Colehill
Hillbutts
Cerne Abbas
Dorset
Winterborne Whitechurch
Sturminster Marshall
Pamphill
Wimborne Minster
Sydling St Nicholas
Piddletrenthide
Cheselbourne
Nether Cerne
Dewlish
Almer
White Lackington
Winterborne Kingston
Winterborne Zelston
Oakley
Godmanstone
Piddlehinton
Corfe Mullen
East End
Merley
Milborne St Andrew
Anderson
Forston
Hill View
Bearwood
Charlton Down
Morden
Broadstone
Grimstone
Puddletown
Tolpuddle
Bere Regis
Bloxworth
East Morden
Lytchett Matravers
Muckleford
Stratton
Athelhampton
Burleston
Affpuddle
Turners Puddle
Slepe
Lytchett Minster
Upton
Waterloo
Bradford Peverell
Charminster
Briants Puddle
Lane End
Wareham Forest
Poole
Dorchester
Tincleton
Holton Heath
Hamworthy
Stinsford
Kingston Maurward
Woodsford
Parkstone
Martinstown
West Stafford
Moreton
Bovington Camp
Sandford
Winterborne Monkton
Whitcombe
Crossways
Northport
Poole Harbour
Brownsea I.
Arne
Winterborne Herringston
West Knighton
Stokeford
Wareham
Broadmayne
East Burton
Wool
Stoborough
Ridge
Warmwell
Owermoigne
East Stoke
West Holme
Stoborough Green
Upwey
Bincombe
Poxwell
East Knighton
Winfrith Newburgh
Broadwey
Littlemoor
Preston
Coombe Keynes
Holworth
Upton
Chaldon Herring or East Chaldon
Norden Heath
Nottington
Overcombe
Osmington
East Creech
Studland
Radipole
Osmington Mills
Ringstead
East Lulworth
West Lulworth
Church Knowle
Corfe Castle
Chickerell
A36
A361
A303
A350
A30
A354
A357
A35
A31
A37
A352
A353
B3092
B3081
B3095
B3089
B3390
B3143
B3142
Frome
Stour
Wylye
Piddle or Trent
Allen
Lydden
Cale
Nadder
TOLL
Ferry

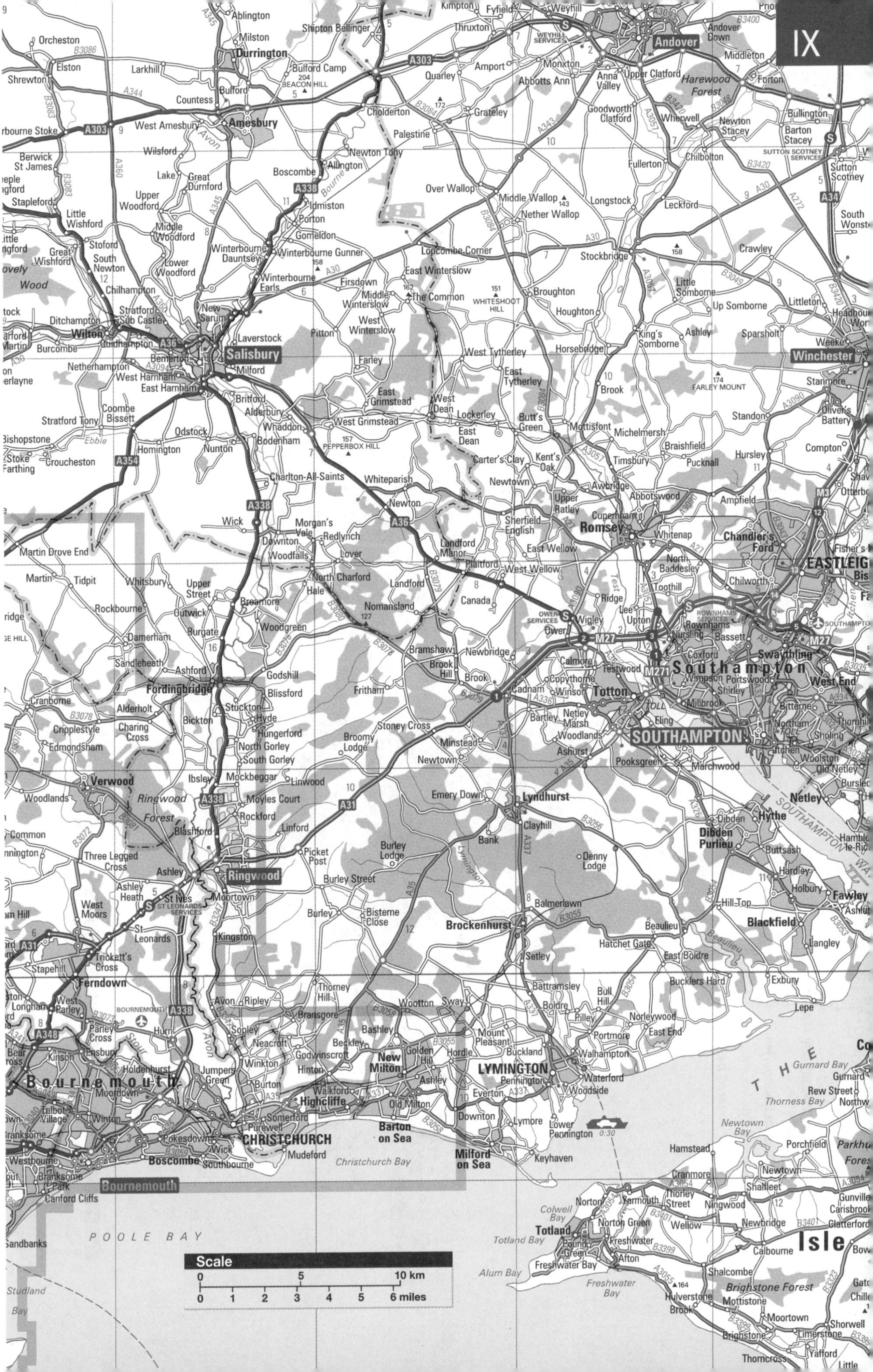
Ablington
Milston
Durrington
Orcheston
Elston
Shrewton
Larkhill
Bulford Camp
Bulford
Countess
Amesbury
West Amesbury
Berwick St James
Wilsford
Lake
Great Durnford
Upper Woodford
Middle Woodford
Lower Woodford
Stapleford
Little Wishford
Great Wishford
Stoford
South Newton
Grovely Wood
Chilhampton
Stratford sub Castle
Ditchampton
Wilton
Quidhampton
Burcombe
Bemerton
Netherhampton
West Harnham
East Harnham
Salisbury
Milford
Laverstock
Old Sarum
Winterbourne Dauntsey
Winterbourne Gunner
Winterbourne Earls
Gomeldon
Porton
Idmiston
Boscombe
Allington
Newton Tony
Cholderton
Shipton Bellinger
Palestine
Quarley
Amport
Thruxton
Kimpton
Fyfield
Weyhill
Monxton
Abbotts Ann
Anna Valley
Upper Clatford
Andover
Andover Down
Middleton
Harewood Forest
Forton
Goodworth Clatford
Wherwell
Newton Stacey
Barton Stacey
Bullington
Sutton Scotney
Chilbolton
Fullerton
Grateley
Over Wallop
Middle Wallop
Nether Wallop
Longstock
Leckford
Stockbridge
Crawley
South Wonston
Lopcombe Corner
East Winterslow
Firsdown
Middle Winterslow
The Common
West Winterslow
Pitton
Farley
Whiteshoot Hill
Broughton
Houghton
Little Somborne
Up Somborne
Littleton
Headbourne Worthy
King's Somborne
Ashley
Sparsholt
Weeke
Winchester
Horsebridge
West Tytherley
East Tytherley
Brook
Farley Mount
Stanmore
Oliver's Battery
Standon
Compton
Hursley
East Grimstead
West Grimstead
West Dean
East Dean
Lockerley
Butt's Green
Mottisfont
Michelmersh
Braishfield
Timsbury
Pucknall
Carter's Clay
Kent's Oak
Awbridge
Abbotswood
Ampfield
Newtown
Upper Ratley
Cupernham
Romsey
Sherfield English
Whitenap
Chandler's Ford
Eastleigh
North Baddesley
Chilworth
Landford Manor
East Wellow
West Wellow
Plaitford
Landford
Canada
Toothill
Ridge
Lee
Upton
Rownhams
Nursling
Bassett
Swaythling
Wigley
Ower
Calmore
Testwood
Totton
Southampton
Coxford
Shirley
Portswood
Millbrook
West End
Bitterne
Woolston
Itchen
Sholing
Old Netley
Netley
Bishopstone
Stoke Farthing
Croucheston
Stratford Tony
Coombe Bissett
Homington
Odstock
Nunton
Britford
Alderbury
Whaddon
Bodenham
Pepperbox Hill
Charlton-All-Saints
Whiteparish
Newton
Wick
Morgan's Vale
Redlynch
Downton
Woodfalls
Lover
North Charford
Hale
Nomansland
Martin Drove End
Martin
Tidpit
Whitsbury
Upper Street
Rockbourne
Outwick
Breamore
Woodgreen
Damerham
Burgate
Sandleheath
Ashford
Fordingbridge
Godshill
Blissford
Stuckton
Hyde
Hungerford
North Gorley
South Gorley
Cranborne
Alderholt
Bickton
Cripplestyle
Charing Cross
Edmondsham
Verwood
Ringwood Forest
Woodlands
Ibsley
Mockbeggar
Linwood
Moyles Court
Rockford
Blashford
Linford
Common
Three Legged Cross
Ashley
Ashley Heath
St Ives
St Leonards
Ringwood
Picket Post
Moortown
West Moors
Kingston
Trickett's Cross
Stapehill
Ferndown
Longham
West Parley
Parley Cross
Bournemouth
Hurn
Ensbury
Kinson
Holdenhurst
Moordown
Talbot Village
Winton
Branksome
Westbourne
Branksome Park
Canford Cliffs
Pokesdown
Boscombe
Southbourne
Wick
Christchurch
Mudeford
Purewell
Somerford
Burton
Jumpers Green
Winkton
Sopley
Neacroft
Avon
Ripley
Bransgore
Thorney Hill
Godwinscroft
Hinton
Walkford
Highcliffe
Bashley
Beckley
New Milton
Golden Hill
Ashley
Old Milton
Barton on Sea
Wootton
Sway
Hordle
Downton
Milford on Sea
Everton
Lymore
Keyhaven
Mount Pleasant
Buckland
Lymington
Pennington
Lower Pennington
Walhampton
Woodside
Boldre
Pilley
Portmore
Norleywood
East End
Battramsley
Bull Hill
Setley
Brockenhurst
Balmerlawn
Bank
Lyndhurst
Clayhill
Emery Down
Denny Lodge
Burley Lodge
Burley Street
Burley
Bisterne Close
Minstead
Newtown
Stoney Cross
Broomy Lodge
Fritham
Bramshaw
Brook Hill
Brook
Newbridge
Cadnam
Copythorne
Winsor
Bartley
Netley Marsh
Woodlands
Ashurst
Eling
Pooksgreen
Marchwood
Dibden
Dibden Purlieu
Hythe
Buttsash
Hardley
Holbury
Fawley
Hill Top
Blackfield
Langley
Beaulieu
Hatchet Gate
East Boldre
Bucklers Hard
Exbury
Lepe
Hamble-le-Rice
Christchurch Bay
Poole Bay
Sandbanks
Studland Bay
Hamstead
Cranmore
Thorley Street
Shalfleet
Newtown
Porchfield
Newtown Bay
Yarmouth
Norton
Norton Green
Ningwood
Newbridge
Wellow
Colwell Bay
Totland
Totland Bay
Freshwater
Pound Green
Afton
Freshwater Bay
Alum Bay
Calbourne
Shalcombe
Brighstone Forest
Hulverstone
Mottistone
Brook
Moortown
Brighstone
Limerstone
Shorwell
Thorncross
Yafford
Gurnard Bay
Gurnard
Rew Street
Thorness Bay
Northwood
Gunville
Carisbrooke
Clatterford
Isle
Scale
0
5
10 km
0
1
2
3
4
5
6 miles

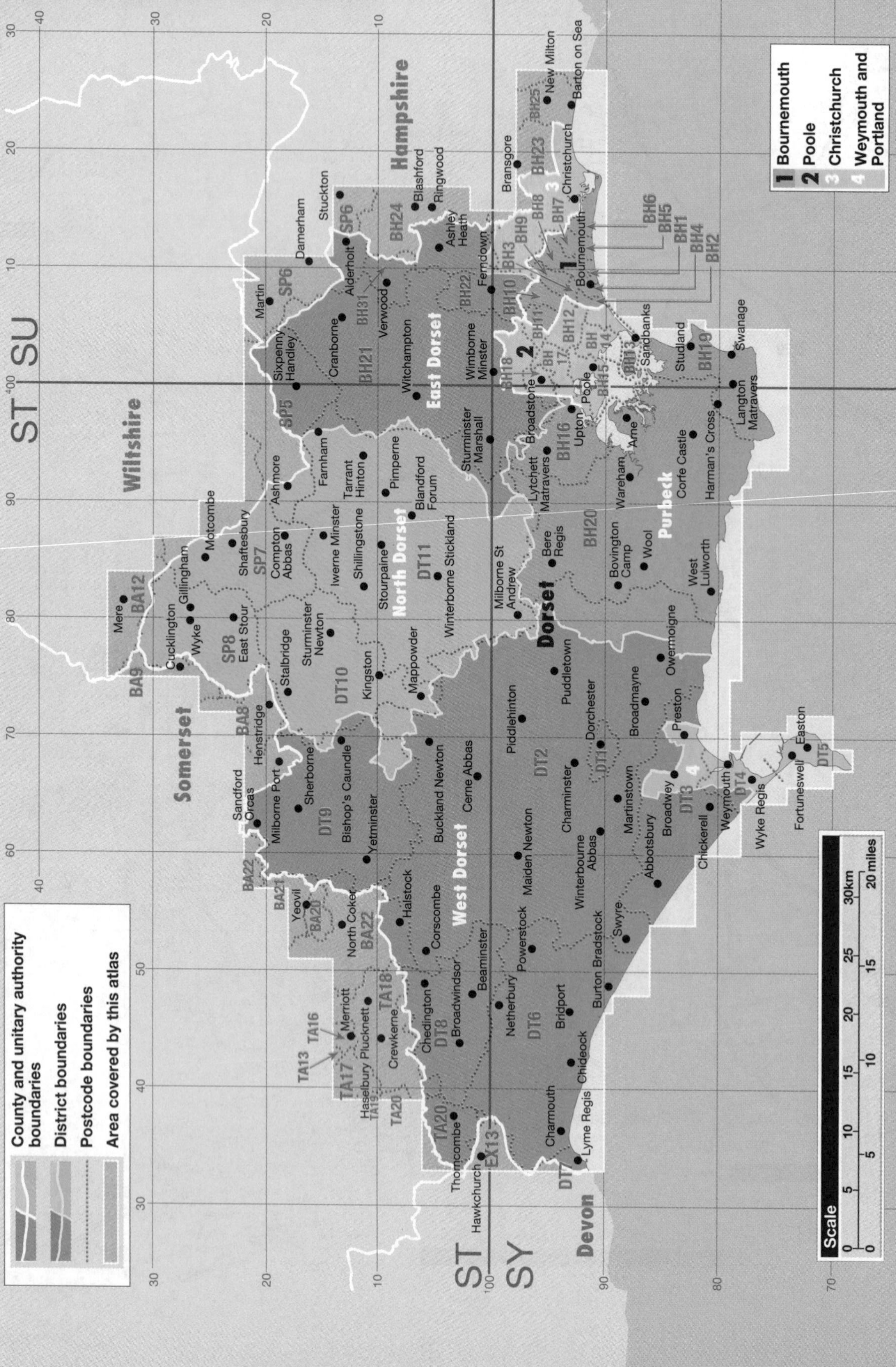

Scale

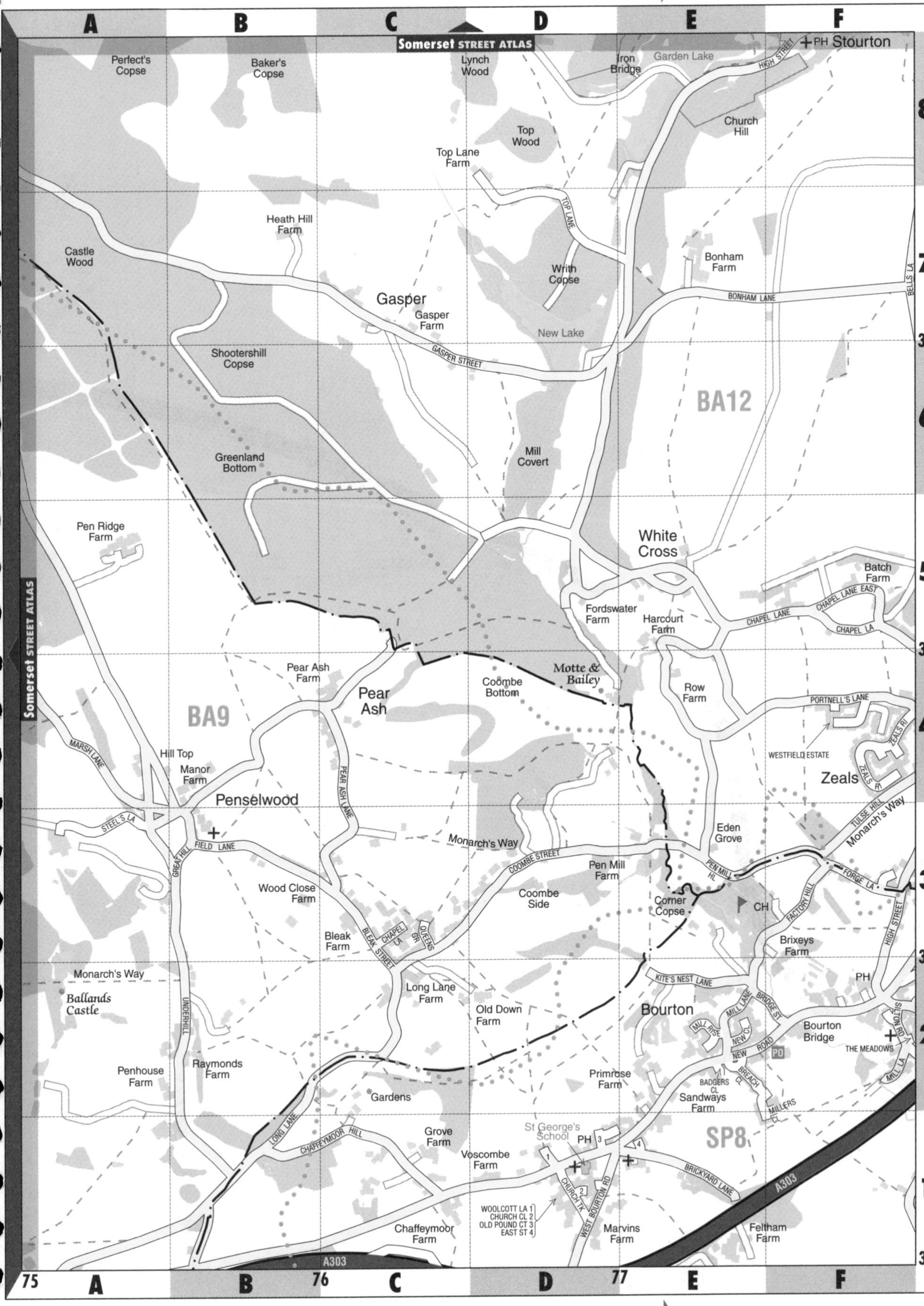

A | B | C | D | E | F

Somerset STREET ATLAS

Somerset STREET ATLAS

Perfect's Copse

Baker's Copse

Lynch Wood

Iron Bridge

Garden Lake

+ PH Stourton

8

Top Wood

Church Hill

Heath Hill Farm

Top Lane Farm

TOP LANE

Bonham Farm

7

Gasper

Writh Copse

BONHAM LANE

BELLS RI

Gasper Farm

GASPER STREET

New Lake

33

Shootershill Copse

BA12

6

Greenland Bottom

Mill Covert

Pen Ridge Farm

White Cross

5

Fordswater Farm

Harcourt Farm

Batch Farm

CHAPEL LANE

CHAPEL LANE EAST

CHAPEL LA

32

Pear Ash Farm

Coombe Bottom

Motte & Bailey

Row Farm

PORTNELL'S LANE

Pear Ash

BA9

ZEALS RI

Westfield Estate

Zeals

4

MARSH LANE

Hill Top Manor Farm

Monarch's Way

Eden Grove

TULSE HILL

Monarch's Way

PEAR ASH LANE

Penselwood

COOMBE STREET

Pen Mill Farm

PEN MILL HL

FORGE LA

3

STEEL'S LA

GREAT HILL

FIELD LANE

Wood Close Farm

Coombe Side

Corner Copse

CH

FACTORY HILL

Brixeys Farm

HIGH STREET

31

Monarch's Way

Bleak Farm

CHAPEL LA DR

QUEENS

KITE'S NEST LANE

PH

Ballands Castle

UNDERHILL

BLEAK STREET

Long Lane Farm

Old Down Farm

Bourton

MILL LANE

BRIDGE ST

Bourton Bridge

MILL LA

2

Penhouse Farm

Raymonds Farm

NEW RD

PO

THE MEADOWS

LONG LANE

Gardens

Grove Farm

Primrose Farm

BADGERS CL

Sandways Farm

BREACH

MILLERS CL

SP8

CHAFFEYMOOR HILL

Voscombe Farm

St George's School

PH 3

4

BRICKYARD LANE

A303

1

Chaffeymoor Farm

WOOLCOTT LA 1
CHURCH CL 2
OLD POUND CT 3
EAST ST 4

CHURCH LA

WEST BOURTON RD

Marvins Farm

Feltham Farm

30

A303

75 | A | B | 76 | C | D | 77 | E | F

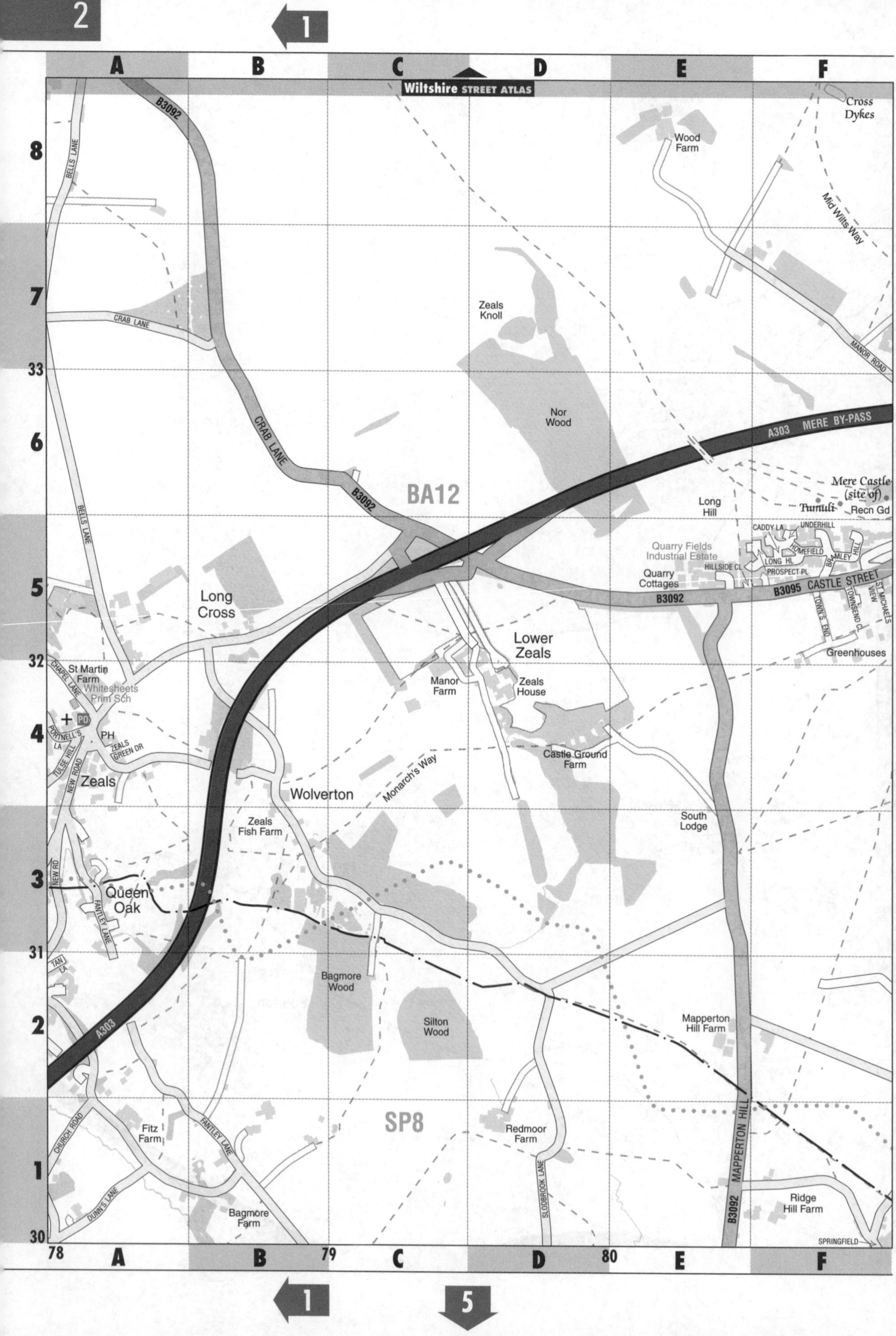

1

A B C D E F

8

7

33

6

5

32

4

3

31

2

1

30

78 79 80

A B C D E F

1

5

B3092

BELLS LANE

CRAB LANE

CRAB LANE

B3092

BA12

Cross Dykes

Wood Farm

Mid Wilts Way

Zeals Knoll

MANOR ROAD

Nor Wood

A303 MERE BY-PASS

Mere Castle (site of)

Tumuli

Recn Gd

Long Hill

CADDY LA

UNDERHILL

HOMEFIELD

LONG HL

BRAMLEY

THE

PROSPECT PL

HILLSIDE CL

Quarry Fields Industrial Estate

Quarry Cottages

B3092

B3095 CASTLE STREET

TOWNS END

TOWNSEND CL

VIEW

ST MICHAELS

Greenhouses

Long Cross

BELLS LANE

Lower Zeals

St Martin Farm

Whitesheets Prim Sch

CHAPEL LANE

PO

PH

PO YNELL'S LA

ZEALS GREEN DR

TULSE HILL

Zeals

NEW ROAD

Manor Farm

Zeals House

Castle Ground Farm

Monarch's Way

Wolverton

Zeals Fish Farm

South Lodge

NEW RD

FANTLEY LANE

Queen Oak

TAN LA

Bagmore Wood

Silton Wood

Mapperton Hill Farm

MAPPERTON HILL

A303

CHURCH ROAD

FANTLEY LANE

SP8

Fitz Farm

Redmoor Farm

SLOObrOOK LANE

DUNN'S LANE

Bagmore Farm

B3092

Ridge Hill Farm

SPRINGFIELD

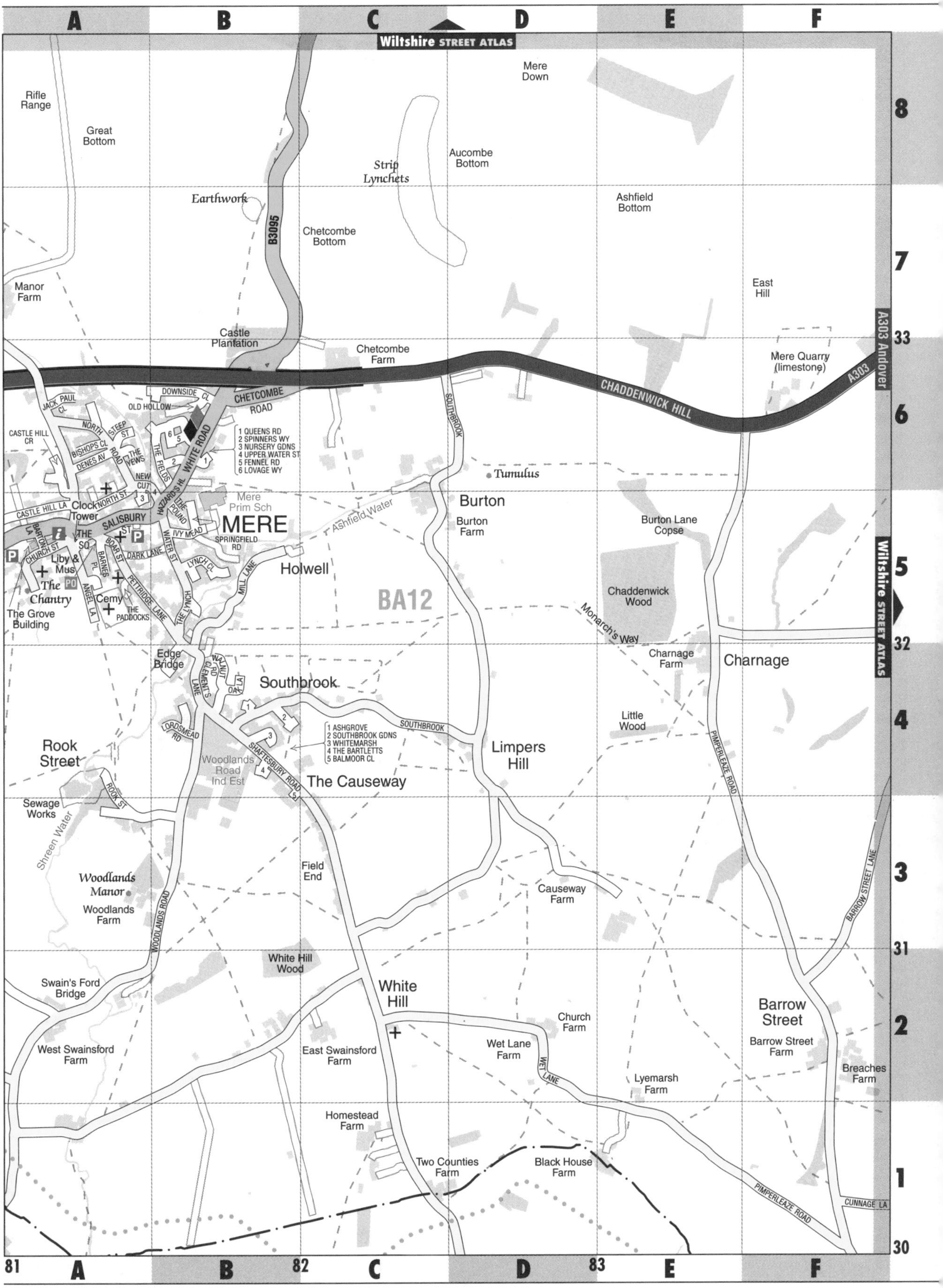

Mere
Down

Strip
Lynchets

Aucombe
Bottom

Ashfield
Bottom

Rifle
Range

Great
Bottom

Earthwork

Chetcombe
Bottom

East
Hill

Mere Quarry
(limestone)

Manor
Farm

Castle
Plantation

Chetcombe
Farm

CHADDENWICK HILL

A303 Andover

33

B3095

DOWNSIDE CL
OLD HOLLOW
CHETCOMBE
ROAD

JACK PAUL
CL

CASTLE HILL
CR

NORTH
STEEP
ST
BISHOPS CL
DENES AV
THE YEWS
THE FIELDS

WHITE ROAD

1 QUEENS RD
2 SPINNERS WY
3 NURSERY GDNS
4 UPPER WATER ST
5 FENNEL RD
6 LOVAGE WY

SOUTHBROOK

6

Tumulus

Burton Lane
Copse

NEW
CUT

NORTH ST
CLOCK
Tower

SALISBURY
ST

Mere
Prim Sch

Burton

Chaddenwick
Wood

5

CASTLE HILL LA

WATER ST
IVY MEAD
SPRINGFIELD
RD

Ashfield Water

Burton
Farm

Monarch's Way

Wiltshire STREET ATLAS

MERE

BARTON
CHURCH ST
THE
SQ

BOAR ST
BARNES
THE LYNCH
MILL LANE

LYNCH CL

DARK LANE

PETTRIDGE LANE

Holwell

BA12

Charnage
Farm

Charnage

Liby &
Mus
PO
The
Chantry
The Grove
Building

NIGEL LA
Cerny

THE
PADDOCKS

32

Little
Wood

Edge
Bridge

WALNUT RD
ST CLEMENTS
LANE
OAK

Southbrook

SOUTHBROOK

Limpers
Hill

PIMPERLEAZE ROAD

4

Rook
Street

CROSSMEAD
RD

SHAFTESBURY ROAD

Woodlands
Road
Ind Est

1 ASHGROVE
2 SOUTHBROOK GDNS
3 WHITEMARSH
4 THE BARTLETTS
5 BALMOOR CL

The Causeway

Causeway
Farm

31

Sewage
Works

Shreen Water

Woodlands
Manor

ROOK ST

WOODLANDS ROAD

Field
End

White Hill
Wood

BARROW STREET LANE

3

White
Hill

Church
Farm

Barrow
Street

2

Woodlands
Farm

Swain's Ford
Bridge

West Swainsford
Farm

East Swainsford
Farm

Wet Lane
Farm

WET LANE

Lyemarsh
Farm

Barrow Street
Farm

Breaches
Farm

Homestead
Farm

Two Counties
Farm

Black House
Farm

PIMPERLEAZE ROAD

CUNNAGE LA

1

30

1

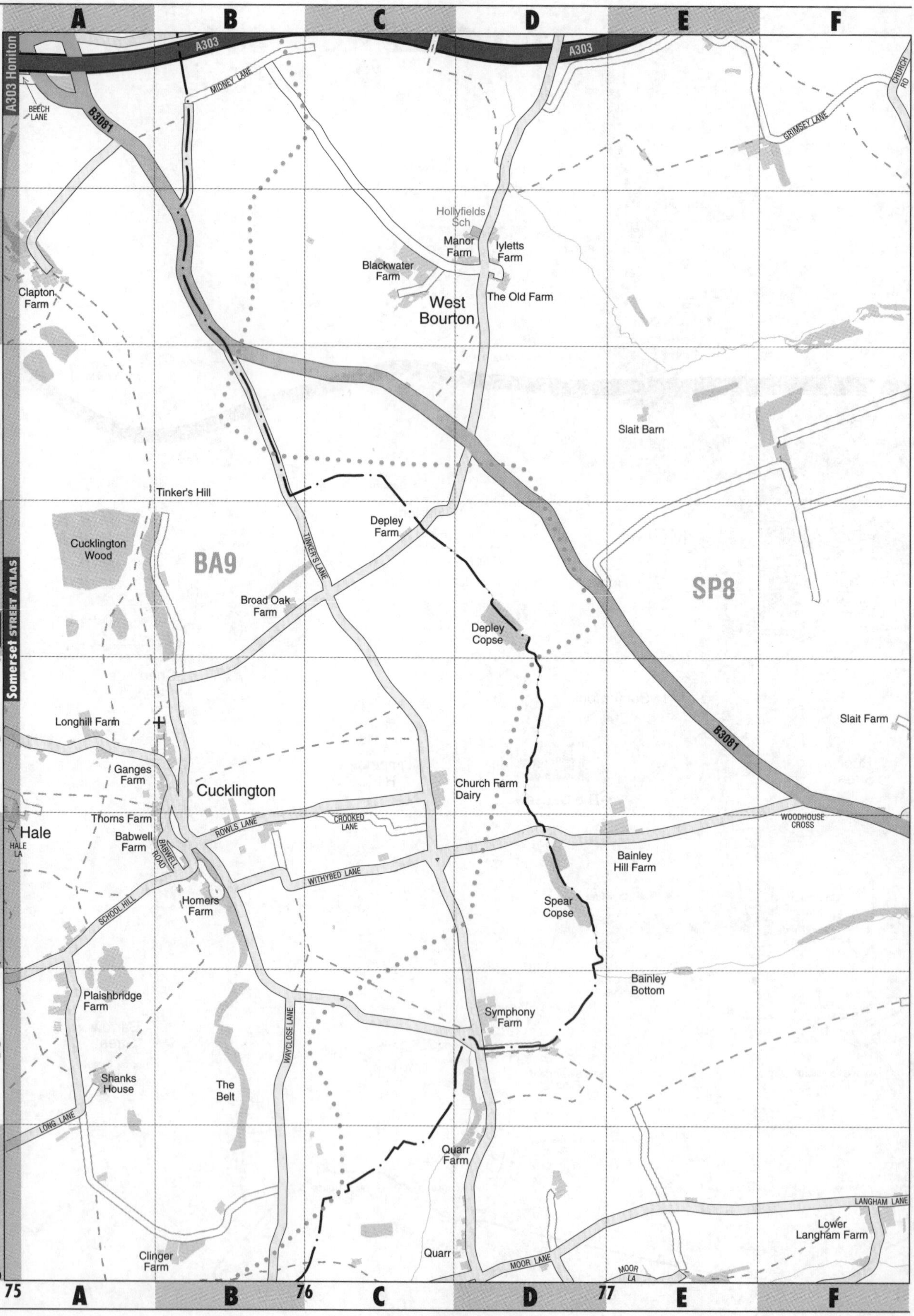
A
B
C
D
E
F
A303
A303
A303 Honiton
BEECH LANE
B3081
MIDNEY LANE
GRIMSEY LANE
CHURCH RD
8
7
29
6
5
28
4
3
27
2
1
26
Hollyfields Sch
Manor Farm
Iyletts Farm
Blackwater Farm
West Bourton
The Old Farm
Clapton Farm
Slait Barn
Tinker's Hill
Cucklington Wood
BA9
Depley Farm
TINKER'S LANE
SP8
Broad Oak Farm
Depley Copse
Somerset STREET ATLAS
Longhill Farm
Slait Farm
B3081
Ganges Farm
Cucklington
Church Farm Dairy
Thorns Farm
Hale
HALE LA
Babwell Farm
BABWELL ROAD
ROWLS LANE
CROOKED LANE
WOODHOUSE CROSS
Bainley Hill Farm
WITHYBED LANE
SCHOOL HILL
Homers Farm
Spear Copse
Bainley Bottom
Plaishbridge Farm
Symphony Farm
WAYCLOSE LANE
Shanks House
The Belt
LONG LANE
Quarr Farm
LANGHAM LANE
Lower Langham Farm
Clinger Farm
Quarr
MOOR LANE
MOOR LA
75
76
77
A
B
C
D
E
F

9

2
6

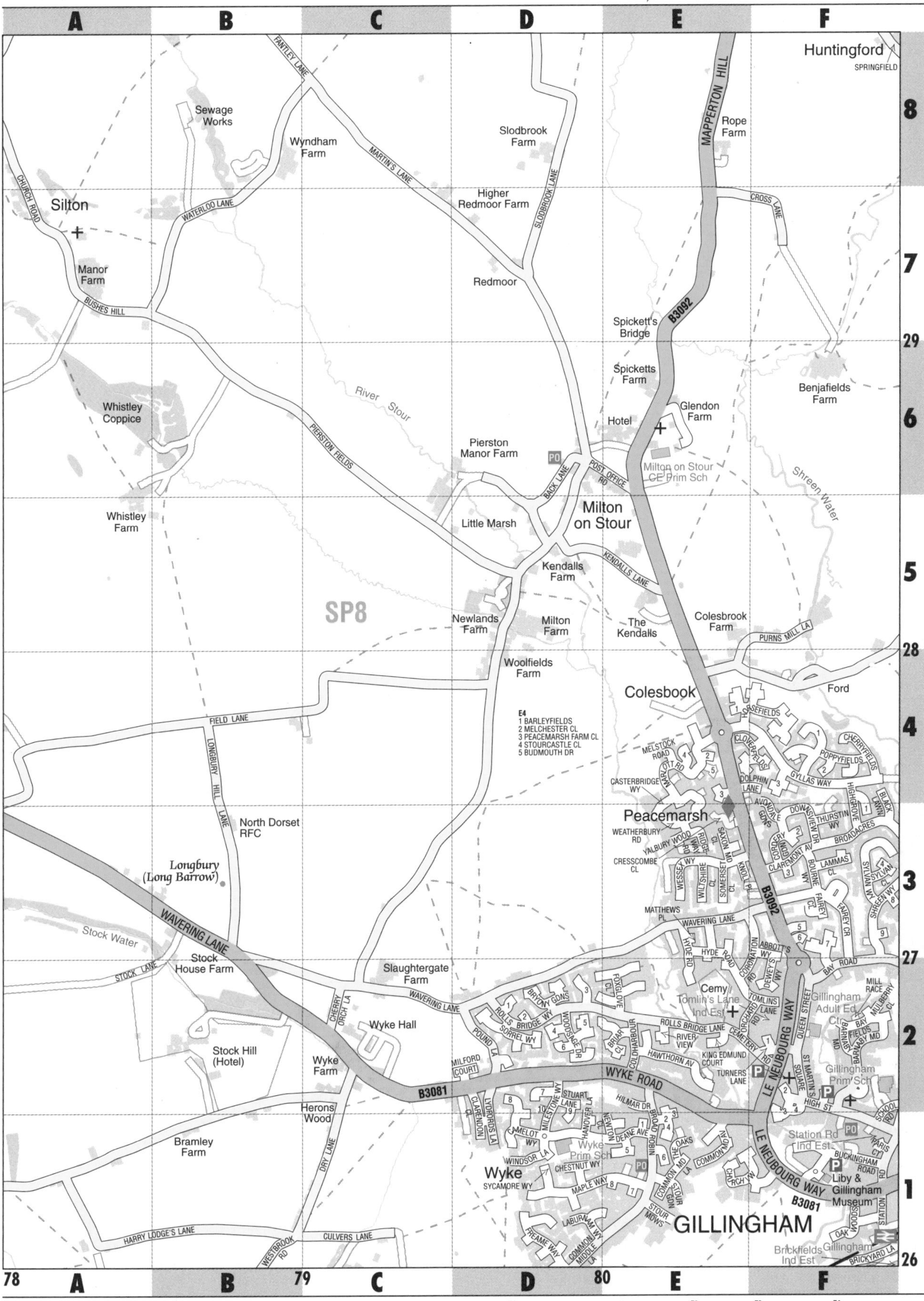

D2
1 YARROW CT
2 BUTTERCUP CL
3 PRIMROSE CL
4 IVY CL
5 CAMPION CL
6 PIMPERNEL CT
7 ORCHARD MEWS
8 PLANTAGENET WY
9 REGENCY CT
10 TUDOR CT

10

E1
1 JESOP CL
2 EDITH CT
3 SYDNEY PL
4 SUTTON CL
5 DAVENANT CL
6 IRIS GDNS
7 JUNIPER GDNS
8 THE LAURELS

6

F2
1 CYPRESS WY
2 CEMETERY RD
3 SOUTH ST
4 THE SQUARE

F3
1 FAIRY BRIDGE WLK
2 ARUN CL
3 ROSEBERRY GDNS
4 SYLVAN CL
5 LODBOURNE TERR
6 LODBOURNE GDNS
7 LODBOURNE GREEN
8 BROOKSIDE
9 SHREEN CL

F4
1 SWALLOWFIELDS
2 HEATHER FIELDS
3 HONEYFIELDS

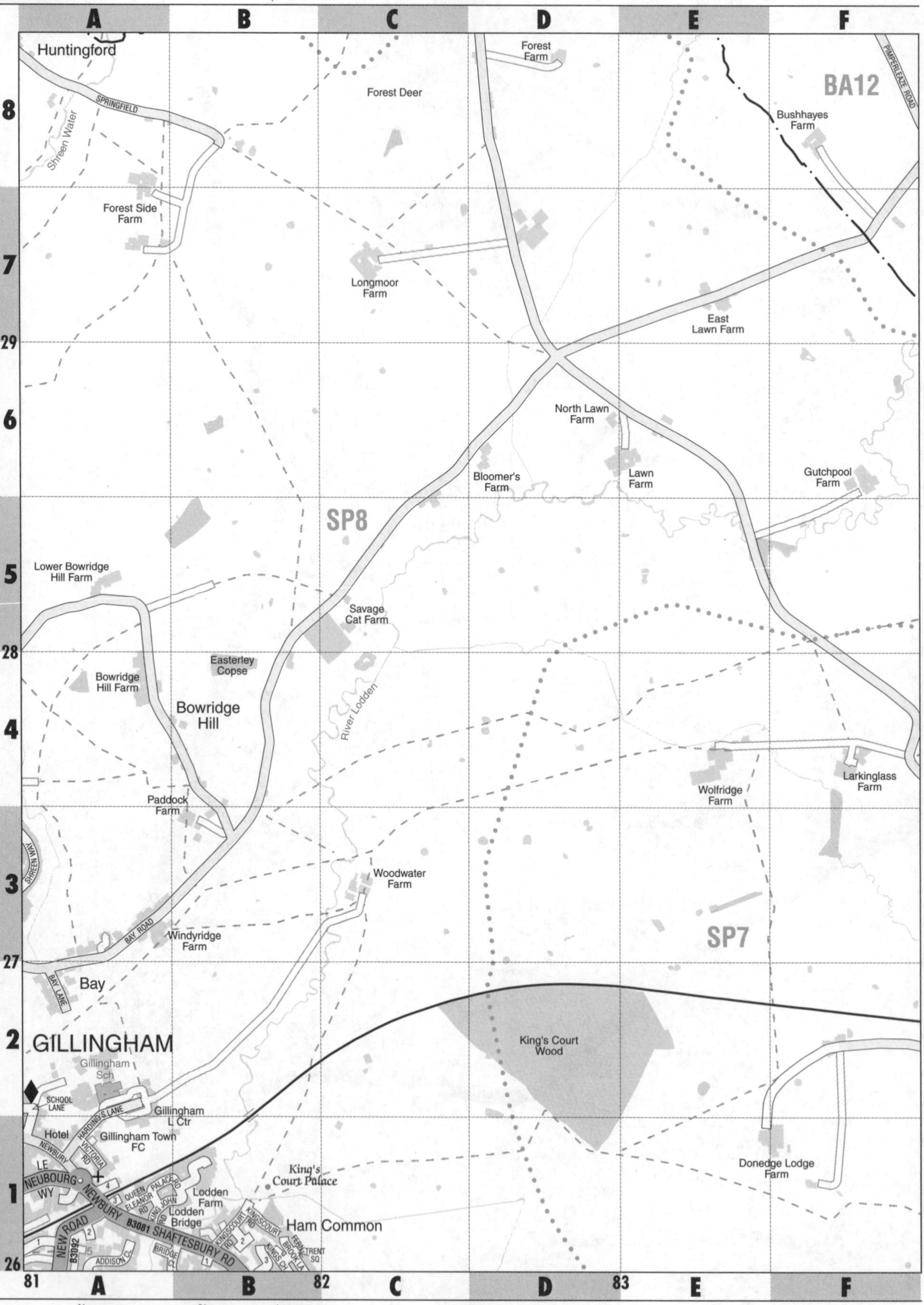

A B C D E F

Huntingford

SPRINGFIELD

Shreen Water

Forest Deer

Forest Farm

BA12

Bushhayes Farm

PIMPERLEAZE ROAD

8

Forest Side Farm

7

Longmoor Farm

East Lawn Farm

29

6

North Lawn Farm

Bloomer's Farm

Lawn Farm

Gutchpool Farm

SP8

Lower Bowridge Hill Farm

5

Savage Cat Farm

28

Easterley Copse

Bowridge Hill Farm

Bowridge Hill

River Lodden

4

Wolfridge Farm

Larkinglass Farm

Paddock Farm

3

Woodwater Farm

SP7

BAY ROAD

Windyridge Farm

27

BAY LANE

SHREEN WAY

Bay

2 GILLINGHAM

Gillingham Sch

SCHOOL LANE

HARDING'S LANE

King's Court Wood

Gillingham L Ctr

Hotel

NEWBURY

Gillingham Town FC

VICTORIA

QUEEN ELEANOR RD

PALACE

KING JOHN

King's Court Palace

Donedge Lodge Farm

1

LE NEUBOURG WY

NEWBURY

NEW ROAD

B3092

ADDISON CL

BRIDGE

B3081 SHAFTESBURY RD

Lodden Farm

Lodden Bridge

KINGSCOURT

FERN LANE

TRENT SQ

Ham Common

26

81 A 82 B C 83 D E F

A1
1 BRICKYARD LA
2 PROSPECT CL
3 ROSE CT
4 RAILWAY TERR
5 Brickfields Ind Est

B1
1 HAM LA
2 KINGSCOURT CL
3 ROOKERY CL

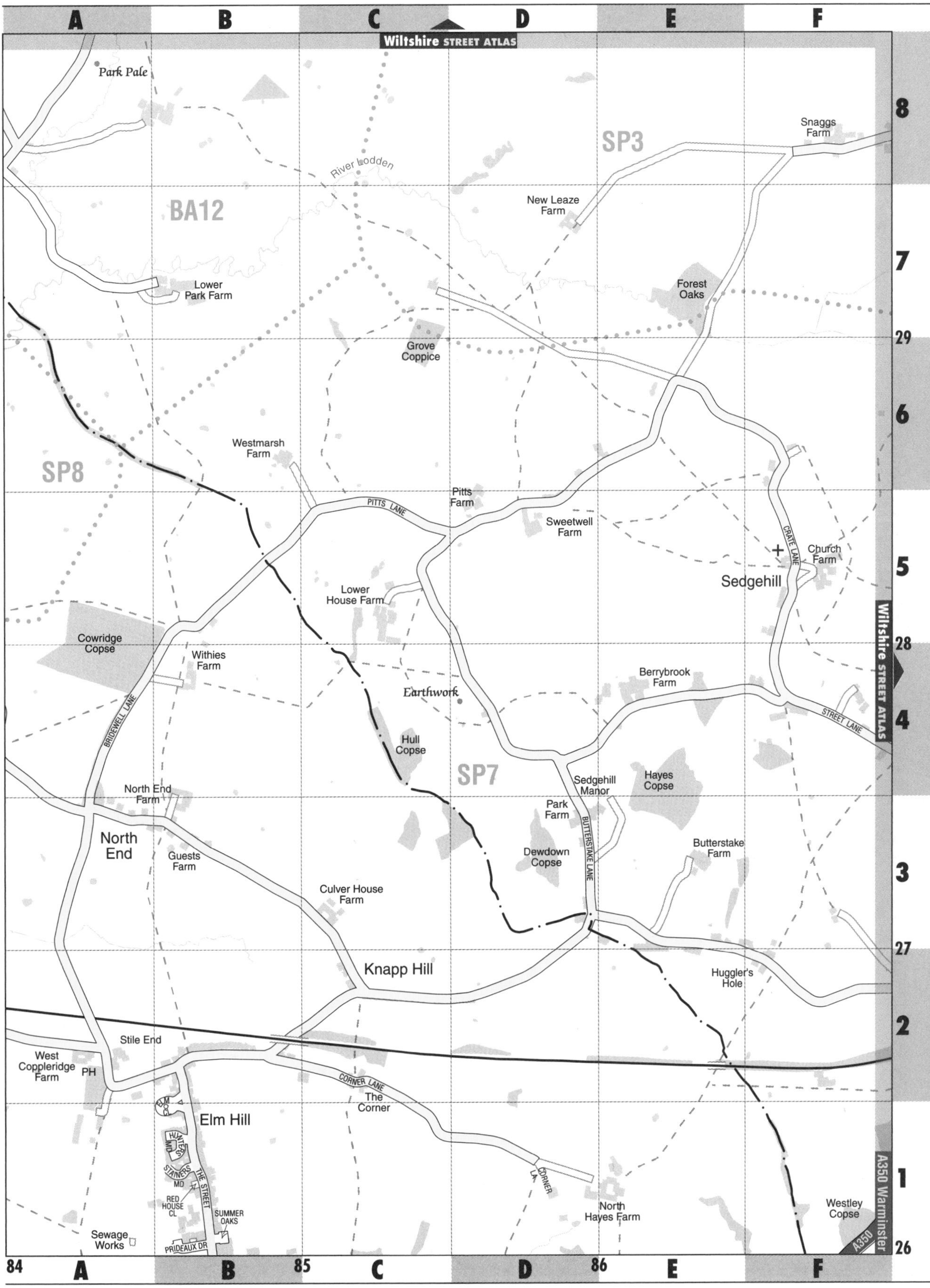
A
B
C
D
E
F
Wiltshire STREET ATLAS
Park Pale
8
Snaggs Farm
SP3
River Lodden
New Leaze Farm
BA12
7
Lower Park Farm
Forest Oaks
Grove Coppice
29
6
Westmarsh Farm
SP8
Pitts Farm
PITTS LANE
Sweetwell Farm
CRATE LANE
Church Farm
5
Sedgehill
Lower House Farm
Cowridge Copse
Withies Farm
28
Berrybrook Farm
Wiltshire STREET ATLAS
Earthwork
BRIDEWELL LANE
STREET LANE
4
Hull Copse
SP7
Sedgehill Manor
Hayes Copse
North End Farm
Park Farm
North End
BUTTERSTAKE LANE
Butterstake Farm
Guests Farm
Dewdown Copse
3
Culver House Farm
27
Knapp Hill
Huggler's Hole
2
Stile End
West Coppleridge Farm
PH
CORNER LANE
The Corner
Elm Hill
ELM CL
HUNTERS MD
STAINERS MD
THE STREET
RED HOUSE CL
SUMMER OAKS
CORNER LA
1
North Hayes Farm
Westley Copse
A350 Warminster
A350
Sewage Works
PRIDEAUX DR
26
84
85
86

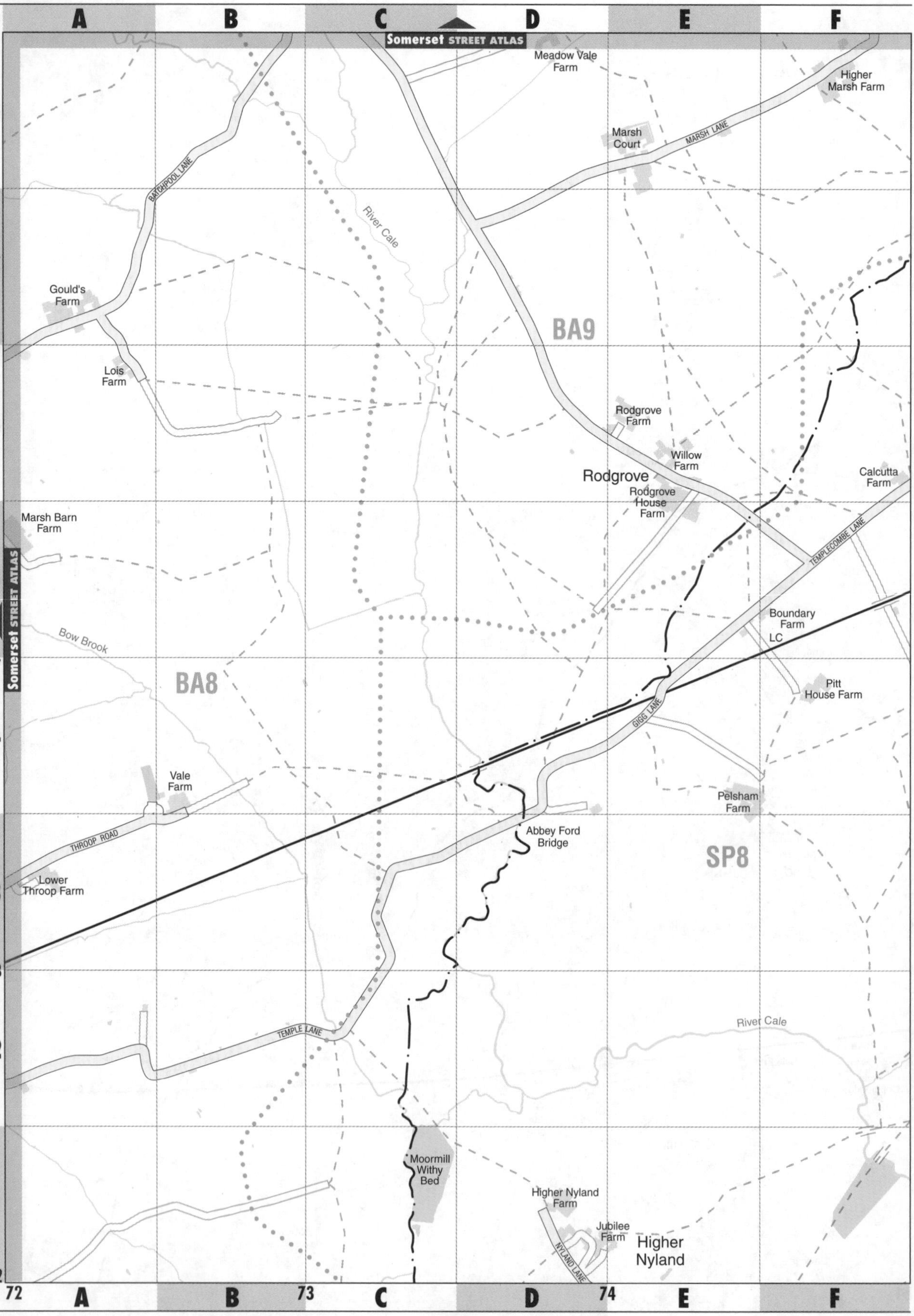

Somerset STREET ATLAS

A B C D E F

8

7

25

6

5

24

4

23

3

2

1

22

72 A B 73 C D 74 E F

Somerset STREET ATLAS

BA9

BA8

SP8

Gould's Farm

Lois Farm

Marsh Barn Farm

Bow Brook

Vale Farm

THROOP ROAD

Lower Throop Farm

TEMPLE LANE

BATCHPOOL LANE

River Cale

Meadow Vale Farm

Marsh Court

MARSH LANE

Higher Marsh Farm

Rodgrove Farm

Willow Farm

Rodgrove

Rodgrove House Farm

Calcutta Farm

TEMPLECOMBE LANE

Boundary Farm
LC

Pitt House Farm

GIGG LANE

Abbey Ford Bridge

Pelsham Farm

Moormill Withy Bed

Higher Nyland Farm

Jubilee Farm

Higher Nyland

NYLAND LANE

River Cale

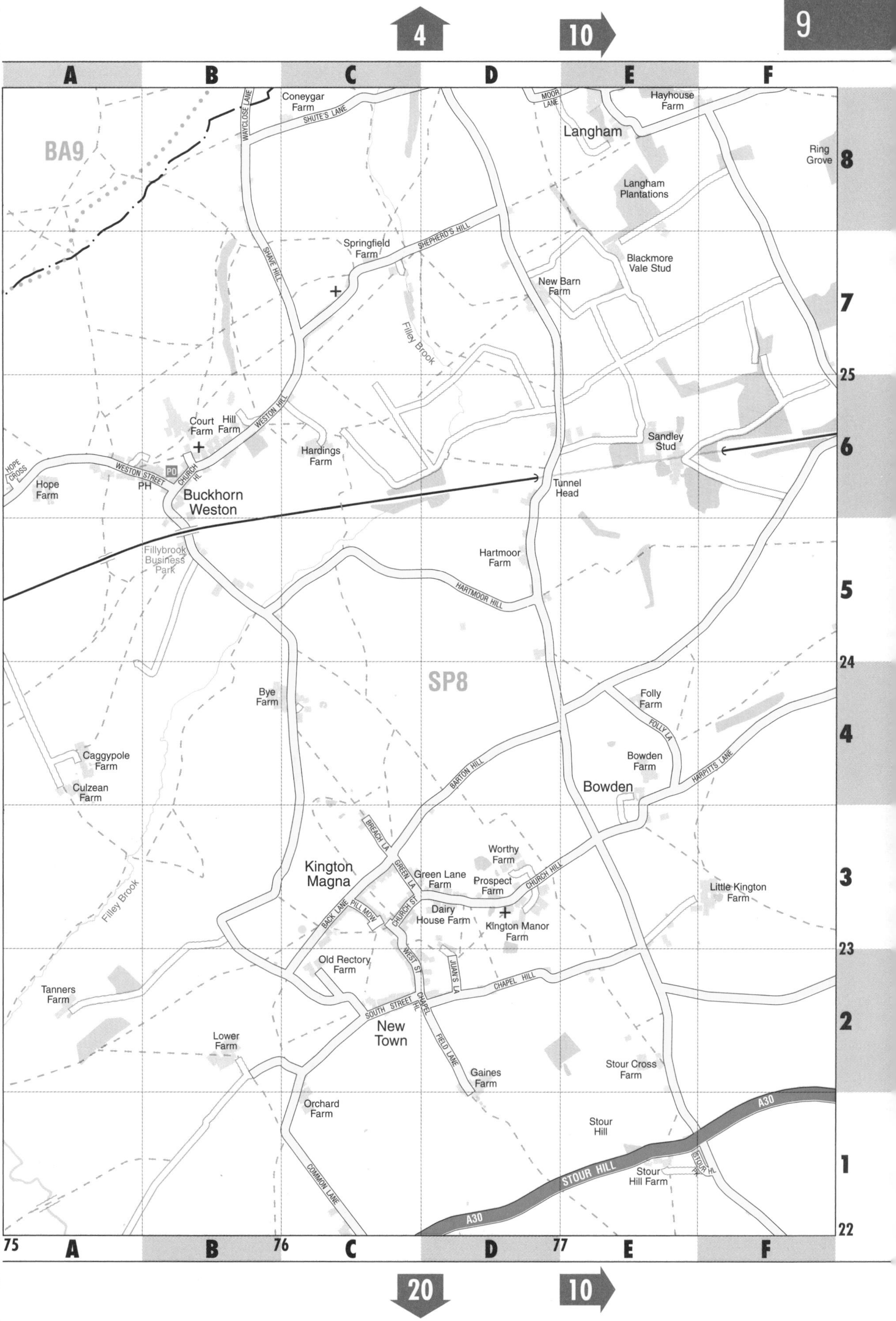
4
10
A
B
C
D
E
F
BA9
Coneygar Farm
SHUTE'S LANE
WAYCLOSE LANE
MOOR LANE
Hayhouse Farm
Langham
Ring Grove
8
Langham Plantations
Springfield Farm
SHEPHERD'S HILL
SHAVE HILL
Blackmore Vale Stud
New Barn Farm
7
Filley Brook
25
Court Farm
Hill Farm
WESTON HILL
Hardings Farm
Sandley Stud
6
HOPE CROSS
Hope Farm
WESTON STREET
PO
CHURCH HL
PH
Buckhorn Weston
Tunnel Head
Fillybrook Business Park
Hartmoor Farm
HARTMOOR HILL
5
24
SP8
Bye Farm
Folly Farm
FOLLY LA
Caggypole Farm
Culzean Farm
Bowden Farm
4
BARTON HILL
Bowden
HARPITTS LANE
BREACH LA
Worthy Farm
Kington Magna
GREEN LA
Green Lane Farm
Prospect Farm
CHURCH HILL
Little Kington Farm
3
Filley Brook
BACK LANE
PILL MDW
CHURCH ST
Dairy House Farm
Kington Manor Farm
23
Old Rectory Farm
WEST ST
JUAN'S LA
CHAPEL HILL
Tanners Farm
SOUTH STREET
CHAPEL HL
2
New Town
Lower Farm
FIELD LANE
Gaines Farm
Stour Cross Farm
Orchard Farm
A30
Stour Hill
1
COMMON LANE
STOUR HILL
Stour Hill Farm
STOUR HL
A30
22
75
76
77
20
10

9
5

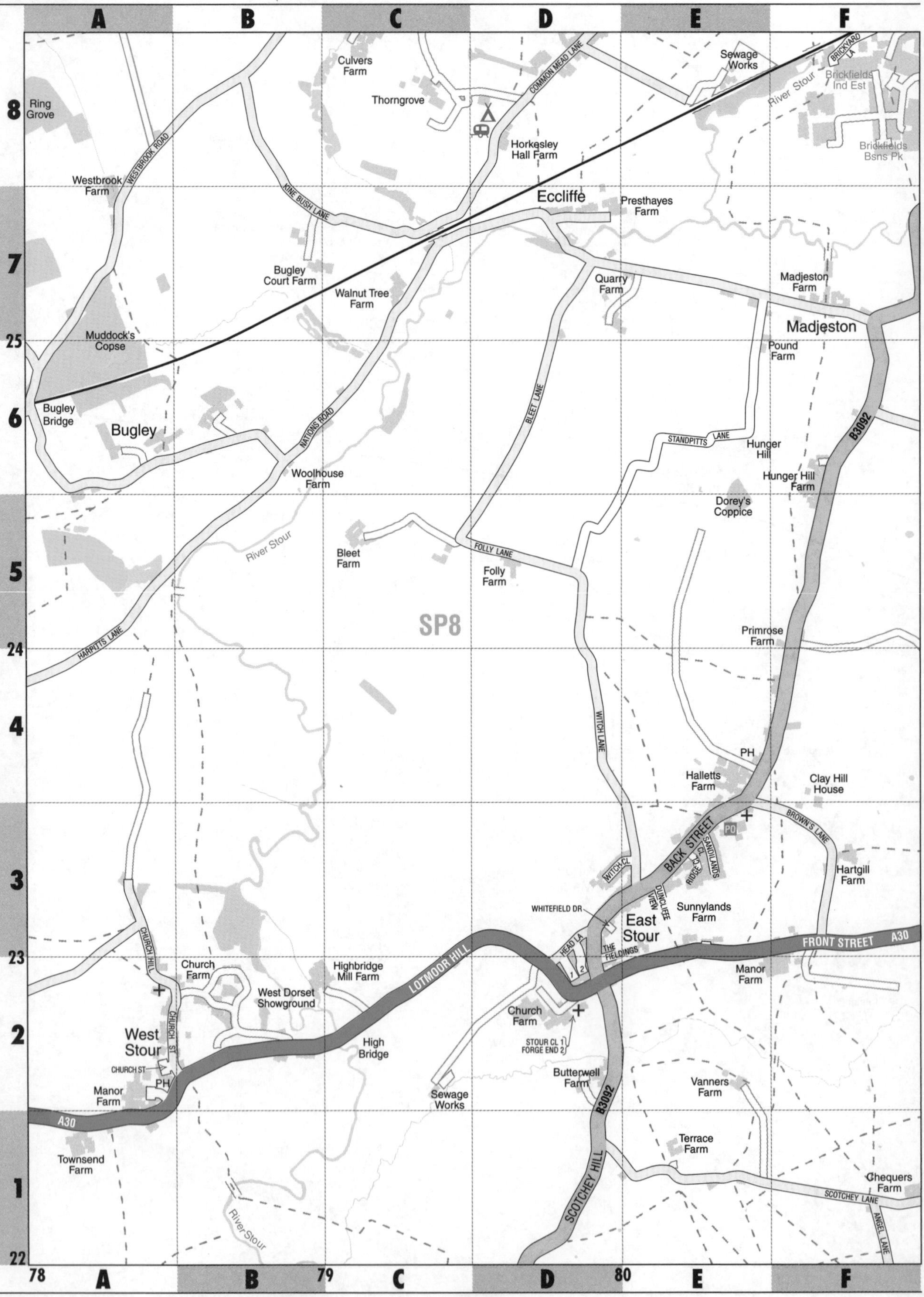
A
B
C
D
E
F
Culvers Farm
Thorngrove
Sewage Works
River Stour
Brickfields Ind Est
BRICKYARD LA
Brickfields Bsns Pk
COMMON MEAD LANE
Ring Grove
WESTBROOK ROAD
Horkesley Hall Farm
Westbrook Farm
KINE BUSH LANE
Eccliffe
Presthayes Farm
Bugley Court Farm
Walnut Tree Farm
Quarry Farm
Madjeston Farm
Madjeston
Muddock's Copse
Pound Farm
Bugley Bridge
Bugley
NATIONS ROAD
BLEET LANE
STANDPITTS LANE
Hunger Hill
Hunger Hill Farm
B3092
Woolhouse Farm
Dorey's Coppice
River Stour
Bleet Farm
FOLLY LANE
Folly Farm
SP8
HARPITTS LANE
Primrose Farm
WITCH LANE
PH
Halletts Farm
Clay Hill House
PO
BROWN'S LANE
BACK STREET
SANDILANDS
RIDGE CL
WITCH CL
Hartgill Farm
WHITEFIELD DR
DUNCLIFFE VIEW
Sunnylands Farm
East Stour
FRONT STREET
A30
HEAD LA
THE FIELDINGS
CHURCH HILL
Church Farm
Highbridge Mill Farm
LOTMOOR HILL
Manor Farm
West Dorset Showground
Church Farm
West Stour
CHURCH ST
High Bridge
STOUR CL 1
FORGE END 2
CHURCH ST
PH
Sewage Works
Butterwell Farm
Vanners Farm
Manor Farm
A30
B3092
Townsend Farm
Terrace Farm
SCOTCHEY HILL
Chequers Farm
SCOTCHEY LANE
ANGEL LANE
River Stour
8
7
25
6
5
24
4
3
23
2
1
22
78
79
80

9
21

6
12

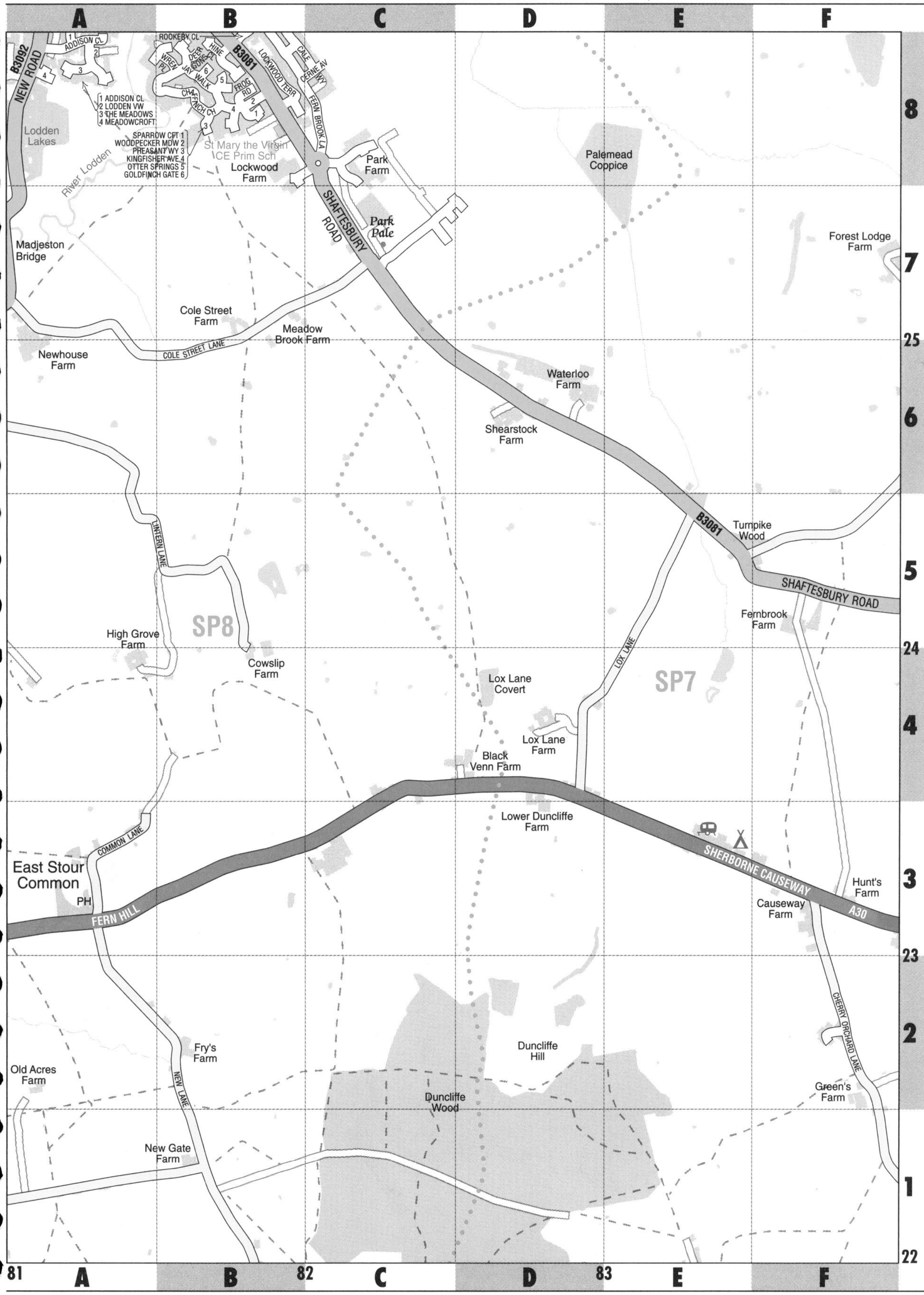
A
B
C
D
E
F
B3092
NEW ROAD
ADDISON CL
ROOKERY CL
HINE
DEER
WREN PL
JAY WALK
FROG RD
CHAFFINCH CH
B3081
LOCKWOOD TERR
CALE WY
CERNE AV
FERN BROOK LA
1 ADDISON CL
2 LODDEN VW
3 THE MEADOWS
4 MEADOWCROFT
SPARROW CFT 1
WOODPECKER MDW 2
PHEASANT WY 3
KINGFISHER AVE 4
OTTER SPRINGS 5
GOLDFINCH GATE 6
Lodden Lakes
St Mary the Virgin CE Prim Sch
Lockwood Farm
Park Farm
Palemead Coppice
River Lodden
Madjeston Bridge
SHAFTESBURY ROAD
Park Pale
Forest Lodge Farm
Cole Street Farm
Meadow Brook Farm
COLE STREET LANE
Newhouse Farm
Waterloo Farm
Shearstock Farm
B3081
Turnpike Wood
LINTERN LANE
SHAFTESBURY ROAD
SP8
Fernbrook Farm
High Grove Farm
Cowslip Farm
LOX LANE
Lox Lane Covert
SP7
Lox Lane Farm
Black Venn Farm
Lower Duncliffe Farm
COMMON LANE
East Stour Common
SHERBORNE CAUSEWAY
PH
Hunt's Farm
Causeway Farm
FERN HILL
A30
CHERRY ORCHARD LANE
Fry's Farm
Duncliffe Hill
Old Acres Farm
NEW LANE
Duncliffe Wood
Green's Farm
New Gate Farm
8
7
25
6
5
24
4
3
23
2
1
22
81
82
83

22
12

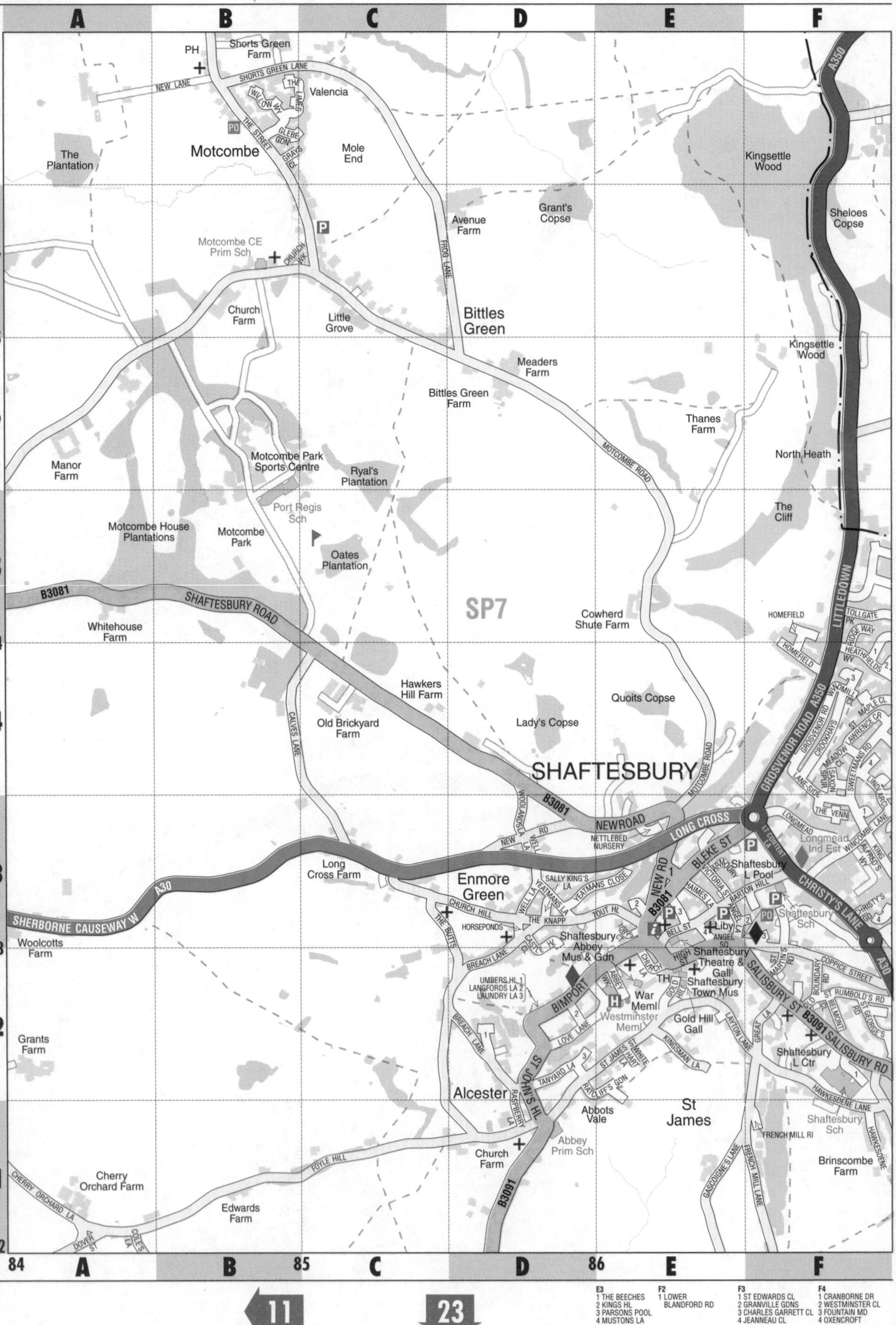

A B C D E F

8
7
25
6
5
24
4
3
23
2
1
22

The Plantation

PH
Shorts Green Farm
Shorts Green Lane
New Lane
WL OW WY
THE LIMES
Valencia
Motcombe
PO
GLEBE GDN
GRAYS CL
THE STREET
CHURCH WY
Motcombe CE Prim Sch
P
Mole End

Avenue Farm
Grant's Copse
FROG LANE
Kingsettle Wood
A350
Sheloes Copse

Church Farm
Little Grove
Bittles Green
Meaders Farm
Kingsettle Wood

Bittles Green Farm
Thanes Farm
North Heath

Manor Farm
Motcombe Park Sports Centre
Ryal's Plantation
MOTCOMBE ROAD
The Cliff

Motcombe House Plantations
Motcombe Park
Port Regis Sch
Oates Plantation
SP7
Cowherd Shute Farm
HOMEFIELD
TOLLGATE
LITTLEDOWN
PK WAY
WYNDHAM
HEATHFIELDS WY
HOMEFIELD

B3081
SHAFTESBURY ROAD
Whitehouse Farm
GROSVENOR RD A350
CROOKHAYS
MAPLE CL
LAWRENCE CR

CALVES LANE
Hawkers Hill Farm
Old Brickyard Farm
Lady's Copse
Quoits Copse
MOTCOMBE ROAD
WYNFORD
MEADOW VIEW
ANSTY CL
SWEETMANS RD
LINZ RD

SHAFTESBURY
B3081
NEW ROAD
WOOLANDS LA
WELL LA
NETTLEBED NURSERY
LONG CROSS
GROSVENOR ROAD A350
STEPHENS
LONGMEAD
WINCOMBE LANE
THE VENN
KING'S

A30
Long Cross Farm
Enmore Green
CHURCH HILL
SALLY KING'S LA
YEATMANS LA
YEATMANS CLOSE
NEW RD
B3081
BLEKE ST
VICTORIA ST
BARTON HILL
HAIMES LA
P
Longmead Ind Est
CHRISTY'S LANE
A30

SHERBORNE CAUSEWAY W
THE BUTTS
THE KNAPP
TOUT HL
Shaftesbury L Pool
BELL ST
Shaftesbury Sch
Christy's

Woolcotts Farm
HORSEPONDS
Shaftesbury Abbey Mus & Gdn
HIGH ST
Shaftesbury Theatre & Gall
Shaftesbury Town Mus
PO
Shaftesbury Sch
COPPICE STREET

BREACH LANE
UMBERS HL 1
LANGFORDS LA 2
LAUNDRY LA 3
BIMPORT
CHURCH
TH
SALISBURY ST
RUMBOLD'S RD
ST GEORGE'S RD
BELMONT

Grants Farm
BREACH LANE
Love Lane
War Meml
H
Westminster Meml
Gold Hill Gall
ABBEY WK
GREAT
LAYTON LANE
B3097 SALISBURY RD
Shaftesbury L Ctr
HAWKESDENE LANE

ST JOHN'S HL
St James Sch
HANNESENE
Shaftesbury Sch

Alcester
TANYARD LA
ST JAMES ST
ST JAMES'S GDN
KINGSMAN LA
Abbots Vale
St James
FRENCH MILL RI

RASPBERRY LA
RATCLIFF'S GDN
Church Farm
Abbey Prim Sch
GASCOIGNES LANE
FRENCH MILL LANE
Brinscombe Farm

Cherry Orchard Farm
FOYLE HILL
B3091
CHERRY ORCHARD LA
DOVER ST
COLES LA
Edwards Farm

84 A 85 B C 86 D E F

E3
1 THE BEECHES
2 KINGS HL
3 PARSONS POOL
4 MUSTONS LA

F2
1 LOWER BLANDFORD RD

F3
1 ST EDWARDS CL
2 GRANVILLE GDNS
3 CHARLES GARRETT CL
4 JEANNEAU CL

F4
1 CRANBORNE DR
2 WESTMINSTER CL
3 FOUNTAIN MD
4 OXENCROFT

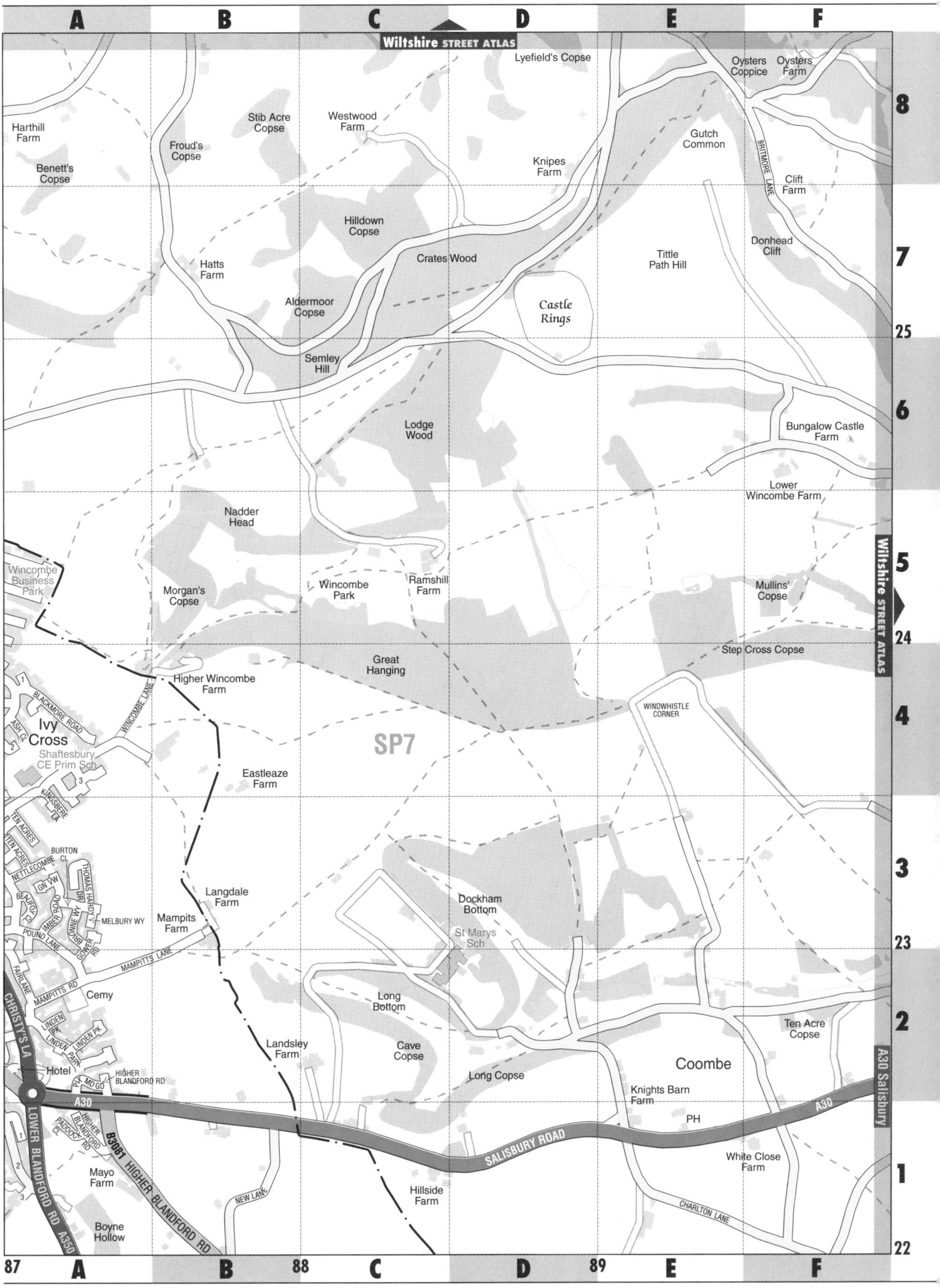

Lyefield's Copse

Oysters Coppice

Oysters Farm

Harthill Farm

Benett's Copse

Froud's Copse

Stib Acre Copse

Westwood Farm

Gutch Common

Knipes Farm

Clift Farm

Hilldown Copse

Crates Wood

Donhead Clift

Hatts Farm

Tittle Path Hill

Aldermoor Copse

Castle Rings

Semley Hill

Bungalow Castle Farm

Lodge Wood

Lower Wincombe Farm

Nadder Head

Morgan's Copse

Wincombe Park

Ramshill Farm

Mullins' Copse

Wincombe Business Park

Step Cross Copse

Great Hanging

Higher Wincombe Farm

WINDWHISTLE CORNER

Ivy Cross

Shaftesbury CE Prim Sch

SP7

Eastleaze Farm

BLACKMORE ROAD

BURTON CL

THOMAS HARDY DR

MELBURY WY

Langdale Farm

Dockham Bottom

NETTLECOMBE

Mampits Farm

St Marys Sch

MAMPITTS LANE

Cemy

Long Bottom

Landsley Farm

Cave Copse

Ten Acre Copse

CHRISTY'S LA

Hotel

HIGHER BLANDFORD RD

Coombe

Long Copse

Knights Barn Farm

A30

PH

A30

LOWER BLANDFORD RD

B3081 HIGHER BLANDFORD RD

NEW LANE

SALISBURY ROAD

White Close Farm

A30 Salisbury

Mayo Farm

Hillside Farm

CHARLTON LANE

Boyne Hollow

A B C D E F

8 7 25 6 5 24 4 3 23 2 1 22

87 A B 88 C D 89 E F

A1
1 BUTTS MD
2 LWR BLANDFORD RD
3 BRINSCOMBE LA

A4
1 HAWTHORN CL
2 SPRINGFIELD CL
3 GREAT GROUND

24

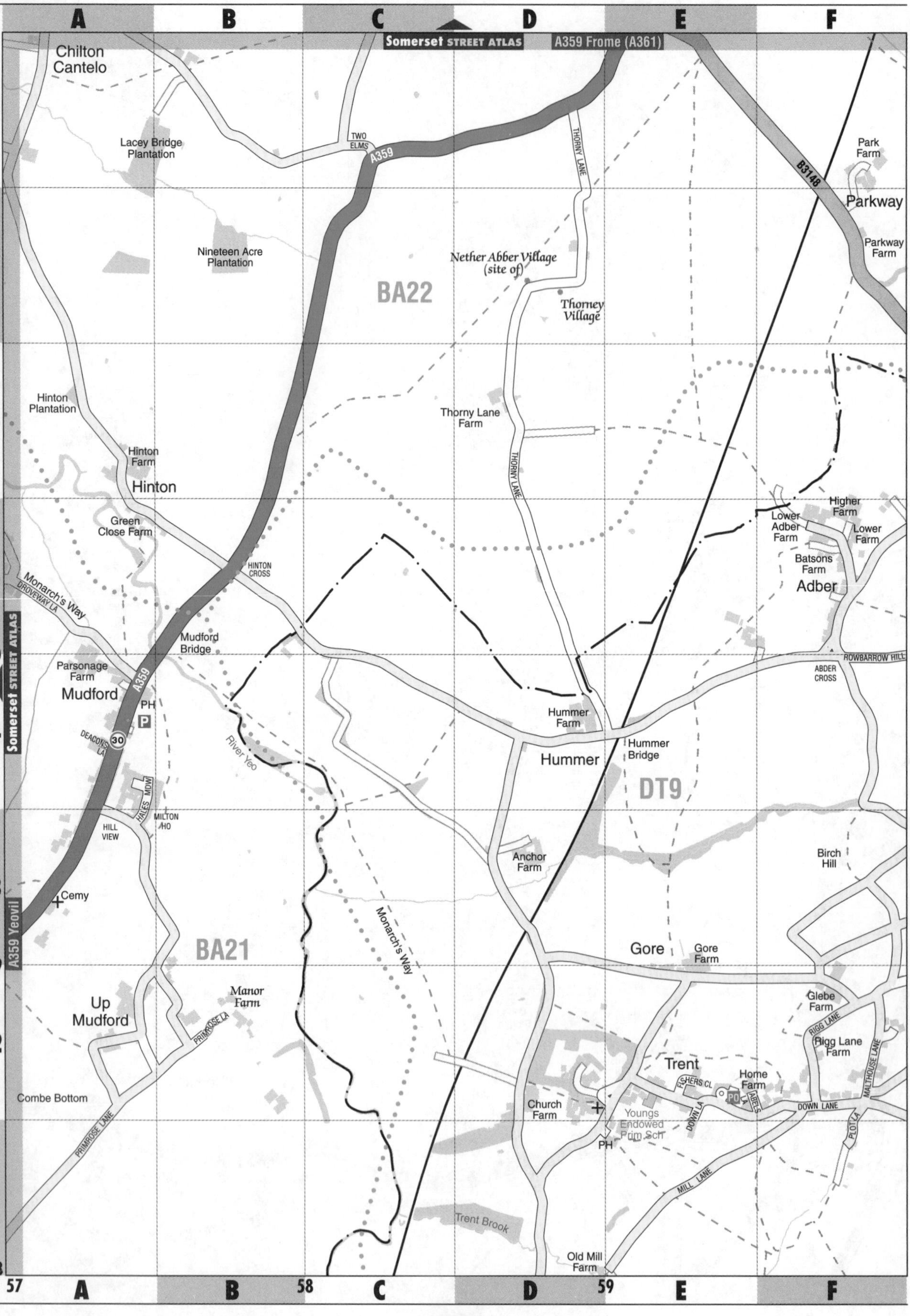

A359 Frome (A361)

Chilton Cantelo

Lacey Bridge Plantation

TWO ELMS

A359

B3148

Park Farm

Parkway

Parkway Farm

Nineteen Acre Plantation

BA22

Nether Abber Village (site of)

Thorney Village

THORNY LANE

Hinton Plantation

Thorny Lane Farm

Hinton Farm

Hinton

Green Close Farm

Higher Farm

Lower Adber Farm

Lower Farm

Batsons Farm

Adber

HINTON CROSS

ROWBARROW HILL

Monarch's Way

DRIVEWAY LA

Mudford Bridge

ABDER CROSS

ABDER CROSS

Parsonage Farm

A359

Mudford

PH

P

DEACONS LA

River Yeo

Hummer Farm

Hummer Bridge

Hummer

DT9

TALES MDW

MILTON HO

HILL VIEW

Anchor Farm

Birch Hill

Cemy

A359 Yeovil

BA21

Monarch's Way

Gore

Gore Farm

Glebe Farm

Up Mudford

Manor Farm

PRIMROSE LA

RIGG LANE

Rigg Lane Farm

MALTHOUSE LANE

Combe Bottom

PRIMROSE LANE

Trent

CHERS CL

Home Farm

PO

DOWN LANE

Church Farm

Youngs Endowed Prim Sch

DONYLL LA

TABEES

PLOT LA

PH

MILL LANE

Trent Brook

Old Mill Farm

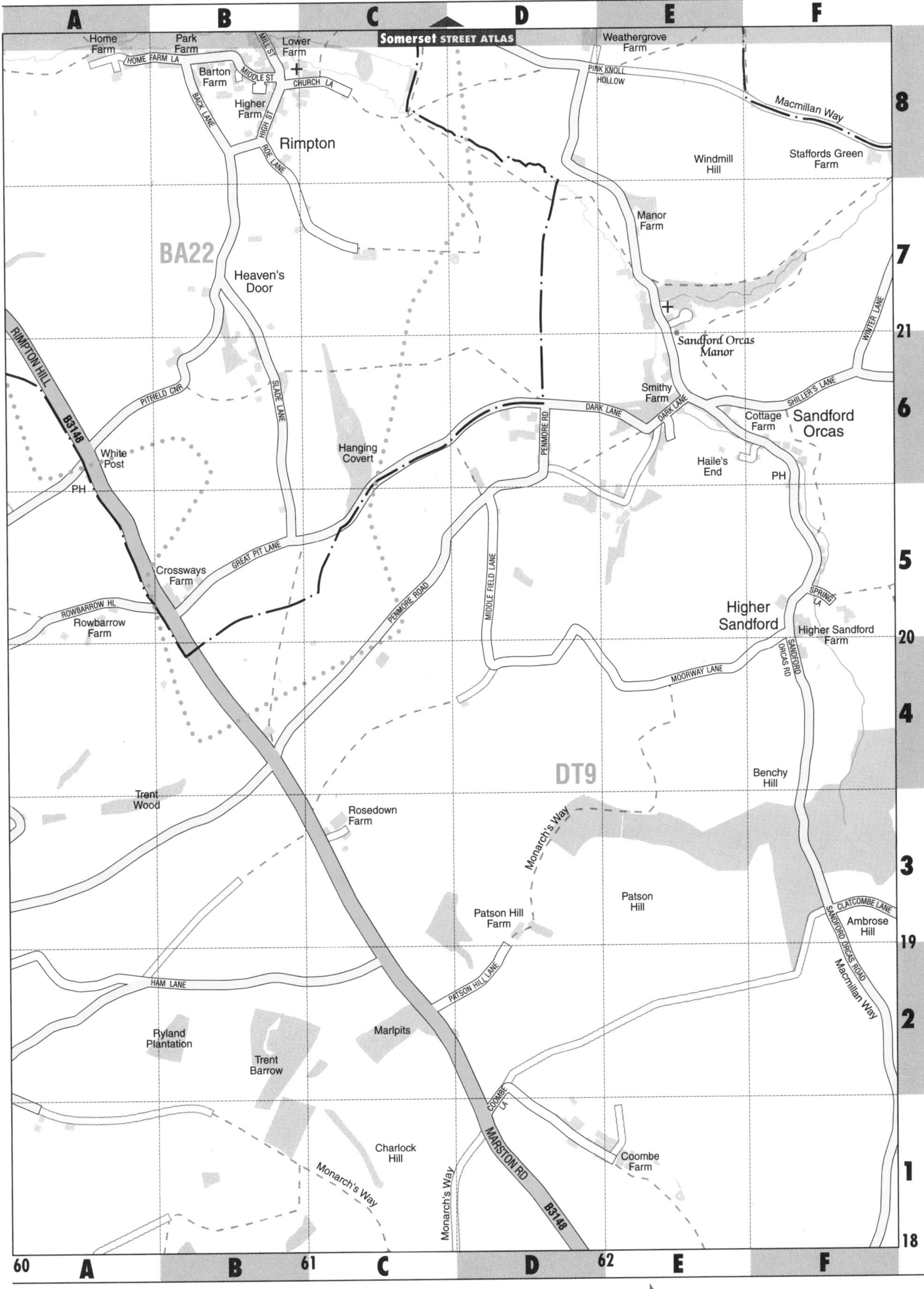

Home Farm
Park Farm
Lower Farm
Weathergrove Farm
PINK KNOLL HOLLOW
Macmillan Way
8

Barton Farm
MIDDLE ST
HOME FARM LA
BACK LANE
HIGH ST
MILL ST
CHURCH LA
ROE LANE
Higher Farm

Windmill Hill
Staffords Green Farm

Rimpton

BA22

Heaven's Door

Manor Farm

7

Sandford Orcas Manor
21

PITRELD CNR
SLADE LANE
Smithy Farm
DARK LANE
DARK LANE
Cottage Farm
SHILLER'S LANE
Sandford Orcas
WINTER LANE
6

White Post
RIMPTON HILL
B3148
PH
Hanging Covert
PENMORE RD
Haile's End
PH

Crossways Farm
GREAT PIT LANE
PENMORE ROAD
MIDDLE FIELD LANE
Higher Sandford
SPRING LA
Higher Sandford Farm
5

ROWBARROW HL
Rowbarrow Farm
MOORWAY LANE
SANDFORD ORCAS RD
20

DT9
Benchy Hill
4

Trent Wood
Rosedown Farm
Monarch's Way
Patson Hill
CLATCOMBE LANE
Ambrose Hill
3

Patson Hill Farm
SANDFORD ORCAS ROAD
Macmillan Way
19

HAM LANE
PATSON HILL LANE
2

Ryland Plantation
Marlpits
Trent Barrow
COOMBE LA
Coombe Farm
1

Charlock Hill
Monarch's Way
Monarch's Way
MARSTON RD
B3148
18

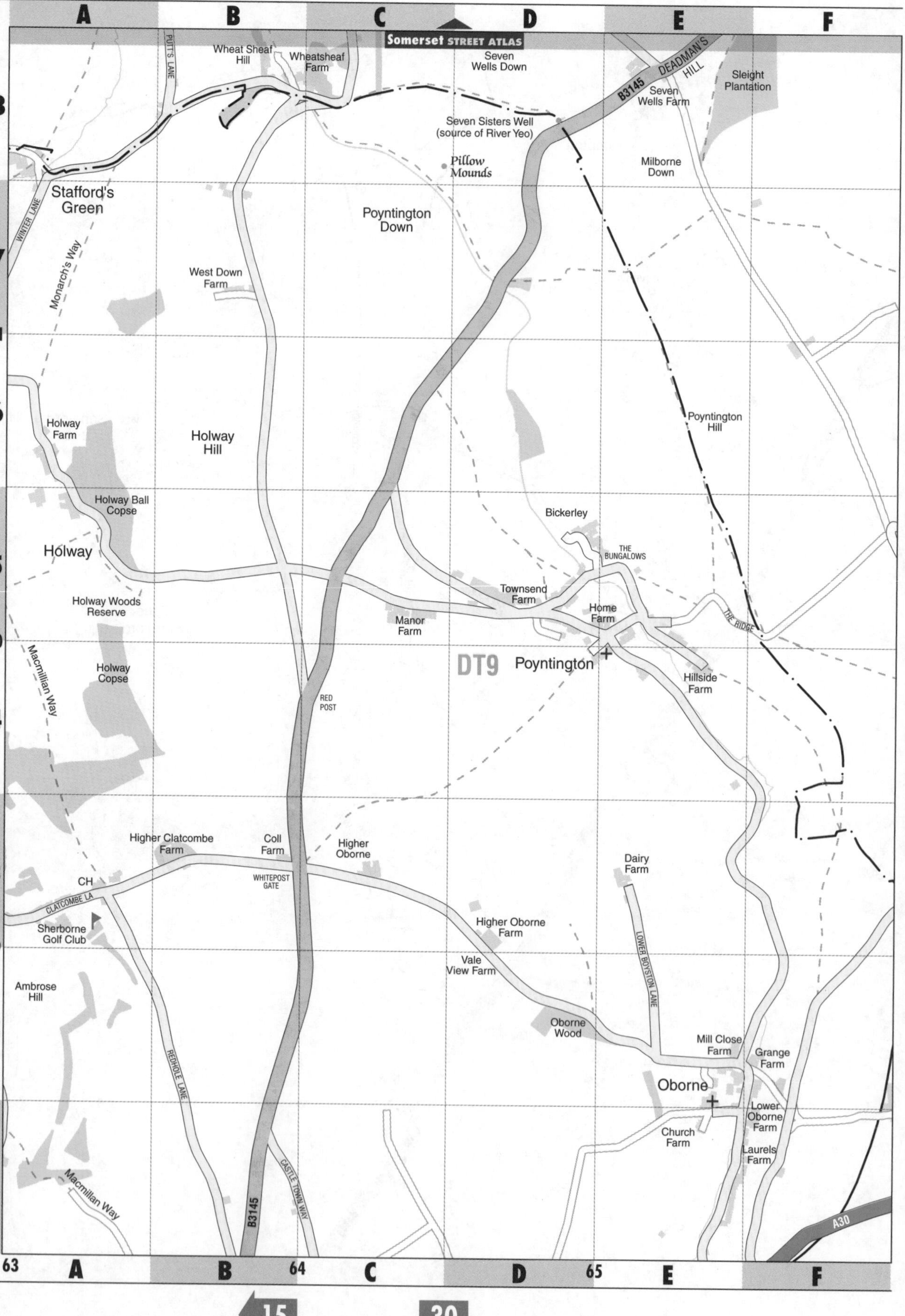

15

Somerset STREET ATLAS

A B C D E F

8

Wheat Sheaf Hill
Wheatsheaf Farm
Seven Wells Down
Sleight Plantation
B3145
DEADMAN'S HILL
Seven Wells Farm

Seven Sisters Well
(source of River Yeo)

Milborne Down

Stafford's Green

Pillow Mounds

Poyntington Down

7

West Down Farm

Monarch's Way
WINTER LANE
PUTT'S LANE

Poyntington Hill

21

6

Holway Farm

Holway Hill

Holway Ball Copse

Bickerley
THE BUNGALOWS

Holway

Townsend Farm

Home Farm

THE RIDGE

5

Holway Woods Reserve

Manor Farm

20

Holway Copse

Macmillan Way

RED POST

DT9 Poyntington

Hillside Farm

4

Higher Clatcombe Farm
Coll Farm
Higher Oborne

Dairy Farm

3

CH
CLATCOMBE LA
WHITEPOST GATE

Sherborne Golf Club

Higher Oborne Farm

LOWER BOYSTON LANE

19

Ambrose Hill

Vale View Farm

2

Oborne Wood

Mill Close Farm

Grange Farm

REDHOLE LANE

Oborne

Lower Oborne Farm

1

Macmillan Way

B3145
CASTLE TOWN WAY

Church Farm

Laurels Farm

A30

18

63 A B 64 C D 65 E F

15

30

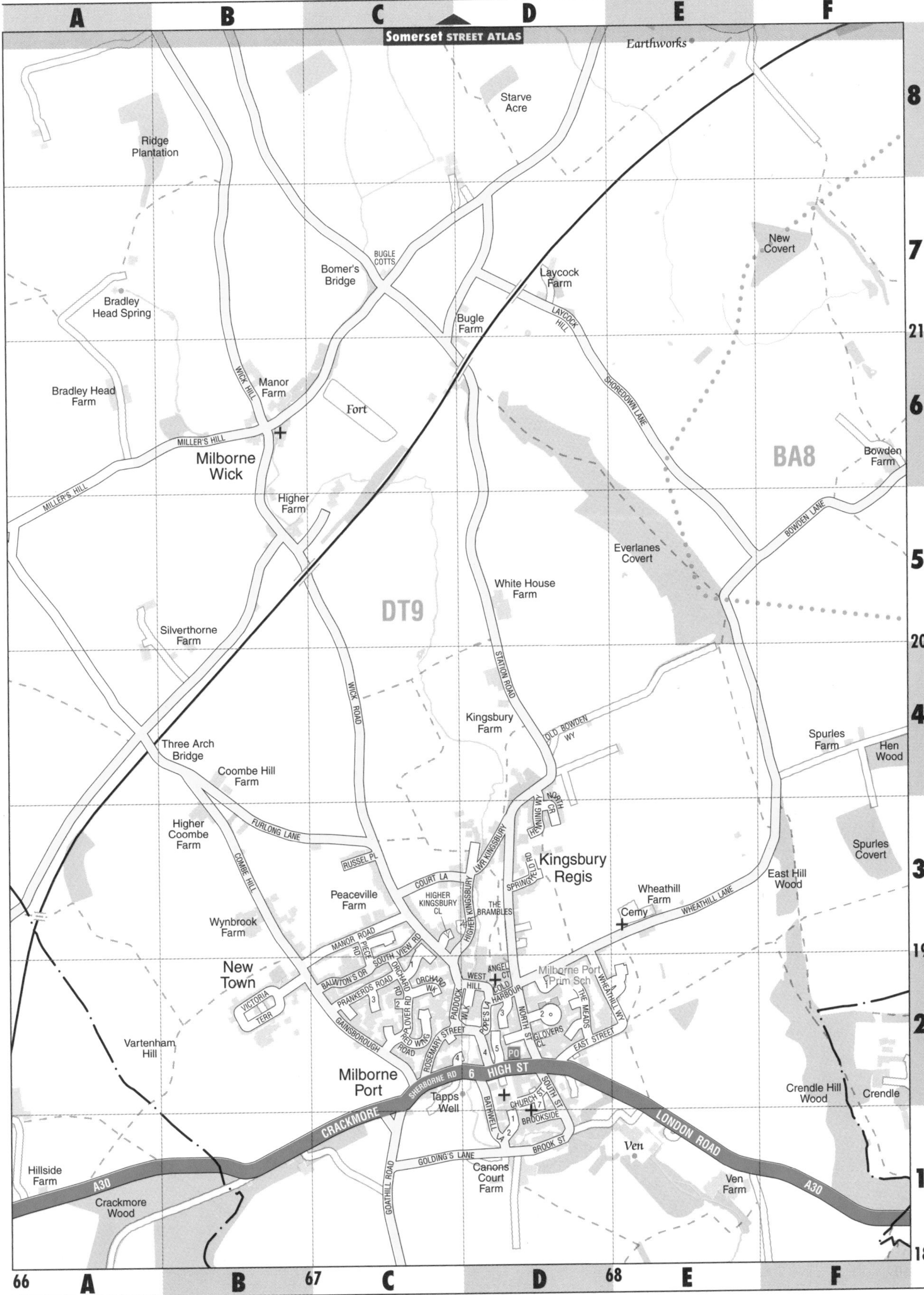

Somerset STREET ATLAS

Earthworks

8

Starve
Acre

Ridge
Plantation

New
Covert

7

BUGLE
COTTS

Bomer's
Bridge

Laycock
Farm

21

Bradley
Head Spring

Bugle
Farm

LAYCOCK
HILL

Bradley Head
Farm

Manor
Farm

Fort

SHOREDOWN LANE

BA8

Bowden
Farm

6

MILLER'S HILL

WICK HILL

Milborne
Wick

MILLER'S HILL

Higher
Farm

BOWDEN LANE

Everlanes
Covert

Bowden Lane

5

White House
Farm

Silverthorne
Farm

DT9

20

WICK ROAD

STATION ROAD

Three Arch
Bridge

Kingsbury
Farm

OLD BOWDEN WY

Spurles
Farm

Hen
Wood

4

Coombe Hill
Farm

FURLONG LANE

Higher
Coombe
Farm

COOMBE HILL

NORTH ST

HEMING WY

Kingsbury
Regis

Spurles
Covert

RUSSEL PL

Peaceville
Farm

COURT LA

HIGHER
KINGSBURY
CL

LWR KINGSBURY

THE
BRAMBLES

SPRINGFIELD RD

Wheathill
Farm

Cemy

East Hill
Wood

3

WHEATHILL LANE

Wynbrook
Farm

MANOR ROAD

HIGHER KINGSBURY

19

New
Town

SOUTH VIEW RD

ORCHARD
WK

WEST
HILL

ANGEL
CT

Milborne Port
Prim Sch

VICTORIA
TERR

BALWTON'S DR

PRANKERDS ROAD

OLD ORCHARD

PADDOCK
WALK

POPE'S LA

LD
HARBOUR

THE
MEADS

WHEATHILL WY

2

GAINSBOROUGH
ROAD

RED WNG

CLOVER RD

NORTH ST

GLOVERS
RD

EAST STREET

Vartenham
Hill

3

ROSEMARY STREET

PO

Milborne
Port

SHERBORNE RD

6 HIGH ST

GOATHILL ROAD

Tapps
Well

BATWELL

CHURCH ST

SOUTH ST

BROOKSIDE

Crendle Hill
Wood

Crendle

CRACKMORE

BROOK ST

Ven

LONDON ROAD

1

Hillside
Farm

A30

GOLDING'S LANE

Canons
Court
Farm

Ven
Farm

A30

Crackmore
Wood

18

C2
1 BAUNTONS CL
2 PLOVER CL
3 PRANKERDS RD
4 LAMBERT CL

31

D1
1 CANNON CT MS
2 PUD BROOK

18 →

D2
1 WHEATHILL CL
2 GLOVERS CL
3 LIMERICK CL
4 LOWER GUNVILLE
5 HIGHER GUNVILLE
6 SANSOME'S HL
7 CHAPEL LA

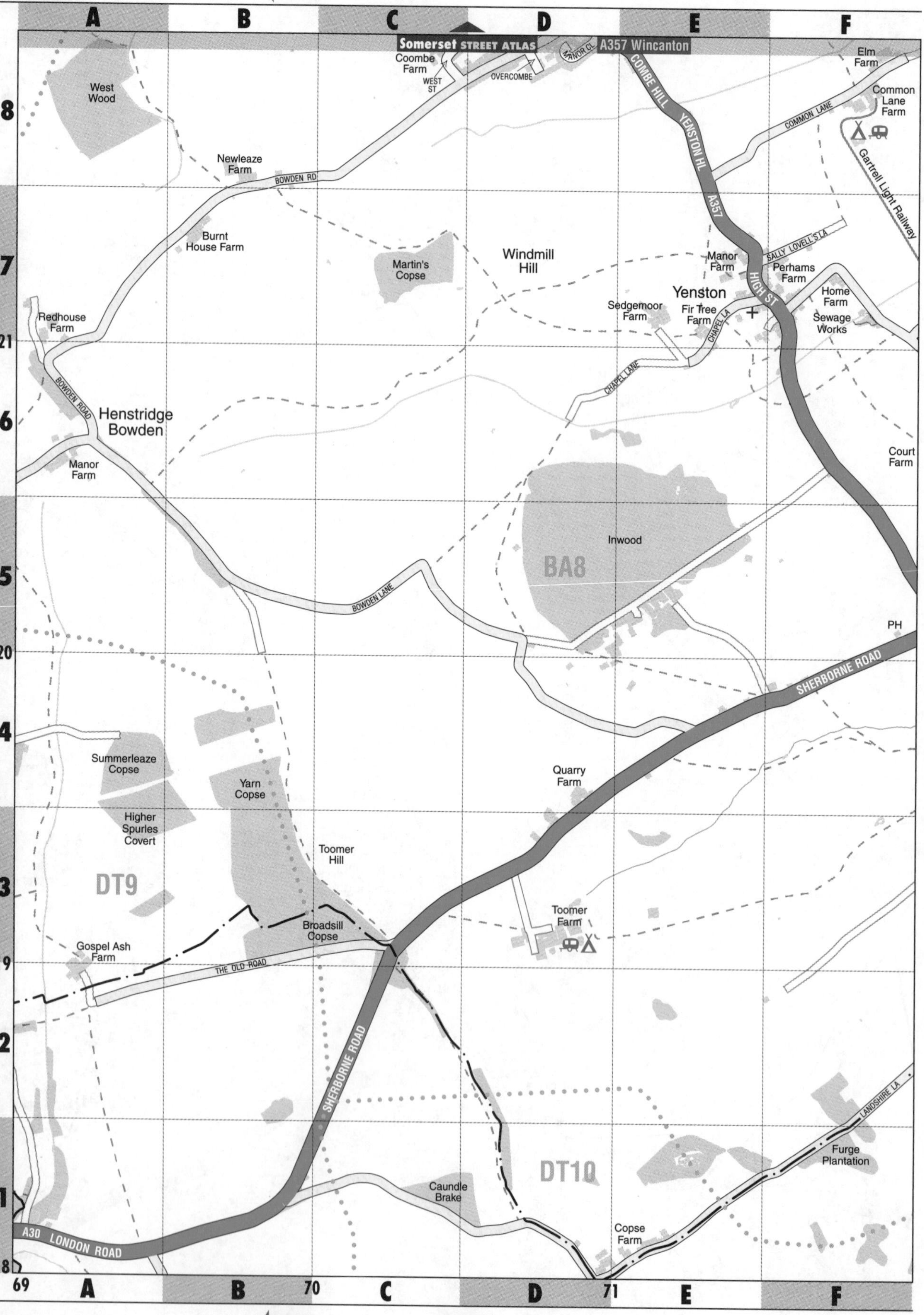

Somerset STREET ATLAS

A357 Wincanton

West Wood

Coombe Farm

WEST ST

OVERCOMBE

MANOR CL

Elm Farm

Common Lane Farm

Common Lane

COMBE HILL

YENSTON HL

Gartrell Light Railway

Newleaze Farm

BOWDEN RD

Burnt House Farm

Martin's Copse

Windmill Hill

A357

Manor Farm

SALLY LOVELL'S LA

Perhams Farm

Redhouse Farm

Yenston

HIGH ST

Home Farm

Sedgemoor Farm

Fir Tree Farm

Sewage Works

BOWDEN ROAD

CHAPEL LA

CHAPEL LANE

Henstridge Bowden

Manor Farm

Court Farm

Inwood

BA8

BOWDEN LANE

PH

SHERBORNE ROAD

Summerleaze Copse

Yarn Copse

Quarry Farm

Higher Spurles Covert

Toomer Hill

DT9

Toomer Farm

Broadsill Copse

Gospel Ash Farm

THE OLD ROAD

SHERBORNE ROAD

Furge Plantation

LANDSHIRE LA

DT10

Caundle Brake

Copse Farm

A30 LONDON ROAD

69 70 71

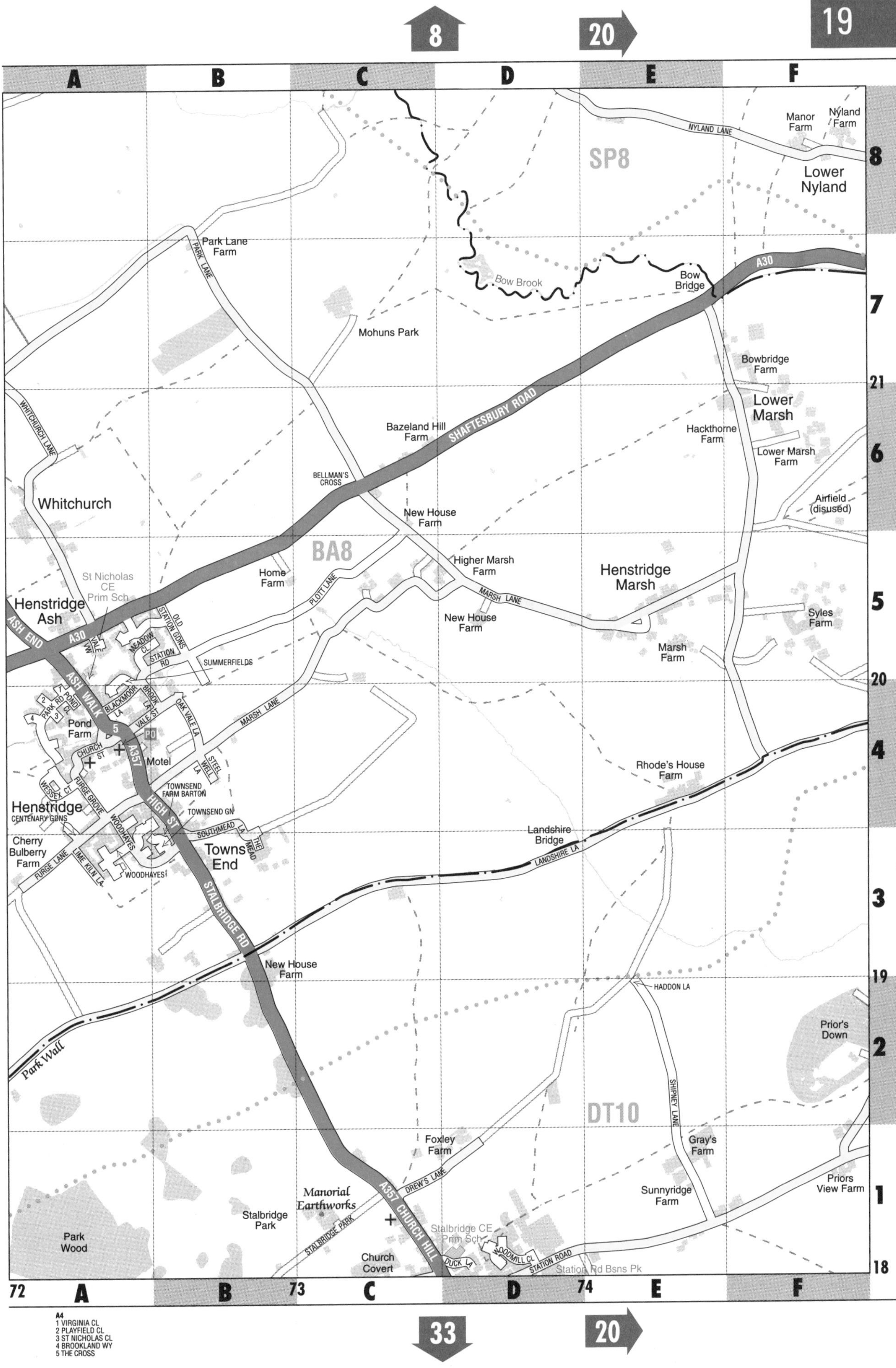

19
9

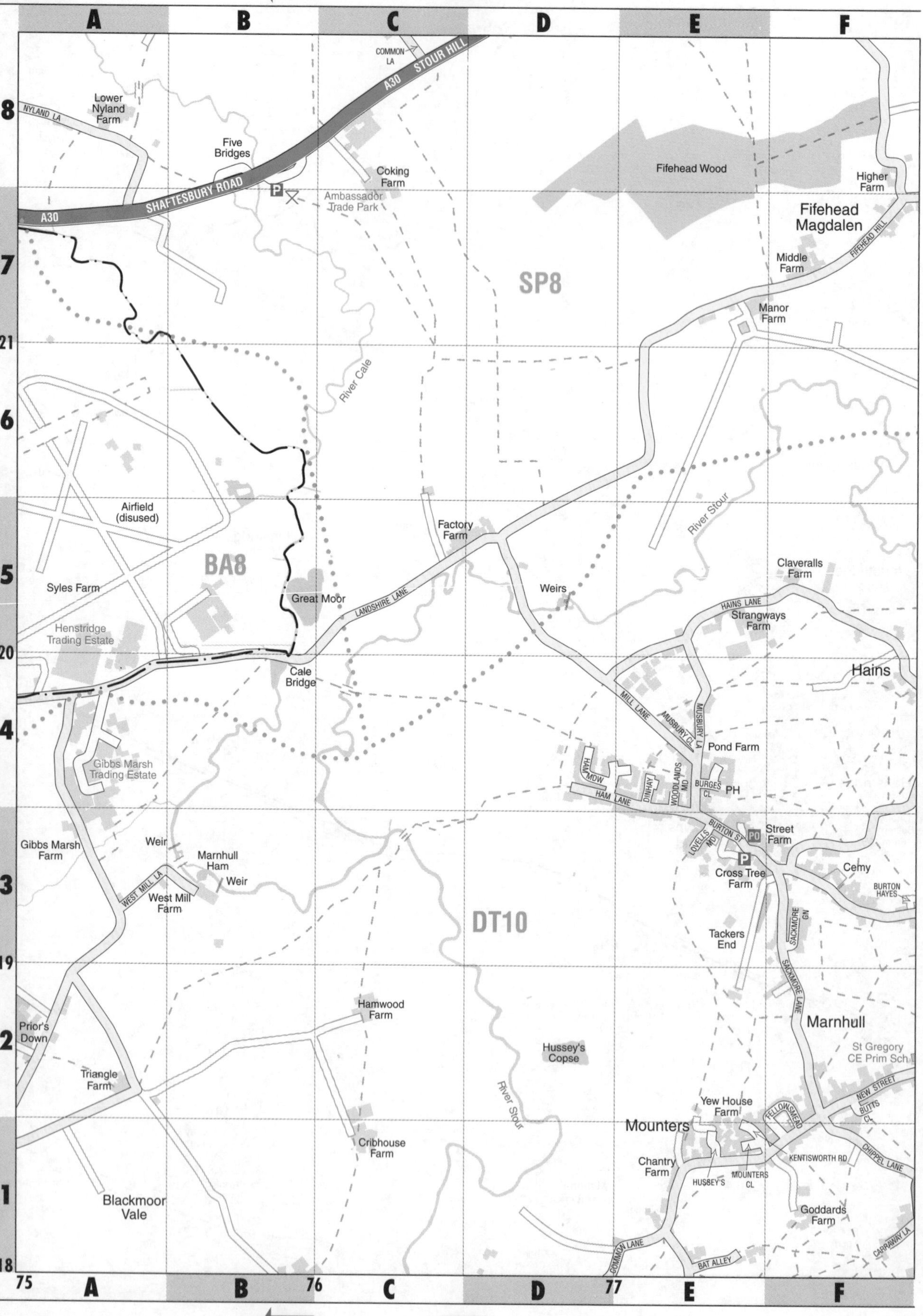
A
B
C
D
E
F
8
7
21
6
5
20
4
3
19
2
1
18
75
76
77
COMMON LA
STOUR HILL
A30
NYLAND LA
Lower Nyland Farm
Five Bridges
SHAFTESBURY ROAD
Coking Farm
Ambassador Trade Park
Fifehead Wood
Higher Farm
Fifehead Magdalen
Middle Farm
FIFEHEAD HILL
Manor Farm
SP8
River Cale
Airfield (disused)
Factory Farm
River Stour
BA8
Syles Farm
Great Moor
LANDSHIRE LANE
Weirs
Claveralls Farm
HAINS LANE
Strangways Farm
Henstridge Trading Estate
Cale Bridge
Hains
MILL LANE
MUSBURY CL
MUSBURY LA
Pond Farm
Gibbs Marsh Trading Estate
HAM MDW
HAM LANE
DINHAY
WOODLANDS MD
BURGES CL
PH
BURTON ST
PO
Street Farm
LOVELLS MD
Gibbs Marsh Farm
Weir
Marnhull Ham
Weir
Cross Tree Farm
Cemy
BURTON HAYES
WEST MILL LA
West Mill Farm
DT10
SACKMORE GN
Tackers End
SACKMORE LANE
Hamwood Farm
Marnhull
Prior's Down
Hussey's Copse
St Gregory CE Prim Sch
Triangle Farm
River Stour
Yew House Farm
FELLOWSMEAD
NEW STREET
BUTTS CL
Mounters
Cribhouse Farm
KENTISWORTH RD
CHIPPEL LANE
Chantry Farm
HUSSEY'S
MOUNTERS CL
Blackmoor Vale
Goddards Farm
CAPPAWAY LA
COMMON LANE
BAT ALLEY

19
34

10
22

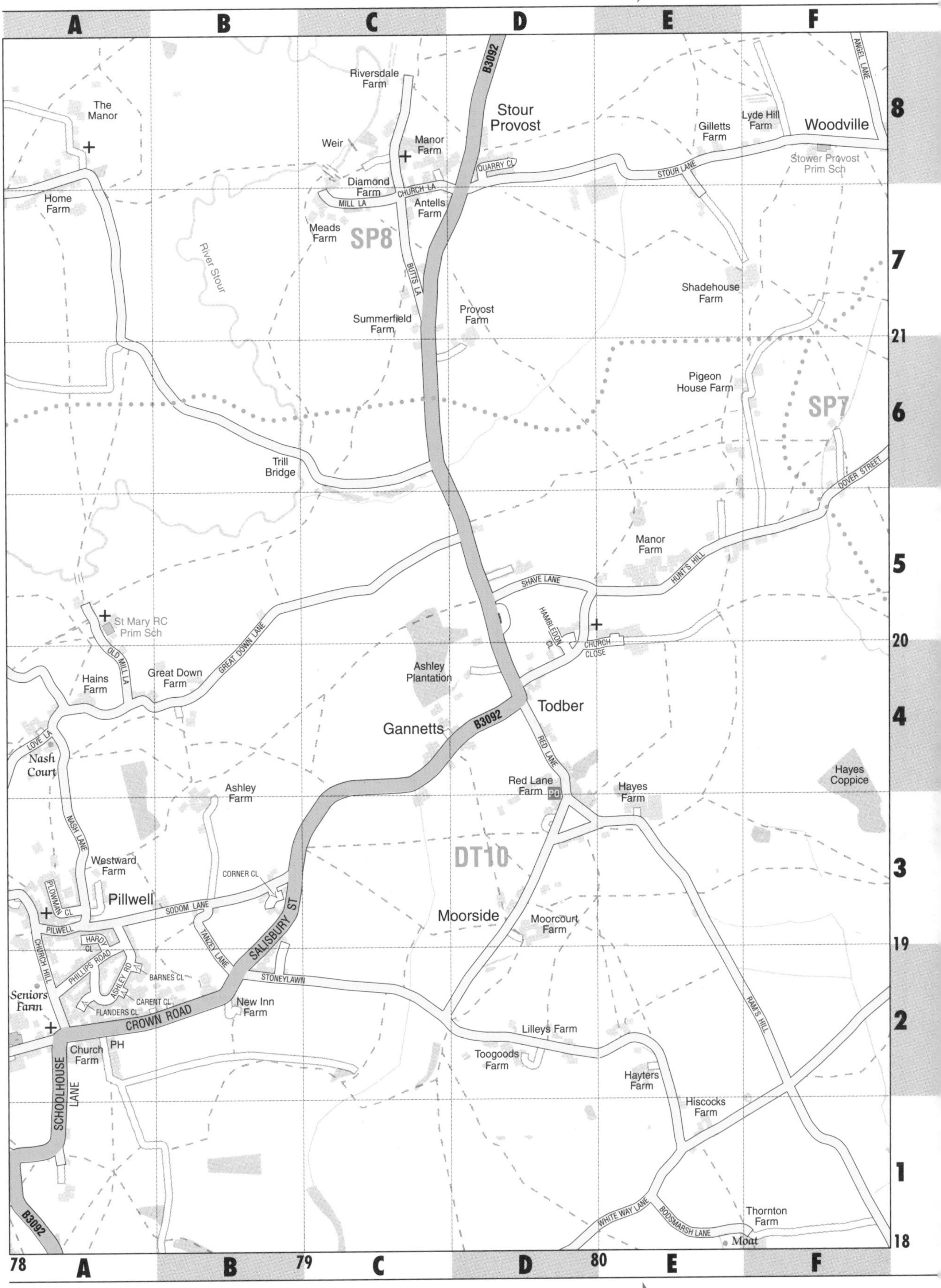
A B C D E F
8
7
21
6
5
20
4
3
19
2
1
18
78 79 80
Riversdale Farm
The Manor
Stour Provost
Weir
Manor Farm
Lyde Hill Farm
Gilletts Farm
Woodville
Stower Provost Prim Sch
QUARRY CL
STOUR LANE
ANGEL LANE
Diamond Farm
CHURCH LA
MILL LA
Antells Farm
Home Farm
Meads Farm
SP8
River Stour
BUTTS LA
B3092
Shadehouse Farm
Summerfield Farm
Provost Farm
Pigeon House Farm
SP7
Trill Bridge
DOVER STREET
Manor Farm
HUNT'S HILL
SHAVE LANE
St Mary RC Prim Sch
HAMBLEDON CL
CHURCH CLOSE
OLD MILL LA
GREAT DOWN LANE
Hains Farm
Great Down Farm
Ashley Plantation
Todber
Gannetts
LOVE LA
Nash Court
RED LANE
Hayes Coppice
Red Lane Farm
PO
Hayes Farm
Ashley Farm
NASH LANE
DT10
Westward Farm
CORNER CL
Pillwell
SODOM LANE
PLOWMAN CL
SALISBURY ST
Moorside
Moorcourt Farm
PILWELL
HARDY CL
CHURCH HILL
PHILLIPS ROAD
TANZEY LANE
ASHLEY RD
BARNES CL
STONEYLAWN
Seniors Farm
CARENT CL
FLANDERS CL
New Inn Farm
CROWN ROAD
RAM'S HILL
Lilleys Farm
Church Farm
PH
Toogoods Farm
Hayters Farm
SCHOOLHOUSE LANE
Hiscocks Farm
WHITE WAY LANE
BODSMARSH LANE
Thornton Farm
Moat

35
22

21
11

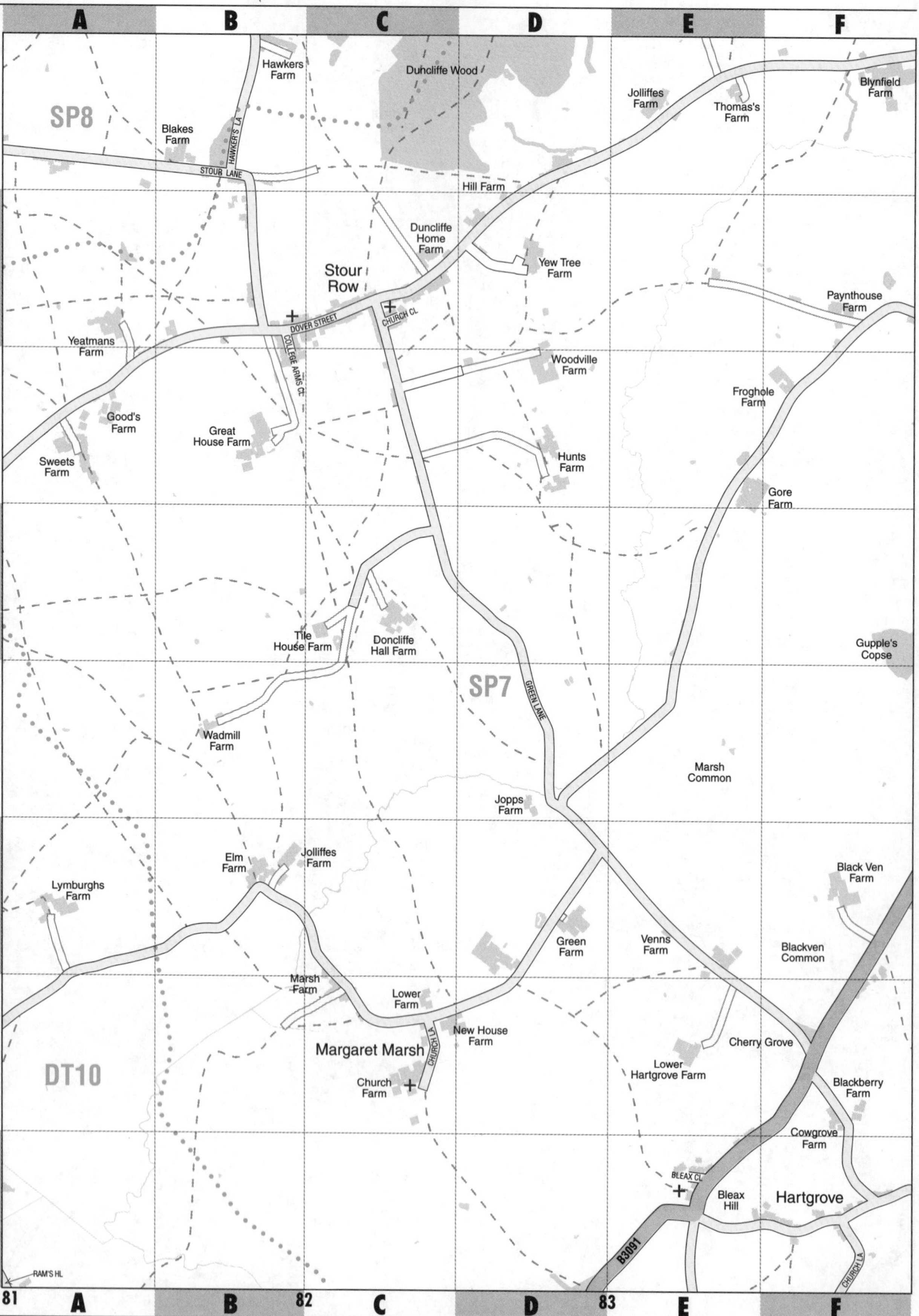

	A	B	C	D	E	F

8

SP8

Hawkers Farm

Duncliffe Wood

Jolliffes Farm

Thomas's Farm

Blynfield Farm

Blakes Farm

STOUR LANE

HAWKER'S LA

Hill Farm

7

Duncliffe Home Farm

Stour Row

Yew Tree Farm

DOVER STREET

CHURCH CL

COLLEGE ARMS CL

Paynthouse Farm

21

Yeatmans Farm

Woodville Farm

Froghole Farm

6

Good's Farm

Great House Farm

Hunts Farm

Gore Farm

Sweets Farm

5

Tile House Farm

Doncliffe Hall Farm

Gupple's Copse

60

SP7

GREEN LANE

4

Wadmill Farm

Marsh Common

Jopps Farm

3

Lymburghs Farm

Elm Farm

Jolliffes Farm

Green Farm

Venns Farm

Black Ven Farm

Blackven Common

19

Marsh Farm

Lower Farm

CHURCH LA

New House Farm

2

DT10

Margaret Marsh

Lower Hartgrove Farm

Cherry Grove

Blackberry Farm

Church Farm

Cowgrove Farm

BLEAX CL

Bleax Hill

Hartgrove

B3091

CHURCH LA

1

18

RAM'S HL

81	A	B	82	C	D	83	E	F

21
36

12
24

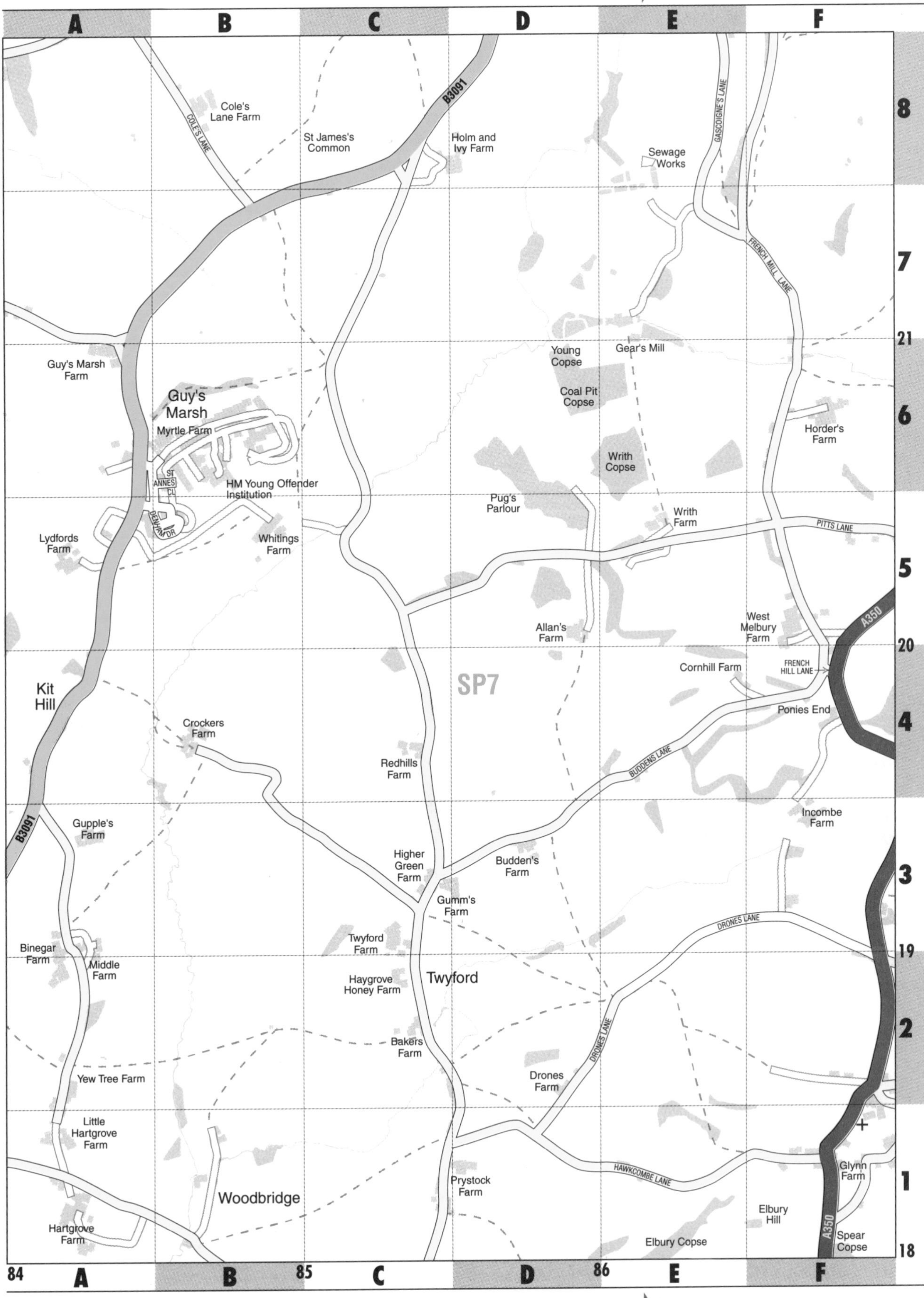
A
B
C
D
E
F
B3091
Cole's Lane Farm
COLE'S LANE
St James's Common
Holm and Ivy Farm
Sewage Works
GASCOIGNE'S LANE
FRENCH MILL LANE
Guy's Marsh Farm
Guy's Marsh
Myrtle Farm
ST ANNES CL
DENHAM DR
HM Young Offender Institution
Young Copse
Gear's Mill
Coal Pit Copse
Horder's Farm
Writh Copse
Pug's Parlour
Writh Farm
PITTS LANE
Lydfords Farm
Whitings Farm
Allan's Farm
West Melbury Farm
A350
Cornhill Farm
FRENCH HILL LANE
SP7
Kit Hill
Crockers Farm
Ponies End
BUDDENS LANE
Redhills Farm
Incombe Farm
Gupple's Farm
Higher Green Farm
Budden's Farm
Gumm's Farm
DRONES LANE
Binegar Farm
Twyford Farm
Middle Farm
Haygrove Honey Farm
Twyford
Bakers Farm
DRONES LANE
Yew Tree Farm
Drones Farm
Little Hartgrove Farm
HAWKCOMBE LANE
Glynn Farm
Woodbridge
Prystock Farm
Elbury Hill
Hartgrove Farm
Elbury Copse
Spear Copse
8
7
21
6
5
20
4
3
19
2
1
18
84
85
86

37
24

23
13

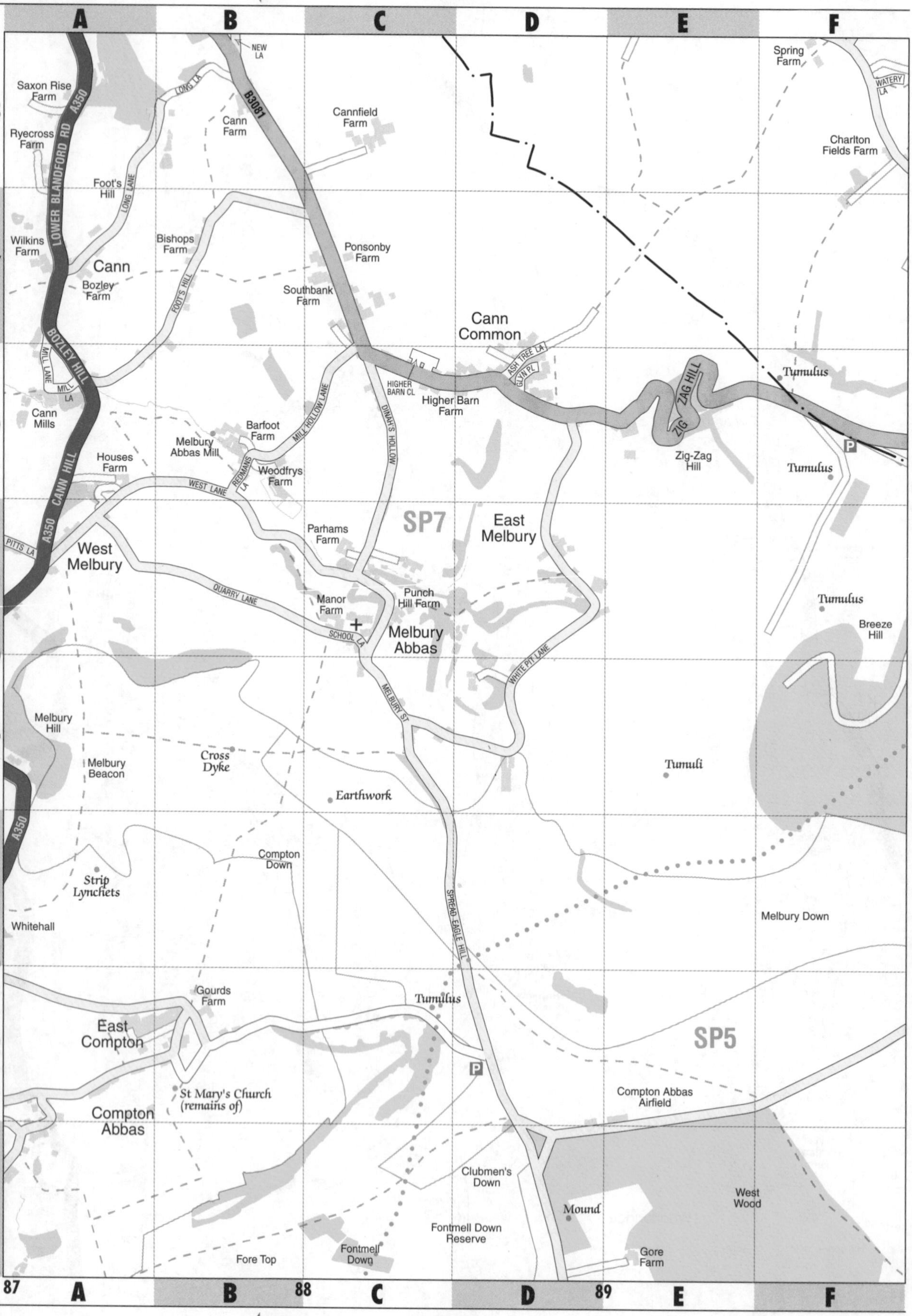
A
B
C
D
E
F
8
7
21
6
5
20
4
3
19
2
1
18
87
88
89
NEW LA
Saxon Rise Farm
Ryecross Farm
LOWER BLANDFORD RD A350
LONG LA
B3081
Cann Farm
Cannfield Farm
Spring Farm
WATERY LA
Charlton Fields Farm
Foot's Hill
LONG LANE
Wilkins Farm
Bishops Farm
Ponsonby Farm
Cann
Bozley Farm
FOOT'S HILL
Southbank Farm
Cann Common
BOZLEY HILL
MILL LANE
MILL LA
ASH TREE LA
GLYN PL
ZIG ZAG HILL
Tumulus
HIGHER BARN CL
Higher Barn Farm
Cann Mills
Barfoot Farm
MILL HOLLOW LANE
DINAH'S HOLLOW
Melbury Abbas Mill
Zig-Zag Hill
Houses Farm
REDMANS LA
Woodfrys Farm
Tumulus
CANN HILL
WEST LANE
SP7
East Melbury
A350
Parhams Farm
PITTS LA
West Melbury
QUARRY LANE
Punch Hill Farm
Tumulus
Manor Farm
Breeze Hill
SCHOOL LA
Melbury Abbas
WHITE PIT LANE
MELBURY ST
Melbury Hill
Melbury Beacon
Cross Dyke
Tumuli
Earthwork
A350
Compton Down
Strip Lynchets
Melbury Down
Whitehall
SPREAD EAGLE HILL
Gourds Farm
Tumulus
East Compton
SP5
St Mary's Church (remains of)
Compton Abbas Airfield
Compton Abbas
Clubmen's Down
West Wood
Mound
Fontmell Down Reserve
Fore Top
Fontmell Down
Gore Farm

23
38

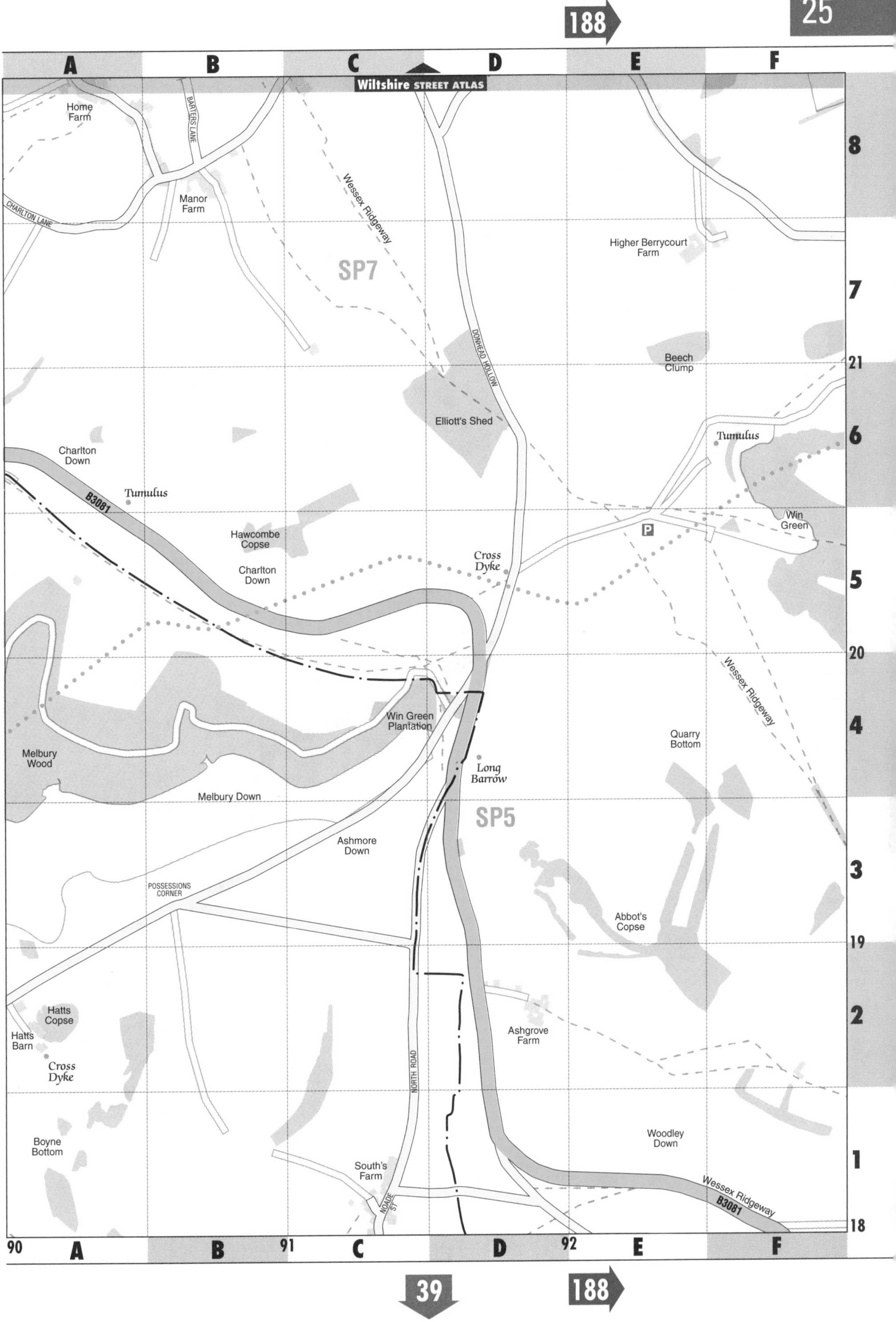

Wiltshire STREET ATLAS

Home Farm

BARTERS LANE

Manor Farm

CHARLTON LANE

Wessex Ridgeway

SP7

Higher Berrycourt Farm

DONHEAD HOLLOW

Beech Clump

Elliott's Shed

Tumulus

Charlton Down

Tumulus

B3081

Hawcombe Copse

Charlton Down

Cross Dyke

P

Win Green

Win Green Plantation

Wessex Ridgeway

Melbury Wood

Quarry Bottom

Melbury Down

Long Barrow

SP5

Ashmore Down

POSSESSIONS CORNER

Abbot's Copse

Hatts Copse

Hatts Barn

Cross Dyke

Ashgrove Farm

NORTH ROAD

Boyne Bottom

Woodley Down

South's Farm

Wessex Ridgeway

B3081

C5
1 BRIGADIER CL
2 HOUNDSTONE CT
3 CELANDINE RD

E5
1 HILLBORNE GDNS
2 THREE CORNER MD
3 PARISH MS

E6
1 TRELLECH CT
2 THE REGENTS
3 DERWENT WY

F6
1 BARLYNCH CT
2 MALVERN CT
3 NETLEY
4 TEWKESBURY

F7
1 FOSSE WY
2 CAMPION WLK
3 WATLING ST
4 GALAHAD CL
5 LANCELOT CL
6 MERLIN CL
7 TRISTRAM CL
8 AKEMAN CL

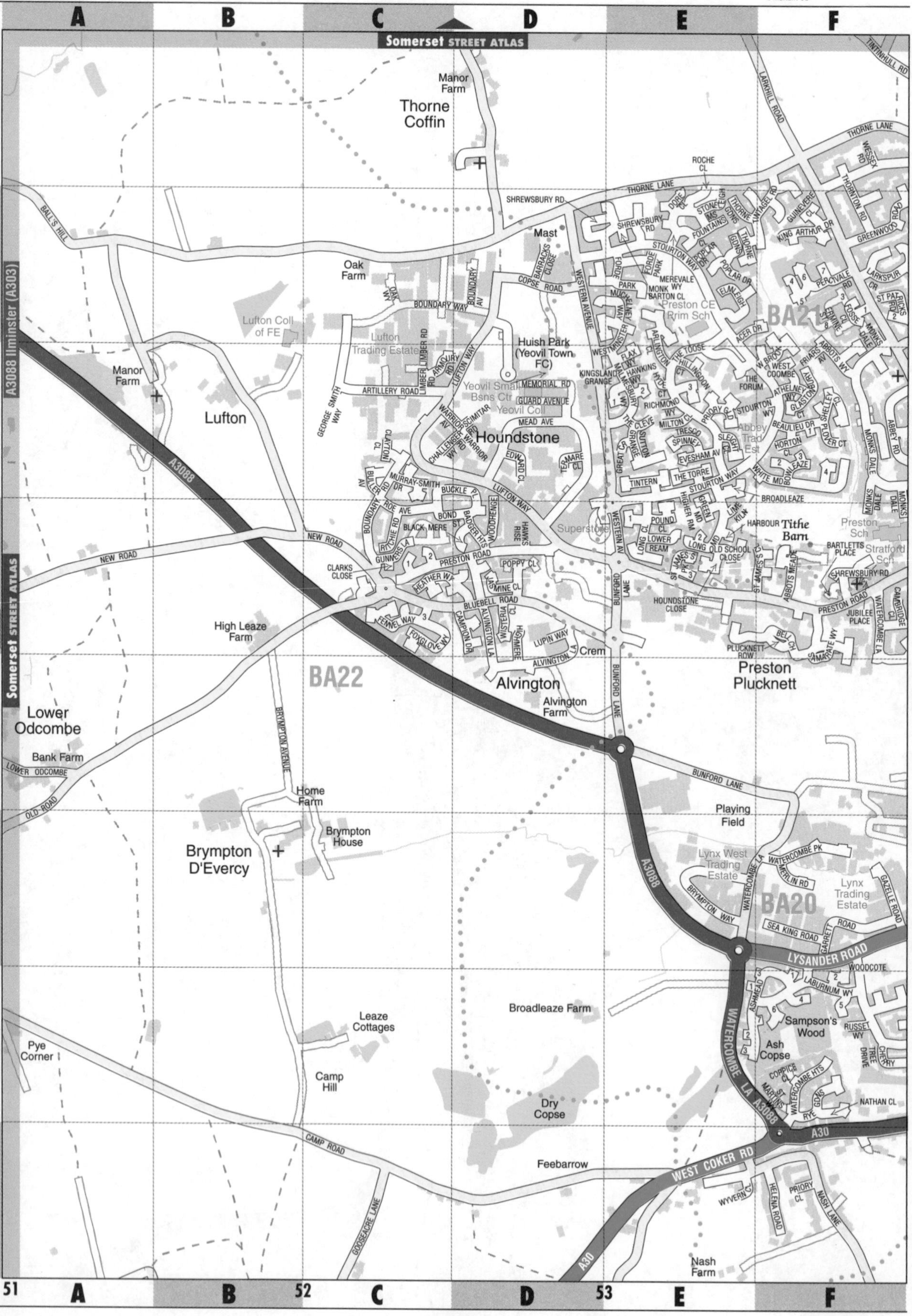

E2
1 FOXCOTE
2 THE FURZE
3 THE CROFT

F2
1 DOWNLEAZE
2 WOODCOTE
3 THE BRIARS
4 OAKLEIGH
5 RIDGEMEAD
6 BIRCHDALE
7 THE SPINNEY

193

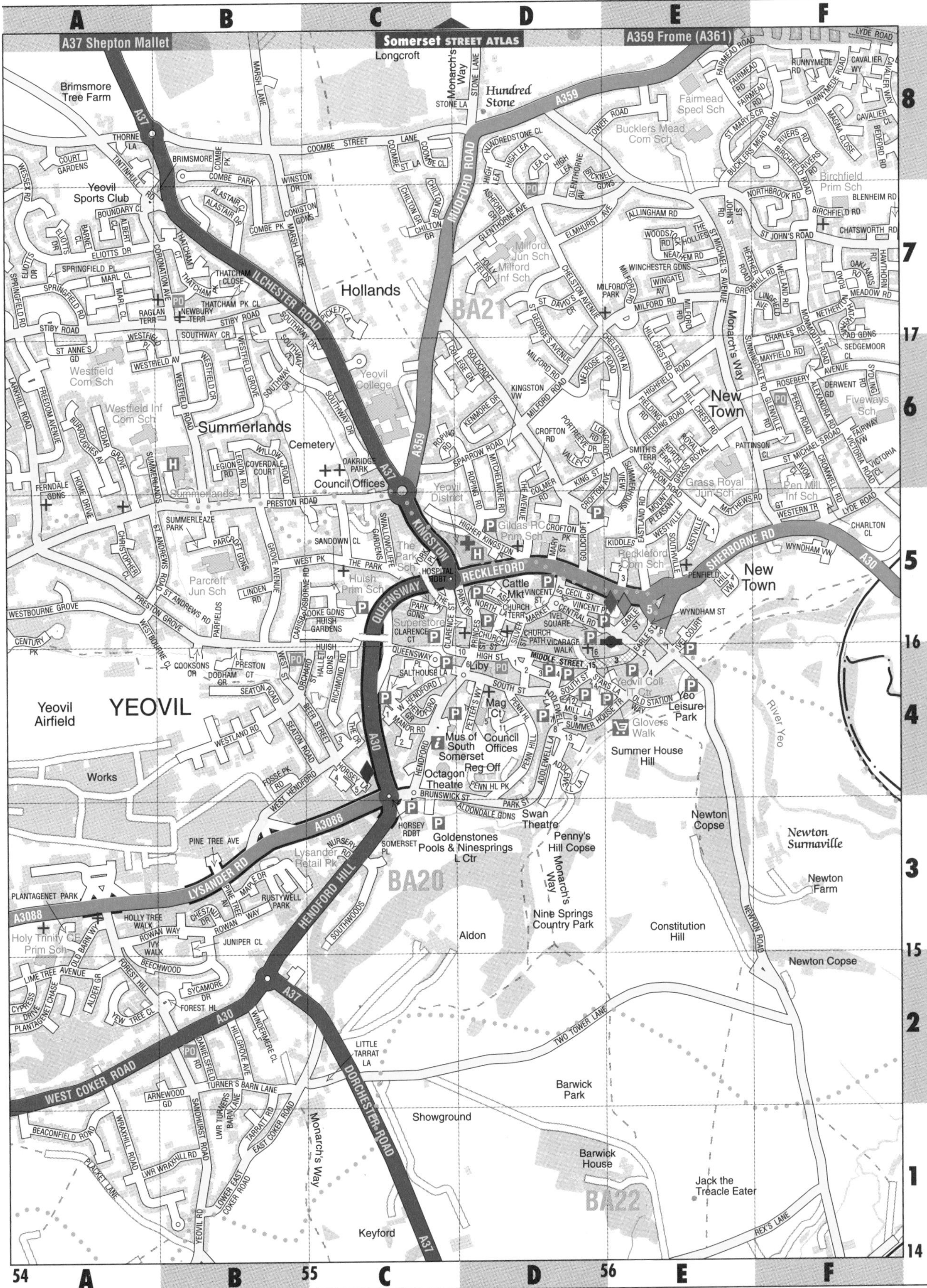

28

E5
1 ST THOMAS CROSS
2 DAMPIER PL
3 DAMPIER ST
4 HILLSIDE TERR
5 WYNDHAM ST
6 SHERBORNE RD

Somerset STREET ATLAS

A37 Shepton Mallet

A359 Frome (A361)

A B C D E F

8

7

YEOVIL

17

6

5

16

4

3

15

2

1

14

1 CORTON CL
2 ADBER CL
3 COMPTON CL
4 SANDLEWOOD CL
5 ASHWOOD DR

TRENT CL
REDWOOD ROAD
BRIAR CL
CONSTABLE CL
GAINSBOROUGH WY
WILTON RD
LYDE ROAD
CAVALIER WY
BEDFORD RD
HERTFORD RD
ROMSEY RD
PO

BLENHEIM RD

ST JOHN'S RD
WELBECK RD
MONTROSE RD
MEADOW RD
WOBURN RD
WENTWORTH RD
MARLBOROUGH RD
ARUNDO RD
LOWTHER
PEMBROKE RD
OXFORD ROAD

BABYLON VIEW

Mark View Bsns Ctr

MEADOW RD
SANDRINGHAM RD
BALMORAL RD
HOWARD RD
LYDE RD
BELVEDERE RD
VALE ROAD
LYDE LA

Sewage Works

ROSEBERY AVE
CLIFTON CL
CAMBORNE PL
CAMBORNE PL

Pen Mill
Yeovil Coll

HERBLAY CL

Pen Mill Trading Estate

Buckland Road

BA21

River Yeo

Compton Road

Sewage Works

Yeovil Pen Mill
FLUSHING MDW

SHERBORNE ROAD

BABYLON HILL

A30

BABYLON HILL

Babylon Hill

CH
Yeovil Golf Club

LEAZE LANE

Tilly's Hill

East Farm

BA20

Park House

UNDERDOWN HOLLOW
Coombe

QUARRY LANE

Manor Farm

FARM ROAD

PETTITTS CL

Cross Wy
CROSS ROAD
QUEENS RD
AMBROSE CL

BISHOPS LANE
MANOR CLOSE
SOUTH VW
NORTH ST
HIGHER WESTBURY
WEST ST

River Yeo

BA22

Yeovil Junction

Yeovil Railway Ctr

Bradford Abbas

CHURCHWELL ST
CHURCH RD
WESSEX DR
WILL LA
PO
St Mary CE Prim Sch

Trent Brook

PH
Glebe Farm
Lower Dairy Farm

CROSS FIELDS
FOLLY LA

Nether Compton

Bucklers Farm

PLUM ORCHARD
Plum Orchard Farm

FLAX LA

Lower Farm

WESTERN ST

ST MICHAELS CL
COMPTON ACRES

Over Compton

Lower Farm

Compton Manor Farm

COMPTON ROAD

Higher Farm

MARL LANE

BABYLON HILL

DT9

Noor Farm

WESSEX DR
BLACK LA
LC

D1
1 BAKEHOUSE LA
2 THE CROSS
3 CHURCHWELL CL

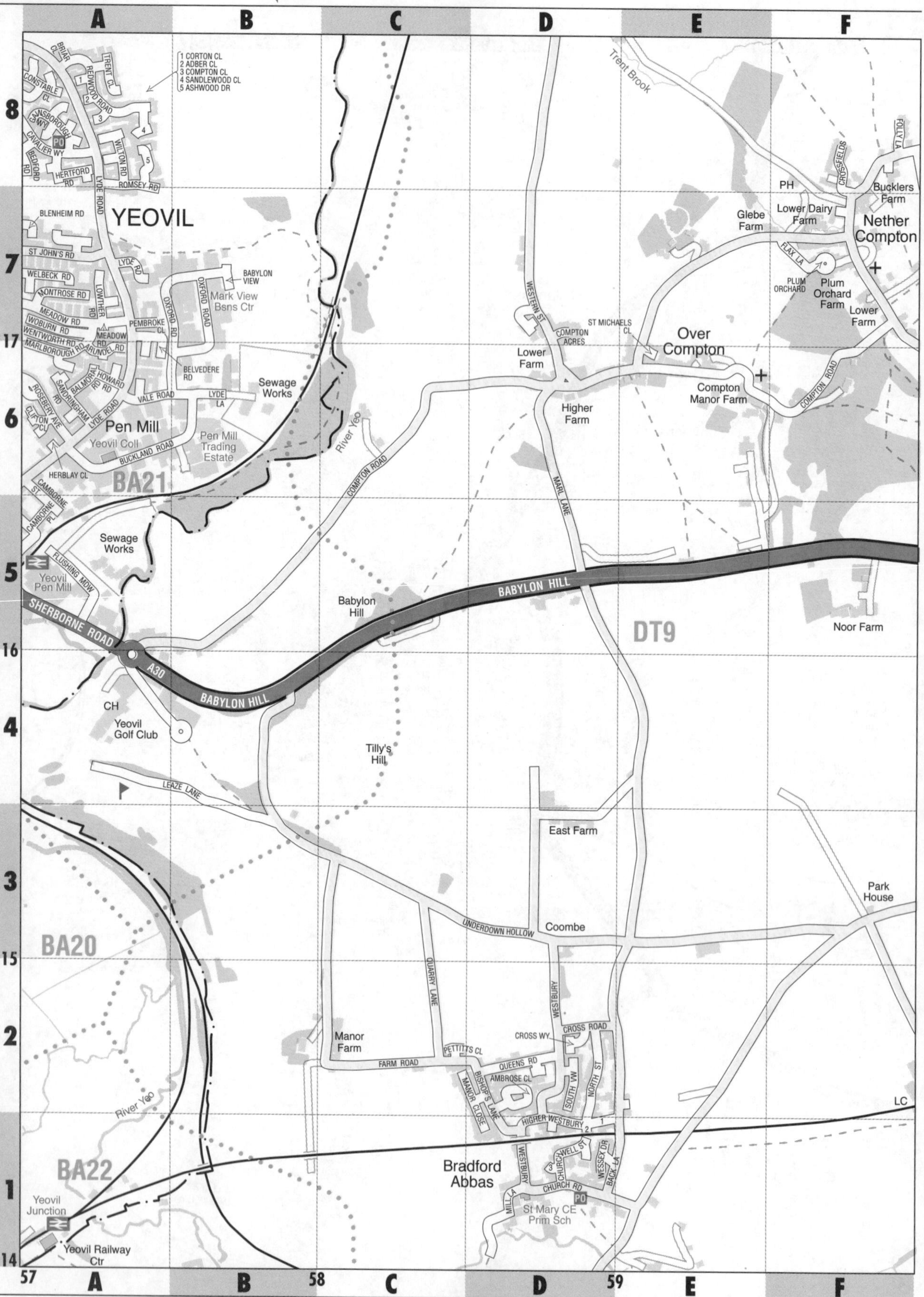

15
30

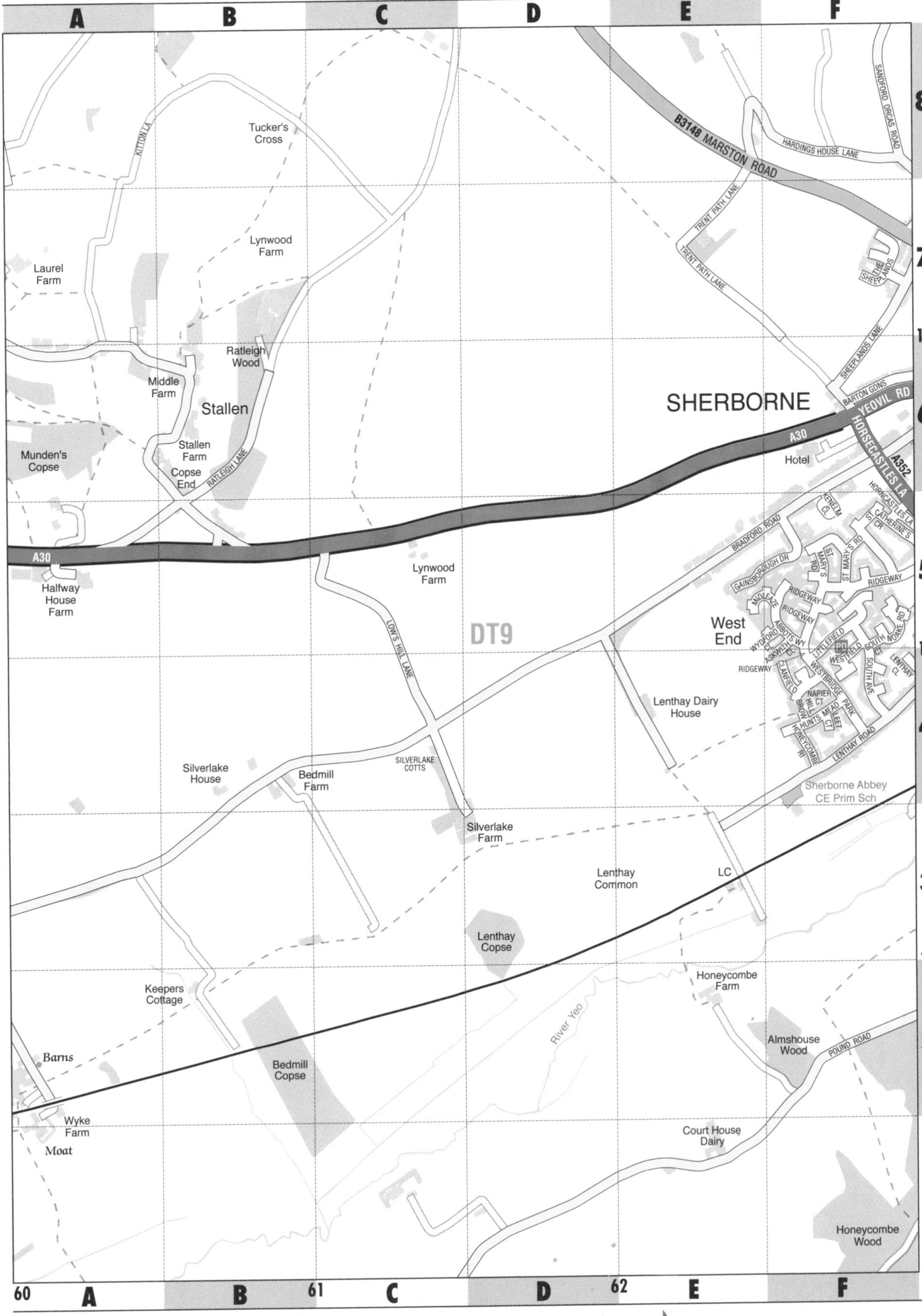
A
B
C
D
E
F
8
7
17
6
5
16
4
3
15
2
1
14
60
61
62
Tucker's Cross
KITTON LA
B3148 MARSTON ROAD
HARDINGS HOUSE LANE
SANDFORD ORCAS ROAD
TRENT PATH LANE
TRENT PATH LANE
Lynwood Farm
Laurel Farm
THE SHEEPLANDS
SHEEPLANDS LANE
Ratleigh Wood
Middle Farm
Stallen
SHERBORNE
BARTON GDNS
YEOVIL RD
A30
HORSECASTLES LA
A352
Hotel
Munden's Copse
Stallen Farm
Copse End
RATLEIGH LANE
KENELM CL
HORNCASTLES LA
ST CATHERINE'S CR
BRADFORD ROAD
A30
Lynwood Farm
GAINSBOROUGH DR
ST MARY'S RD
ST MARY'S RD
RIDGEWAY
Halfway House Farm
MIDLEAZE
RIDGEWAY
RIDGEWAY
West End
LITTLEFIELD
ABBOTS WY
WYDFORD CL
ASKWITH CL
WESTFIELD
SOUTH CT
NOAKE RD
LENTHAY CL
DT9
LOW'S HILL LANE
RIDGEWAY
CLAYFIELD
WESTBRIDGE PARK
SOUTH AVE
Lenthay Dairy House
NAPIER CT
BROW HILL
HUNTS MEAD
LEET CT
HONEYCOMBE RI
LENTHAY ROAD
Silverlake House
Bedmill Farm
SILVERLAKE COTTS
Sherborne Abbey CE Prim Sch
Silverlake Farm
Lenthay Common
LC
Lenthay Copse
Honeycombe Farm
Keepers Cottage
River Yeo
Almshouse Wood
POUND ROAD
Barns
Bedmill Copse
Wyke Farm
Moat
Court House Dairy
Honeycombe Wood

194
30

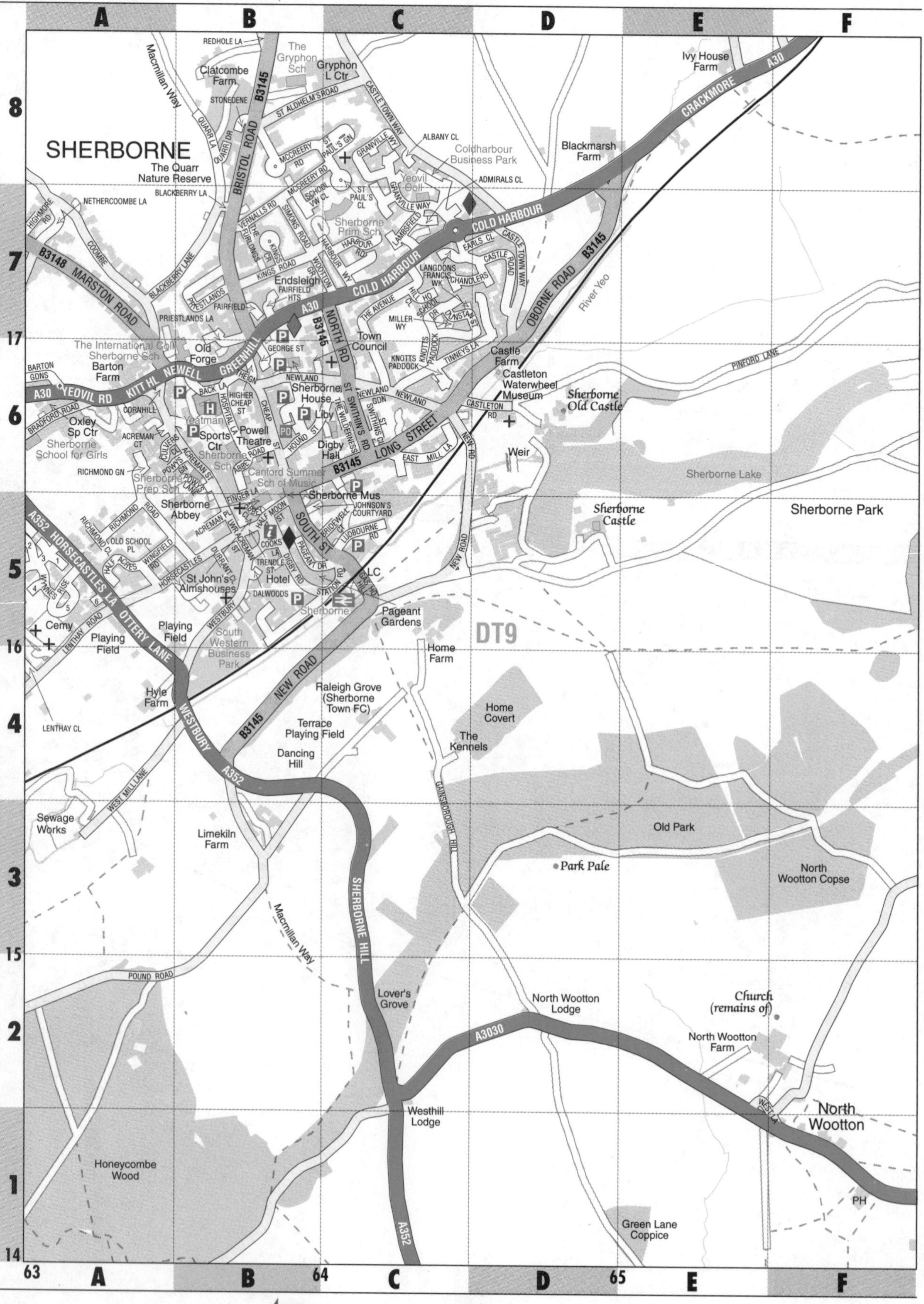

17
32

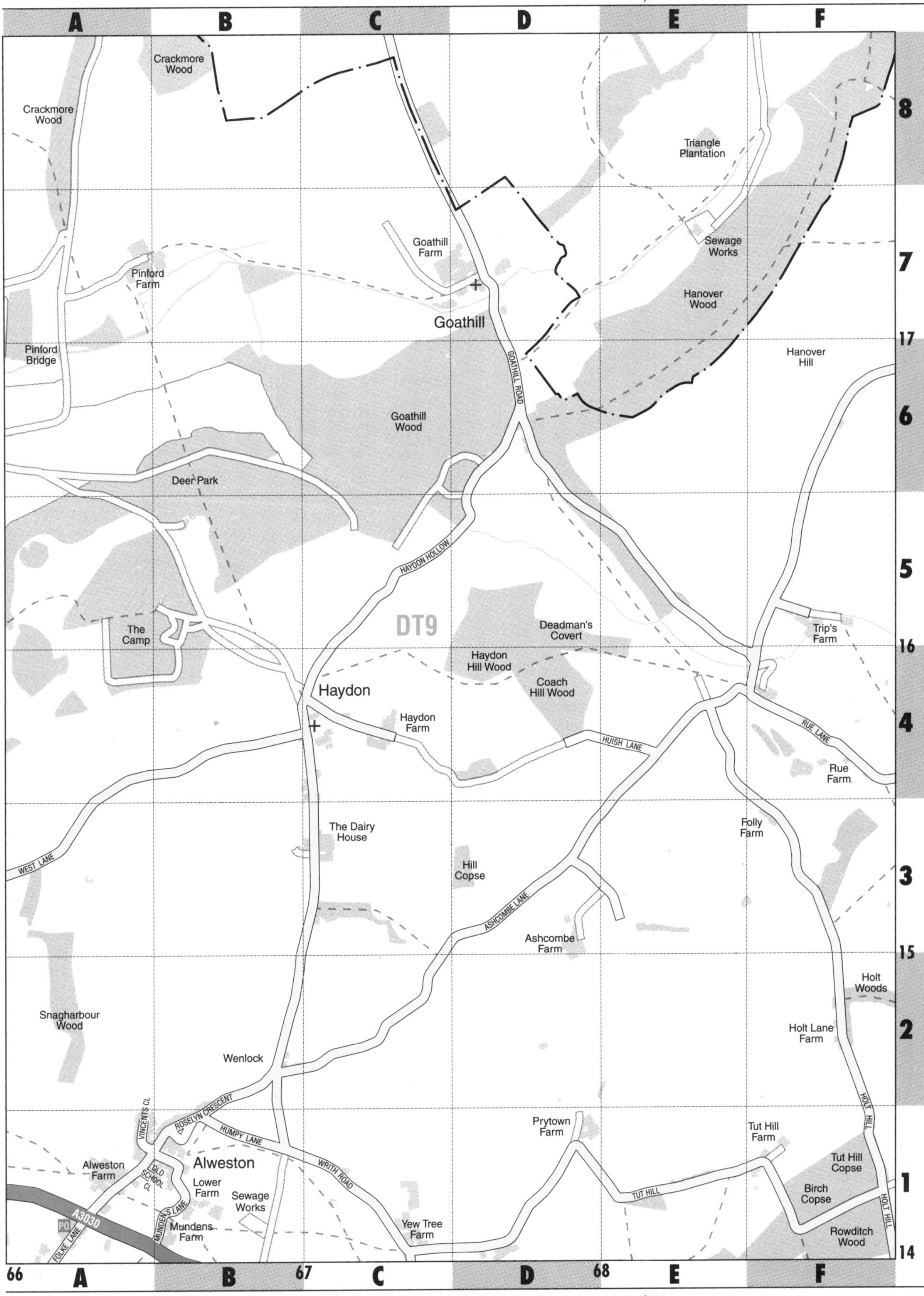
A B C D E F
8
7
17
6
5
16
4
3
15
2
1
14
66 67 68
Crackmore Wood
Triangle Plantation
Goathill Farm
Pinford Farm
Sewage Works
Hanover Wood
Goathill
Pinford Bridge
GOATHILL ROAD
Hanover Hill
Goathill Wood
Deer Park
HAYDON HOLLOW
DT9
Deadman's Covert
The Camp
Trip's Farm
Haydon Hill Wood
Coach Hill Wood
Haydon
Haydon Farm
HUISH LANE
RUE LANE
Rue Farm
The Dairy House
Folly Farm
WEST LANE
Hill Copse
ASHCOMBE LANE
Ashcombe Farm
Holt Woods
Snagharbour Wood
Holt Lane Farm
Wenlock
HOLT HILL
VINCENTS CL
ROSELYN CRESCENT
Prytown Farm
Tut Hill Farm
HUMPY LANE
Tut Hill Copse
Alweston
Alweston Farm
OLD SCHOOL CL
WRITH ROAD
Birch Copse
Lower Farm
Sewage Works
TUT HILL
HOLT HILL
A3030
PO
MUNDENS LANE
Mundens Farm
Yew Tree Farm
Rowditch Wood
FOLKE LANE

195
32

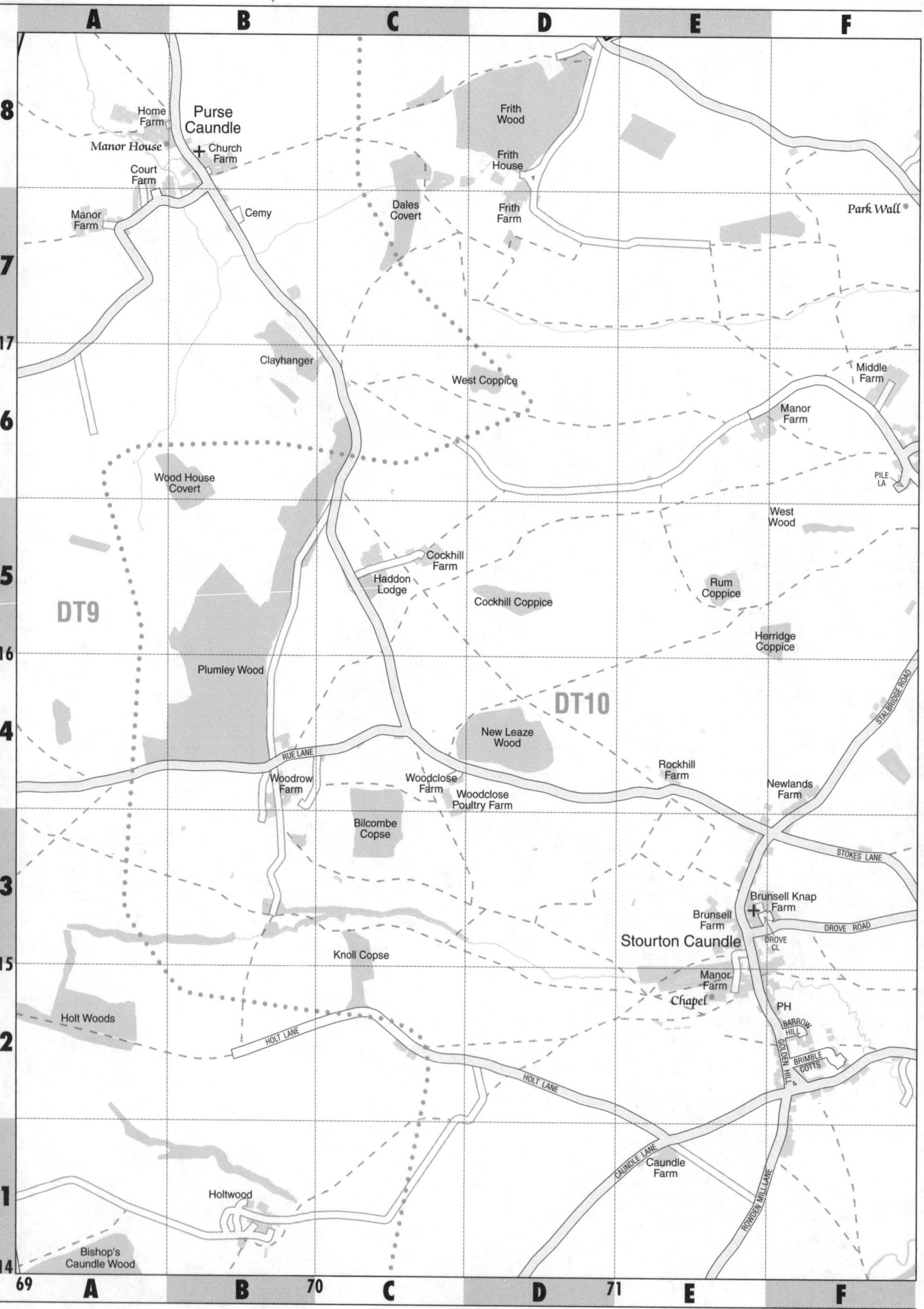

Home
Farm

Purse
Caundle

Manor House

+ Church
Farm

Court
Farm

Cemy

Manor
Farm

Frith
Wood

Frith
House

Frith
Farm

Park Wall

Dales
Covert

Clayhanger

17

West Coppice

Middle
Farm

Manor
Farm

PILE
LA

Wood House
Covert

West
Coppice

West
Wood

DT9

Cockhill
Farm

Haddon
Lodge

Cockhill Coppice

Rum
Coppice

Herridge
Coppice

16

Plumley Wood

DT10

New Leaze
Wood

RUE LANE

Woodrow
Farm

Woodclose
Farm

Rockhill
Farm

Newlands
Farm

STALBRIDGE ROAD

Woodclose
Poultry Farm

Bilcombe
Copse

STOKES LANE

Brunsell Knap
Farm

+

DROVE ROAD

Brunsell
Farm

DROVE
CL

Knoll Copse

15

Stourton Caundle

Manor
Farm

Chapel

PH

BARROW
HILL

Holt Woods

HOLT LANE

GOLDEN HILL

BRIMBLE
COTTS

HOLT LANE

Holtwood

Caundle
Farm

CAUNDLE LANE

ROWDEN MILL LANE

Bishop's
Caundle Wood

19
34

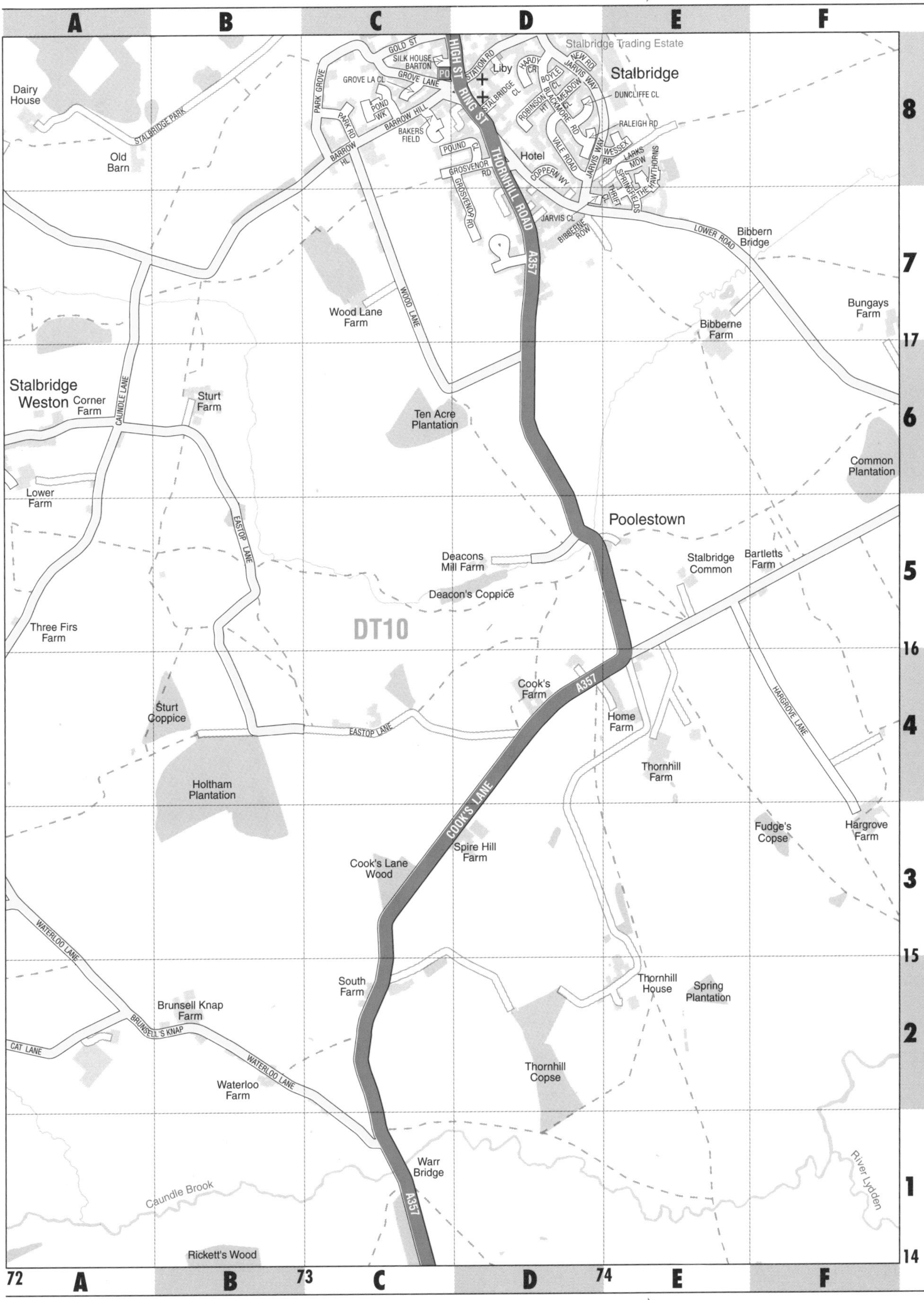
A
B
C
D
E
F
Stalbridge Trading Estate
Stalbridge
GOLD ST
SILK HOUSE BARTON
PO
HIGH ST
STATION RD
Liby
HARDY CR
NEW RD
JARVIS WAY
GROVE LA CL
GROVE LANE
PARK GROVE
POND WK
RING ST
STALBRIDGE CL
BOYLE CL
MEADOW CL
BLACKMORE RD
ROBINSON HT
DUNCLIFFE CL
RALEIGH RD
PARK RD
BARROW HILL
BAKERS FIELD
POUND CL
THORNHILL ROAD
Hotel
VALE ROAD
WESSEX RD
LARKS MDW
THE HAWTHORNS
BARROW HL
GROSVENOR RD
COPPERN WY
SPRINGFIELDS
THRIFT CL
JARVIS CL
BIBBERNE ROW
LOWER ROAD
Dairy House
STALBRIDGE PARK
Old Barn
Bibbern Bridge
A357
Wood Lane Farm
WOOD LANE
Bungays Farm
Bibberne Farm
Stalbridge Weston
Corner Farm
CAUNDLE LANE
Sturt Farm
Ten Acre Plantation
Common Plantation
Lower Farm
EASTOP LANE
Poolestown
Deacons Mill Farm
Stalbridge Common
Bartletts Farm
Deacon's Coppice
Three Firs Farm
DT10
Cook's Farm
A357
Home Farm
HARGROVE LANE
Sturt Coppice
EASTOP LANE
Holtham Plantation
Thornhill Farm
COOK'S LANE
Spire Hill Farm
Fudge's Copse
Hargrove Farm
Cook's Lane Wood
WATERLOO LANE
South Farm
Thornhill House
Spring Plantation
Brunsell Knap Farm
BRUNSELL'S KNAP
CAT LANE
WATERLOO LANE
Waterloo Farm
Thornhill Copse
Warr Bridge
Caundle Brook
River Lydden
A357
Rickett's Wood
8
7
17
6
5
16
4
3
15
2
1
14
72
73
74

196
34

A · B · C · D · E · F

8

Gomershay
Farm

Bibbern Brook

River Stour

Common Lane

Pleck

Crosses
Farm

Walton
Elm

Shepherds
Close Farm

Mowes La

Antells
Farm

Common Lane

Cox Hill

Yardgrove
Farm

7

Hewletts
Farm

King's Mill
Farm

Cox Hill

Bungays
Farm

Grove
Farm

17

King's Mill
Bridge

KING'S MILL ROAD

6

LOWER ROAD

River Lydden

Weirs

Cutt Mill Lane

BAGBER
CROSSROADS

Halletts
Farm

Cutt Mill

Joyce's
Coppice

Marsh
Farm

Lower
Bagber
Farm

5

Lower Ryalls
Farm

DT10

Pentridge Lane

Pentridge
Farm

16

Ryalls
Farm

Bagber
Wood

Pentridge Lane

Lovell's
Coppice

4

Bagber
Bridge

Bagber
House
Farm

Manor
Farm

Stour Valley Way

Stalbridge Lane

River Lydden

3

Rushay
Farm

Blackwater
Bridge

15

Ash Tree
Farm

Queen's
Coppice

2

Pleak
House
Farm

Longacres
Farm

Mullins'
Farm

Oaks
Farm

Stalbridge La

Meadow
Farm

Horsehill
Farm

Medieval Village
of Colber (site of)

1

Perry
Farm

Higher
Farm

Oaklea
Farm

Bagber
Common

14

75   A · B · 76 · C · D · 77 · E · F

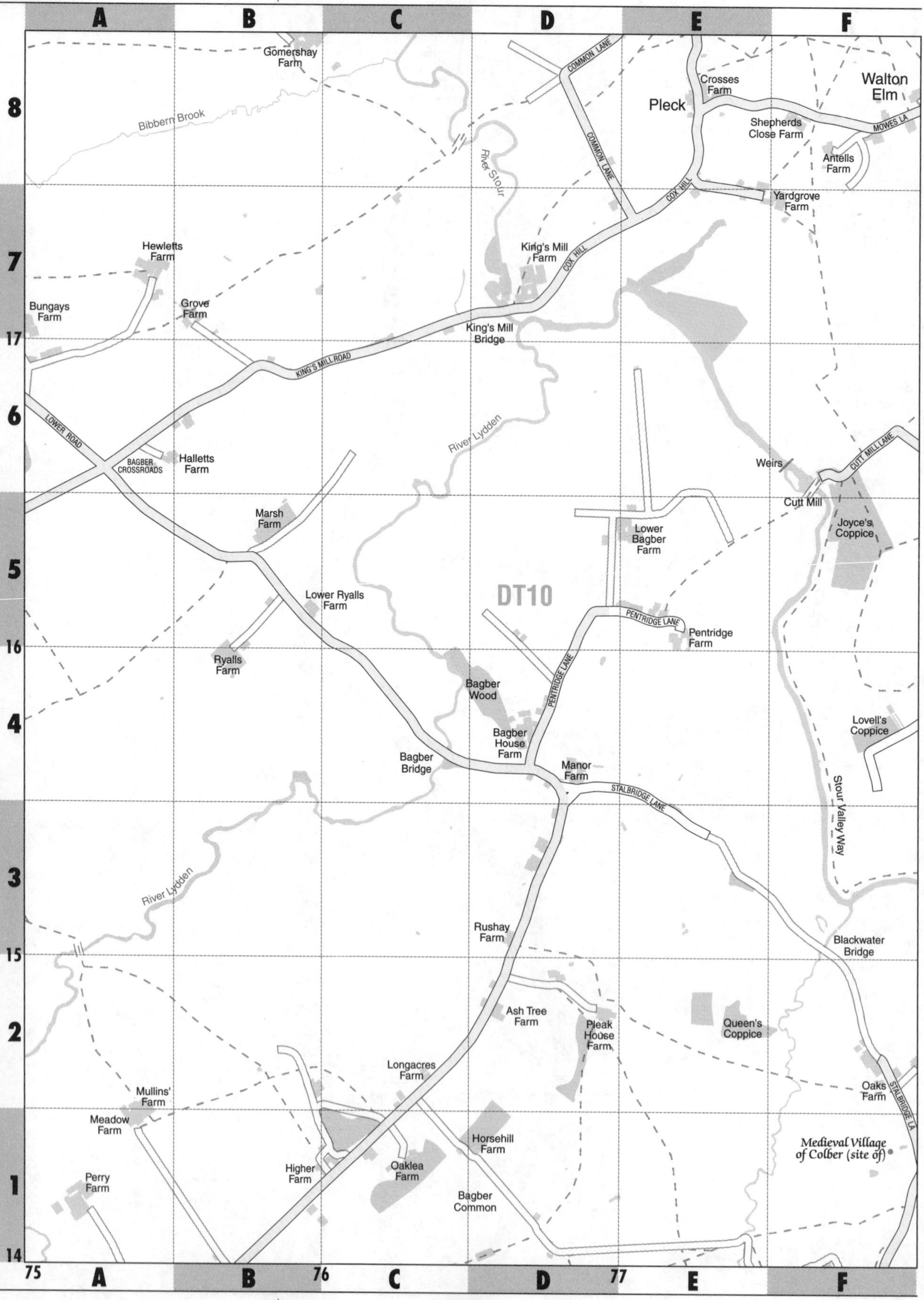

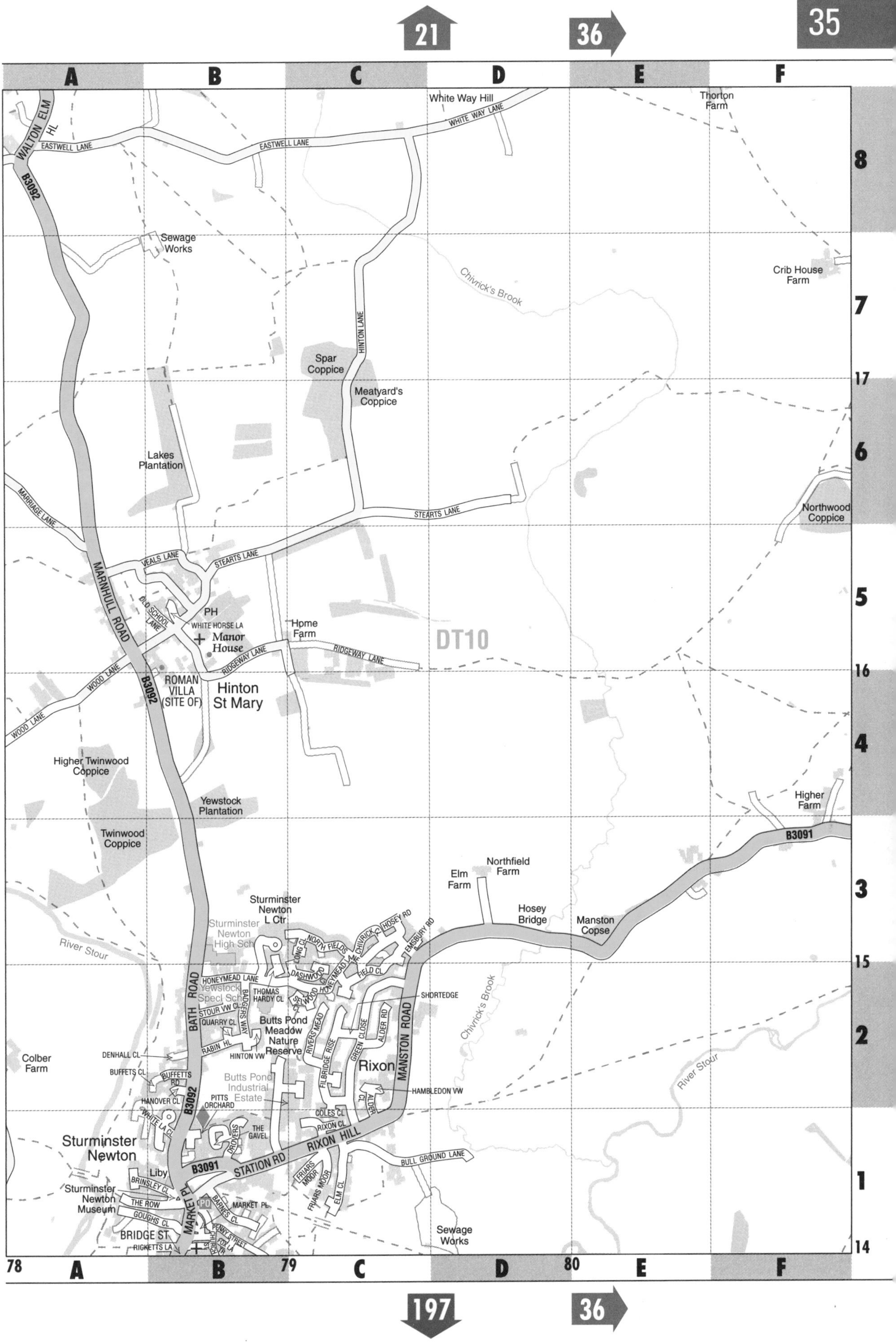
21
36
A
B
C
D
E
F
8
7
17
6
5
16
4
3
15
2
1
14
78
79
80
197
White Way Hill
WHITE WAY LANE
Thorton Farm
WALTON ELM
HL
EASTWELL LANE
B3092
Sewage Works
Crib House Farm
Chivrick's Brook
HINTON LANE
Spar Coppice
Meatyard's Coppice
Lakes Plantation
MARRIAGE LANE
STEARTS LANE
Northwood Coppice
VEALS LANE
MARNHULL ROAD
OLD SCHOOL LANE
PH
WHITE HORSE LA
Manor House
Home Farm
RIDGEWAY LANE
DT10
WOOD LANE
ROMAN VILLA (SITE OF)
Hinton St Mary
Higher Twinwood Coppice
Yewstock Plantation
Higher Farm
Twinwood Coppice
B3091
Northfield Farm
Elm Farm
Sturminster Newton L Ctr
Hosey Bridge
Manston Copse
Sturminster Newton High Sch
River Stour
HOSEY RD
EMSBURY RD
CHIVRICK
NORTH FIELDS
LONG CL
HONEYMEAD LANE
DASHWOOD
FIELD CL
BATH ROAD
Yewstock Specl Sch
THOMAS HARDY CL
BADGERS WAY
SHORTEDGE
STOUR VW CL
QUARRY CL
Butts Pond Meadow Nature Reserve
RIVERS MEAD
GREEN CLOSE
ALDER RD
MANSTON ROAD
RABIN HL
HINTON VW
Colber Farm
DENHALL CL
BUFFETS CL
BUFFETTS RD
Butts Pond Industrial Estate
FILBRIDGE RISE
Rixon
HAMBLEDON VW
HANOVER CL
PITTS ORCHARD
COLES CL
WHITE LA CL
RIXON CL
RIXON HILL
THE GAVEL
DROVERS
Sturminster Newton
BULL GROUND LANE
B3091
STATION RD
FRIARS MOOR
ELM CL
Liby
BRINSLEY CL
Sturminster Newton Museum
THE ROW
GOUGHS CL
MARKET PL
PO
BARNES CL
MARKET PL
BRIDGE ST
PENNY STREET
FOX LA
CHURCH ST
RICKETTS LA
Sewage Works

35
22

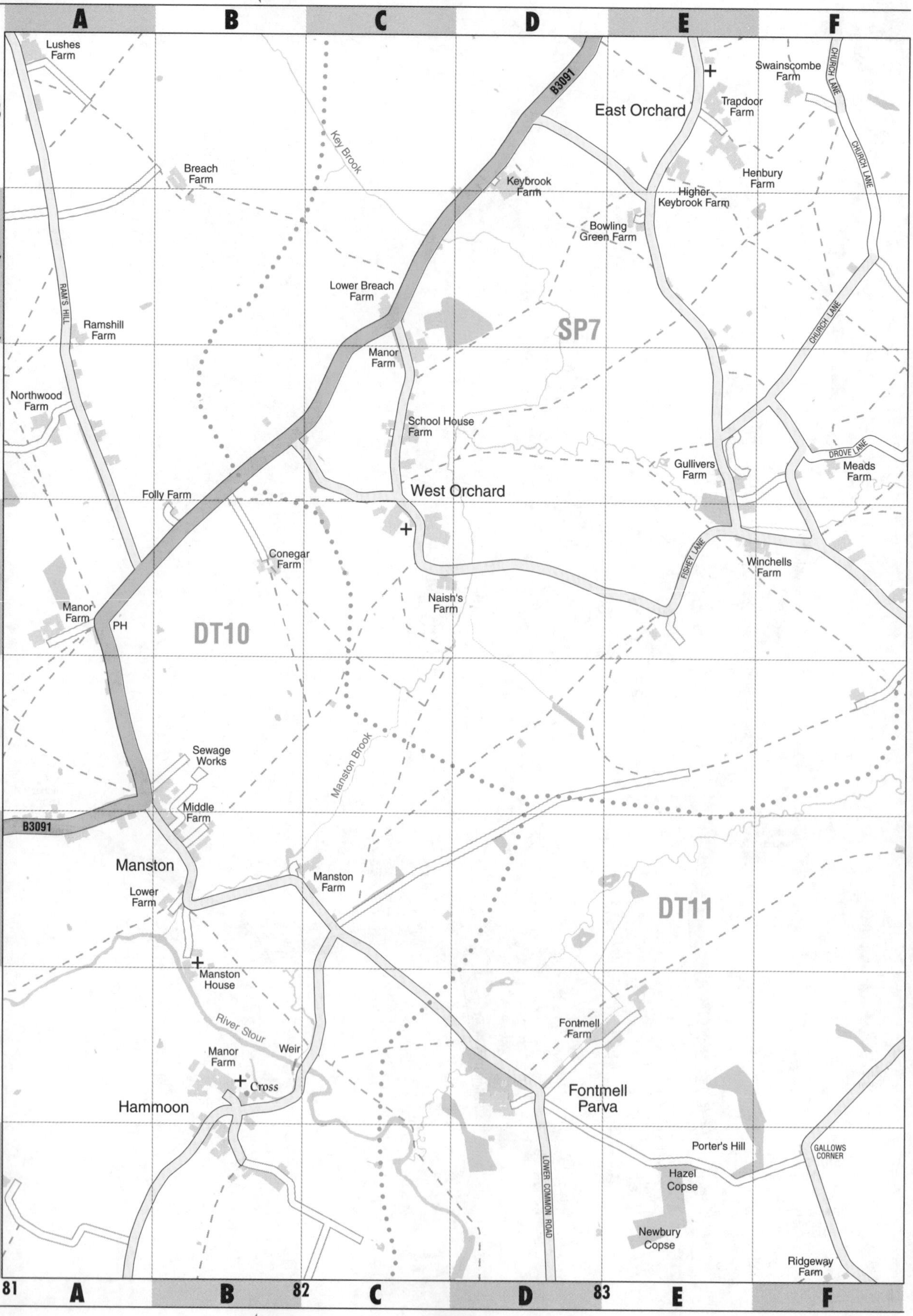

A B C D E F

8

Lushes Farm

B3091

East Orchard

Swainscombe Farm

CHURCH LANE

Breach Farm

Keybrook Farm

Trapdoor Farm

Key Brook

Henbury Farm

7

RAM'S HILL

Ramshill Farm

Lower Breach Farm

Bowling Green Farm

Higher Keybrook Farm

SP7

17

Manor Farm

6

Northwood Farm

School House Farm

CHURCH LANE

DROVE LANE

Meads Farm

Folly Farm

West Orchard

Gullivers Farm

FISHEY LANE

5

Conegar Farm

Winchells Farm

Naish's Farm

16

Manor Farm

PH

DT10

4

Sewage Works

Manston Brook

Middle Farm

B3091

3

Manston

Manston Farm

DT11

Lower Farm

15

Manston House

River Stour

Fontmell Farm

2

Manor Farm

Weir

Cross

Fontmell Parva

Hammoon

LOWER COMMON ROAD

Porter's Hill

GALLOWS CORNER

Hazel Copse

1

Newbury Copse

Ridgeway Farm

14

81 A B 82 C D 83 E F

23
38

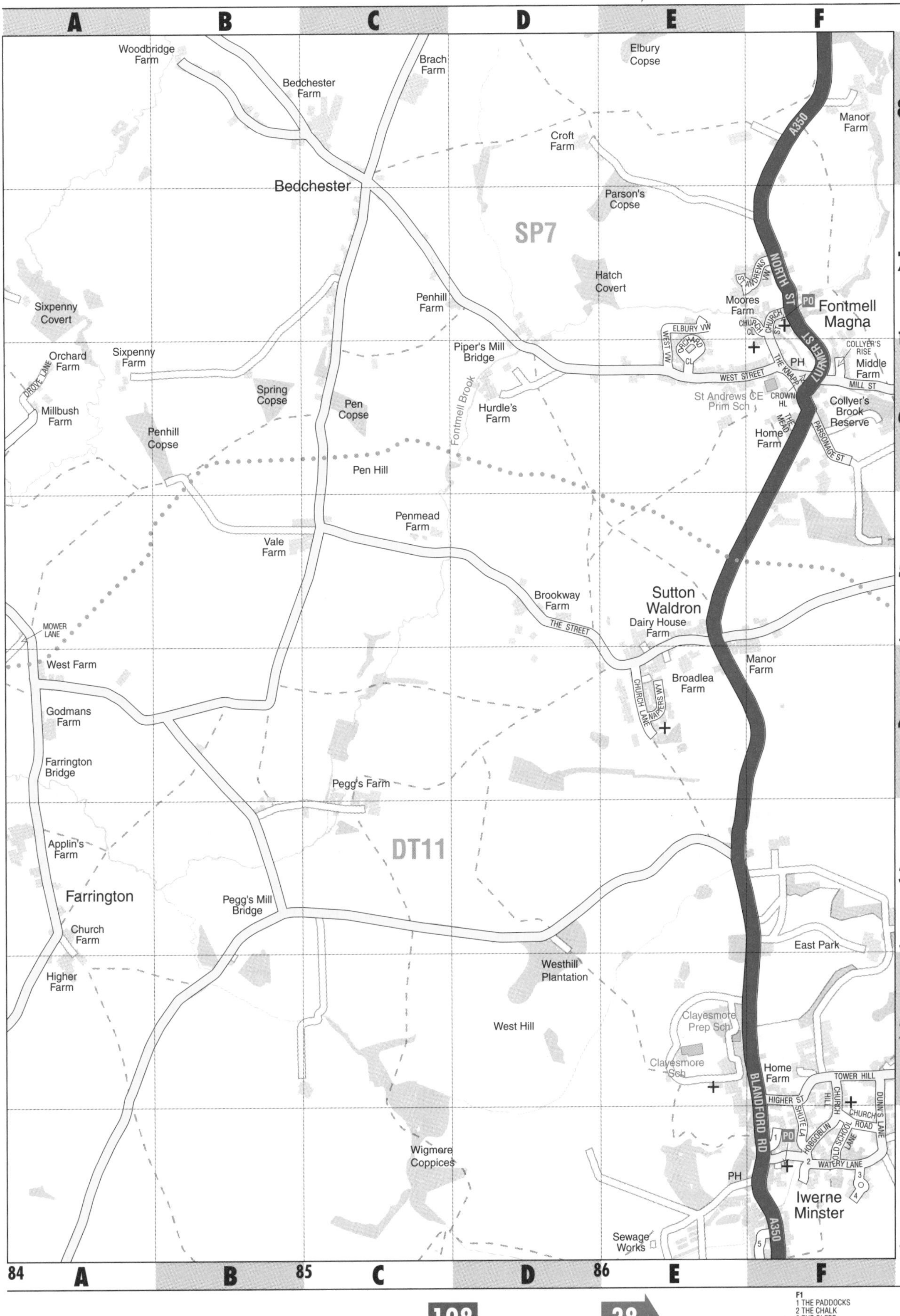
A
B
C
D
E
F
Woodbridge Farm
Bedchester Farm
Brach Farm
Elbury Copse
Manor Farm
Croft Farm
Bedchester
Parson's Copse
SP7
A350
NORTH ST
Hatch Covert
Sixpenny Covert
Penhill Farm
Moores Farm
Fontmell Magna
PO
PH
ST ANDREWS VW
ELBURY VW
WEST VW
ORCHARD CL
CHURCH CL
CHURCH ST
WEST STREET
THE KNAPP
CROWN HL
MILL ST
COLLYER'S RISE
Middle Farm
St Andrews CE Prim Sch
Collyer's Brook Reserve
Orchard Farm
Sixpenny Farm
Piper's Mill Bridge
DROVE LANE
Spring Copse
Pen Copse
Hurdle's Farm
Millbush Farm
Penhill Copse
Fontmell Brook
THE MEAD
Home Farm
PARSONAGE ST
Pen Hill
Penmead Farm
Vale Farm
Brookway Farm
Sutton Waldron
Dairy House Farm
THE STREET
MOWER LANE
West Farm
Manor Farm
Broadlea Farm
Godmans Farm
CHURCH LANE
NAPIERS WAY
Farrington Bridge
Peggs Farm
Applin's Farm
DT11
Farrington
Pegg's Mill Bridge
Church Farm
East Park
Higher Farm
Westhill Plantation
Claysmore Prep Sch
West Hill
Clayesmore Sch
Home Farm
TOWER HILL
HIGHER ST
SHUTE LA
HILL
CHURCH
CHURCH ROAD
DUNN'S LANE
BLANDFORD RD
HOBGOBLIN
OLD SCHOOL LANE
WATERY LANE
Wigmore Coppices
PH
Iwerne Minster
Sewage Works
A350
8
7
17
6
5
16
4
3
15
2
1
14
84
85
86
F1
1 THE PADDOCKS
2 THE CHALK
3 THE GLEBE
4 GLEBE CT
5 OAKWOOD DR

198
38

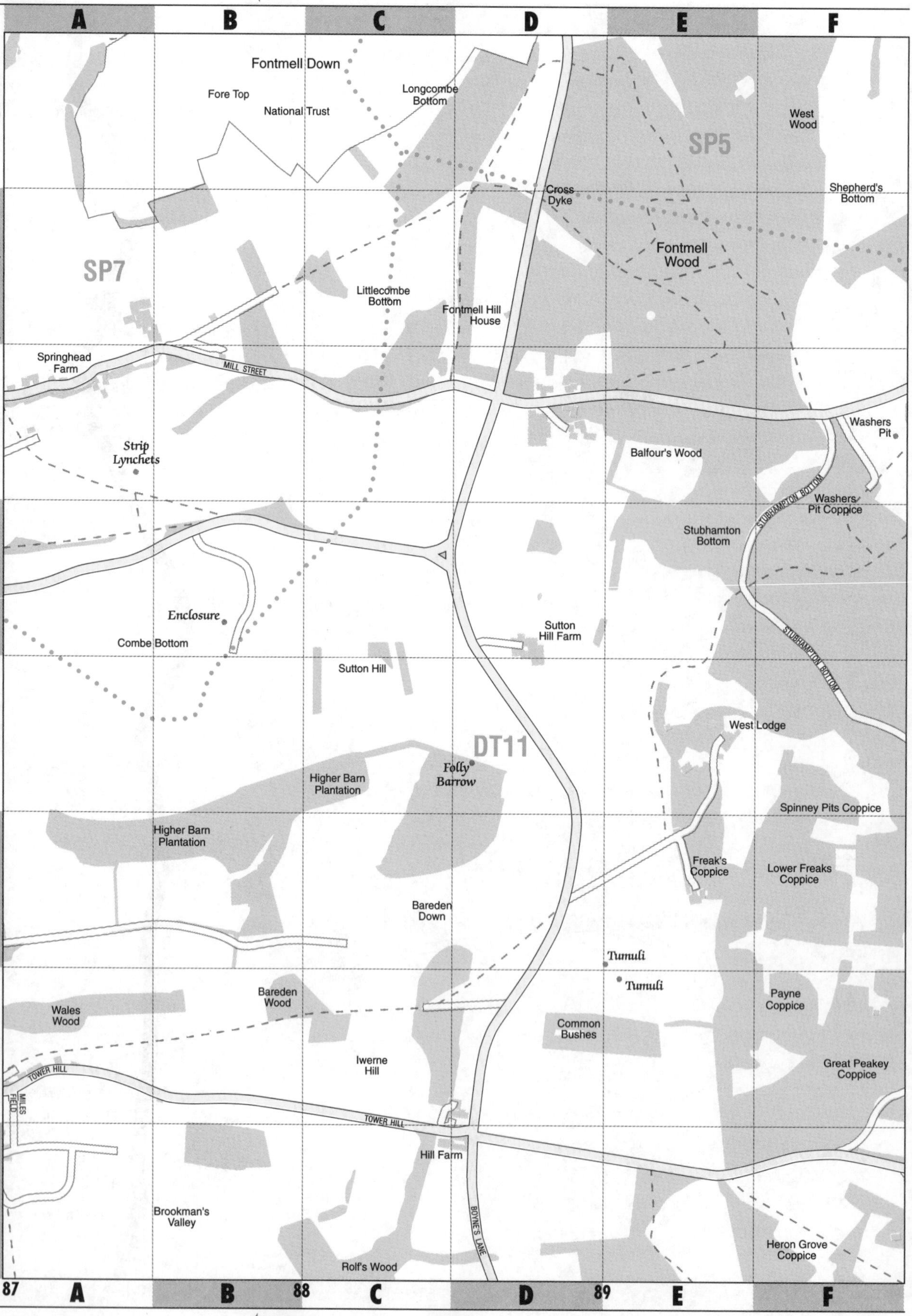

A B C D E F

8

Fontmell Down

Fore Top

National Trust

Longcombe Bottom

SP5

West Wood

Cross Dyke

Shepherd's Bottom

7

SP7

Fontmell Wood

Littlecombe Bottom

Fontmell Hill House

17

Springhead Farm

MILL STREET

6

Washers Pit

Strip Lynchets

Balfour's Wood

Washers Pit Coppice

STUBHAMPTON BOTTOM

Stubhamton Bottom

5

Enclosure

Combe Bottom

STUBHAMPTON BOTTOM

16

Sutton Hill Farm

Sutton Hill

West Lodge

4

DT11

Higher Barn Plantation

Folly Barrow

Spinney Pits Coppice

Higher Barn Plantation

Freak's Coppice

Lower Freaks Coppice

3

Bareden Down

Tumuli

15

Tumuli

Payne Coppice

Bareden Wood

Wales Wood

2

Common Bushes

Great Peakey Coppice

TOWER HILL

Iwerne Hill

MILES FIELD

TOWER HILL

BOYNE'S LANE

1

Hill Farm

Brookman's Valley

Heron Grove Coppice

14

Rolf's Wood

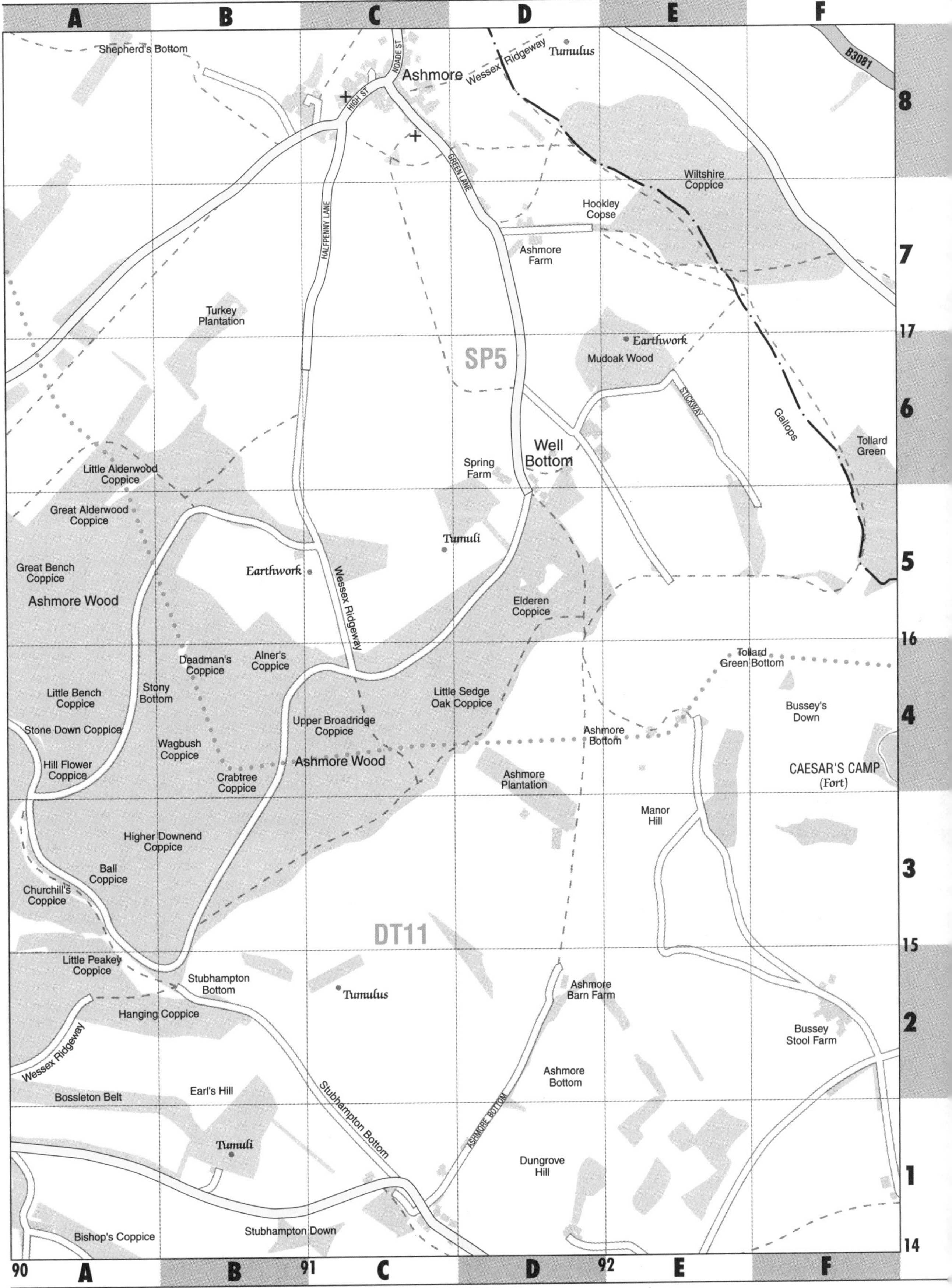

B3081

A B C D E F

8

Shepherd's Bottom

Ashmore
Wessex Ridgeway
Tumulus

High St

ROADE ST

GREEN LANE

Wiltshire
Coppice

7

HALFPENNY LANE

Hookley
Copse

Ashmore
Farm

Turkey
Plantation

SP5

Earthwork

17

Mudoak Wood

6

Gallops

Well
Bottom

STICKWAY

Tollard
Green

Little Alderwood
Coppice

Spring
Farm

Great Alderwood
Coppice

Tumuli

Earthwork

Wessex Ridgeway

Great Bench
Coppice

Elderen
Coppice

5

Ashmore Wood

16

Tollard
Green Bottom

Deadman's
Coppice

Alner's
Coppice

Bussey's
Down

Little Bench
Coppice

Stony
Bottom

Little Sedge
Oak Coppice

4

Stone Down Coppice

Upper Broadridge
Coppice

Ashmore
Bottom

CAESAR'S CAMP
(Fort)

Wagbush
Coppice

Hill Flower
Coppice

Ashmore Wood

Crabtree
Coppice

Ashmore
Plantation

Higher Downend
Coppice

Manor
Hill

3

Ball
Coppice

15

Churchill's
Coppice

DT11

Little Peakey
Coppice

Stubhampton
Bottom

Ashmore
Barn Farm

2

Hanging Coppice

Tumulus

Bussey
Stool Farm

Wessex Ridgeway

Ashmore
Bottom

Earl's Hill

Bossleton Belt

Stubhampton Bottom

ASHMORE BOTTOM

Tumuli

Dungrove
Hill

1

Bishop's Coppice

Stubhampton Down

90 A B 91 C D 92 E F 14

A | B | C | D | E | F

8

Long Copse

Burwood

Pound Farm

BELLOWS CROSS

Ashes Farm

Cranborne Middle Sch

Paul's Copse

SP6

Cranborne

7

GRUGS LA

PENNY'S LANE

Holwell Farm

Jordan Hill Plantation

CHURCHILL DRIVE

Old Claygrounds

HIGH ST
THE SQ
CRANE ST
WATER ST

Cranborne Manor Gardens

WIMBORNE ST
SWAN ST
CHURCH ST

PO
PH

PENNY'S MD
FRIDAY'S HERON

Cranborne Manor

Cranborne CE First Sch

CASTLE ST

HABGRUS FIELD

Higher Holwell Farm

B3078

13

CASTLE HL LA

CASTLE CL

CASTLE HL LA

6

B3078

Castle Hill

River Crane

Lower Holwell

Hill Wood

Motte & Bailey

MILL LANE

Gilham's Copse

Fir Copse

HARE LANE

5

Cranborne Copse

Castle Hill Wood

Mill Farm

Bottom Copse

Long Copse

Great Rhymes Copse

12

Lower Farm

Barnfield Farm

BH21

Little Rhymes Copse

Woodward's Copse

4

Edmondsham House & Gardens

Furze Common Copse

Mill Copse

MILL LA

Common Copse

Cook's Moor

Edmondsham

3

Pert Copse

Wingsdown

Upper Farm

11

Hobbys Copse

Smallbridge Farm

Chalybeate Spring

Maldry Wood

Sandy's Hill

Pinnocks Moor Bridge

Dorset Heavy Horse Centre

2

Smallbridge Copse

Deer Park Ponds

Sutton Copse

Pains Moor Copse

River Crane

Westworth Farm

1

B3081

Great Rough Copse

HORTON RD

Sutton Holms Reserve

Sutton Farm

Birches Copse

10

05 | A | B | 06 | C | D | 07 | E | F

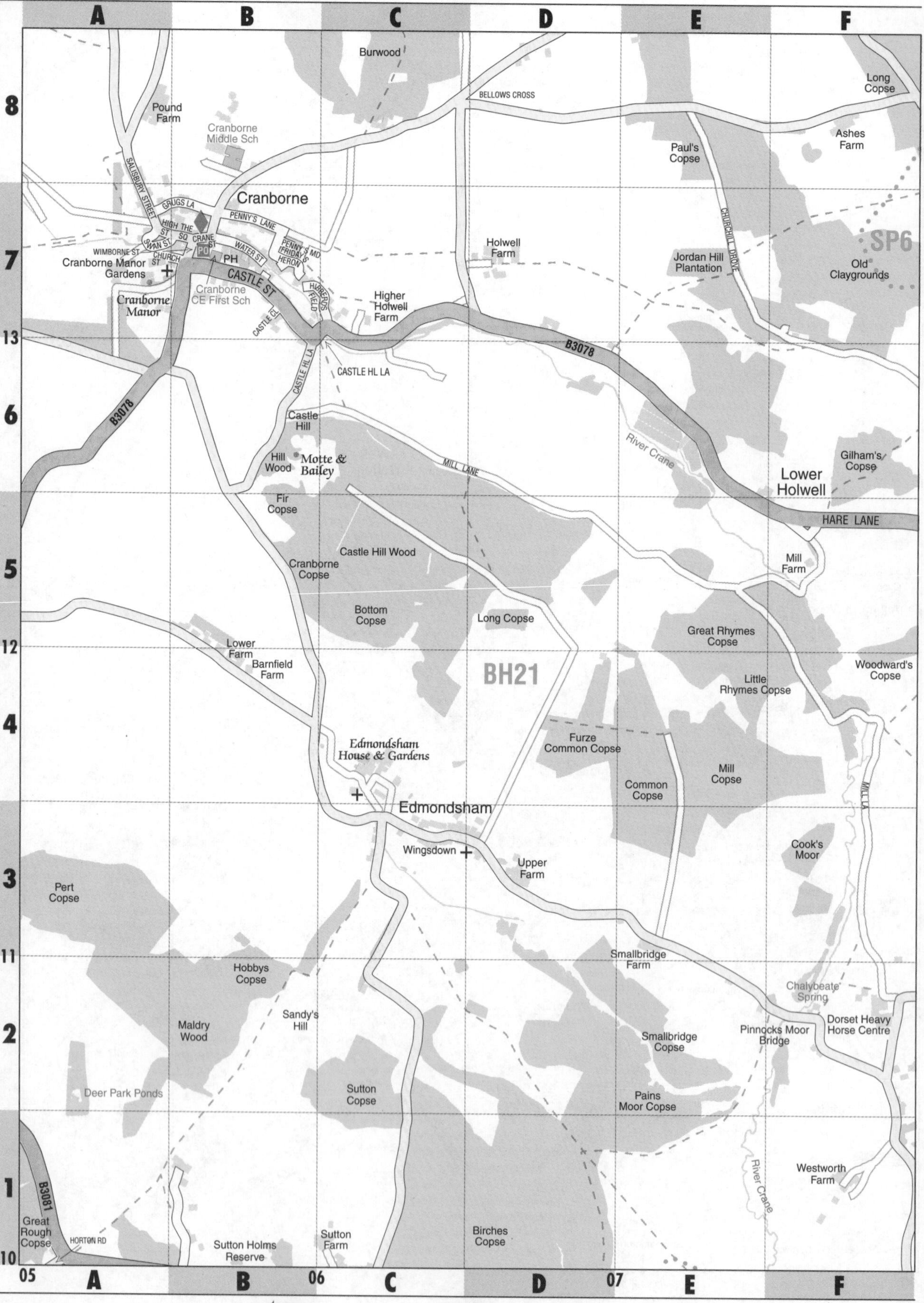

190
42

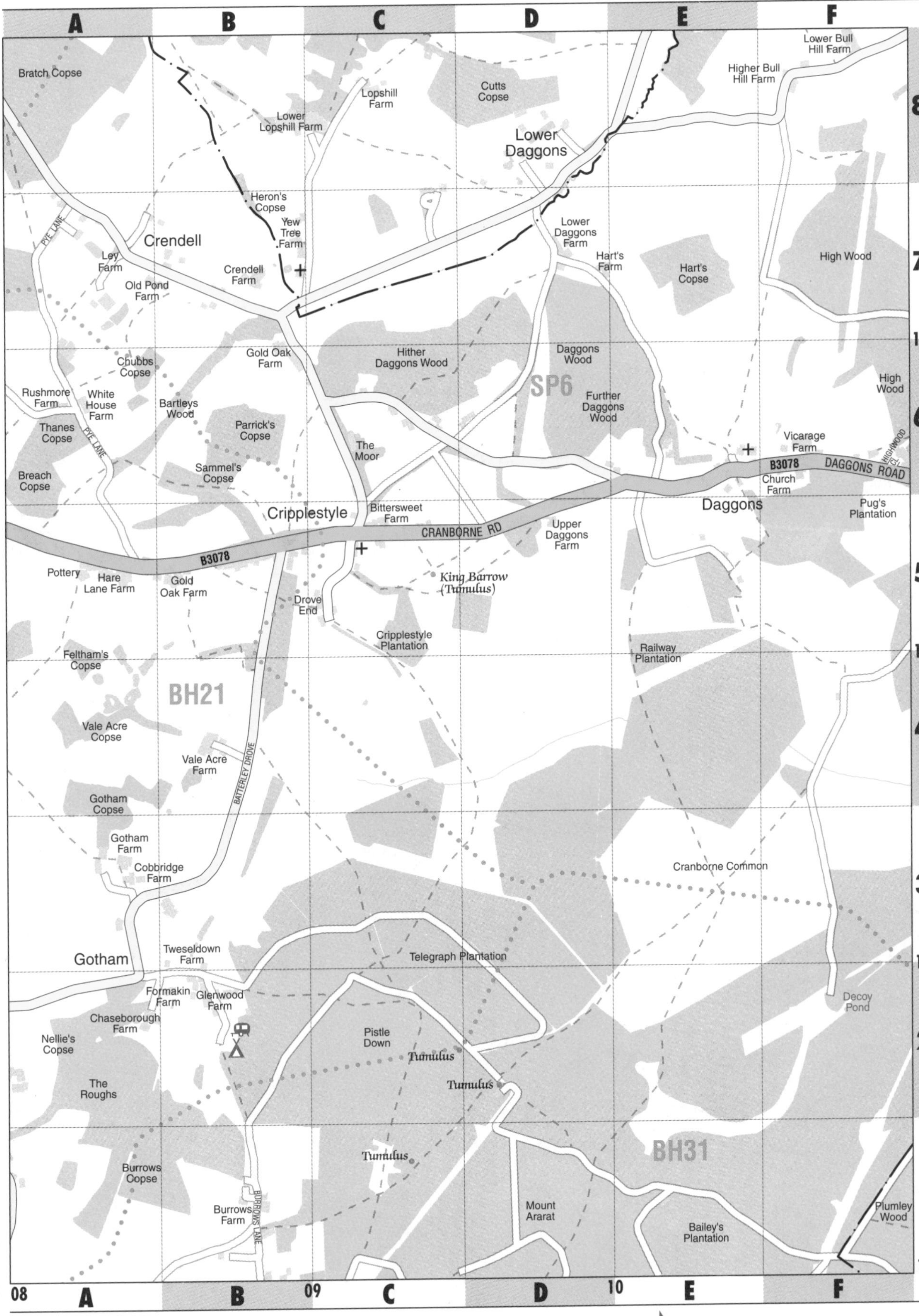
A
B
C
D
E
F
8
7
13
6
5
12
4
3
11
2
1
10
08
09
10
Bratch Copse
Lopshill Farm
Lower Lopshill Farm
Cutts Copse
Lower Bull Hill Farm
Higher Bull Hill Farm
Lower Daggons
Heron's Copse
Yew Tree Farm
Crendell
PYE LANE
Ley Farm
Old Pond Farm
Crendell Farm
Lower Daggons Farm
Hart's Farm
Hart's Copse
High Wood
Gold Oak Farm
Hither Daggons Wood
Daggons Wood
SP6
Further Daggons Wood
High Wood
Chubbs Copse
Rushmore Farm
White House Farm
Bartleys Wood
Parrick's Copse
Thanes Copse
The Moor
Vicarage Farm
HIGHWOOD CL
B3078
DAGGONS ROAD
Church Farm
Breach Copse
Sammel's Copse
Cripplestyle
Bittersweet Farm
Daggons
Pug's Plantation
CRANBORNE RD
Upper Daggons Farm
Pottery
Hare Lane Farm
Gold Oak Farm
Drove End
King Barrow (Tumulus)
Cripplestyle Plantation
Railway Plantation
Feltham's Copse
BH21
Vale Acre Copse
Vale Acre Farm
BATTERLEY DROVE
Gotham Copse
Gotham Farm
Cobbridge Farm
Cranborne Common
Gotham
Tweseldown Farm
Telegraph Plantation
Formakin Farm
Glenwood Farm
Decoy Pond
Chaseborough Farm
Nellie's Copse
Pistle Down
Tumulus
Tumulus
The Roughs
Tumulus
BH31
Burrows Copse
BURROWS LANE
Burrows Farm
Mount Ararat
Bailey's Plantation
Plumley Wood

45
42

41

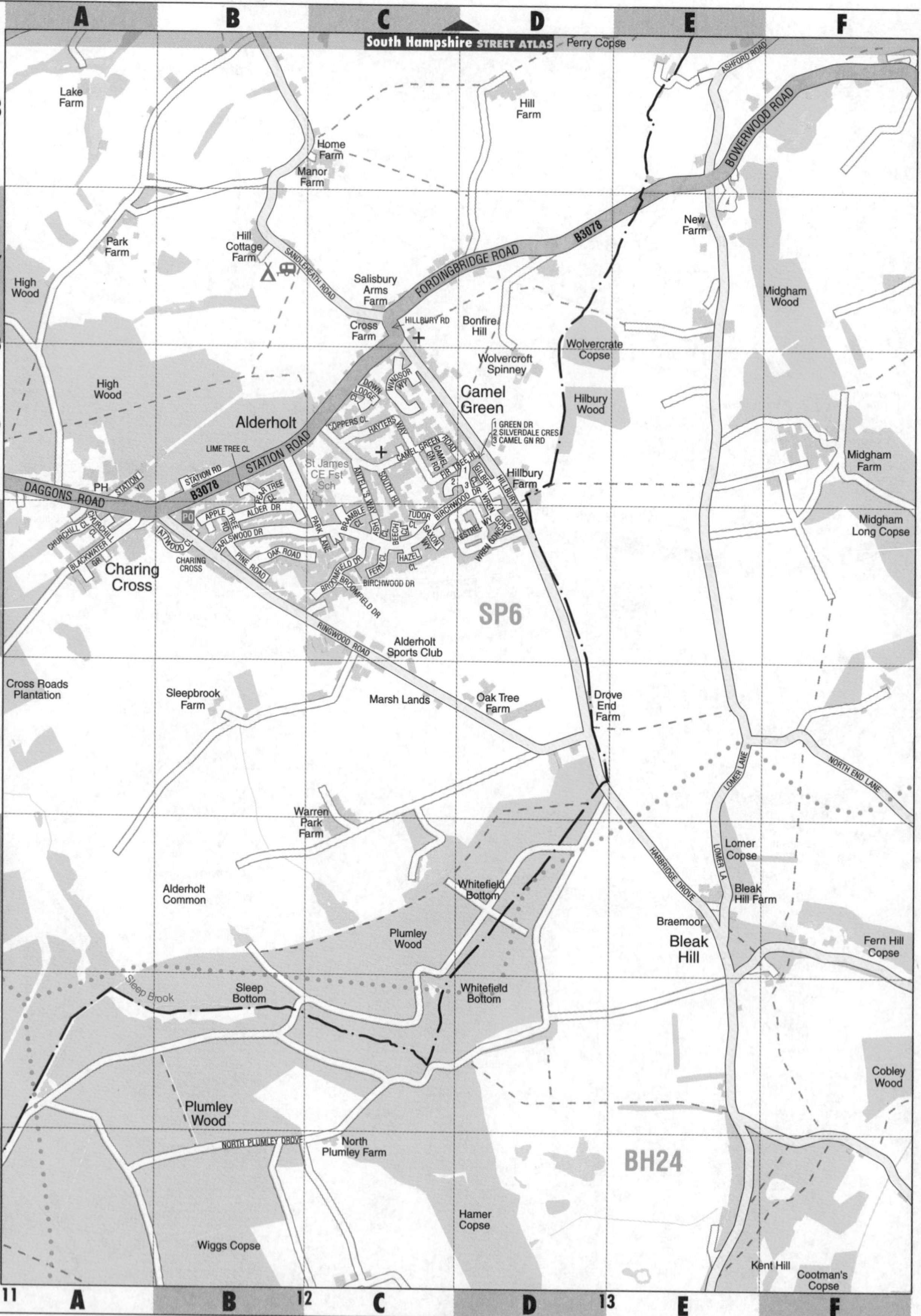
South Hampshire STREET ATLAS
A
B
C
D
E
F
8
7
6
5
4
3
2
1
13
12
11
10
Perry Copse
Lake Farm
Hill Farm
Home Farm
Manor Farm
ASHFORD ROAD
BOWERWOOD ROAD
New Farm
B3078
FORDINGBRIDGE ROAD
Park Farm
Hill Cottage Farm
SANDLEHEATH ROAD
High Wood
Salisbury Arms Farm
Midgham Wood
Cross Farm
HILLBURY RD
Bonfire Hill
Wolvercrate Copse
Wolvercroft Spinney
High Wood
Camel Green
Hilbury Wood
Alderholt
STATION ROAD
LIME TREE CL
COPPERS CL
HAYTERS WAY
DOWN LODGE CL
WINDSOR WY
1 GREEN DR
2 SILVERDALE CRES
3 CAMEL GN RD
Midgham Farm
St James CE Fst Sch
Hillbury Farm
HILLBURY ROAD
DAGGONS ROAD
PH
STATION YD
STATION RD
PEAR TREE CL
ALDER DR
APPLE TREE RD
EARLSWOOD DR
CHURCHILL CL
BLACKWATER GR
ATTWOOD CL
CHARING CROSS
Charing Cross
PINE ROAD
OAK ROAD
PARK LANE
ANTELL'S WAY
SOUTH HL
BRAMBLE CL
BEECH CL
TUDOR CL
HAZEL CL
FERN CL
BIRCHWOOD DR
BROOMFIELD DR
KESTREL WY
WREN GDNS
GILBERT CL
FIR TREE HL
Midgham Long Copse
SP6
RINGWOOD ROAD
Alderholt Sports Club
Cross Roads Plantation
Sleepbrook Farm
Marsh Lands
Oak Tree Farm
Drove End Farm
NORTH END LANE
LOMER LANE
Warren Park Farm
Lomer Copse
LOMER LA
HARBRIDGE DROVE
Alderholt Common
Whitefield Bottom
Bleak Hill Farm
Braemoor
Plumley Wood
Bleak Hill
Fern Hill Copse
Sleep Brook
Sleep Bottom
Whitefield Bottom
Cobley Wood
Plumley Wood
NORTH PLUMLEY DROVE
North Plumley Farm
BH24
Hamer Copse
Wiggs Copse
Kent Hill
Cootman's Copse

41
46

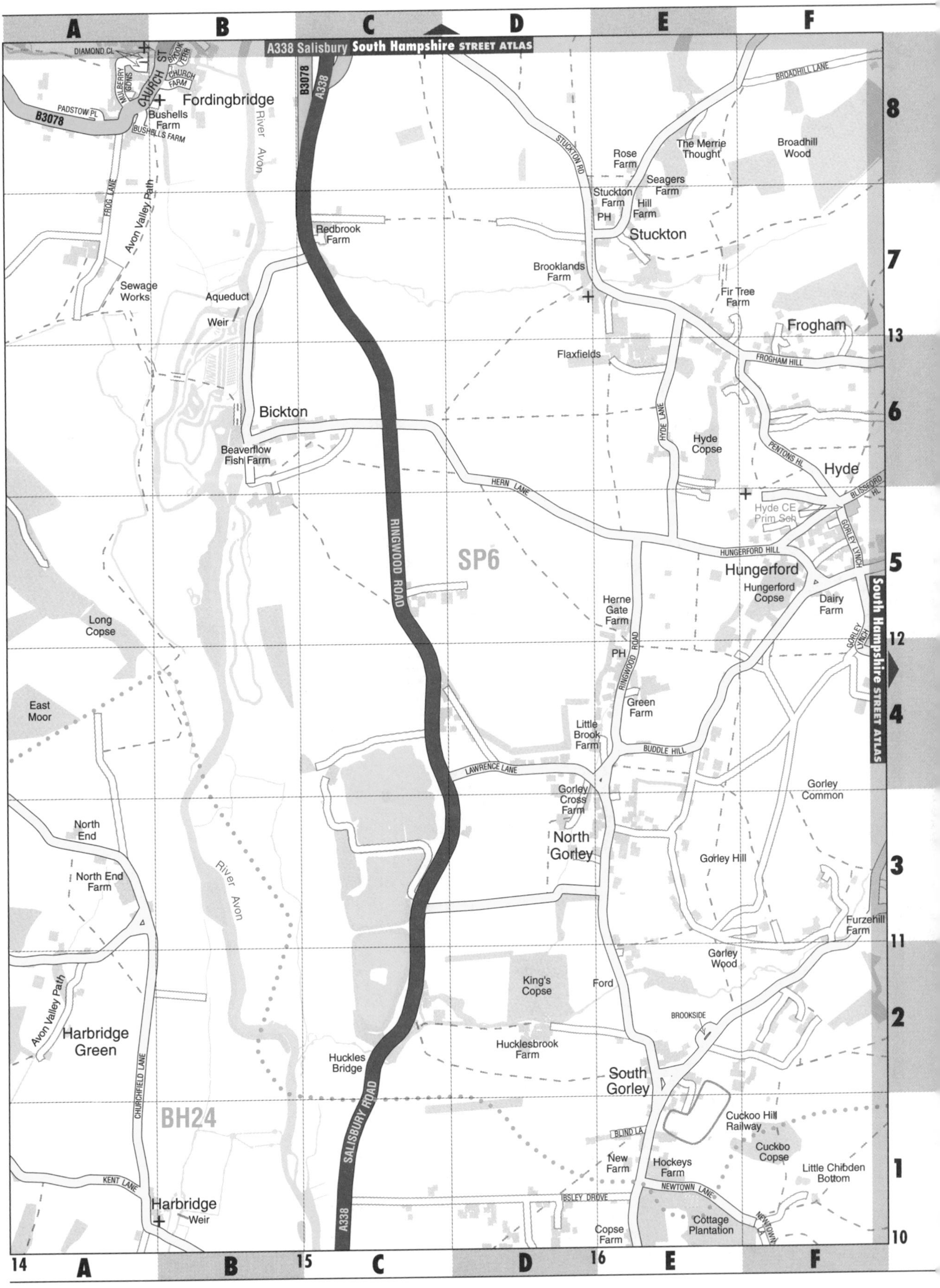

A338 Salisbury **South Hampshire** STREET ATLAS

BROADHILL LANE

Fordingbridge

DIAMOND CL

MULBERRY GDNS
CHURCH ST
BROOK TERR
CHURCH FARM

Bushells Farm
BUSHELLS FARM

PADSTOW PL

B3078

FROG LANE

Avon Valley Path

River Avon

Sewage Works

Aqueduct

Weir

Redbrook Farm

Rose Farm

The Merrie Thought

Broadhill Wood

STUCKTON RD

Seagers Farm

Stuckton Farm PH

Hill Farm

Stuckton

Brooklands Farm

Fir Tree Farm

Frogham

13

FROGHAM HILL

Flaxfields

Bickton

HYDE LANE

Hyde Copse

PENTONS HL

Hyde

BLISSFORD HL

6

Beaverflow Fish Farm

RINGWOOD ROAD

HERN LANE

Hyde CE Prim Sch

GORLEY LYNCH

SP6

HUNGERFORD HILL

Hungerford

Hungerford Copse

Dairy Farm

5

Long Copse

Herne Gate Farm

GORLEY LYNCH

12

PH

RINGWOOD ROAD

Green Farm

East Moor

Little Brook Farm

BUDDLE HILL

Gorley Common

4

LAWRENCE LANE

Gorley Cross Farm

North Gorley

Gorley Hill

North End

North End Farm

Avon Valley Path

River Avon

Gorley Wood

Furzehill Farm

11

CHURCHFIELD LANE

King's Copse

Ford

3

Huckles Bridge

Hucklesbrook Farm

BROOKSIDE

2

BH24

Harbridge Green

SALISBURY ROAD

South Gorley

BLIND LA

Cuckoo Hill Railway

Cuckbo Copse

Little Chibden Bottom

New Farm

Hockeys Farm

NEWTOWN LANE

NEWTOWN LA

KENT LANE

Harbridge

Weir

A338

IBSLEY DROVE

Copse Farm

Cottage Plantation

10

8

7

1

47

← 201
40 ↑

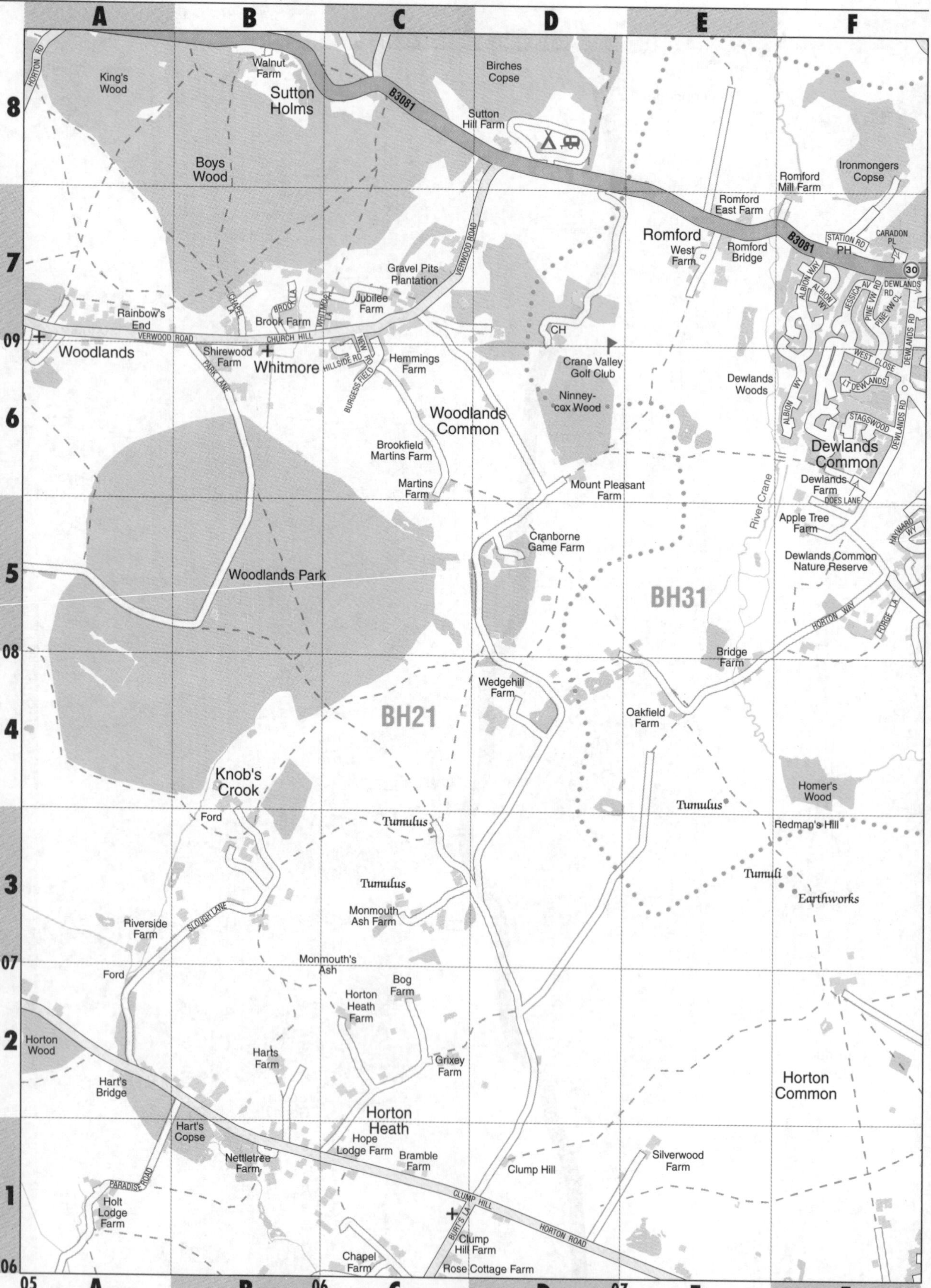

A · **B** · **C** · **D** · **E** · **F**

HORTON RD

King's Wood

Walnut Farm

Sutton Holms

Boys Wood

Birches Copse

B3081

Sutton Hill Farm

Romford Mill Farm

Ironmongers Copse

Romford East Farm

Romford

West Farm

Romford Bridge

B3081

STATION RD

CARADON PL

PH

30

8

7

Gravel Pits Plantation

VERWOOD ROAD

ALBION WY

ALBION WAY

JESSICA AV

PINE VW RD

DEWLANDS RD

Rainbow's End

VERWOOD ROAD

CHAPEL LA

BROOK LA

Brook Farm

LA MOOR

Jubilee Farm

CH

PINE VW CL

DEWLANDS RD

09

+ Woodlands

Shirewood Farm

PARK LANE

+ Whitmore

HILLSIDE RD

CHURCH HILL

BURGESS FIELD LA

Hemmings Farm

CH

Crane Valley Golf Club

WEST CLOSE

DEWLANDS

Dewlands Woods

STAGSWOOD

Dewlands Common

6

Woodlands Common

Ninney-cox Wood

▶

DEWLANDS RD

HAYWARD WY

Brookfield Martins Farm

Martins Farm

Mount Pleasant Farm

Dewlands Farm

DOES LANE

Apple Tree Farm

5

Woodlands Park

Cranborne Game Farm

River Crane

BH31

Dewlands Common Nature Reserve

HORTON WAY

FORGE LA

08

Bridge Farm

4

Wedgehill Farm

Oakfield Farm

BH21

Knob's Crook

Tumulus

Homer's Wood

Ford

Tumulus

Tumulus

Redman's Hill

3

Tumulus

Tumuli

Earthworks

Riverside Farm

SLOUGH LANE

Monmouth Ash Farm

07

Monmouth's Ash

Ford

Horton Heath Farm

Bog Farm

2

Horton Wood

Harts Farm

Grixey Farm

Horton Common

Hart's Bridge

PARADISE ROAD

Hart's Copse

Horton Heath

Hope Lodge Farm

Bramble Farm

Clump Hill

Silverwood Farm

1

Nettletree Farm

CLUMP HILL

BURT'S LA

HORTON ROAD

Holt Lodge Farm

+

Clump Hill Farm

06

Chapel Farm

Rose Cottage Farm

41
46

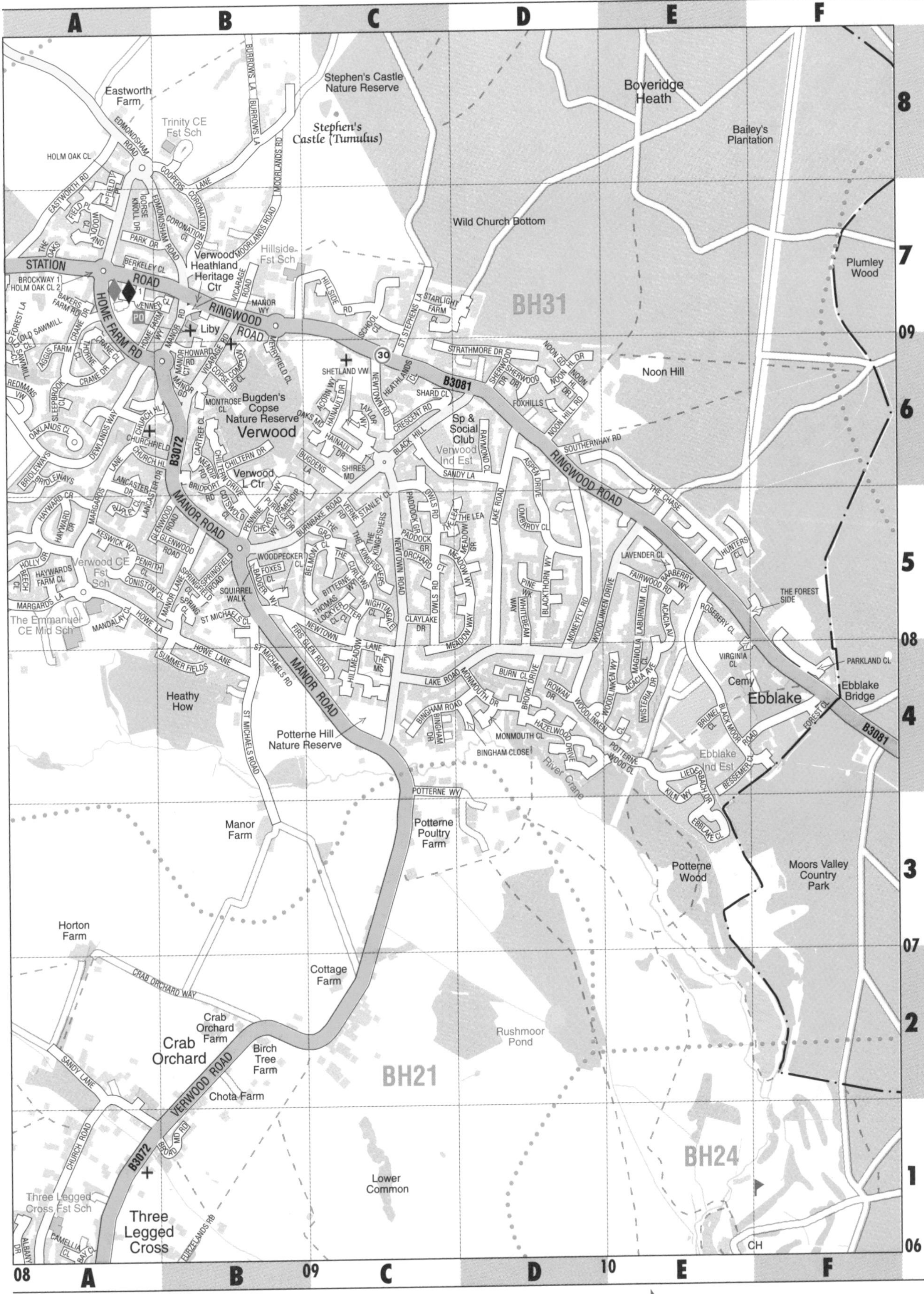
Eastworth Farm
Trinity CE Fst Sch
Stephen's Castle Nature Reserve
Stephen's Castle (Tumulus)
Boveridge Heath
Bailey's Plantation
Wild Church Bottom
Plumley Wood
Hillside Fst Sch
Verwood Heathland Heritage Ctr
BH31
STATION ROAD
RINGWOOD ROAD
HOME FARM RD
MANOR ROAD
B3072
B3081
Liby
Noon Hill
Bugden's Copse Nature Reserve
Verwood
Verwood L Ctr
Sp & Social Club
Verwood Ind Est
Verwood CE Fst Sch
The Emmanuel CE Mid Sch
Heathy How
Potterne Hill Nature Reserve
Cemy
Ebblake
Ebblake Bridge
Ebblake Ind Est
River Crane
Manor Farm
Potterne Poultry Farm
Potterne Wood
Moors Valley Country Park
Horton Farm
Cottage Farm
Crab Orchard Farm
Crab Orchard
Birch Tree Farm
Chota Farm
Rushmoor Pond
BH21
BH24
Lower Common
Three Legged Cross Fst Sch
Three Legged Cross
VERWOOD ROAD
CRAB ORCHARD WAY
SANDY LANE
CHURCH ROAD
CH

53
46

45
42

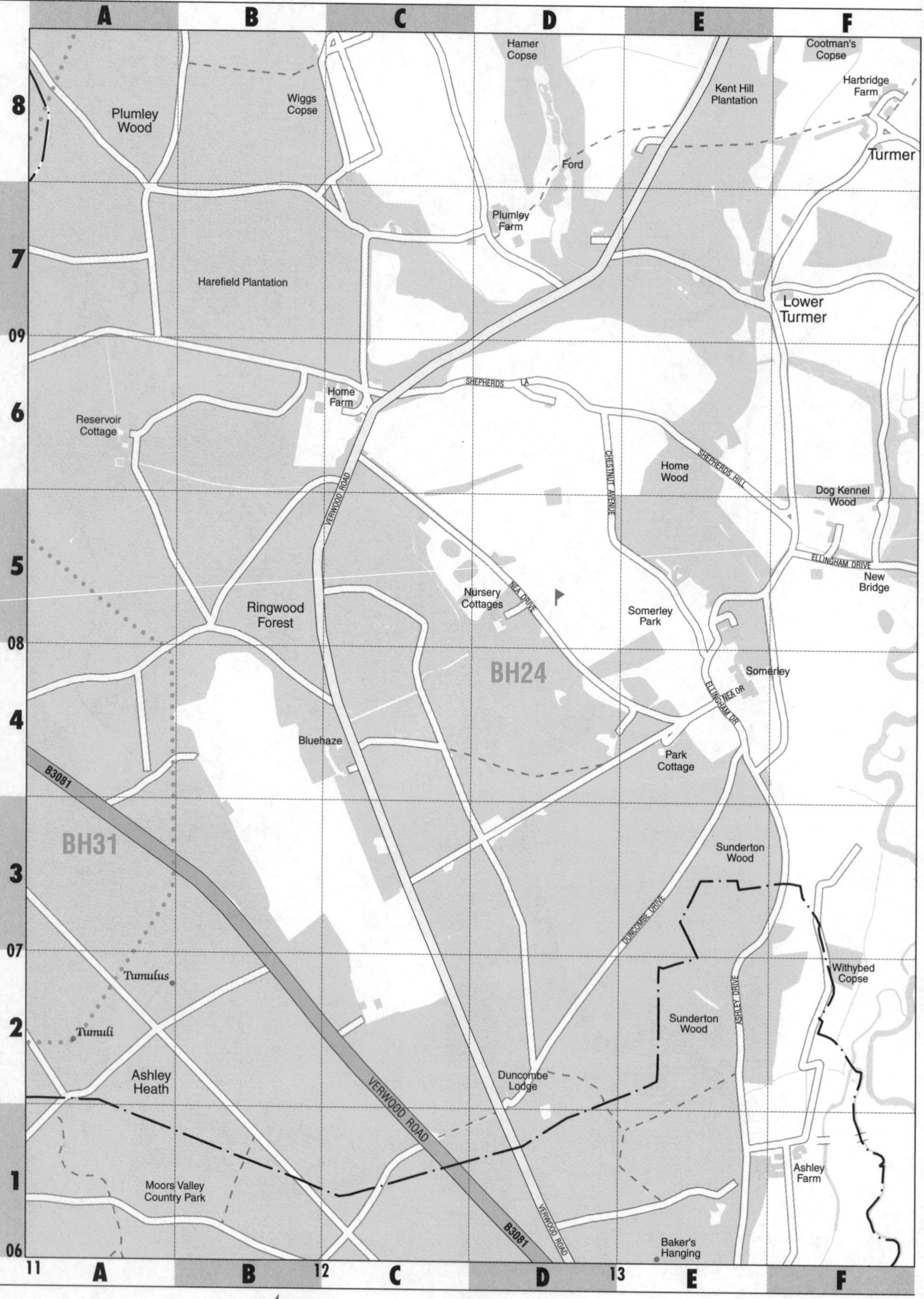

A B C D E F

8

Plumley Wood

Wiggs Copse

Hamer Copse

Kent Hill Plantation

Cootman's Copse

Harbridge Farm

Ford

Turmer

7

Plumley Farm

Harefield Plantation

Lower Turmer

09

SHEPHERDS LA

6

Reservoir Cottage

Home Farm

Home Wood

SHEPHERDS HILL

CHESTNUT AVENUE

Dog Kennel Wood

ELLINGHAM DRIVE

New Bridge

5

VERWOOD ROAD

Nursery Cottages

NEA DRIVE

Somerley Park

Somerley

Ringwood Forest

BH24

08

4

Bluehaze

ELLINGHAM DR

Park Cottage

BH31

B3081

3

Sunderton Wood

DUNCOMBE DRIVE

07

Withybed Copse

Tumulus

2

Tumuli

Sunderton Wood

ASHLEY DRIVE

Ashley Heath

Duncombe Lodge

VERWOOD ROAD

1

Moors Valley Country Park

Ashley Farm

Baker's Hanging

B3081

VERWOOD ROAD

06

11   A   B   12   C   D   13   E   F

45
54

43

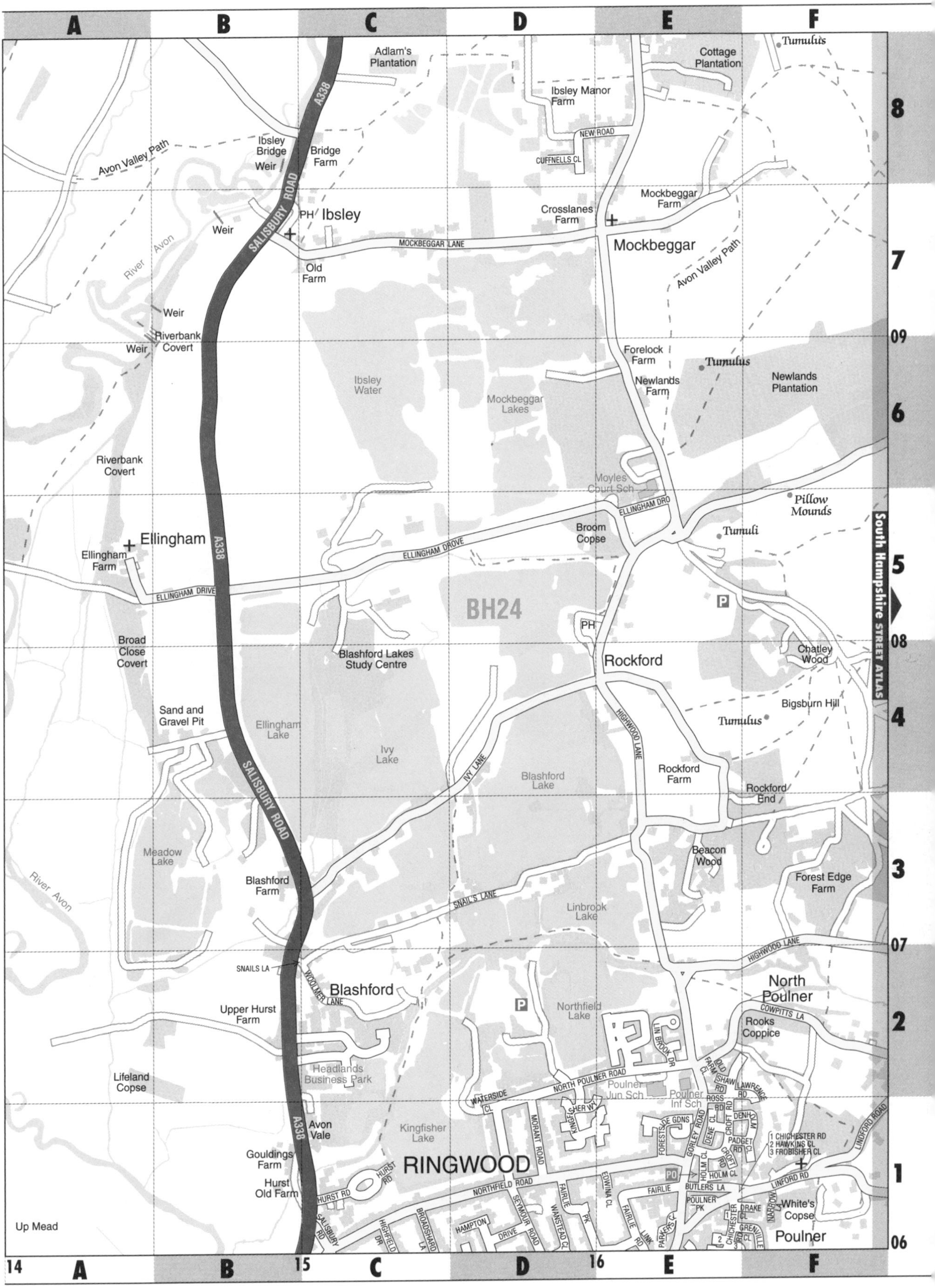

A
B
C
D
E
F
8
7
6
5
4
3
2
1
09
08
07
06
14
15
16
Tumulus
Adlam's Plantation
Cottage Plantation
Ibsley Manor Farm
A338
NEW ROAD
CUFFNELLS CL
Avon Valley Path
Ibsley Bridge
Weir
Bridge Farm
PH
Ibsley
SALISBURY ROAD
Mockbeggar Farm
Crosslanes Farm
Mockbeggar
MOCKBEGGAR LANE
River Avon
Old Farm
Weir
Riverbank Covert
Forelock Farm
Tumulus
Newlands Farm
Newlands Plantation
Ibsley Water
Mockbeggar Lakes
Riverbank Covert
Moyles Court Sch
ELLINGHAM DRO
Pillow Mounds
Broom Copse
Tumuli
Ellingham
Ellingham Farm
ELLINGHAM DROVE
ELLINGHAM DRIVE
BH24
P
PH
Broad Close Covert
Blashford Lakes Study Centre
Rockford
Chatley Wood
Bigsburn Hill
Tumulus
Sand and Gravel Pit
Ellingham Lake
Ivy Lake
HIGHWOOD LANE
IVY LANE
Blashford Lake
Rockford Farm
Rockford End
Meadow Lake
Beacon Wood
River Avon
Blashford Farm
SNAIL'S LANE
Linbrook Lake
Forest Edge Farm
HIGHWOOD LANE
SNAILS LA
WOOLMER LANE
Blashford
North Poulner
P
Northfield Lake
COWPITTS LA
Upper Hurst Farm
LIN BROOK DR
Rooks Coppice
Headlands Business Park
NORTH POULNER ROAD
Poulner Jun Sch
Poulner Inf Sch
Lifeland Copse
WATERSIDE CL
SHAW RD
LAWRENCE RD
ROSS RD
Avon Vale
Kingfisher Lake
MORANT ROAD
GORLEY ROAD
HOLM CL
1 CHICHESTER RD
2 HAWKINS CL
3 FROBISHER CL
LINFORD ROAD
Gouldings Farm
HURST RD
RINGWOOD
Hurst Old Farm
NORTHFIELD ROAD
EDWINA CL
FAIRLIE
BUTLERS LA
LINFORD RD
White's Copse
SALISBURY RD
HIGHFIELD DR
BROADSHARD LA
HAMPTON DRIVE
SEYMOUR ROAD
WANSTEAD CL
PK
LINK RD
PARKERS CL
POULNER PK
DRAKE CL
GRENVILLE RD
NARROW LA
Poulner
Up Mead
South Hampshire STREET ATLAS

55

211
200
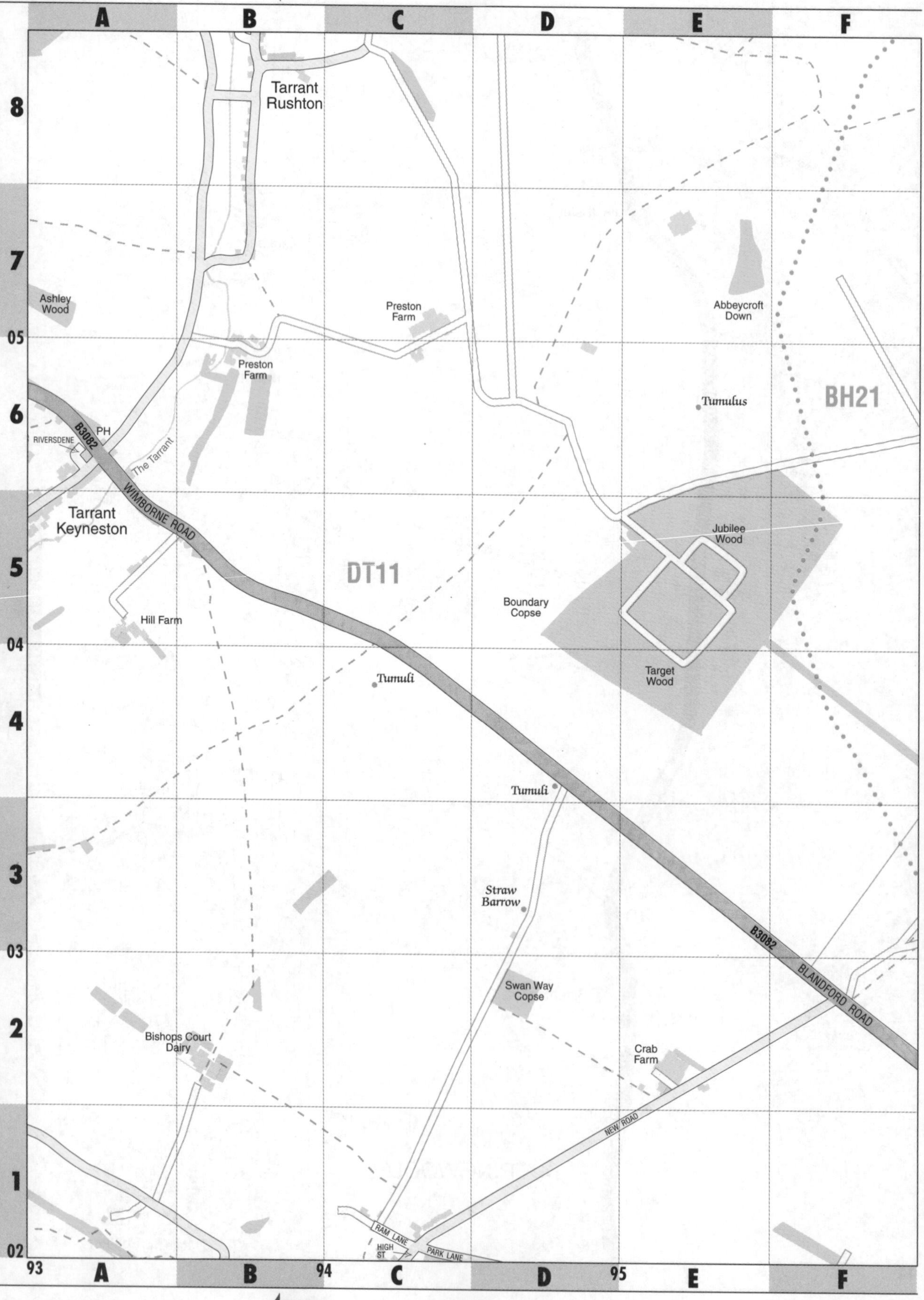
A
B
C
D
E
F
8
7
05
6
5
04
4
3
03
2
1
02
93
94
95
Tarrant
Rushton
Ashley
Wood
Preston
Farm
Abbeycroft
Down
Preston
Farm
Tumulus
BH21
PH
RIVERSDENE
B3082
The Tarrant
Tarrant
Keyneston
WIMBORNE ROAD
Jubilee
Wood
DT11
Boundary
Copse
Hill Farm
Target
Wood
Tumuli
Tumuli
Straw
Barrow
B3082
BLANDFORD ROAD
Swan Way
Copse
Bishops Court
Dairy
Crab
Farm
NEW ROAD
RAM LANE
HIGH
ST
PARK LANE
211
56

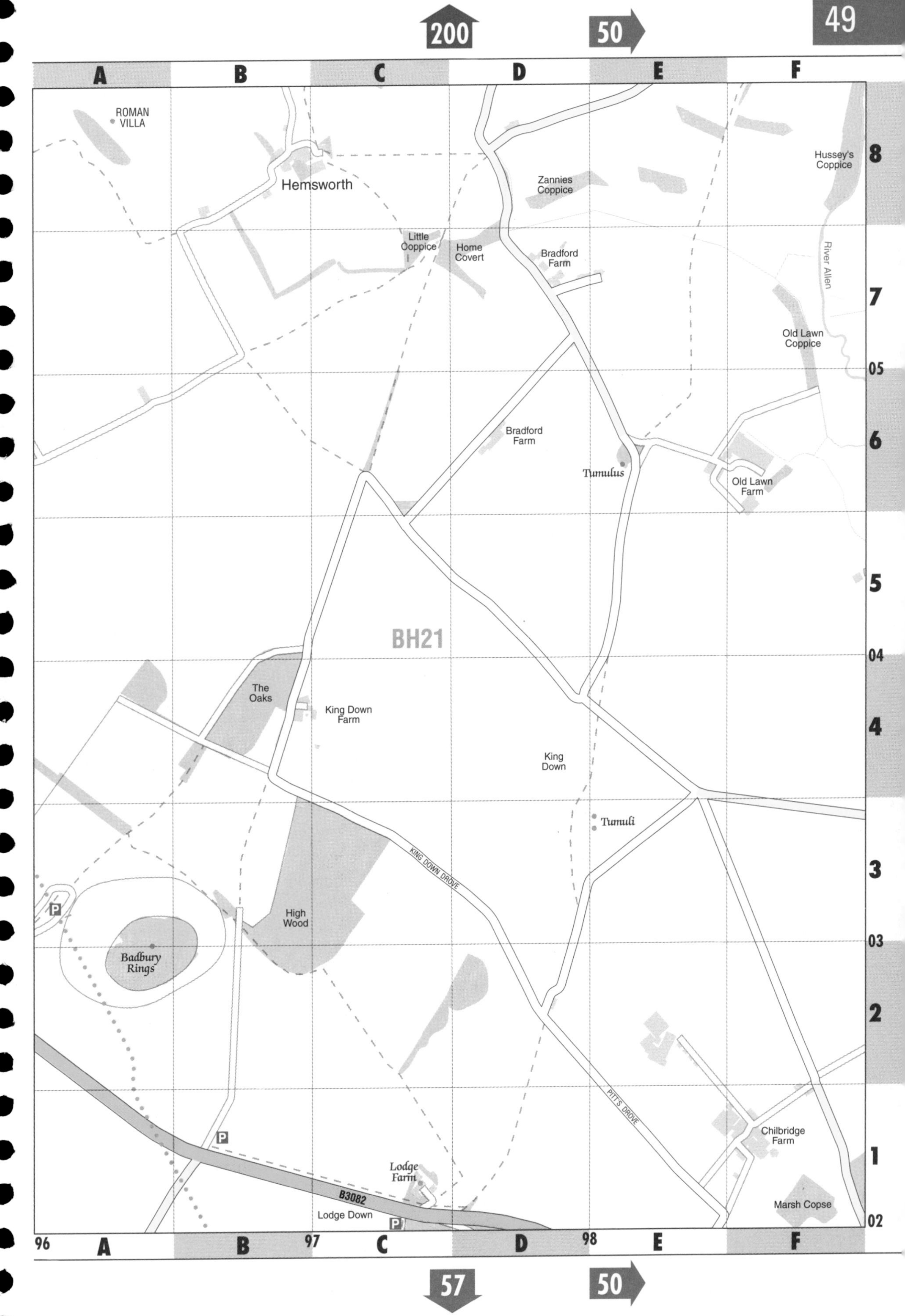
200
50
A
B
C
D
E
F
ROMAN VILLA
Hemsworth
Zannies Coppice
Hussey's Coppice
Little Coppice
Home Covert
Bradford Farm
River Allen
Old Lawn Coppice
Bradford Farm
Tumulus
Old Lawn Farm
BH21
The Oaks
King Down Farm
King Down
Tumuli
KING DOWN DROVE
High Wood
Badbury Rings
P
PITT'S DROVE
Chilbridge Farm
Lodge Farm
B3082
Lodge Down
Marsh Copse
8
7
05
6
5
04
4
3
03
2
1
02
96
97
98
57
50

49
201

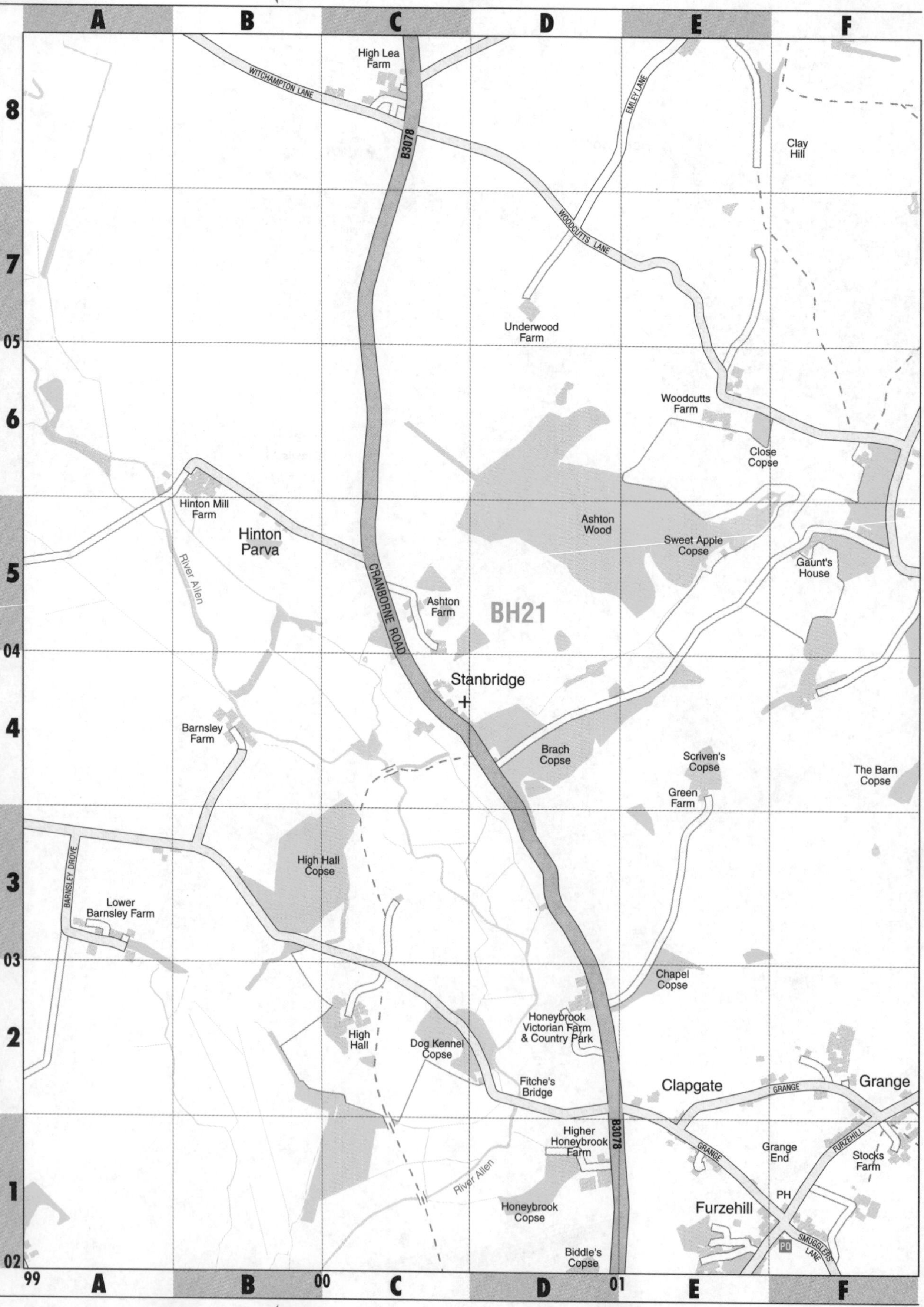
A
B
C
D
E
F
8
7
05
6
5
04
4
3
03
2
1
02
99
00
01
High Lea Farm
WITCHAMPTON LANE
B3078
EMLEY LANE
Clay Hill
WOODCUTTS LANE
Underwood Farm
Woodcutts Farm
Close Copse
Hinton Mill Farm
Hinton Parva
River Allen
Ashton Wood
Sweet Apple Copse
Gaunt's House
CRANBORNE ROAD
Ashton Farm
BH21
Stanbridge
Barnsley Farm
Brach Copse
Scriven's Copse
The Barn Copse
Green Farm
BARNSLEY DROVE
High Hall Copse
Lower Barnsley Farm
Chapel Copse
Honeybrook Victorian Farm & Country Park
High Hall
Dog Kennel Copse
Fitche's Bridge
Clapgate
GRANGE
Grange
Higher Honeybrook Farm
B3078
GRANGE
Grange End
FURZEHILL
Stocks Farm
River Allen
Honeybrook Copse
PH
Furzehill
PO
SMUGGLERS LANE
Biddle's Copse

58
49
59

201
52

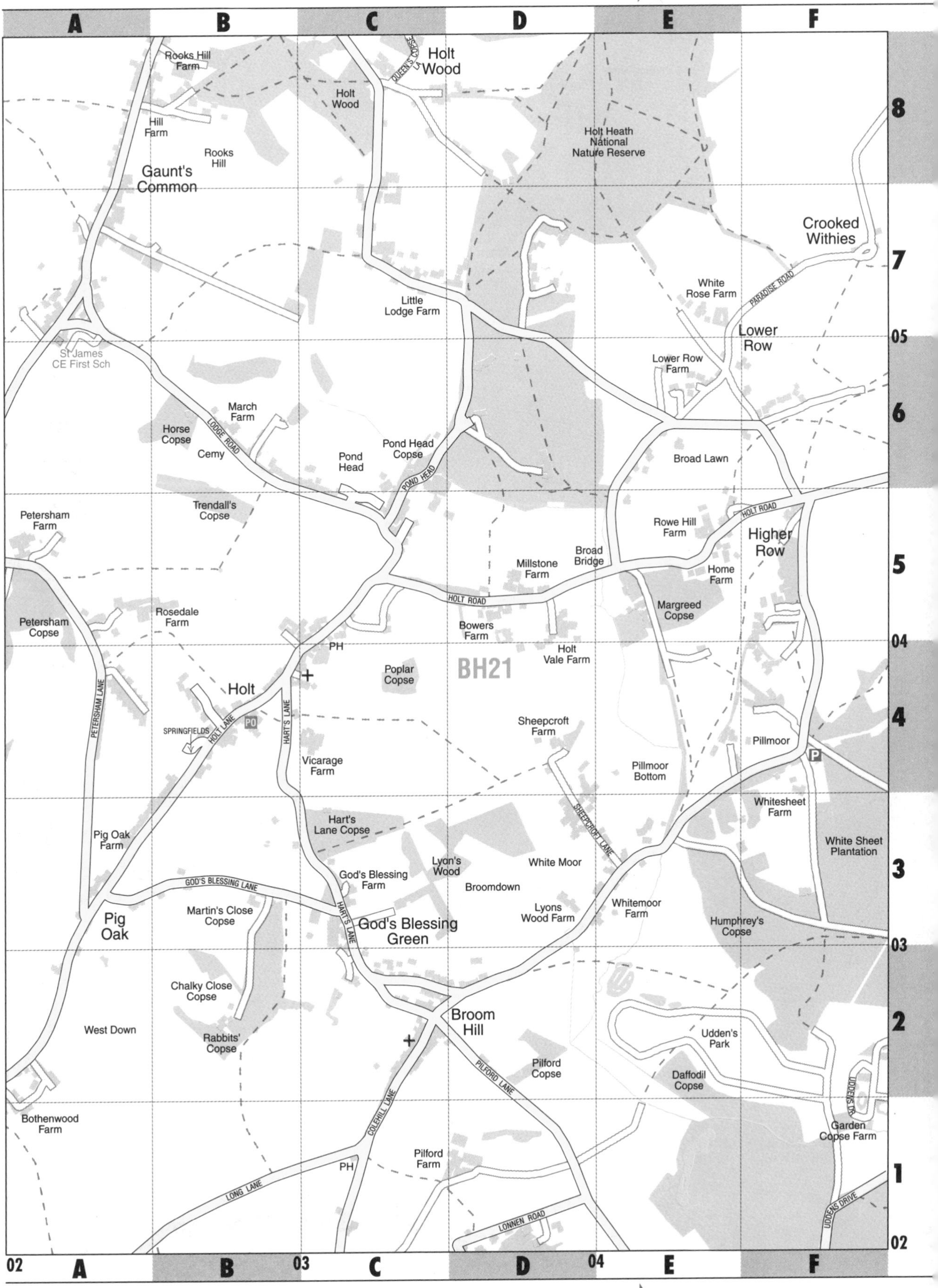
A
B
C
D
E
F
Rooks Hill Farm
Queen's Copse La
Holt Wood
Holt Wood
Hill Farm
Rooks Hill
Gaunt's Common
Holt Heath National Nature Reserve
Crooked Withies
White Rose Farm
Paradise Road
Little Lodge Farm
Lower Row
Lower Row Farm
St James CE First Sch
March Farm
Horse Copse
Lodge Road
Cemy
Pond Head Copse
Pond Head
Pond Head
Broad Lawn
Petersham Farm
Trendall's Copse
Holt Road
Rowe Hill Farm
Higher Row
Broad Bridge
Millstone Farm
Home Farm
Holt Road
Margreed Copse
Rosedale Farm
Petersham Copse
Bowers Farm
PH
Holt Vale Farm
Poplar Copse
BH21
Holt
Petersham Lane
Hart's Lane
Springfields
Holt Lane
PO
Sheepcroft Farm
Pillmoor
P
Vicarage Farm
Pillmoor Bottom
Whitesheet Farm
Hart's Lane Copse
Sheepcroft Lane
Pig Oak Farm
White Sheet Plantation
Lyon's Wood
White Moor
God's Blessing Lane
God's Blessing Farm
Broomdown
Martin's Close Copse
Hart's Lane
Lyons Wood Farm
Whitemoor Farm
Pig Oak
God's Blessing Green
Humphrey's Copse
Chalky Close Copse
Broom Hill
West Down
Rabbits' Copse
Udden's Park
Pilford Copse
Pilford Lane
Daffodil Copse
Uddens Dr
Bothenwood Farm
Colehill Lane
Garden Copse Farm
Pilford Farm
PH
Long Lane
Lonnen Road
Uddens Drive
8
7
05
6
5
04
4
3
03
2
1
02
02
03
04

59
52
60

51
44

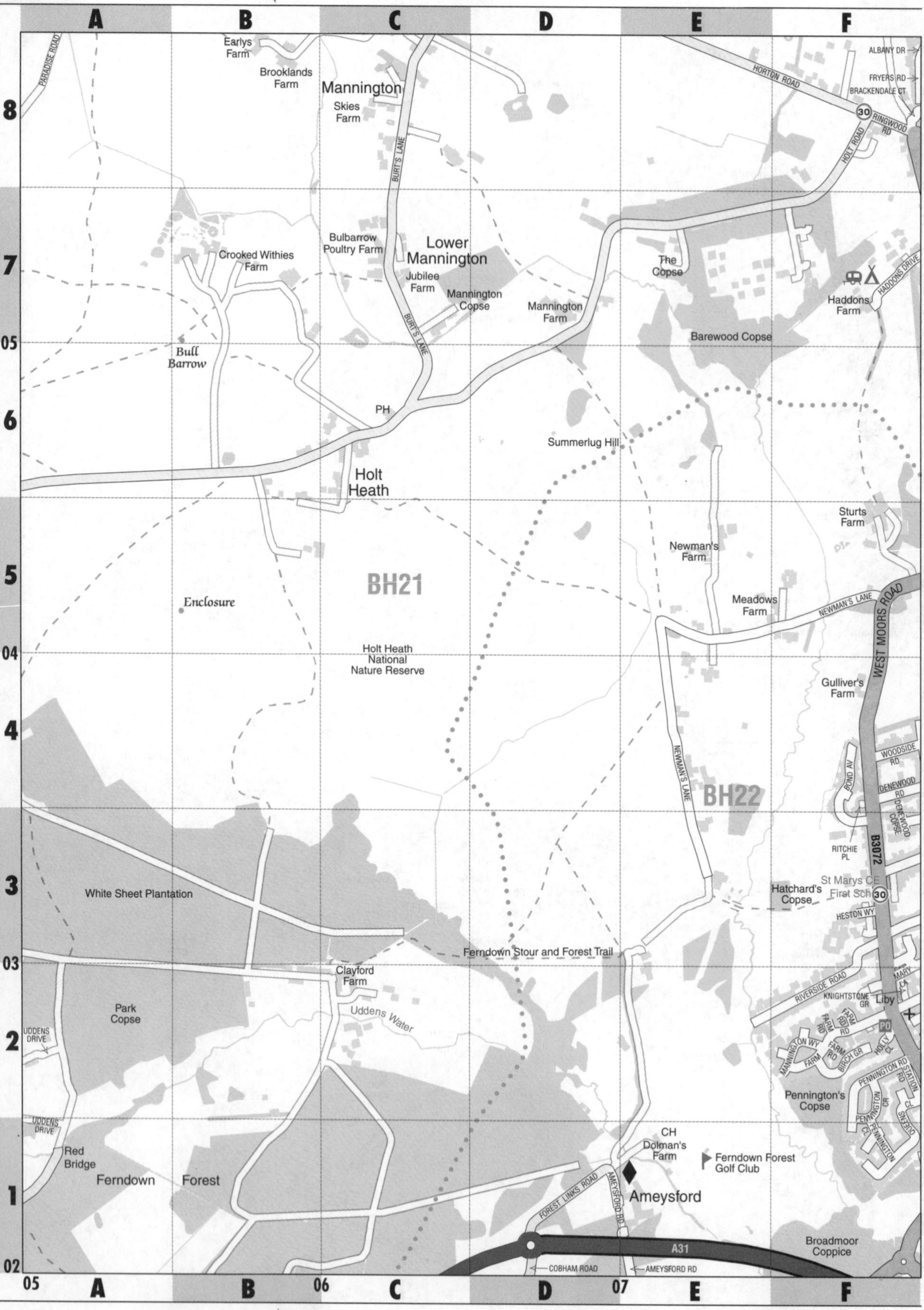

A B C D E F

8

7

05

6

5

04

4

3

03

2

01

02

05 A B 06 C D 07 E F

Earlys Farm

Brooklands Farm

Mannington

Skies Farm

Bulbarrow Poultry Farm

Crooked Withies Farm

Lower Mannington

Jubilee Farm

Mannington Copse

Mannington Farm

BURT'S LANE

The Copse

Barewood Copse

HORTON ROAD

ALBANY DR

FRYERS RD
BRACKENDALE CT

30
RINGWOOD RD

HOLT ROAD

HADDONS DRIVE

Haddons Farm

Bull Barrow

PH

Holt Heath

Summerlug Hill

Sturts Farm

Newman's Farm

Meadows Farm

NEWMAN'S LANE

WEST MOORS ROAD

BH21

Enclosure

Holt Heath National Nature Reserve

Gulliver's Farm

WOODSIDE RD

BOND AV

DENEWOOD RD

DENEWOOD COPSE

B3072

RITCHIE PL

BH22

White Sheet Plantation

NEWMAN'S LANE

Hatchard's Copse

St Marys CE First Sch 30

HESTON WY

Ferndown Stour and Forest Trail

RIVERSIDE ROAD

KNIGHTSTONE GR

Liby

Clayford Farm

Uddens Water

UDDENS DRIVE

Park Copse

MANNINGTON WY

FARM RD

BRICK GR

PENNINGTON RD

STATION RD

SNEED RD

Pennington's Copse

UDDENS DRIVE

Red Bridge

Ferndown Forest

CH
Dolman's Farm

Ferndown Forest Golf Club

FOREST LINKS ROAD

AMEYSFORD RD

Ameysford

Broadmoor Coppice

A31

COBHAM ROAD

AMEYSFORD RD

45
54

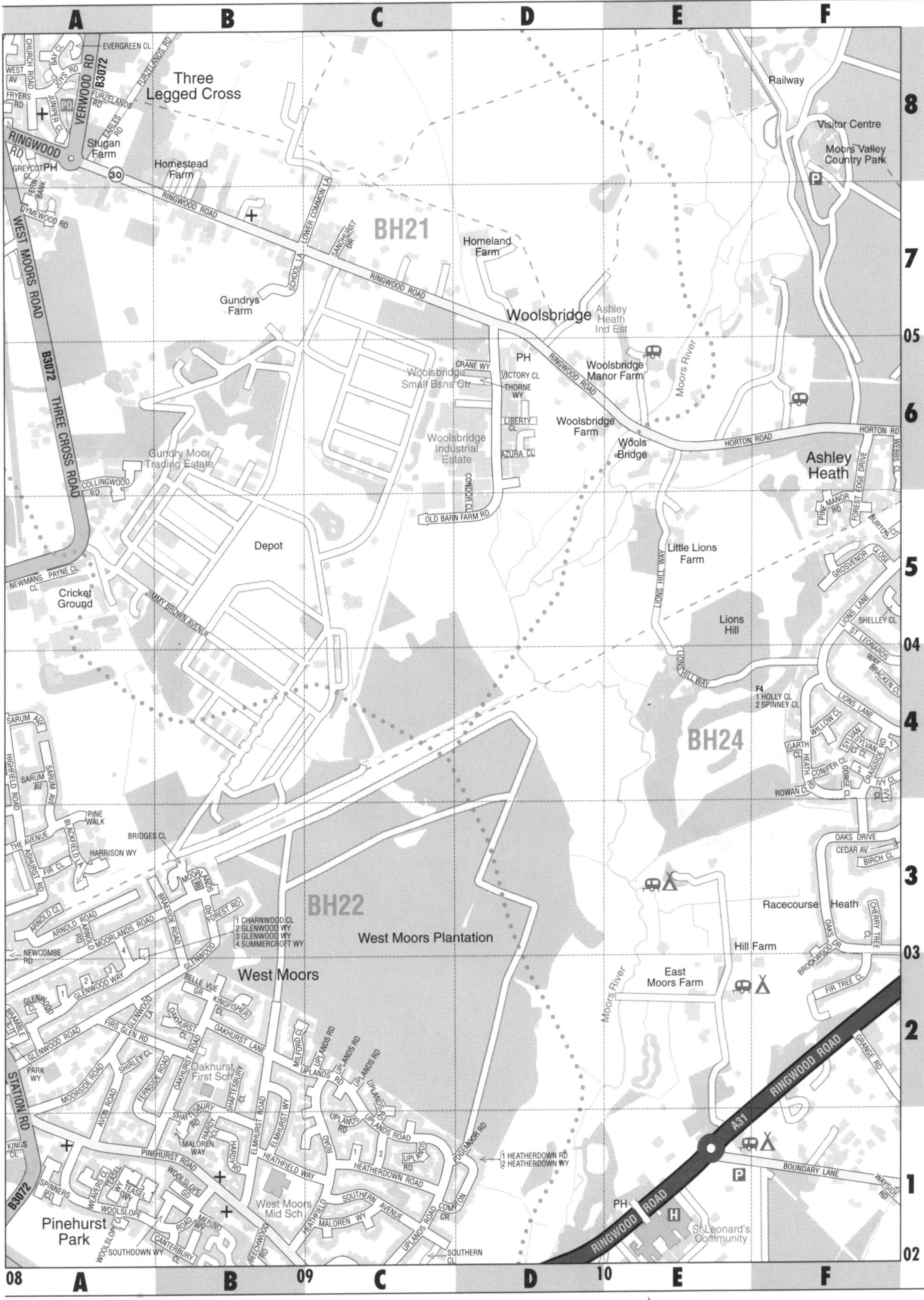
A
B
C
D
E
F
8
7
6
5
4
3
2
1
05
04
03
02
08
09
10
Three Legged Cross
EVERGREEN CL
CHURCH ROAD
BAY CL
JOYS RD
WEST AV
FRYERS RD
JUNIPER CL
VERWOOD RD
B3072
FURZELANDS RD
FURZELANDS RD
EARLES RD
Stugan Farm
RINGWOOD RD
GREYCOT CL
PH
FERN BANK
30
Homestead Farm
RINGWOOD ROAD
DYMEWOOD RD
WEST MOORS ROAD
B3072
THREE CROSS ROAD
LOWER COMMON LA
SCHOOL LA
SANDHURST DR
BH21
Homeland Farm
RINGWOOD ROAD
Gundrys Farm
Woolsbridge
Ashley Heath Ind Est
CRANE WY
PH
Woolsbridge Small Bsns Ctr
VICTORY CL
THORNE WY
LIBERTY CL
AZURA CL
Woolsbridge Industrial Estate
CONDOR CL
OLD BARN FARM RD
RINGWOOD ROAD
Woolsbridge Manor Farm
Moors River
Woolsbridge Farm
Wools Bridge
HORTON ROAD
HORTON RD
Railway
Visitor Centre
Moors Valley Country Park
P
Ashley Heath
WEBBS CL
FOREST EDGE DRIVE
PINE MANOR RD
BURTON CL
Gundry Moor Trading Estate
COLLINGWOOD RD
Depot
Little Lions Farm
LIONS HILL WAY
GROSVENOR CLOSE
NEWMANS CL
PAYNE CL
Cricket Ground
JIMMY BROWN AVENUE
Lions Hill
LIONS LANE
SHELLEY CL
ST LEONARDS WAY
BRACKEN CL
LIONS HILL WAY
F4
1 HOLLY CL
2 SPINNEY CL
LIONS LANE
WILLOW CL
SYLVAN CL
CRAIGSIDE RD
GARTH CL
HEATH RD
CONIFER CL
GORSE CL
IVY CL
ROWAN CL
BH24
SARUM AVE
SARUM AV
SARUM AVE
HIGHFIELD ROAD
PINE WALK
BLACKFIELD LA
BRIDGES CL
THE AVENUE
ASHURST RD
HARRISON WY
FIR CL
MOORLANDS RISE
FOREST RD
BRAESIDE ROAD
ARNOLD CL
ARNOLD ROAD
ARNOLD RD
MOORLANDS ROAD
BH22
1 CHARNWOOD CL
2 GLENWOOD WY
3 GLENWOOD WY
4 SUMMERCROFT WY
West Moors Plantation
OAKS DRIVE
CEDAR AV
BIRCH CL
Racecourse Heath
CHERRY TREE CL
OAKS DR
BROCKWOOD CR
Hill Farm
FIR TREE CL
NEWCOMBE RD
GLENWOOD
GLENWOOD WAY
West Moors
BELLE VUE GR
KINGFISHER CL
East Moors Farm
Moors River
GLENWOOD CL
BRAMBLE CT
GLENWOOD ROAD
FIRS GLEN RD
GLENWOOD LA
OAKHURST CL
OAKHURST LANE
MILFORD CL
UPLANDS RD
UPLANDS RD
UPLANDS RD
GRANGE RD
RINGWOOD ROAD
PARK WY
STATION RD
MOORSIDE ROAD
AVON ROAD
SHIRLEY CL
FERNSIDE ROAD
OAKHURST ROAD
Oakhurst First Sch
SHAFTESBURY CL
UPLANDS RD
UPLANDS RD
SHAFTESBURY RD
HARDY CL
MALOREN WAY
HARDY RD
ELMHURST ROAD
ELMHURST WY
UPLANDS ROAD
HEATHFIELD WAY
HEATHERDOWN ROAD
UPLANDS RD
EDGEMOOR RD
1 HEATHERDOWN RD
2 HEATHERDOWN WY
A31
BOUNDARY LANE
WAYSIDE RD
P
KINGS CL
PINEHURST ROAD
B3072
SPINNERS CL
WEAVERS CL
TEASEL WY
TEASEL
WOOLSLOPE GD
WOOLSLOPE
WOOLSLOPE CL
ROAD
MERINO WY
CANTERBURY CL
SOUTHDOWN WY
West Moors Mid Sch
BEECHWOOD RD
HEATHFIELD
SOUTHERN AVENUE
MALOREN WY
UPLANDS ROAD
COMPTON CR
SOUTHERN CL
Pinehurst Park
PH
RINGWOOD ROAD
H
St Leonard's Community

61
54
62

53
46

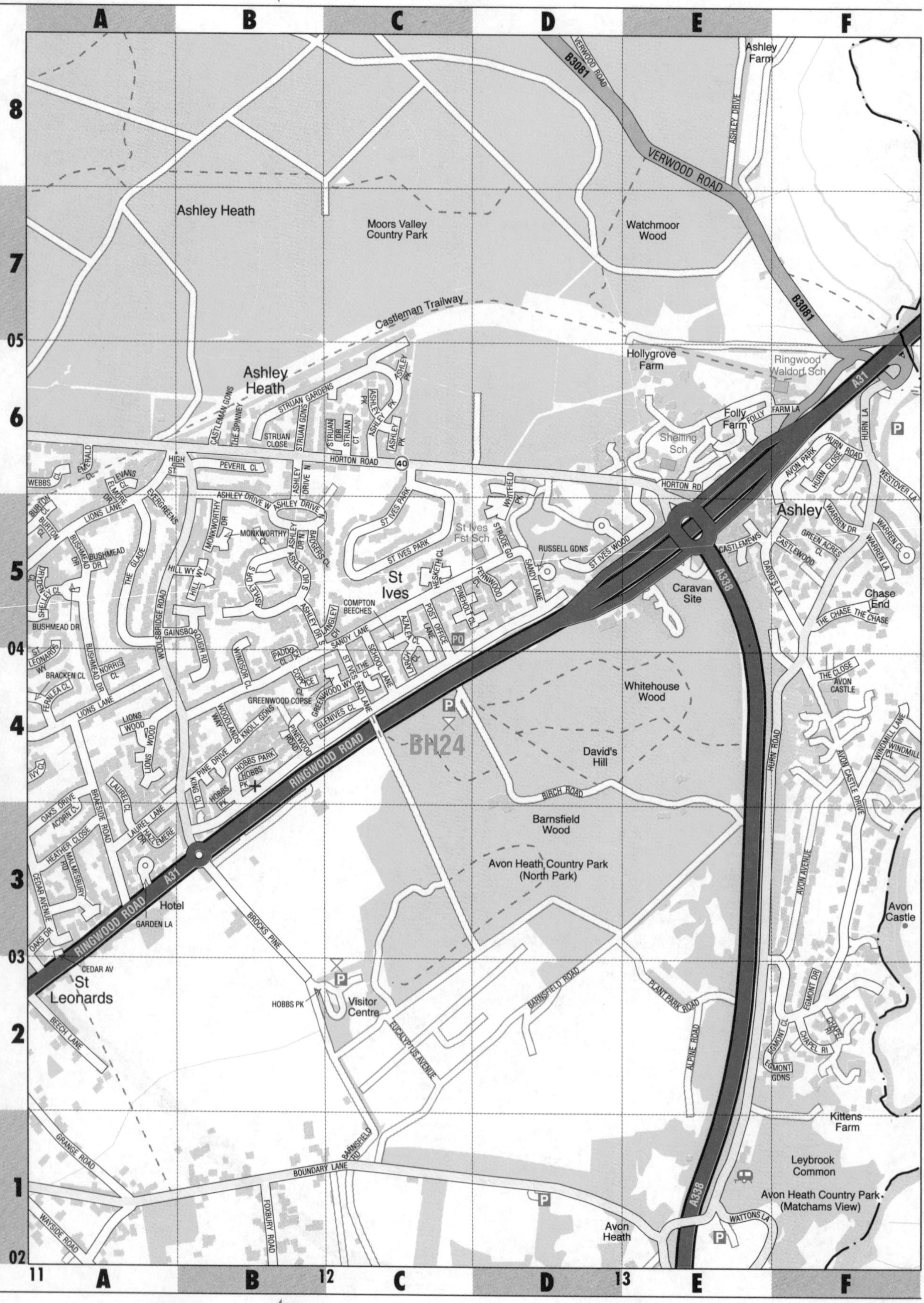
A
B
C
D
E
F
8
7
05
6
5
04
4
3
03
2
1
02
11
12
13
Ashley Farm
VERWOOD ROAD
B3081
ASHLEY DRIVE
Ashley Heath
Moors Valley Country Park
Watchmoor Wood
Castleman Trailway
Hollygrove Farm
Ringwood Waldorf Sch
A31
Ashley Heath
CASTLEMAN GDNS
THE SPINNEY
STRUAN GARDENS
STRUAN CLOSE
STRUAN GDNS
STRUAN DR
STRUAN CT
ASHLEY PK
Folly Farm
FOLLY FARM LA
HURN LA
Shelling Sch
HORTON ROAD
40
HORTON RD
PEVERIL CL
HIGH ST
EVERALD CL
WEBBS CL
EVANS CL
ELMORE DR
BURTON CL
LIONS LANE
EVERGREENS
ASHLEY DRIVE W
ASHLEY DRIVE N
ASHLEY DRIVE
MONKWORTHY DR
MONKWORTHY CL
BADGERS CL
ST IVES PARK
WHITFIELD PK
St Ives Fst Sch
STRODE GD
RUSSELL GDNS
ST IVES WOOD
AVON PARK
HURN ROAD
HURN CLOSE
WESTOVER LA
Ashley
WARREN DR
WARREN CL
WARREN LA
GREEN ACRES CL
CASTLEMEWS
CASTLEWOOD
DAVID'S LA
BUSHMEAD DR
BUSHMEAD
THE GLADE
HILL WY
St Ives
HESKETH CL
FERNWOOD CL
PINEHOLT CL
SANDY LANE
Caravan Site
A338
Chase End
THE CHASE
COMPTON BEECHES
GAINSBOROUGH RD
WOOLSBRIDGE ROAD
SHELLEY CL
DRYDEN CL
BUSHMEAD DR
ST LEONARDS WY
BRACKEN CL
FERNLEA CL
NORRIS CL
WINDSOR CL
PADDOCK CL
LANGLEY CH
SANDY LANE
AZALEA CL
LARCH CL
POST OFFICE LANE
SCHOOL LANE
PO
THE CLOSE
AVON CASTLE
COPSE CL
ST IVES END LANE
GREENWOOD WY
GREENWOOD COPSE
GLENIVES CL
LIONS LANE
Whitehouse Wood
WOODLANDS WAY
KNOLL GDNS
PINEWOOD ROAD
LIONS WOOD
P
BH24
RINGWOOD ROAD
David's Hill
WINDMILL LANE
WINDMILL CL
HURN ROAD
AVON CASTLE DRIVE
IVY CL
PINE DRIVE
HOBBS PARK
HOBBS PK
KING CL
OAKS DRIVE
ACORN CL
BRAESIDE ROAD
LAUREL CL
LAUREL LANE
HAZEL DR
EMERE
BIRCH ROAD
Barnsfield Wood
HEATHER CLOSE
MALMESBURY RD
CEDAR AVENUE
A31
Avon Heath Country Park (North Park)
AVON AVENUE
Hotel
GARDEN LA
BROCKS PINE
Avon Castle
OAKS DR
RINGWOOD ROAD
CEDAR AV
St Leonards
HOBBS PK
Visitor Centre
BARNSFIELD ROAD
PLANT PARK ROAD
EGMONT DR
EGMONT CL
CHAPEL RI
EGMONT GDNS
BEECH LANE
EUCALYPTUS AVENUE
ALPINE ROAD
Kittens Farm
GRANGE ROAD
BARNSFIELD RD
Leybrook Common
BOUNDARY LANE
Avon Heath Country Park (Matchams View)
FOXBURY ROAD
WATTONS LA
WAYSIDE ROAD
Avon Heath

62
53
63

B7 1 THE SWEEP 2 STAR LA 3 FURLONG MEWS 4 PEDDLARS WK 5 COTTAGE MEWS 6 EBENEZER LA 7 GOOSEBERRY LA 8 DEWEYS LA

B8 1 LINDEN GDNS 2 MANOR GDNS 3 ORCHARD MD

C6 1 HARRY BARROW CL 2 CHARING CL 3 WATERLOO WY 4 SOUTHFIELD MS

D6 1 CROW ARCH LA 2 JOYCE DICKSON CL

D8 1 BEECHCROFT LA 2 BEECHCROFT MS 3 WANSTEAD CL 4 Lumby Dr Mobile Home Pk

E6 1 OLD STACKS GDNS 2 THE CLOISTERS 3 SANDERLINGS

E8 1 WHITEHART FIELDS 2 PIPERS ASH 3 RALEIGH CL 4 CUNNINGHAM CL 5 MERRYWEATHER EST

F6 1 HOLMWOOD GARTH 2 ASHBURN GARTH 3 FOREST HILLS CT

47

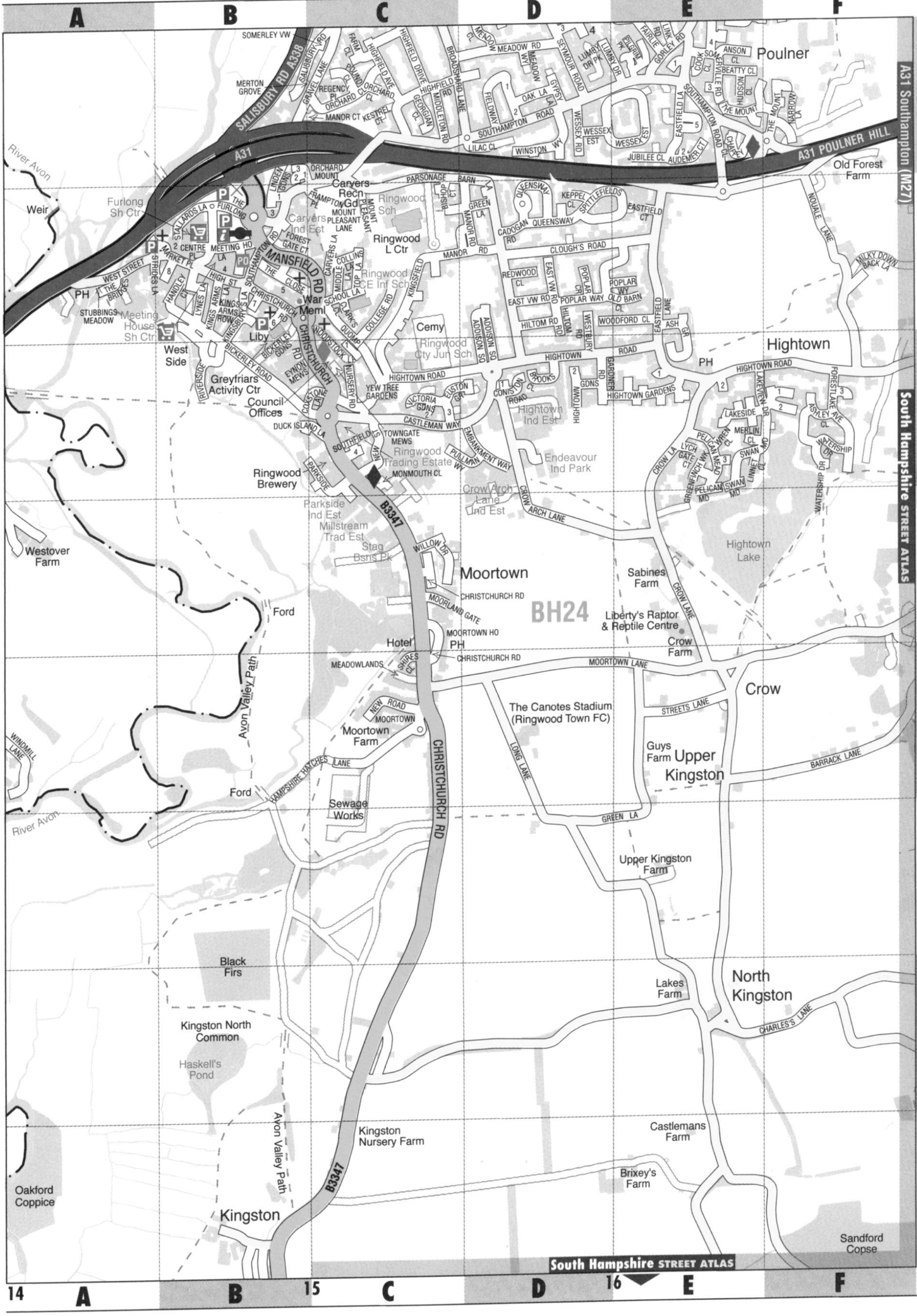

63

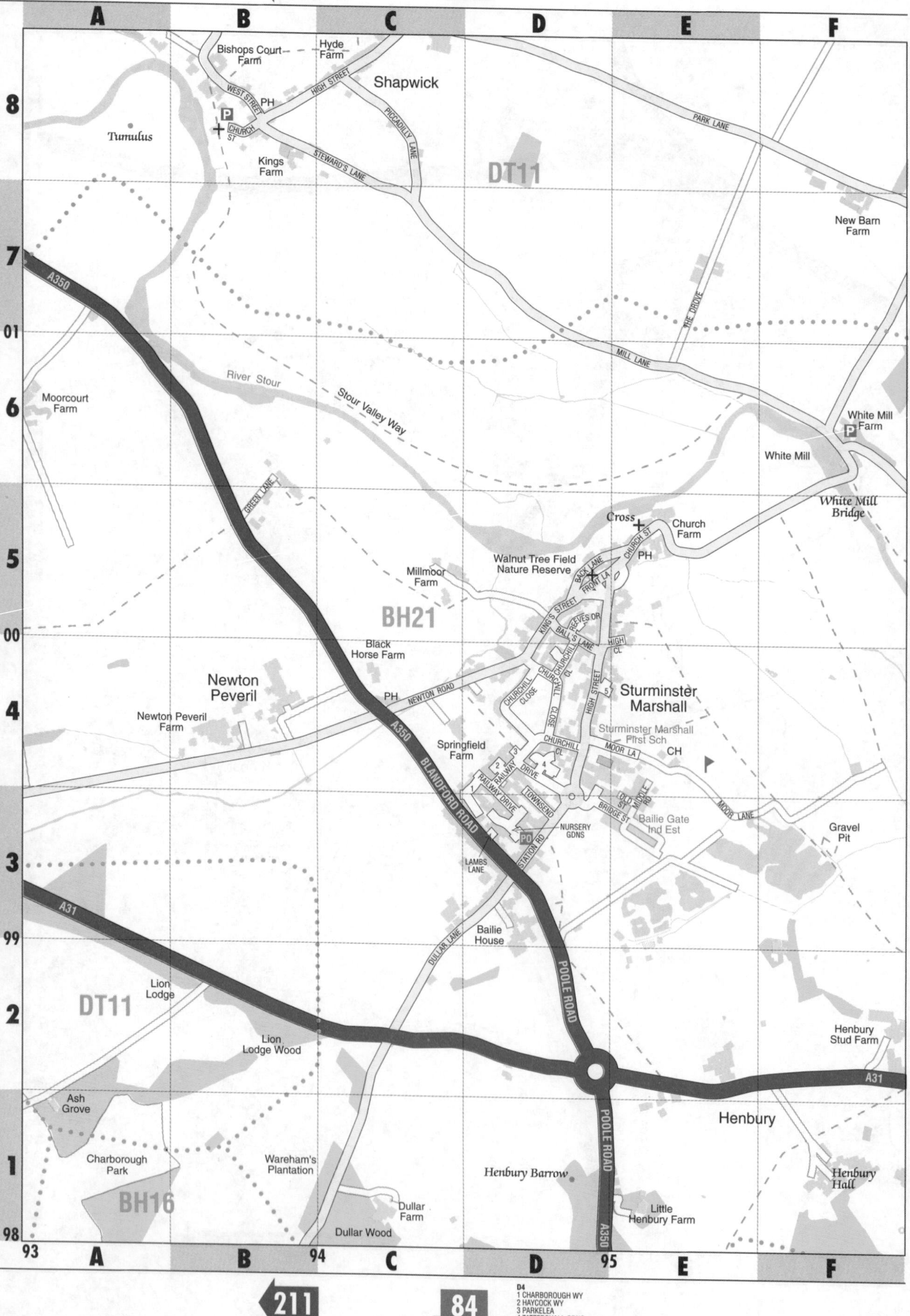

← 211
↑ 48

Shapwick

Bishops Court Farm
Hyde Farm
WEST STREET
PH
HIGH STREET
P
CHURCH ST
Kings Farm
STEWARD'S LANE
PICCADILLY LANE

DT11

Turnulus

New Barn Farm

PARK LANE

A350

THE DRIVE

01

River Stour
Stour Valley Way

MILL LANE

White Mill Farm
P

Moorcourt Farm

6

White Mill

GREEN LANE

White Mill Bridge

Cross
Church Farm
CHURCH ST

5

Millmoor Farm

Walnut Tree Field Nature Reserve
BACK LANE
FRONT LA
PH

BH21

KING'S STREET
REEVES DR
BALL'S LANE
HIGH CL

Black Horse Farm

CHURCHILL CLOSE
TRIM CL
CHURCHILL CL
HIGH STREET

Sturminster Marshall

Newton Peveril

PH
NEWTON ROAD

Sturminster Marshall Plrst Sch
CH

Newton Peveril Farm

A350

Springfield Farm

CHURCHILL CL
MOOR LA
OLD ST
MIDDLE RD

00

4

RAILWAY DRIVE
RAILWAY DRIVE
TOWNSEND
BRIDGE ST

MOOR LANE

BLANDFORD ROAD

PO

NURSERY GDNS

Bailie Gate Ind Est

Gravel Pit

3

LAMBS LANE

STATION RD

Bailie House

DULLAR LANE

99

A31

POOLE ROAD

Henbury Stud Farm

DT11

Lion Lodge

2

A31

Lion Lodge Wood

Ash Grove

Henbury

POOLE ROAD

Charborough Park

Wareham's Plantation

Henbury Barrow

A350

Henbury Hall

1

BH16

Dullar Farm

Little Henbury Farm

98

Dullar Wood

93
A
B
94
C
D
95
E
F

← 211
↓ 84

D4
1 CHARBOROUGH WY
2 HAYCOCK WY
3 PARKELEA
4 TATTERSHALL GDNS
5 SHERIDEN WY

49
58

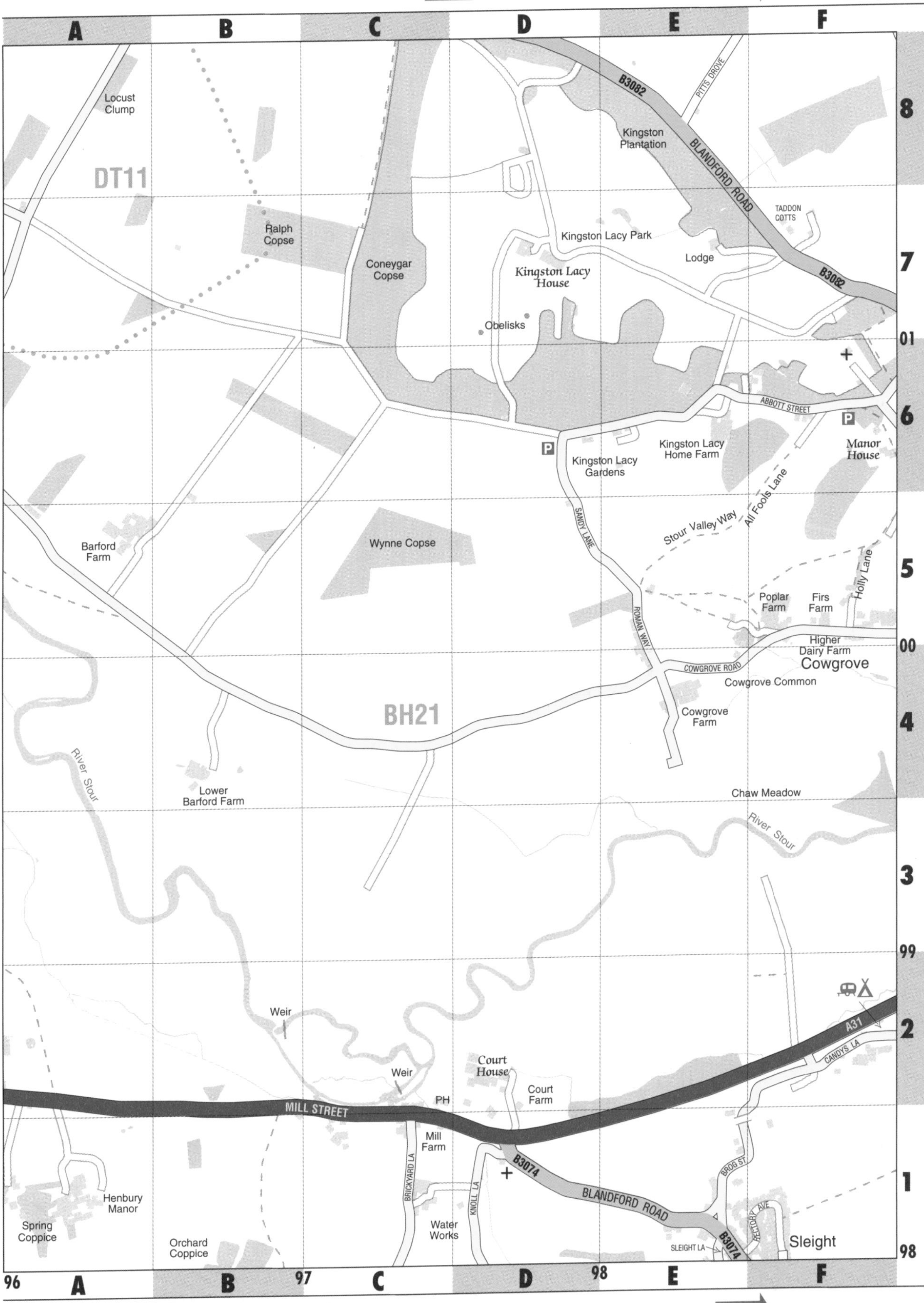

A
B
C
D
E
F
8
7
01
6
5
00
4
3
99
2
1
98
96
97
98
Locust Clump
DT11
Ralph Copse
Coneygar Copse
B3082
PITTS DROVE
Kingston Plantation
BLANDFORD ROAD
TADDON COTTS
Kingston Lacy Park
Lodge
Kingston Lacy House
Obelisks
ABBOTT STREET
Manor House
Kingston Lacy Home Farm
Kingston Lacy Gardens
SANDY LANE
All Fools Lane
Stour Valley Way
Barford Farm
Wynne Copse
Holly Lane
Poplar Farm
Firs Farm
ROMAN WAY
Higher Dairy Farm
Cowgrove
COWGROVE ROAD
Cowgrove Common
BH21
Cowgrove Farm
River Stour
Lower Barford Farm
Chaw Meadow
River Stour
A31
CANDYS LA
Weir
Weir
Court House
Court Farm
PH
MILL STREET
Mill Farm
B3074
BLANDFORD ROAD
BROG ST
BRICKYARD LA
KNOLL LA
RECTORY AVE
Henbury Manor
Spring Coppice
Orchard Coppice
Water Works
SLEIGHT LA
B3074
Sleight

85
58

49 57 50

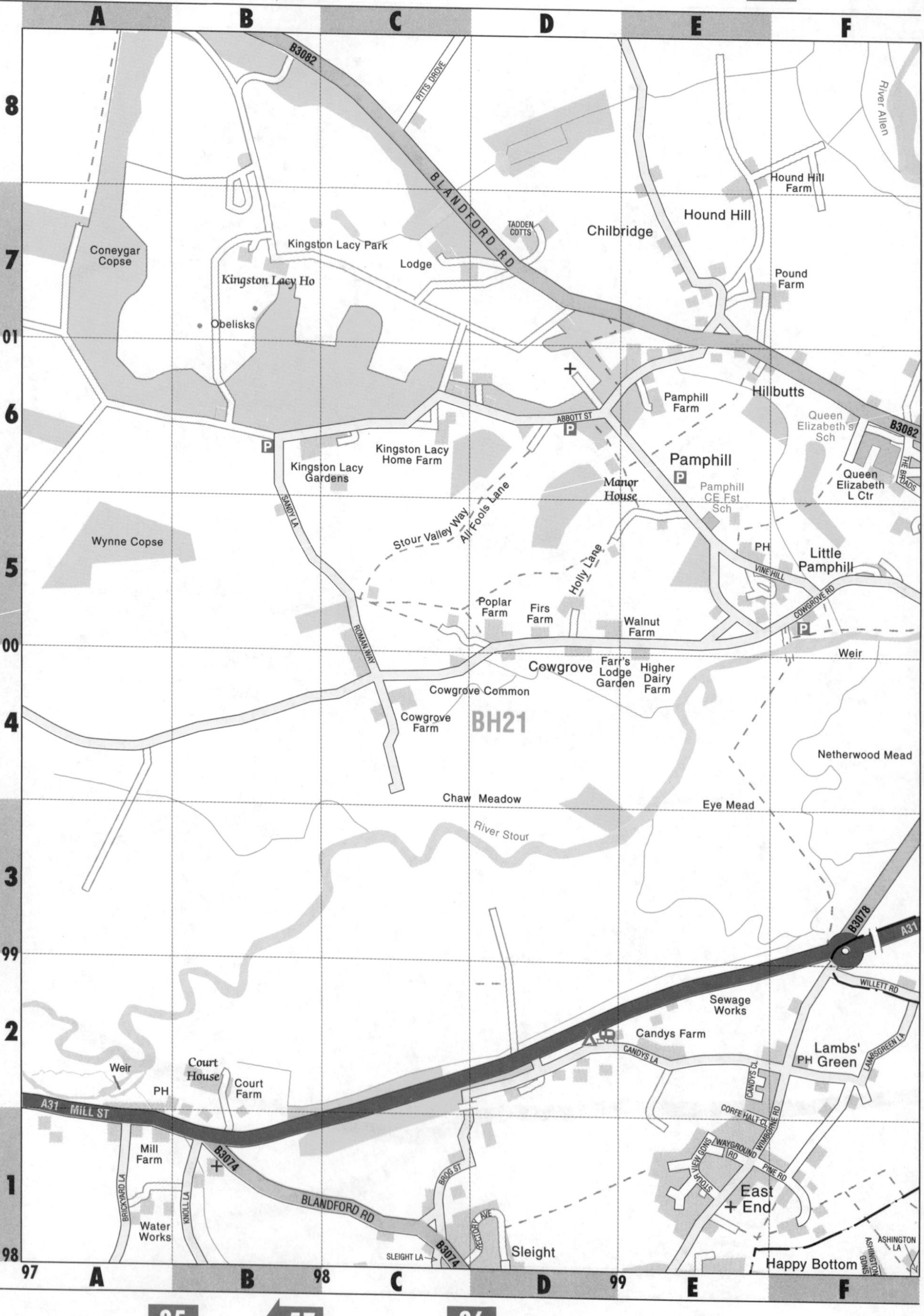

A
B
C
D
E
F
8
7
01
6
5
00
4
3
99
2
1
98
97
98
99
B3082
PITTS DROVE
BLANDFORD RD
River Allen
Hound Hill Farm
Hound Hill
Chilbridge
TADDEN COTTS
Kingston Lacy Park
Coneygar Copse
Lodge
Kingston Lacy Ho
Pound Farm
Obelisks
Hillbutts
Pamphill Farm
ABBOTT ST
Queen Elizabeth's Sch
B3082
Kingston Lacy Home Farm
Pamphill
Kingston Lacy Gardens
Manor House
Pamphill CE Fst Sch
Queen Elizabeth L Ctr
THE BROADS
SANDY LA
Stour Valley Way
All Fools Lane
Wynne Copse
PH
Little Pamphill
Holly Lane
VINE HILL
COWGROVE RD
Poplar Farm
Firs Farm
Walnut Farm
ROMAN WAY
Weir
Cowgrove
Farr's Lodge Garden
Higher Dairy Farm
Cowgrove Common
Cowgrove Farm
BH21
Netherwood Mead
Chaw Meadow
Eye Mead
River Stour
B3078
A31
WILLETT RD
Sewage Works
Candys Farm
CANDYS LA
Lambs' Green
PH
LAMBSGREEN LA
Weir
Court House
PH
Court Farm
CANDYS CL
A31 MILL ST
CORFE HALT CL
WIMBORNE RD
Mill Farm
B3074
WAYGROUND RD
PINE RD
STOUR VIEW GDNS
BROG ST
BRICKYARD LA
KNOLL LA
BLANDFORD RD
East End
Water Works
RECTORY AVE
ASHINGTON LA
ASHINGTON GDNS
SLEIGHT LA
B3074
Sleight
Happy Bottom

85 57 86

B6
1 FARMERS WLK
2 COWDRYS FIELD
3 KNOBCROOK RD
4 SHEPPARDS FIELD
5 CULVERHAYES CL

50

B5
1 HAMILTON CT
2 BARTLEY CT
3 PRIORS WLK
4 CROWN CT
5 KINGSMEAD CT
6 CHURCH ST
7 CORNMARKET CL
8 WEST STREET CT
9 THREE LIONS CL
10 WESTFIELD
11 MORAY CT
12 The Priest's House Mus

C5
1 GULLIVER CT
2 HELIC HO
3 MARLBOROUGH CT
4 QUEENSMEAD
5 MILLBANK HO
6 JESSOPP HO

60 51

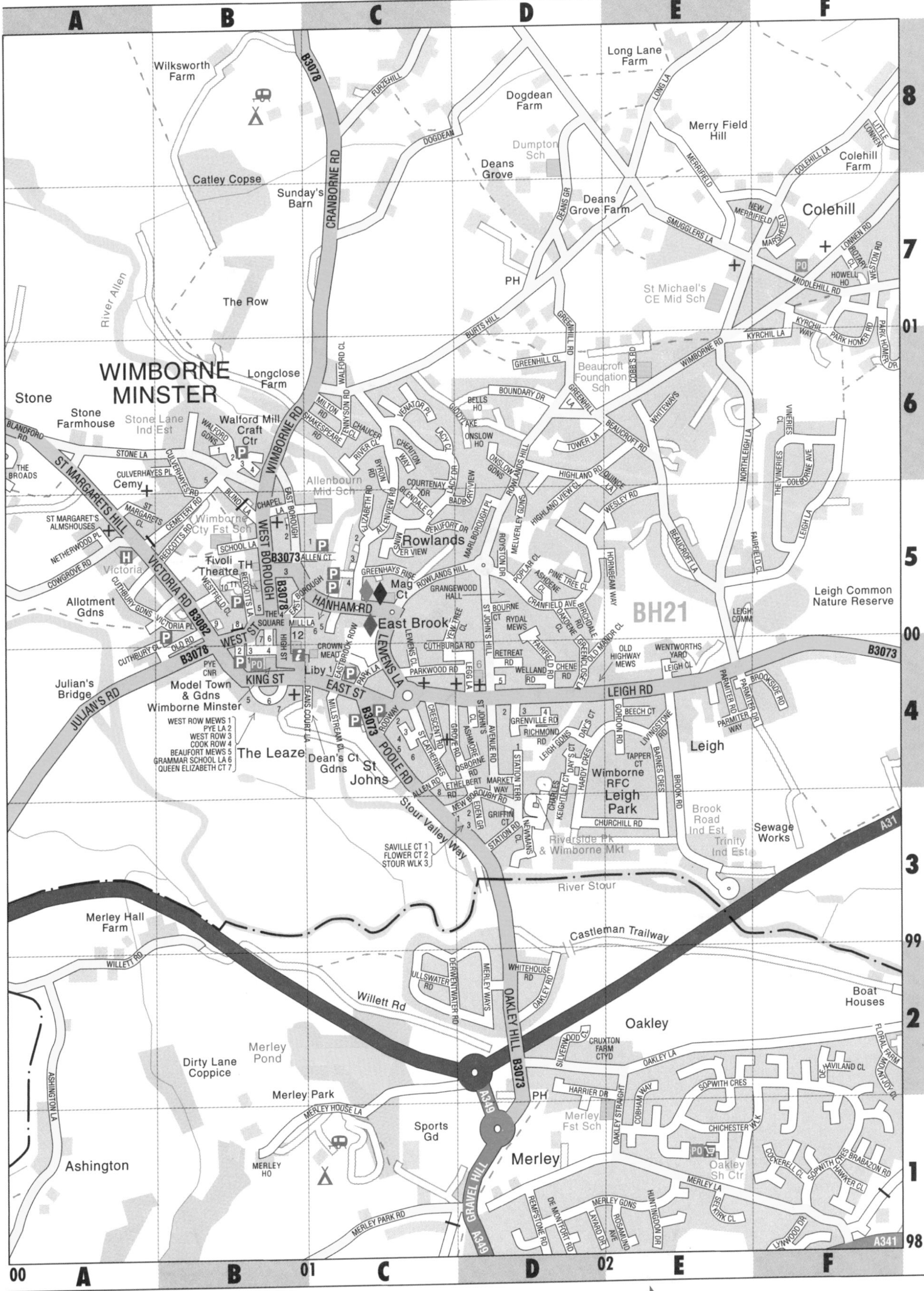

C4
1 QUARTERJACK MEWS
2 SHAMROCK CT
3 STEVENSONS CL
4 BROADWAY PK
5 COPPERCOURT LEAZE
6 BROADWAY GDNS
7 ROBINS CT
8 RIVERSDALE

87

D4
1 INGRAM WLK
2 MOORHILLS
3 MEADOW CT
4 CROMWELL RD
5 HARLESTON VILLAS
6 St John's CE Fst Sch

60

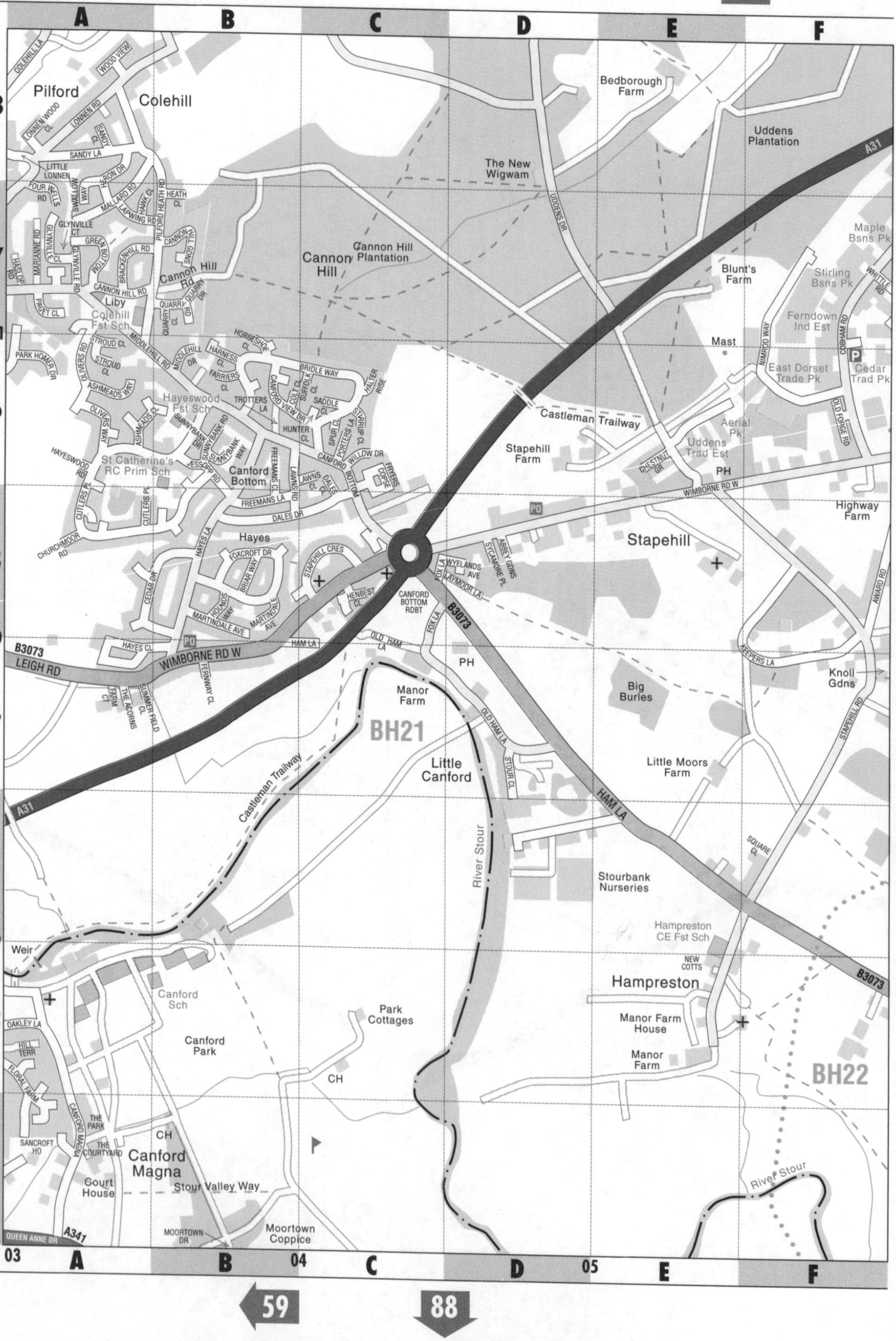
51
59
52
A
B
C
D
E
F
8
7
01
6
5
00
4
3
99
2
1
98
03
04
05
Pilford
Colehill
Bedborough Farm
Uddens Plantation
A31
The New Wigwam
Cannon Hill
Cannon Hill Plantation
Cannon Hill Rd
Liby
Colehill Fst Sch
Blunt's Farm
Maple Bsns Pk
Stirling Bsns Pk
Ferndown Ind Est
Mast
East Dorset Trade Pk
Cedar Trad Pk
Hayeswood Fst Sch
Castleman Trailway
Stapehill Farm
Aerial Pk
Uddens Trad Est
PH
St Catherine's RC Prim Sch
Canford Bottom
Highway Farm
Hayes
Stapehill
CANFORD BOTTOM RDBT
B3073
LEIGH RD
WIMBORNE RD W
Manor Farm
BH21
Big Burles
Knoll Gdns
Little Canford
Little Moors Farm
HAM LA
River Stour
Stourbank Nurseries
Hampreston CE Fst Sch
Weir
Canford Sch
Hampreston
Park Cottages
Manor Farm House
Manor Farm
Canford Park
CH
BH22
Canford Magna
Court House
Stour Valley Way
Moortown Coppice
A341
QUEEN ANNE DR

52 62 53

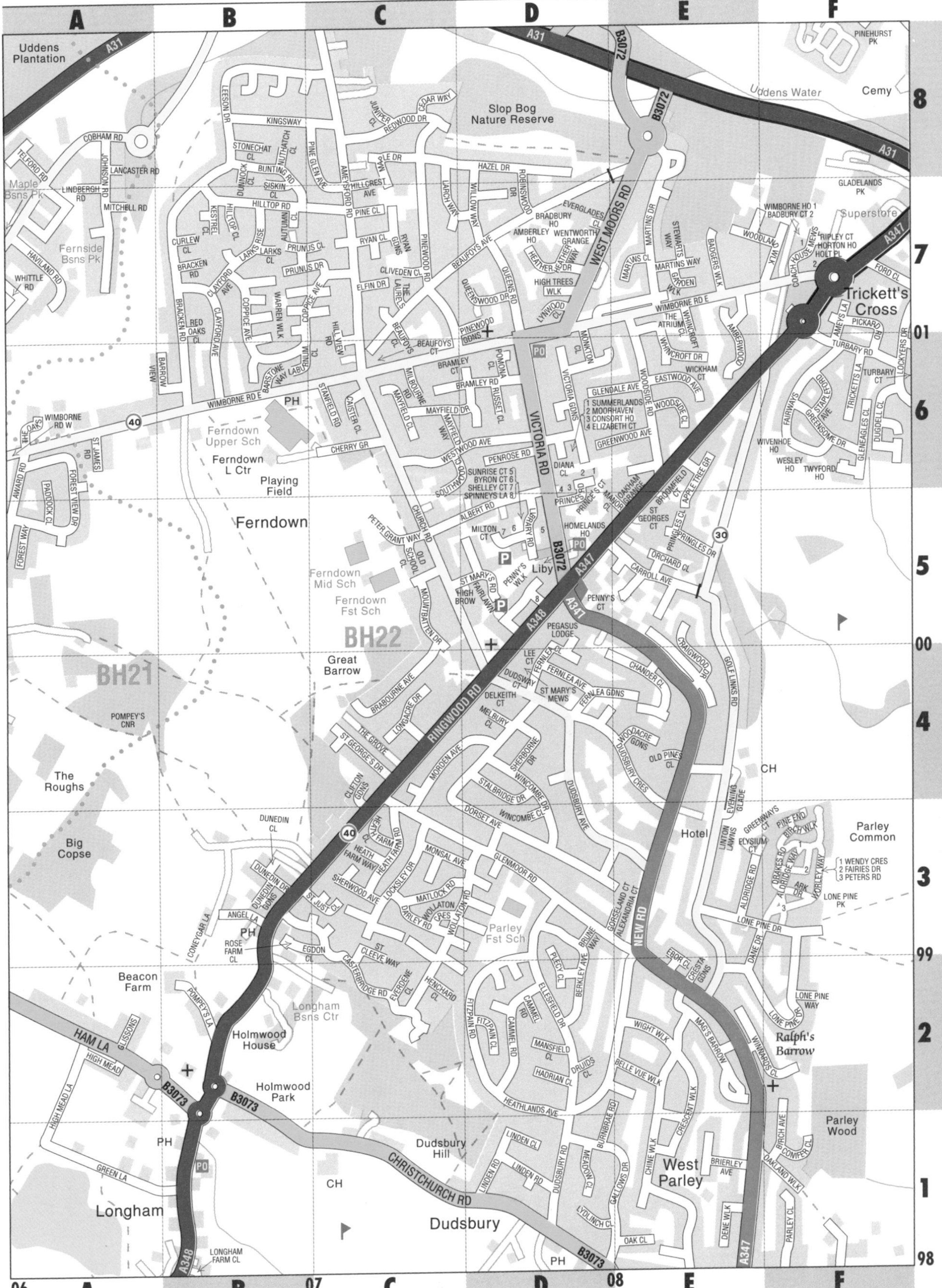
A
B
C
D
E
F
8
7
01
6
5
00
4
3
99
2
1
98
06
07
08
Uddens Plantation
A31
Slop Bog Nature Reserve
B3072
Uddens Water
Cemy
PINEHURST PK
GLADELANDS PK
Superstore
Trickett's Cross
A347
COBHAM RD
LANCASTER RD
JOHNSON RD
TELFORD RD
Maple Bsns Pk
LINDBERGH RD
MITCHELL RD
Fernside Bsns Pk
HAVILAND RD
WHITTLE RD
KINGSWAY
LEESON DR
STONECHAT CL
NUTHATCH CL
BUNTING RD
SISKIN CL
DUNNOCK CL
HILLTOP RD
CURLEW CL
KESTREL CL
HILLTOP CL
LARKS RISE
LARKS CL
AUTUMN CL
PRUNUS CL
PRUNUS DR
BRACKEN RD
CLAYFORD AVE
COPPICE AVE
WARREN WLK
RED OAKS CL
BARROW VIEW
BARNSTONE WAY
LABURNUM CL
JUNIPER CL
CEDAR WAY
REDWOOD DR
PINE GLEN AVE
AMEYSFORD RD
HILLCREST AVE
PINE CL
RYAN CL
RYAN GDNS
CLIVEDEN CL
ELFIN DR
THE LAURELS
HILL VIEW RD
PINEWOOD RD
LARCH WAY
WILLOW WAY
HAZEL DR
ROBINSWOOD DR
BEAUFOYS AVE
BEAUFOYS CL
BEAUFOYS CT
QUEENSWOOD DR
QUEENS RD
PINEWOOD GDNS
EVERGLADES CL
BRADBURY HO
AMBERLEY HO
WENTWORTH GRANGE
HEATHER DR
HEATHER WAY
HIGH TREES WLK
LYNWOOD CT
WEST MOORS RD
MARTINS DR
MARTINS CL
STEWARTS WAY
MARTINS WAY
GARDEN WLK
BADGERS WLK
WOODLAND WLK
WIMBORNE HO 1
BADBURY CT 2
COACH HOUSE MEWS
1 RIPLEY CT
2 HORTON HO
HOLT PL
FORD CL
AMEYS LA
PICKARD RD
LOCKYERS DR
TURBARY RD
TURBARY CT
WIMBORNE RD E
THE ATRIUM
WHINCROFT CL
WHINCROFT DR
AMBERWOOD
MONKTON CL
WICKHAM CT
EASTWOOD AVE
PO
BRAMLEY CT
BRAMLEY RD
POMONA CL
RUSSET CL
MILBOURNE RD
MAYFIELD DR
MAYFIELD CL
MAYFIELD WAY
VICTORIA GDNS
GLENDALE AVE
1 SUMMERLANDS
2 MOORHAVEN
3 CONSORT HO
4 ELIZABETH CT
WOODSIDE RD
WOODSIDE CL
GREENWOOD AVE
STAPLEFORD AVE
FAIRWAYS
TRICKETTS LA
DUDGELL CL
GREENSOME DR
GLENEAGLES CL
WIVENHOE HO
WESLEY HO
TWYFORD HO
PH
40
WIMBORNE RD W
THE OAKS
ST JAMES RD
STANFIELD RD
CAISTER CL
Ferndown Upper Sch
CHERRY GR
Ferndown L Ctr
Playing Field
AWARD RD
PADDOCK CL
FOREST VIEW DR
FOREST WAY
WESTWOOD AVE
PENROSE RD
SOUTHWOOD CL
SUNRISE CT 5
BYRON CT 6
SHELLEY CT 7
SPINNEYS LA 8
DIANA CL
PRINCE'S CT
PRINCE'S RD
OAKHAM GRANGE
MANOR CL
BROOMFIELD CT
APPLE TREE GR
ST GEORGES CT
PRINGLES CL
PRINGLES DR
30
ALBERT RD
VICTORIA RD
B3072
Ferndown
PETER GRANT WAY
CHURCH RD
OLD SCHOOL CL
MILTON CT
LIBRARY RD
HOMELANDS HO
Liby
A347
ORCHARD CL
CARROLL AVE
Ferndown Mid Sch
Ferndown Fst Sch
MOUNTBATTEN DR
ST MARY'S RD
FAIRLAWN
HIGH BROW
PENNY'S WLK
PENNY'S CT
A348
PEGASUS LODGE
CRAIGWOOD DR
GOLF LINKS RD
BH22
BH21
Great Barrow
LEE CT
FERNLEA CL
FERNLEA AVE
DUDSWAY CT
ST MARY'S MEWS
FERNLEA GDNS
CHANDER CL
DELKEITH CT
MELBURY CL
BRABOURNE AVE
LONGACRE DR
RINGWOOD RD
POMPEY'S CNR
THE GROVE
ST GEORGE'S DR
MORDEN AVE
SHERBORNE DR
WOODACRE GDNS
OLD PINES CL
DUDSBURY CRES
CH
The Roughs
STALBRIDGE DR
WINCOMBE DR
WINCOMBE CL
DUDSBURY AVE
CLIFTON GDNS
DORSET AVE
EVENING GLADE
Hotel
LINTON LAWNS
GREENWAYS CT
ELYSIUM CT
PINE END
BIRCH WLK
Parley Common
Big Copse
DUNEDIN CL
HEATH FARM CL
HEATH FARM RD
HEATH FARM WAY
MONSAL AVE
GLENMOOR RD
ALDRIDGE RD
DRAKES RD
ALDRIDGE WAY
WORLEY WAY
1 WENDY CRES
2 FAIRIES DR
3 PETERS RD
ARK DR
LONE PINE PK
DUNEDIN DR
DUNEDIN GDNS
SHERWOOD AVE
LOCKSLEY DR
MATLOCK RD
WOLLATON CRES
WOLLATON RD
DARLEY RD
ST JUST CL
GORSELAND CT
ALEXANDRIA CT
NEW RD
LONE PINE DR
DANE DR
ANGEL LA
CONEYGAR LA
ROSE FARM CL
EGDON CL
ST CLEEVE WAY
Parley Fst Sch
PLECY CL
BERKLEY AVE
BRUNE WAY
EBOR CL
CRESTA GDNS
Beacon Farm
POMPEY'S LA
CASTERBRIDGE RD
EVERDENE CL
HENCHARD CL
FITZPAIN RD
ELLESFIELD DR
CAMMEL RD
LONE PINE WAY
Longham Bsns Ctr
FITZPAIN CL
HAM LA
GLISSONS
HIGH MEAD
Holmwood House
MANSFIELD CL
WIGHT WLK
MAC'S BARROW
WINNARDS CL
Ralph's Barrow
HIGH MEAD LA
B3073
Holmwood Park
HADRIAN CL
DRUIDS CL
BELLE VUE WLK
HEATHLANDS AVE
CRESCENT WLK
BURNBRAE RD
BIRCH AVE
CONIFER CL
Parley Wood
PH
LINDEN CL
LINDEN RD
DUDSBURY RD
MEADOW CL
GALLOWS DR
CHINE WLK
Dudsbury Hill
West Parley
BRIERLEY AVE
OAKLAND WLK
GREEN LA
PO
CH
CHRISTCHURCH RD
LYDLINCH CL
Longham
Dudsbury
DENE WLK
PARLEY CL
OAK CL
LONGHAM FARM CL

89 62

53 61 54

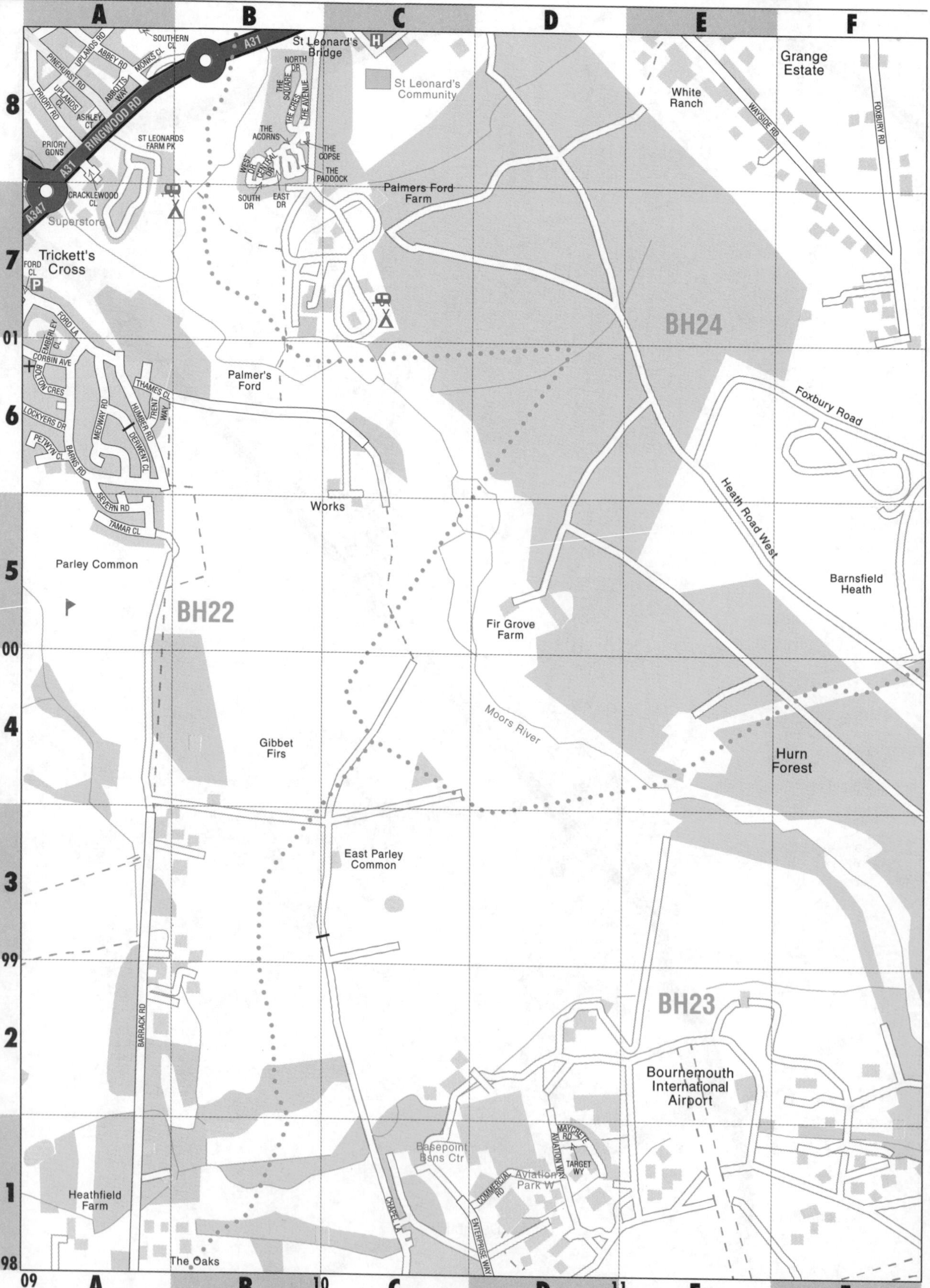
A
B
C
D
E
F
8
7
01
6
5
00
4
3
99
2
1
98
09
10
11
SOUTHERN CL
A31
St Leonard's Bridge
St Leonard's Community
Grange Estate
White Ranch
WAYSIDE RD
FOXBURY RD
PINEHURST RD
UPLANDS RD
ABBEY RD
MONKS CL
PRIORY RD
UPLANDS CL
ABBOTTS WAY
ASHLEY CT
RINGWOOD RD
PRIORY GDNS
ST LEONARDS FARM PK
NORTH DR
THE SQUARE
THE CRES
THE AVENUE
THE ACORNS
THE COPSE
THE PADDOCK
WEST DR
CENTRAL DR
SOUTH DR
EAST DR
Palmers Ford Farm
A347
CRACKLEWOOD CL
Superstore
Trickett's Cross
FORD CL
BH24
FORD LA
EMBERLEY CL
CORBIN AVE
BOLTON CRES
Palmer's Ford
THAMES CL
TRENT WAY
HUMBER RD
MEDWAY RD
DERWENT CL
LOCKYERS DR
PETWYN CL
BARNS RD
Foxbury Road
Works
SEVERN RD
TAMAR CL
Heath Road West
Parley Common
Barnsfield Heath
BH22
Fir Grove Farm
Moors River
Gibbet Firs
Hurn Forest
East Parley Common
BH23
BARRACK RD
Bournemouth International Airport
MAYCREETE RD
AVIATION WAY
Basepoint Bsns Ctr
TARGET WY
Aviation Park W
COMMERCIAL RD
CHAPEL LA
ENTERPRISE WAY
Heathfield Farm
The Oaks

61 90

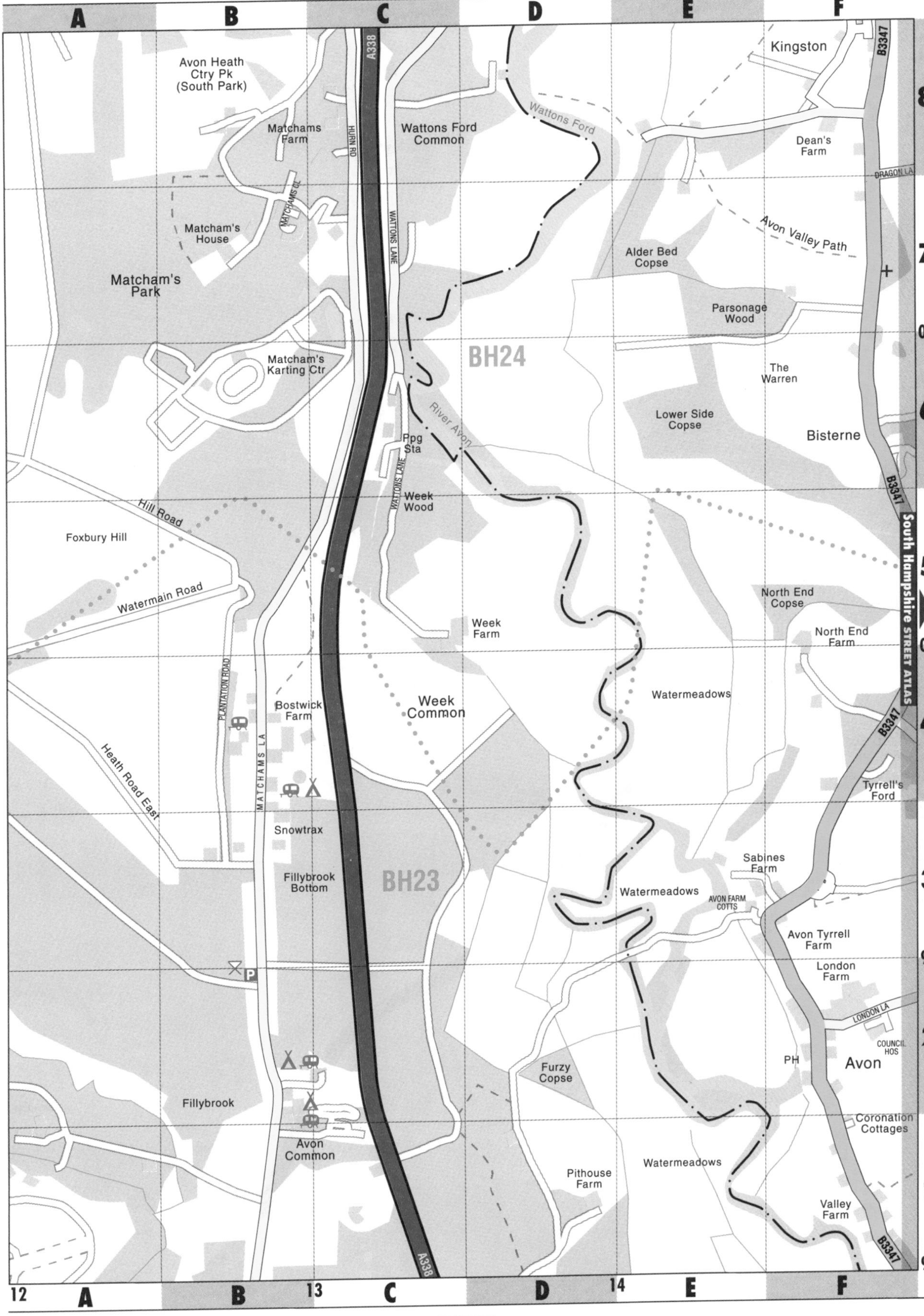

A B C D E F

8

Kingston

Avon Heath
Ctry Pk
(South Park)

Matchams
Farm

Wattons Ford
Common

Wattons Ford

Dean's
Farm

DRAGON LA

Matcham's
House

7

Alder Bed
Copse

Avon Valley Path

Matcham's
Park

Parsonage
Wood

01

BH24

The
Warren

6

Matcham's
Karting Ctr

River Avon

Lower Side
Copse

Bisterne

Hill Road

Ppg
Sta

Week
Wood

Foxbury Hill

5

North End
Copse

South Hampshire STREET ATLAS

Watermain Road

Week
Farm

North End
Farm

00

Heath Road East

Bostwick
Farm

Week
Common

Watermeadows

4

B3347

Tyrrell's
Ford

Snowtrax

BH23

Sabines
Farm

3

Fillybrook
Bottom

Watermeadows

AVON FARM
COTTS

Avon Tyrrell
Farm

London
Farm

99

LONDON LA

2

Fillybrook

PH

COUNCIL
HOS

Avon

Furzy
Copse

Coronation
Cottages

Avon
Common

Pithouse
Farm

Watermeadows

1

Valley
Farm

B3347

98

12 A B 13 C D 14 E F

202

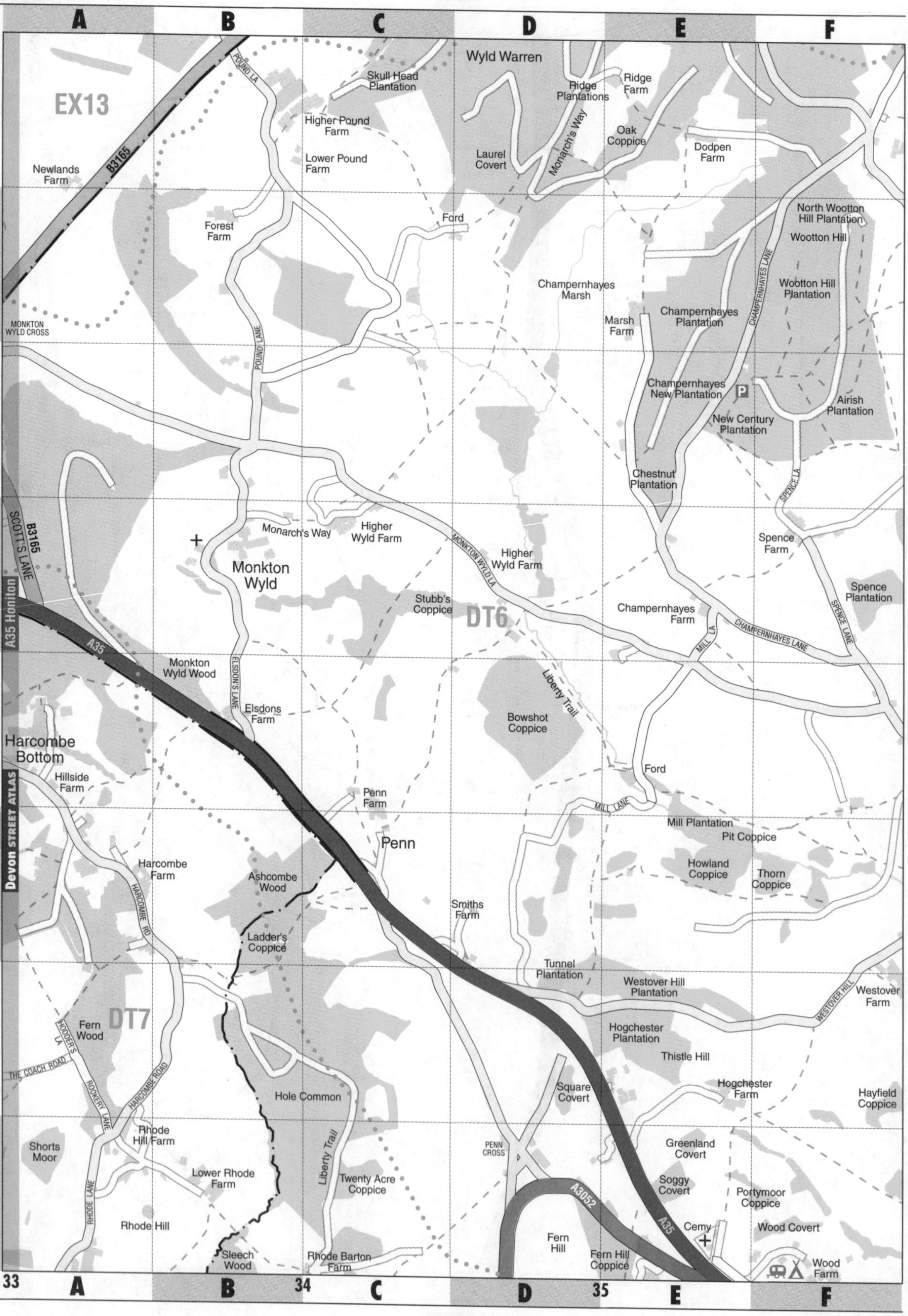

A
B
C
D
E
F
8
7
97
6
5
96
4
3
95
2
1
94
33
34
35
EX13
DT6
DT7
Wyld Warren
Skull Head Plantation
Ridge Plantations
Ridge Farm
Higher Pound Farm
Lower Pound Farm
Oak Coppice
Dodpen Farm
Laurel Covert
Monarch's Way
Newlands Farm
B3165
POUND LA
Ford
Forest Farm
North Wootton Hill Plantation
Wootton Hill
Wootton Hill Plantation
Champernhayes Marsh
Champernhayes Plantation
Marsh Farm
CHAMPERNHAYES LANE
MONKTON WYLD CROSS
POUND LANE
Champernhayes New Plantation
New Century Plantation
Airish Plantation
Chestnut Plantation
SPENCE LA
SCOTT'S LANE
Monarch's Way
Higher Wyld Farm
Spence Farm
Monkton Wyld
MONKTON WYLD LA
Higher Wyld Farm
Stubb's Coppice
Champernhayes Farm
Spence Plantation
A35 Honiton
A35
MILL LA
CHAMPERNHAYES LANE
SPENCE LANE
Monkton Wyld Wood
Liberty Trail
ELSDON'S LANE
Elsdons Farm
Bowshot Coppice
Harcombe Bottom
Hillside Farm
Ford
Penn Farm
MILL LANE
Mill Plantation
Pit Coppice
Penn
Harcombe Farm
Ashcombe Wood
Howland Coppice
Thorn Coppice
Devon STREET ATLAS
HARCOMBE RD
Smiths Farm
Ladder's Coppice
Tunnel Plantation
Westover Hill Plantation
Westover Farm
WESTOVER HILL
Fern Wood
RODDER'S LA
Hogchester Plantation
Thistle Hill
THE COACH ROAD
HARCOMBE ROAD
ROOKERY LANE
Hole Common
Square Covert
Hogchester Farm
Hayfield Coppice
Shorts Moor
Rhode Hill Farm
PENN CROSS
Greenland Covert
Lower Rhode Farm
Liberty Trail
Twenty Acre Coppice
Soggy Covert
Portymoor Coppice
RHODE LANE
Rhode Hill
A3052
Cemy
Wood Covert
Fern Hill
Fern Hill Coppice
Sleech Wood
Rhode Barton Farm
Wood Farm

96

202
66

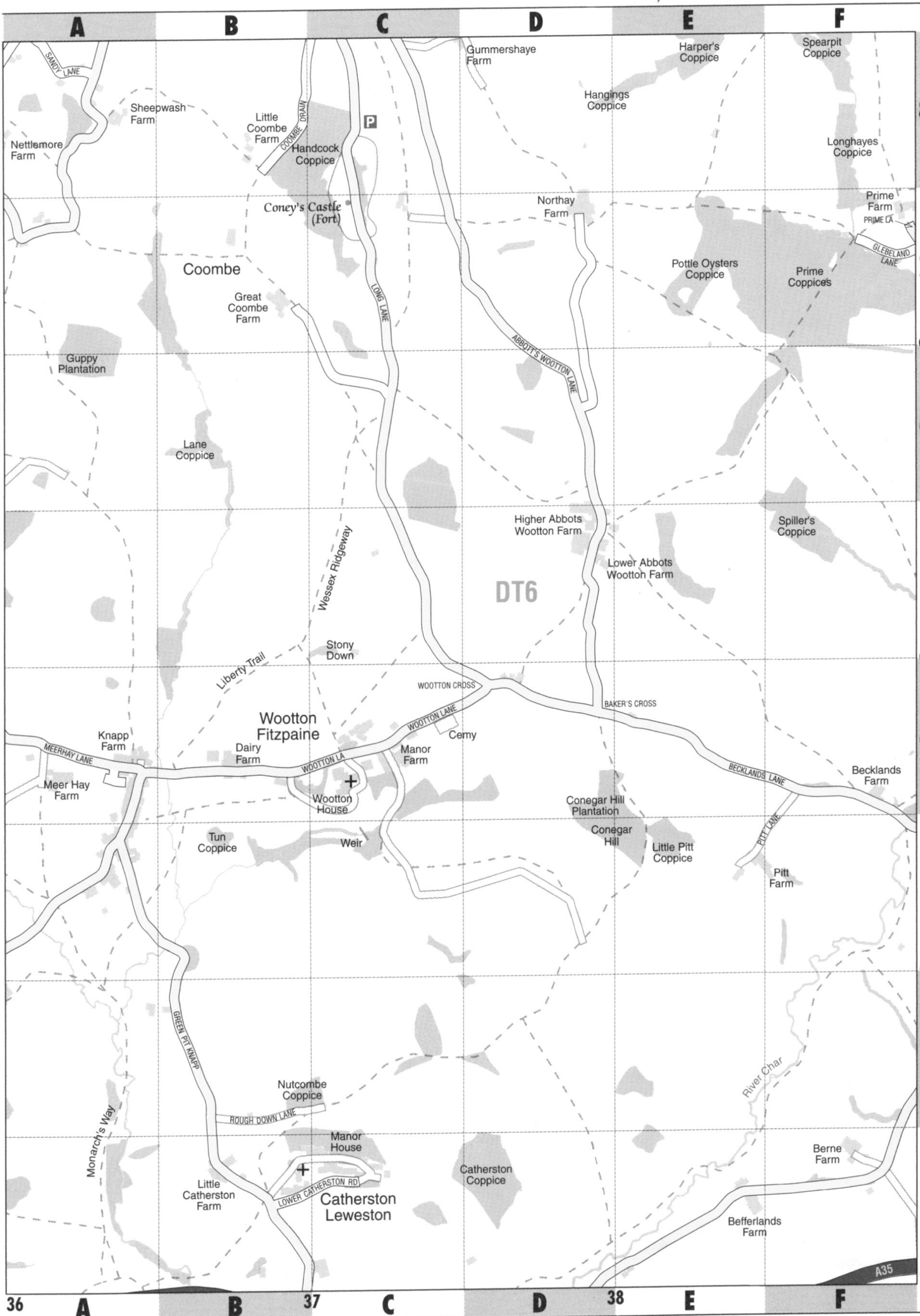
A
B
C
D
E
F
8
7
97
6
5
96
4
3
95
2
1
94
36
37
38
SANDY LANE
Sheepwash Farm
Nettlemore Farm
Little Coombe Farm
COOMBE DRAIN
Handcock Coppice
P
Coney's Castle (Fort)
Gummershaye Farm
Harper's Coppice
Hangings Coppice
Spearpit Coppice
Longhayes Coppice
Prime Farm
PRIME LA
GLEBELAND LANE
Northay Farm
Pottle Oysters Coppice
Prime Coppices
Coombe
Great Coombe Farm
LONG LANE
ABBOTT'S WOOTTON LANE
Guppy Plantation
Lane Coppice
Higher Abbots Wootton Farm
Spiller's Coppice
Wessex Ridgeway
Lower Abbots Wootton Farm
DT6
Stony Down
Liberty Trail
WOOTTON CROSS
BAKER'S CROSS
Wootton Fitzpaine
WOOTTON LANE
Cemy
Knapp Farm
MEERHAY LANE
Dairy Farm
WOOTTON LA
Manor Farm
Meer Hay Farm
Wootton House
BECKLANDS LANE
Becklands Farm
Conegar Hill Plantation
Conegar Hill
Little Pitt Coppice
PITT LANE
Tun Coppice
Weir
Pitt Farm
GREEN PIT KNAPP
River Char
Monarch's Way
Nutcombe Coppice
ROUGH DOWN LANE
Manor House
Berne Farm
Catherston Coppice
Little Catherston Farm
LOWER CATHERSTON RD
Catherston Leweston
Befferlands Farm
A35

97
66

65
203

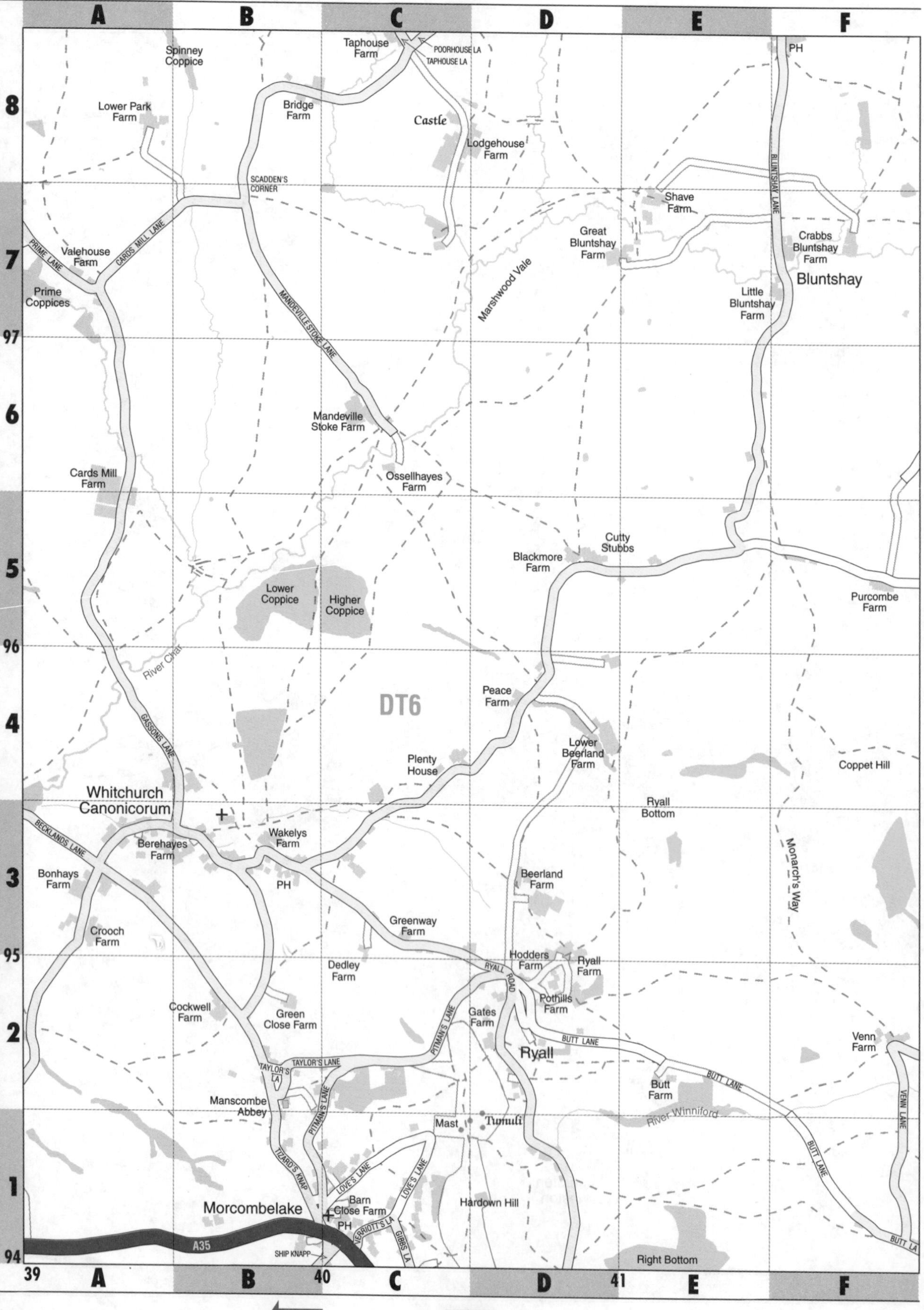
A
B
C
D
E
F
8
7
97
6
5
96
4
3
95
2
1
94
39
40
41
Spinney Coppice
Taphouse Farm
POORHOUSE LA
TAPHOUSE LA
PH
Lower Park Farm
Bridge Farm
Castle
Lodgehouse Farm
SCADDEN'S CORNER
Shave Farm
BLUNTSHAY LANE
PRIME LANE
CARDS MILL LANE
Valehouse Farm
Prime Coppices
Great Bluntshay Farm
Crabbs Bluntshay Farm
Marshwood Vale
Bluntshay
Little Bluntshay Farm
MANDEVILLE STOKE LANE
Mandeville Stoke Farm
Cards Mill Farm
Ossellhayes Farm
Cutty Stubbs
Blackmore Farm
Lower Coppice
Higher Coppice
Purcombe Farm
River Char
DT6
Peace Farm
GASSONS LANE
Lower Beerland Farm
Plenty House
Coppet Hill
Whitchurch Canonicorum
Ryall Bottom
BECKLANDS LANE
Berehayes Farm
Wakelys Farm
Monarch's Way
Bonhays Farm
PH
Beerland Farm
Crooch Farm
Greenway Farm
Hodders Farm
Ryall Farm
Dedley Farm
RYALL ROAD
Pothills Farm
Cockwell Farm
Green Close Farm
Gates Farm
PITMAN'S LANE
BUTT LANE
Venn Farm
Ryall
TAYLOR'S LA
TAYLOR'S LANE
Butt Farm
Manscombe Abbey
PITMAN'S LANE
Mast
Tumuli
River Winniford
VENN LANE
TIZARD'S KNAP
LOVE'S LANE
LOVE'S LANE
BUTT LANE
Barn Close Farm
Hardown Hill
Morcombelake
PH
VERRIOTT'S LA
GIBBS LA
BUTT LA
A35
SHIP KNAPP
Right Bottom

65
98

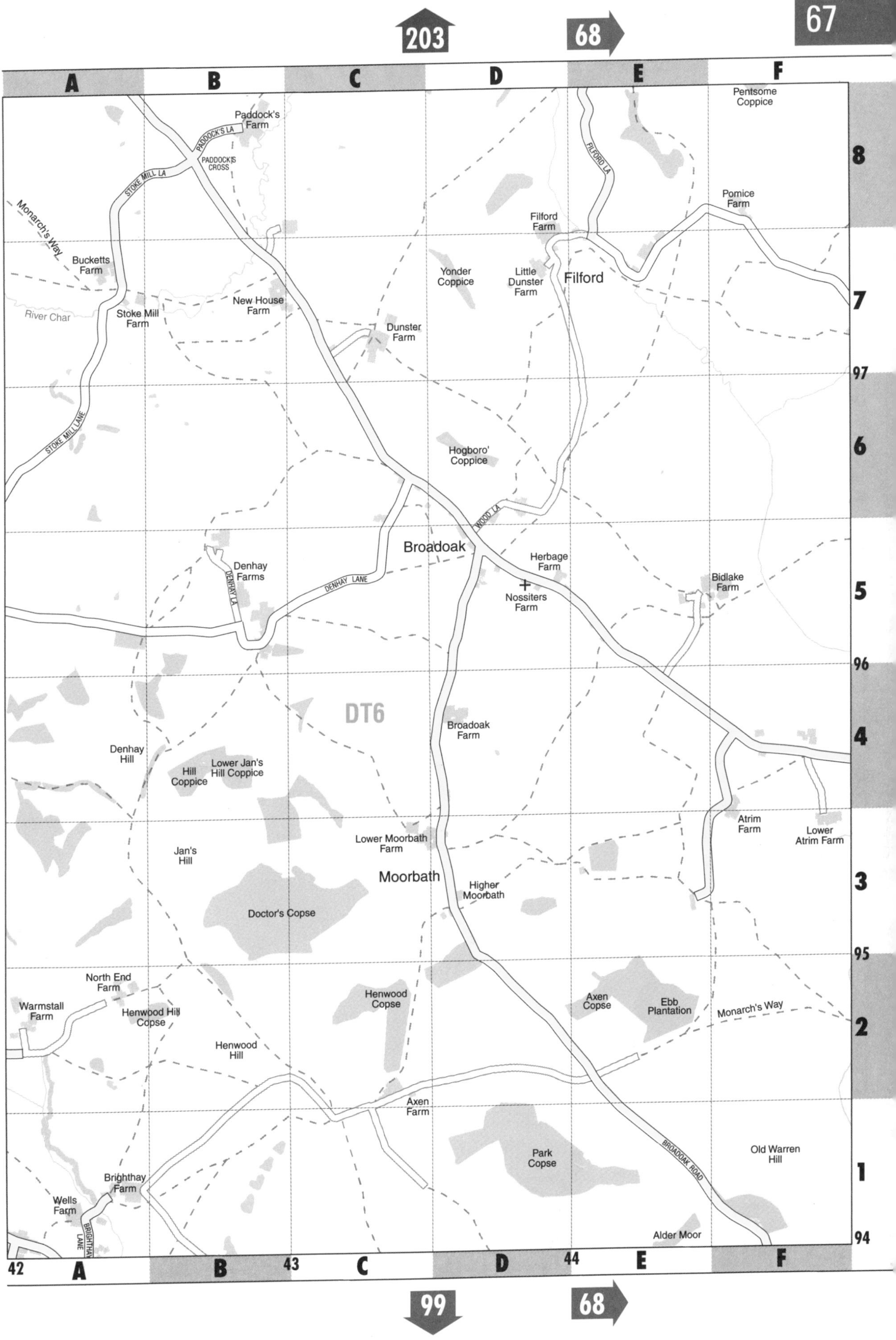

203
68
A
B
C
D
E
F
Pentsome Coppice
Paddock's Farm
PADDOCK'S LA
PADDOCK'S CROSS
STOKE MILL LA
Monarch's Way
FILFORD LA
Pomice Farm
Filford Farm
Bucketts Farm
Yonder Coppice
Little Dunster Farm
Filford
New House Farm
Stoke Mill Farm
River Char
Dunster Farm
STOKE MILL LANE
Hogboro' Coppice
WOOD LA
Broadoak
Herbage Farm
Denhay Farms
DENHAY LA
DENHAY LANE
Bidlake Farm
Nossiters Farm
DT6
Broadoak Farm
Denhay Hill
Hill Coppice
Lower Jan's Hill Coppice
Atrim Farm
Lower Atrim Farm
Lower Moorbath Farm
Jan's Hill
Moorbath
Higher Moorbath
Doctor's Copse
North End Farm
Henwood Copse
Axen Copse
Ebb Plantation
Monarch's Way
Warmstall Farm
Henwood Hill Copse
Henwood Hill
Axen Farm
BROADOAK ROAD
Old Warren Hill
Park Copse
Brighthay Farm
Wells Farm
BRIGHTHAY LANE
Alder Moor
8
7
97
6
5
96
4
3
95
2
1
94
42
43
44
99
68

A B C D E F

8

Higher Kingsland Farm
Kershay Farms
Nurserymead Coppice
Shatcombe Coppice
B3162
Long Bottom Coppice
Salway Ash CE Prim Sch
Kingsland
WHITHAY LA
Higher Kershay Farm
Lower Kershay Farm
Perhay Farm
SLAPE HILL
PH
Myrtle Farm
Waytown
White House Farm
Way Farm
Oxbridge
Oxbridge Farm

7

STRONGATE LA
Strongate Farm
WHITHAY LANE
Brinsham Farm
Marlis Farm
Elwell Lodge
Camesworth

97

Church Grounds
Ash Farm
SALWAY DR
PITCHERS
Pineapple Bsns Pk
Pineapple Farm
PINEAPPLE LANE
Higher Ford Farm
Elwell Farms
Higher Elwell Farm
Snailscroft Farm
Foxmoor Coppice

6

Hill Farm
PH
Salwayash
Lambrook
Lambrook Farm
River Brit
Bingham's Farm

5

Broadenham Farm
Ash Lane Farm
ASH LANE
Ash
Seaview Farm
DT6
Higher Ash Farm
Higher Wooth Farm

96

Limbury
Ashleigh Farm
Sewage Works

4

Atrim
Colly Farm
Wooth Old Farm
Wooth Farm
Wooth

3

Dottery
Higher Pymore Farm
PYMORE LANE
Lower Ash Farm
Watford Lane
Watford Farm

95

Bilshay Farm
BILSHAY LANE
Monarch's Way
Middle Pymore Farm
MORDAGE GROVE
OLD THREAD MILL
SOUTH ROAD
THREAD MILL LA
Factory
PH
PYMORE ROAD
Gore Cross Business Park
GORE CROSS
A3066
BLIND LANE CL
GORE LANE
TOWNSEND WY

2

New Close Farm
DOTTERY ROAD
Washingpool Farm
Lower Pymore Farm
Pymore
Queenwell
CORBIN WAY
RIDGEWAY
HILLVIEW
BEAMINSTER ROAD
The Sir John Colfox Sch
DOCKRAMS
PAGEANT'S CL
BANTON SHARD
KINGS WILLIAMS HEAD
COURT
VILLAGE RD
TRINITY WY

1

River Simene
B3162
Seymour Farm
River Brit
DODHAM'S LANE
ST ANDREW'S ROAD
KNIGHTSTONE RI
FISHNER LA

94

45 A B 46 C D 47 E F

F1
1 FISHWEIR FIELDS
2 ACER AVE
3 WHITE CL
4 SPRING CL
5 GORE CROSS WY
6 BATH ORCHARD

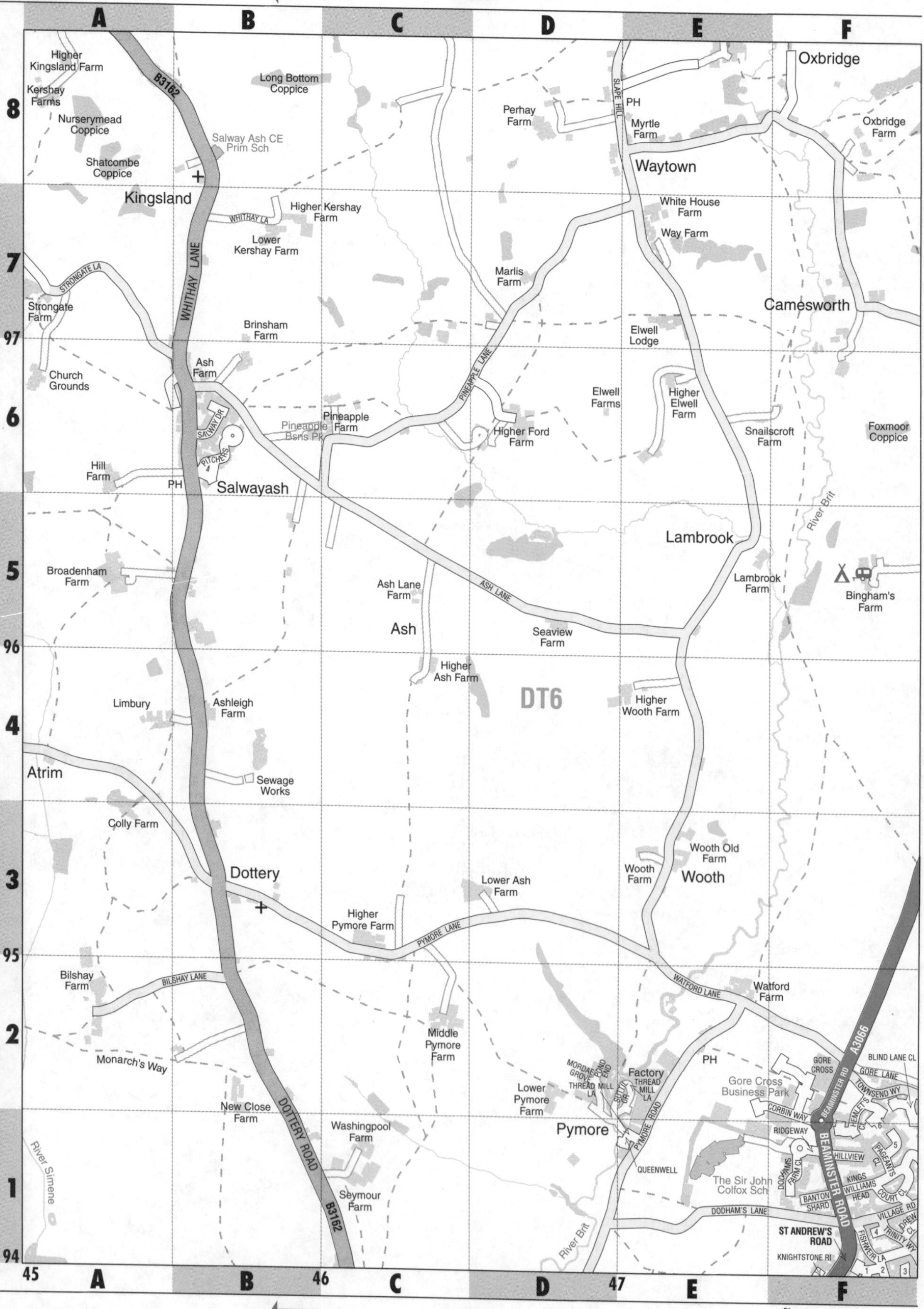

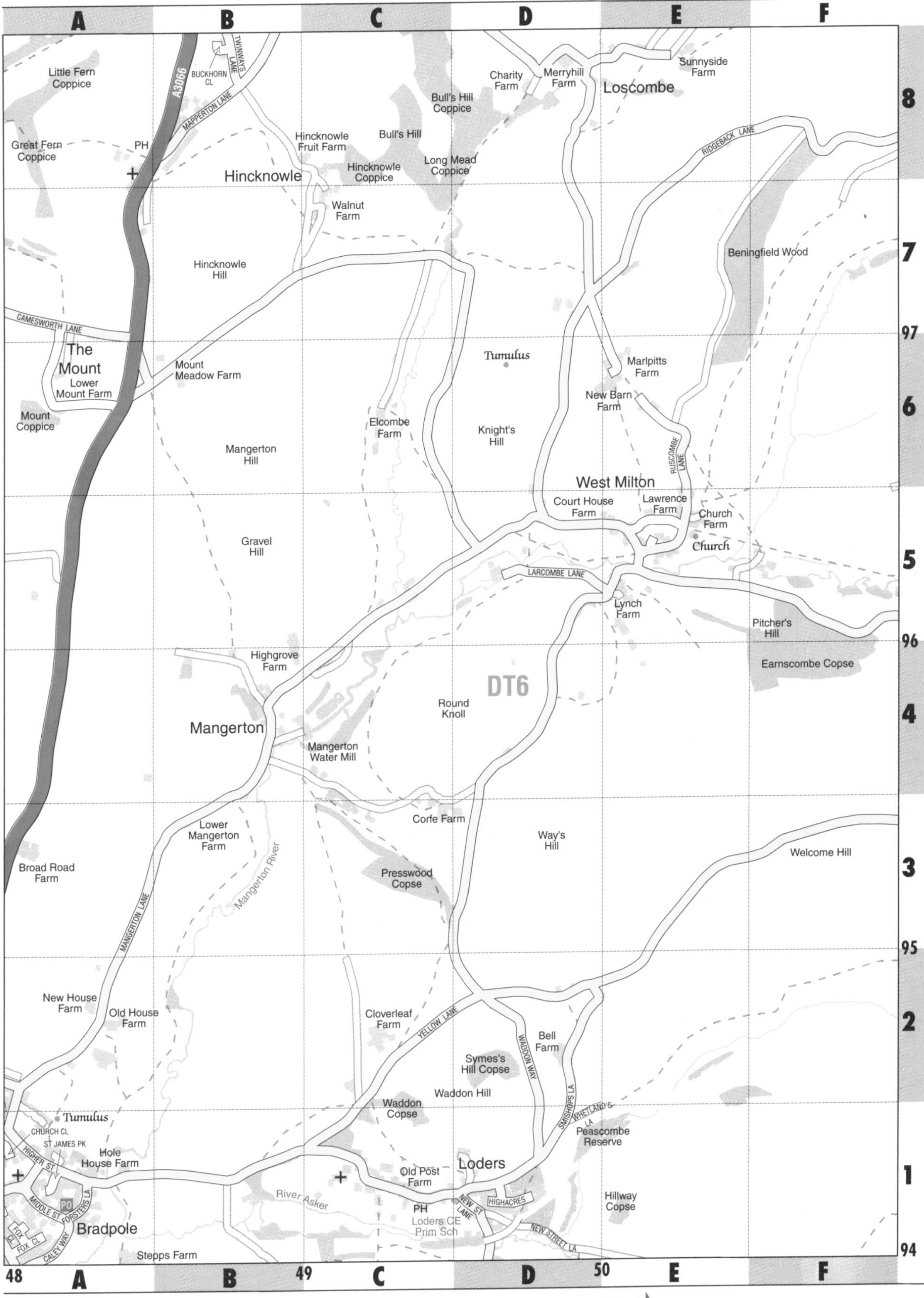

A   B   C   D   E   F

8
7
97
6
5
96
4
3
95
2
1
94

Little Fern Coppice
BUCKHORN CL
TWINWAY'S LANE
MAPPERTON LANE
A3066
Great Fern Coppice
PH
Hincknowle Fruit Farm
Bull's Hill
Bull's Hill Coppice
Charity Farm
Merryhill Farm
Sunnyside Farm
Loscombe
RIDGEBACK LANE
Hincknowle
Hincknowle Coppice
Long Mead Coppice
Walnut Farm
Hincknowle Hill
CAMESWORTH LANE
Beningfield Wood
The Mount
Lower Mount Farm
Mount Meadow Farm
Tumulus
Marlpitts Farm
Mount Coppice
Elcombe Farm
Knight's Hill
New Barn Farm
Mangerton Hill
West Milton
RUSCOMBE LANE
Gravel Hill
Court House Farm
Lawrence Farm
Church Farm
Church
LARCOMBE LANE
Lynch Farm
Pitcher's Hill
Highgrove Farm
Earnscombe Copse
DT6
Mangerton
Round Knoll
Mangerton Water Mill
Lower Mangerton Farm
Corfe Farm
Way's Hill
Welcome Hill
Broad Road Farm
MANGERTON LANE
Mangerton River
Presswood Copse
New House Farm
Old House Farm
Cloverleaf Farm
YELLOW LANE
Bell Farm
WADDON WAY
Symes's Hill Copse
Waddon Hill
SMISKOP'S LA
WHETLAND'S LA
Peascombe Reserve
Tumulus
CHURCH CL
ST JAMES PK
Hole House Farm
Waddon Copse
HIGHER ST
PO
Old Post Farm
Loders
HIGHACRES
Hillway Copse
FOX CL
MIDDLE ST
FORSTERS LA
CALEYS WAY
Bradpole
River Asker
PH
Loders CE Prim Sch
NEW ST
NEW LANE
NEW STREET LA
Stepps Farm

69
205

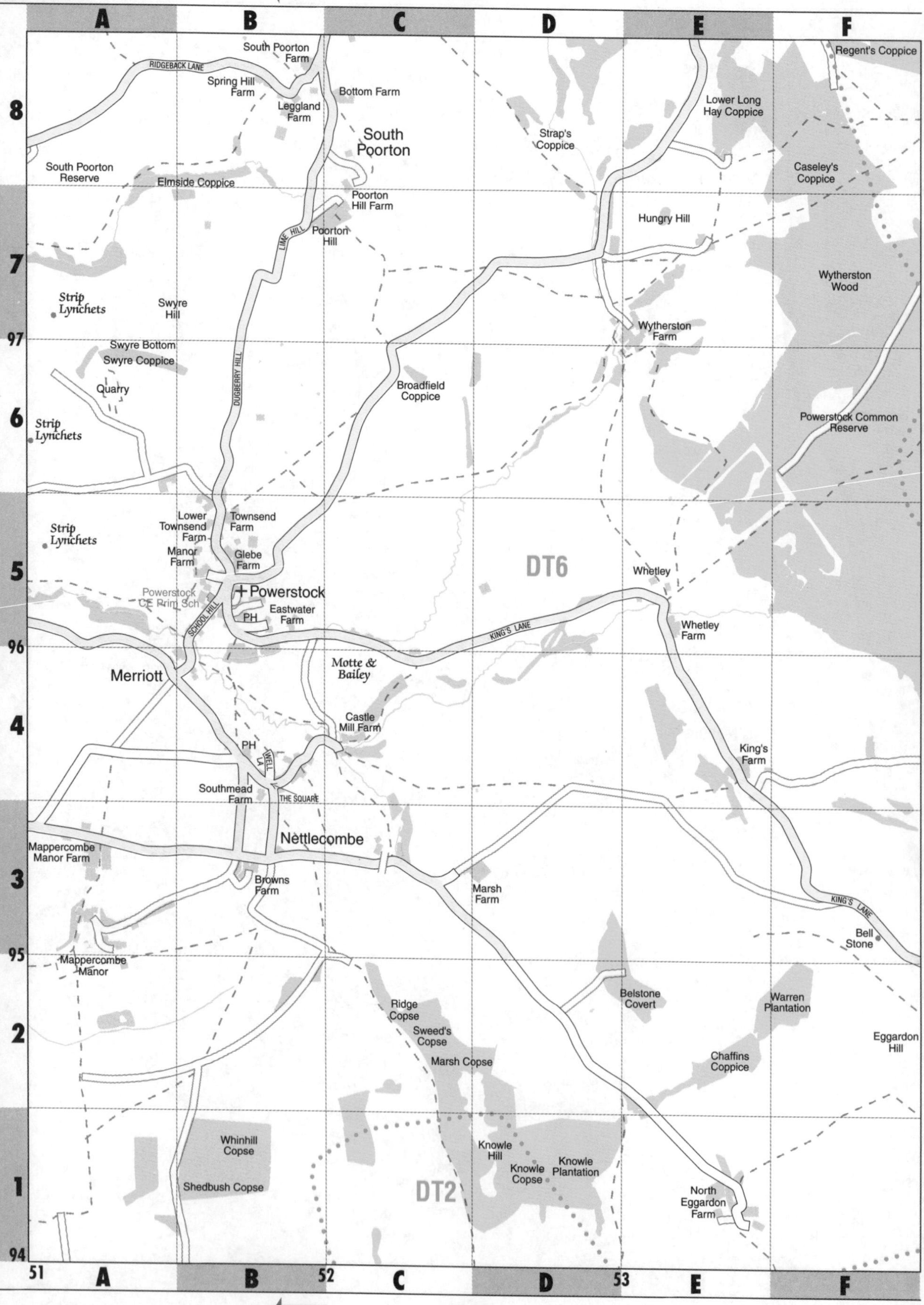

A B C D E F

8

RIDGEBACK LANE

South Poorton Farm

Spring Hill Farm

Leggland Farm

Bottom Farm

South Poorton

Regent's Coppice

Lower Long Hay Coppice

Strap's Coppice

Caseley's Coppice

South Poorton Reserve

Elmside Coppice

Poorton Hill Farm

LIME HILL

Poorton Hill

Hungry Hill

Wytherston Wood

7

97

Strip Lynchets

Swyre Hill

Swyre Bottom

Swyre Coppice

DUGBERRY HILL

Broadfield Coppice

Wytherston Farm

Powerstock Common Reserve

6

Quarry

Strip Lynchets

Lower Townsend Farm

Townsend Farm

Manor Farm

Glebe Farm

DT6

Whetley

5

Strip Lynchets

Powerstock CE Prim Sch

+ Powerstock

PH

Eastwater Farm

King's Lane

Whetley Farm

96

Merriott

Motte & Bailey

King's Farm

4

PH

WELL LA

Castle Mill Farm

Southmead Farm

THE SQUARE

Nettlecombe

King's Farm

95

Mappercombe Manor Farm

Browns Farm

Marsh Farm

KING'S LANE

Bell Stone

3

Mappercombe Manor

Ridge Copse

Sweed's Copse

Marsh Copse

Belstone Covert

Warren Plantation

Chaffins Coppice

Eggardon Hill

2

Whinhill Copse

Shedbush Copse

DT2

Knowle Hill

Knowle Copse

Knowle Plantation

North Eggardon Farm

1

94

51 A B 52 C D 53 E F

205
72

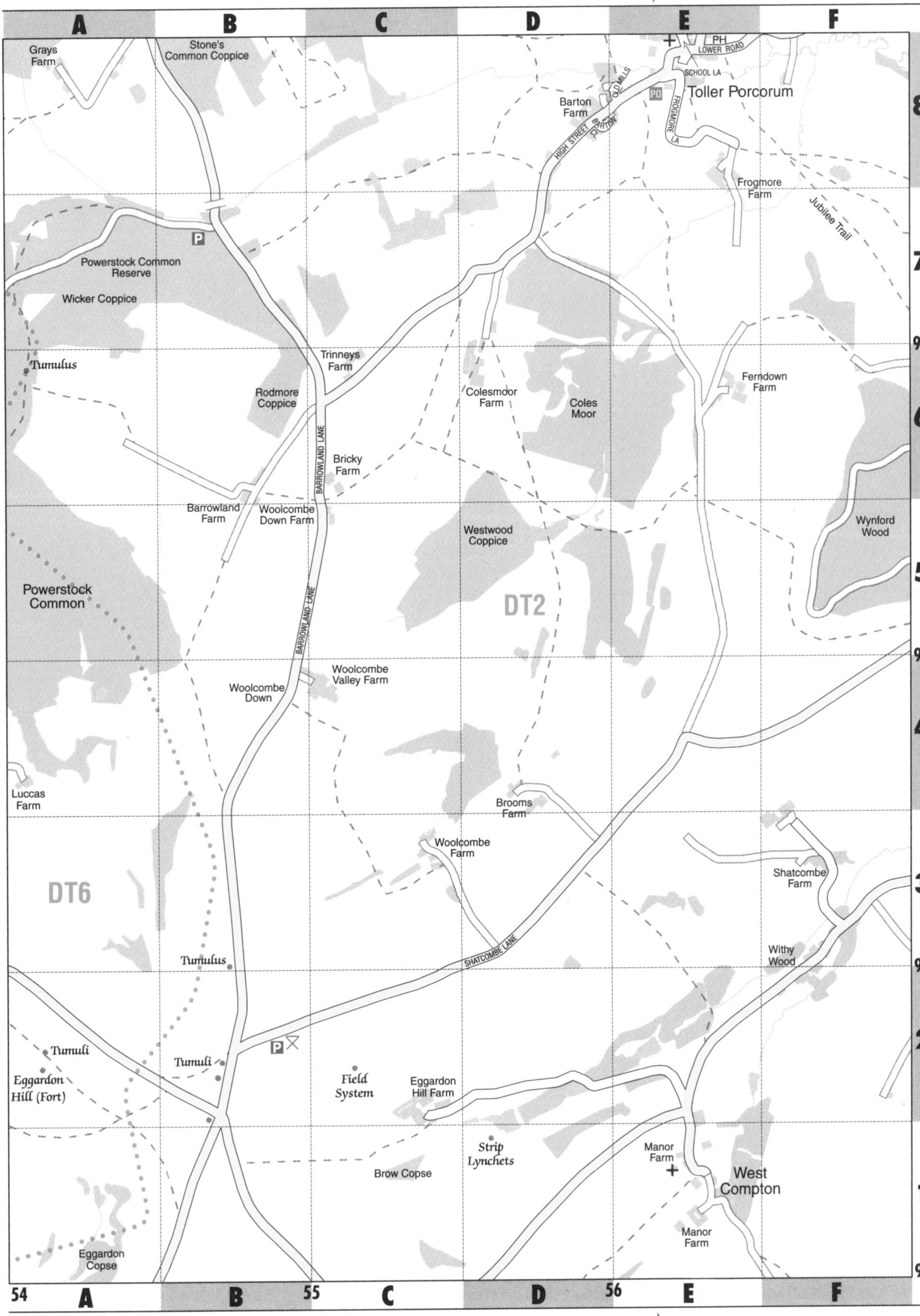
A
B
C
D
E
F
Grays Farm
Stone's Common Coppice
PH
LOWER ROAD
SCHOOL LA
OLD MILLS
PO
Toller Porcorum
Barton Farm
HIGH STREET
BARTON CL
FROGMORE LA
Frogmore Farm
Jubilee Trail
8
P
Powerstock Common Reserve
Wicker Coppice
7
Trinneys Farm
97
Tumulus
Rodmore Coppice
Colesmoor Farm
Coles Moor
Ferndown Farm
6
BARROWLAND LANE
Bricky Farm
Barrowland Farm
Woolcombe Down Farm
Westwood Coppice
Wynford Wood
5
Powerstock Common
DT2
96
Woolcombe Valley Farm
Woolcombe Down
4
Luccas Farm
Brooms Farm
Woolcombe Farm
DT6
Shatcombe Farm
3
SHATCOMBE LANE
Withy Wood
Tumulus
95
2
Tumuli
Eggardon Hill (Fort)
Tumuli
Field System
Eggardon Hill Farm
Strip Lynchets
Manor Farm
Brow Copse
West Compton
1
Manor Farm
Eggardon Copse
94
54
55
56

103
72

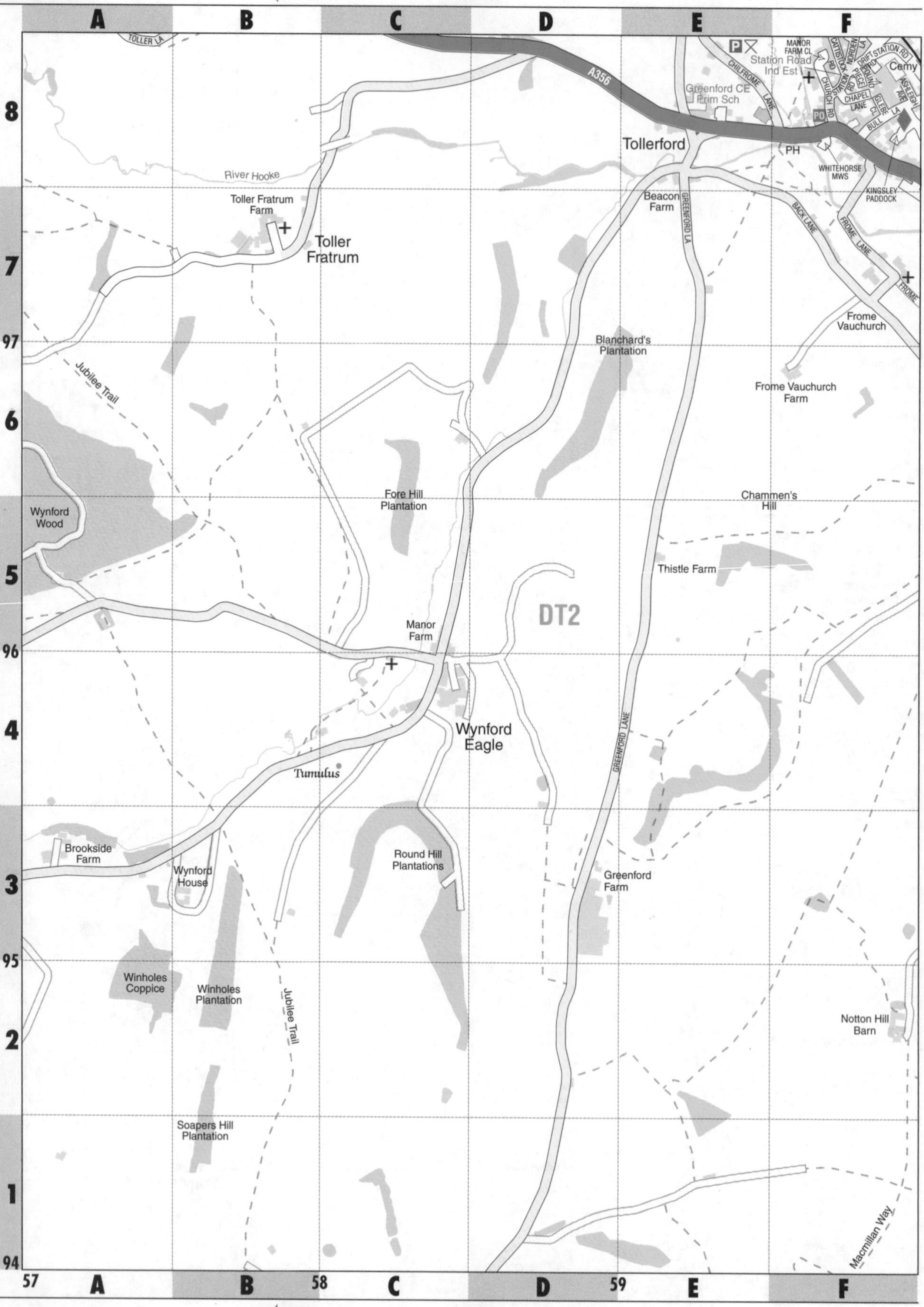

71
206

A B C D E F

8

Station Road Ind Est
Greenford CE Prim Sch
Tollerford
PH
MANOR FARM CL
Cemy
CHAPEL LANE
BULL
WHITEHORSE MWS
KINGSLEY PADDOCK
CHILFROME LANE

River Hooke

Toller Fratrum Farm
Toller Fratrum

7

Beacon Farm
GREENFORD LA
BACK LANE
FROME LANE
Frome Vauchurch
FROME

97

Jubilee Trail

Blanchard's Plantation

Frome Vauchurch Farm

6

Fore Hill Plantation

Chammen's Hill

Wynford Wood

5

Thistle Farm

DT2

96

Manor Farm

4

Wynford Eagle

GREENFORD LANE

Tumulus

Brookside Farm

3

Wynford House

Round Hill Plantations

Greenford Farm

95

Winholes Coppice

Winholes Plantation

Jubilee Trail

2

Notton Hill Barn

1

Soapers Hill Plantation

Macmillan Way

94

57 A B 58 C D 59 E F

71
104

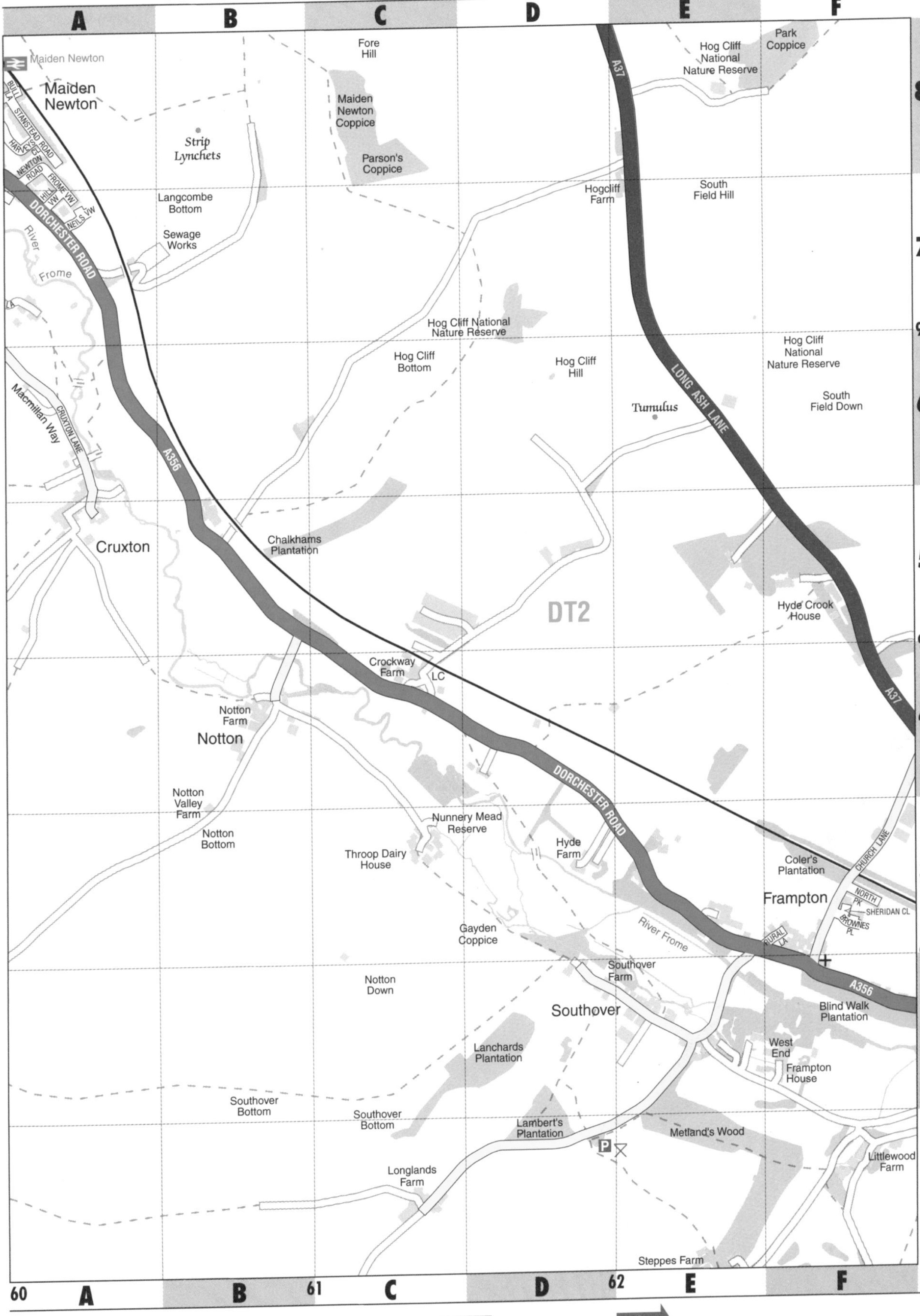

A B C D E F

8

Maiden Newton

Maiden
Newton

BULL LA
STANSTEAD ROAD
HARVEY LA
NEWTON
ROAD
FROME TW
ELM VW
NELS VW

DORCHESTER ROAD

River
Frome

Macmillan Way

CRUXTON LANE

A356

Cruxton

Fore
Hill

Maiden
Newton
Coppice

Parson's
Coppice

Strip
Lynchets

Langcombe
Bottom

Sewage
Works

Chalkhams
Plantation

Hog Cliff
Bottom

Hog Cliff National
Nature Reserve

Hog Cliff
Hill

Hogcliff
Farm

A37

Hog Cliff
National
Nature Reserve

Park
Coppice

South
Field Hill

LONG ASH LANE

Tumulus

Hog Cliff
National
Nature Reserve

South
Field Down

Hyde Crook
House

DT2

A37

8

7

97

6

5

96

Crockway
Farm

LC

Notton
Farm

Notton

Notton
Valley
Farm

Notton
Bottom

DORCHESTER ROAD

Nunnery Mead
Reserve

Throop Dairy
House

Hyde
Farm

Gayden
Coppice

River Frome

Coler's
Plantation

Frampton

CHURCH LANE

NORTH
PK
SHERIDAN CL
BROWNES
PL
RURAL LA

Blind Walk
Plantation

A356

4

3

95

2

Notton
Down

Southover

Southover
Farm

West
End

Frampton
House

Lanchards
Plantation

Southover
Bottom

Southover
Bottom

Lambert's
Plantation

P

Metland's Wood

Littlewood
Farm

Longlands
Farm

Steppes Farm

1

94

73
207

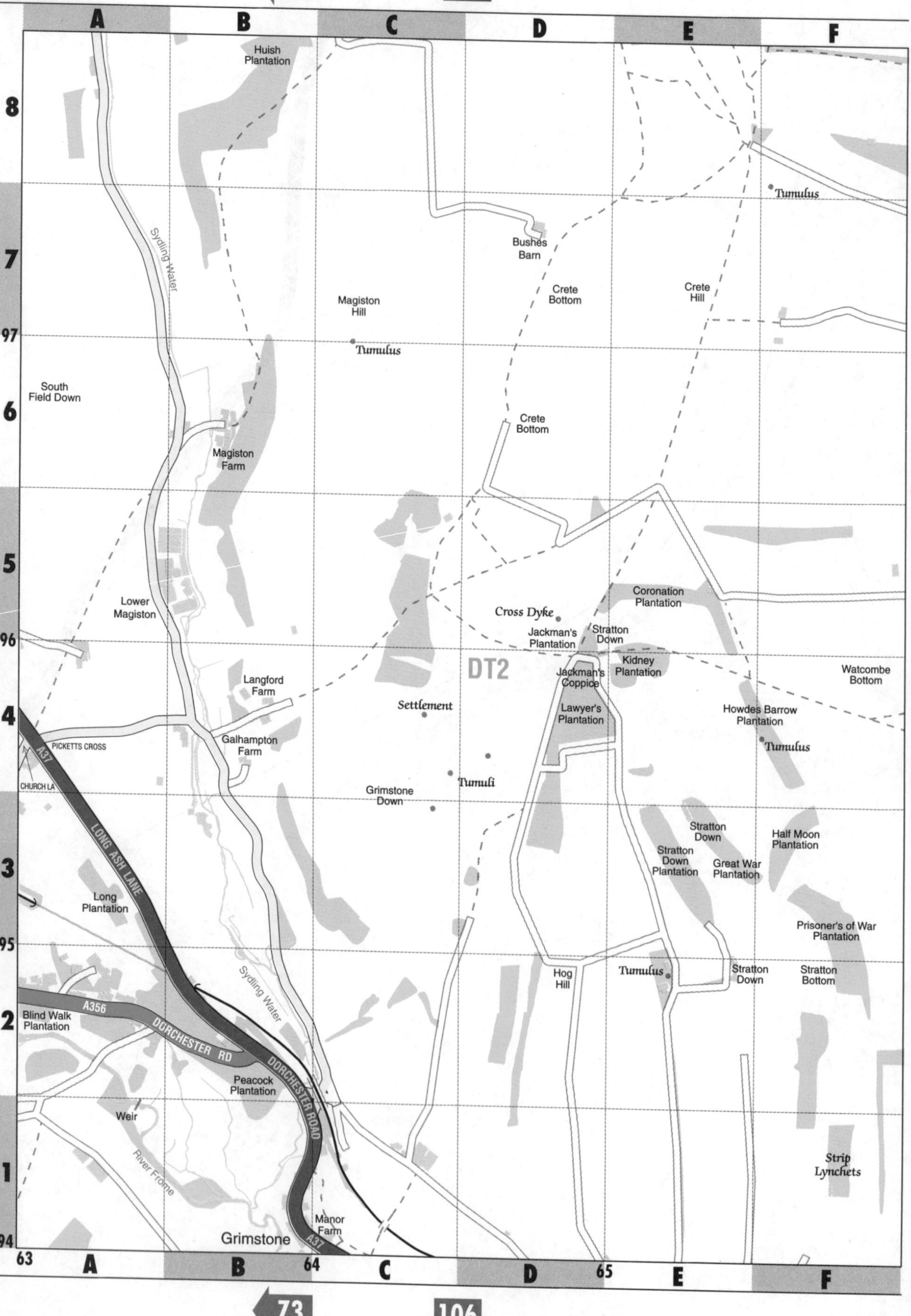
A
B
C
D
E
F
8
7
97
6
5
96
4
3
95
2
1
94
63
64
65
Huish Plantation
Sydling Water
Bushes Barn
Crete Bottom
Crete Hill
Tumulus
Magiston Hill
Tumulus
South Field Down
Crete Bottom
Magiston Farm
Lower Magiston
Coronation Plantation
Cross Dyke
Jackman's Plantation
Stratton Down
Kidney Plantation
DT2
Watcombe Bottom
Langford Farm
Jackman's Coppice
Settlement
Lawyer's Plantation
Howdes Barrow Plantation
Tumulus
PICKETTS CROSS
A37
Galhampton Farm
CHURCH LA
Tumuli
Grimstone Down
LONG ASH LANE
Stratton Down
Half Moon Plantation
Stratton Down Plantation
Great War Plantation
Long Plantation
Prisoner's of War Plantation
Sydling Water
Hog Hill
Tumulus
Stratton Down
Stratton Bottom
A356
Blind Walk Plantation
DORCHESTER RD
DORCHESTER ROAD
Peacock Plantation
Weir
River Frome
Strip Lynchets
Manor Farm
Grimstone
A37

73
106

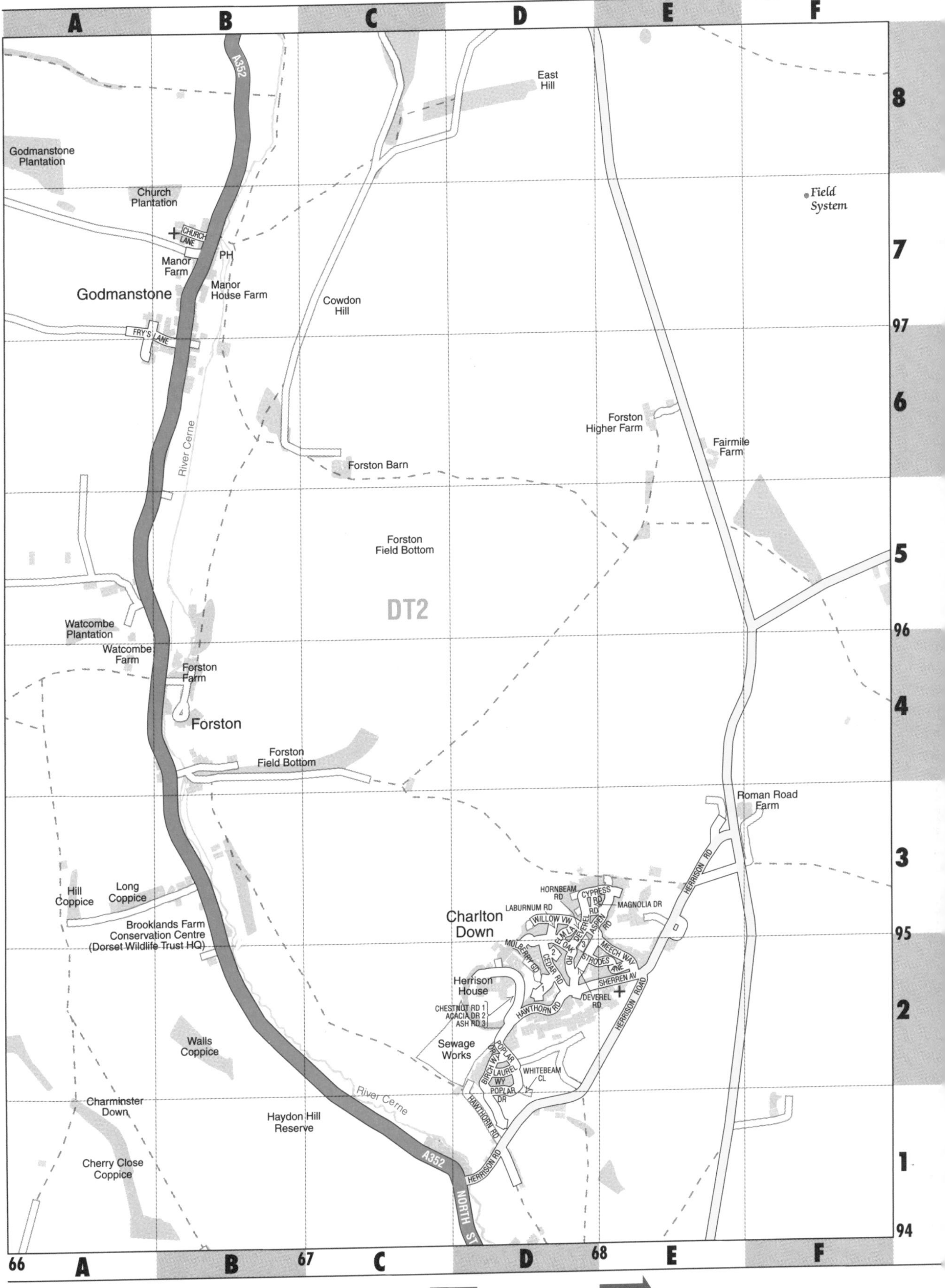

A   B   C   D   E   F

8

Godmanstone Plantation

East Hill

Church Plantation

Field System

7

CHURCH LANE
Manor Farm
PH
Manor House Farm

Godmanstone

Cowdon Hill

97

FRY'S LANE

River Cerne

6

Forston Higher Farm

Fairmile Farm

Forston Barn

Forston Field Bottom

5

DT2

Watcombe Plantation

96

Watcombe Farm

Forston Farm

4

Forston

Forston Field Bottom

Roman Road Farm

3

Hill Coppice

Long Coppice

HORNBEAM RD
CYPRESS RD
MAGNOLIA DR

Brooklands Farm Conservation Centre (Dorset Wildlife Trust HQ)

LABURNUM RD
WILLOW VW

Charlton Down

MEECH WAY

95

MULBERRY CFT
CEDAR RD
STRODES LANE

SHERREN AV

Herrison House

HERRISON ROAD

DEVEREL RD

CHESTNUT RD 1
ACACIA DR 2
ASH RD 3

HAWTHORN RD

2

Walls Coppice

Sewage Works

POPLAR
BIRCH WY
LAUREL WY
POPLAR DR

WHITEBEAM CL

Charminster Down

River Cerne

HAWTHORN RD

1

Cherry Close Coppice

Haydon Hill Reserve

A352

HERRISON RD

NORTH ST

94

75
208

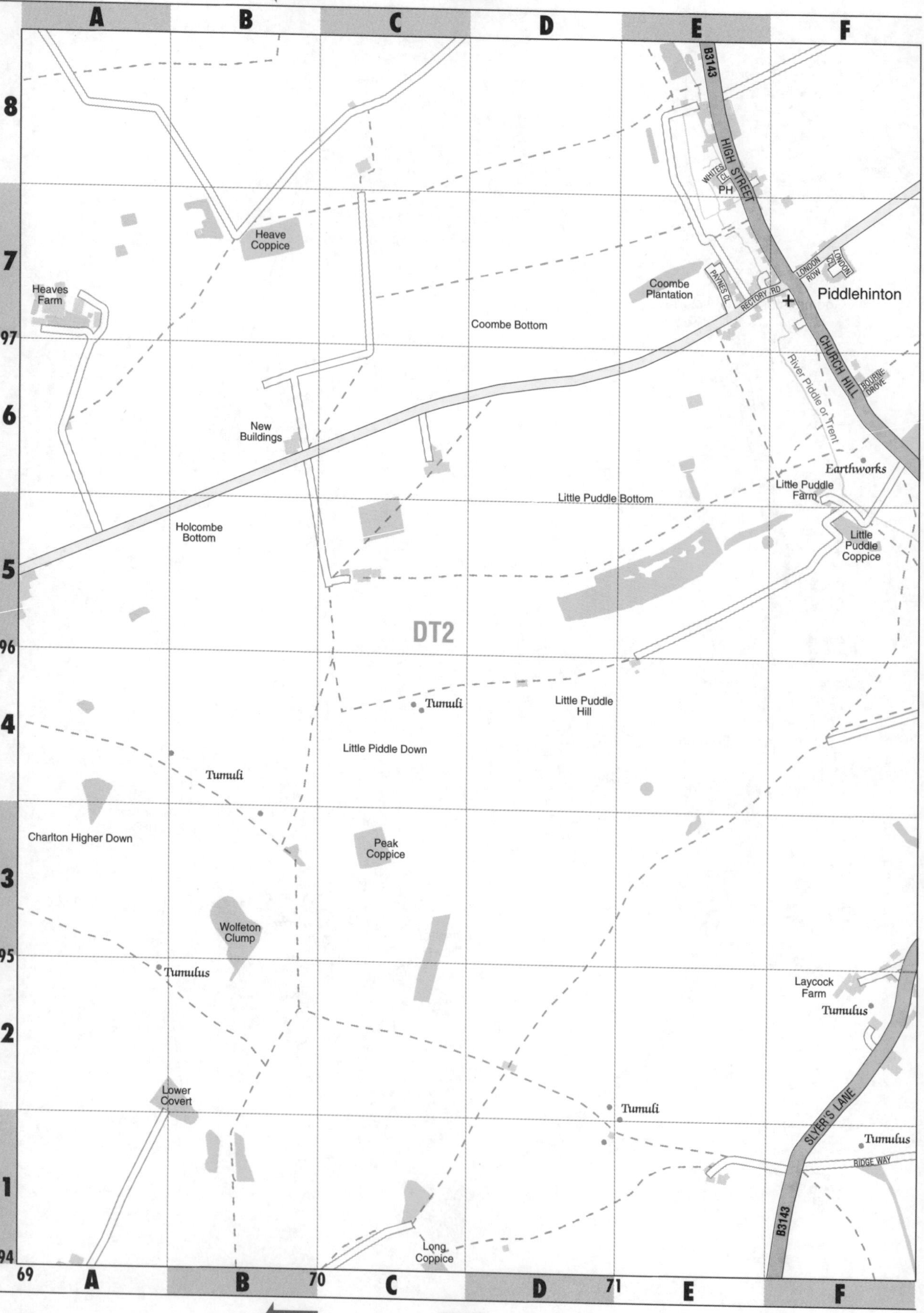
A
B
C
D
E
F
8
7
97
6
5
96
4
3
95
2
1
94
69
70
71
B3143
HIGH STREET
WHITES CL
PH
LONDON ROW
LONDON CL
PAYNES CL
RECTORY RD
Piddlehinton
CHURCH HILL
BOURNE DROVE
River Piddle or Trent
Heave Coppice
Heaves Farm
Coombe Plantation
Coombe Bottom
New Buildings
Earthworks
Little Puddle Farm
Little Puddle Bottom
Holcombe Bottom
Little Puddle Coppice
DT2
Tumuli
Little Puddle Hill
Little Piddle Down
Tumuli
Charlton Higher Down
Peak Coppice
Wolfeton Clump
Tumulus
Laycock Farm
Tumulus
Lower Covert
Tumuli
SLYER'S LANE
Tumulus
RIDGE WAY
B3143
Long Coppice

75
108

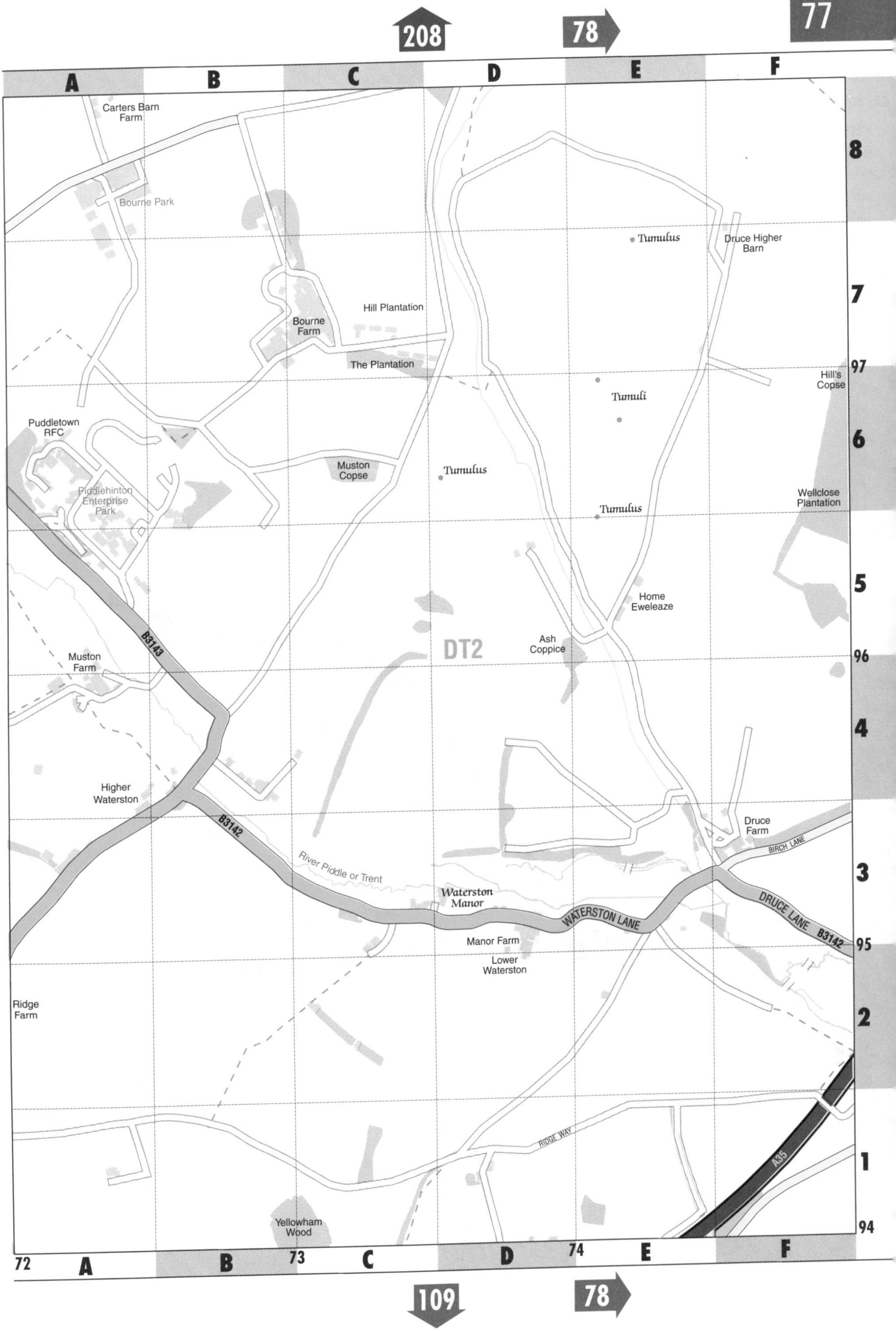
208
78
A
B
C
D
E
F
Carters Barn Farm
Bourne Park
Tumulus
Druce Higher Barn
8
7
Hill Plantation
Bourne Farm
The Plantation
97
Hill's Copse
Tumuli
Puddletown RFC
6
Muston Copse
Tumulus
Piddlehinton Enterprise Park
Wellclose Plantation
Tumulus
5
Home Eweleaze
B3143
Muston Farm
DT2
Ash Coppice
96
4
Higher Waterston
Druce Farm
B3142
BIRCH LANE
3
River Piddle or Trent
Waterston Manor
WATERSTON LANE
DRUCE LANE
B3142
Manor Farm
95
Lower Waterston
Ridge Farm
2
RIDGE WAY
1
A35
Yellowham Wood
94
72
A
B
73
C
D
74
E
F
109
78

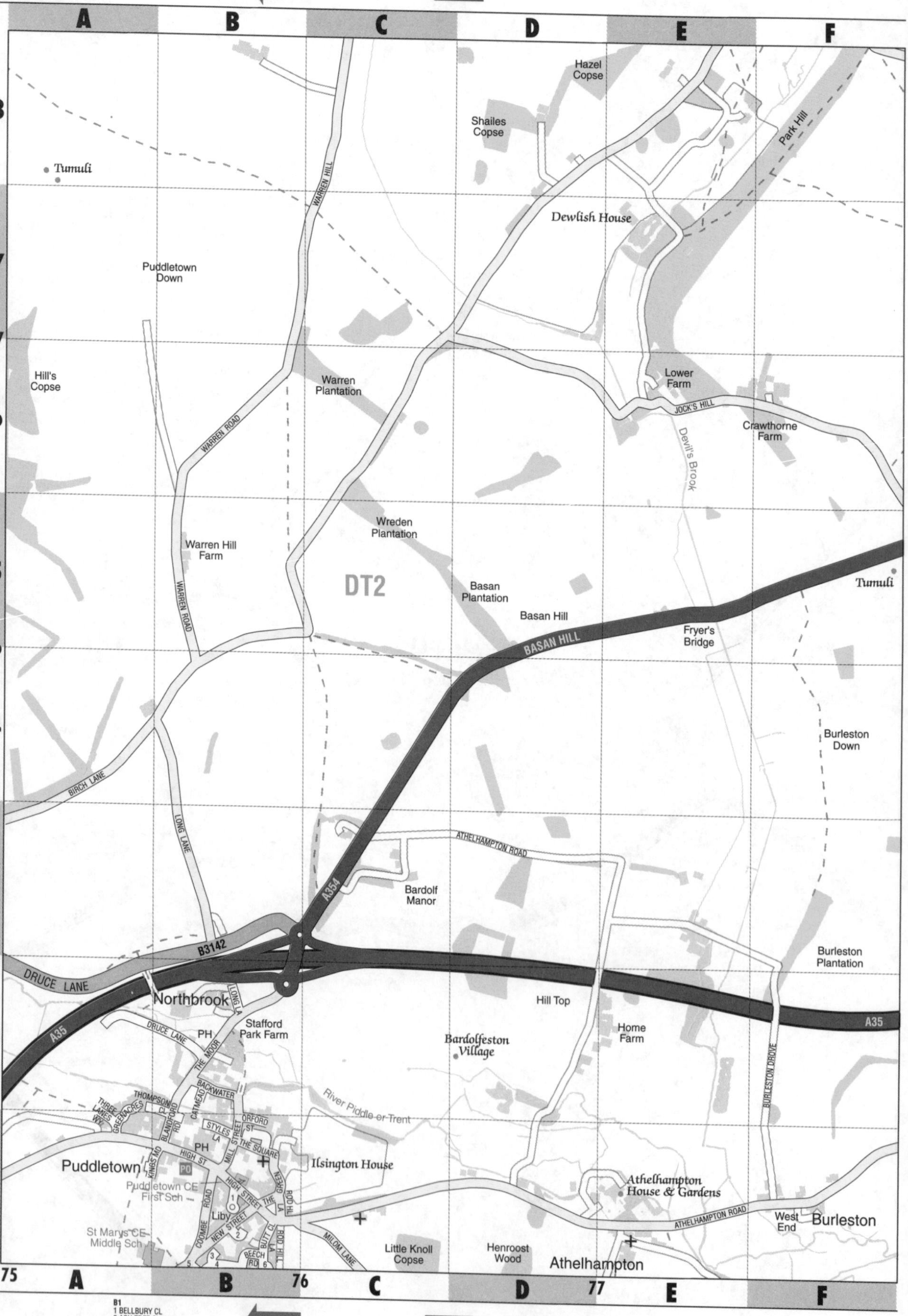

77
209

A **B** **C** **D** **E** **F**

8
Tumuli
Hazel Copse
Shailes Copse
Park Hill
Dewlish House

7
Puddletown Down

97
Hill's Copse
Warren Plantation
Lower Farm
Jock's Hill
Crawthorne Farm

6
WARREN ROAD
Devil's Brook

Warren Hill Farm
Wreden Plantation
DT2
Basan Plantation
Basan Hill
Tumuli

5
WARREN ROAD
BASAN HILL
Fryer's Bridge

96

4
BIRCH LANE
Burleston Down

LONG LANE

3
A354
Athelhampton Road
Bardolf Manor
Burleston Plantation

95
B3142
DRUCE LANE
Hill Top
A35

2
A35
Northbrook
Druce Lane
PH
Stafford Park Farm
The Moor
Bardolfeston Village
Home Farm
Burleston Drive

THREE LANES WAY
GREENACRES
THOMPSON CLOSE
CATSHEAD
BACKWATER
BLANDFORD CLOSE
STYLES LA
HIGH STREET
MILL STREET
ORFORD ST
The Square
River Piddle or Trent

1
Puddletown
KINGS RD
PH
PO
HIGH ST
NEW STREET
THE LA
Liby
Ilsington House
Athelhampton House & Gardens
West End
Burleston

COOMBE LANE
Puddletown CE First Sch
St Marys CE Middle Sch
BEECH RD
BUTT CL
MILOM LANE
Little Knoll Copse
Henroost Wood
Athelhampton
ATHELHAMPTON ROAD

94
75 **A** **B** 76 **C** **D** 77 **E** **F**

B1
1 BELLBURY CL
2 ASH TREE CL
3 WILLOUGHBY CL
4 BRYMER RD
5 WHITE HILL
6 CHAPEL VIEW

209
80

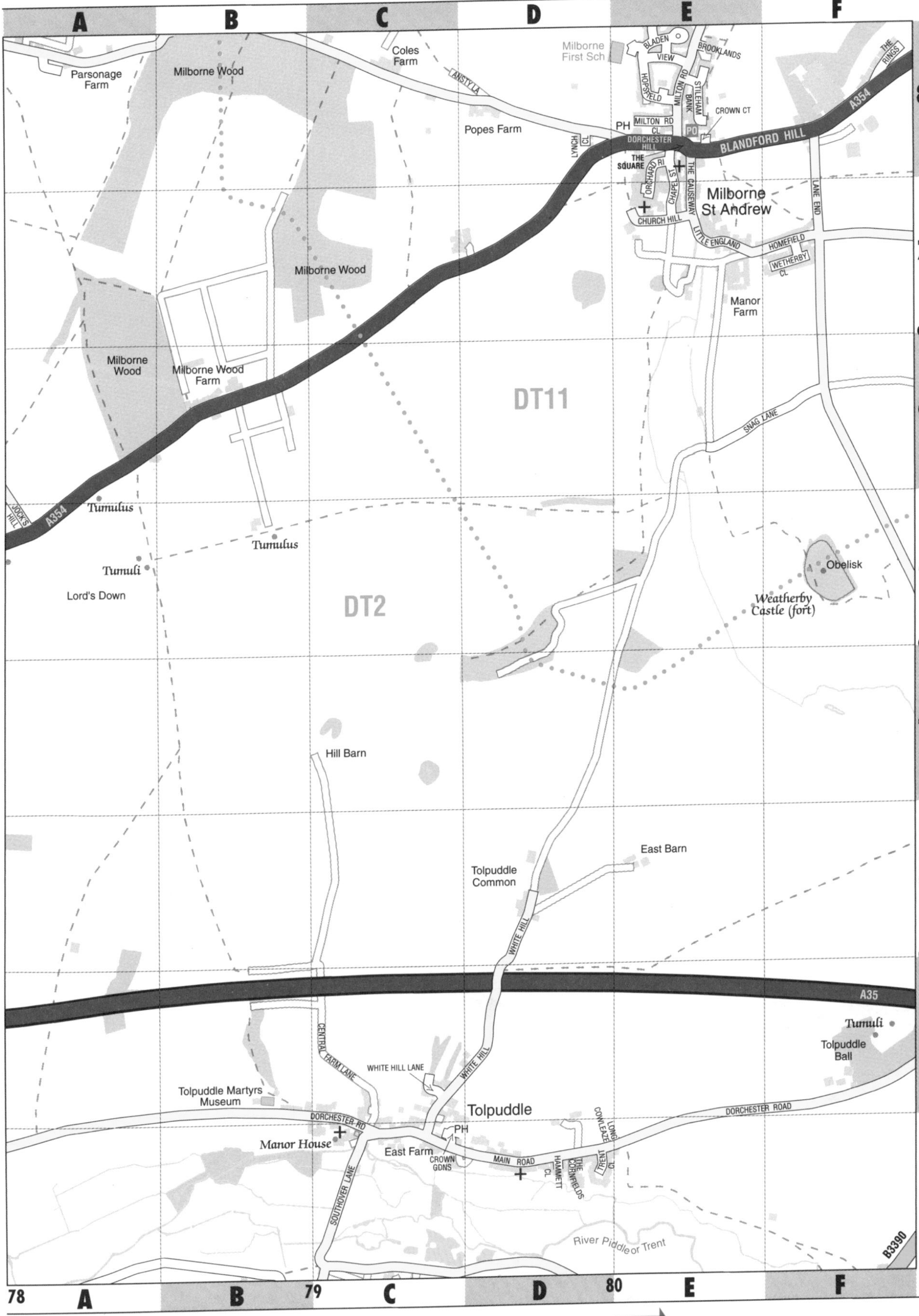
Parsonage Farm
Milborne Wood
Coles Farm
ANSTY LA
Milborne First Sch
BLADEN VIEW
BROOKLANDS
HOPSFIELD
MILTON RD
STILEHAM BANK
CROWN CT
THE RINGS
A354
PH
MILTON RD CL
PO
Popes Farm
LYNCH CL
DORCHESTER HILL
BLANDFORD HILL
THE SQUARE
ORCHARD RI
CHAPEL ST
THE CAUSEWAY
Milborne St Andrew
CHURCH HILL
LITTLE ENGLAND
HOMEFIELD
WETHERBY CL
LANE END
Milborne Wood
Manor Farm
Milborne Wood
Milborne Wood Farm
DT11
SNAG LANE
JOCK'S HILL
Tumulus
Tumulus
Tumuli
Lord's Down
DT2
Obelisk
Weatherby Castle (fort)
Hill Barn
East Barn
Tolpuddle Common
WHITE HILL
A35
Tumuli
Tolpuddle Ball
CENTRAL FARM LANE
WHITE HILL LANE
WHITE HILL
Tolpuddle Martyrs Museum
Tolpuddle
DORCHESTER RD
Manor House
PH
LONG CONLEAZE
DORCHESTER ROAD
East Farm
CROWN GDNS
MAIN ROAD
HAMMETT CL
THE CORNFIELDS
TRENT CL
SOUTHOVER LANE
River Piddle or Trent
B3390
A B C D E F
8 7 97 6 5 96 4 3 95 2 1 94
78 79 80

111
80

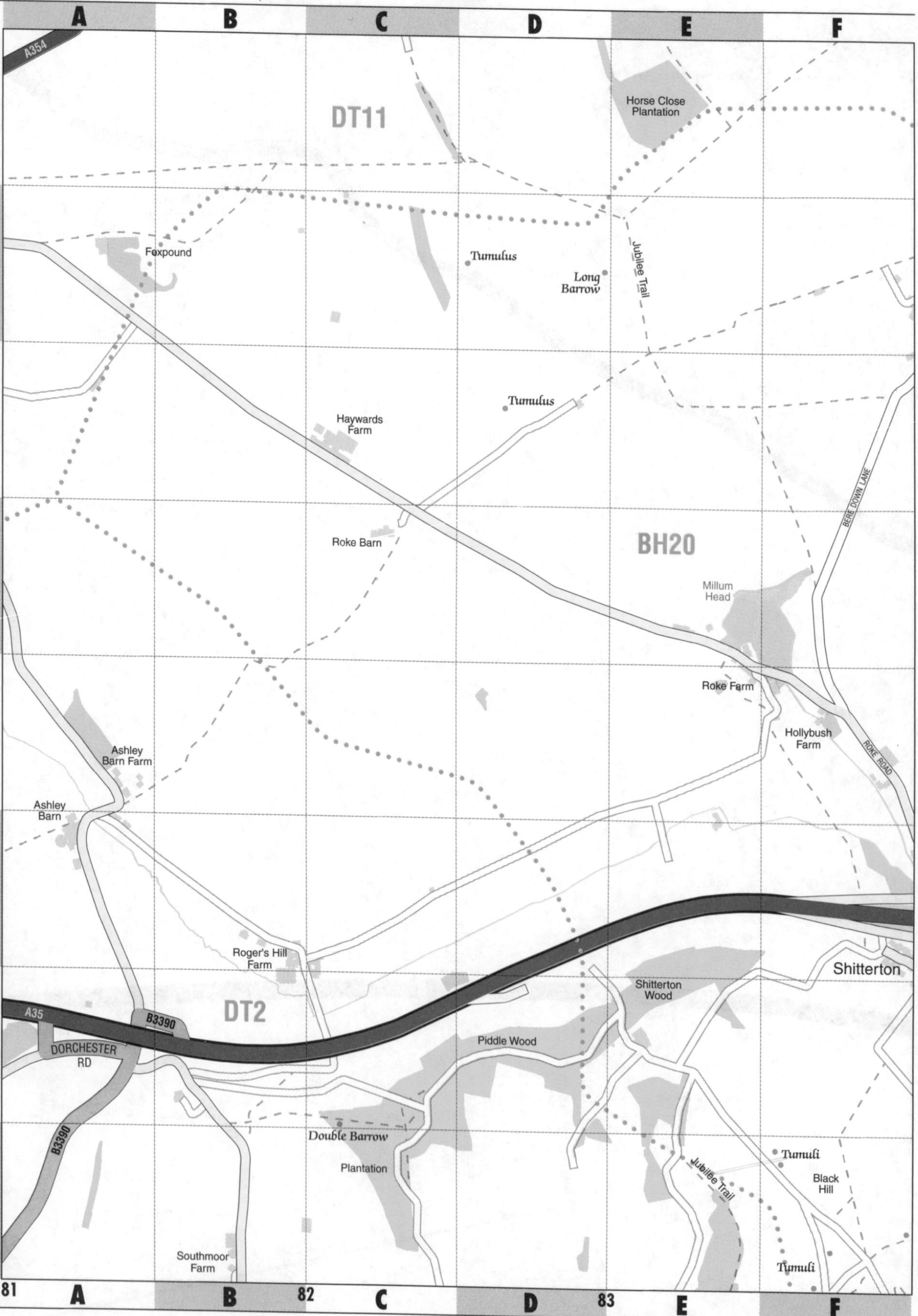

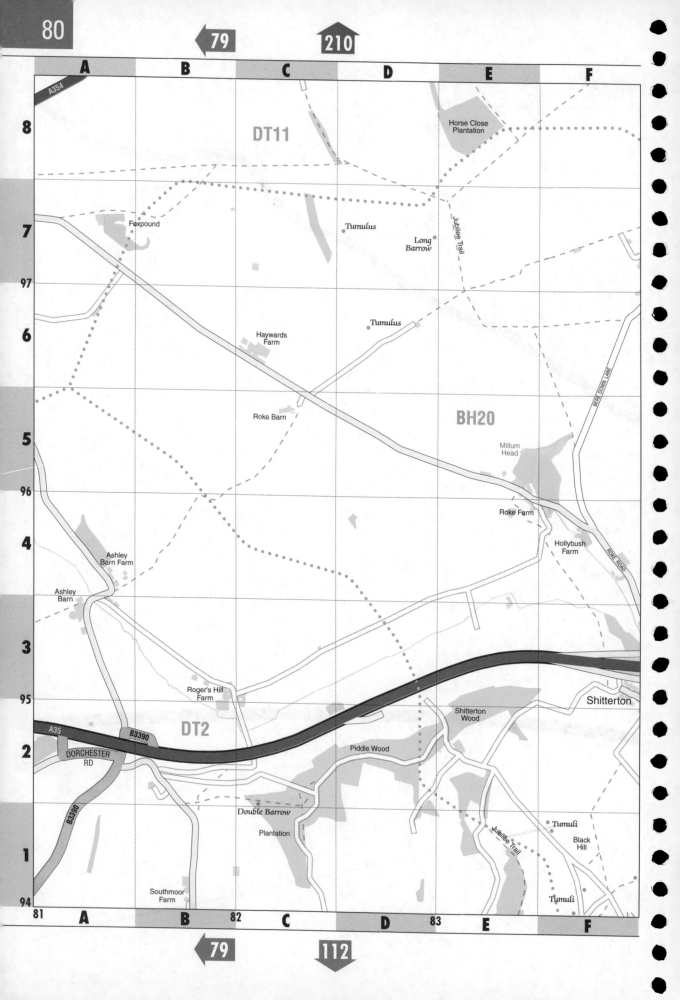

A354

DT11

Horse Close
Plantation

Foxpound

Tumulus

Long
Barrow

Jubilee Trail

Haywards
Farm

Tumulus

Roke Barn

BH20

Millum
Head

Roke Farm

Hollybush
Farm

BERE DOWN LANE

ROKE ROAD

Ashley
Barn Farm

Ashley
Barn

Roger's Hill
Farm

Shitterton

Shitterton
Wood

A35

B3390

DT2

DORCHESTER
RD

Piddle Wood

B3390

Double Barrow

Plantation

Jubilee Trail

Tumuli

Black
Hill

Southmoor
Farm

Tumuli

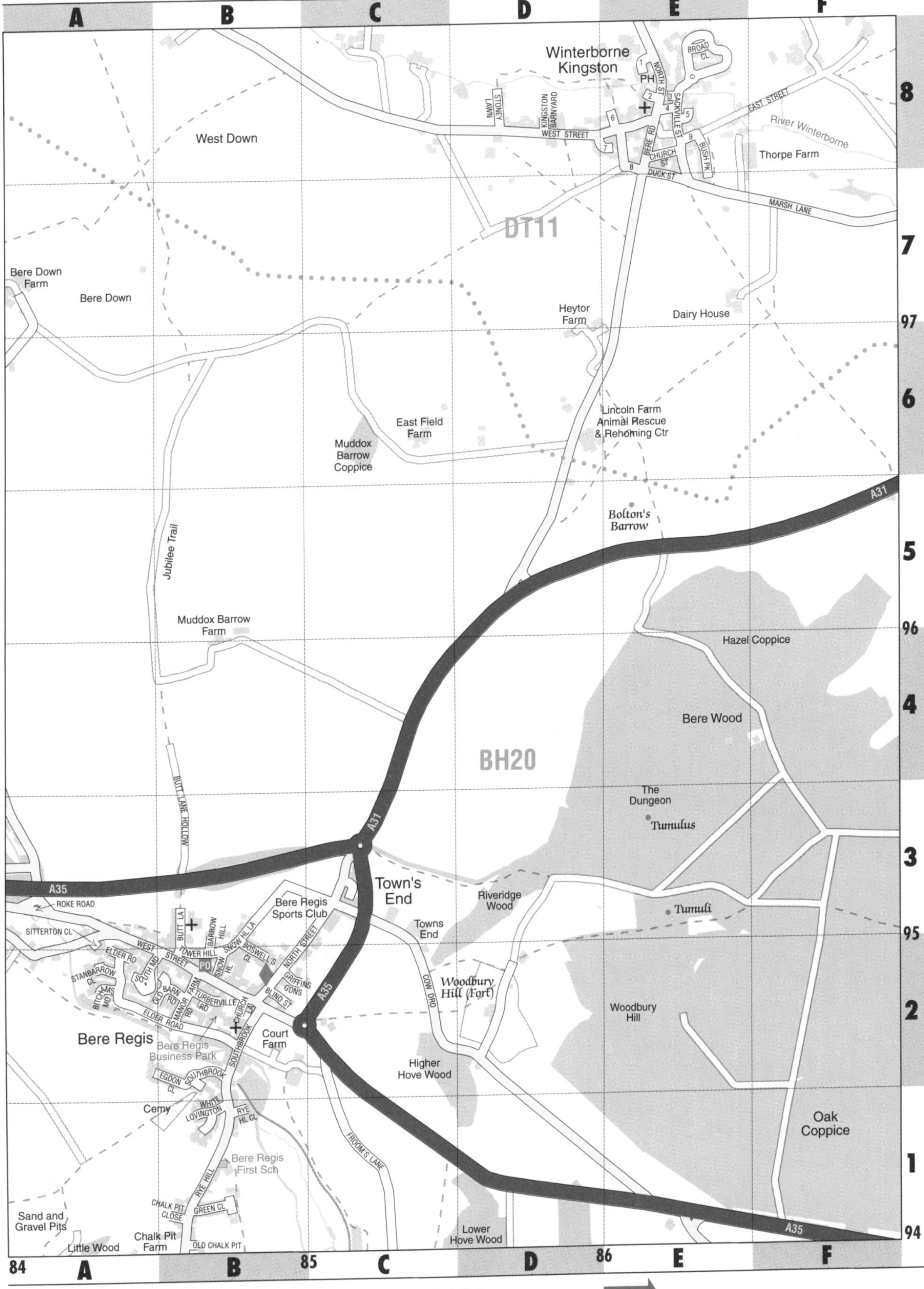

210

82

E8
1 WIND WHISTLE FM
2 CLYPETTS
3 PITCHER CL
4 NOAH HENVILLE CNR
5 WARES CL
6 PLUMBLEY MDWS
7 ORCHARD LA
8 BAGWOOD RD
9 EAST ST

A B C D E F

8
7
97
6
5
96
4
3
95
2
1
94

Winterborne
Kingston

BROAD CL

PH

NORTH ST
SACKVILLE ST
STONEY
LAWN
KINGSTON BARNYARD
WEST STREET
BERE RD
CHURCH
DUCK ST
BUSH PK

East Street

River Winterborne

Thorpe Farm

DT11

West Down

Bere Down
Farm

Bere Down

Heytor
Farm

Dairy House

East Field
Farm

Muddox
Barrow
Coppice

Lincoln Farm
Animal Rescue
& Rehoming Ctr

MARSH LANE

A31

Bolton's
Barrow

Jubilee Trail

Hazel Coppice

Muddox Barrow
Farm

BH20

Bere Wood

BUTT LANE HOLLOW

A31

The
Dungeon

Tumulus

Town's
End

Riveridge
Wood

Tumuli

A35

ROKE ROAD

SITTERTON CL

Bere Regis
Sports Club

Towns
End

Woodbury
Hill (Fort)

Woodbury
Hill

CON DRO

BUTT LA
BARROW HILL
SNOW HL LA
BOSWELL'S CL
NORTH STREET
LOWER HILL
WEST STREET
SOUTH MD
GRIFFINS GDNS
BLIND ST
TURBERVILLE RD
CHURCH
SOUTHBROOK

STANBARROW CL
ELDER RD
MANOR FARM
BARN RD
BITCH'S MD
ELDER ROAD

PO

Bere Regis

Bere Regis
Business Park

Court
Farm

Higher
Hove Wood

LEGDON CL
SOUTHBROOK CL
WHITE LOVINGTON
RYE HL CL
RYE HILL

Cemy

Oak
Coppice

Bere Regis
First Sch

FROM'S LANE

Sand and
Gravel Pits

CHALK PIT CLOSE
GREEN CL

A35

Little Wood

Chalk Pit
Farm

Old Chalk Pit

Lower
Hove Wood

A35

84 A B 85 C D 86 E F

113

82

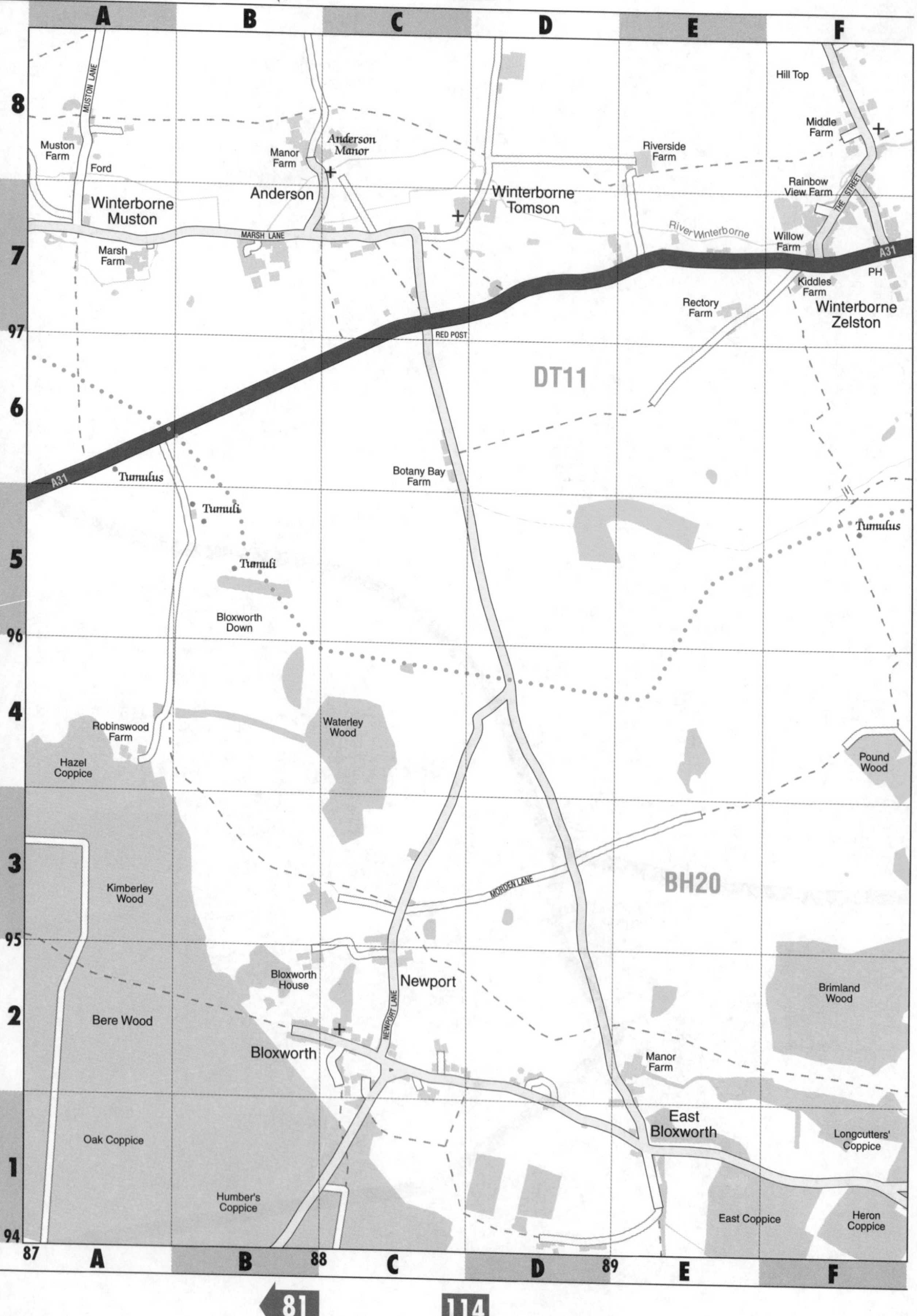

81
211

A B C D E F

8

Hill Top

Muston Farm

Ford

Middle Farm

Manor Farm

Anderson Manor

Riverside Farm

Rainbow View Farm

THE STREET

Winterborne Muston

Anderson

Winterborne Tomson

7

MARSH LANE

River Winterborne

Willow Farm

A31

PH

Marsh Farm

RED POST

Kiddles Farm

Winterborne Zelston

97

Rectory Farm

DT11

6

A31

Tumulus

Botany Bay Farm

Tumulus

Tumuli

5

Tumuli

96

Bloxworth Down

4

Robinswood Farm

Waterley Wood

Pound Wood

Hazel Coppice

3

Kimberley Wood

MORDEN LANE

BH20

Brimland Wood

95

Bloxworth House

Newport

2

Bere Wood

NEWPORT LANE

Manor Farm

Bloxworth

East Bloxworth

Longcutters' Coppice

1

Oak Coppice

East Coppice

Heron Coppice

Humber's Coppice

94

87 **A** 88 **B** **C** 89 **D** **E** **F**

81
114

211
84

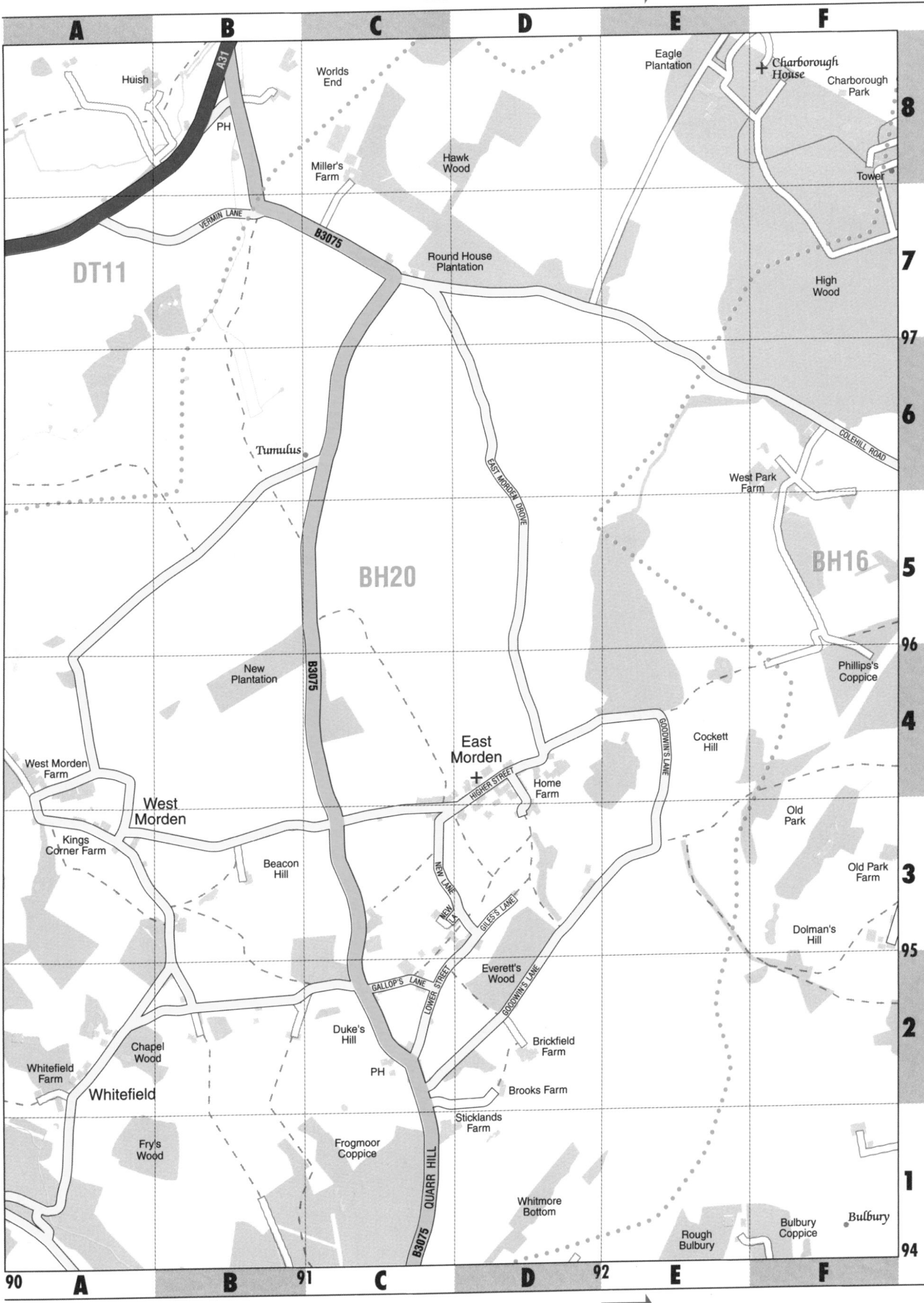
A
B
C
D
E
F
8
7
97
6
5
96
4
3
95
2
1
94
90
91
92
Huish
PH
A31
Worlds End
Miller's Farm
Hawk Wood
Eagle Plantation
Charborough House
Charborough Park
Tower
VERMIN LANE
B3075
DT11
Round House Plantation
High Wood
COLEHILL ROAD
Tumulus
EAST MORDEN DROVE
West Park Farm
BH20
BH16
New Plantation
Phillips's Coppice
GOODWIN'S LANE
Cockett Hill
East Morden
West Morden Farm
HIGHER STREET
Home Farm
West Morden
Kings Corner Farm
Old Park
Beacon Hill
NEW LANE
Old Park Farm
GILES'S LANE
Dolman's Hill
Everett's Wood
GALLOP'S LANE
LOWER STREET
Duke's Hill
Chapel Wood
Brickfield Farm
Whitefield Farm
PH
Whitefield
Brooks Farm
Sticklands Farm
Fry's Wood
Frogmoor Coppice
QUARR HILL
Whitmore Bottom
Bulbury
Bulbury Coppice
Rough Bulbury

115
84

83
56

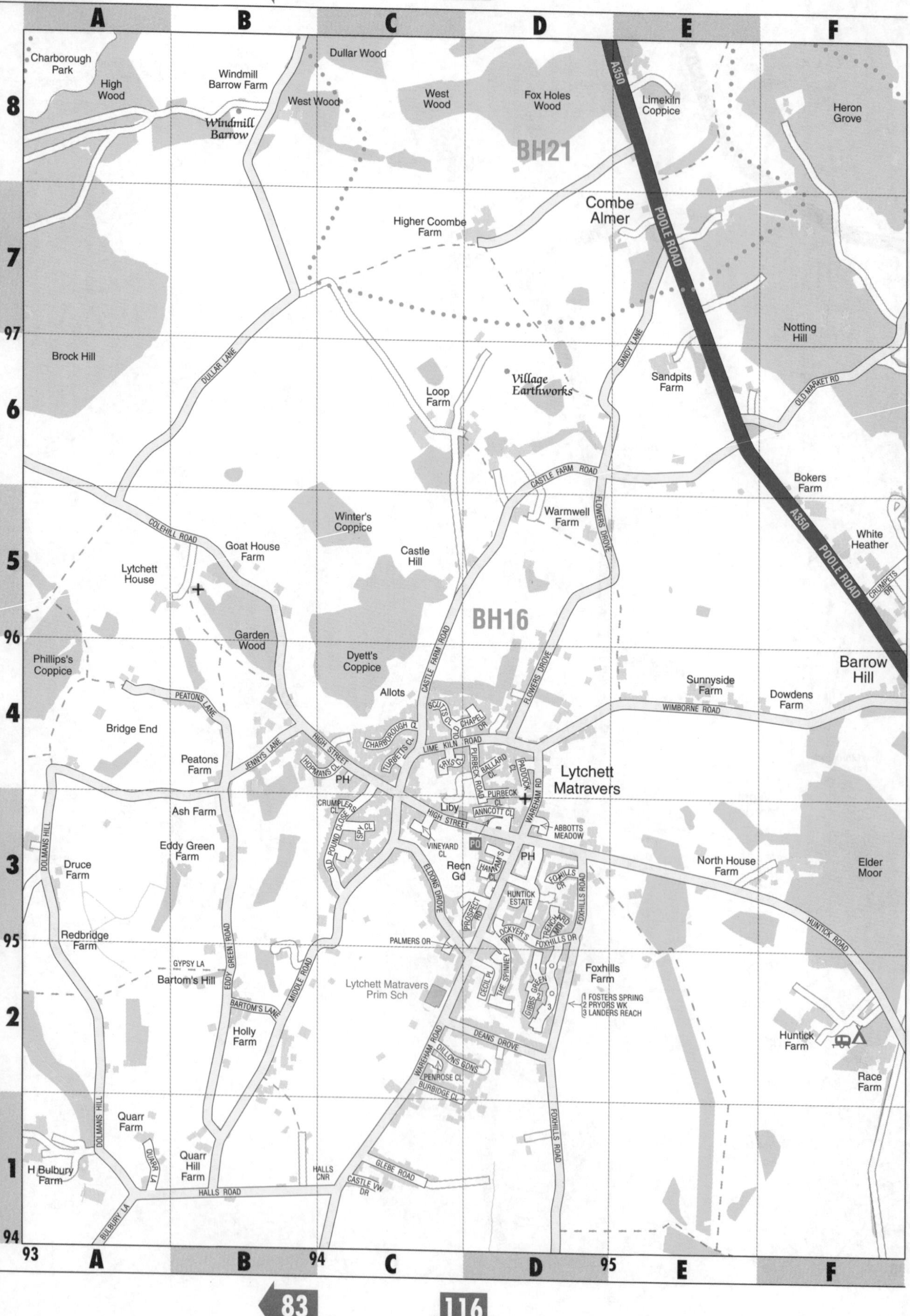
A
B
C
D
E
F
8
7
97
6
5
96
4
3
95
2
1
94
93
94
95
Charborough Park
High Wood
Windmill Barrow Farm
Windmill Barrow
Dullar Wood
West Wood
West Wood
Fox Holes Wood
BH21
A350
Limekiln Coppice
Heron Grove
Combe Almer
POOLE ROAD
Higher Coombe Farm
Notting Hill
Brock Hill
DULLAR LANE
SANDY LANE
Sandpits Farm
OLD MARKET RD
Loop Farm
Village Earthworks
CASTLE FARM ROAD
Bokers Farm
Warmwell Farm
FLOWERS DROVE
Winter's Coppice
COLEHILL ROAD
Goat House Farm
Castle Hill
Lytchett House
White Heather
CRUMPETS DR
BH16
Garden Wood
Phillips's Coppice
Dyett's Coppice
CASTLE FARM ROAD
FLOWERS DROVE
Barrow Hill
Allots
Sunnyside Farm
Dowdens Farm
WIMBORNE ROAD
PEATONS LANE
Bridge End
SCUTTS CL
CHAPEL DR
CHARBOROUGH CL
HIGH STREET
JENNYS LANE
LIME KILN ROAD
TURBETTS CL
FRYS CL
PURBECK ROAD
BALLARD CL
PADDOCK CL
Peatons Farm
HOPMANS CL
PH
Lytchett Matravers
PURBECK CL
WAREHAM RD
CRUMPLERS CL
Liby
ANNCOTT CL
Ash Farm
OLD POUND CLOSE
SPY CL
HIGH STREET
ABBOTTS MEADOW
VINEYARD CL
PO
PH
Eddy Green Farm
DOLMANS HILL
Druce Farm
Recn Gd
HAYWARD'S CL
FOXHILLS CR
North House Farm
Elder Moor
ELDONS DROVE
HUNTICK ESTATE
FOXHILLS ROAD
PROSPECT RD
HUNTICK ROAD
LOCKYER'S WY
FRENCH MILL LA
FOXHILLS DR
Redbridge Farm
PALMERS OR
GYPSY LA
EDDY GREEN ROAD
Bartom's Hill
MIDDLE ROAD
Lytchett Matravers Prim Sch
CECIL PL
THE SPINNEY
GIBBS GREEN
Foxhills Farm
1 FOSTERS SPRING
2 PRYORS WK
3 LANDERS REACH
BARTOM'S LANE
Holly Farm
DEANS DROVE
WAREHAM ROAD
Huntick Farm
DILLONS GDNS
PENROSE CL
BURBIDGE CL
Race Farm
Quarr Farm
FOXHILLS ROAD
QUARR LA
Quarr Hill Farm
H Bulbury Farm
HALLS CNR
GLEBE ROAD
HALLS ROAD
CASTLE VW DR
BULBURY LA

83
116

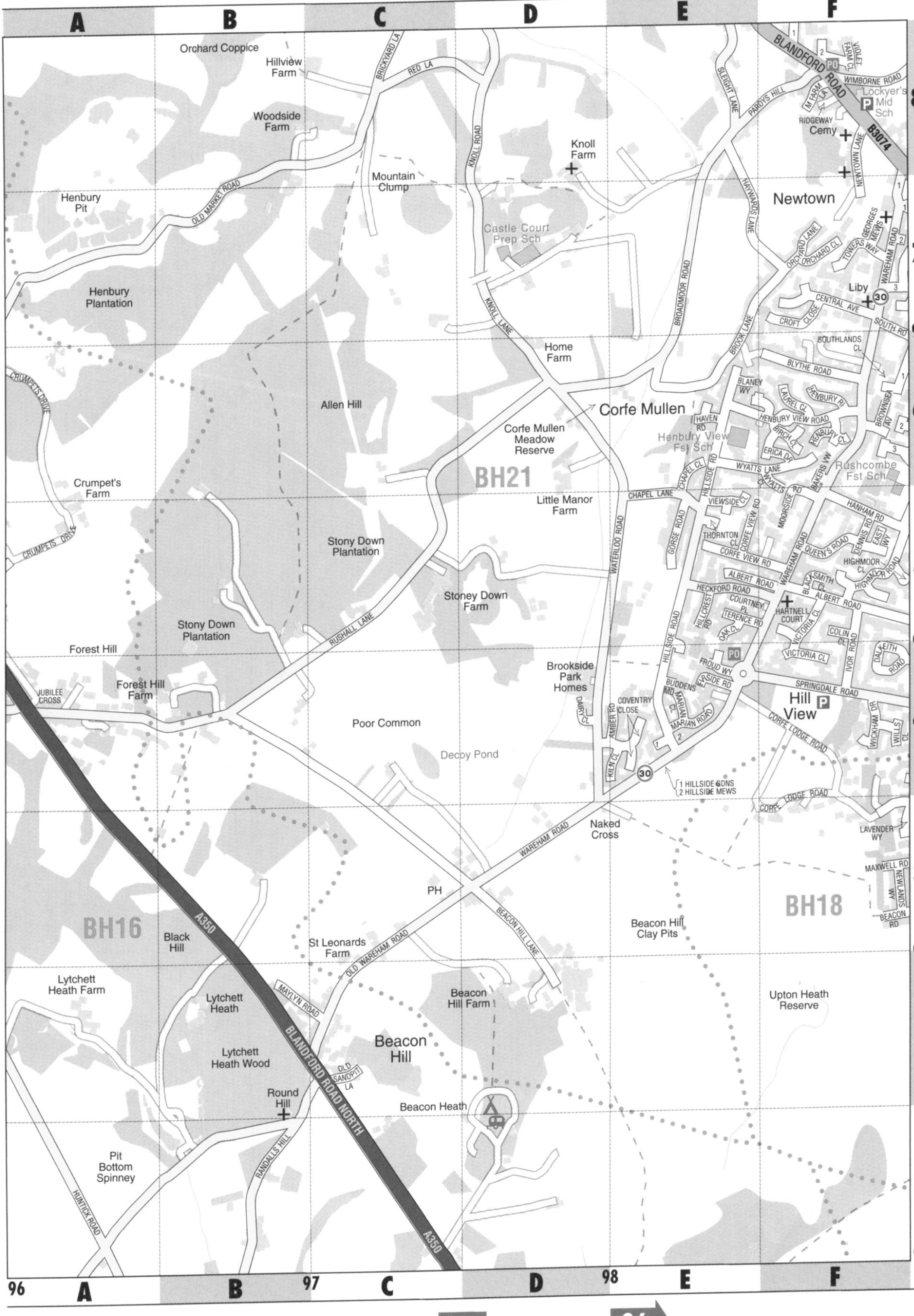

57 85 58

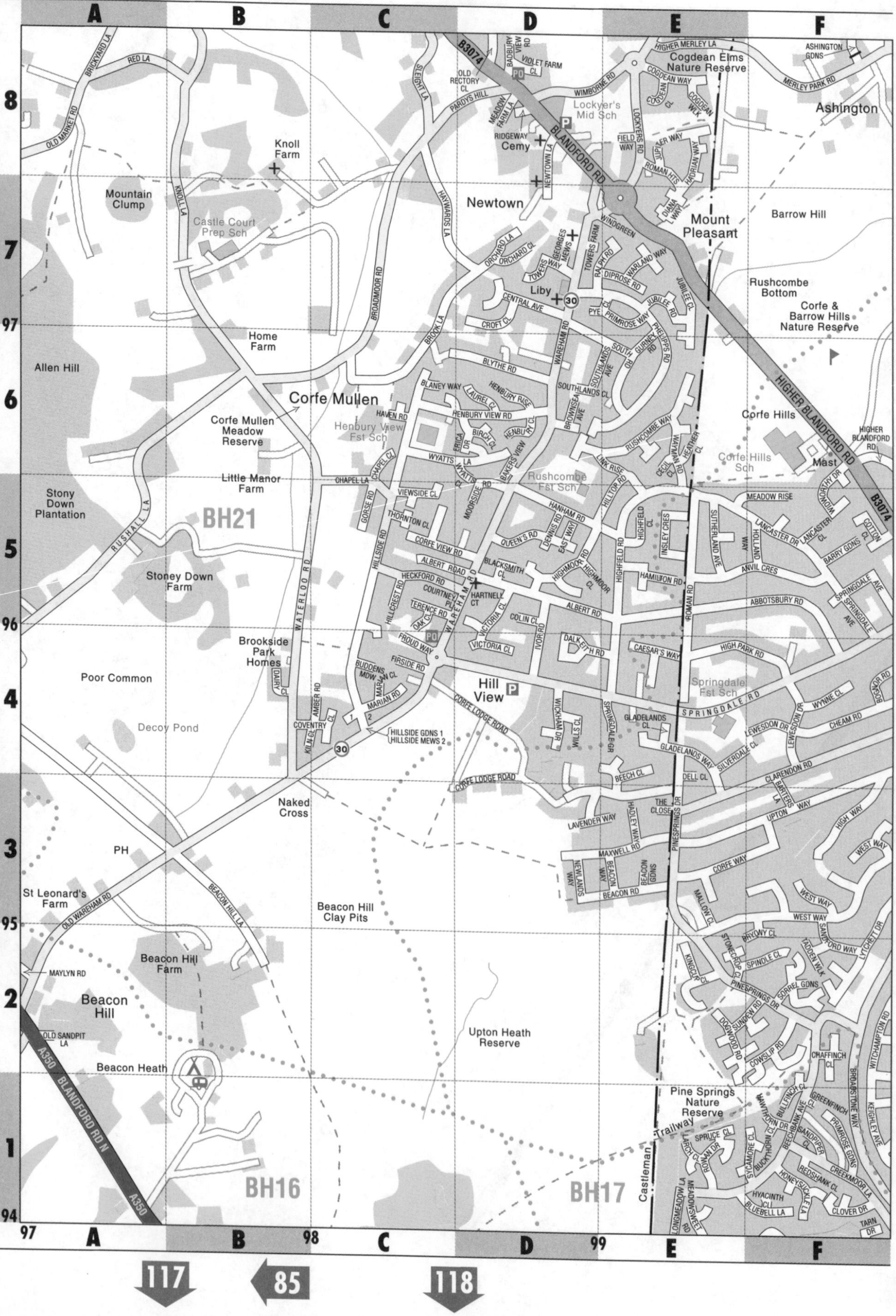
A
B
C
D
E
F
8
7
97
6
5
96
4
3
95
2
1
94
97
98
99
B3074
HIGHER MERLEY LA
Cogdean Elms
Nature Reserve
ASHINGTON GDNS
MERLEY PARK RD
Ashington
RED LA
BRICKYARD LA
OLD MARKET RD
BADBURY VIEW RD
VIOLET FARM CL
OLD RECTORY CL
PARDYS HILL
SLEIGHT LA
WIMBORNE RD
COGDEAN WAY
COGDEAN CL
COGDEAN WLK
Lockyer's
Mid Sch
MEADOW FARM LA
RIDGEWAY
Cemy
NEWTOWN LA
BLANDFORD RD
FIELD WAY
LOCKYERS RD
JUPITER WAY
ROMAN HTS
HADRIAN WAY
DIANA WAY
Knoll
Farm
Mountain
Clump
KNOLL LA
Castle Court
Prep Sch
HAYWARDS LA
Newtown
Mount
Pleasant
Barrow Hill
WINDGREEN
ORCHARD LA
ORCHARD CL
GEORGES MEWS
TOWERS FARM
TOWERS WAY
RALPH RD
WARLAND WAY
DIPROSE RD
JUBILEE CL
JUBILEE RD
Rushcombe
Bottom
Corfe &
Barrow Hills
Nature Reserve
BROADMOOR RD
Liby
30
CENTRAL AVE
PYE CL
PRIMROSE WAY
CROFT CL
BROOK LA
Home
Farm
WAREHAM RD
SOUTHLANDS AVE
SOUTH RD
GURNEY RD
PHILLIPPS RD
Allen Hill
BLYTHE RD
BLANEY WAY
LAUREL CL
HENBURY RISE
SOUTHLANDS CL
HIGHER BLANDFORD RD
Corfe Mullen
HAVEN RD
HENBURY VIEW RD
BROWNSEA AVE
RUSHCOMBE WAY
Corfe Hills
Corfe Mullen
Meadow
Reserve
Henbury View
Fst Sch
ERICA DR
BIRCH CL
HENBURY CL
WAYMAN RD
HEATHER CL
CECIL CL
Corfe Hills
Sch
HIGHER BLANDFORD RD
Mast
WYATTS LA
WYATTS CL
BAKERS VIEW
LINK RISE
Little Manor
Farm
CHAPEL LA
CHAPEL CL
Rushcombe
Fst Sch
HILLTOP RD
MEADOW RISE
WOODWORTHY DR
Stony
Down
Plantation
VIEWSIDE CL
MOORSIDE RD
HANHAM RD
HIGHFIELD CL
INSLEY CRES
SUTHERLAND AVE
COTTON CL
BH21
GORSE RD
THORNTON CL
DENNIS RD
EAST WAY
HOLLAND WAY
LANCASTER DR
LANCASTER CL
RUSHALL LA
HILLSIDE RD
CORFE VIEW RD
QUEEN'S RD
HIGHFIELD RD
BARRY GDNS
ALBERT ROAD
BLACKSMITH CL
HIGHMOOR RD
HIGHMOOR CL
ANVIL CRES
Stoney Down
Farm
HECKFORD RD
WATERLOO RD
HAMILTON RD
SPRINGDALE AVE
COURTNEY PL
HARTNELL CT
ROMAN RD
ABBOTSBURY RD
HILLCREST RD
TERENCE RD
VICTORIA CL
ALBERT RD
OAK CL
COLIN CL
IVOR RD
SPRINGDALE AVE
Brookside
Park
Homes
FROUD WAY
VICTORIA CL
DALKEITH RD
CAESAR'S WAY
HIGH PARK RD
DAIRY CL
FIRSIDE RD
Poor Common
BUDDENS MDW
MARIAN CL
MARIAN RD
Hill
View
Springdale
Fst Sch
AMBER RD
SPRINGDALE RD
WYNNE CL
COVENTRY CL
KILN CL
CORFE LODGE ROAD
WICKHAM DR
WILLS CL
SPRINGDALE GR
GLADELANDS CL
LEWESDON DR
CHEAM RD
HILLSIDE GDNS 1
HILLSIDE MEWS 2
Decoy Pond
GLADELANDS WAY
SILVERDALE CL
LEWESDON DR
CLARENDON RD
BEECH CL
DELL CL
CORFE LODGE ROAD
Naked
Cross
THE CLOSE
BARTERS LA
UPTON WAY
HIGH WAY
LAVENDER WAY
HADLEY WAY
PINESPRINGS DR
PH
MAXWELL RD
WEST WAY
NEWLANDS WAY
BEACON WAY
BEACON GDNS
CORFE WAY
St Leonard's
Farm
OLD WAREHAM RD
BEACON HILL LA
BEACON RD
Beacon Hill
Clay Pits
MALLOW CL
WEST WAY
WEST WAY
SANDFORD WAY
LYTCHETT DR
BRYONY CL
STONECROP CL
TADDEN WLK
KINGCUP CL
SPINDLE CL
Beacon Hill
Farm
MAYLYN RD
SORREL GDNS
PINESPRINGS DR
Beacon
Hill
OLD SANDPIT LA
DOGWOOD RD
SUNDEW RD
COWSLIP RD
CHAFFINCH CL
WITCHAMPTON RD
Upton Heath
Reserve
A350
BLANDFORD RD N
Beacon Heath
Pine Springs
Nature
Reserve
Trailway
Castleman
SPRUCE CL
HAWTHORN DR
BULLFINCH CL
BEECHBANK AVE
GREENFINCH CL
BROADSTONE WAY
KEIGHLEY AVE
LARCH CL
ROWAN DR
SYCAMORE CL
BUCKTHORN CL
SANDPIPER CL
PRIMROSE GDNS
REDSHANK CL
CREEKMOOR LA
HYACINTH CL
HONEYSUCKLE LA
BLUEBELL LA
CLOVER DR
LONGMEADOW LA
MEADOWSWEET RD
TARN DR
BH16
BH17
A350

117 85 118

59
88

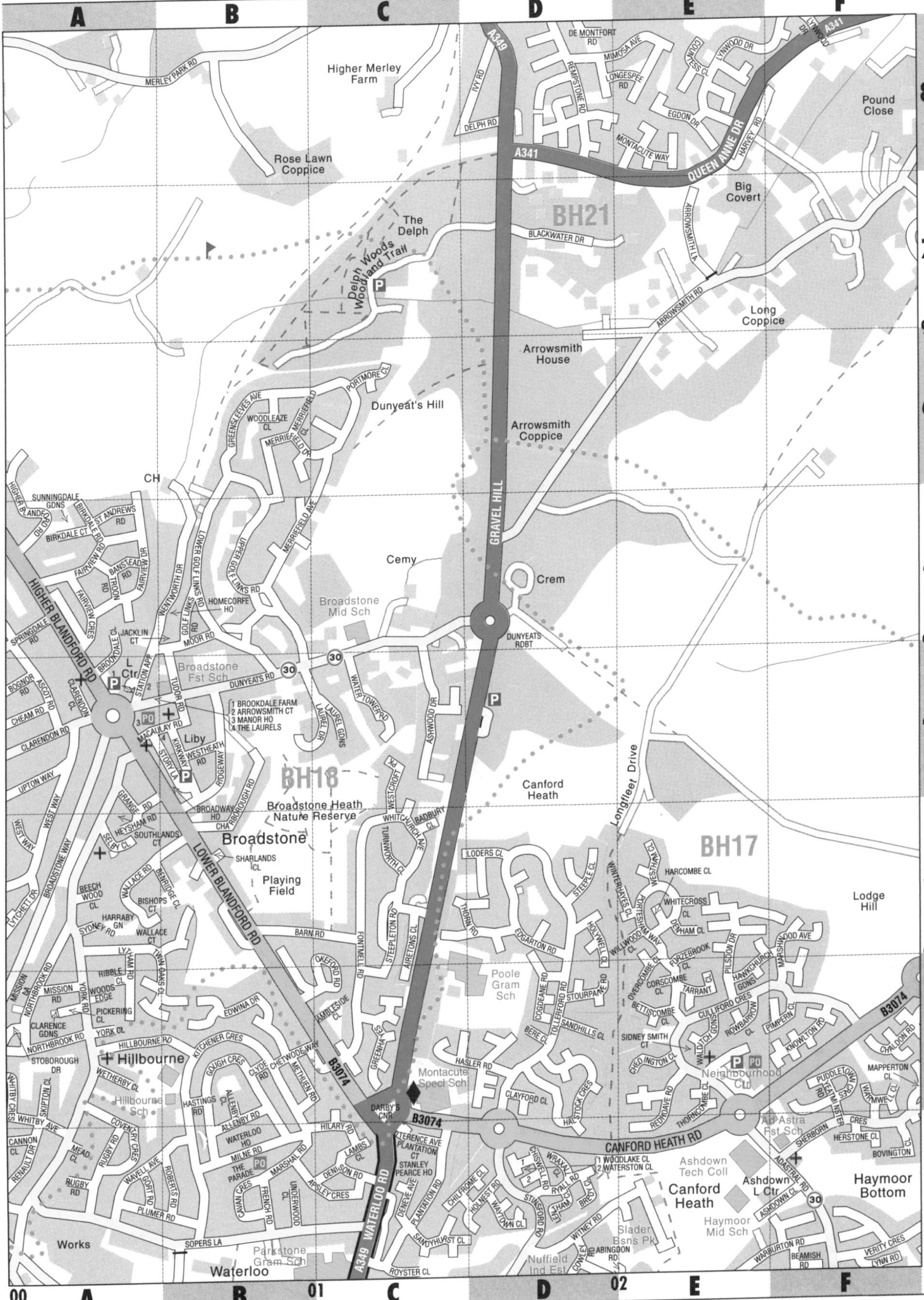
A
B
C
D
E
F
8
7
97
6
5
96
4
3
95
2
1
94
00
01
02
Higher Merley Farm
MERLEY PARK RD
Rose Lawn Coppice
The Delph
Delph Woods Woodland Trail
A349
A341
DE MONTFORT RD
MIMOSA AVE
REMPSTONE RD
LONGESPEE RD
COUNTESS CL
LYNWOOD DR
EGDON DR
MONTACUTE WAY
QUEEN ANNE DR
HARVEY RD
IVY RD
DELPH RD
Pound Close
Big Covert
BH21
BLACKWATER DR
ARROWSMITH LA
ARROWSMITH RD
Long Coppice
Arrowsmith House
Dunyeat's Hill
Arrowsmith Coppice
PORTMORE CL
GREENSLEEVES AVE
WOODLEAZE CL
MERRIEFIELD CL
MERRIEFIELD DR
MERRIEFIELD AVE
CH
SUNNINGDALE GDNS
HIGHER BLANDFORD RD
BIRKDALE RD
ST ANDREWS RD
BIRKDALE CT
FAIRVIEW RD
BANSTEAD RD
FAIRVIEW DR
FAIRVIEW CRES
TROON RD
WENTWORTH DR
LOWER GOLF LINKS RD
UPPER GOLF LINKS RD
GRAVEL HILL
Cemy
Crem
Broadstone Mid Sch
HOMECORFE HO
GOLF LINKS RD
MOOR RD
JACKLIN CT
SPRINGDALE RD
BROOKDALE CL
DUNYEATS RDBT
L Ctr
Broadstone Fst Sch
STATION APP
TUDOR RD
DUNYEATS RD
1 BROOKDALE FARM
2 ARROWSMITH CT
3 MANOR HO
4 THE LAURELS
WATERTOWER RD
LAUREL DR
LAUREL GDNS
ASHWOOD DR
BOGNOR RD
ASCOT RD
CLARENDON CL
CHEAM RD
CLARENDON RD
MACAULAY RD
KIRKWAY
Liby
WESTHEATH RD
RIDGEWAY
STORY LA
BH18
UPTON WAY
WEST WAY
GRANGE RD
HEYSHAM RD
BROADWAY HO
CHALLONBOROUGH RD
Broadstone Heath Nature Reserve
WESTCROFT PK
Canford Heath
Longfleet Drive
BH17
Broadstone
SELBY CL
SOUTHLANDS CT
SHARLANDS CL
LOWER BLANDFORD RD
BROADSTONE WAY
WHITCHURCH AVE
BADBURY CL
TURNWORTH CL
LODERS CL
WINTERHAYES CL
WESTHAM CL
HARCOMBE CL
Playing Field
BEECH WOOD CL
WALLACE RD
BENBRIDGE CL
BISHOPS CT
HARRABY GN
SYDNEY RD
WALLACE CT
LYTCHETT DR
THORN RD
STEEPLE CL
PORTESHAM WAY
WHITECROSS CL
DENHAM CL
Lodge Hill
STEEPLETON RD
AIRETONS CL
BARN RD
FONTMELL RD
EDGARTON RD
HOLYWELL CL
WILLWOOD CL
FORZEBROOK CL
PILSDON DR
HAWKCHURCH GDNS
MARSHWOOD AVE
LYTHAM RD
LYNN OAKS CL
RIBBLE CL
MISSION LA
NORTHBROOK RD
MISSION RD
WOODS EDGE
PICKERING CL
YORK RD
OKEFORD RD
AMBLESIDE CL
Poole Gram Sch
COGDEANE RD
TOLLERFORD RD
STOURPAINE RD
OVERCOMBE CL
CORSCOMBE CL
TARRANT CL
BETTISCOMBE CL
CULLIFORD CRES
ROWBARROW CL
PIMPERN CL
KNOWLTON RD
B3074
EDWINA DR
CLARENCE GDNS
YORK CL
NORTHBROOK RD
HILLBOURNE RD
Hillbourne
STOBOROUGH DR
KITCHENER CRES
CHETWODE WAY
CLYDE RD
METHUEN RD
GREENHAM
SANDHILLS CL
BERE CL
SIDNEY SMITH CT
CHEDINGTON CL
WALDITCH GDNS
Neighbourhood Ctr
CHALDON RD
MAPPERTON CL
WHITBY CRES
SKIPTON CL
WETHERBY CL
Hillbourne Sch
HASTINGS RD
GOUGH CRES
ALLENBY CL
ALLENBY RD
HASLER RD
Montacute Specl Sch
CLAYFORD CL
HAYSTOCK CRES
REDGRAVE RD
THORNCOMBE CL
PUDDLETOWN CRES
HEATHMINSTER CRES
WARMWELL CL
DARBY'S CNR
WHITBY AVE
COVENTRY CRES
WATERLOO HO
HILARY RD
LAMBS CL
TERENCE AVE
PLANTATION CT
STANLEY PEARCE HO
CANFORD HEATH RD
1 WOODLAKE CL
2 WATERSTON CL
Ad Astra Fst Sch
SHERBORN CRES
HERSTONE CL
BOVINGTON CL
CANNON CL
RENAULT DR
MEAD RD
RUGBY RD
WAVELL AVE
GORT RD
ROBERTS RD
MILNE RD
THE PARADE
MARSHAL RD
DENISON RD
APSLEY CRES
CAVAN CRES
FRENCH RD
UNDERWOOD CL
WATERLOO RD
DENEVE AVE
PLANTATION RD
CHILFROME CL
HOLNEST RD
WAYTOWN CL
CHISWELL RD
WRAXALL CL
RYALL RD
STINSFORD RD
BREDY CL
Ashdown Tech Coll
Canford Heath
Ashdown L Ctr
ADASTRAL RD
ASHDOWN CL
Haymoor Bottom
PLUMER RD
Works
SOPERS LA
Parkstone Gram Sch
Waterloo
SANDYHURST CL
ROYSTER CL
WITNEY RD
COWLEY RD
ABINGDON RD
Slader Bsns Pk
Nuffield Ind Est
Haymoor Mid Sch
WARBURTON RD
BEAMISH RD
VERITY CRES
LYNN RD
30

119
88

87
60

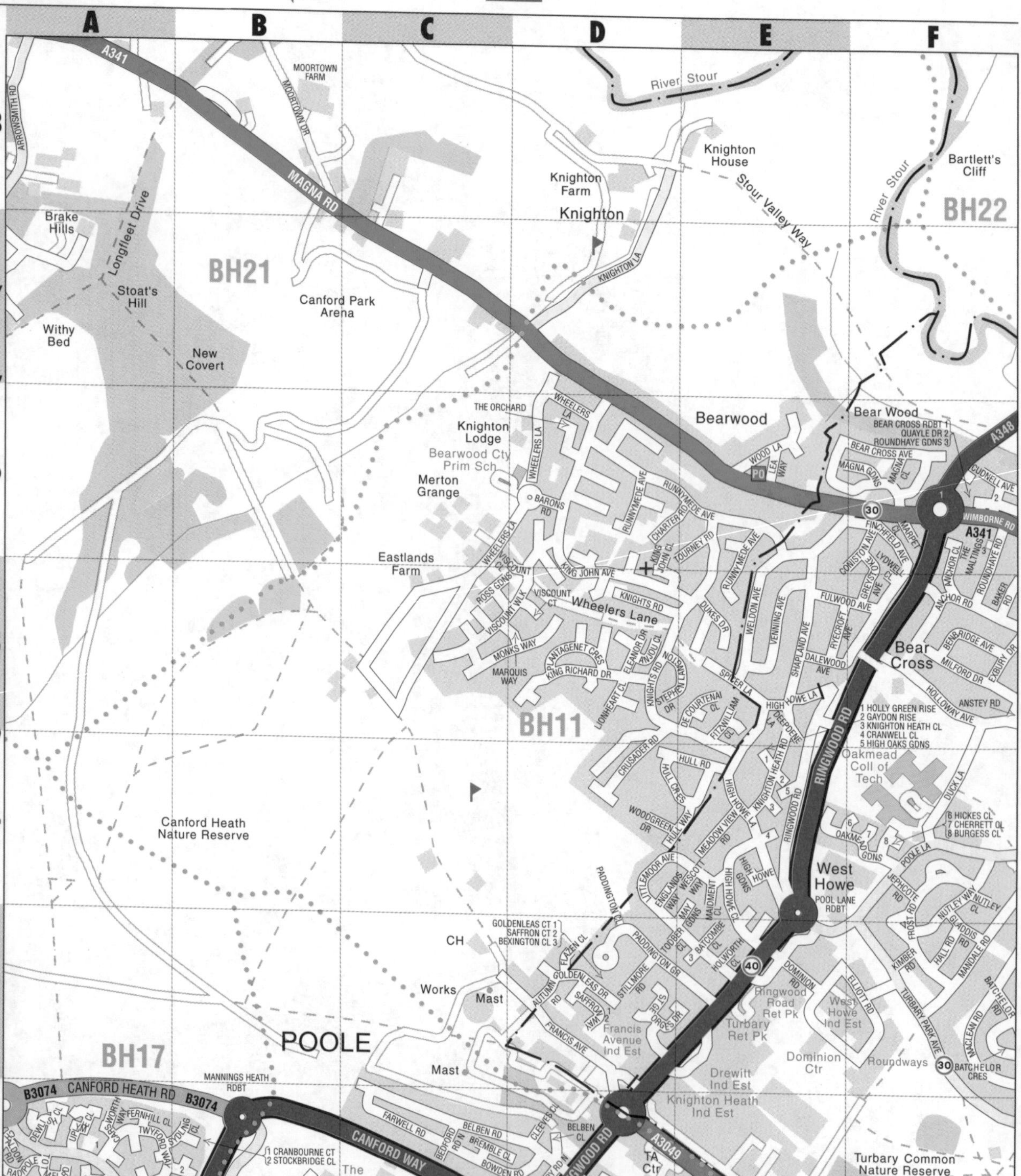
A
B
C
D
E
F
8
7
97
6
5
96
4
3
95
2
1
94
03
04
05
A341
MAGNA RD
ARROWSMITH RD
MOORTOWN FARM
MOORTOWN DR
River Stour
Knighton House
Knighton Farm
Knighton
Stour Valley Way
Bartlett's Cliff
BH22
Brake Hills
Longfleet Drive
Stoat's Hill
Withy Bed
BH21
Canford Park Arena
New Covert
KNIGHTON LA
Bearwood
Bear Wood
BEAR CROSS RDBT 1
QUAYLE DR 2
ROUNDHAYE GDNS 3
BEAR CROSS AVE
MAGNA GDNS
WOOD LA
LEA WAY
A348
CUDNELL AVE
WIMBORNE RD
THE ORCHARD
WHEELERS LA
Knighton Lodge
Bearwood Cty Prim Sch
Merton Grange
BARONS RD
RUNNYMEDE AVE
CHARTER RD
TOURNEY RD
FINCHFIELD AVE
Eastlands Farm
VISCOUNT CT
KING JOHN AVE
KINGS JOHN CL
ROSS GDNS
VISCOUNT WLK
KNIGHTS RD
Wheelers Lane
DUKES DR
WELDON AVE
VENNING AVE
FULWOOD AVE
CONISTON AVE
LYDWELL CL
ANCHOR CL
THE MALTINGS
ROUNDHAYE RD
ANCHOR RD
BAKER RD
Bear Cross
BENBRIDGE AVE
MILFORD DR
EXBURY DR
HOLLOWAY AVE
ANSTEY RD
MONKS WAY
PLANTAGENET CRES
MARQUIS WAY
KING RICHARD DR
ELEANOR DR
ANJOU CL
STEPHEN LANGTON DR
SPICER LA
SHAPLAND AVE
RYECROFT AVE
DALEWOOD AVE
HOWE LA
HIGH HOWE LA
DEEPDENE LA
LIONHEART CL
DE COURTENAI CL
FITZWILLIAM CL
BH11
1 HOLLY GREEN RISE
2 GAYDON RISE
3 KNIGHTON HEATH CL
4 CRANWELL CL
5 HIGH OAKS GDNS
RINGWOOD RD
Oakmead Coll of Tech
DUCK LA
CRUSADER RD
HULL RD
HULL CRES
KNIGHTON HEATH RD
WOODGREEN DR
HULL WAY
MEADOW VIEW RD
6 HICKES CL
7 CHERRETT CL
8 BURGESS CL
OAKMEAD GDNS
POOLE LA
Canford Heath Nature Reserve
LITTLEMOOR AVE
ENGLANDS WAY
WESCOTT WAY
HIGH GDNS
HIGH HOWE CL
West Howe
POOL LANE RDBT
JEPHCOTE RD
FROST RD
NUTLEY WAY
NUTLEY CL
GLADDIS RD
HALL RD
MANDALE RD
KIMBER RD
BATCHELOR RD
GOLDENLEAS CT 1
SAFFRON CT 2
BEXINGTON CL 3
CH
PADDINGTON CL
FLAZEN CL
TOOGOOD WAY
BATCOMBE CL
MAIDMENT CL
HOLWORTH CL
PADDINGTON GR
STILLMORE RD
ST GEORGES DR
GOLDENLEAS DR
AUTUMN RD
SAFFRON WAY
FRANCIS AVE
Works
Mast
Francis Avenue Ind Est
Ringwood Road Ret Pk
Turbary Ret Pk
DOMINION RD
ELLIOTT RD
West Howe Ind Est
TURBARY PARK AVE
MACLEAN RD
Dominion Ctr
Roundways
BATCHELOR CRES
POOLE
BH17
Mast
Drewitt Ind Est
Knighton Heath Ind Est
MANNINGS HEATH RDBT
B3074
CANFORD HEATH RD
FERNHILL CL
TWYFORD WAY
SYDLING CL
UPTON CL
FARWELL RD
BELBEN RD
BREMBLE CL
BEDFORD RD N
BOWDEN RD
CLEEVES CL
BELBEN CL
1 CRANBOURNE CT
2 STOCKBRIDGE CL
CANFORD WAY
RINGWOOD RD
A3049
TA Ctr
Turbary Common Nature Reserve
RADIPOLE RD
HOOKE CL
MAPPERTON CL
SUTTON CL
HENBURY CL
SHERBORN CRES
CHALBURY CL
SOUTHBROOK CL
VANTAGE WAY
The Fulcrum Ctr
HUDSON CL
BEDFORD RD S
DOLBERY RD N
ALDERNEY RDBT
LEWY CRES
LEYLAND RD
Discovery Court Bsns Ctr
WALLISDOWN RD
Alderney
BH12
LYON RD
IVAMY PL
DOWNEY CL
TOZER CL
RIGGS GDNS
TURBARY HTS
CANFORD AVE
NOBLE CL
EVANS CL
WEBB'S WAY
TEMPLER CL
BASCOTT RD
ST HELIER RD
ST BRELADES AVE
RALEIGH RD
BENBOW CRES
JERSEY RD
GUERNSEY RD
FIRMAIN RD
CORBIERE AVE
Bourne Bottom
Haymoor Bottom
YARROW CL
DORSET WAY
YARROW RD
MANNINGS HEATH RD
Broom Road Bsns Pk
BROOM RD
DOLBERY RD S
B3068
PORTELET CL
THRUSH RD
Superstore
The Courtyard
Alderney
ALDERNEY AVE
Winchelsea Specl Sch
KEYES CL
HAWKINS RD
FROBISHER AVE
SCOTT RD
SCOTT CL
FRASER RD
MOSSLEY AVE
HILLSIDE RD
VERITY CRES
Tower Park
LING RD
CALLUNA RD
HERBERT AVE
MANOR AVE
HERM RD
EVERING GDNS
EVERING AVE
Manorside Comb Sch
PLEMONT CL
Bourne Valley Nature Reserve
A3049

87
120

61
90

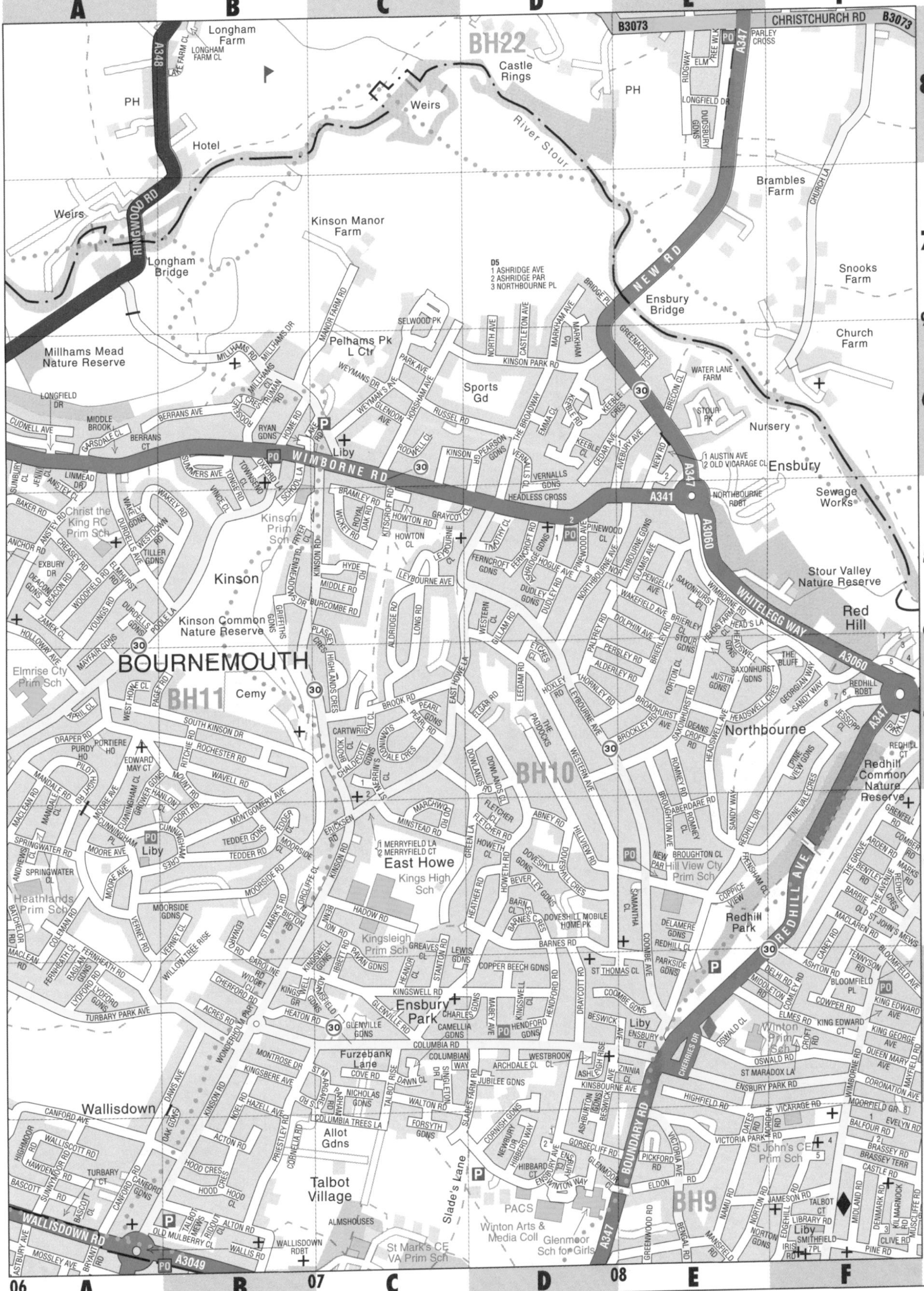

121
90

D1
1 HARTMOOR GDNS
2 GLENMOOR GDNS

F1
1 EVELYN MEWS
2 ST JOHN'S GDNS
3 NORWAY CL
4 VICTORIA PARK PL
5 LAMPTON GDNS
6 ALEXANDER GDNS
7 MELGATE CL
8 KINGSLEY HO

F4
1 REDHILL PARK HOMES
2 WHEATPLOT PARK HOMES
3 KINGFISHER PARK HOMES
4 RIVERSIDE
5 WIMBORNE RD
6 MAGNOLIA HO
7 WISTERIA HO
8 LABURNUM HO

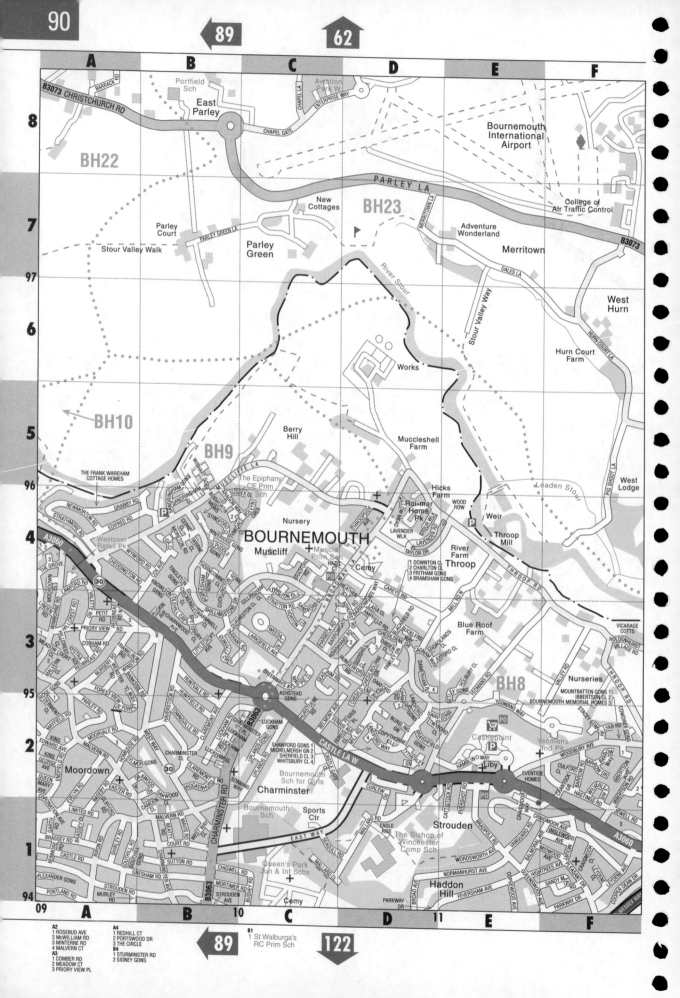

A2
1 ROSEBUD AVE
2 McWILLIAM RD
3 MINTERNE RD
4 MALVERN CT
A3
1 COMBER RD
2 MEADOW CT
3 PRIORY VIEW PL

A4
1 REDHILL CT
2 PORTSWOOD DR
3 THE CIRCLE
B4
1 STURMINSTER RD
2 SIDNEY GDNS

B1
1 St Walburga's
RC Prim Sch

63
92

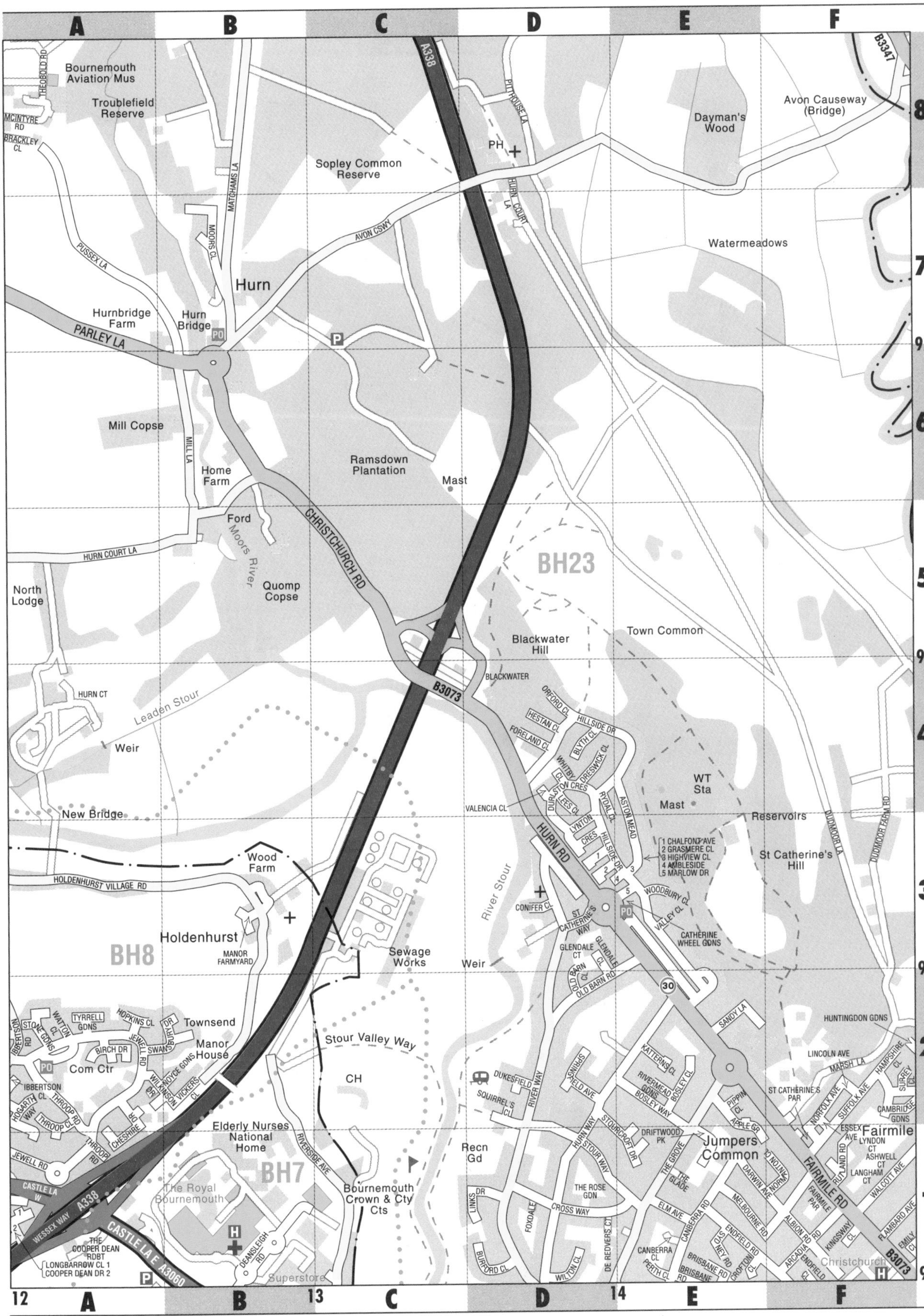
A
B
C
D
E
F
Bournemouth Aviation Mus
Troublefield Reserve
THEOBOLD RD
MCINTYRE RD
BRACKLEY CL
Sopley Common Reserve
PH
PITTHOUSE LA
HURN COURT LA
Dayman's Wood
Avon Causeway (Bridge)
B3347
A338
MATCHAMS LA
MOORS CL
PUSSEX LA
AVON CSWY
Watermeadows
Hurn
Hurnbridge Farm
Hurn Bridge
PARLEY LA
Mill Copse
MILL LA
Home Farm
Ramsdown Plantation
Mast
Ford
Moors River
HURN COURT LA
CHRISTCHURCH RD
BH23
North Lodge
Quomp Copse
Blackwater Hill
Town Common
BLACKWATER
B3073
HURN CT
Leaden Stour
Weir
ORFORD CL
HESTAN CL
HILLSIDE DR
FORELAND CL
BLYTH CL
WHITBY CL
DRESWICK CL
DURLSTON CRES
LEES CL
VALENCIA CL
RYDAL CL
ASTON MEAD
LYNTON CRES
HILLSIDE DR
WT Sta
Mast
Reservoirs
New Bridge
HURN RD
1 CHALFONT AVE
2 GRASMERE CL
3 HIGHVIEW CL
4 AMBLESIDE
5 MARLOW DR
St Catherine's Hill
DUDMOOR LA
DUDMOOR FARM RD
Wood Farm
HOLDENHURST VILLAGE RD
River Stour
CONIFER CL
ST CATHERINE'S WAY
WOODBURY CL
VALLEY CL
CATHERINE WHEEL GDNS
Holdenhurst
BH8
MANOR FARMYARD
Sewage Works
GLENDALE CT
GLENDALE CL
OLD BARN CL
OLD BARN RD
Weir
30
SANDY LA
HUNTINGDON GDNS
Townsend
TYRRELL GDNS
HOPKINS CL
WATTON CL
STONE GDNS
JEWELL RD
SWANS
Manor House
BIRCH DR
Com Ctr
Stour Valley Way
SPRINGS FIELD AVE
KATTERNS CL
RIVERMEAD GDNS
BOSLEY CL
BOSLEY WAY
LINCOLN AVE
MARSH LA
HAMPSHIRE CL
IBBERTSON CL
HOGARTH WAY
THROOP CL
THROOP RD
VICKERS CL
WILKINSON DR
CHESHIRE DR
CH
DUKESFIELD
SQUIRREL'S CL
RIVER WAY
PIPPIN CL
APPLE GR
ST CATHERINE'S PAR
NORFOLK AVE
SUFFOLK AVE
SURREY CL
CAMBRIDGE GDNS
ESSEX AVE
Fairmile
LYNDON CT
ASHWELL CT
LANGHAM CT
WALCOTT AVE
Elderly Nurses National Home
RIVERSIDE AVE
Recn Gd
HURN WAY
STOUR WAY
STOURCROFT DR
DRIFTWOOD PK
THE GROVE
THE GLADE
Jumpers Common
DARWIN AVE
NORTON CL
FAIRMILE RD
JEWELL RD
CASTLE LA W
BH7
The Royal Bournemouth
Bournemouth Crown & Cty Cts
THE ROSE GDN
CROSS WAY
ELM AVE
CANBERRA RD
MELBOURNE RD
ENDFIELD RD
ALBION RD
FAIRMILE PAR
KINGSWAY
FLAMBARD AVE
WESSEX WAY
A338
CASTLE LA E A3060
THE COOPER DEAN RDBT
1 LONGBARROW CL
2 COOPER DEAN DR
DEANSLEIGH RD
Superstore
LINKS DR
FOXDALE
BURFORD CL
WILTON CL
DE REDVERS CT
CANBERRA CL
PERTH CL
BRISBANE RD
CROFTON CL
Christchurch
B3073
8
7
97
6
5
96
4
3
95
2
1
94
12
13
14

123
92

91

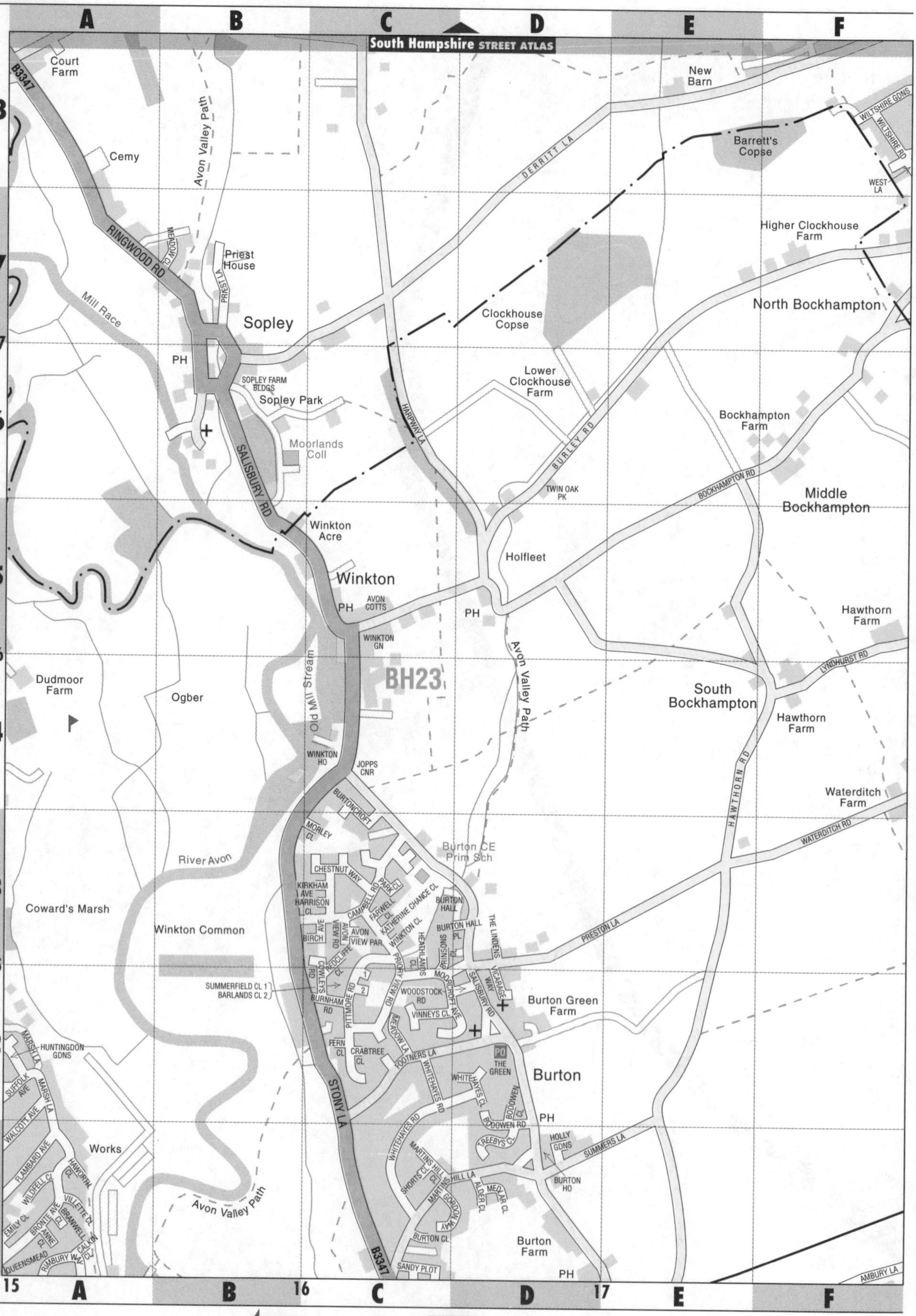
A
B
C
D
E
F
South Hampshire STREET ATLAS
8
7
97
6
5
96
4
3
95
2
1
94
15
16
17
Court Farm
B3347
Cemy
Avon Valley Path
New Barn
Barrett's Copse
WILTSHIRE GDNS
WILTSHIRE RD
WEST LA
DERRITT LA
Higher Clockhouse Farm
RINGWOOD RD
MEADOW CL
Priest House
PRIEST LA
Mill Race
Sopley
North Bockhampton
Clockhouse Copse
PH
SOPLEY FARM BLDGS
Sopley Park
Lower Clockhouse Farm
HARPWAY LA
Bockhampton Farm
Moorlands Coll
SALISBURY RD
BURLEY RD
TWIN OAK PK
BOCKHAMPTON RD
Middle Bockhampton
Winkton Acre
Holfleet
Winkton
AVON COTTS
Hawthorn Farm
WINKTON GN
BH23
LYNDHURST RD
Dudmoor Farm
Ogber
Old Mill Stream
South Bockhampton
Hawthorn Farm
WINKTON HO
JOPPS CNR
HAWTHORN RD
Waterditch Farm
BURTONCROFT
MORLEY CL
Burton CE Prim Sch
WATERDITCH RD
River Avon
CHESTNUT WAY
PARK CL
KIRKHAM AVE
HARRISON CL
CAMPBELL RD
FARWELL CL
KATHERINE CHANCE CL
BURTON HALL
Coward's Marsh
BIRCH AVE
AVON VIEW RD
AVON VIEW PAR
WINKTON CL
HEATHLANDS CL
BURTON HALL PL
ROBINSONS WAY
THE LINDENS
PRESTON LA
Winkton Common
REDCLIFFE CL
PRIORY VIEW RD
COWLEYS RD
SUMMERFIELD CL 1
BARLANDS CL 2
BURNHAM RD
PITTMORE RD
WOODSTOCK RD
MOORCROFT AVE
VICARAGE WAY
Burton Green Farm
VINNEYS CL
MEADOW LA
HUNTINGDON GDNS
MARSH LA
FERN CL
CRABTREE CL
FOOTNERS LA
THE GREEN
Burton
SUFFOLK AVE
WALCOTT AVE
WHITEHAYES RD
WHITEHAYES CL
BODOWEN CL
BODOWEN RD
STONY LA
FLAMBARD AVE
Works
WHITEHAYES RD
TREEBYS CL
HOLLY GDNS
SUMMERS LA
HAWORTH CL
WILDFELL CL
MARTINS HILL CL
SHORTS CL
HILL LA
BURTON HO
VILLETTE CL
BRONTE AVE
BRANWELL CL
MARTINS HILL LA
ALDER CL
MEDLAR CL
GORDON WAY
EMILY CL
ANNIE CL
Avon Valley Path
Burton Farm
CALKIN CL
QUEENSMEAD
RIMBURY WAY
BURTON CL
SANDY PLOT
B3347
PH
AMBURY LA

91

124

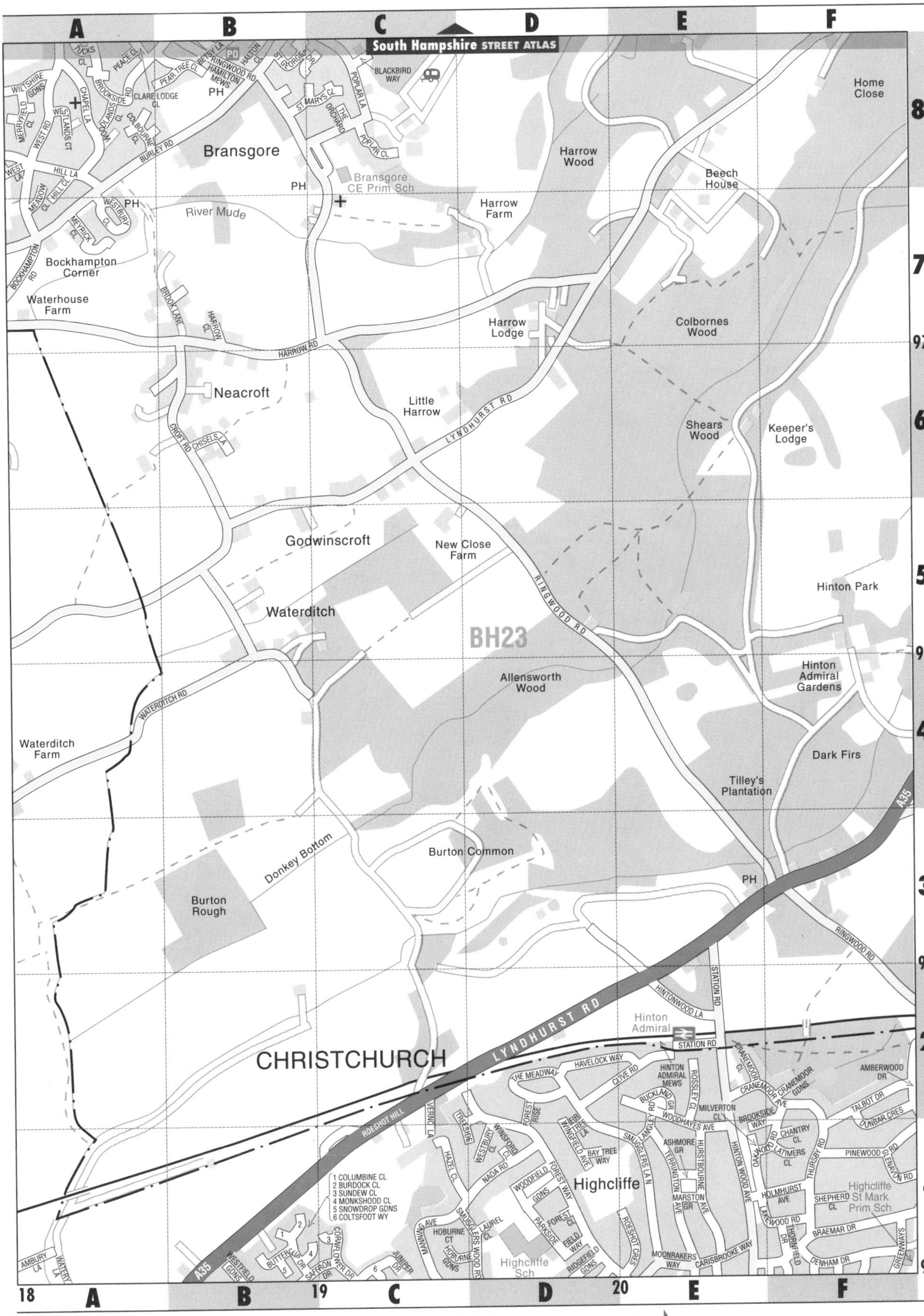

South Hampshire STREET ATLAS

8

7

97

6

5

96

4

95

3

2

1

94

Home Close

Bransgore

Harrow Wood

Beech House

River Mude

Harrow Farm

Bockhampton Corner

Colbornes Wood

Waterhouse Farm

Harrow Lodge

Neacroft

Little Harrow

Shears Wood

Keeper's Lodge

Hinton Park

Godwinscroft

New Close Farm

Hinton Admiral Gardens

Waterditch

BH23

Dark Firs

Allensworth Wood

Waterditch Farm

Tilley's Plantation

PH

Donkey Bottom

Burton Common

Burton Rough

Station Rd

Hintonwood La

Hinton Admiral

Station Rd

CHRISTCHURCH

LYNDHURST RD

The Meadway

Havelock Way

Clive Rd

Amberwood Dr

Talbot Dr

Dunbar Cres

Pinewood Rd

Highcliffe St Mark Prim Sch

Highcliffe

1 COLUMBINE CL
2 BURDOCK CL
3 SUNDEW CL
4 MONKSHOOD CL
5 SNOWDROP GDNS
6 COLTSFOOT WY

Highcliffe Sch

Braemar Dr

Denham Dr

18   A   B   19   C   D   20   E   F

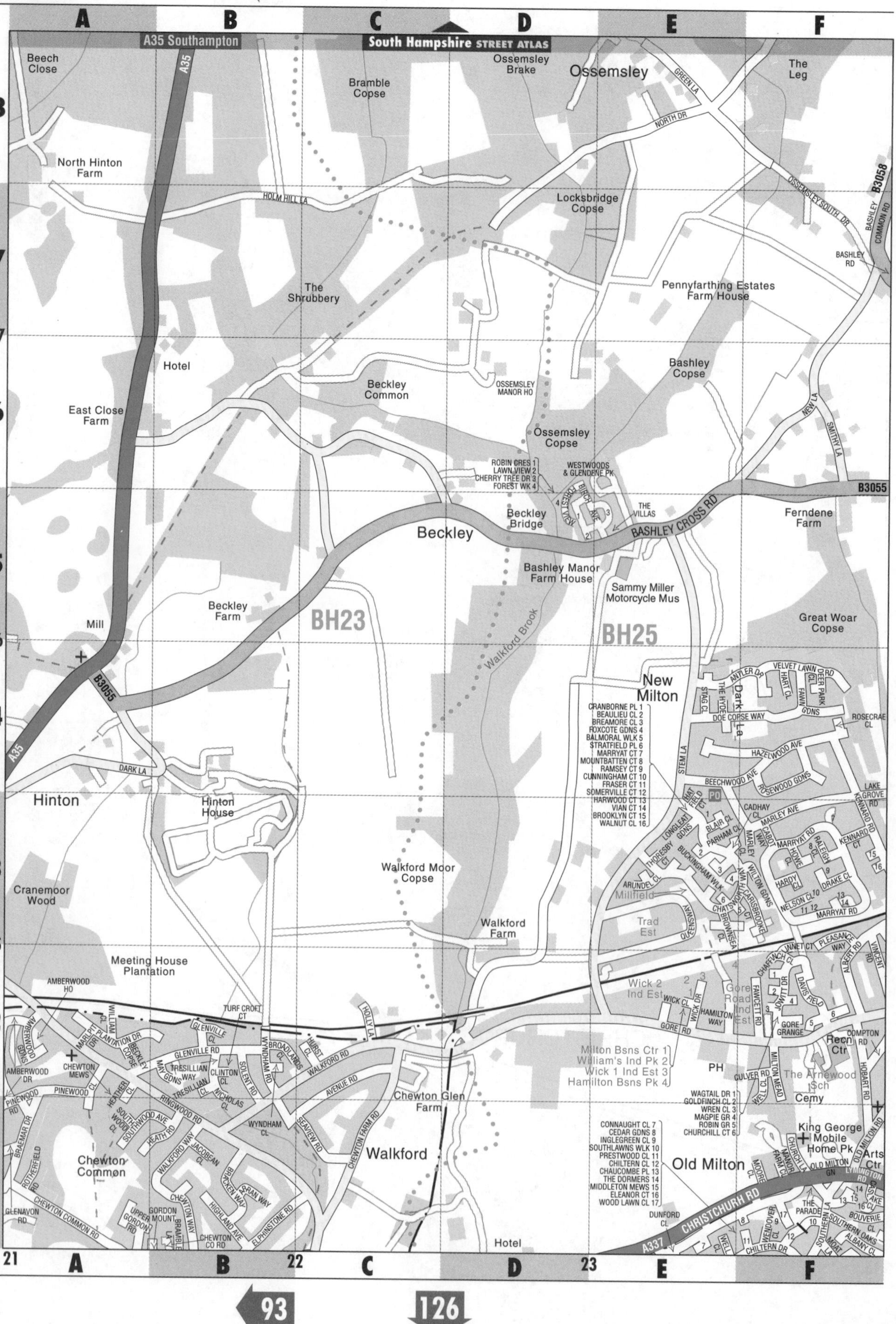

South Hampshire STREET ATLAS

A35 Southampton

A35

8

Beech
Close

North Hinton
Farm

HOLM HILL LA

Bramble
Copse

Ossemsley
Brake

Ossemsley

Locksbridge
Copse

The
Leg

B3058

OSSEMSLEY SOUTH DR

BASHLEY
RD

BASHLEY COMMON RD

7

97

The
Shrubbery

NORTH DR

GREEN LA

Pennyfarthing Estates
Farm House

6

Hotel

East Close
Farm

Beckley
Common

OSSEMSLEY
MANOR HO

Ossemsley
Manor Ho

Ossemsley
Copse

Bashley
Copse

NEW LA

SMITH LA

B3055

Ferndene
Farm

ROBIN CRES 1
LAWN VIEW 2
CHERRY TREE DR 3
FOREST WK 4

WESTWOODS
& GLENDENE PK

THE
VILLAS

BASHLEY CROSS RD

Beckley

Beckley
Bridge

5

Beckley
Farm

BH23

Mill

B3055

A35

96

Bashley Manor
Farm House

Walkford Brook

Sammy Miller
Motorcycle Mus

BH25

New
Milton

Great Woar
Copse

VELVET LAWN

ANTLER DR

DEER PARK

4

DARK LA

CRANBORNE PL 1
BEAULIEU CL 2
BREAMORE CL 3
FOXCOTE GDNS 4
BALMORAL WLK 5
STRATFIELD PL 6
MARRYAT CT 7
MOUNTBATTEN CT 8
RAMSEY CT 9
CUNNINGHAM CT 10
FRASER CT 11
SOMERVILLE CT 12
HARWOOD CT 13
VIAN CT 14
BROOKLYN CT 15
WALNUT CL 16

HART CL

FAWN
GDNS

ROSECRAE
CL

STAG CL

THE HYDE

STEM LA

DOE CORSE WAY

HAZELWOOD AVE

LAKE
GROVE

KENNARD RD

BEECHWOOD AVE

ROSEWOOD GDNS

CADHAY

PO

MARLEY AVE

KENNARD
RD

Hinton

Hinton
House

3

Cranemoor
Wood

Walkford Moor
Copse

Walkford
Farm

Millfield

Trad
Est

THORESBY
CT

LONGLEAT
GDNS

BLAIR CL

PARHAM CL

ARUNDEL

BUCKINGHAM WLK

CHATSWORTH
GLOUCESTERBROOKE

MARLEY
CL

WILTON
GDNS

HARDY
CL

NELSON CL
MARRYAT RD

DRAKE CL

95

Meeting House
Plantation

AMBERWOOD
HO

TURF CROFT
CT

HOLLY LA

Wick 2
Ind Est

CHAFFINCH CL

HAMILTON
WAY

Wick CL

GORE RD

GORE
RD

FAWCETT RD

JOHN ST

DAISY FIELD

JINNET CT

PLEASANCE
WAY

VINCENT
CL

ALBERT RD

Gore
Road
Ind Est

Recn
Ctr

GORE
GRANGE

DOMPTON
RD

2

AMBERWOOD
DR

BRAEMAR DR

ROTHERFIELD RD

WILLOW

MARLPIT

PLANTATION DR

GLENVILLE RD

BROADLANDS

CLINTON CL

LYNWYNDHAM RD

SOLENT RD

HURST

WALKFORD RD

AVENUE RD

Chewton Glen
Farm

Milton Bsns Ctr 1
William's Ind Pk 2
Wick 1 Ind Est 3
Hamilton Bsns Pk 4

PH

MILTON MEAD

CULVER RD

The Arnewood
Sch

Cemy

HOBART RD

HEXTHORN

CHEWTON
MEWS

PINEWOOD
RD

PINEWOOD

TRESILLIAN
WAY

TRESILLIAN

RINGWOOD RD

NICHOLAS
CL

WYNDHAM
CL

SEAVIEW RD

WAGTAIL DR 1
GOLDFINCH CL 2
WREN CL 3
MAGPIE GR 4
ROBIN GR 5
CHURCHILL CT 6

PENSHURST
CL

CONNAUGHT CL 7
CEDAR GDNS 8
INGLEGREEN CL 9
SOUTHLAWNS WLK 10
PRESTWOOD CL 11
CHILTERN CL 12
CHAUCOMBE PL 13
THE DORMERS 14
MIDDLETON MEWS 15
ELEANOR CT 16
WOOD LAWN CL 17

King George
Mobile
Home Pk

Arts
Ctr

1

GLENAVON
RD

CHEWTON COMMON RD

Chewton
Common

GORDON
GORDON RD

UPPER MOUNT
BRAMBLE

ELPHINSTONE RD

HIGHLAND AVE

BRAN WAY

HEATH RD

JACOBEAN
CL

SOUTHWOOD AVE

WALKFORD WAY

CHEWTON FARM RD

Walkford

Old Milton

DUNFORD
CL

OLD MILTON
GN

MOORE CL

FERNHILL LA

WELLS

CHILTERN DR

THE
PARADE

WILLMORE
CL

SOUTHERN OAKS

MODEL

ALBANY CL

BOUVERIE

A337

CHRISTCHURCH RD

Hotel

94

A   B   22   C   D   23   E   F

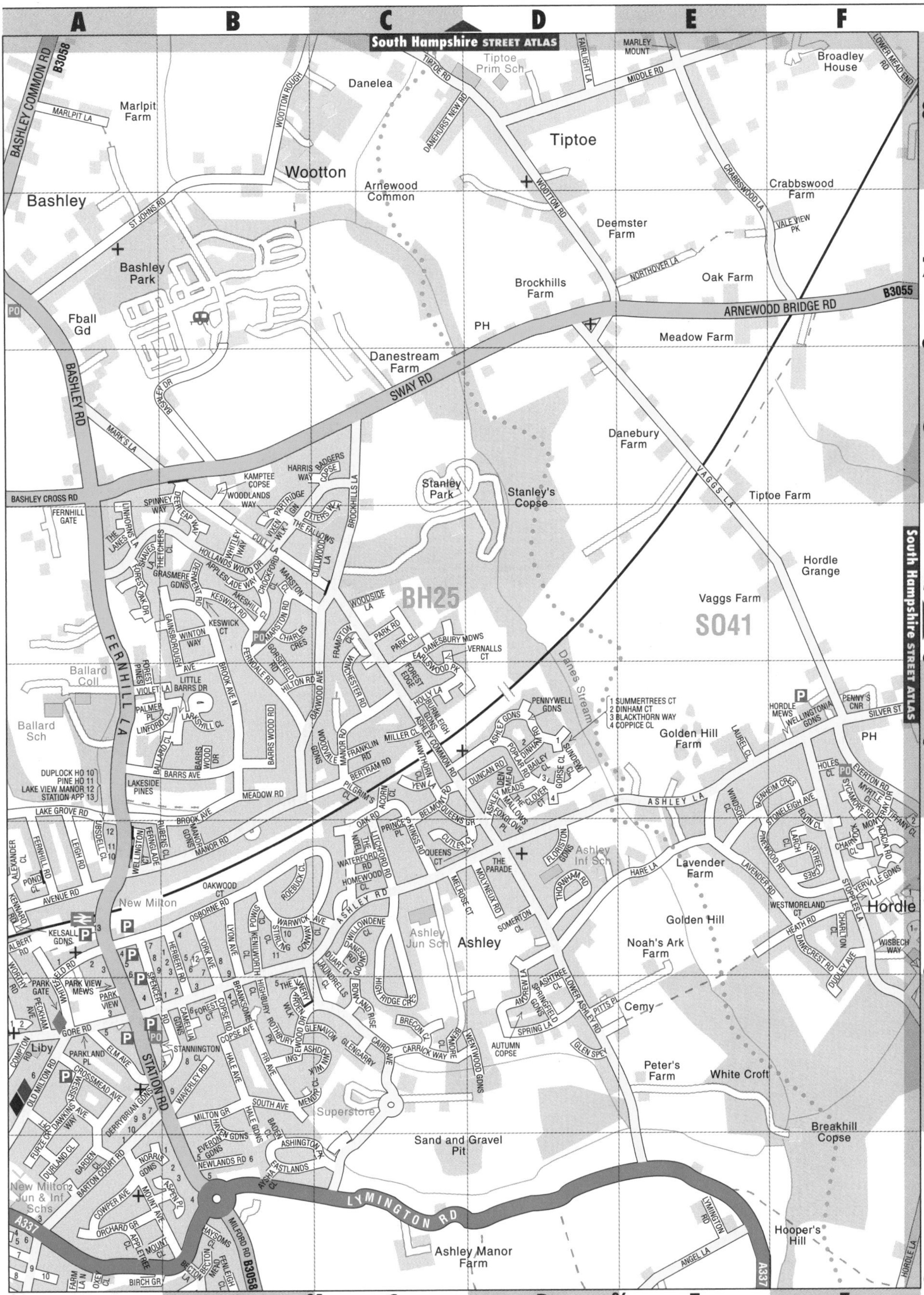

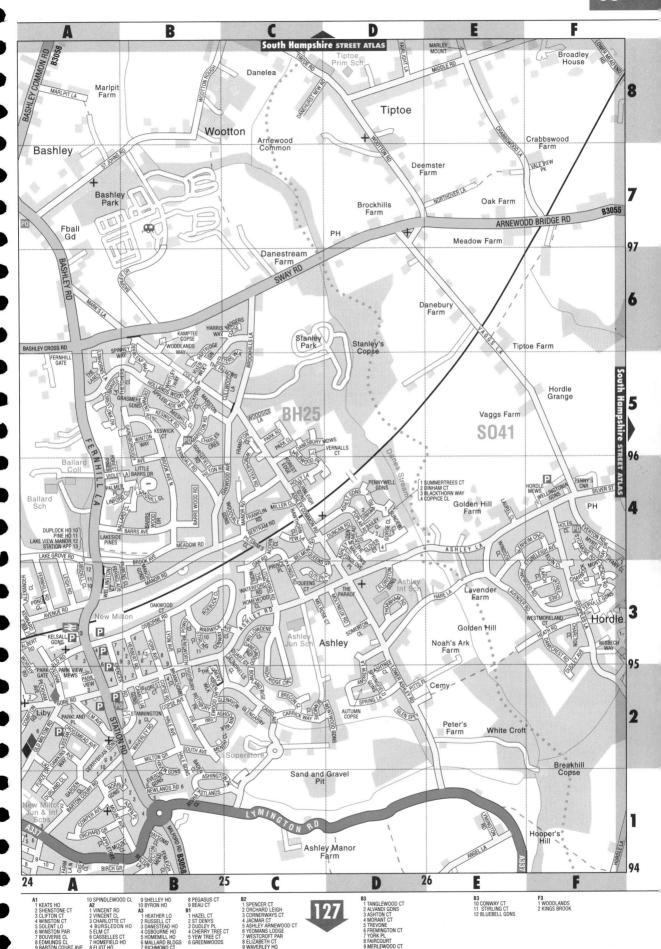

South Hampshire STREET ATLAS

127

64

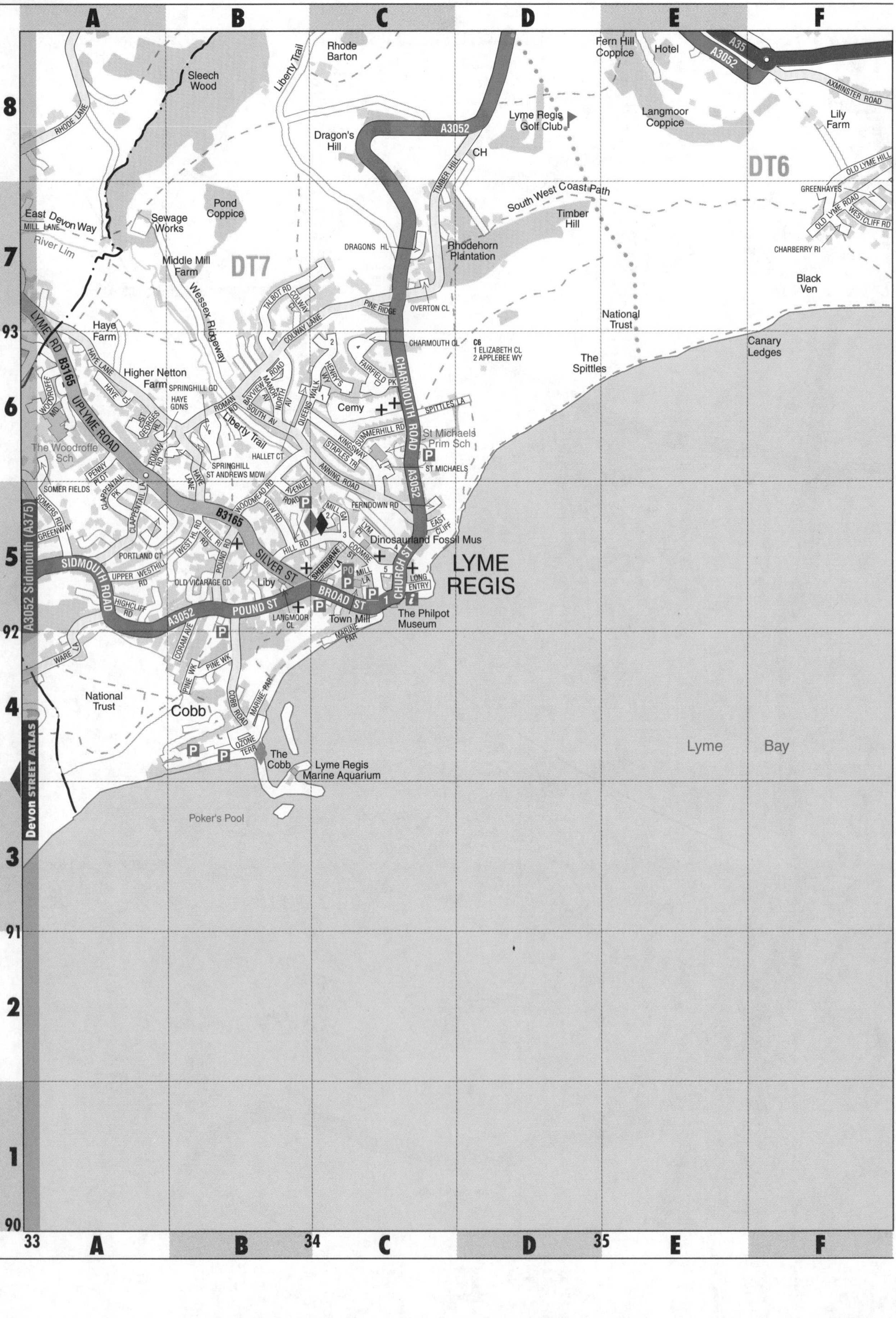

C6
1 ELIZABETH CL
2 APPLEBEE WY

LYME REGIS

Lyme Bay

DT7

DT6

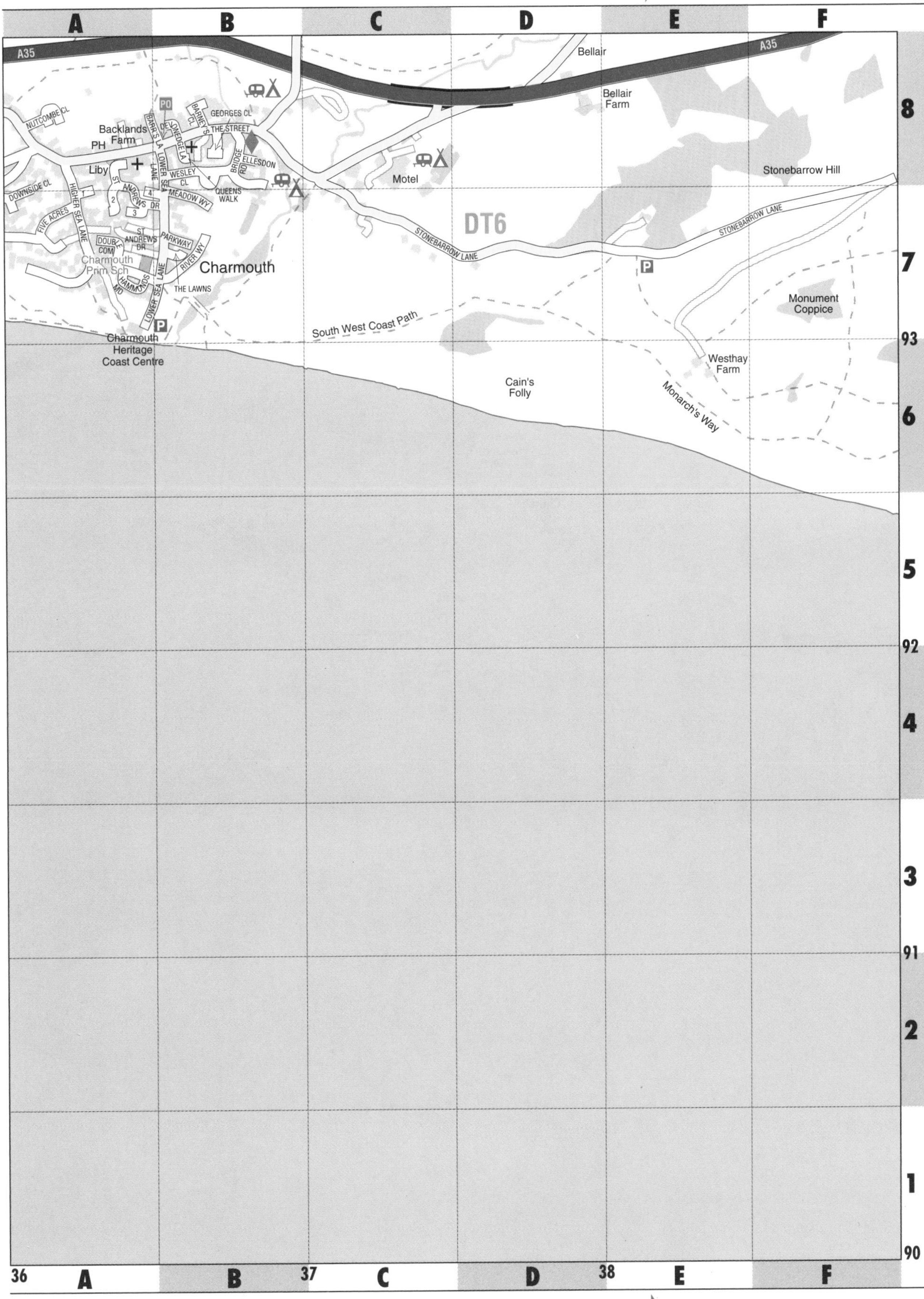

97
66

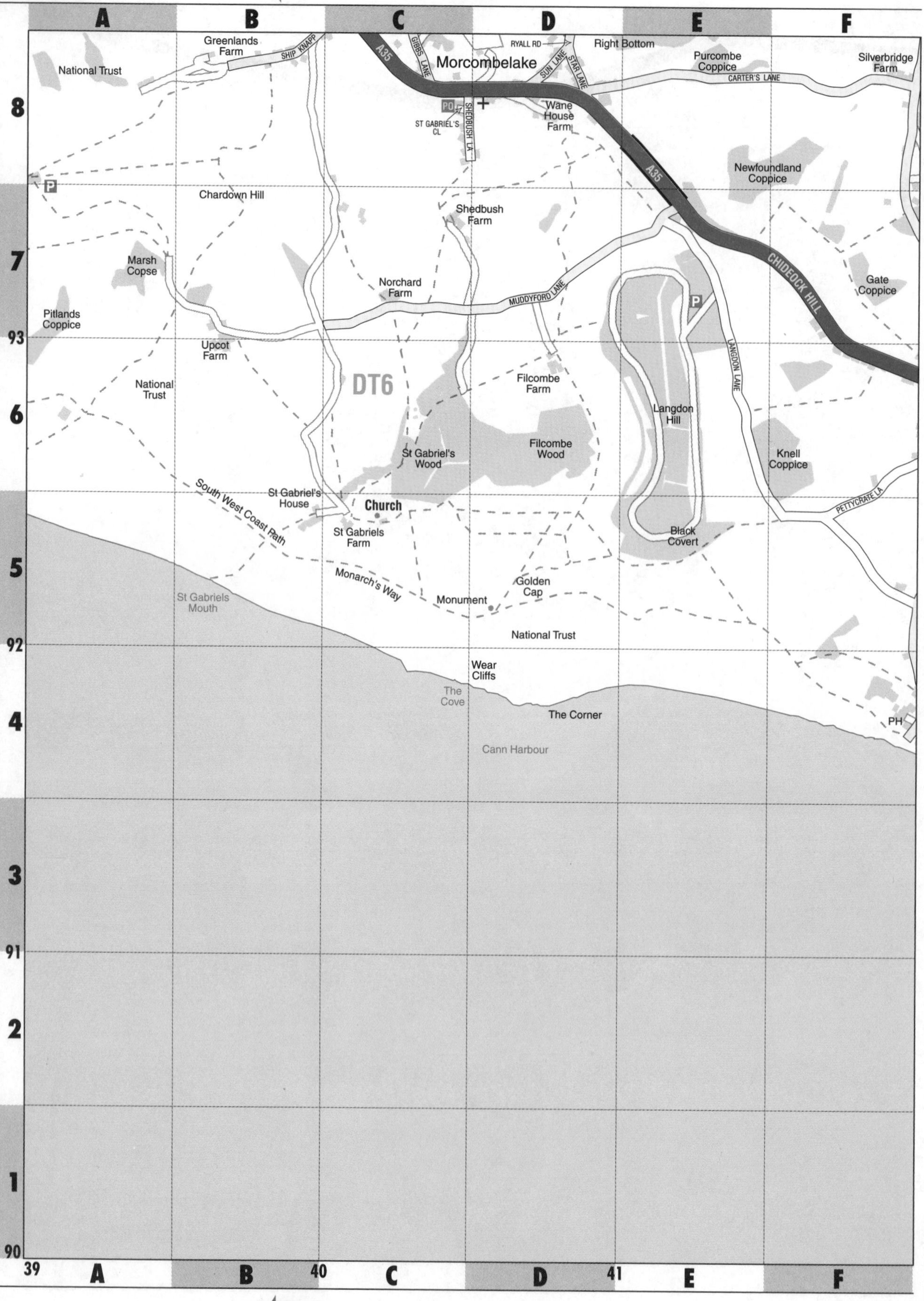

A
B
C
D
E
F
8
7
93
6
5
92
4
3
91
2
1
90
39
40
41
Greenlands Farm
SHIP KNAPP
National Trust
A35
GIBBS LANE
RYALL RD
Morcombelake
SUN LANE
STAR LANE
Right Bottom
Purcombe Coppice
CARTER'S LANE
Silverbridge Farm
PO
ST GABRIEL'S CL
SHEDBUSH LA
Wane House Farm
Newfoundland Coppice
P
Chardown Hill
Shedbush Farm
Marsh Copse
Norchard Farm
MUDDYFORD LANE
CHIDEOCK HILL
Gate Coppice
Pitlands Coppice
Upcot Farm
LANGDON LANE
DT6
National Trust
Filcombe Farm
Langdon Hill
St Gabriel's Wood
Filcombe Wood
Knell Coppice
South West Coast Path
St Gabriel's House
Church
PETTYCRATE LA
St Gabriels Farm
Black Covert
Monarch's Way
Golden Cap
St Gabriels Mouth
Monument
National Trust
Wear Cliffs
The Cove
The Corner
PH
Cann Harbour

97

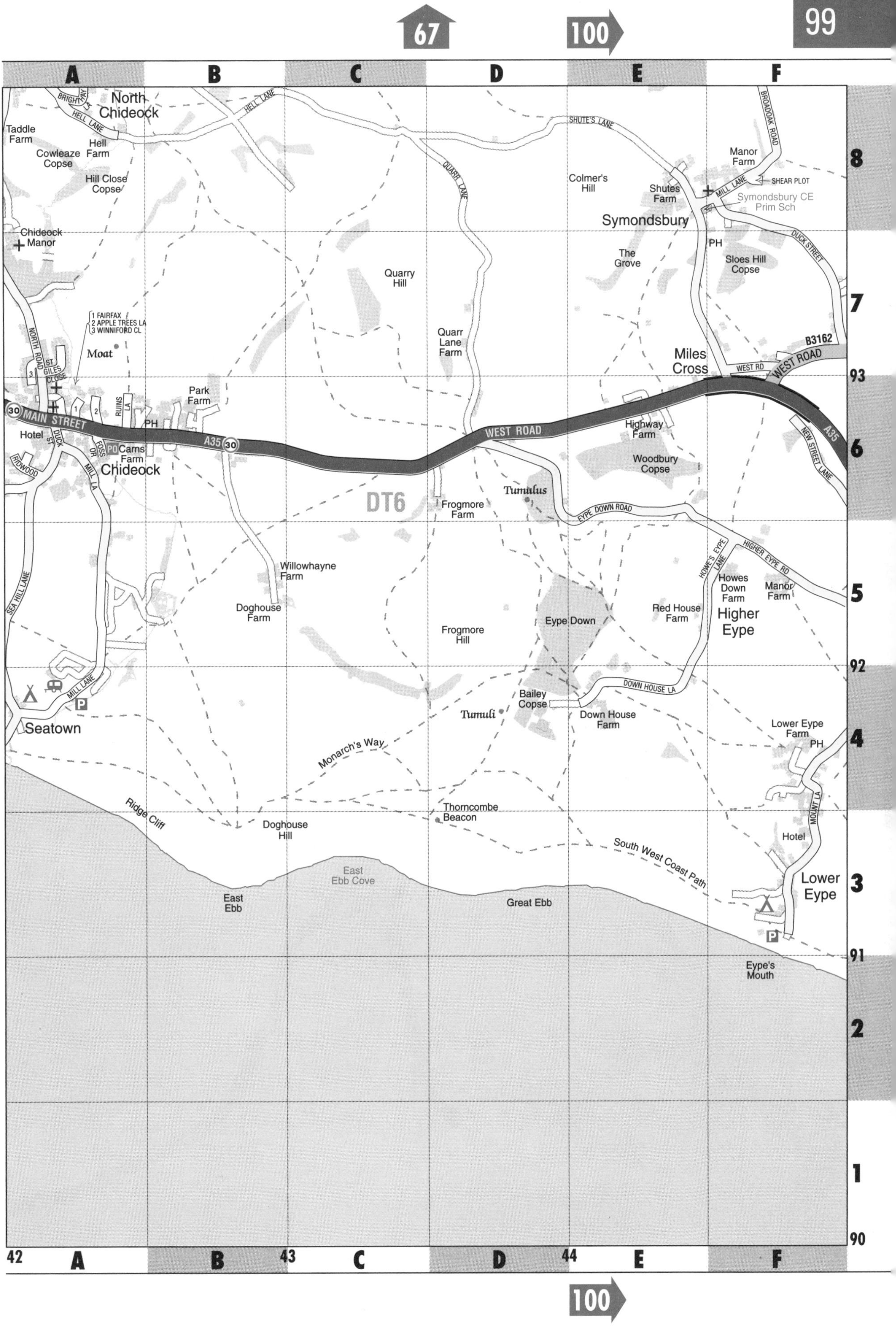
67
100
A
B
C
D
E
F
North Chideock
Taddle Farm
Hell Farm
Cowleaze Copse
Hill Close Copse
Chideock Manor
HELL LANE
BRIGHT WAY
SHUTE'S LANE
BROADOAK ROAD
Manor Farm
SHEAR PLOT
MILL LANE
Symondsbury CE Prim Sch
Colmer's Hill
Shutes Farm
Symondsbury
QUARR LANE
DUCK STREET
The Grove
PH
Sloes Hill Copse
Quarry Hill
1 FAIRFAX
2 APPLE TREES LA
3 WINNIFORD CL
NORTH ROAD
Quarr Lane Farm
Moat
Miles Cross
B3162
WEST RD
WEST ROAD
ST GILES CLOSE
Park Farm
RUINS LA
MAIN STREET
Hotel
PH
Highway Farm
A35
NEW STREET LANE
DUCK ST
FOSS DR
PO
Carns Farm
Chideock
RIDWOOD
MILL LA
Woodbury Copse
Tumulus
DT6
Frogmore Farm
EYPE DOWN ROAD
HOWE'S EYPE LANE
HIGHER EYPE RD
Willowhayne Farm
Howes Down Farm
Manor Farm
SEA HILL LANE
Doghouse Farm
Frogmore Hill
Eype Down
Red House Farm
Higher Eype
MILL LANE
DOWN HOUSE LA
Bailey Copse
Tumuli
Down House Farm
Seatown
Lower Eype Farm
Monarch's Way
Ridge Cliff
Thorncombe Beacon
Doghouse Hill
MOUNT LA
Hotel
South West Coast Path
East Ebb Cove
East Ebb
Great Ebb
Lower Eype
Eype's Mouth
8
7
93
6
5
92
4
3
91
2
1
90
42
43
44
100

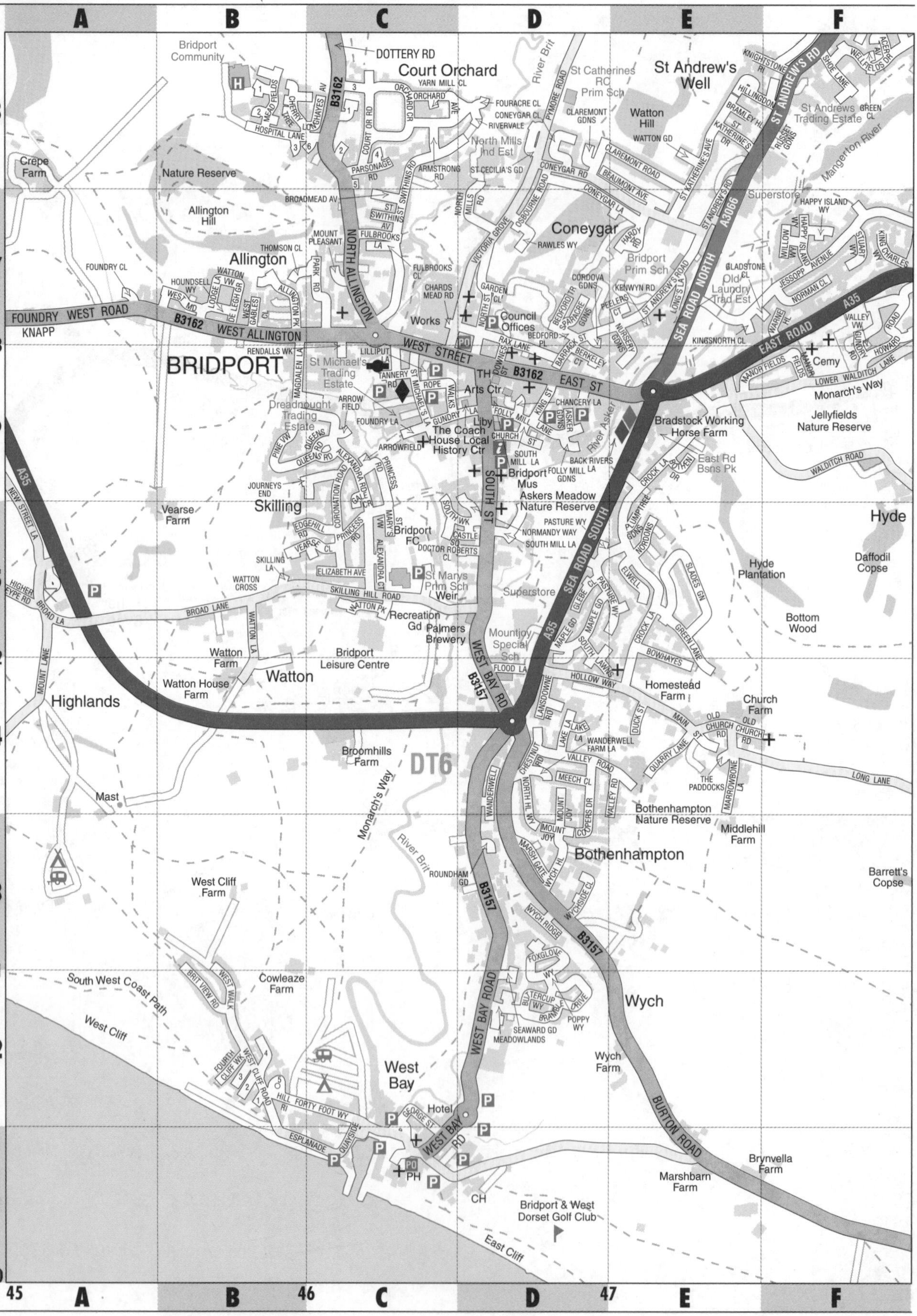

B8
1 LAUREL CL
2 ST LUKE'S CT
3 ALLINGTON GDNS
← 99

C8
1 HILLVIEW EST
2 DIMENTS GDNS
3 ALLINGTON MD
4 VICARAGE CT
5 BIDDLECOME ORCH
6 TRUSTIN CL
↑ 68

B2
1 FIRST CLIFF WK
2 SECOND CLIFF WK
3 THIRD CLIFF WK
4 MEADWAY
5 HILL CL
← 99

69
102

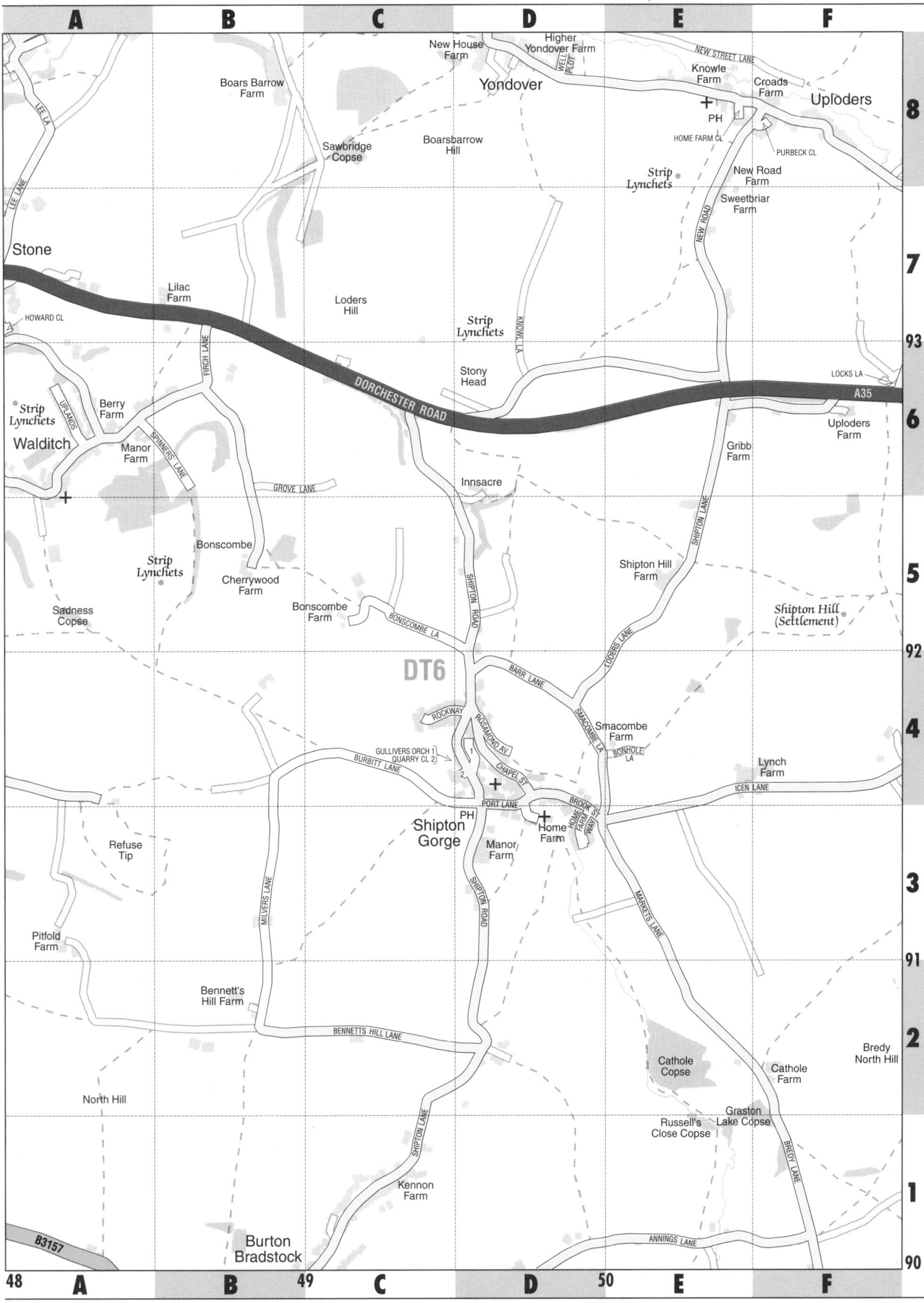
A
B
C
D
E
F
New House Farm
Higher Yondover Farm
WELL PLOT
NEW STREET LANE
Boars Barrow Farm
Yondover
Knowle Farm
Croads Farm
Uploders
LEE LA
PH
HOME FARM CL
PURBECK CL
Sawbridge Copse
Boarsbarrow Hill
Strip Lynchets
New Road Farm
Sweetbriar Farm
LEE LANE
NEW ROAD
Stone
Lilac Farm
Loders Hill
HOWARD CL
Strip Lynchets
KNOWL LA
FIRCH LANE
Stony Head
LOCKS LA
DORCHESTER ROAD
A35
Strip Lynchets
Berry Farm
UPLANDS
Walditch
Manor Farm
SPINNERS' LANE
Uploders Farm
Gribb Farm
Innsacre
GROVE LANE
SHIPTON LANE
Bonscombe
Strip Lynchets
Cherrywood Farm
Shipton Hill Farm
SHIPTON ROAD
Sadness Copse
Bonscombe Farm
BONSCOMBE LA
Shipton Hill (Settlement)
LODERS LANE
DT6
BARR LANE
ROCKWAY
ROSAMOND AV
SMACOMBE LA
Smacombe Farm
BONHOLE LA
GULLIVERS ORCH 1
QUARRY CL 2
BURBITT LANE
CHAPEL ST
Lynch Farm
ICEN LANE
PORT LANE
BROOK ST
PH
Shipton Gorge
Home Farm
HOME FARM WAY
Manor Farm
Refuse Tip
SHIPTON ROAD
MARKETS LANE
MILVERS LANE
Pitfold Farm
Bennett's Hill Farm
BENNETTS HILL LANE
Cathole Copse
Catholе Farm
Bredy North Hill
North Hill
Graston Lake Copse
Russell's Close Copse
SHIPTON LANE
BREDY LANE
Kennon Farm
B3157
Burton Bradstock
ANNINGS LANE
8
7
93
6
5
92
4
3
91
2
1
90
48
49
50
A
B
C
D
E
F

128
102

101
70

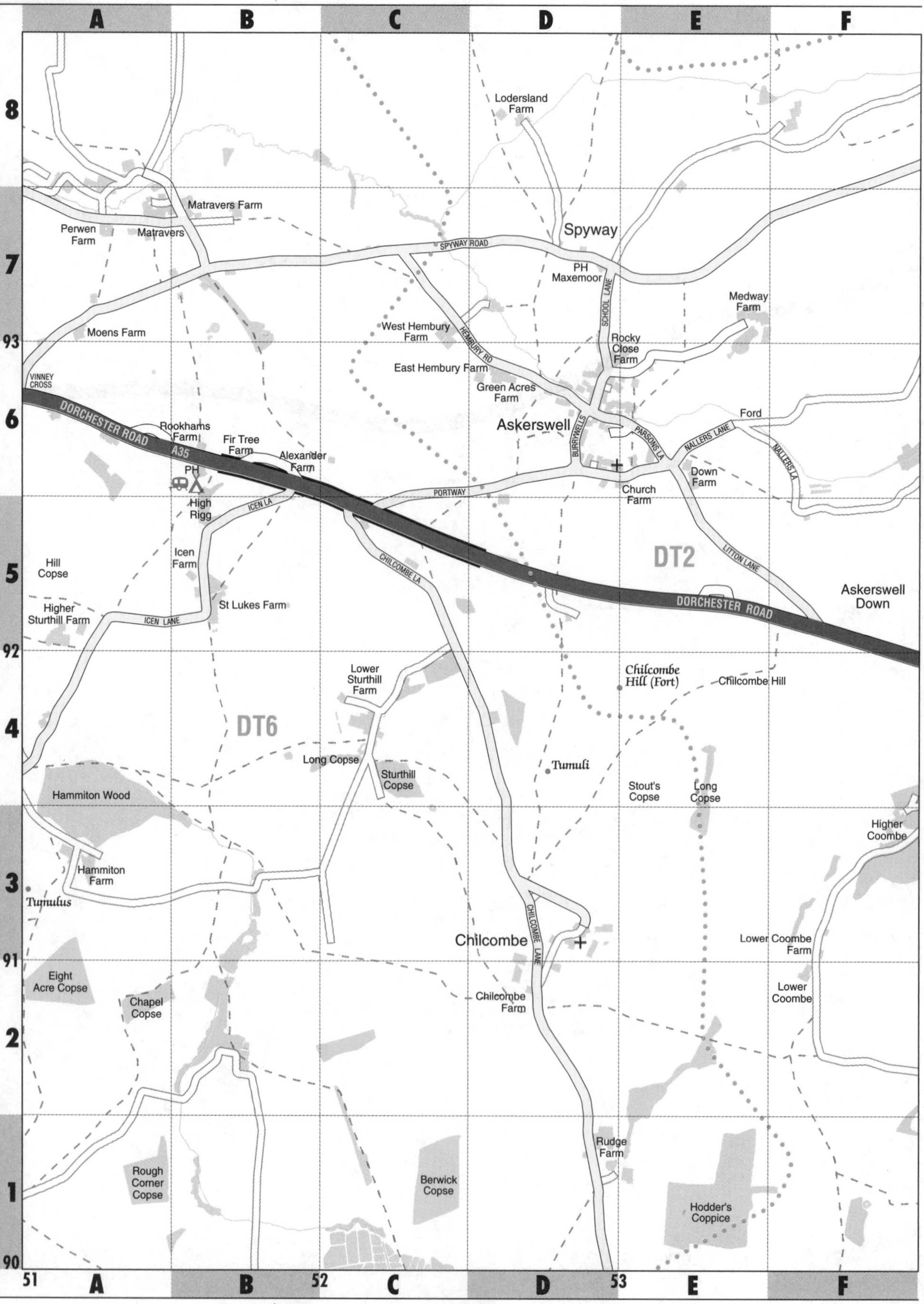

A B C D E F

8

Lodersland Farm

Matravers Farm

Spyway

Perwen Farm

Matravers

7

SPYWAY ROAD

PH Maxemoor

SCHOOL LANE

Medway Farm

93

Moens Farm

West Hembury Farm

Rocky Close Farm

HEMBURY RD

East Hembury Farm

Green Acres Farm

Ford

VINNEY CROSS

6

DORCHESTER ROAD

A35

Rookhams Farm

Fir Tree Farm

Alexander Farm

Askerswell

BURYWELLS

PARSONS LA

NALLERS LANE

NALLERS LA

Down Farm

PH

High Rigg

ICEN LA

PORTWAY

Church Farm

DT2

LITTON LANE

5

Hill Copse

Icen Farm

CHILCOMBE LA

DORCHESTER ROAD

Askerswell Down

Higher Sturthill Farm

ICEN LANE

St Lukes Farm

92

Lower Sturthill Farm

Chilcombe Hill (Fort)

Chilcombe Hill

4

DT6

Long Copse

Sturthill Copse

Tumuli

Stout's Copse

Long Copse

Higher Coombe

Hammiton Wood

3

Tumulus

Hammiton Farm

CHILCOMBE LANE

Chilcombe

Lower Coombe Farm

91

Eight Acre Copse

Chapel Copse

Chilcombe Farm

Lower Coombe

2

Rudge Farm

1

Rough Corner Copse

Berwick Copse

Hodder's Coppice

90

51 A B 52 C D 53 E F

71
104
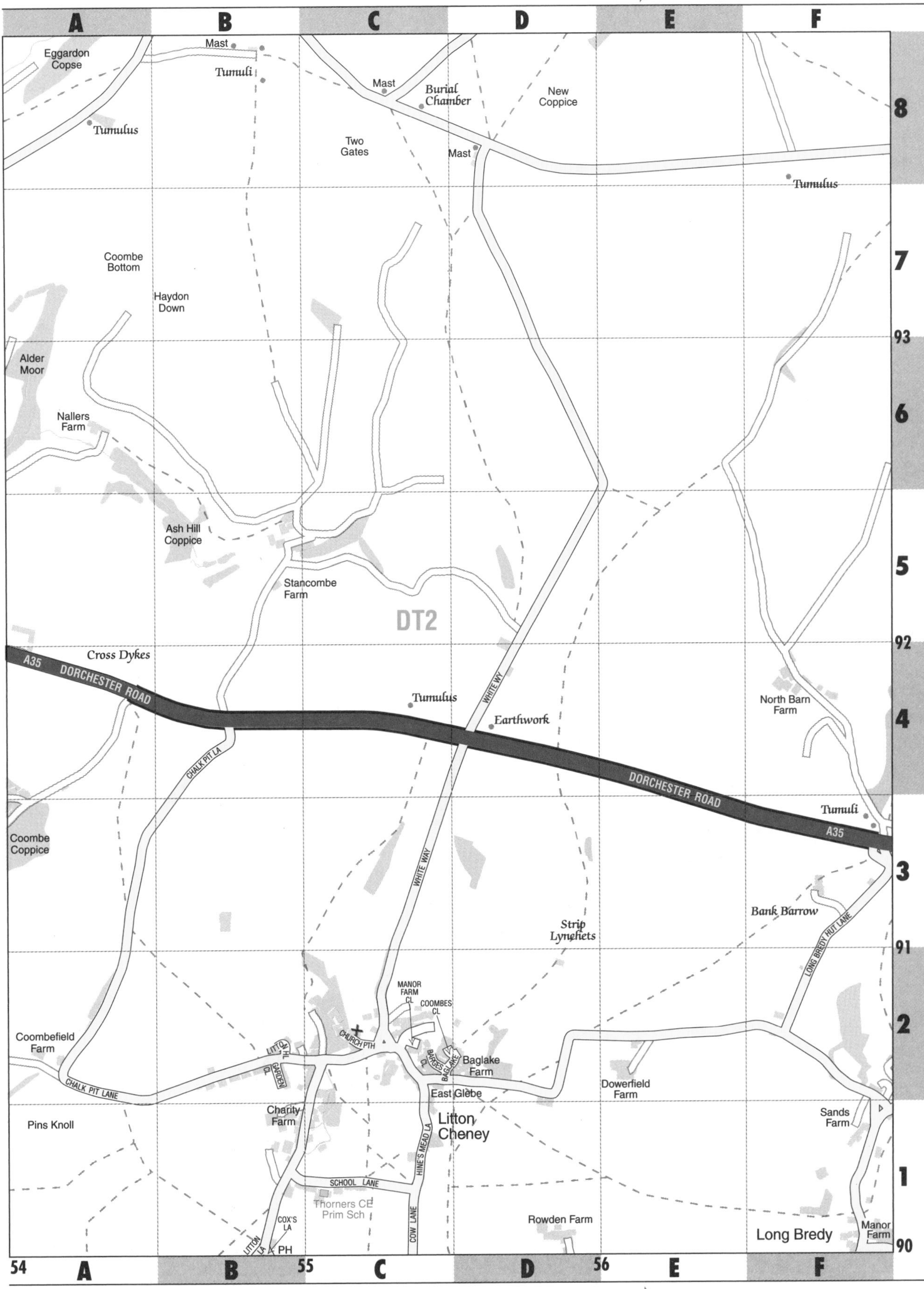
Eggardon Copse
Mast
Tumuli
Tumulus
Mast
Burial Chamber
New Coppice
Two Gates
Mast
Tumulus
Coombe Bottom
Haydon Down
Alder Moor
Nallers Farm
Ash Hill Coppice
Stancombe Farm
DT2
Cross Dykes
A35
DORCHESTER ROAD
Tumulus
WHITE WY
Earthwork
North Barn Farm
CHALK PIT LA
DORCHESTER ROAD
Tumuli
A35
Coombe Coppice
WHITE WAY
Bank Barrow
Strip Lynchets
LONG BREDY HUT LANE
MANOR FARM CL
COOMBES CL
CHURCH PTH
Coombefield Farm
LITTON HL
GARDEN CL
BARGES CL
BAGLAKE
Baglake Farm
CHALK PIT LANE
East Glebe
Dowerfield Farm
Pins Knoll
Charity Farm
Litton Cheney
Sands Farm
HINE'S MEAD LA
SCHOOL LANE
Thorners CE Prim Sch
COX'S LA
COW LANE
Rowden Farm
Long Bredy
Manor Farm
LITTON LA
PH
A B C D E F
8 7 93 6 5 92 4 3 91 2 1 90
54 55 56
130
104

103
72

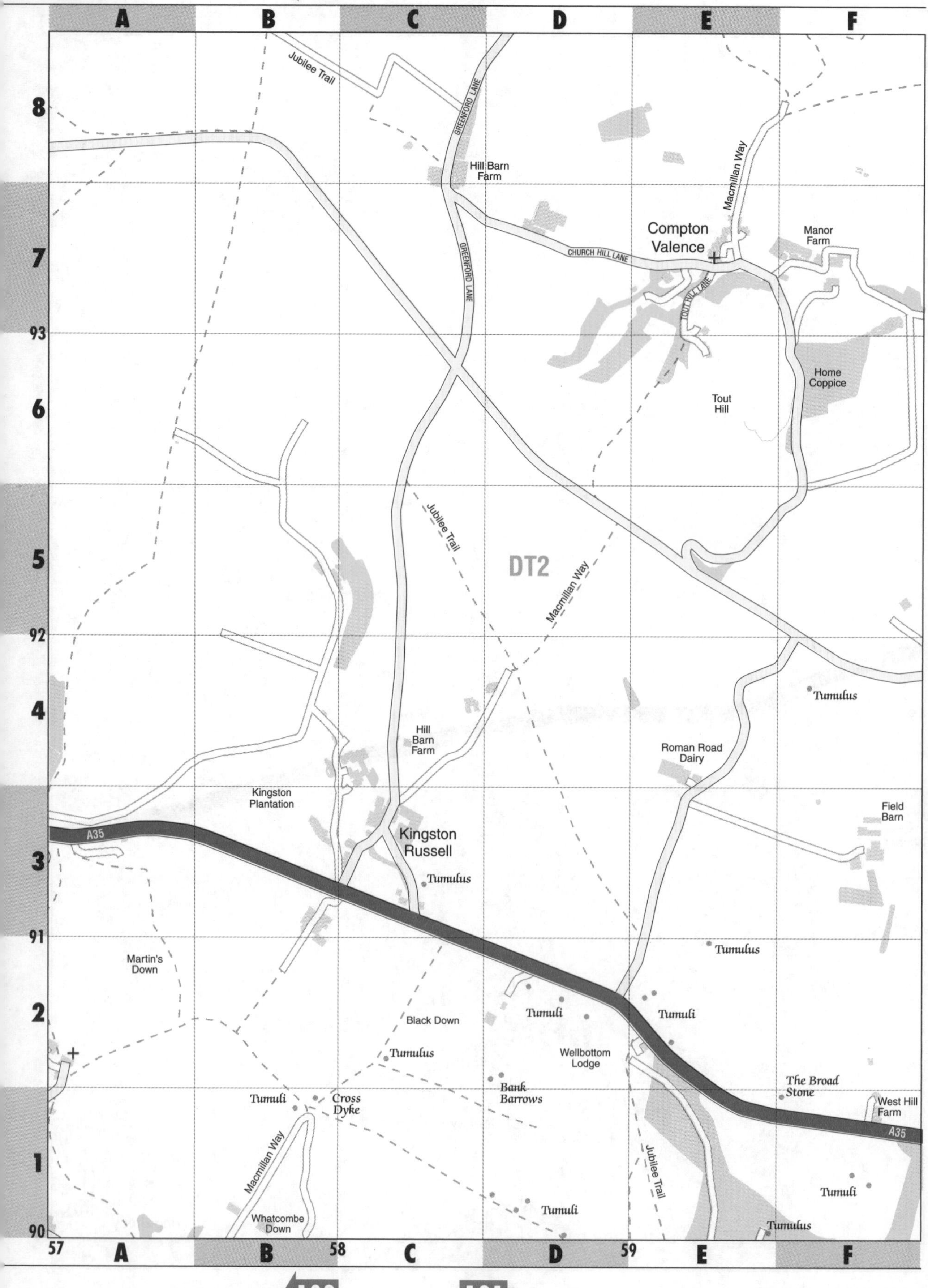
A
B
C
D
E
F
8
7
93
6
5
92
4
3
91
2
1
90
57
58
59
Jubilee Trail
GREENFORD LANE
Hill Barn Farm
Macmillan Way
Compton Valence
CHURCH HILL LANE
Manor Farm
TOUT HILL LANE
Home Coppice
Tout Hill
DT2
Macmillan Way
Jubilee Trail
Tumulus
Hill Barn Farm
Roman Road Dairy
Kingston Plantation
Field Barn
A35
Kingston Russell
Tumulus
Tumulus
Martin's Down
Tumuli
Tumuli
Black Down
Tumulus
Wellbottom Lodge
Bank Barrows
The Broad Stone
Tumuli
Cross Dyke
West Hill Farm
A35
Macmillan Way
Jubilee Trail
Tumuli
Tumuli
Whatcombe Down
Tumulus

103
131

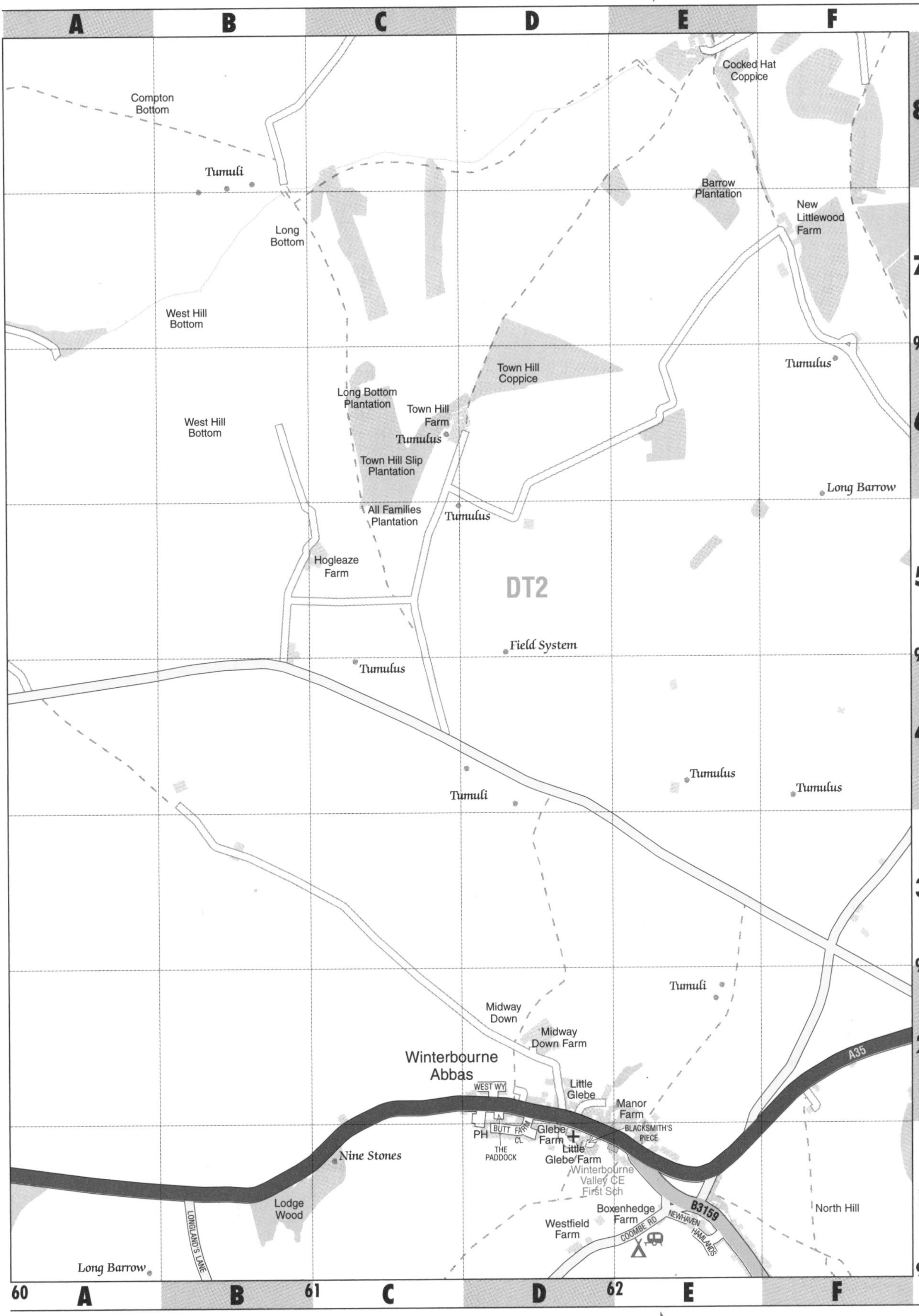

73
106

A B C D E F

8
7
93
6
5
92
4
91
3
2
1
90

Cocked Hat Coppice

Compton Bottom

Tumuli

Long Bottom

Barrow Plantation

New Littlewood Farm

West Hill Bottom

Town Hill Coppice

Tumulus

West Hill Bottom

Long Bottom Plantation

Town Hill Farm

Tumulus

Town Hill Slip Plantation

Long Barrow

All Families Plantation

Tumulus

DT2

Hogleaze Farm

Field System

Tumulus

Tumulus

Tumulus

Tumuli

Tumulus

Tumuli

A35

Tumuli

Midway Down

Midway Down Farm

Winterbourne Abbas

Little Glebe

Manor Farm

WEST WY

BUTT FARM CL

PH

BLACKSMITH'S PIECE

Glebe Farm

Nine Stones

THE PADDOCK

Little Glebe Farm

Winterbourne Valley CE First Sch

B3159

Lodge Wood

Boxenhedge Farm

North Hill

Westfield Farm

COOMBE RD

NEWHAVEN

HAYLANDS

Long Barrow

LONGLAND'S LANE

60 A B 61 C D 62 E F

105
74

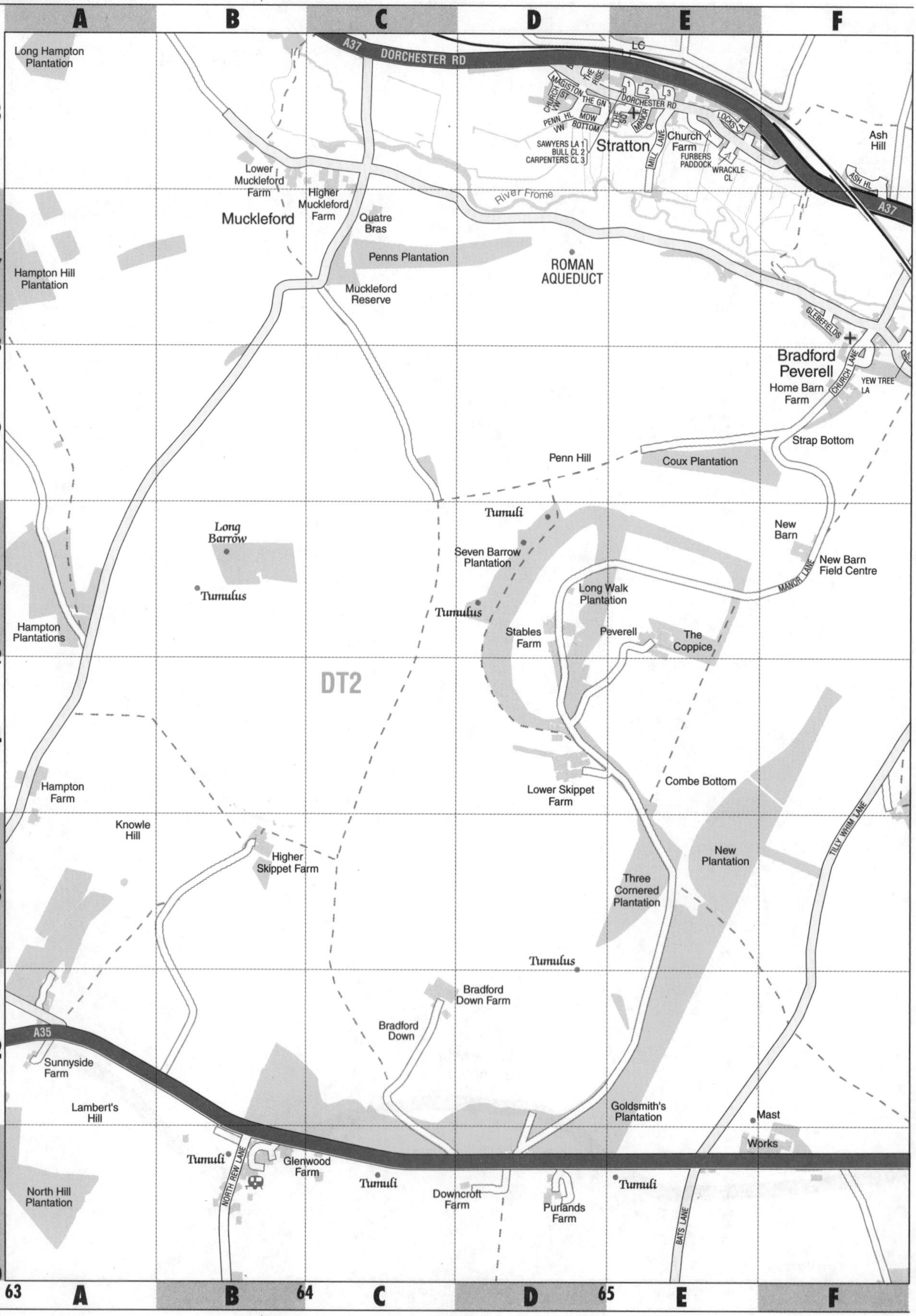

A | B | C | D | E | F

8

Long Hampton
Plantation

A37 DORCHESTER RD

LC

CHURCH ST
MAGISTON
THE GN
1 2 3
DORCHESTER RD
THE RISE
PENN HL
VW
MDW
BOTTOM
LOCKS A
SAWYERS LA 1
BULL CL 2
CARPENTERS CL 3
Stratton
MILL LANE
MANOR
Church
Farm
FURBERS
PADDOCK
WRACKLE
CL

Ash
Hill

A37

Lower
Muckleford
Farm

Higher
Muckleford
Farm

Muckleford

Quatre
Bras

River Frome

7

Hampton Hill
Plantation

Penns Plantation

ROMAN
AQUEDUCT

GLEBEFIELDS

Muckleford
Reserve

Bradford
Peverell

93

Home Barn
Farm

YEW TREE
LA

CHURCH LANE

6

Penn Hill

Coux Plantation

Strap Bottom

New
Barn

New Barn
Field Centre

Long
Barrow

Tumuli

Seven Barrow
Plantation

Long Walk
Plantation

MANOR LANE

5

Tumulus

Tumulus

Stables
Farm

Peverell

The
Coppice

92

Hampton
Plantations

DT2

4

Hampton
Farm

Lower Skippet
Farm

Combe Bottom

TILLY WHIM LANE

Knowle
Hill

Higher
Skippet Farm

New
Plantation

3

Three
Cornered
Plantation

91

Tumulus

A35

Bradford
Down Farm

2

Sunnyside
Farm

Bradford
Down

Goldsmith's
Plantation

Mast

Lambert's
Hill

Works

NORTH PEW LANE

Tumuli

Glenwood
Farm

Tumuli

Downcroft
Farm

Purlands
Farm

Tumuli

BATS LANE

1

North Hill
Plantation

90

63 | A | B | 64 | C | D | 65 | E | F

75
108

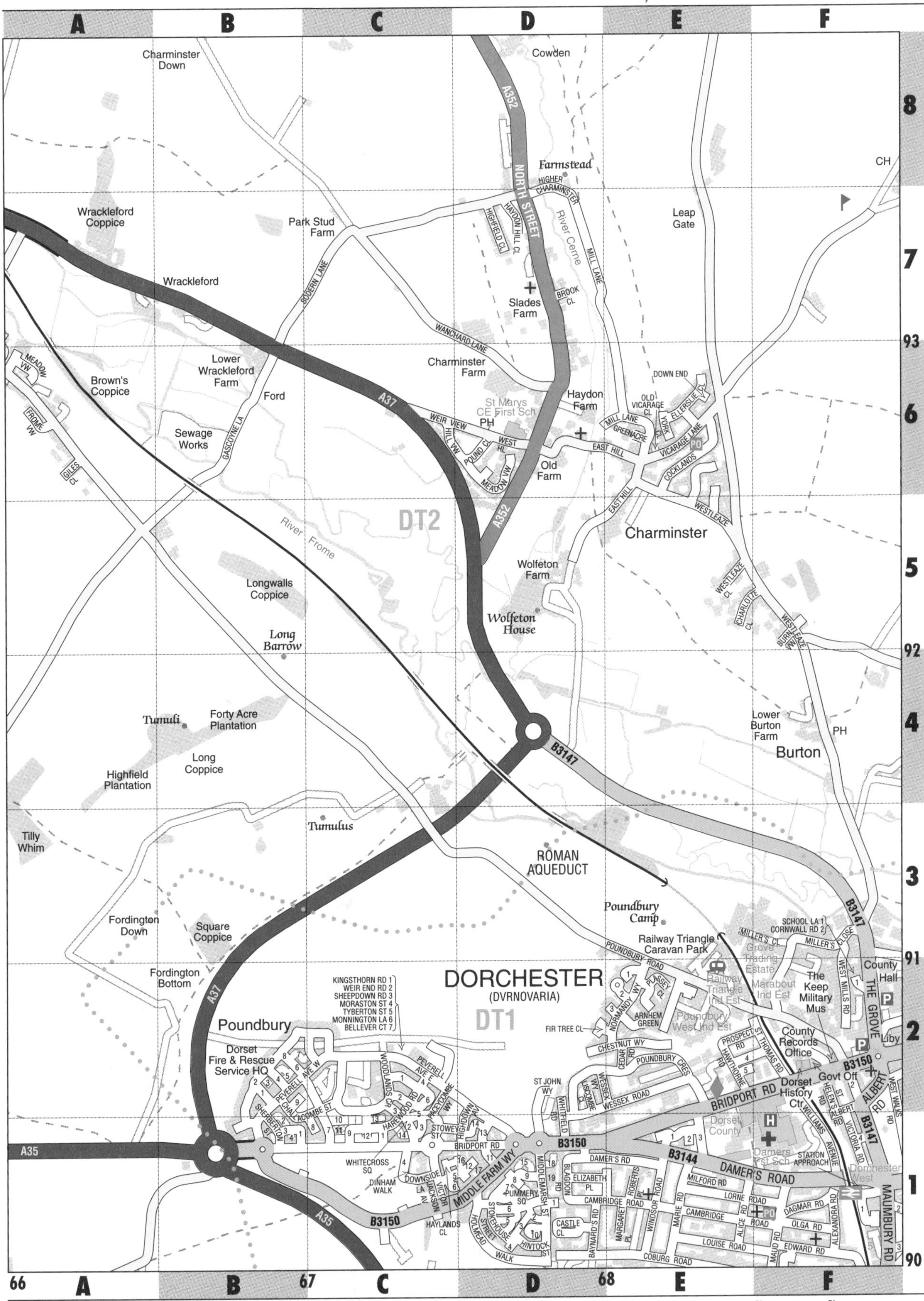

B1
1 BEECHWOOD LA
2 SHAPLEY CT
3 CHERRYBROOK LA
4 YARDWORTHY

B2
1 WESTCOTT ST
2 GREAT CRANFORD ST
3 DARTMEET CT
4 STANNON ST
5 HEXWORTHY CT
6 DUNNABRIDGE ST
7 OAKERY CT
8 DUNNABRIDGE SQ
9 RUNDLESTONE CT

C1
1 ELVASTONE ST
2 ACONBURY AVE
3 KING'S PITT
4 BILLINGSMOOR LA
5 NETHERTON ST
6 BRISTON CL
7 LYDGATE ST
8 HERMITAGE CT
9 HESSARY ST
10 TAVITON CT
11 BABENY WK
12 LOWER BLAKEMERE RD
13 DEWSALL PL
14 MERRIVALE

D1
1 CAMBRIDGE WK
2 WISHAY ST
3 ASHINGTON ST
4 CHASEBOROUGH SQ
5 BARLAKE CT
6 BURRATON SQ
7 CASEBERRY CT
8 BROOKHOUSE ST
9 STOWCASTLE ST
10 WELLAND CT
11 NANTILLO ST
12 PENDRUFFLE LA
13 WINDSLADE ST
14 PENBUGLE YD
15 PITCOTE LA
16 TINTERN LA
17 PENHALE WK
18 SPRINGHAM WK
19 EVERSHOT WK

134
108

E1
1 FOURGATES RD
2 COWLEY CL
3 GLOUCESTER RD

E2
1 WYVERN RD
2 MALTA CL
3 HOLLY CL
4 MOUNTAIN ASH RD
5 HAWTHORN CL

F1
1 GREAT WESTERN RD
2 FAIRFIELD RD
3 UPPER FAIRFIELD RD
4 WESTOVER RD
5 Great Western Ind Ctr

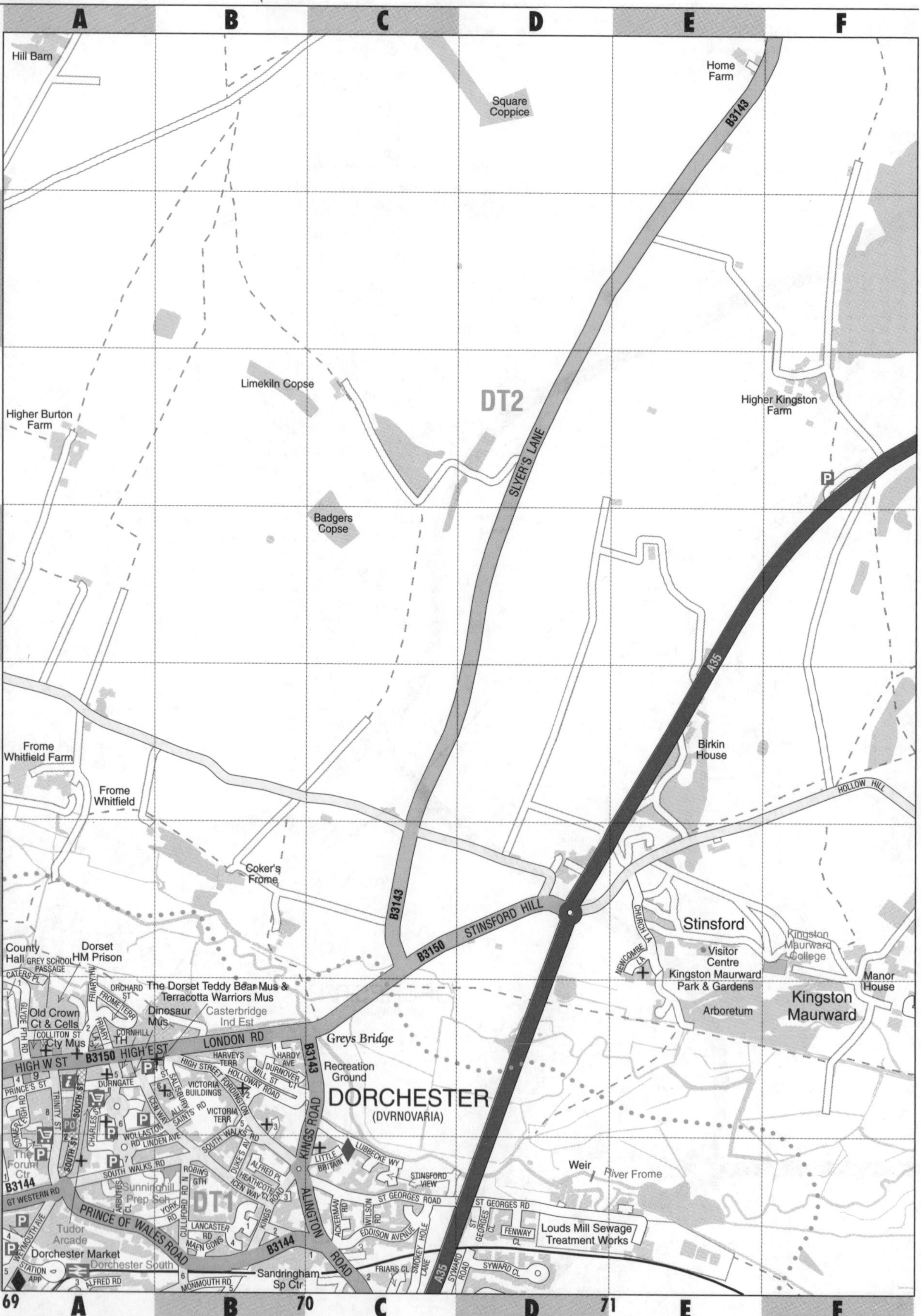

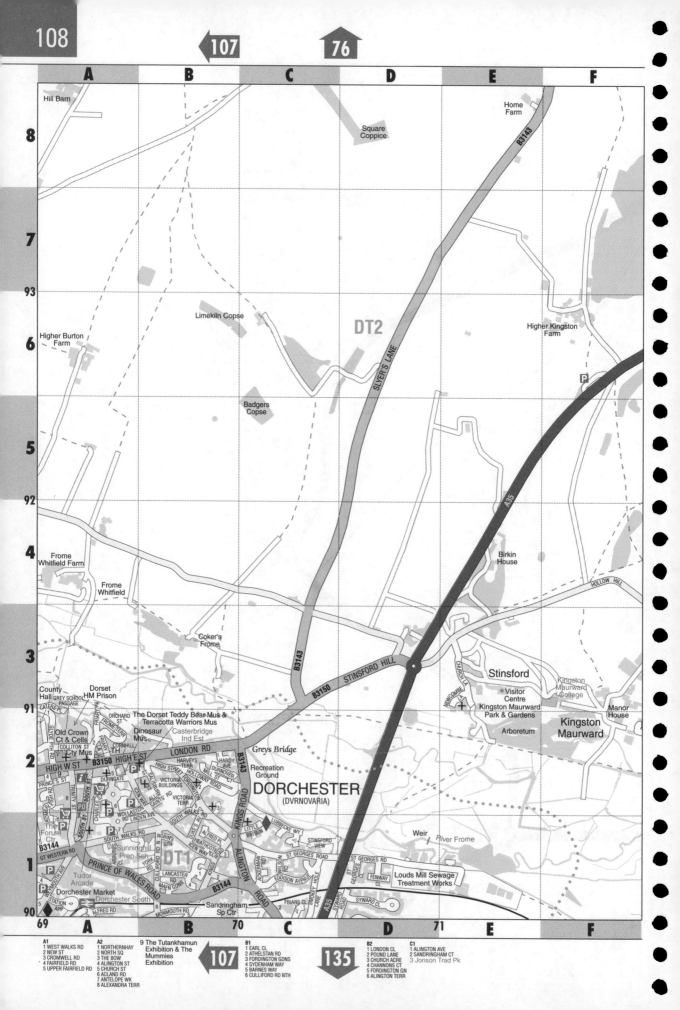

107
76

A B C D E F

8
7
93
6
5
92
4
3
91
2
1
90

Hill Barn

Square
Coppice

Home
Farm

B3143

DT2

Higher Kingston
Farm

Limekiln Copse

Higher Burton
Farm

SLYER'S LANE

Badgers
Copse

P

A35

Birkin
House

HOLLOW HILL

Frome
Whitfield Farm

Frome
Whitfield

Coker's
Frome

B3143

STINSFORD HILL

B3150

Stinsford

Visitor
Centre
Kingston Maurward
Park & Gardens

Kingston
Maurward
College

Manor
House

Kingston
Maurward

CHURCH LA

NEWCOMBE LA

Arboretum

County
Hall GREY SCHOOL
PASSAGE
CATERS PL
Dorset
HM Prison

Old Crown
Ct & Cells
COLLITON ST
Cty Mus
ORCHARD
ST
CORNHILL
TH
The Dorset Teddy Bear Mus &
Terracotta Warriors Mus
Dinosaur
Mus
Casterbridge
Ind Est

LONDON RD
Greys Bridge

HIGH W ST
B3150 HIGH E ST
HARVEYS
TERR
HARDY
AVE
DURNOVER
ST
B3143
Recreation
Ground

HIGH STREET
FORDINGTON

HOLLOWAY
ROAD

MILL
ST

DORCHESTER
(DVRNOVARIA)

PRINCE'S ST
TRINITY ST
DURNGATE
SALT LANE
ALL
SAINTS
RD
VICTORIA
BUILDINGS
VICTORIA
TERR
i
PO
CHARLES ST
SOUTH ST
ICEN WAY
WOLLASTON
RD LINDEN AVE
SOUTH WALKS RD
DUKE'S AVE
ALFRED PL
HEATHCOTE RD

KINGS ROAD

Little
Britain
LUBBECKE WY

Weir
River Frome

The
Forum
Ctr
B3144
GT WESTERN RD
PRINCE OF WALES ROAD
ARBUTUS CL
Sunninghill
Prep Sch
DT1
ROBINS
GTH
CULLIFORD RD
YORK
RD
LANCASTER
RD
MAEN GDNS

ALINGTON ROAD
ALKERMAN RD
WILSON
RD
ICEN WAY CL
EDDISON AVENUE
SMOKEY HOLE LANE
FRIARS CL
ST GEORGES RD
ST GEORGES ROAD
STINSFORD
VIEW

GEORGES
RD
FENWAY
CL
SYWARD CL
Louds Mill Sewage
Treatment Works

Tudor
Arcade
Dorchester Market
Dorchester South
STATION
APP
P
WEYMOUTH AVE
ALFRED RD
MONMOUTH RD
B3144
Sandringham
Sp Ctr

69 A 70 B C 71 D E F

A1
1 WEST WALKS RD
2 NEW ST
3 CROMWELL RD
4 FAIRFIELD RD
5 UPPER FAIRFIELD RD

A2
1 NORTHERNHAY
2 NORTH SQ
3 THE BOW
4 ALINGTON ST
5 CHURCH ST
6 ACLAND RD
7 ANTELOPE WK
8 ALEXANDRA TERR

9 The Tutankhamun
Exhibition & The
Mummies
Exhibition

B1
1 EARL CL
2 ATHELSTAN RD
3 FORDINGTON GDNS
4 SYDENHAM WAY
5 BARNES WAY
6 CULLIFORD RD NTH

B2
1 LONDON CL
2 POUND LANE
3 CHURCH ACRE
4 CHANNONS CT
5 FORDINGTON GN
6 ALINGTON TERR

C1
1 ALINGTON AVE
2 SANDRINGHAM CT
3 Jonson Trad Pk

107
135

77
110

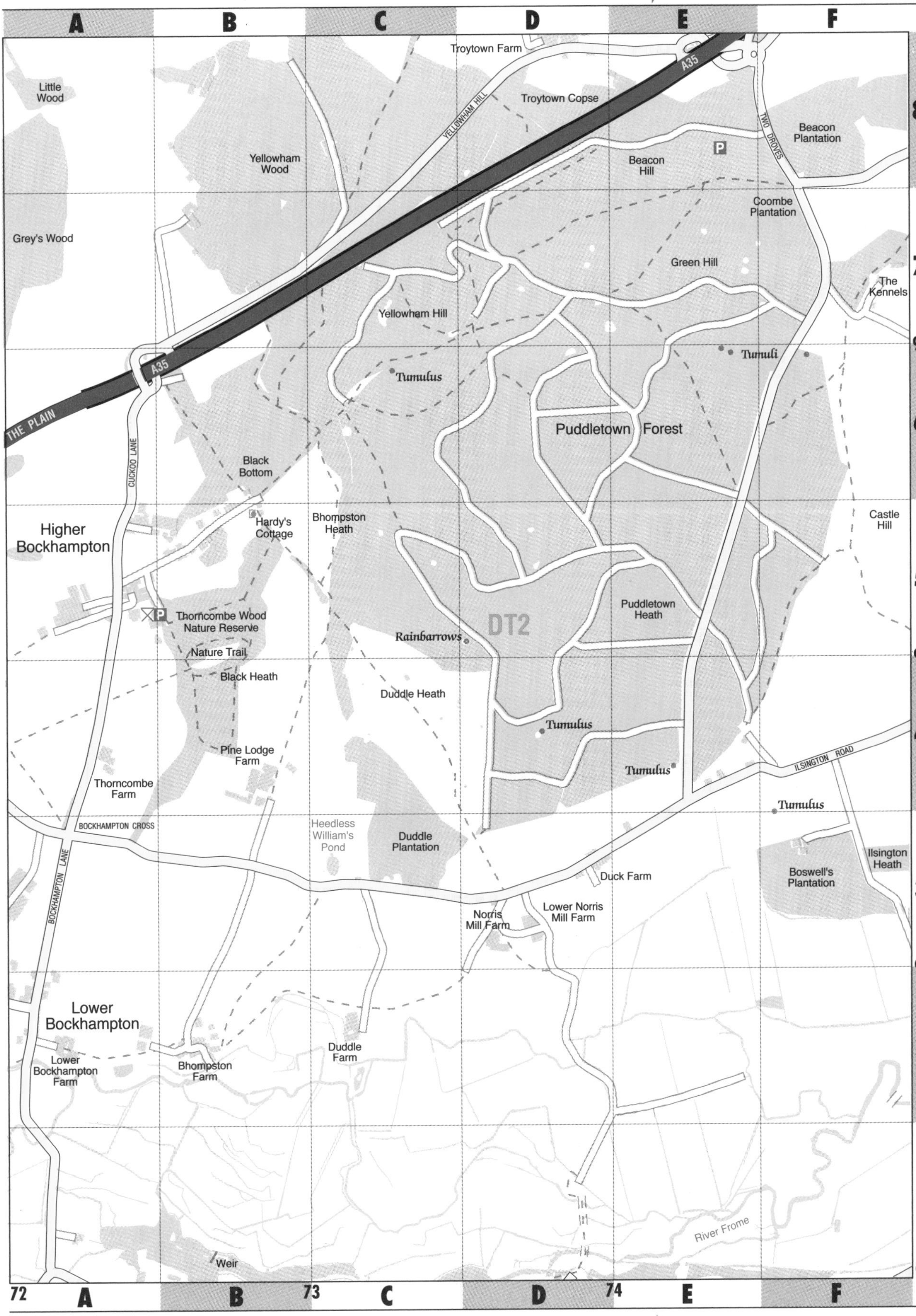
A B C D E F
8
7
6
5
4
3
2
1
93
92
91
90
72
73
74
Troytown Farm
Little Wood
Troytown Copse
A35
Yellowham Wood
Yellowham Hill
Two Droves
Beacon Plantation
Beacon Hill
Grey's Wood
Coombe Plantation
Green Hill
The Kennels
Yellowham Hill
Tumuli
Tumulus
The Plain
Puddletown Forest
Cuckoo Lane
Black Bottom
Higher Bockhampton
Hardy's Cottage
Bhompston Heath
Castle Hill
Thorncombe Wood Nature Reserve
Puddletown Heath
Nature Trail
Rainbarrows
DT2
Black Heath
Duddle Heath
Tumulus
Pine Lodge Farm
Tumulus
Ilsington Road
Thorncombe Farm
Tumulus
Bockhampton Cross
Heedless William's Pond
Duddle Plantation
Ilsington Heath
Duck Farm
Boswell's Plantation
Bockhampton Lane
Norris Mill Farm
Lower Norris Mill Farm
Lower Bockhampton
Lower Bockhampton Farm
Bhompston Farm
Duddle Farm
River Frome
Weir

136
110

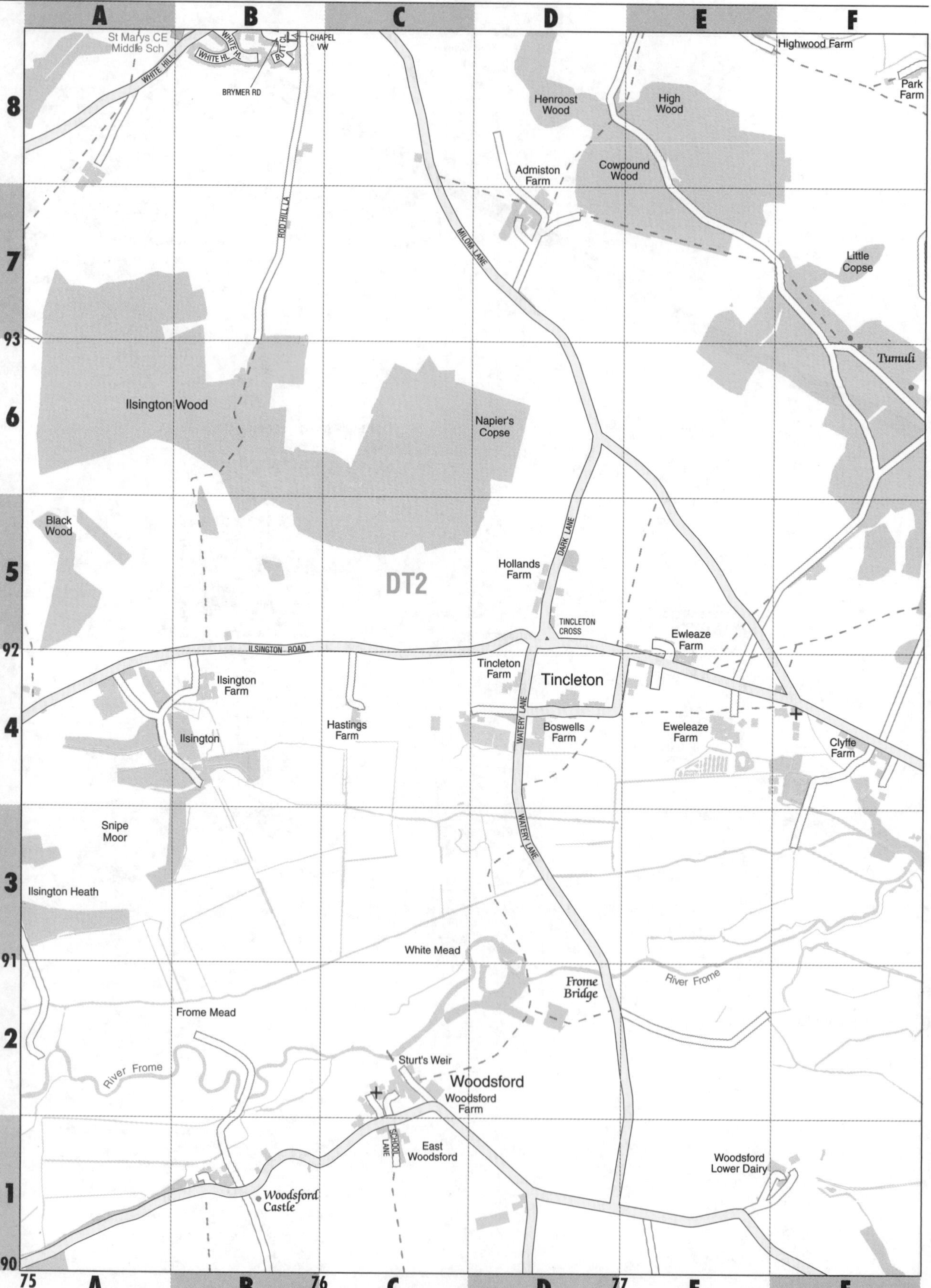

109
78

St Marys CE
Middle Sch

WHITE HILL

WHITE HL

CHAPEL
VW

BRYMER RD

BROTHILL LA

MILOR LANE

Highwood Farm

Park
Farm

Henroost
Wood

High
Wood

Admiston
Farm

Cowpound
Wood

Little
Copse

Ilsington Wood

Napier's
Copse

Tumuli

DARK LANE

Black
Wood

DT2

Hollands
Farm

TINCLETON
CROSS

Ewleaze
Farm

ILSINGTON ROAD

Tincleton
Farm

Tincleton

Ilsington
Farm

Hastings
Farm

Ilsington

WATERY LANE

Boswells
Farm

Eweleaze
Farm

Clyffe
Farm

Snipe
Moor

Ilsington Heath

WATERY LANE

White Mead

River Frome

Frome
Bridge

Frome Mead

River Frome

Sturt's Weir

Woodsford

Woodsford
Farm

SCHOOL LANE

East
Woodsford

Woodsford
Lower Dairy

Woodsford
Castle

109
137

79
112

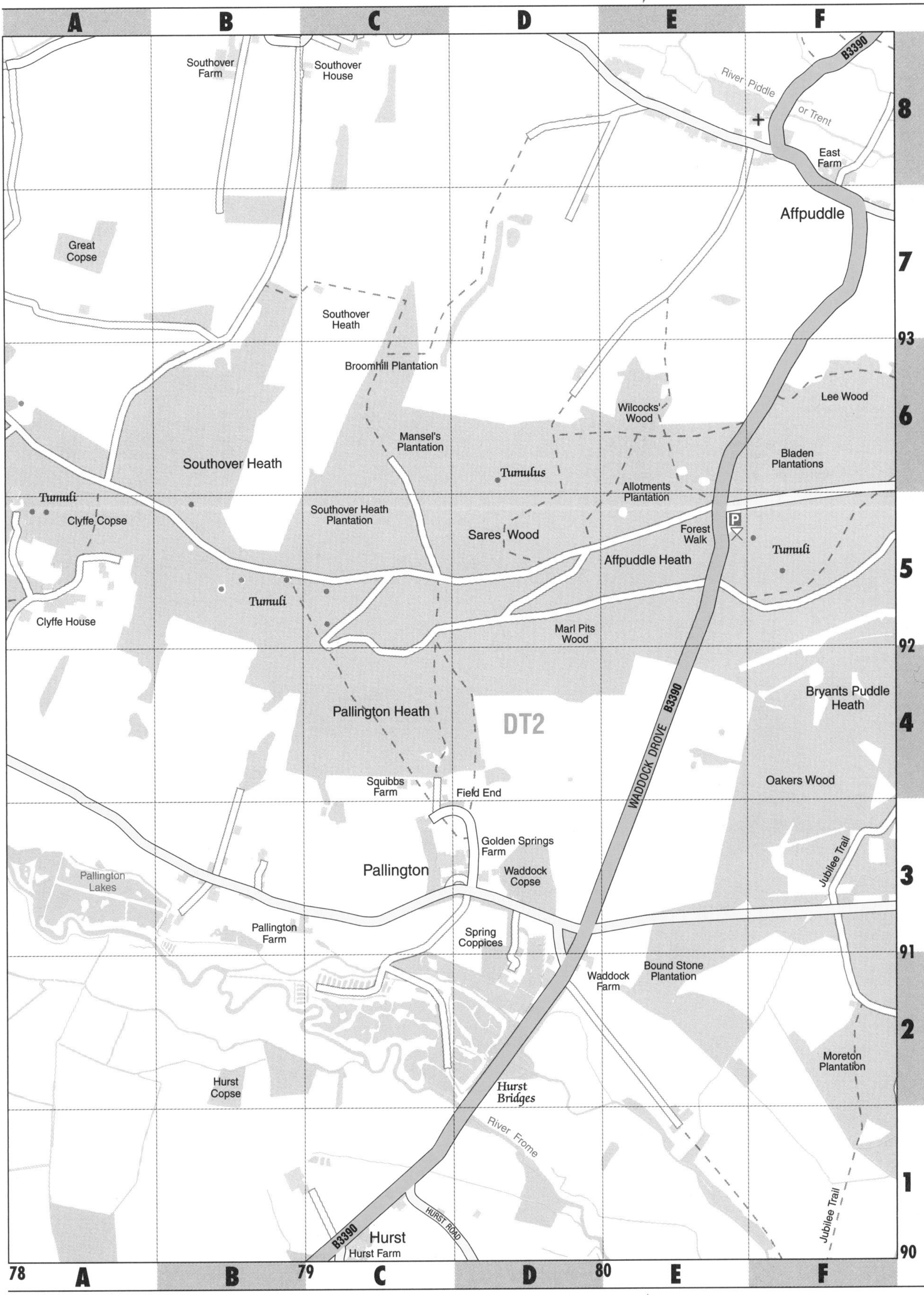
A
B
C
D
E
F
Southover Farm
Southover House
River Piddle or Trent
B3390
East Farm
Affpuddle
Great Copse
Southover Heath
Broomhill Plantation
Lee Wood
Wilcocks' Wood
Mansel's Plantation
Bladen Plantations
Southover Heath
Tumulus
Allotments Plantation
Tumuli
Clyffe Copse
Southover Heath Plantation
Sares Wood
Forest Walk
Tumuli
Affpuddle Heath
Tumuli
Clyffe House
Marl Pits Wood
Bryants Puddle Heath
Pallington Heath
DT2
WADDOCK DROVE
B3390
Oakers Wood
Squibbs Farm
Field End
Golden Springs Farm
Jubilee Trail
Pallington Lakes
Pallington
Waddock Copse
Pallington Farm
Spring Coppices
Waddock Farm
Bound Stone Plantation
Moreton Plantation
Hurst Copse
Hurst Bridges
River Frome
Jubilee Trail
HURST ROAD
B3390
Hurst
Hurst Farm
8
7
93
6
5
92
4
3
91
2
1
90
78
79
80

138
112

← 111
80

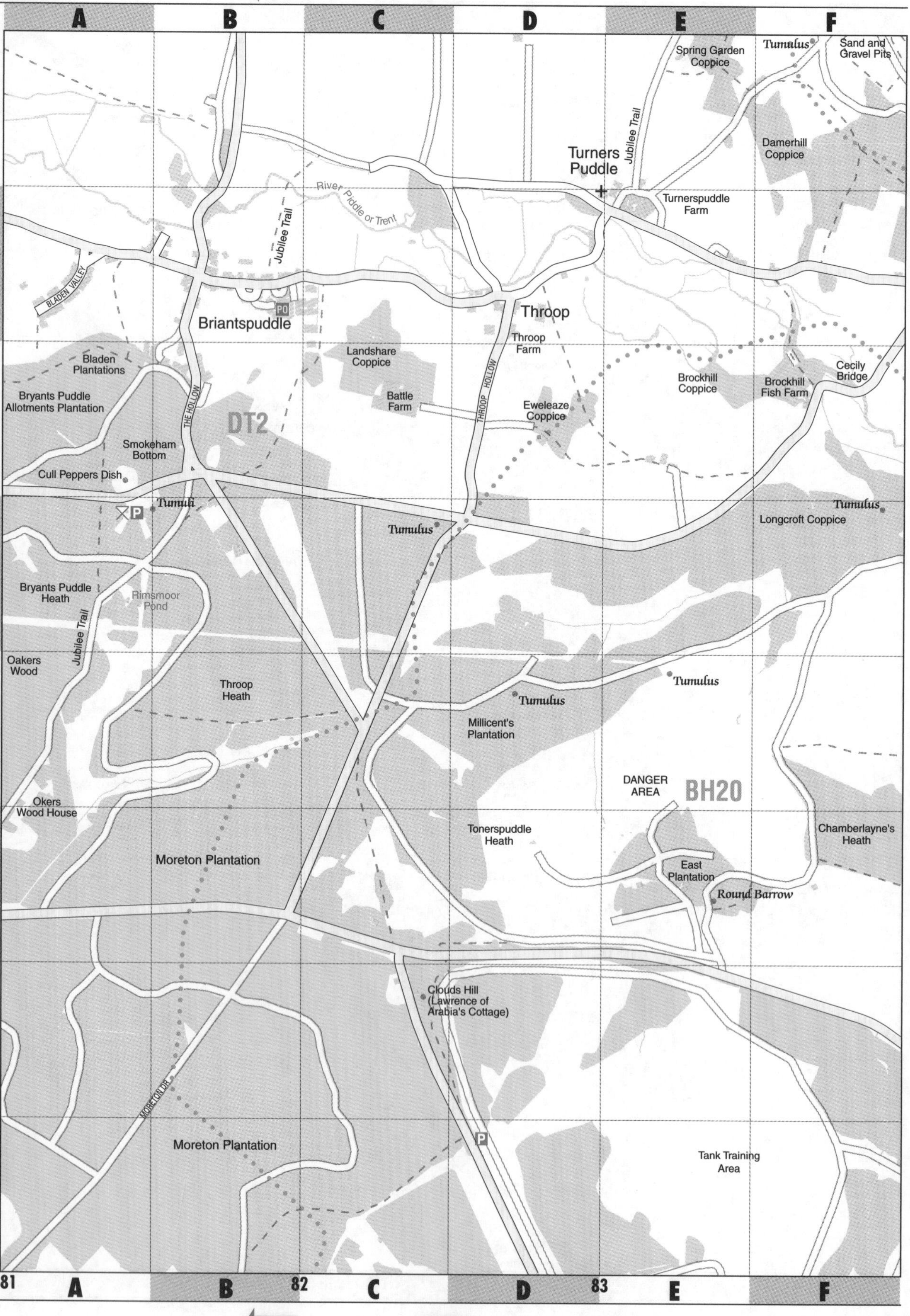

A B C D E F

8

7

93

6

5

92

4

3

91

2

1

90

Bladen Plantations
Bryants Puddle Allotments Plantation
Bladen Valley
Briantspuddle
PO
THE HOLLOW
DT2
Smokeham Bottom
Cull Peppers Dish
Tumuli
Bryants Puddle Heath
Rimsmoor Pond
Oakers Wood
Jubilee Trail
Throop Heath
Okers Wood House
Moreton Plantation
MORETON DR
Moreton Plantation

River Piddle or Trent
Jubilee Trail
Landshare Coppice
Battle Farm
Tumulus
Millicent's Plantation
Tumulus
Tonerspuddle Heath
Clouds Hill (Lawrence of Arabia's Cottage)
P

Spring Garden Coppice
Tumulus
Sand and Gravel Pits
Damerhill Coppice
Turners Puddle
Jubilee Trail
Turnerspuddle Farm
Throop
Throop Farm
THROOP HOLLOW
Eweleaze Coppice
Brockhill Coppice
Cecily Bridge
Brockhill Fish Farm
Tumulus
Longcroft Coppice
Tumulus
DANGER AREA
BH20
Chamberlayne's Heath
East Plantation
Round Barrow
Tank Training Area

81 A B 82 C D 83 E F

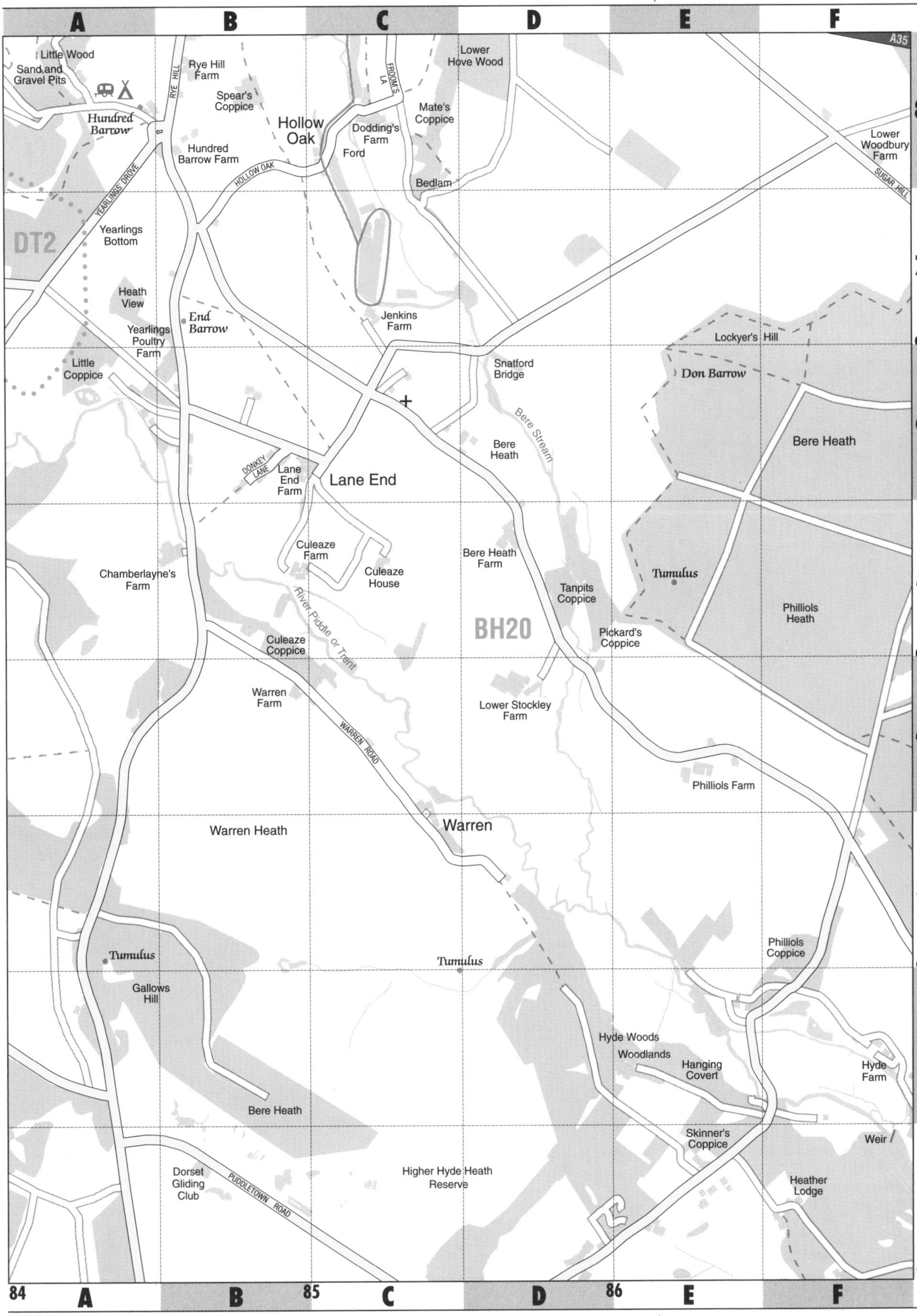

A B C D E F

A35

Little Wood
Sand and
Gravel Pits
Hundred
Barrow

RYE HILL
Rye Hill
Farm
Spear's
Coppice
Hundred
Barrow Farm

HOLLOW OAK
Hollow
Oak

FROOM'S LA
Dodding's
Farm
Ford

Lower
Hove Wood
Mate's
Coppice
Bedlam

Lower
Woodbury
Farm

SUGAR HILL

8

DT2
YEARLINGS DRIVE
Yearlings
Bottom

Heath
View

Yearlings
Poultry
Farm

Little
Coppice

End
Barrow

Jenkins
Farm

Snatford
Bridge

Bere Stream

Lockyer's Hill

Don Barrow

Bere Heath

7

93

6

DONKEY LANE
Lane
End
Farm
Lane End

Culeaze
Farm
Culeaze
House

Bere
Heath

Bere Heath
Farm

Tanpits
Coppice

Tumulus

Bere Heath

Philliols
Heath

5

Chamberlayne's
Farm

Culeaze
Coppice

River Piddle or Trent

Warren
Farm

WARREN ROAD

BH20

Pickard's
Coppice

Lower Stockley
Farm

92

Warren Heath

Warren

Philliols Farm

4

Tumulus
Gallows
Hill

Tumulus

Philliols
Coppice

91

Hyde Woods
Woodlands

Hanging
Covert

Hyde
Farm

2

Bere Heath

Dorset
Gliding
Club

PUDDLETOWN ROAD

Higher Hyde Heath
Reserve

Skinner's
Coppice

Weir

Heather
Lodge

1

90

84 A B 85 C D 86 E F

113
82

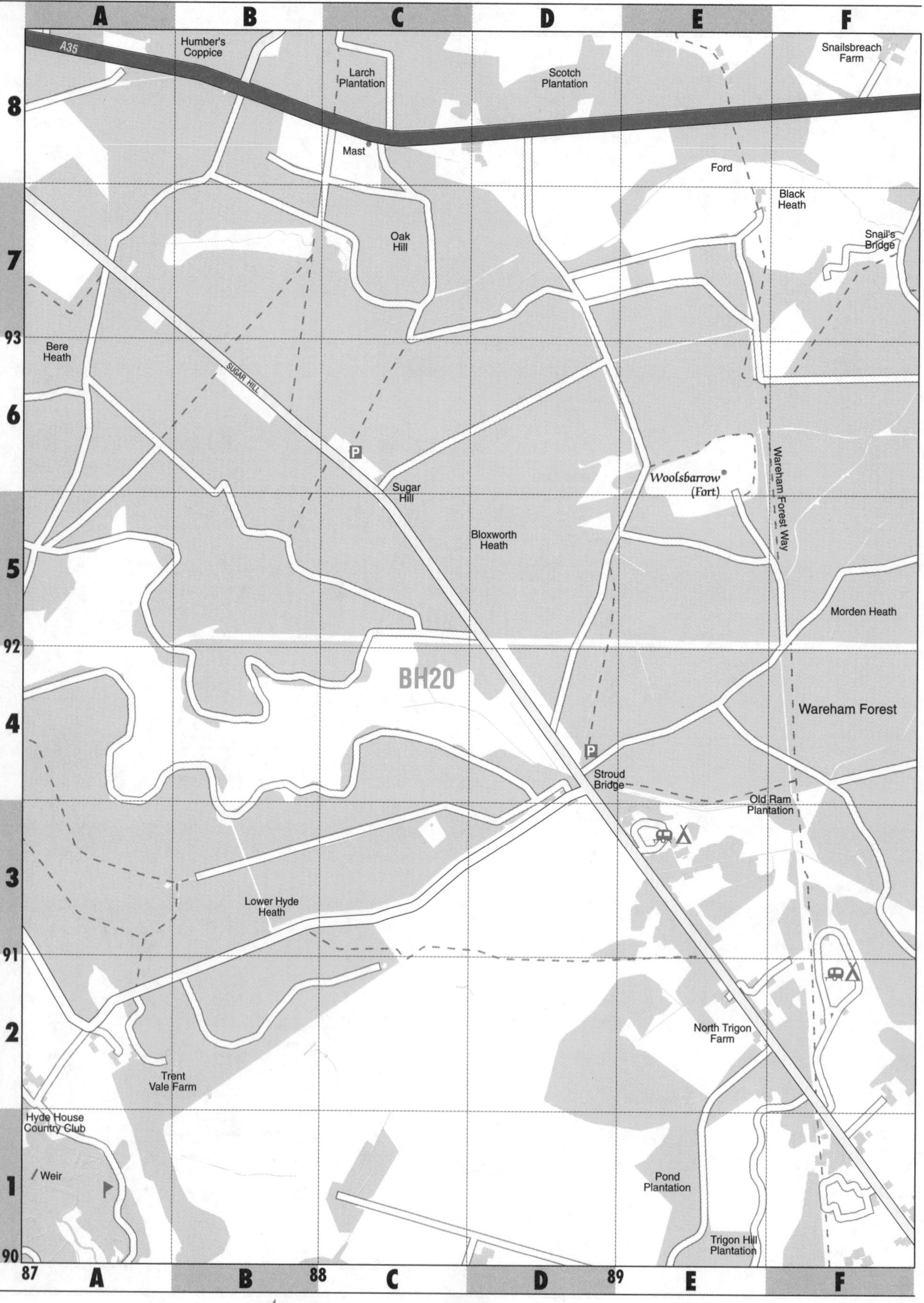

A B C D E F

A35

Humber's
Coppice

Larch
Plantation

Scotch
Plantation

Snailsbreach
Farm

8

Mast

Ford

Black
Heath

Snail's
Bridge

Oak
Hill

7

93

Bere
Heath

SUGAR HILL

Woolsbarrow
(Fort)

Wareham Forest Way

6

P

Sugar
Hill

Bloxworth
Heath

Morden Heath

5

92

BH20

Wareham Forest

4

P

Stroud
Bridge

Old Ram
Plantation

3

Lower Hyde
Heath

91

North Trigon
Farm

2

Trent
Vale Farm

Hyde House
Country Club

Pond
Plantation

1

Weir

Trigon Hill
Plantation

90

87 A B 88 C D 89 E F

83
116

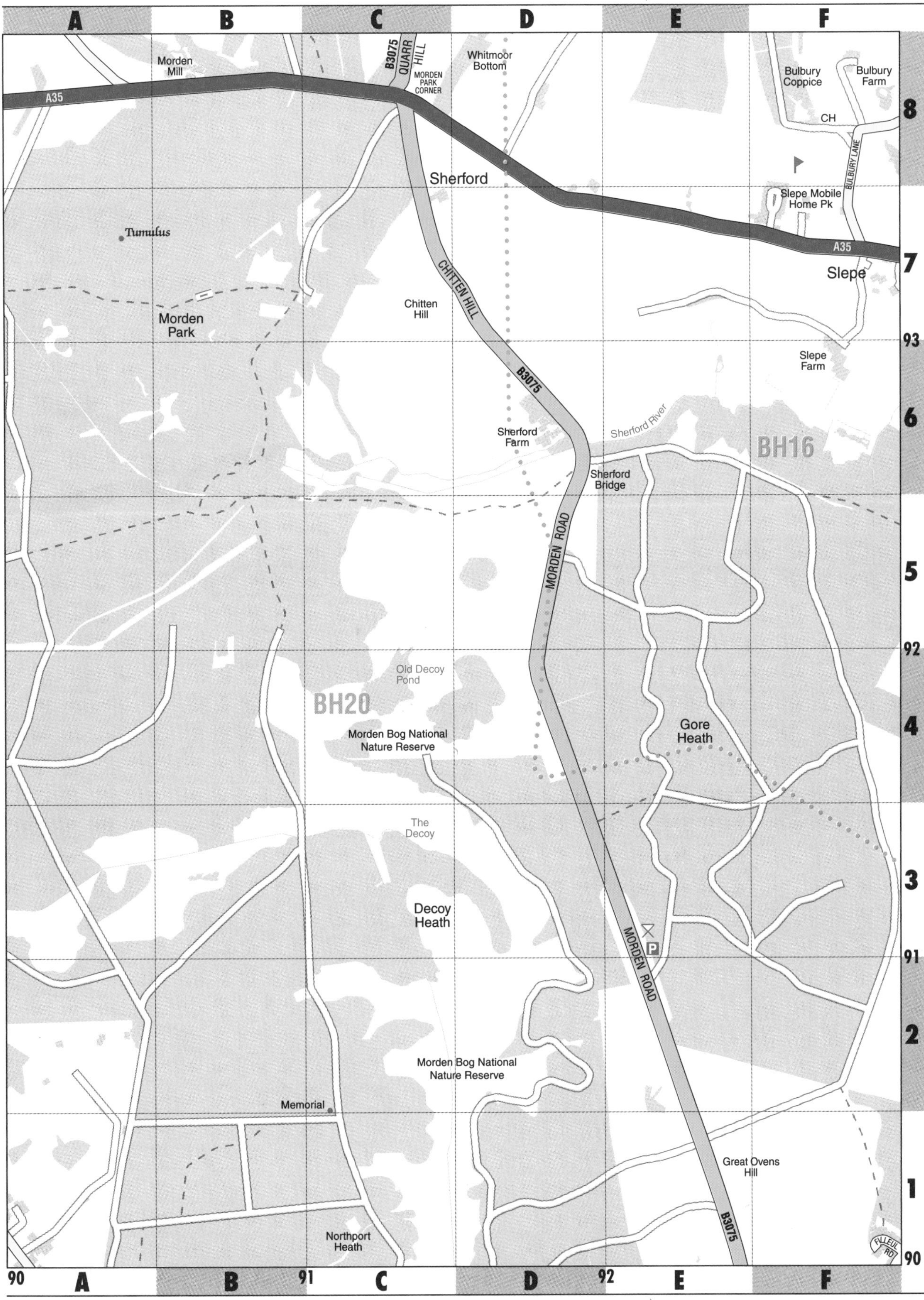
A
B
C
D
E
F
Morden Mill
A35
B3075
QUARR HILL
MORDEN PARK CORNER
Whitmoor Bottom
Bulbury Coppice
Bulbury Farm
CH
BULBURY LANE
8
Sherford
Slepe Mobile Home Pk
Tumulus
A35
7
Slepe
CHITTEN HILL
Chitten Hill
Morden Park
93
Slepe Farm
B3075
6
Sherford River
BH16
Sherford Farm
Sherford Bridge
MORDEN ROAD
5
92
Old Decoy Pond
BH20
Gore Heath
4
Morden Bog National Nature Reserve
The Decoy
3
Decoy Heath
P
MORDEN ROAD
91
2
Morden Bog National Nature Reserve
Memorial
Great Ovens Hill
1
B3075
Northport Heath
FULLEUL RD
90
90
A
B
91
C
D
92
E
F

142
116

115 84

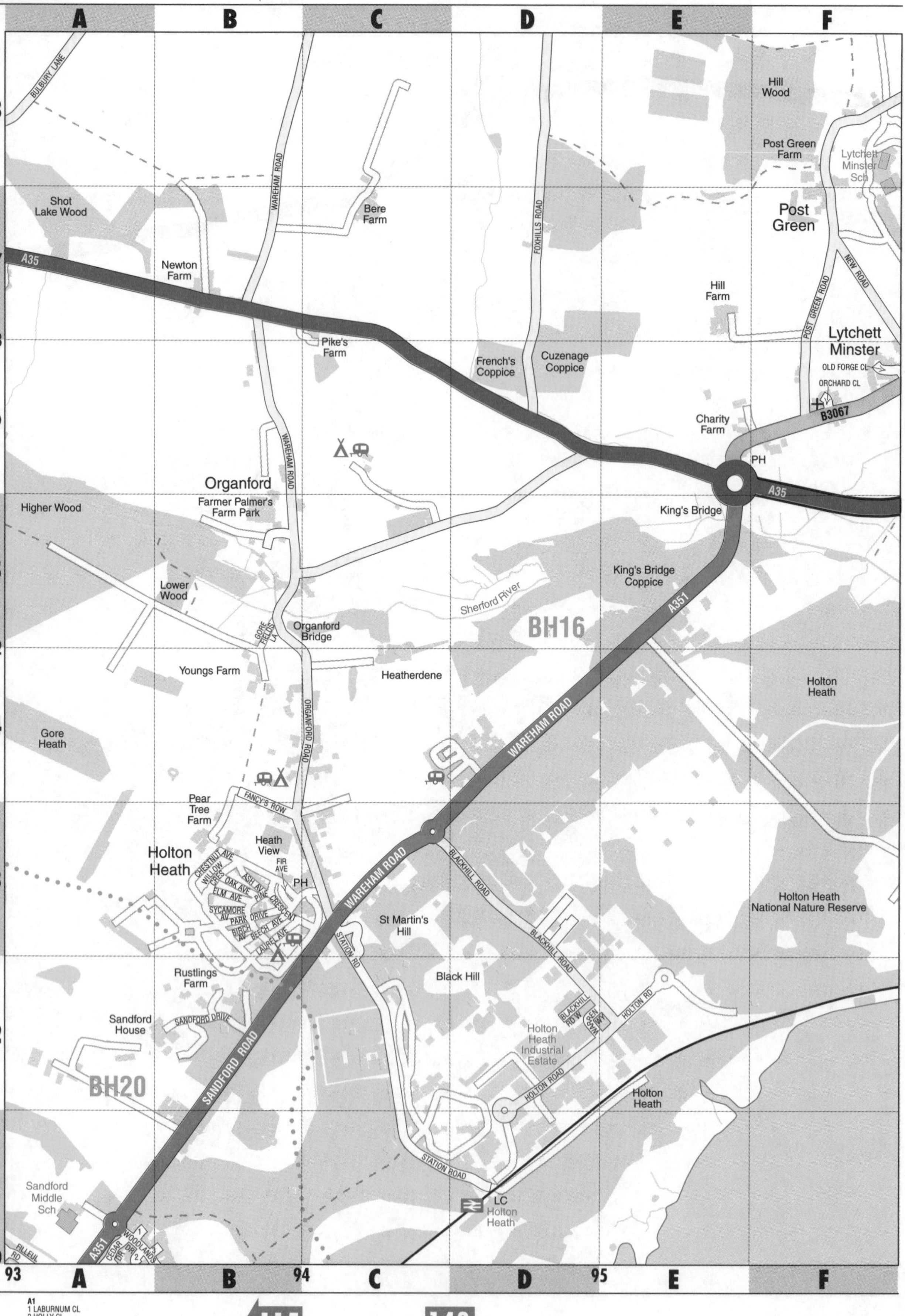

A B C D E F

8

Bulbury Lane

Hill Wood

Shot Lake Wood

Post Green Farm

Lytchett Minster Sch

7
A35

Newton Farm

Bere Farm

Foxhills Road

Post Green

New Road

93

Pike's Farm

French's Coppice

Cuzenage Coppice

Hill Farm

Post Green Road

Lytchett Minster

OLD FORGE CL
ORCHARD CL
B3067

6

Charity Farm

PH

Organford

Wareham Road

Farmer Palmer's Farm Park

King's Bridge

A35

Higher Wood

King's Bridge Coppice

A351

5

Lower Wood

Sherford River

BH16

Holton Heath

92

Organford Bridge

Organford Road

Youngs Farm

Heatherdene

4

Gore Heath

Wareham Road

Holton Heath National Nature Reserve

Pear Tree Farm

FANCY'S ROW

Heath View

Blackhill Road

Holton Heath

CHESTNUT LANE
WILLOW
OAK AVE
ELM AVE
FIR AVE
PH

3

Holton Heath

SYCAMORE AV
BIRCH DRIVE
BEECH AVE
PARK
ASH AVE
CRESCENT

LAUREL AVE

St Martin's Hill

Black Hill

BLACKHILL RD W
ASH CL

HOLTON RD

91

Rustlings Farm

STATION RD

Holton Heath Industrial Estate

HOLTON ROAD

2

Sandford House

SANDFORD DRIVE

SANDFORD ROAD

BH20

Holton Heath

1

Sandford Middle Sch

A351

WOOD MEAD
CEDAR DR
2

STATION ROAD

LC
Holton Heath

PILLEUL RD

90

93 A B 94 C D 95 E F

A1
1 LABURNUM CL
2 HOLLY CL
3 ALDER CL

C7
7 ST NEOTS CL
1 DORCHESTER RD
2 GREENWAY CRES
3 OAKLEY GDNS
4 SEABANK CL
5 PINEWOOD CL
6 OASIS MEWS

C8
1 HICKORY CL
2 GURJUN CL

D7
1 BEACON RD
2 FOXGLOVES
3 STUART CL
4 CORONATION AVE
5 EGDON CT
6 THE TRIANGLE
7 DARIAN CT
8 MOOR LAND PK

D8
1 DOUSSIE CL
2 RICHARD CL
3 KESTREL CL
4 BELL HEATHER CL

85

E7
1 SHIRLEY RD
2 Upton Cross Mobile Home Park
3 ELIZABETH RD
4 CHRIS CRES
5 MAPLE LO

118

6 LLEWELLIN CT
7 BRIARSWOOD RD
8 MEADOWS DR
9 DAVENPORT CL
10 PRESTON CL

E8
1 DOUGLAS CL
2 TURBARY CT
3 MEADOW BANK
4 MEADOWS CL

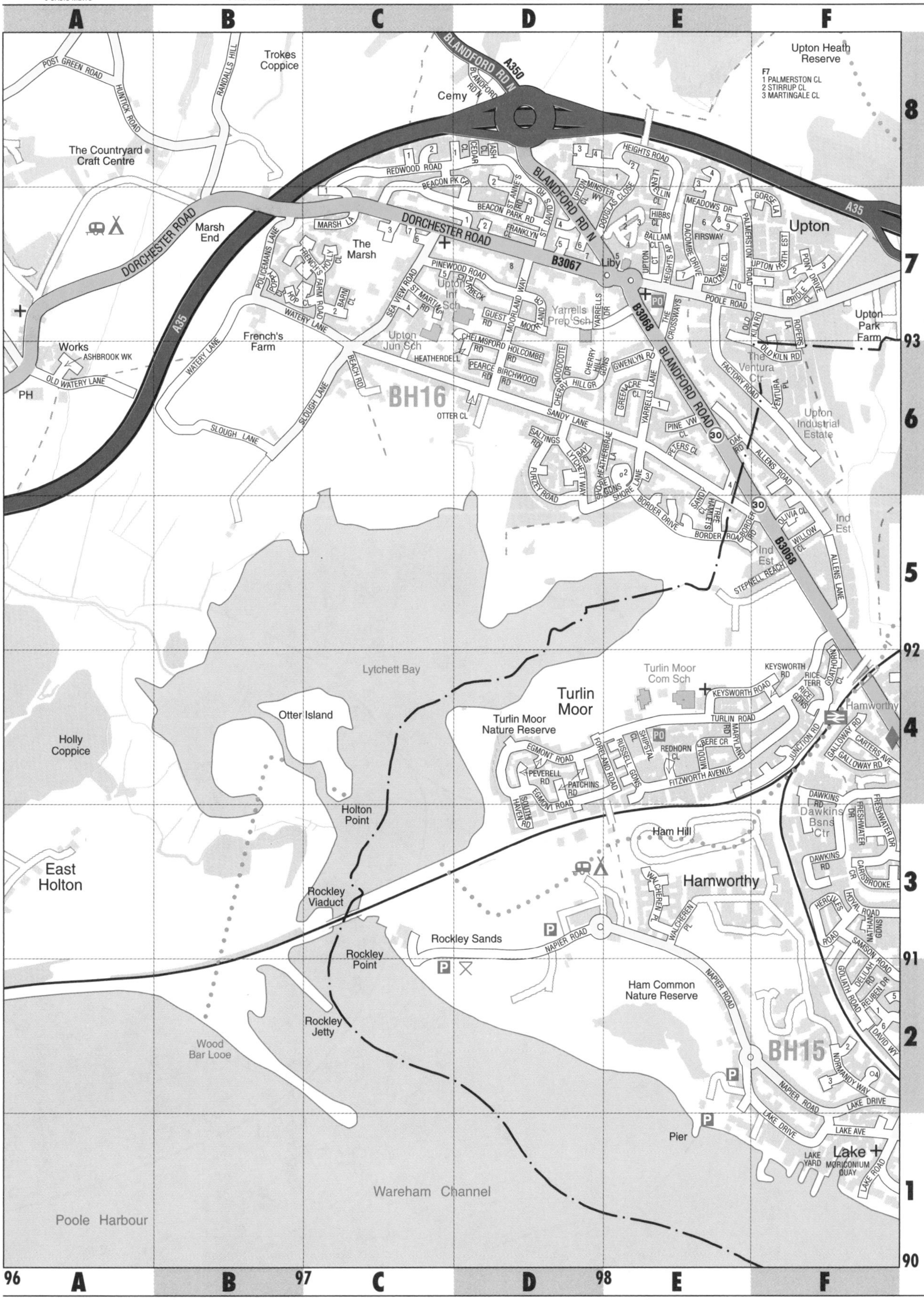

144

118

E6
1 YARRELLS CL
2 SHORE AVE
3 SHORE CL
4 OLD BOUND RD

F2
1 SOLOMON WY
2 FORT CUMBERLAND CL
3 KANGAW PL
4 SALERNO PL
5 CARMEL CL
6 BENJAMIN RD

85 117 86

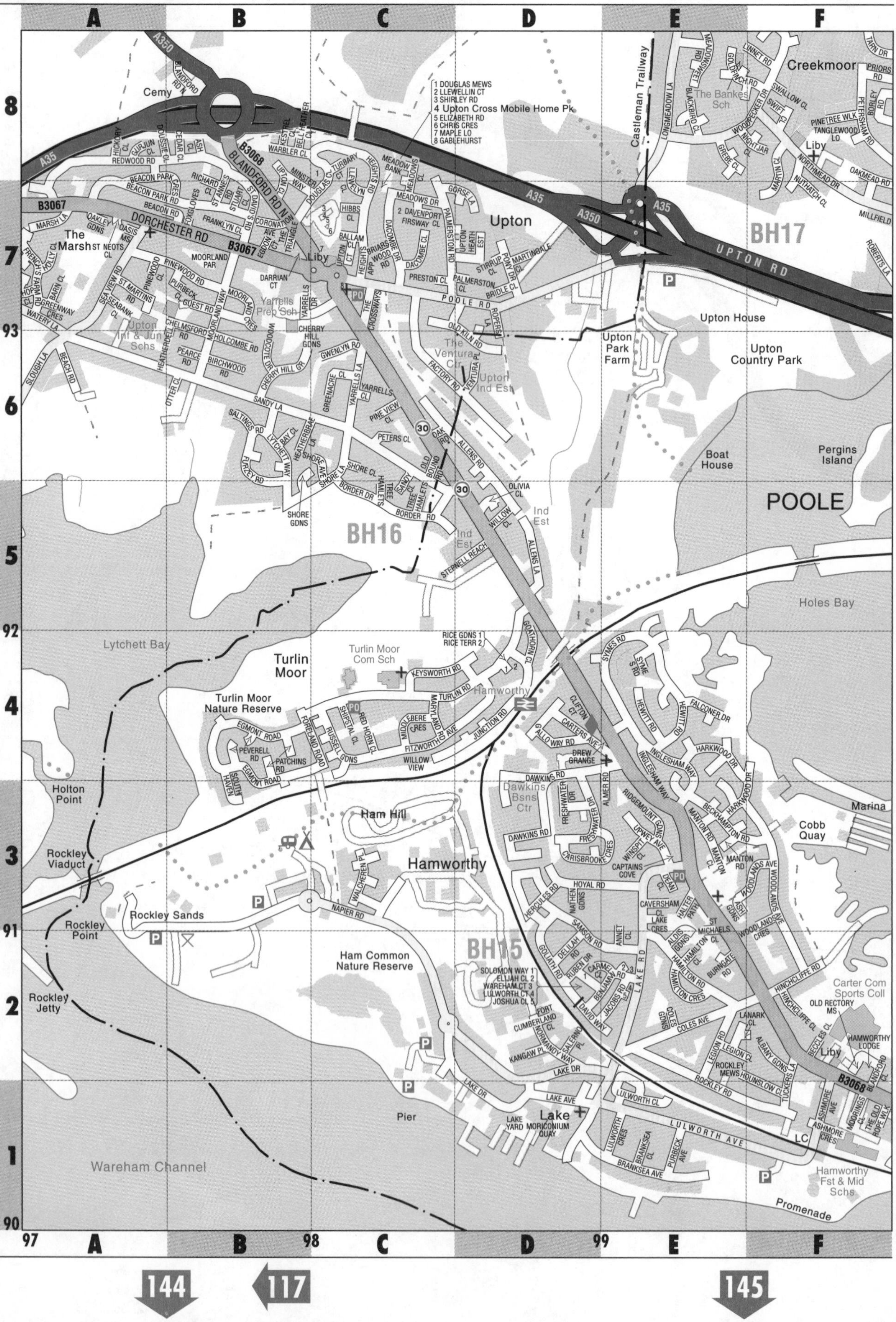
A B C D E F
8 7 6 5 4 3 2 1
93 92 91 90
97 98 99
Cemy
A350
A35
B3068
B3067
BLANDFORD RD N
1 DOUGLAS MEWS
2 LLEWELLIN CT
3 SHIRLEY RD
4 Upton Cross Mobile Home Pk
5 ELIZABETH RD
6 CHRIS CRES
7 MAPLE LO
8 GABLEHURST
Castleman Trailway
Creekmoor
The Bankes Sch
LONGMEADOW LA
Liby
BH17
UPTON RD
REDWOOD RD
BEACON PARK RD
DORCHESTER RD
The Marsh
Upton
Yarrells Prep Sch
Upton Inf & Jun Schs
POOLE RD
Upton House
Upton Park Farm
Upton Country Park
The Ventura Ctr
Upton Ind Est
SANDY LA
Boat House
Pergins Island
POOLE
BH16
Ind Est
ALLENS LA
STERNELL REACH
Holes Bay
Lytchett Bay
Turlin Moor
Turlin Moor Com Sch
Turlin Moor Nature Reserve
Hamworthy
EGMONT ROAD
FORELAND ROAD
Dawkins Bsns Ctr
Holton Point
Ham Hill
Hamworthy
Rockley Viaduct
Rockley Sands
Rockley Point
NAPIER RD
Marina
Cobb Quay
Ham Common Nature Reserve
BH15
Rockley Jetty
Carter Com Sports Coll
Pier
Lake
LAKE DR
LULWORTH AVE
BRANKSEA AVE
Wareham Channel
Hamworthy Fst & Mid Schs
Promenade

144 117 145

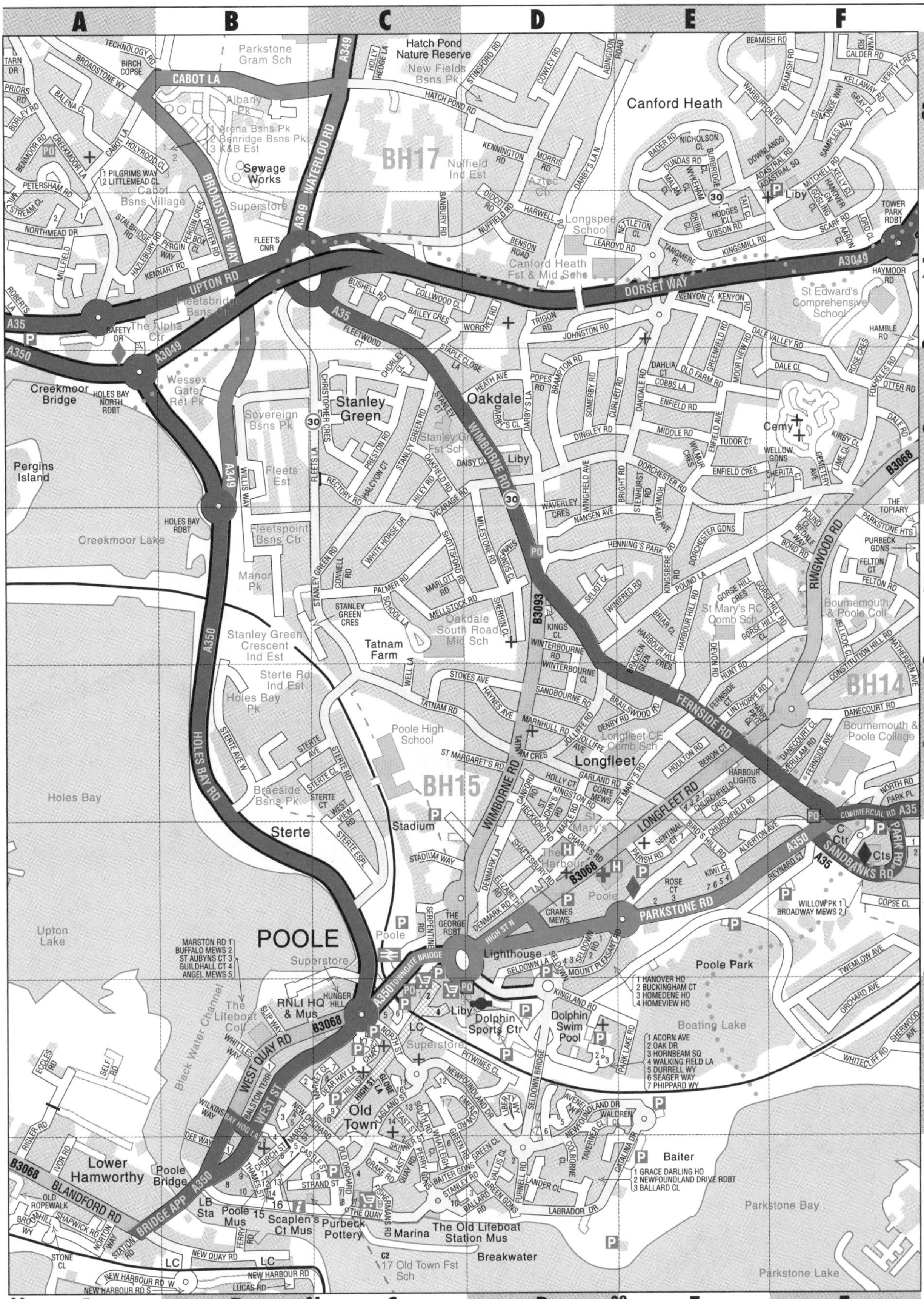

B1
1 BARBERS PILES
2 ST JAMES CL
3 POPLAR CL
4 LEVET'S LA
5 NEW ST
6 ST GEORGE'S ALMSHOS
7 CINNAMON LA
8 BARBERS WHARF
9 BARBERS GATE
10 YEATMANS OLD MILL
11 THAMES MEWS
12 SARUM ST
13 GRAND PAR
14 PARADISE ST
15 Local History Ctr
16 Custom House

145

C1
1 PROSPEROUS ST
2 DANIEL GDNS
3 THE SEED WAREHOUSE
4 DRAKE CT
5 TAYLOR'S BLDGS
6 RODNEY CT
7 QUAY POINT
8 THE KIOSKS
9 Dolphin Quays

146

10 EAST QUAY

C2
1 Towngate Sh Ctr
2 FALKLAND SQ
3 Dolphin Sh Ctr
4 KINGLAND CRES
5 WINCHESTER PL
6 VANGUARD RD
7 MALTHOUSE

120

8 OLD TOWN MEWS
9 CARTER'S LA
10 THE OLD BREWERY
11 THE BROMBYS
12 EMERSON CL
13 NELSON CT
14 LAGLAND CT
15 GRENVILLE CT
16 GLOBE LA
17 Old Town Fst Sch

E3
1 BIRDS HILL GDNS
2 CHURCHFIELD CT
3 THE MALTINGS
4 LANSDELL CT
5 GARDENS CT
6 SUNNINGDALE
7 PARK VIEW

E4
1 BANCROFT CT
2 CROWE HILL CT
3 MERTON CT
4 THOROGOOD CT

F7
1 GREENFIELDS
2 HANDLEY LODGE
3 SHILLINGSTONE GDNS
4 CASHMOOR CL
5 BROADMAYNE RD
6 ROWE GDNS
7 ALDER HEIGHTS

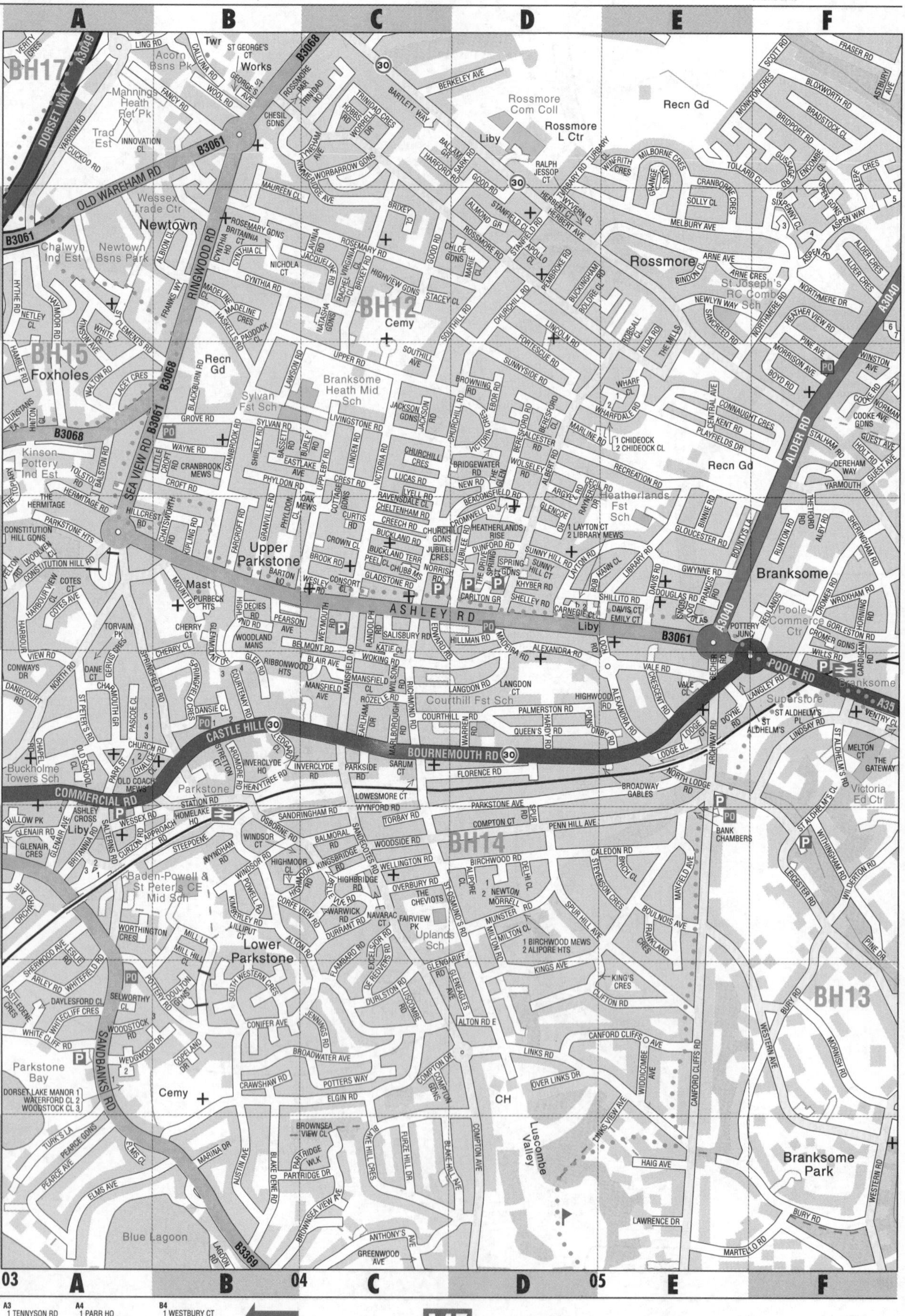

A3
1 TENNYSON RD
2 MENTONE RD
3 CLARENCE RD
4 BRANDWOOD CT

A4
1 PARR HO
2 FRINTON CT
3 ST PETER'S CT
4 SINCLAIR CT
5 ELDON CT

B4
1 WESTBURY CT
2 CHALBURY CT
3 HIGHFIELD HO
4 FAR ENDS

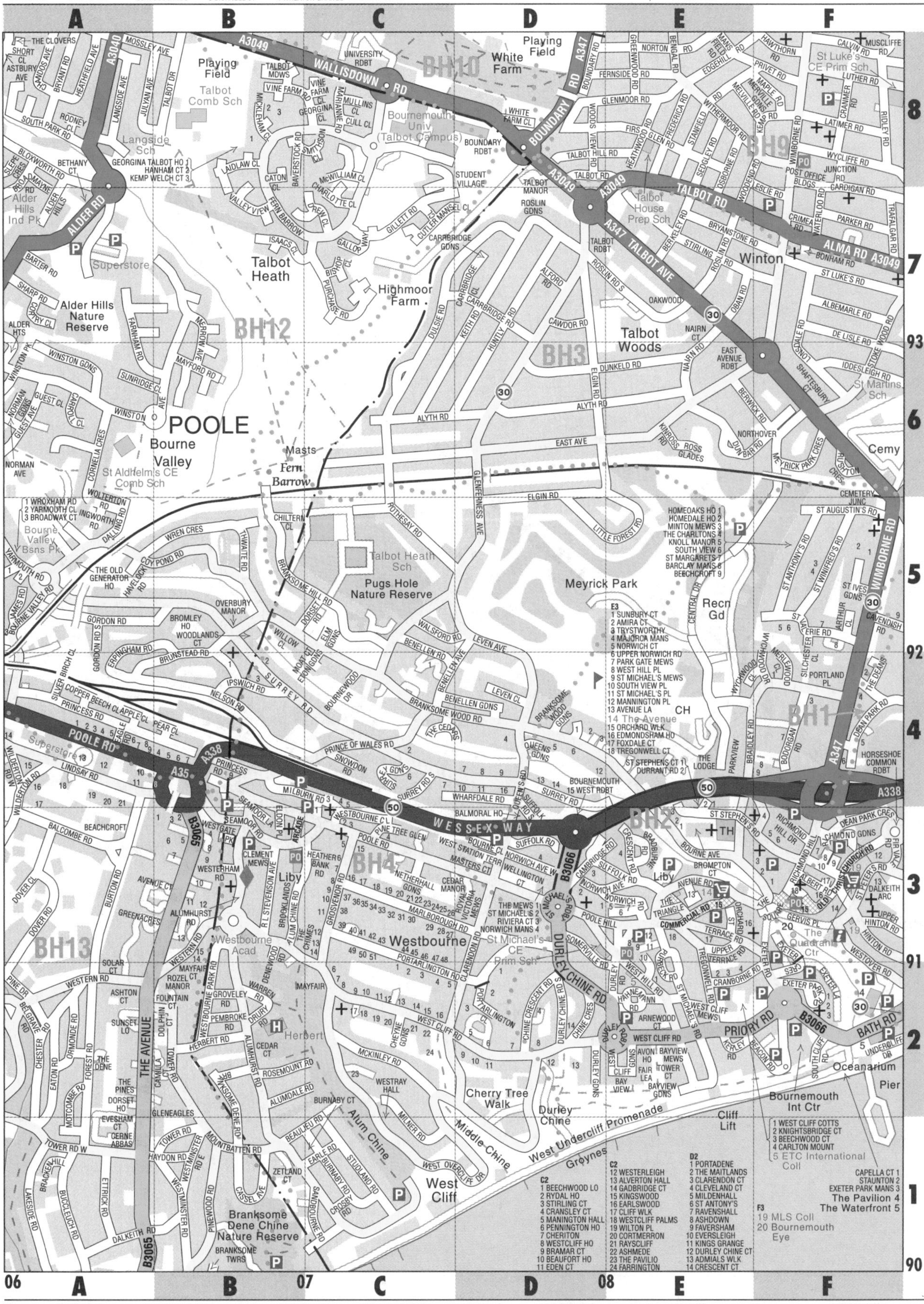

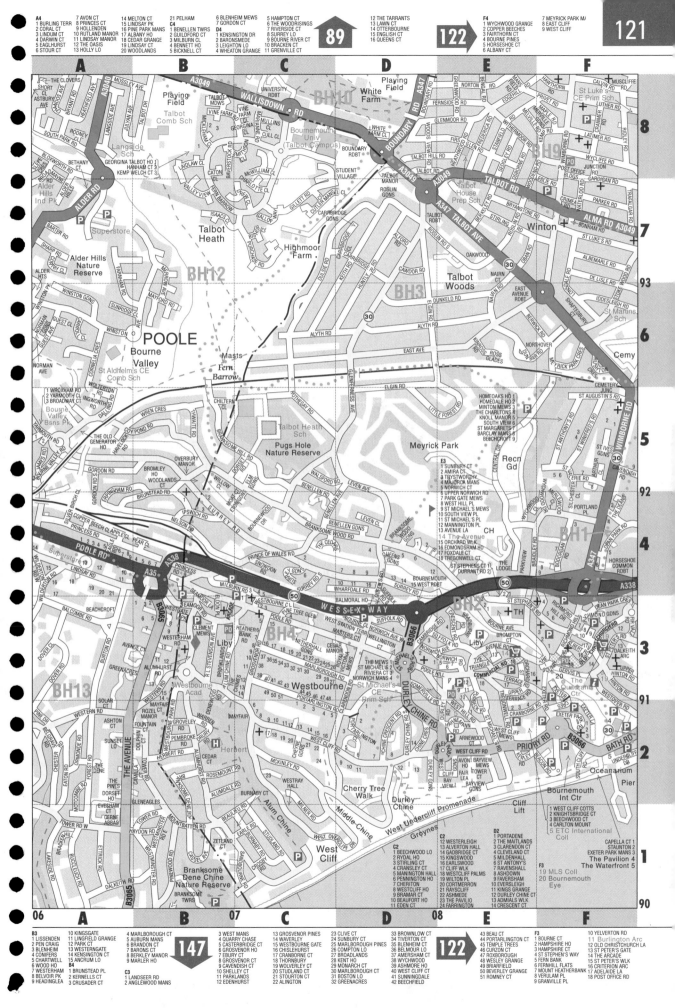

A5
1 CULFORD CT
2 APSLEY CT
3 TRELOEN CT
4 RAVANA CT
5 HOMELEIGH HO
6 BEECHEY CT
7 WELLINGTON CT
8 MORINGTON CT
9 PARSONAGE CT

B5
1 HAMILTON CT
2 MOORLEA
3 PORCHESTER CT

121

C5
1 OPHIR GDNS
2 METHUEN CL
3 LOWTHER GDNS
4 THE LANE LOTHER GDNS
5 STEWART CL
6 HENVILLE RD
7 MALMESBURY PARK PL
8 WESLEY CL

90

E5
1 ST ANN'S CT
2 ST GEORGE'S CT
3 ST DAVID'S CT
4 ST JOHN'S CT

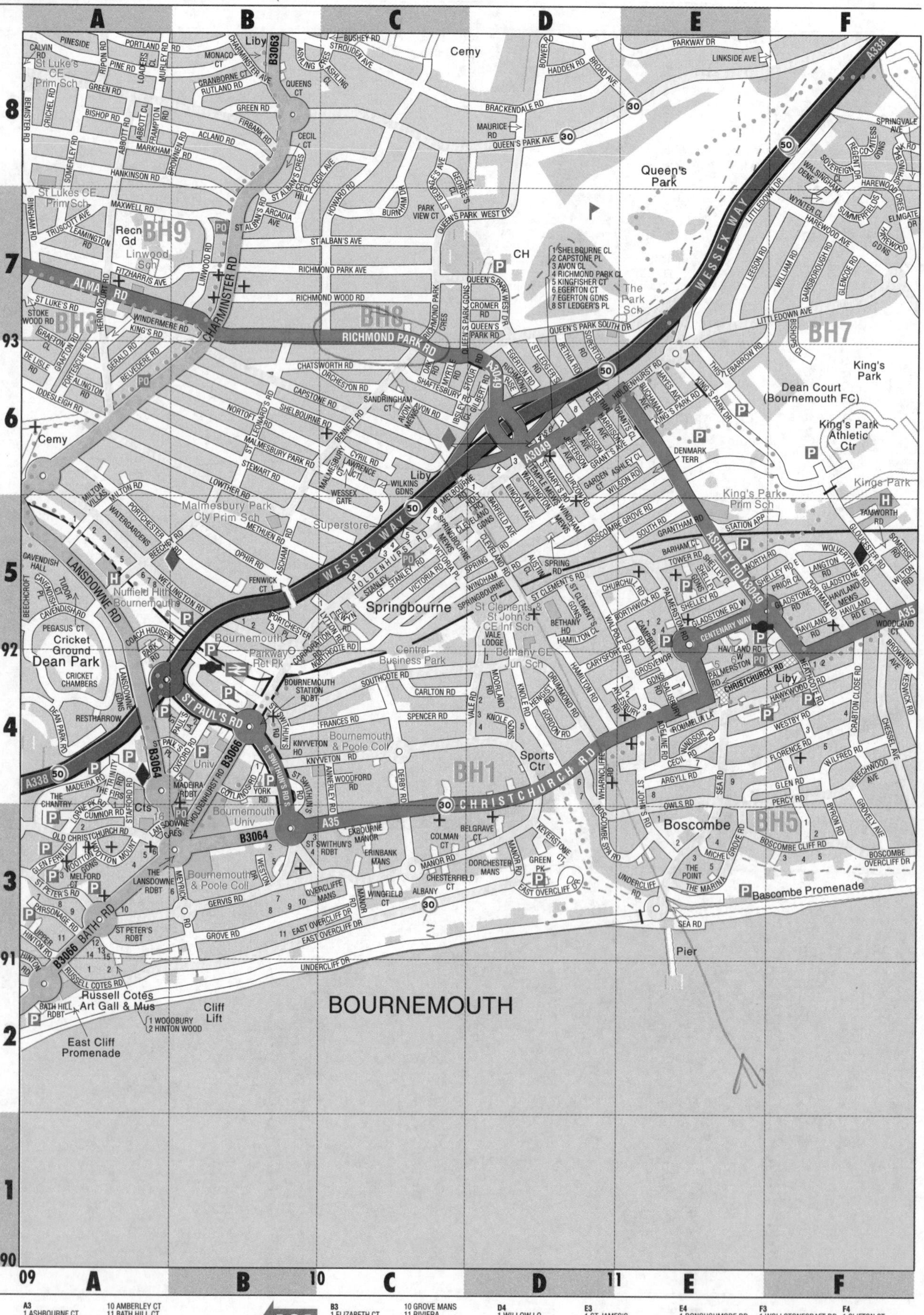

A3
1 ASHBOURNE CT
2 TRINITY
3 ST PETERS CT
4 PINE GRANGE
5 BUCKINGHAM MANS
6 JACEY HO
7 THE PINNACLE
8 ALEXANDRA LODGE
9 QUEENSBURY MANS
10 AMBERLEY CT
11 BATH HILL CT
12 LITTLE FOREST MANS
13 THE FARTHINGS CT
14 FOREST HO
15 BERNE CT
16 Bournemouth & Poole Coll

121

B3
1 ELIZABETH CT
2 BOURNEMOUTH HO
3 CODOGAN CT
4 BURFORD CT
5 GRANGE CT
6 GARDEN HO
7 ATHELNEY CT
8 GROSVENOR CT
9 EDEN CT
10 GROVE MANS
11 RIVIERA

B4
1 KILMARNOCK RD
2 HOMELIFE HO
3 LANDSDOWNE MS

D4
1 WILLOW LO
2 GROSVENOR CT
3 PINE MANS
4 VALE MONS
5 KNOLE CT
6 COURTLEIGH MANOR
7 GORSECLIFF CT

E3
1 ST JAMES'S
2 MARINA CT
3 MERMAID CT
4 SAN REMO TWRS
5 MARINA TWRS

E4
1 DONOUGHMORE RD
2 RANDOLPH RD
3 THE CRESCENT
4 CARNARVON RD
5 Royal Arc
6 Soveriegn Ctr
7 HORACE RD
8 ARGYLL MANS
9 FAIRHAVEN CT

F3
1 WOLLSTONECRAFT RD
2 CLEASBY GRANGE
3 LAVERSTOCK
4 OCEAN HTS
5 CARLINFORD

F4
1 CLIFTON CT
2 HEATHCOTE CT
3 GRANTLEY RD
4 THESSALY CT
5 ST GEORGES MANS
6 WATKIN RD

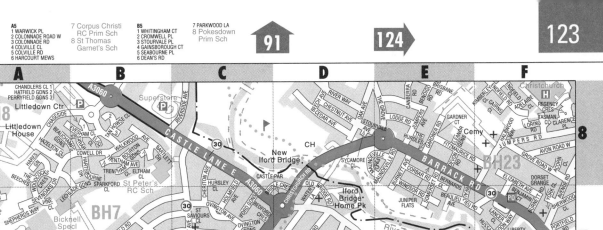

A5
1 WARWICK PL
2 COLONNADE ROAD W
3 COLONNADE RD
4 COLVILLE CL
5 COLVILLE RD
6 HARCOURT MEWS

7 Corpus Christi
RC Prim Sch
8 St Thomas
Garnet's Sch

B5
1 WHITINGHAM CT
2 CROMWELL PL
3 STOURVALE PL
4 GAINSBOROUGH CT
5 SEABOURNE PL
6 DEAN'S RD

7 PARKWOOD LA
8 Pokesdown
Prim Sch

91

124

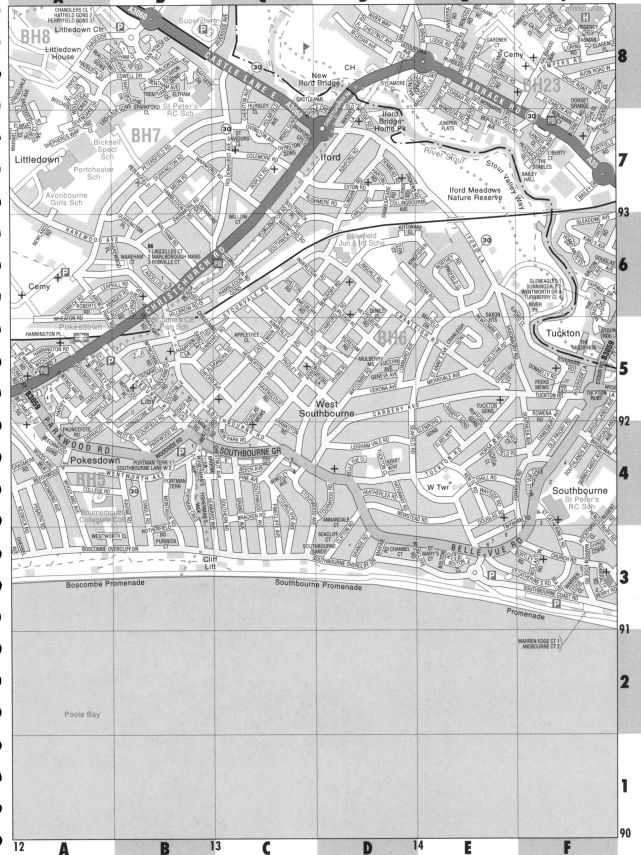

A4
1 Anglo-European
Coll of Chiropractic

C4
1 ST MICHAELS CT
2 CARBERY ROW
3 CARBERY LA
4 STOURWOOD MANS
5 SOUTHBOURNE LANE E
6 SOUTHBOURNE LANE CENTRAL

124

E3
1 WINDSOR MANS
2 ETON MANS
3 BOLTON CT
4 THE PARADE
5 SOUTHBOURNE CROSS ROADS
6 BELLE VUE MANS
7 INGARTH
8 AUDRAYTON CT

F4
1 FOXHOLES
2 BELLE VUE GDNS
3 BRACKEN LODGE
4 COMPTON CT

A5
1 MARINA VIEW
2 THE MOORINGS
3 SWAN GN
4 KINGFISHERS
5 WATERMEAD
6 MALMSBURY CL

A6
1 HOMESTOUR HO
2 ORCHARD MEWS
3 ST ANDREWS
4 RIVERLAND CT

123 ◀

A7
1 WINSTON CT
2 KENILWORTH CT
3 ARTHUR LA
4 MULBERRY CT
5 MITRE CT

92

B6
1 POUND LA
2 MILLHAMS STREET N
3 THE CLOISTERS
4 PRIORY VIEW CT
5 SILVER ST

E6
1 FRANCESCA LO
2 GILLION CT
3 ROSEDALE CL
4 Mudeford
  Inf Sch

E7
1 STRETE MOUNT
2 PUREWELL CT
3 COURT CL
4 FRANCESCA GRANGE
5 FRANCESCA CT

F8
1 SOUTHDOWN CT
2 MALVERN CT
3 PURBECK CT
4 MENDIP CT
5 CHILTERN CT
6 COTSWOLD CT

7 QUANTOCK CT
8 PENNINE CT
9 WENLOCK CT

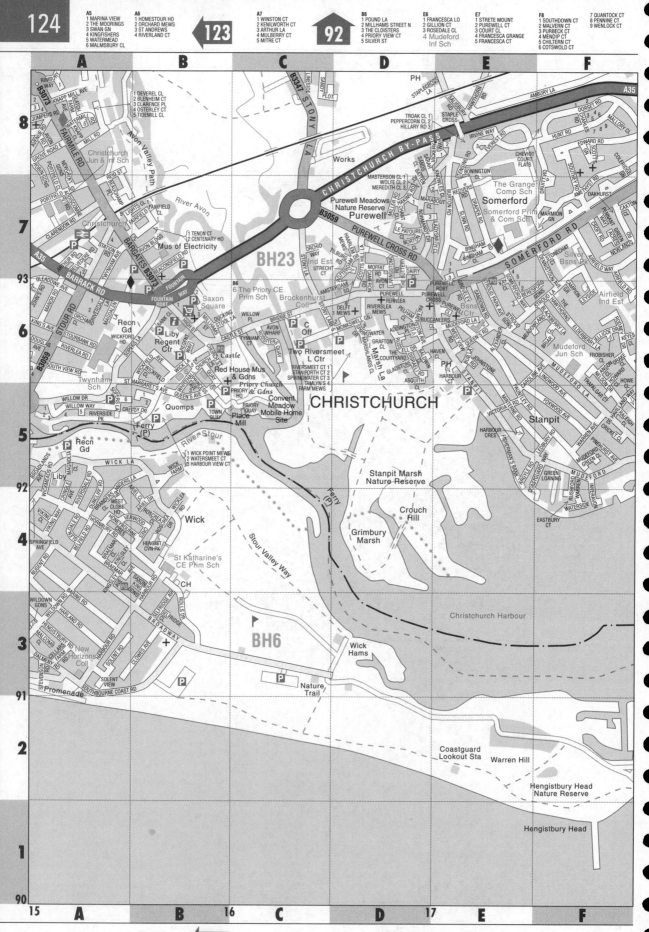

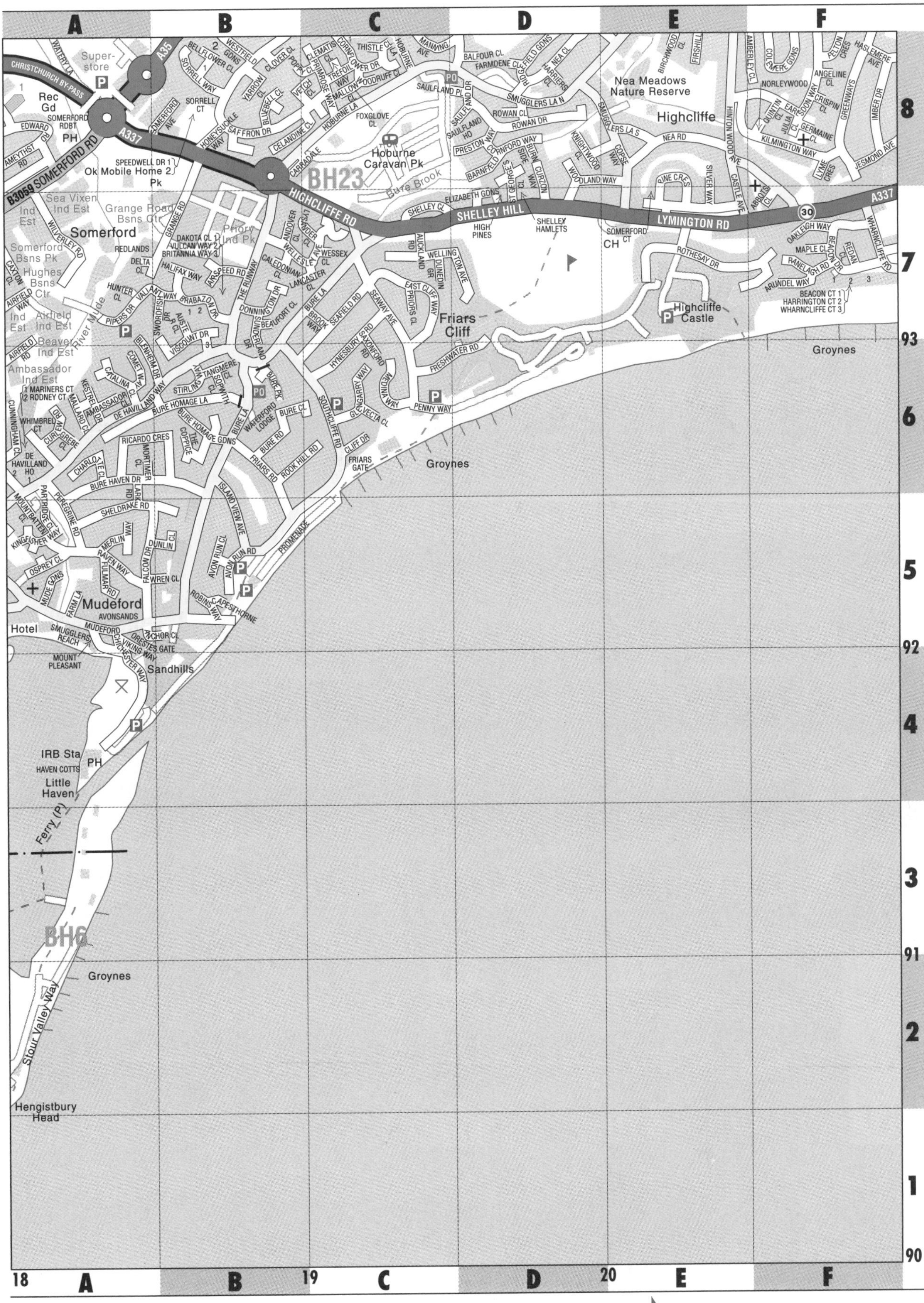

125
94

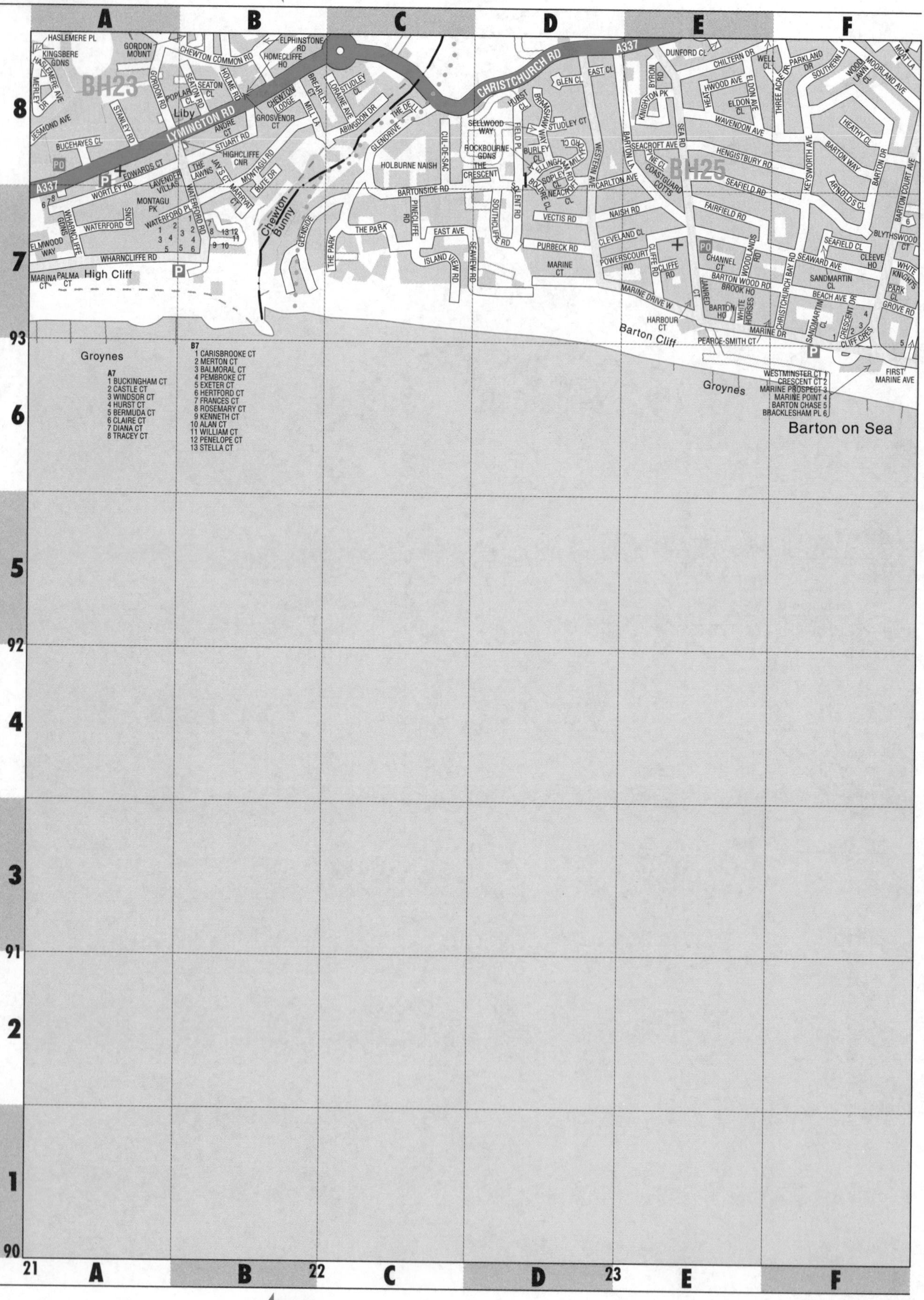

Groynes

A7
1 BUCKINGHAM CT
2 CASTLE CT
3 WINDSOR CT
4 HURST CT
5 BERMUDA CT
6 CLAIRE CT
7 DIANA CT
8 TRACEY CT

B7
1 CARISBROOKE CT
2 MERTON CT
3 BALMORAL CT
4 PEMBROKE CT
5 EXETER CT
6 HERTFORD CT
7 FRANCES CT
8 ROSEMARY CT
9 KENNETH CT
10 ALAN CT
11 WILLIAM CT
12 PENELOPE CT
13 STELLA CT

WESTMINSTER CT 1
CRESCENT CT 2
MARINE PROSPECT 3
MARINE POINT 4
BARTON CHASE 5
BRACKLESHAM PL 6

Barton on Sea

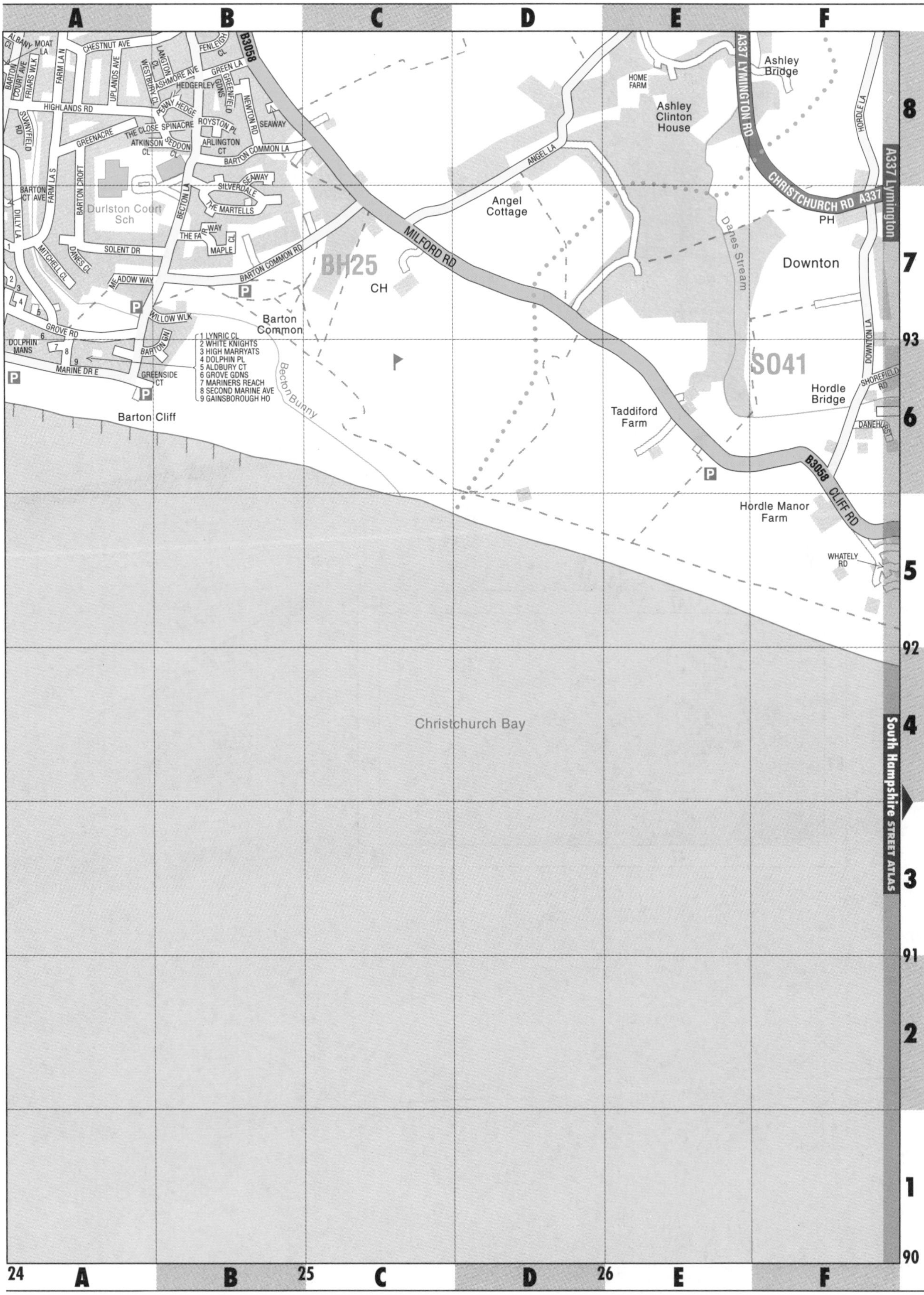

A   B   C   D   E   F

8
7
93
6
5
92
4
3
91
2
1
90

ALBANY MOAT LA
BARTON COURT CL
CHESTNUT AVE
FRIARS WLK
FARM LA N
LANGTON CL
UPLANDS AVE
FENLEIGH CL
GREEN LA
NEWTON RD
B3058
HIGHLANDS RD
WESTBURY CL
ASHMORE AVE
HEDGERLEY
PENNY HEDGE
GREENFIELD
SEAWAY
GREENACRE
THE CLOSE
SPINACRE
ROYSTON PL
ARLINGTON CT
BARTON COMMON LA
SEAWAY
SUNNYFIELD RD
ATKINSON CL
SEDDON CL
SILVERDALE
DILLY LA
BECTON LA
Durlston Court Sch
THE MARTELLS
BARTON CT AVE
FARM LA S
BARTON CROFT
MITCHELL CL
DANES CL
MEADOW WAY
THE FAIRWAY
MAPLE CL
SOLENT DR
WILLOW WLK
BARTON COMMON RD
P
P
BH25
MILFORD RD
CH
GROVE RD
BARTON
Barton Common
Angel Cottage
Angel La
A337 LYMINGTON RD
Ashley Bridge
HORDLE LA
HOME FARM
Ashley Clinton House
CHRISTCHURCH RD A337
A337 Lymington
PH
Downton
DOLPHIN MANS
P
GREENSIDE CT
P
1 LYNRIC CL
2 WHITE KNIGHTS
3 HIGH MARRYATS
4 DOLPHIN PL
5 ALDBURY CT
6 GROVE GDNS
7 MARINERS REACH
8 SECOND MARINE AVE
9 GAINSBOROUGH HO
MARINE DR E
Becton Bunny
SO41
DOWNTON LA
SHOREFIELD RD
Hordle Bridge
DANEHURST
Barton Cliff
Danes Stream
Taddiford Farm
P
B3058 CLIFF RD
Hordle Manor Farm
WHATELY RD

Christchurch Bay

24   A   B   25   C   D   26   E   F

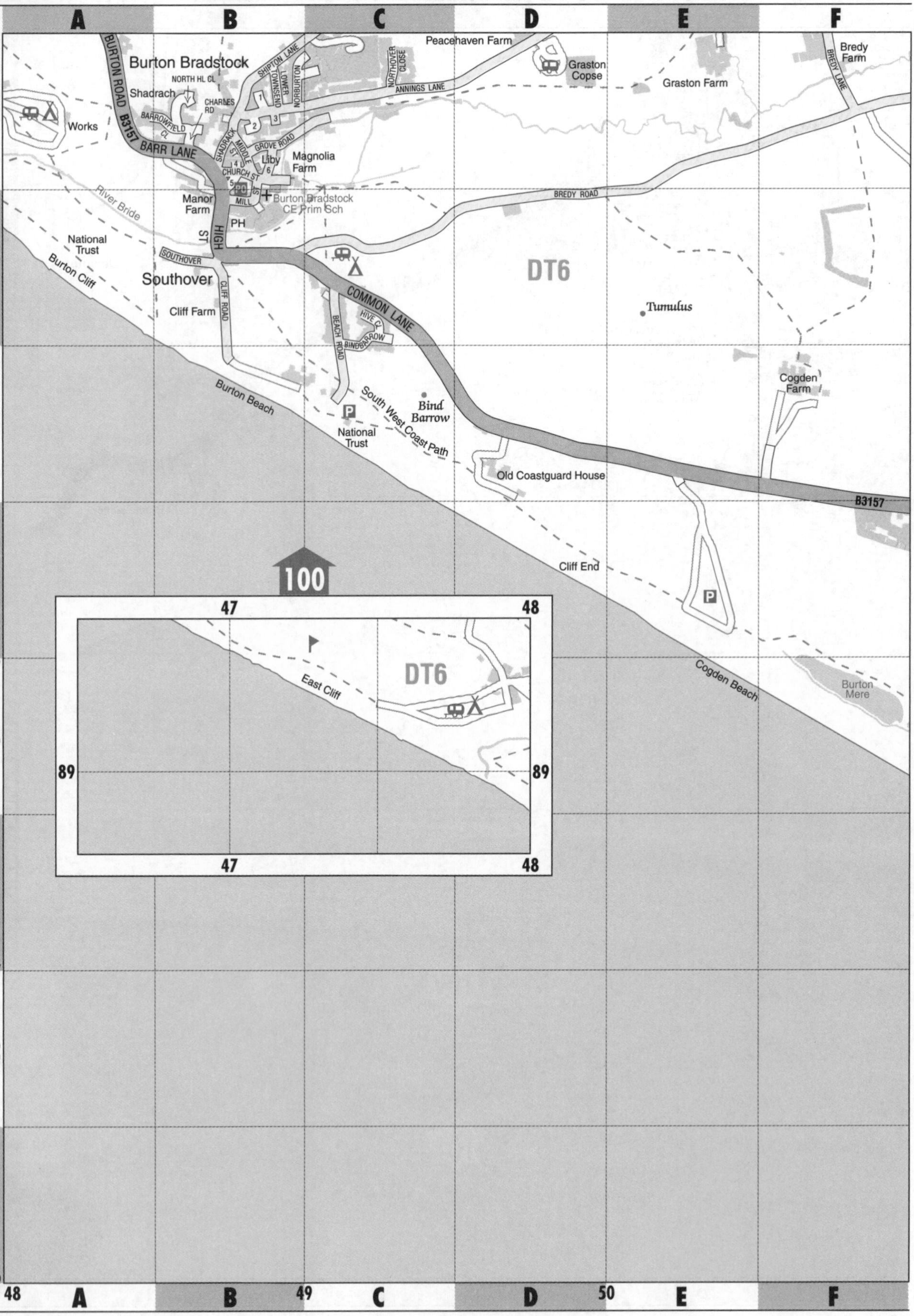

B8
1 HOWARTH CL
2 SOUTH ANNINGS
3 GROVE ORCHARD
4 ST LAWRENCE
5 DONKEY LA
6 DARBY LA

102
130

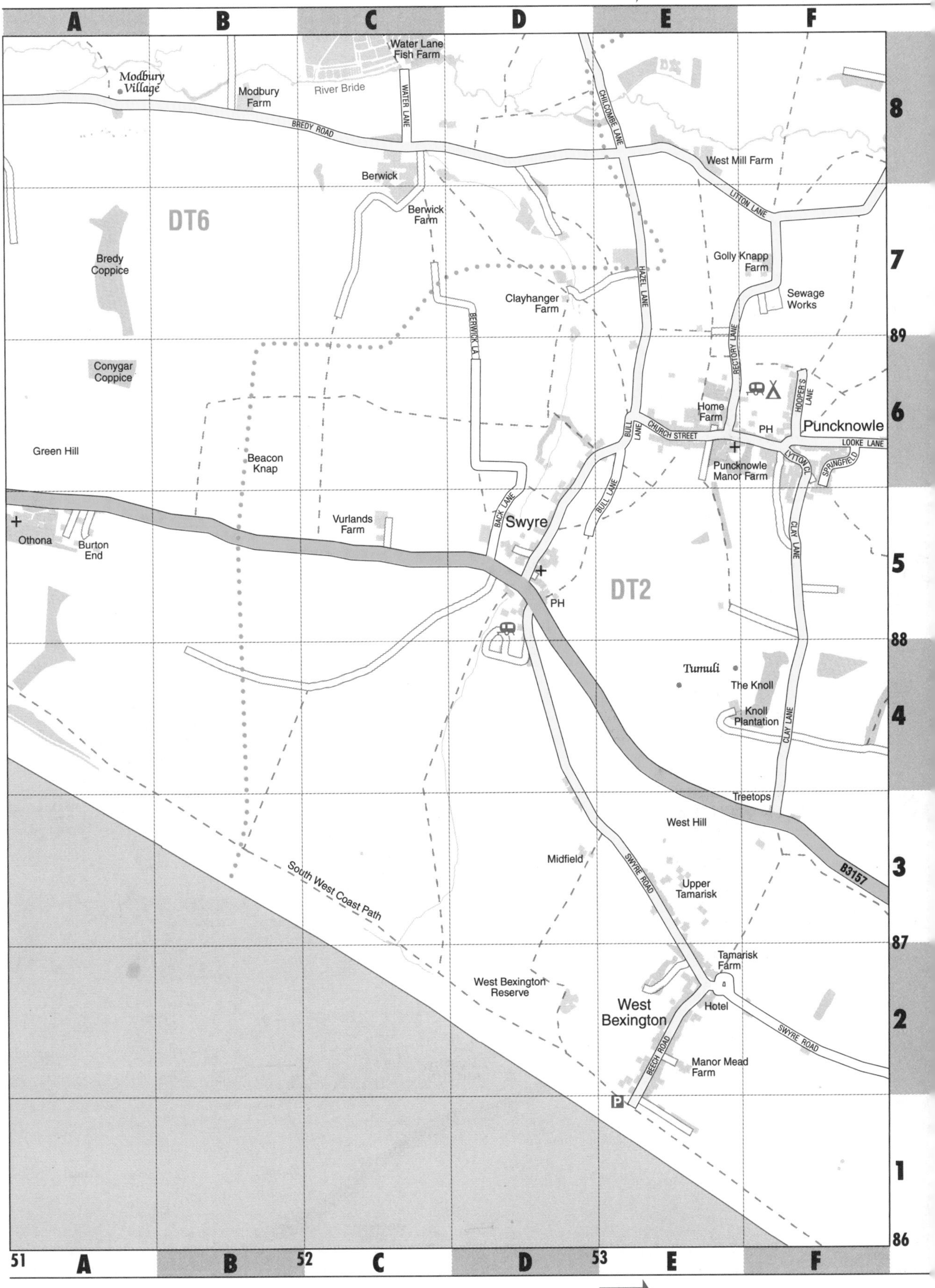
A
B
C
D
E
F
Water Lane Fish Farm
Modbury Village
Modbury Farm
River Bride
WATER LANE
BREDY ROAD
CHILCOMBE LANE
8
West Mill Farm
Berwick
LYTTON LANE
Berwick Farm
DT6
Bredy Coppice
HAZEL LANE
Golly Knapp Farm
7
Clayhanger Farm
Sewage Works
BERWICK LA
89
RECTORY LANE
Conygar Coppice
HOOPER'S LANE
Home Farm
6
BULL LANE
CHURCH STREET
PH
Puncknowle
LOOKE LANE
Green Hill
Beacon Knap
Puncknowle Manor Farm
LYTTON CL
SPRINGFIELD
BACK LANE
BULL LANE
Othona
Burton End
Vurlands Farm
Swyre
CLAY LANE
5
DT2
PH
88
Tumuli
The Knoll
Knoll Plantation
CLAY LANE
4
Treetops
West Hill
Midfield
SWYRE ROAD
3
B3157
South West Coast Path
Upper Tamarisk
87
Tamarisk Farm
West Bexington Reserve
West Bexington
Hotel
2
SWYRE ROAD
BEECH ROAD
Manor Mead Farm
P
1
86
51
A
B
52
C
D
53
E
F

130

129
103

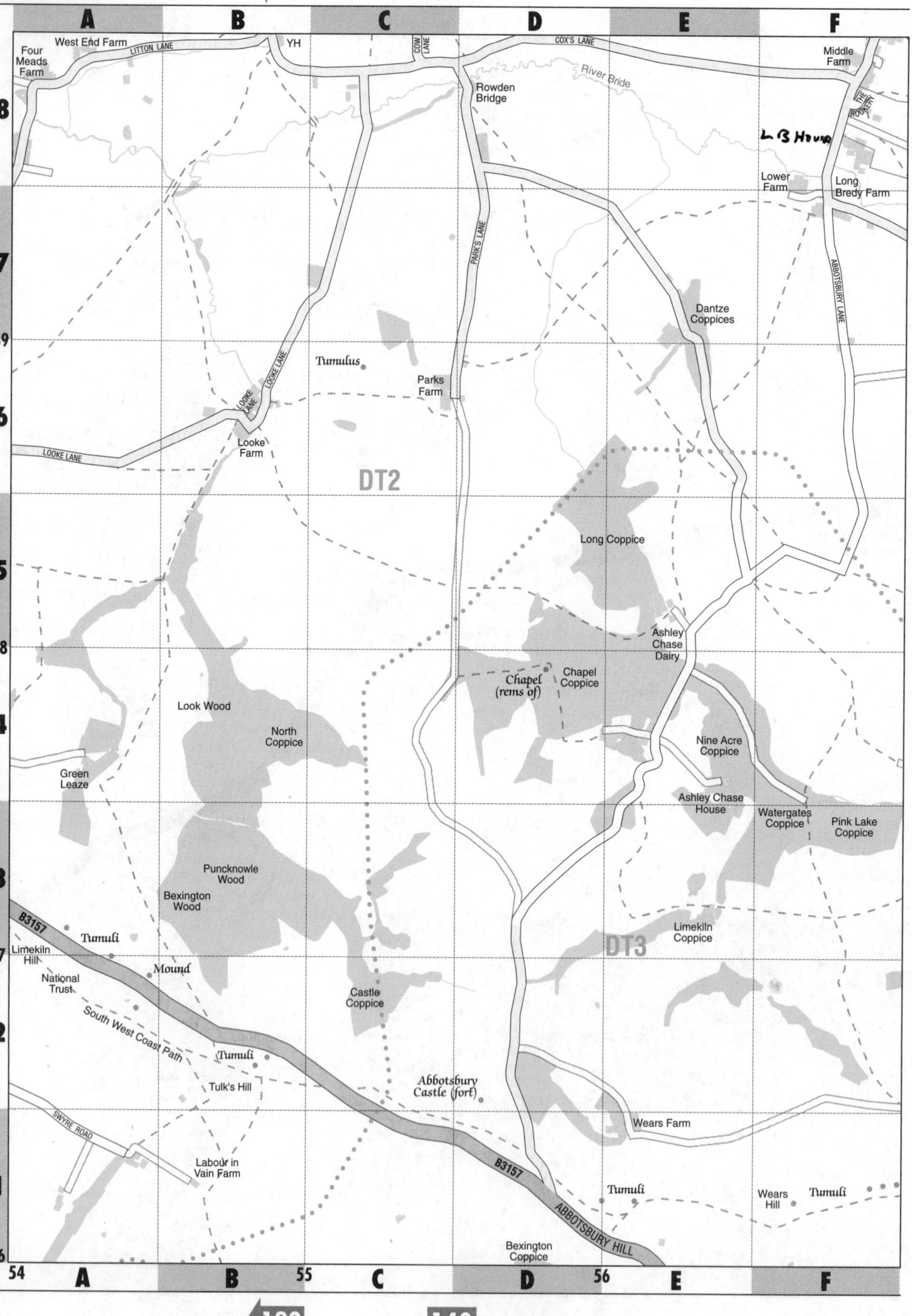

A | B | C | D | E | F

8

Four Meads Farm
West End Farm
LITTON LANE
YH
COW LANE
COX'S LANE
River Bride
Middle Farm
THE ROOKERY
Rowden Bridge
L B House
PARK'S LANE
Lower Farm
Long Bredy Farm

7

ABBOTSBURY LANE

89

Dantze Coppices

Tumulus
LOOKE LANE
Parks Farm

6

LOOKE LANE
Looke Farm

LOOKE LANE

DT2

Long Coppice

5

Ashley Chase Dairy

88

Look Wood
Chapel (rems of)
Chapel Coppice

4

North Coppice
Nine Acre Coppice

Green Leaze
Ashley Chase House
Watergates Coppice
Pink Lake Coppice

Puncknowle Wood
Bexington Wood
Limekiln Coppice

3

B3157
DT3

87

Limekiln Hill
Tumuli
Mound
National Trust
Castle Coppice
South West Coast Path

2

Tumuli
Abbotsbury Castle (fort)
Wears Farm
Tulk's Hill

SWYRE ROAD

1

Labour in Vain Farm
B3157
Tumuli
Wears Hill
Tumuli
ABBOTSBURY HILL

86

Bexington Coppice

54 | A | B | 55 | C | D | 56 | E | F

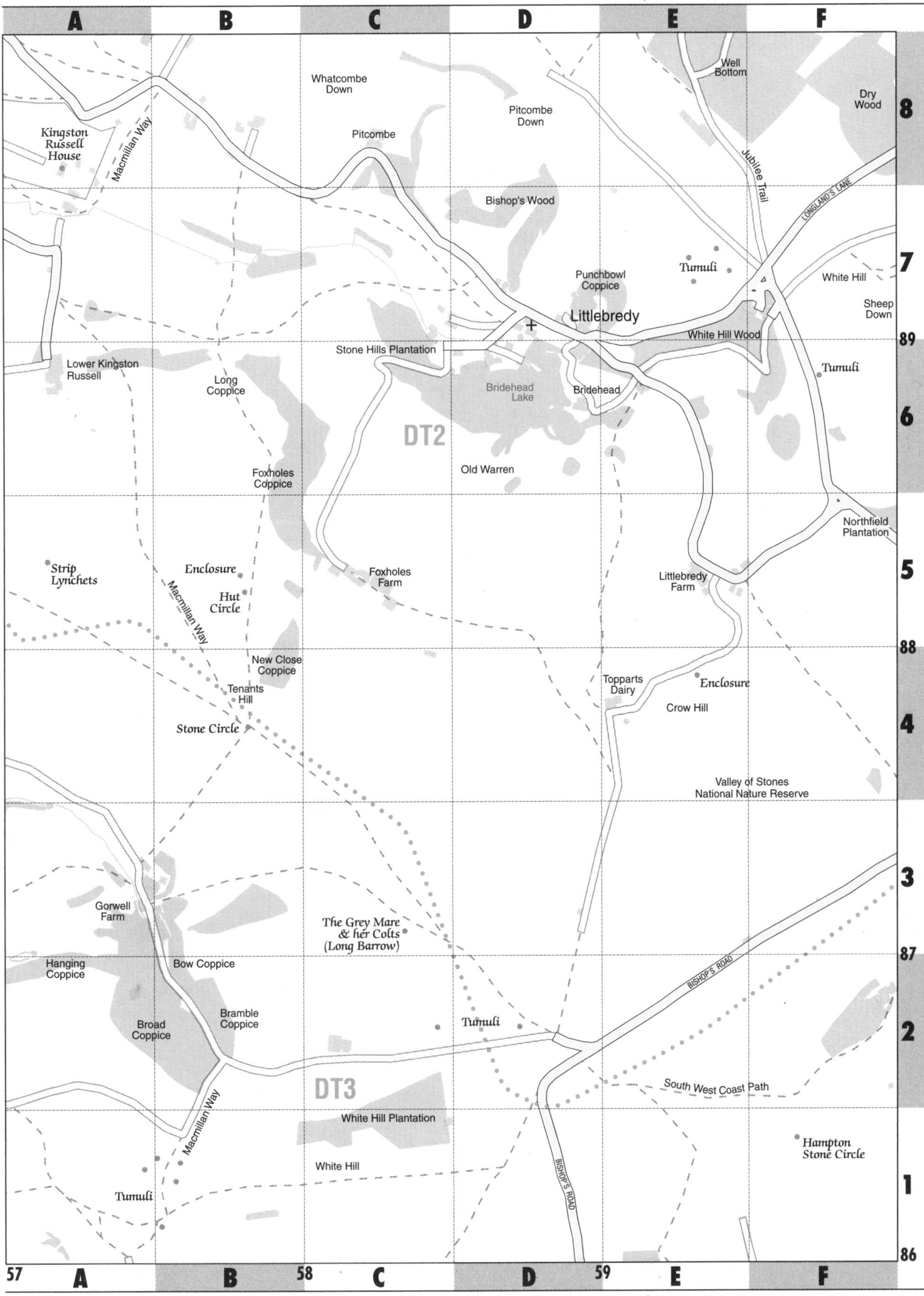

104
132

A B C D E F

Well
Bottom

Dry
Wood

8

Kingston
Russell
House

Whatcombe
Down

Pitcombe
Down

Jubilee Trail

Macmillan Way

Pitcombe

Bishop's Wood

Longland's Lane

Punchbowl
Coppice

Tumuli

White Hill

7

Littlebredy

White Hill Wood

Sheep
Down

89

Lower Kingston
Russell

Stone Hills Plantation

Long
Coppice

Bridehead
Lake

Bridehead

Tumuli

DT2

6

Foxholes
Coppice

Old Warren

Northfield
Plantation

Strip
Lynchets

Enclosure

Foxholes
Farm

Littlebredy
Farm

5

Macmillan Way

Hut
Circle

New Close
Coppice

88

Tenants
Hill

Topparts
Dairy

Enclosure

Stone Circle

Crow Hill

4

Valley of Stones
National Nature Reserve

Gorwell
Farm

3

The Grey Mare
& her Colts
(Long Barrow)

Bishop's Road

87

Hanging
Coppice

Bow Coppice

Bramble
Coppice

Tumuli

2

Broad
Coppice

DT3

Macmillan Way

White Hill Plantation

South West Coast Path

Bishop's Road

Hampton
Stone Circle

White Hill

Tumuli

1

86

131
105

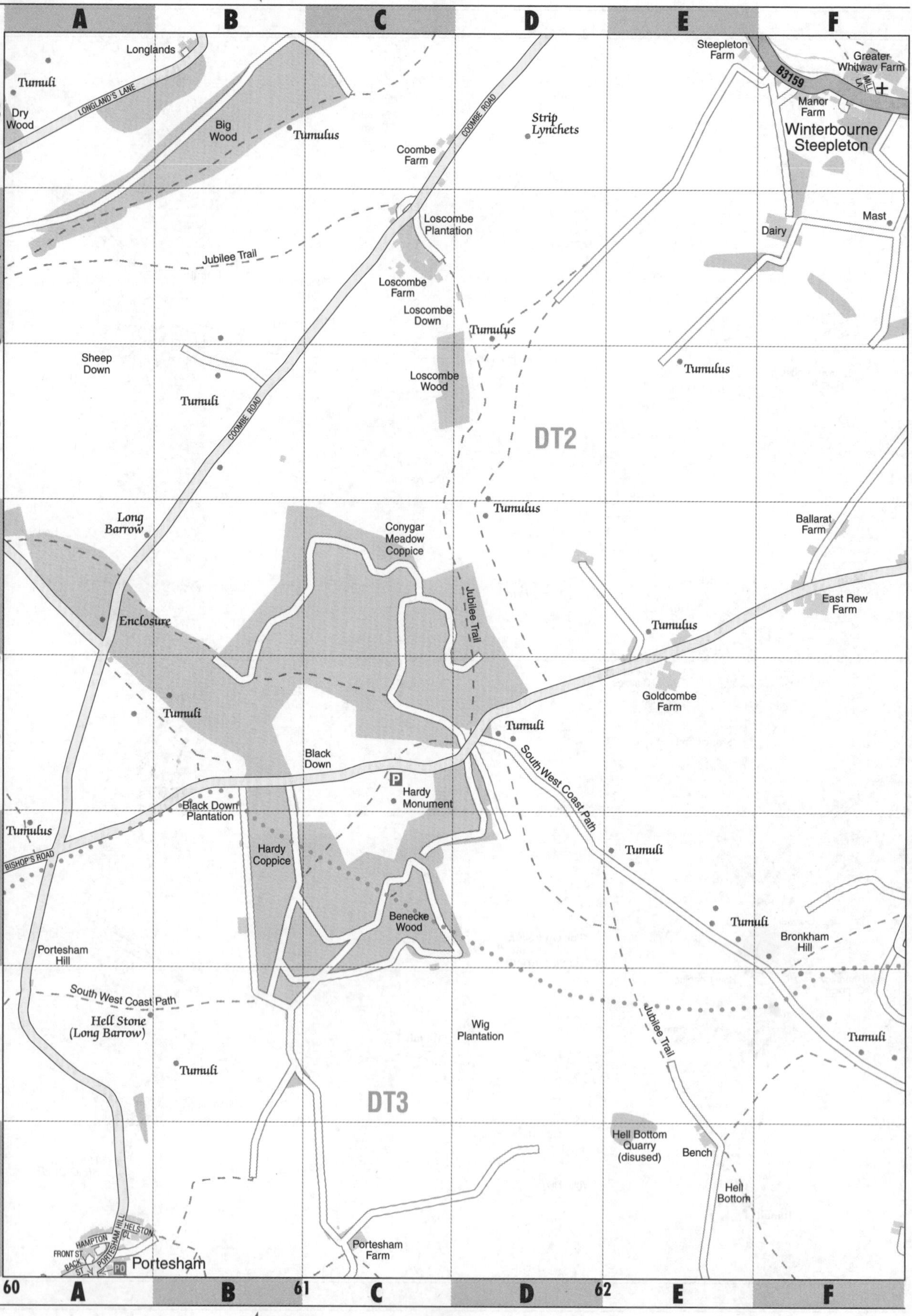

A B C D E F

8

Longlands

Tumuli

Dry
Wood

Longland's Lane

Big
Wood

Tumulus

Coombe
Farm

Strip
Lynchets

Steepleton
Farm

Greater
Whitway Farm

B3159

Manor
Farm

Winterbourne
Steepleton

7

Jubilee Trail

Loscombe
Plantation

Loscombe
Farm

Dairy

Mast

89

Sheep
Down

Tumuli

Coombe Road

Loscombe
Down

Loscombe
Wood

Tumulus

Tumulus

6

DT2

5

Long
Barrow

Enclosure

Conygar
Meadow
Coppice

Jubilee Trail

Tumulus

Tumulus

Ballarat
Farm

East Rew
Farm

88

Tumuli

Black
Down

Tumuli

Goldcombe
Farm

4

P

Hardy
Monument

South West Coast Path

Tumuli

3

Tumulus

BISHOP'S ROAD

Black Down
Plantation

Hardy
Coppice

Benecke
Wood

Tumuli

Tumuli

Bronkham
Hill

87

Portesham
Hill

South West Coast Path

Hell Stone
(Long Barrow)

Wig
Plantation

Jubilee Trail

Tumuli

2

Tumuli

DT3

Hell Bottom
Quarry
(disused)

Bench

Hell
Bottom

1

HAMPTON HILL

HELSTON
CL

FRONT ST

BACK
ST

PO

Portesham

Portesham
Farm

86

60   **A**   **B**   61   **C**   **D**   62   **E**   **F**

131
150

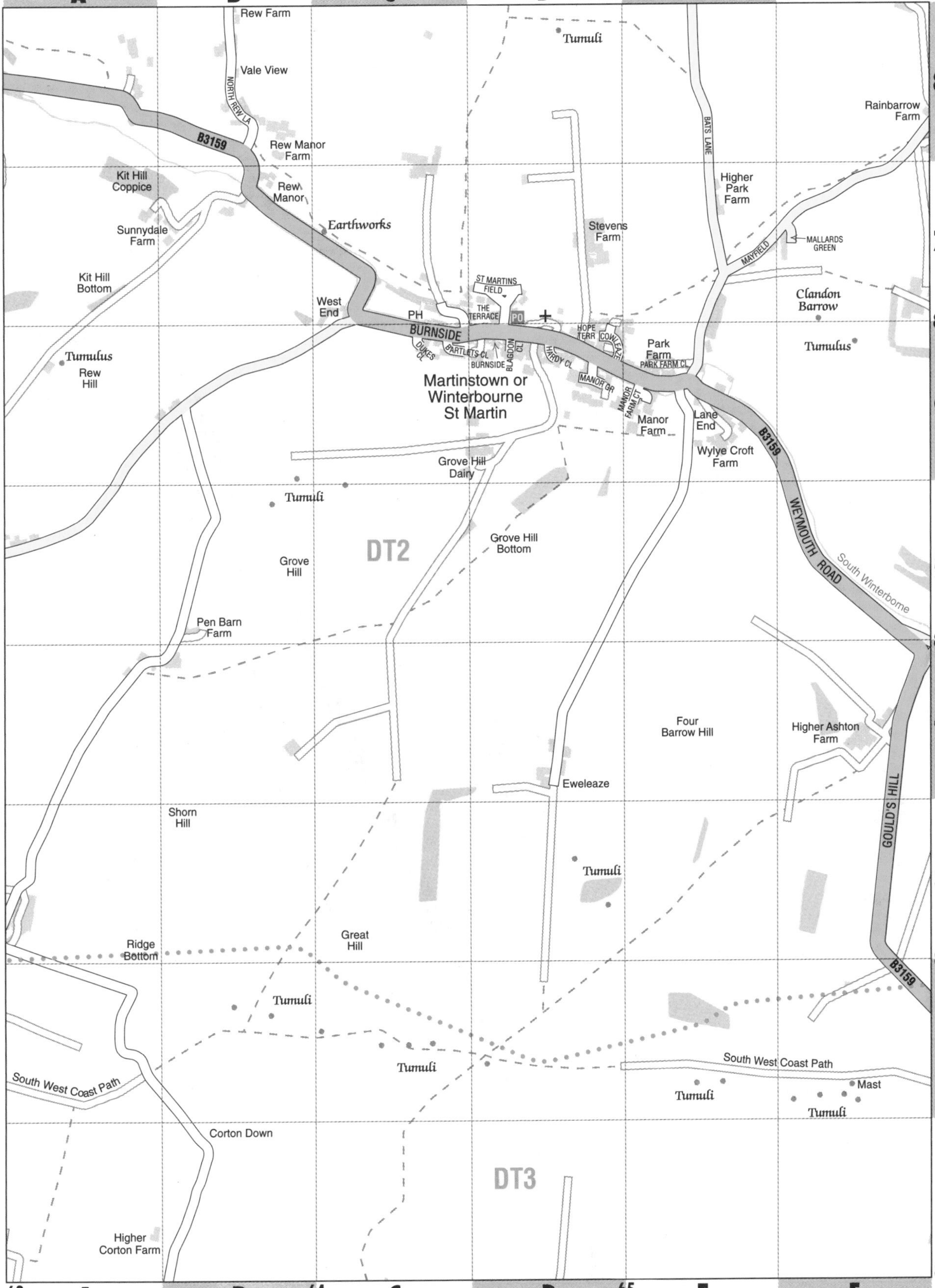
106
134
A
B
C
D
E
F
Rew Farm
Tumuli
Vale View
NORTH REW LA
B3159
Rew Manor
Farm
BATS LANE
Rainbarrow
Farm
Kit Hill
Coppice
Rew
Manor
Higher
Park
Farm
Earthworks
Stevens
Farm
Sunnydale
Farm
MAYFIELD
MALLARDS
GREEN
Kit Hill
Bottom
ST MARTINS
FIELD
West
End
THE
TERRACE
PO
Clandon
Barrow
PH
BURNSIDE
HOPE
TERR
COWLEAZE
Park
Farm
PARK FARM CL
Tumulus
DUKES
CL
BARTLETS CL
BURNSIDE
BLAGDON
CL
HARDY CL
Tumulus
Rew
Hill
Martinstown or
Winterbourne
St Martin
MANOR GR
MANOR
FARM CT
Manor
Farm
Lane
End
Wylye Croft
Farm
Grove Hill
Dairy
Tumuli
Grove Hill
Bottom
DT2
Grove
Hill
WEYMOUTH ROAD
South Winterborne
Pen Barn
Farm
Four
Barrow Hill
Higher Ashton
Farm
Eweleaze
GOULD'S HILL
Shorn
Hill
Tumuli
Great
Hill
Ridge
Bottom
Tumuli
Tumuli
South West Coast Path
Mast
Tumuli
Tumuli
South West Coast Path
Corton Down
DT3
Higher
Corton Farm
8
7
89
6
5
88
4
3
87
2
1
86
63
64
65
151
134

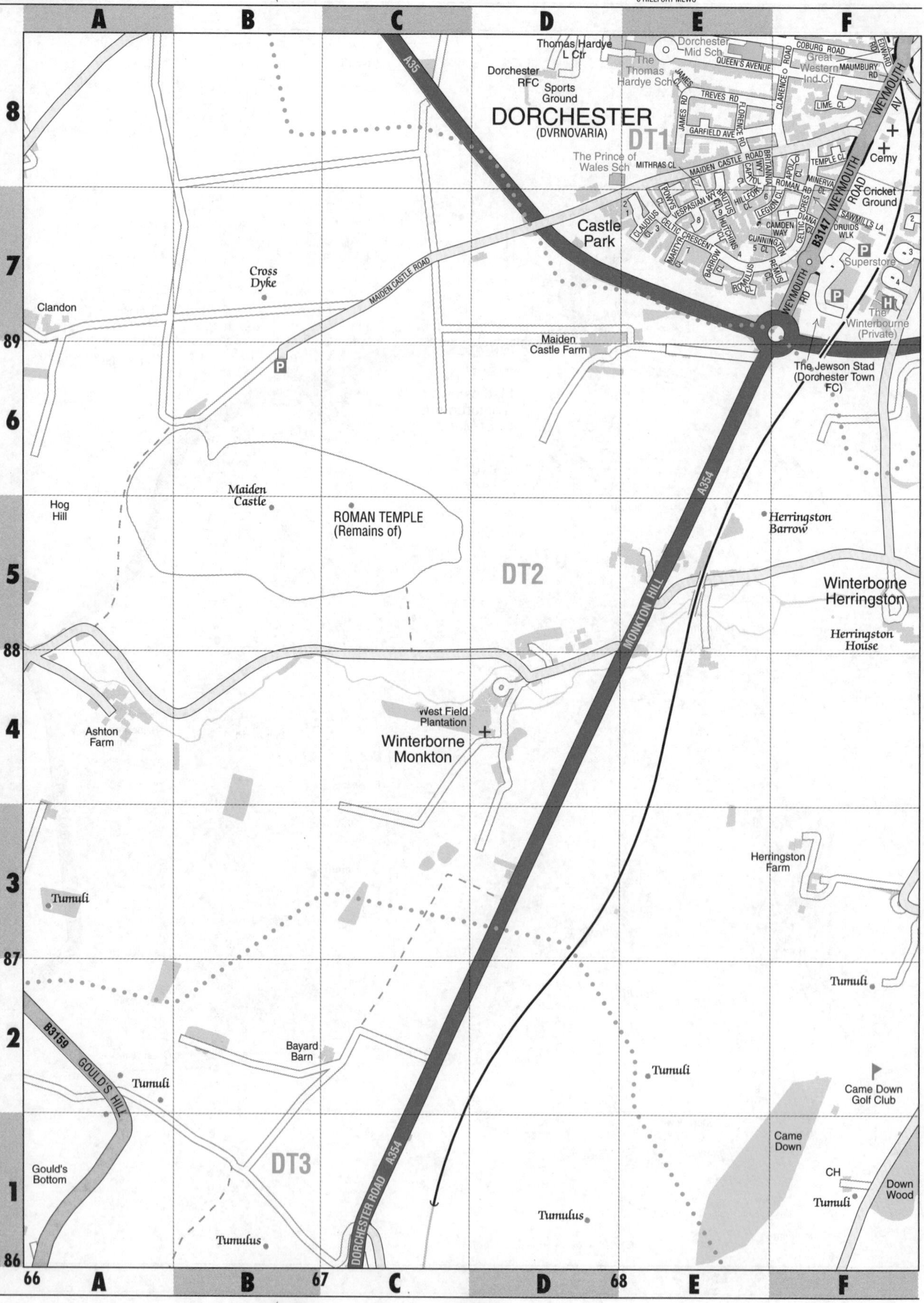

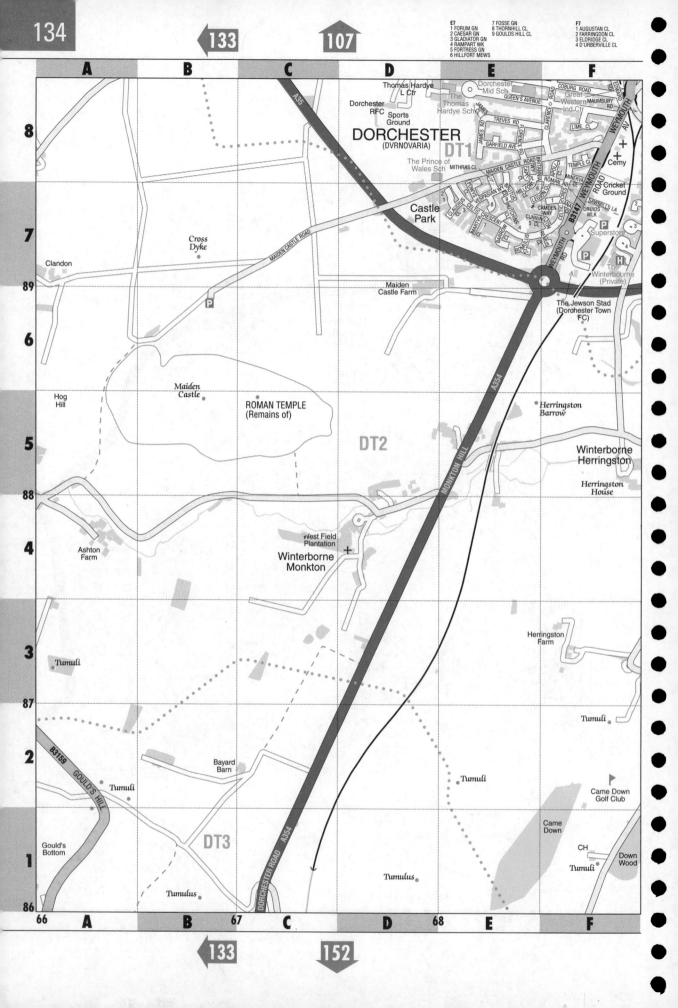

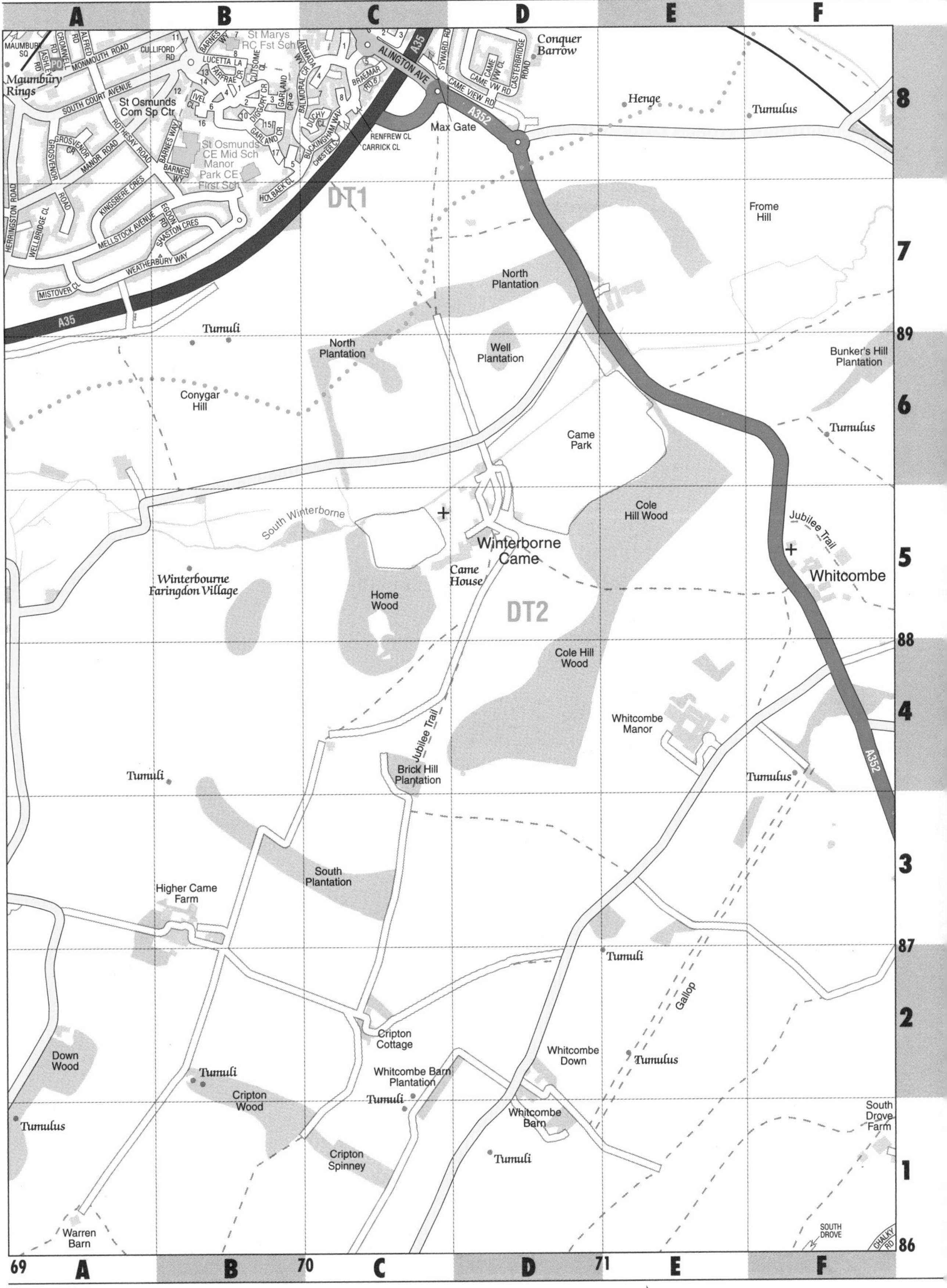

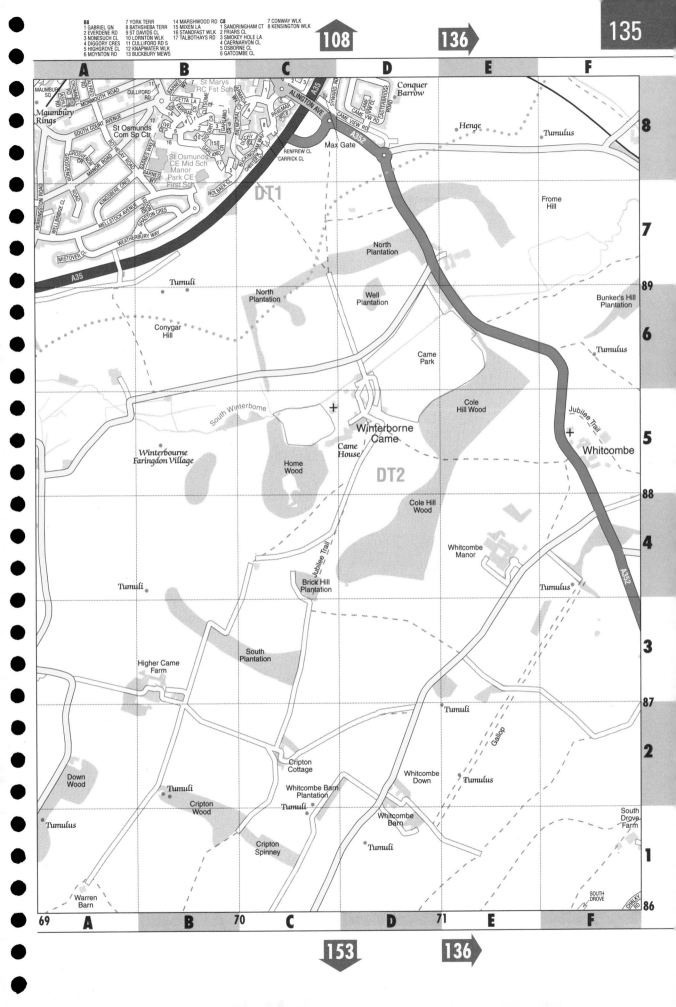

108
136
136

B8
1 GABRIEL GN
2 EVERDENE RD
3 NONESUCH CL
4 DIGGORY CRES
5 HIGHGROVE CL
6 MOYNTON RD
7 YORK TERR
8 BATHSHEBA TERR
9 ST DAVIDS CL
10 LORNTON WLK
11 CULLIFORD RD S
12 KNAPWATER WLK
13 BUCKBURY MEWS
14 MARSHWOOD RD
15 MIXEN LA
16 STANDFAST WLK
17 TALBOTHAYS RD

C8
1 SANDRINGHAM CT
2 FRIARS CL
3 SMOKEY HOLE LA
4 CAERNARVON CL
5 OSBORNE CL
6 GATCOMBE CL
7 CONWAY WLK
8 KENSINGTON WLK

← 135
109

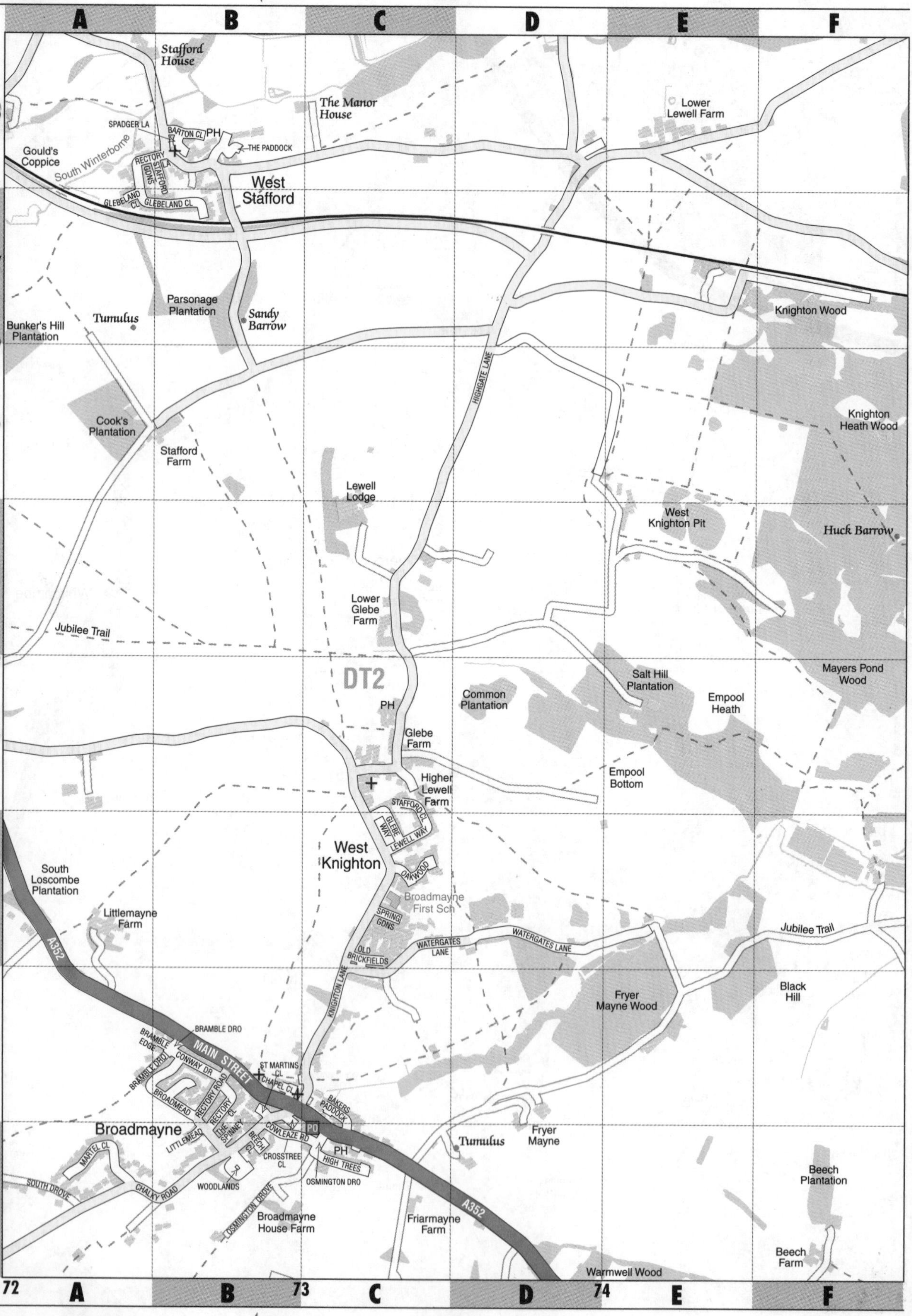

A   B   C   D   E   F

8

Stafford House

The Manor House

Lower Lewell Farm

SPADGER LA
BARTON CL
PH
THE PADDOCK

Gould's Coppice

South Winterborne

RECTORY GDNS

West Stafford

GLEBELAND CL
GLEBELAND CL

7

Parsonage Plantation

Knighton Wood

Bunker's Hill Plantation

Tumulus

Sandy Barrow

89

HIGHGATE LANE

6

Cook's Plantation

Stafford Farm

Knighton Heath Wood

Lewell Lodge

West Knighton Pit

Huck Barrow

5

Lower Glebe Farm

Jubilee Trail

88

DT2

Salt Hill Plantation

Mayers Pond Wood

PH

Common Plantation

Empool Heath

4

Glebe Farm

Empool Bottom

Higher Lewell Farm

STAFFORD CL
GLEBE WAY
LEWELL WAY

West Knighton

OAKWOOD

3

South Loscombe Plantation

Littlemayne Farm

SPRING GDNS

Broadmayne First Sch

Jubilee Trail

A352

OLD BRICKFIELDS

WATERGATES LANE
WATERGATES LANE

87

KNIGHTON LANE

Black Hill

2

BRAMBLE DRO

MAIN STREET

BRAMBLE EDGE

CONWAY DR

Fryer Mayne Wood

BRAMBLE DRO

BROADMEAD

ST MARTINS CL
CHAPEL CL

RECTORY ROAD

BAKERS PADDOCK

Broadmayne

MARTEL CL

LITTLEMEAD

THE SPINNEY

BEECH

COWLEAZE RD

PO

Tumulus

Fryer Mayne

Beech Plantation

CROSSTREE CL

HIGH TREES

PH

SOUTH DROVE

CHALKY ROAD

WOODLANDS

OSMINGTON DRO

OSMINGTON DRO

1

Broadmayne House Farm

Friarmayne Farm

A352

Beech Farm

86

72   A   B   73   C   D   74   E   F

Warmwell Wood

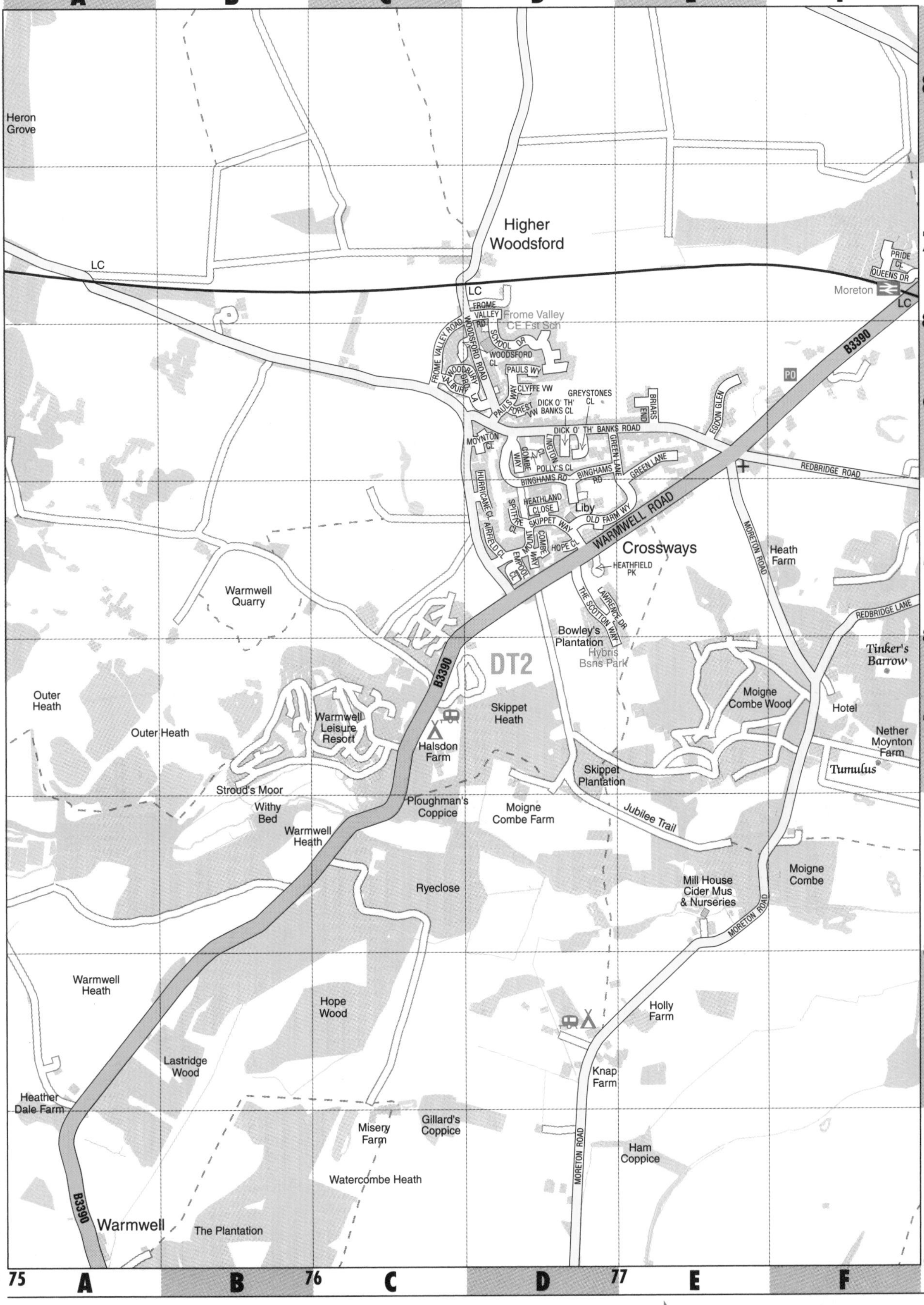

110
138

A   B   C   D   E   F

8

Heron Grove

7

Higher Woodsford

LC

LC

PRIDE CL
QUEENS DR
Moreton
LC

89

FROME VALLEY ROAD
WOODSFORD ROAD
SCHOOL DR
Frome Valley
CE Fst Sch
WOODSFORD CL
PAULS WY

B3390

PO

6

VICARAGE
WOODBURY
FROME VALLEY RD

CLYFFE VW
DICK O' TH'
VAN BANKS CL
PAULS WAY
CREST
GREYSTONES
CL
BRIARS
END

GORDON GLEN

MOYNTON
CL
POLLY'S CL
LINGTON CL
DICK O' TH' BANKS ROAD
GREEN LANE
COMBE WAY
BINGHAMS RD
BINGHAMS
RD
Green Lane

REDBRIDGE ROAD

HURRICANE PL
SPITFIRE
AIRFIELD
HEATHLAND
CLOSE
SKIPPET WAY
OLD FARM WY
Liby

WARMWELL ROAD

Crossways

Heath Farm

5

COMBE
WAY
EMPTOL WY
HOPE CL
HEATHFIELD
PK

MORETON ROAD

Warmwell Quarry

LAWRENCE DR
THE SCOTTISH WAY

88

Bowley's Plantation

Hybris Bsns Park

REDBRIDGE LANE

Tinker's Barrow

Outer Heath

B3390

DT2

Skippet Heath

Moigne Combe Wood

Hotel

4

Outer Heath

Warmwell Leisure Resort

Halsdon Farm

Skippet Plantation

Nether Moynton Farm

Tumulus

Stroud's Moor

Withy Bed

Ploughman's Coppice

Moigne Combe Farm

Jubilee Trail

Moigne Combe

3

Warmwell Heath

Ryeclose

Mill House Cider Mus & Nurseries

MORETON ROAD

87

Warmwell Heath

Hope Wood

Holly Farm

2

Lastridge Wood

Heather Dale Farm

Misery Farm

Gillard's Coppice

Knap Farm

B3390

Watercombe Heath

Ham Coppice

1

Warmwell

The Plantation

86

155
138

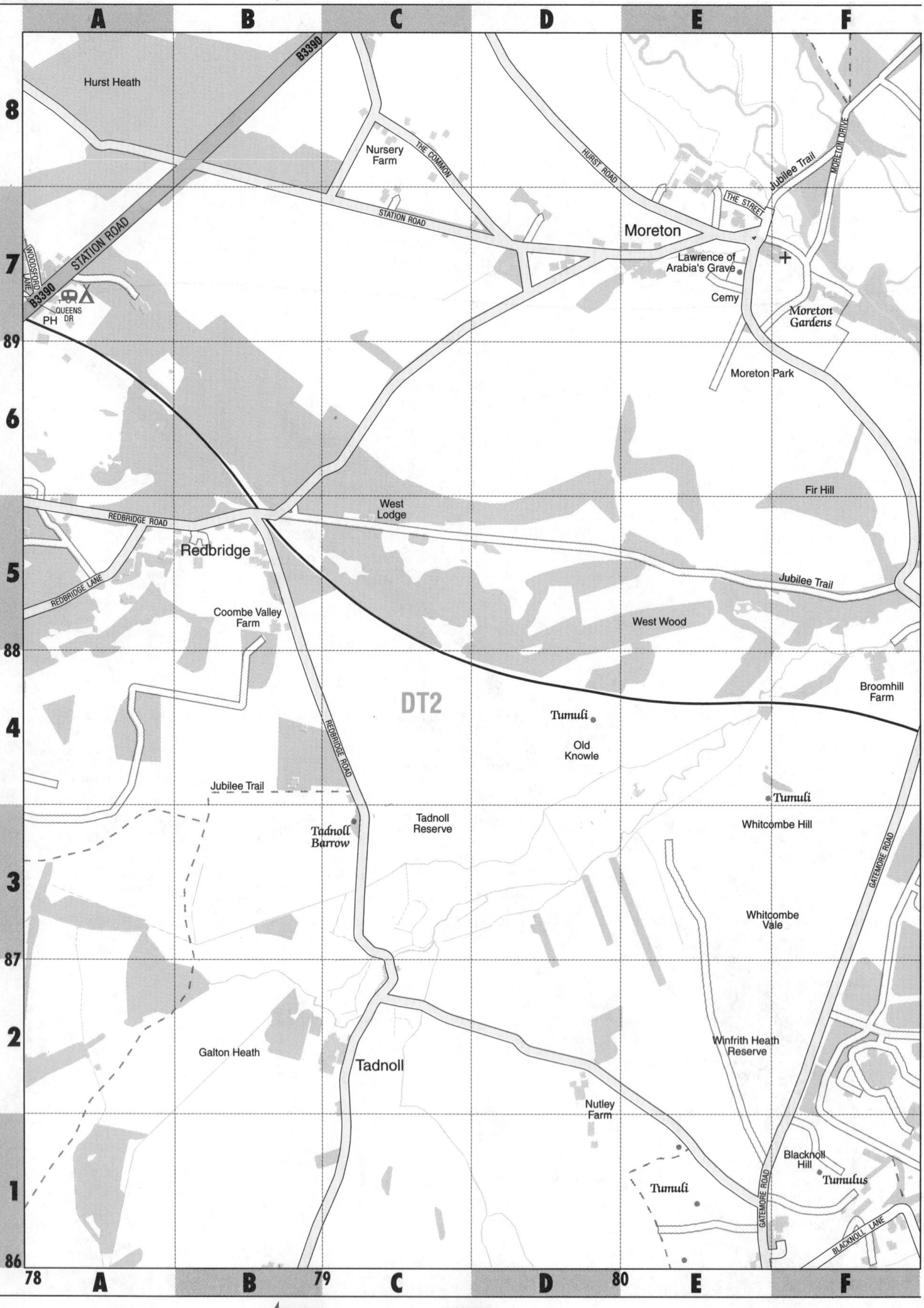

137
111

A **B** **C** **D** **E** **F**

Hurst Heath

B3390

8

Nursery
Farm

THE COMMON

STATION ROAD

HURST ROAD

THE STREET

Jubilee Trail

MORETON DRIVE

Moreton

7

WOODSFORD LANE

STATION ROAD

B3390

Lawrence of
Arabia's Grave

Cemy

Moreton
Gardens

QUEENS
DR

PH

89

Moreton Park

6

Fir Hill

REDBRIDGE ROAD

West
Lodge

Jubilee Trail

Redbridge

5

REDBRIDGE LANE

Coombe Valley
Farm

West Wood

88

DT2

Broomhill
Farm

4

REDBRIDGE ROAD

Tumuli

Old
Knowle

Tumuli

Jubilee Trail

Whitcombe Hill

Tadnoll
Barrow

Tadnoll
Reserve

3

Whitcombe
Vale

87

GATEMORE ROAD

2

Galton Heath

Tadnoll

Winfrith Heath
Reserve

Nutley
Farm

Blacknoll
Hill

1

Tumuli

GATEMORE ROAD

Tumulus

BLACKNOLL LANE

86

78 **A** **B** **79** **C** **D** **80** **E** **F**

137
156

112
140

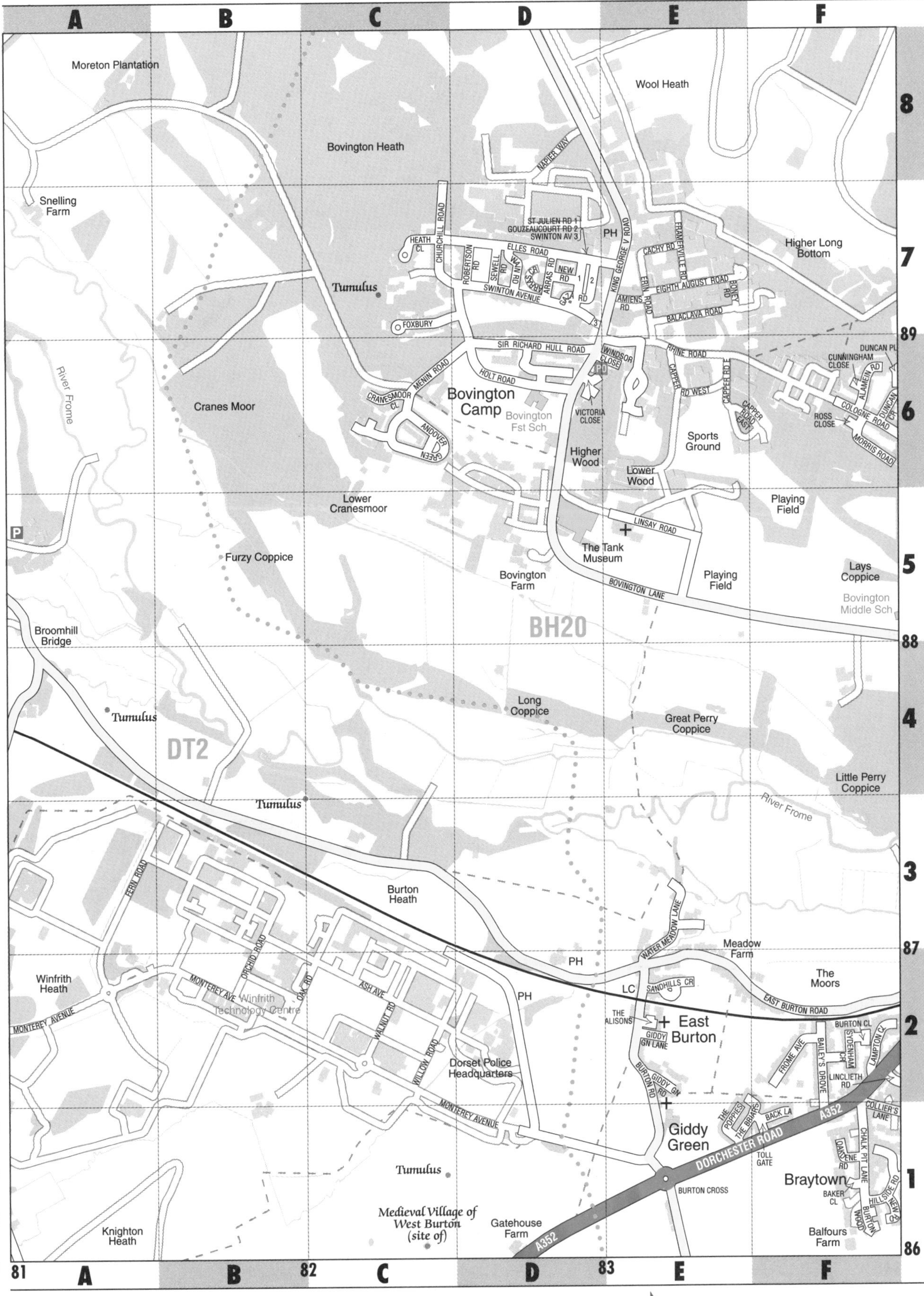
A
B
C
D
E
F
8
7
89
6
5
88
4
3
87
2
1
86
81
82
83
Moreton Plantation
Wool Heath
Bovington Heath
Snelling Farm
NAPIER WAY
ST JULIEN RD 1
GOUZEAUCOURT RD 2
SWINTON AV 3
PH
KING GEORGE V ROAD
FRAMERVILLE RD
Higher Long Bottom
HEATH CL
CHURCHILL ROAD
ELLES ROAD
ROBERTSON RD
SEWELL RD
NEW RD
CACHY RD
ERIN ROAD
EIGHTH AUGUST ROAD
BONEY RD
Tumulus
SWINTON AVENUE
ARRAS RD
AMIENS RD
BALACLAVA ROAD
FOXBURY
SIR RICHARD HULL ROAD
WINDSOR CLOSE
RHINE ROAD
DUNCAN PL
CUNNINGHAM CLOSE
ALAMEIN RD
River Frome
MENIN ROAD
HOLT ROAD
PO
CAPPER RD WEST
CAPPER RD E
CAPPER ROAD EAST
CRANESMOOR CL
Bovington Camp
Bovington Fst Sch
VICTORIA CLOSE
ROSS CLOSE
COLOGNE ROAD
DUNCAN CR
Cranes Moor
ANDOVER GREEN
Higher Wood
Sports Ground
MORRIS ROAD
Lower Wood
Lower Cranesmoor
Playing Field
P
LINSAY ROAD
The Tank Museum
Furzy Coppice
Bovington Farm
Playing Field
Lays Coppice
BOVINGTON LANE
Bovington Middle Sch
BH20
Broomhill Bridge
Long Coppice
Great Perry Coppice
Tumulus
DT2
Little Perry Coppice
Tumulus
River Frome
FERN ROAD
Burton Heath
WATER MEADOW LANE
ORCHID ROAD
Meadow Farm
Winfrith Heath
PH
MONTEREY AVE
Winfrith Technology Centre
OAK RD
ASH AVE
PH
LC
SANDHILLS CR
The Moors
EAST BURTON ROAD
MONTEREY AVENUE
THE ALISONS
East Burton
GIDDY GN LANE
BURTON CL
SYDENHAM CR
LAMPTON CL
FROME AVE
BAILEY'S DROVE
WALNUT RD
WILLOW ROAD
Dorset Police Headquarters
BURTON RD
GIDDY GN RD
LINCLIETH RD
MONTEREY AVENUE
THE POPPIES
THE BRIARS
BACK LA
A352
COLLIER'S LANE
Giddy Green
DORCHESTER ROAD
TOLL GATE
OAKDENE RD
CHALK PIT LANE
Tumulus
BURTON CROSS
Braytown
HILLSIDE RD
Medieval Village of West Burton (site of)
Gatehouse Farm
BAKER CL
BURTON WOOD
Knighton Heath
A352
Balfours Farm
81
A
B
82
C
D
83
E
F

157
140

A B C D E F

8

Stoke
Heath

CH

Grants
Farm

7

Tumuli

Longthorns
Farm

RIDDLETOWN ROAD

89

Woolbridge
Heath

Birch Wood

Great
Plantation

Sand and
Gravel Pit

Lower Long
Bottom

6

DUNCAN CRES

COLOGNE ROAD

Monkey
World Ape
Rescue
Centre

Battery
Bank

Sand and
Gravel Pits

5

Bovington
Middle Sch

Eight Acre Wood
Nature Reserve

Hethfelton

88

BOVINGTON LA

COLOGNE RD

LYTCHETT LANE

TOUT HILL

LYTCHETT LANE

Tout
Hill

BH20

4

Stokeford Common

Holly Wood

PH

Stokeford

3

A352

River Frome

Wool
Bridge

Stony
Weir

Hethfelton
Farm

87

LC

Wool

East Burton Rd

DORCHESTER ROAD

PH

HYDE
RD

STATION RD

P

PO

1 JEREMY CL
2 BINDON WY
3 THE CROSS

Bindon Abbey
(rems)

Church

2

St Marys RC
First Sch

Liby

MEADOW LANE

BREACH FIELD

HIGH ST CL

HIGH ST CL

HIGH ST

KING ST

Manor
Farm

Wool

East Stoke Fen
Reserve

Manor
Farm

COLLIER'S LANE

FOLLY LA

KNOWLE HL

DUCK ST

B3071

CHURCH LANE

Wool CE
First Sch

BINDON LANE

East
Stoke

LWR HILLSIDE RD

Braytown

LULWORTH ROAD

MEADOW

1

Quarr
Hill

Cole
Wood

Inglewood
Farm

86

84 A B 85 C D 86 E F

A1
1 KNOWLE WOOD KNAP
2 VICARAGE CL
3 HILLSIDE RD

A2
1 CEDAR CL
2 COTTAGE CL
3 LINCLIETH RD
4 BREACH FIELD
5 LOCKS PIECE
6 THE SQUARE

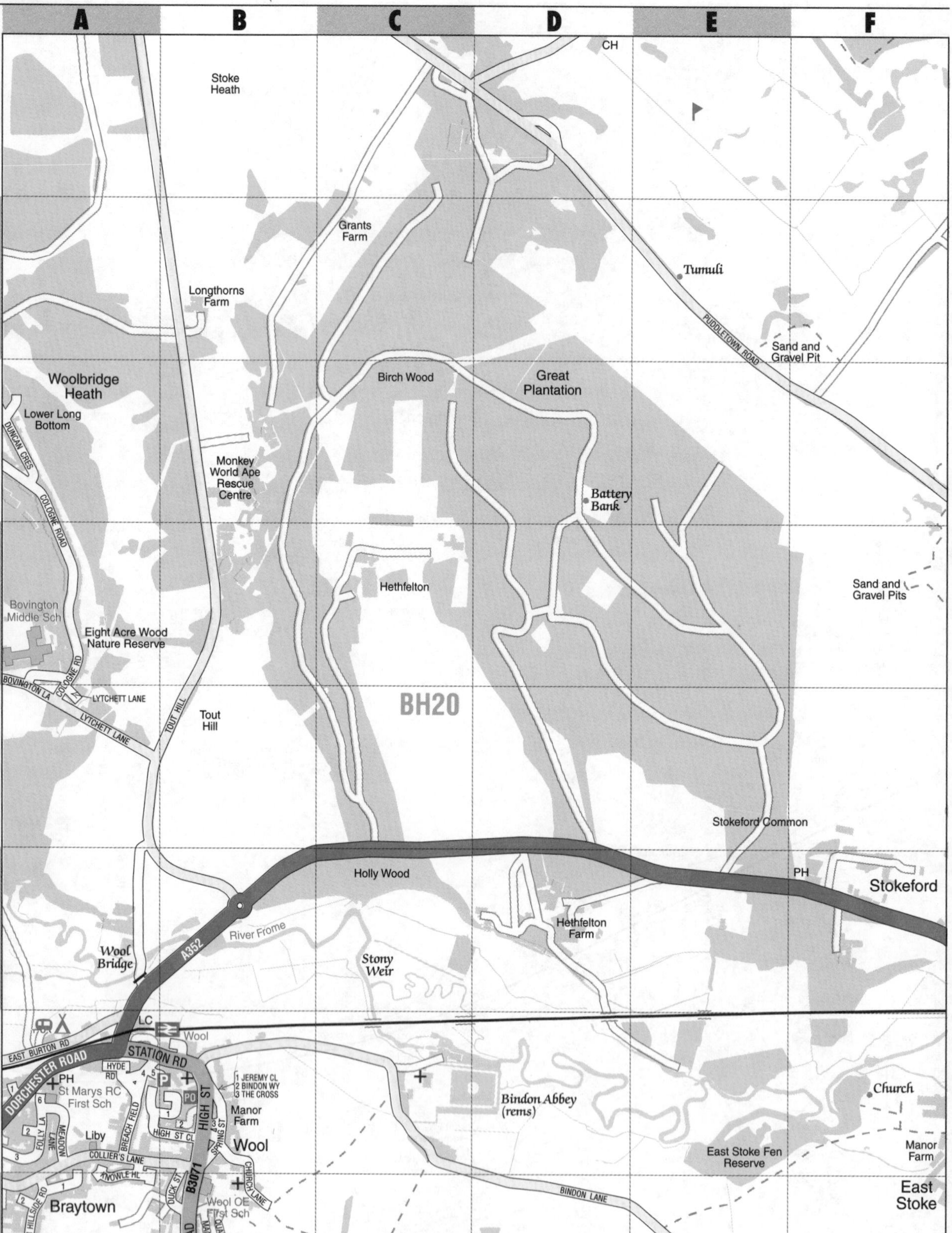

114
142

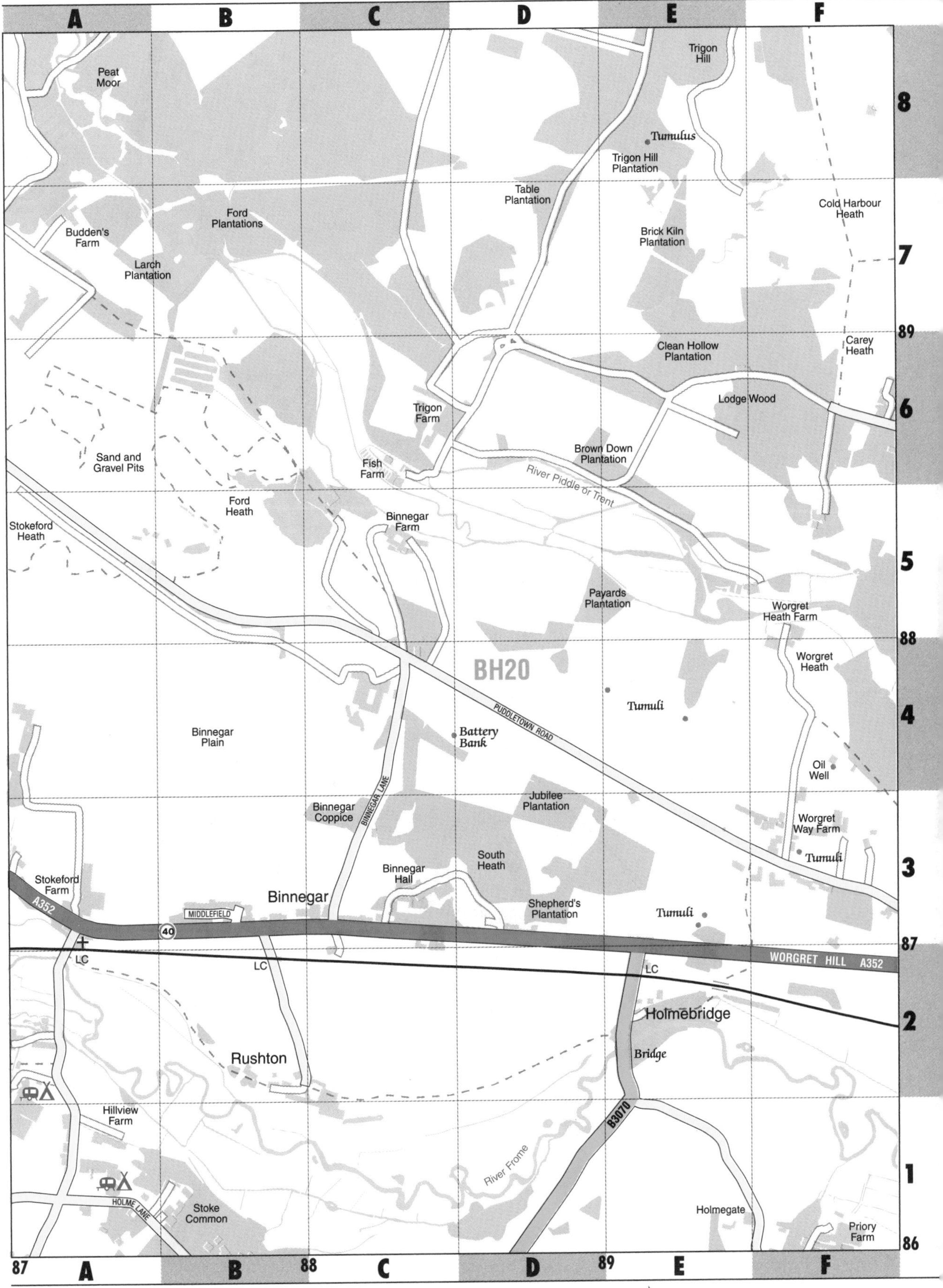
A
B
C
D
E
F
Peat Moor
Trigon Hill
Tumulus
Trigon Hill Plantation
Table Plantation
Cold Harbour Heath
Budden's Farm
Ford Plantations
Brick Kiln Plantation
Larch Plantation
Clean Hollow Plantation
Carey Heath
Lodge Wood
Trigon Farm
Sand and Gravel Pits
Fish Farm
Brown Down Plantation
River Piddle or Trent
Ford Heath
Binnegar Farm
Stokeford Heath
Payards Plantation
Worgret Heath Farm
Worgret Heath
BH20
Tumuli
Puddletown Road
Battery Bank
Binnegar Plain
Oil Well
Jubilee Plantation
Binnegar Coppice
Binnegar Lane
Worgret Way Farm
Tumuli
South Heath
Binnegar Hall
Stokeford Farm
Binnegar
Shepherd's Plantation
Tumuli
A352
Middlefield
40
LC
LC
LC
Worgret Hill A352
Holmebridge
Bridge
Rushton
Hillview Farm
B3070
River Frome
Holme Lane
Stoke Common
Holmegate
Priory Farm
8
7
89
6
5
88
4
3
87
2
1
86
87
88
89

159
142

141
115

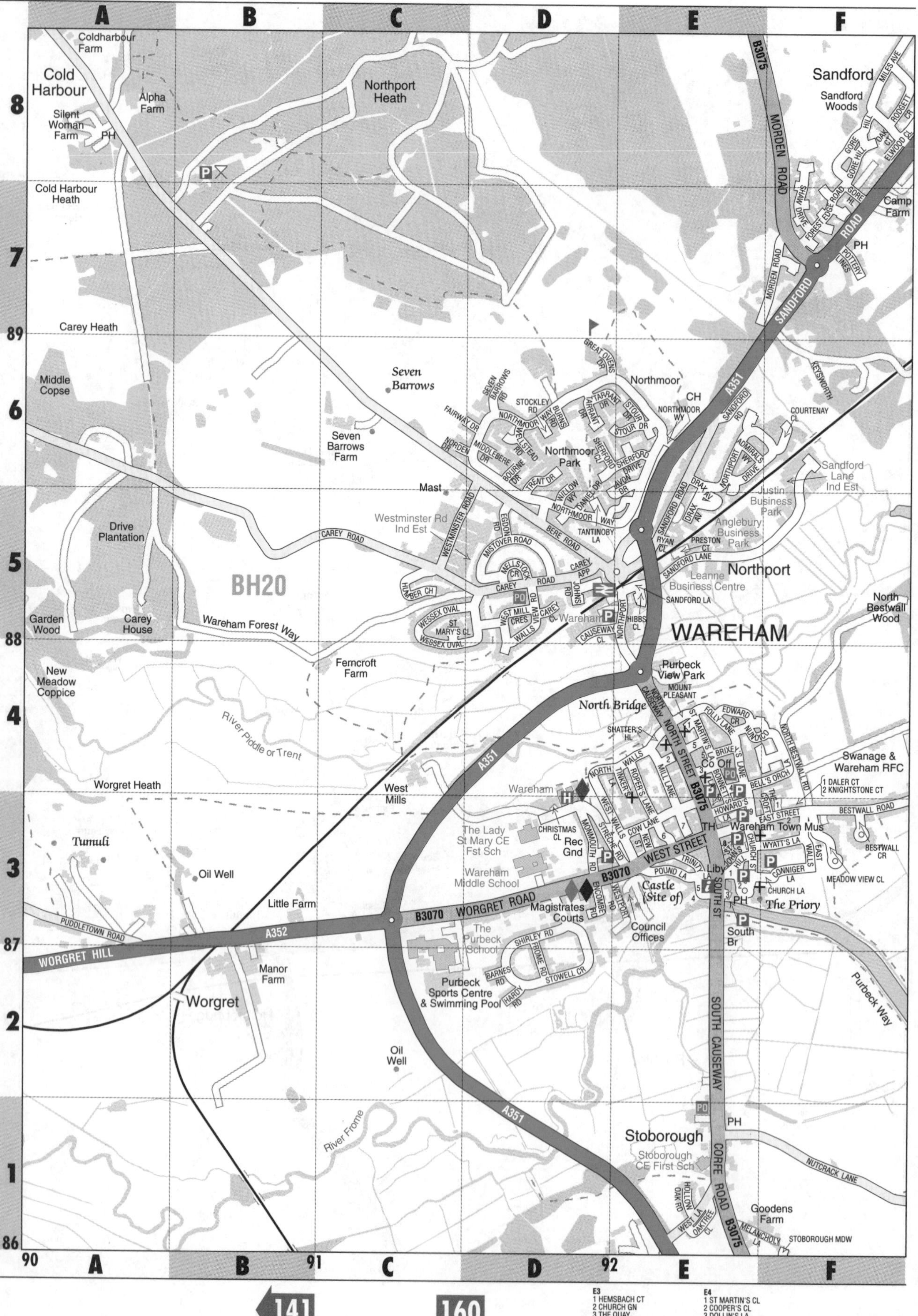

141
160

E3
1 HEMSBACH CT
2 CHURCH GN
3 THE QUAY
4 ABBOT'S QUAY
5 TANNER'S LA
6 ST MICHAEL'S RD
7 HILLARD CT
8 REMPSTONE SHOPPING ARCADE
9 MORETON'S LA

E4
1 ST MARTIN'S CL
2 COOPER'S CL
3 DOLLIN'S LA
4 CARRION LA
5 KENNINGTON SQ
6 CONCHES CT

116
144

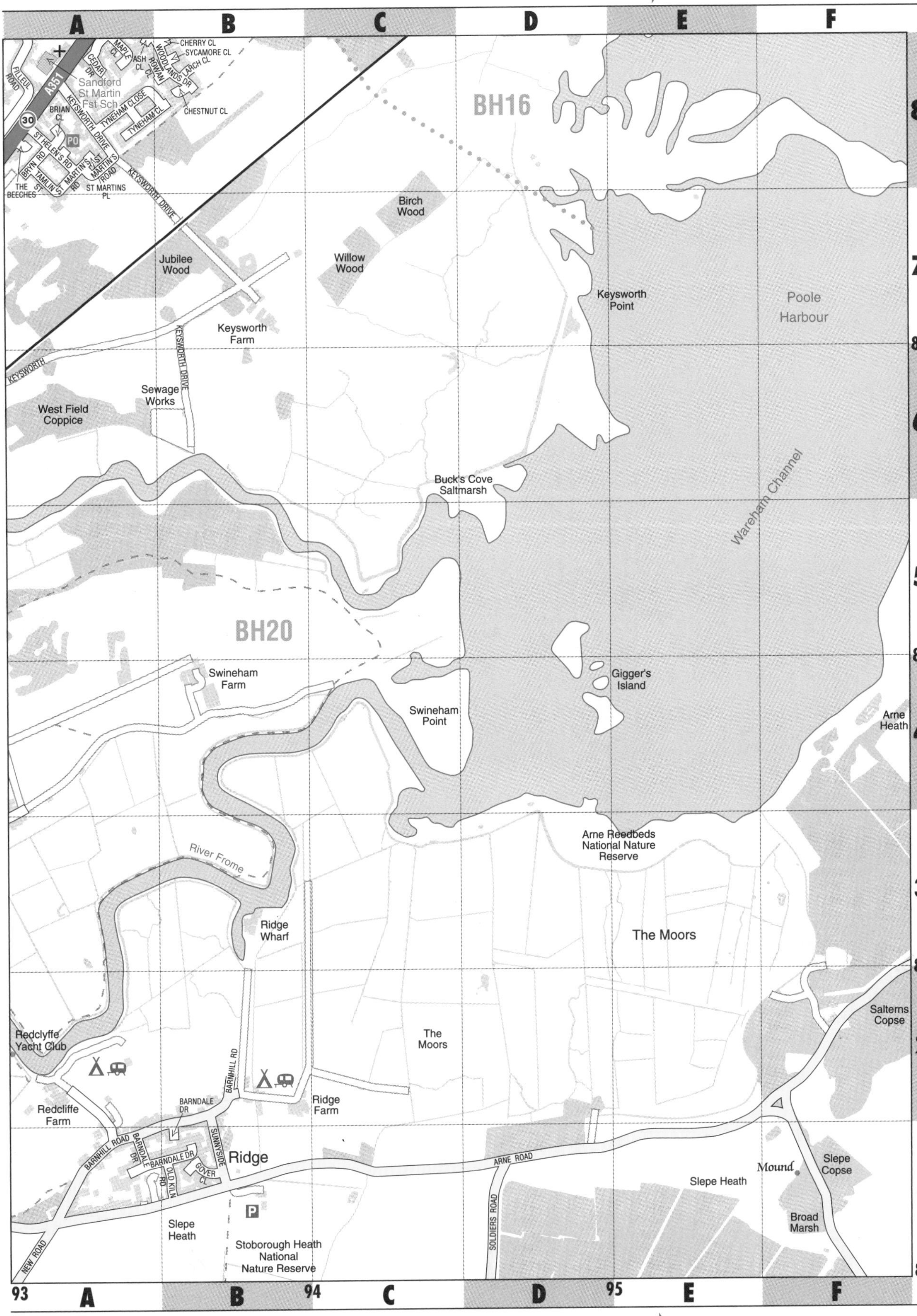
A
B
C
D
E
F
8
7
89
6
5
88
4
3
87
2
1
86
93
94
95
CHERRY CL
SYCAMORE CL
ARCH CL
MAPLE CL
CEDAR DR
ASH CL
ROWAN
WOODLANDS DR
FILLEUL ROAD
A351
Sandford
St Martin
Fst Sch
TYNEHAM CLOSE
TYNEHAM CL
CHESTNUT CL
BRIAN CL
KEYSWORTH DRIVE
30
PO
ST HELEN'S RD
BRYN RD
TAMLIN ST
ST MARTIN'S RD
EAST ST MARTIN'S ROAD
THE BEECHES
ST MARTINS PL
BH16
Birch
Wood
Willow
Wood
Jubilee
Wood
Keysworth
Farm
Keysworth
Point
Poole
Harbour
KEYSWORTH
West Field
Coppice
Sewage
Works
Buck's Cove
Saltmarsh
Wareham Channel
BH20
Swineham
Farm
Gigger's
Island
Swineham
Point
Arne
Heath
Arne Reedbeds
National Nature
Reserve
River Frome
Ridge
Wharf
The Moors
Salterns
Copse
The
Moors
Redclyffe
Yacht Club
BARNHILL RD
Redcliffe
Farm
BARNDALE DR
Ridge
Farm
BARNHILL ROAD
SUNNYSIDE
Ridge
GOVER CL
OLD KILN RD
ARNE ROAD
SOLDIERS ROAD
Slepe Heath
Mound
Slepe
Copse
P
Slepe
Heath
Broad
Marsh
Stoborough Heath
National
Nature Reserve
NEW ROAD

161
144

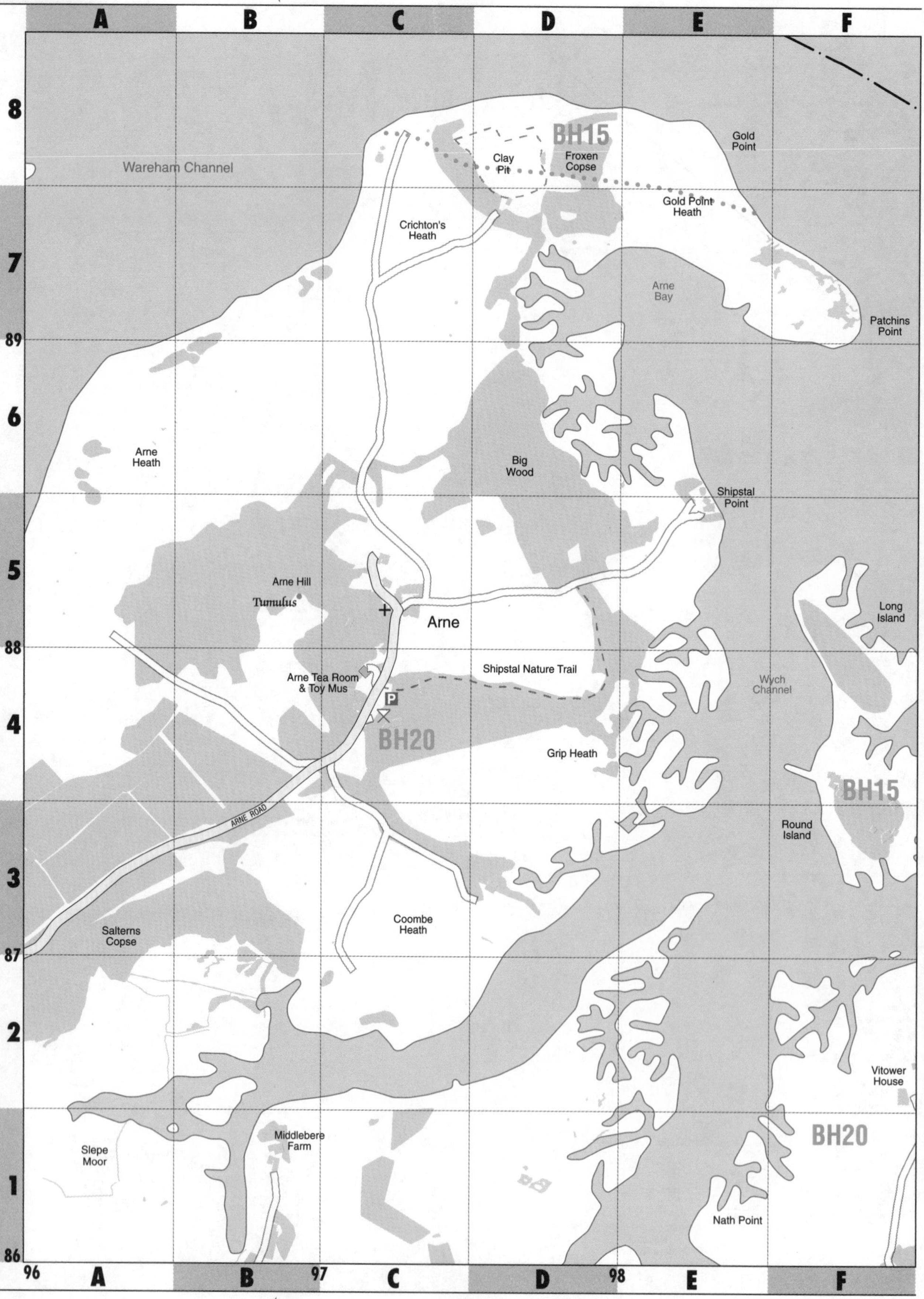

143
117
118

A   B   C   D   E   F

8

Wareham Channel

BH15

Gold
Point

Clay
Pit

Froxen
Copse

Gold Point
Heath

Crichton's
Heath

7

Arne
Bay

89

Patchins
Point

6

Arne
Heath

Big
Wood

Shipstal
Point

5

Arne Hill

Tumulus

Long
Island

Arne

88

Shipstal Nature Trail

Arne Tea Room
& Toy Mus

Wych
Channel

P

4

BH20

Grip Heath

BH15

ARNE ROAD

Round
Island

3

Salterns
Copse

Coombe
Heath

87

2

Vitower
House

BH20

1

Slepe
Moor

Middlebere
Farm

Nath Point

86

96   A   B   97   C   D   98   E   F

118 146 119

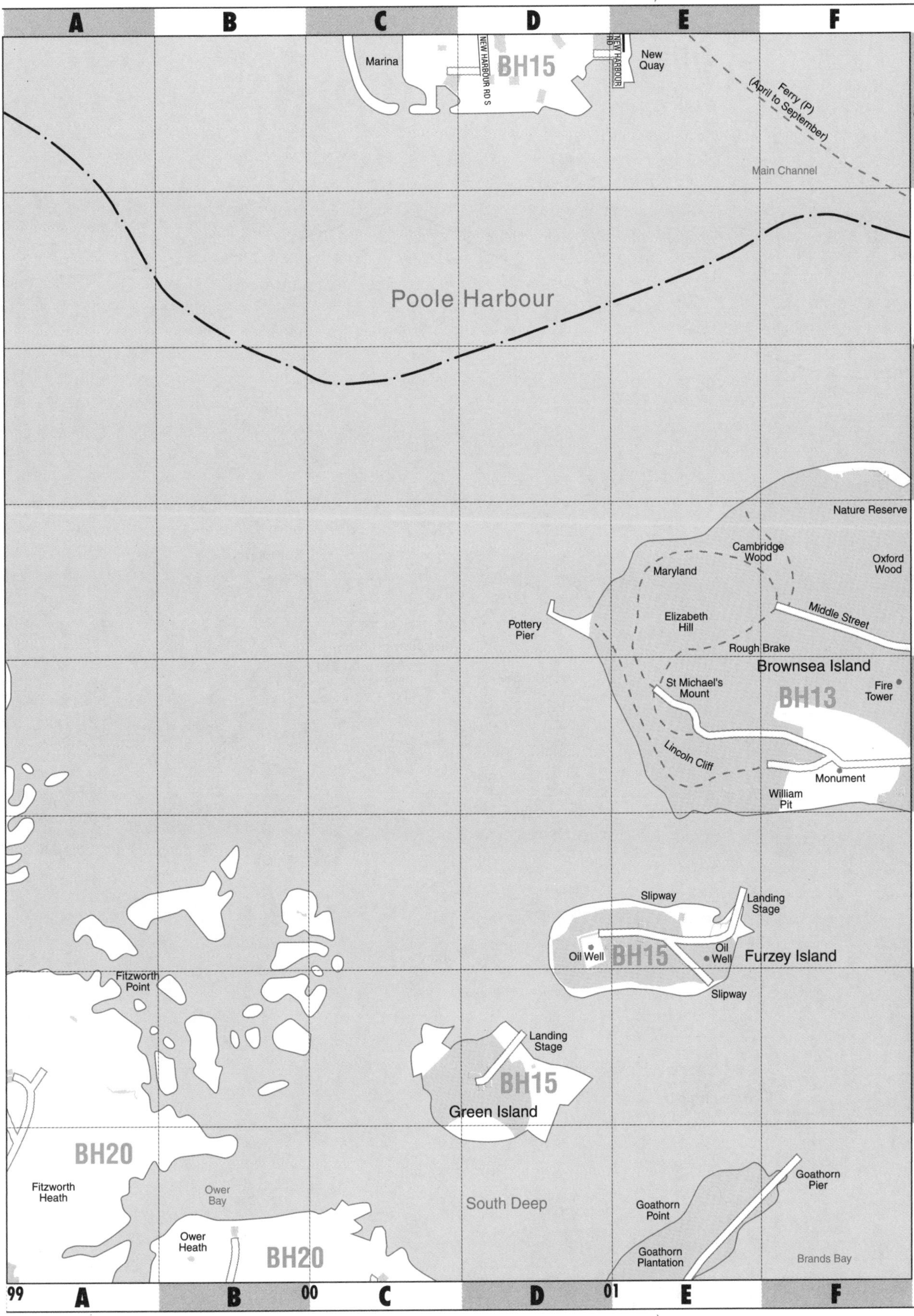
A
B
C
D
E
F
Marina
NEW HARBOUR RD S
BH15
NEW HARBOUR RD
New Quay
Ferry (P) (April to September)
Main Channel
8
7
Poole Harbour
89
6
Nature Reserve
Cambridge Wood
Oxford Wood
Maryland
5
Elizabeth Hill
Middle Street
Pottery Pier
Rough Brake
88
Brownsea Island
St Michael's Mount
Fire Tower
BH13
4
Lincoln Cliff
Monument
William Pit
3
Slipway
Landing Stage
Oil Well
BH15
Oil Well
Furzey Island
87
Fitzworth Point
Slipway
Landing Stage
2
BH15
Green Island
BH20
Goathorn Pier
Fitzworth Heath
Ower Bay
South Deep
Goathorn Point
1
Ower Heath
BH20
Goathorn Plantation
Brands Bay
86
99
00
01

163 146

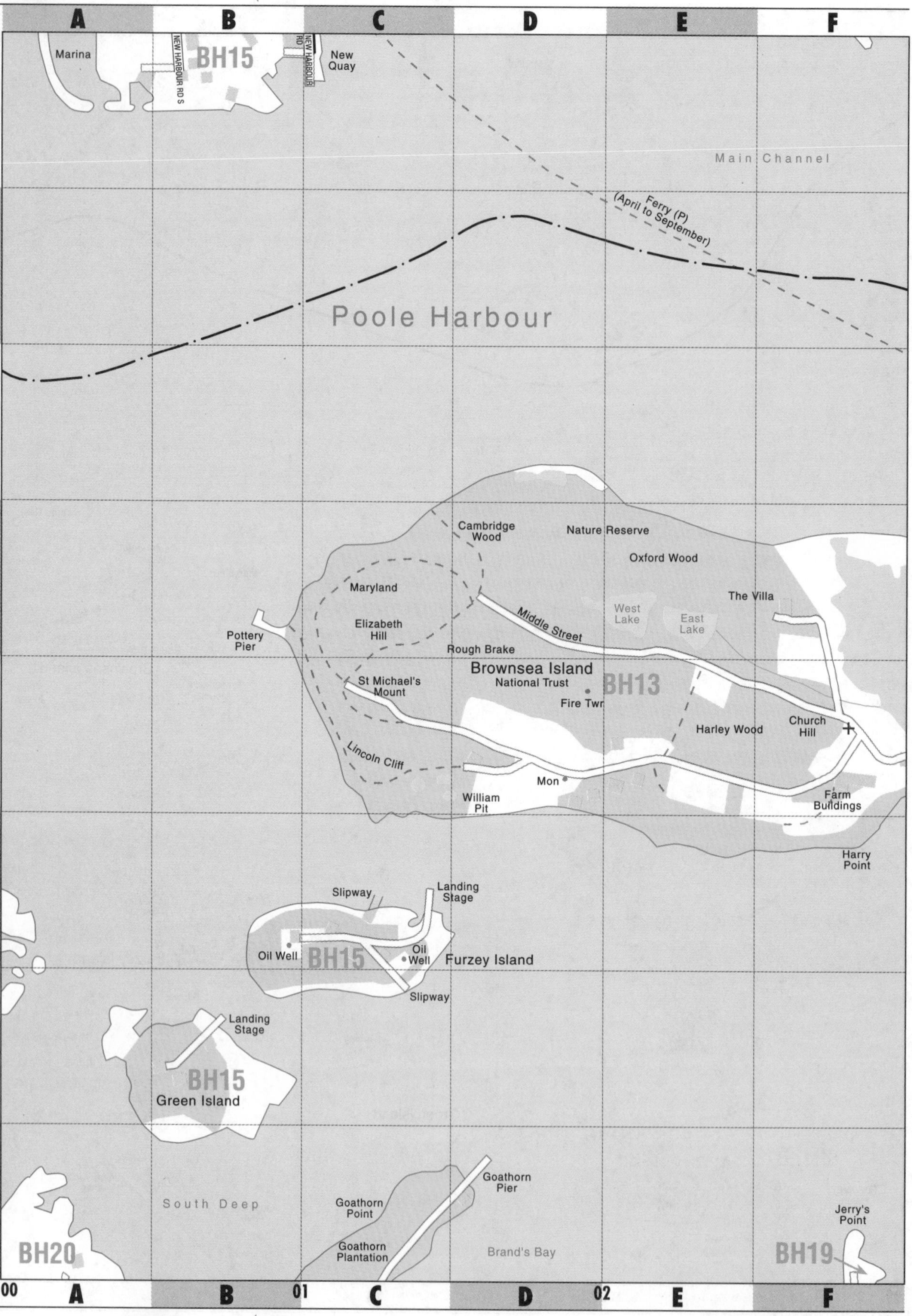

Marina

BH15

New Quay

NEW HARBOUR RD S

NEW HARBOUR RD

Main Channel

Ferry (P)
(April to September)

Poole Harbour

Cambridge Wood

Nature Reserve

Oxford Wood

The Villa

Maryland

West Lake

East Lake

Pottery Pier

Elizabeth Hill

Middle Street

Rough Brake

Brownsea Island
National Trust

BH13

St Michael's Mount

Fire Twr

Harley Wood

Church Hill

Lincoln Cliff

Mon

Harry Point

William Pit

Farm Buildings

Slipway

Landing Stage

Oil Well

BH15

Oil Well

Furzey Island

Slipway

Landing Stage

BH15

Green Island

South Deep

Goathorn Point

Goathorn Pier

Goathorn Plantation

Brand's Bay

Jerry's Point

BH20

BH19

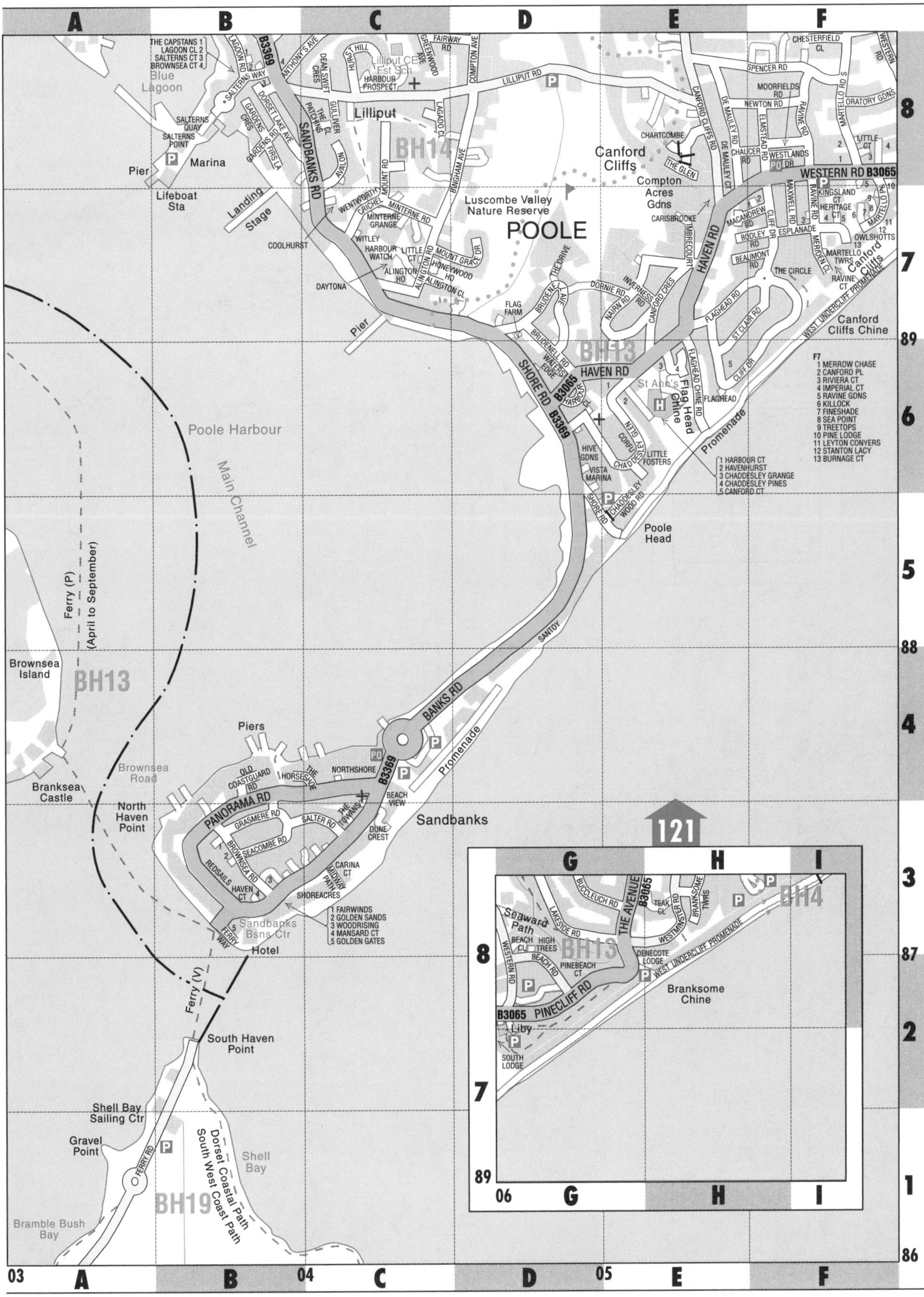

F8
1 KENILWORTH CT
2 BRACKENS WAY
3 STONELEIGH
4 BRANKSOME CT
5 MARTELLO HO

F7
1 MERROW CHASE
2 CANFORD PL
3 RIVIERA CT
4 IMPERIAL CT
5 RAVINE GDNS
6 KILLOCK
7 FINESHADE
8 SEA POINT
9 TREETOPS
10 PINE LODGE
11 LEYTON CONYERS
12 STANTON LACY
13 BURNAGE CT

1 HARBOUR CT
2 HAVENHURST
3 CHADDESLEY GRANGE
4 CHADDESLEY PINES
5 CANFORD CT

1 FAIRWINDS
2 GOLDEN SANDS
3 WOODRISING
4 MANSARD CT
5 GOLDEN GATES

121

130

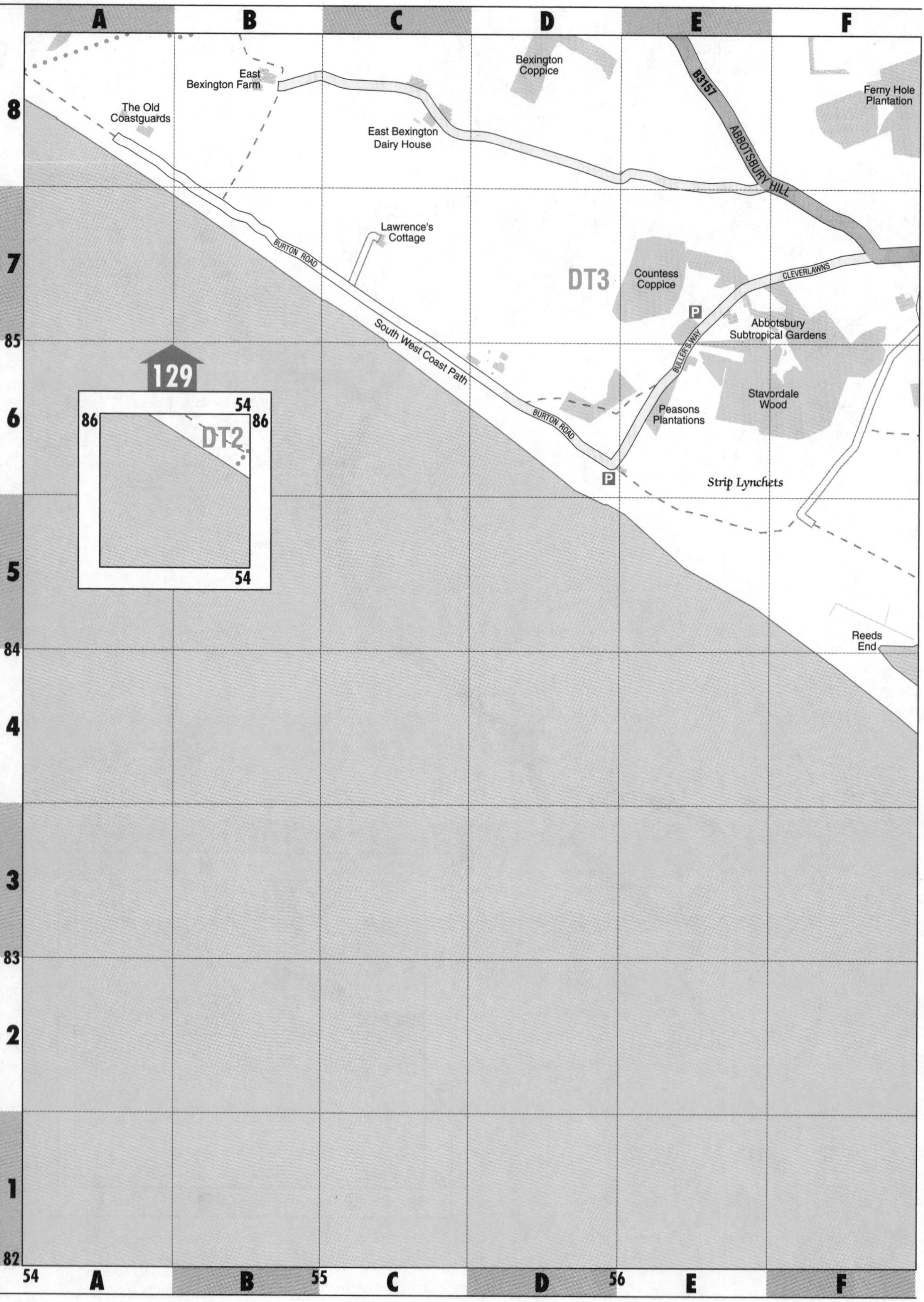
A
B
C
D
E
F
East
Bexington Farm
Bexington
Coppice
Ferny Hole
Plantation
B3157
ABBOTSBURY HILL
The Old
Coastguards
East Bexington
Dairy House
Lawrence's
Cottage
BURTON ROAD
DT3
Countess
Coppice
CLEVERLAWNS
BULLER'S WAY
Abbotsbury
Subtropical Gardens
South West Coast Path
129
54
86
86
DT2
54
Peasons
Plantations
Stavordale
Wood
BURTON ROAD
Strip Lynchets
Reeds
End
8
7
85
6
5
84
4
3
83
2
1
82
54
55
56

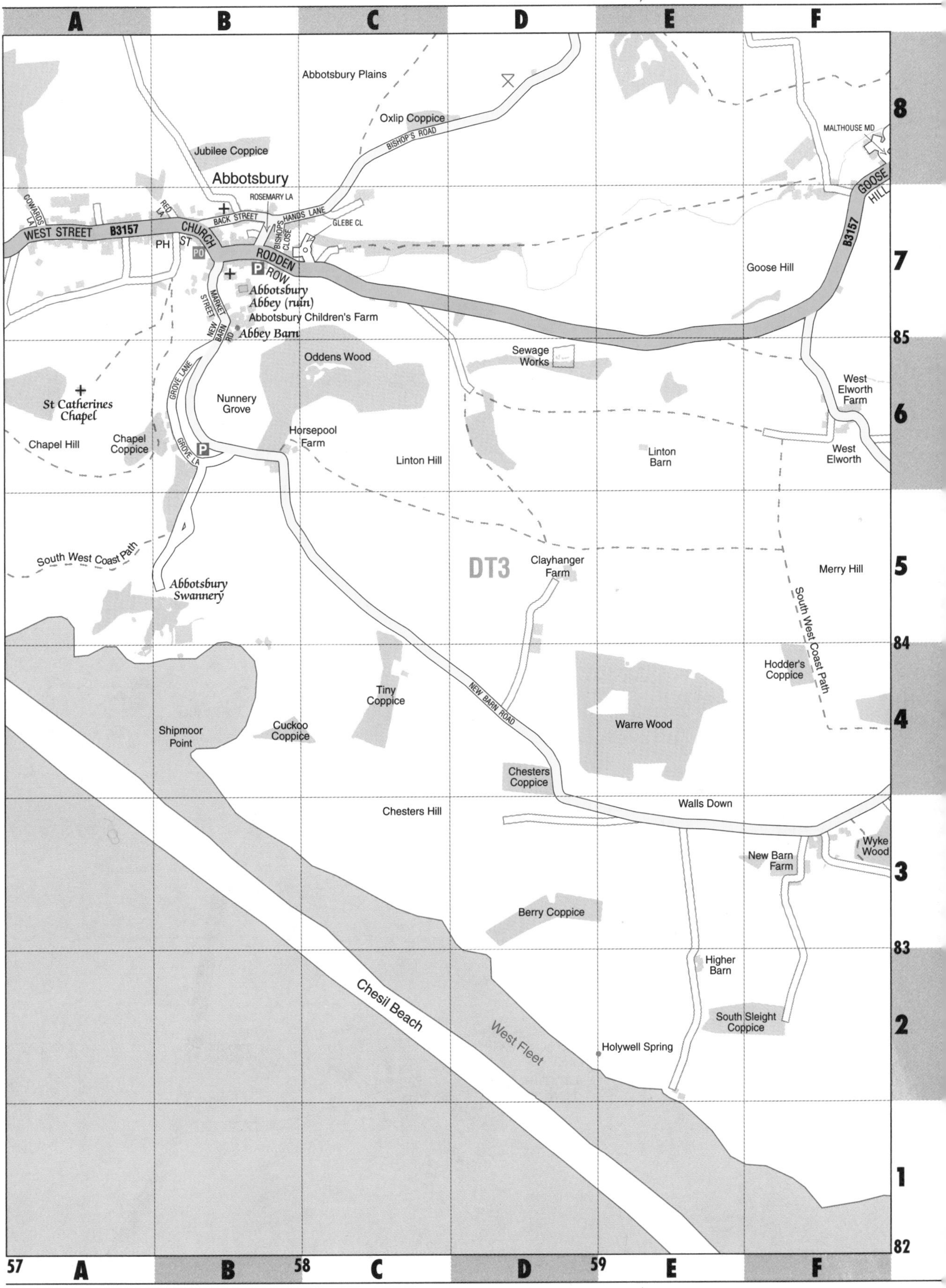
A
B
C
D
E
F
8
7
85
6
5
84
4
3
83
2
1
82
57
58
59
Abbotsbury Plains
Oxlip Coppice
BISHOP'S ROAD
Jubilee Coppice
Abbotsbury
ROSEMARY LA
COWARDS LA
RED LA
BACK STREET
HANDS LANE
GLEBE CL
WEST STREET
B3157
CHURCH ST
PH
PO
BISHOPS CLOSE
RODDEN ROW
P
Abbotsbury Abbey (ruin)
MARKET STREET
NEW BARN RD
Abbotsbury Children's Farm
Abbey Barn
MALTHOUSE MD
GOOSE HILL
B3157
Goose Hill
Sewage Works
Oddens Wood
GROVE LANE
Nunnery Grove
St Catherines Chapel
Chapel Hill
Chapel Coppice
GROVE LA
P
Horsepool Farm
Linton Hill
West Elworth Farm
Linton Barn
West Elworth
South West Coast Path
DT3
Clayhanger Farm
Merry Hill
Abbotsbury Swannery
South West Coast Path
Hodder's Coppice
Tiny Coppice
NEW BARN ROAD
Warre Wood
Shipmoor Point
Cuckoo Coppice
Chesters Coppice
Walls Down
Chesters Hill
Wyke Wood
New Barn Farm
Berry Coppice
Higher Barn
Chesil Beach
West Fleet
South Sleight Coppice
Holywell Spring
A
B
C
D
E
F

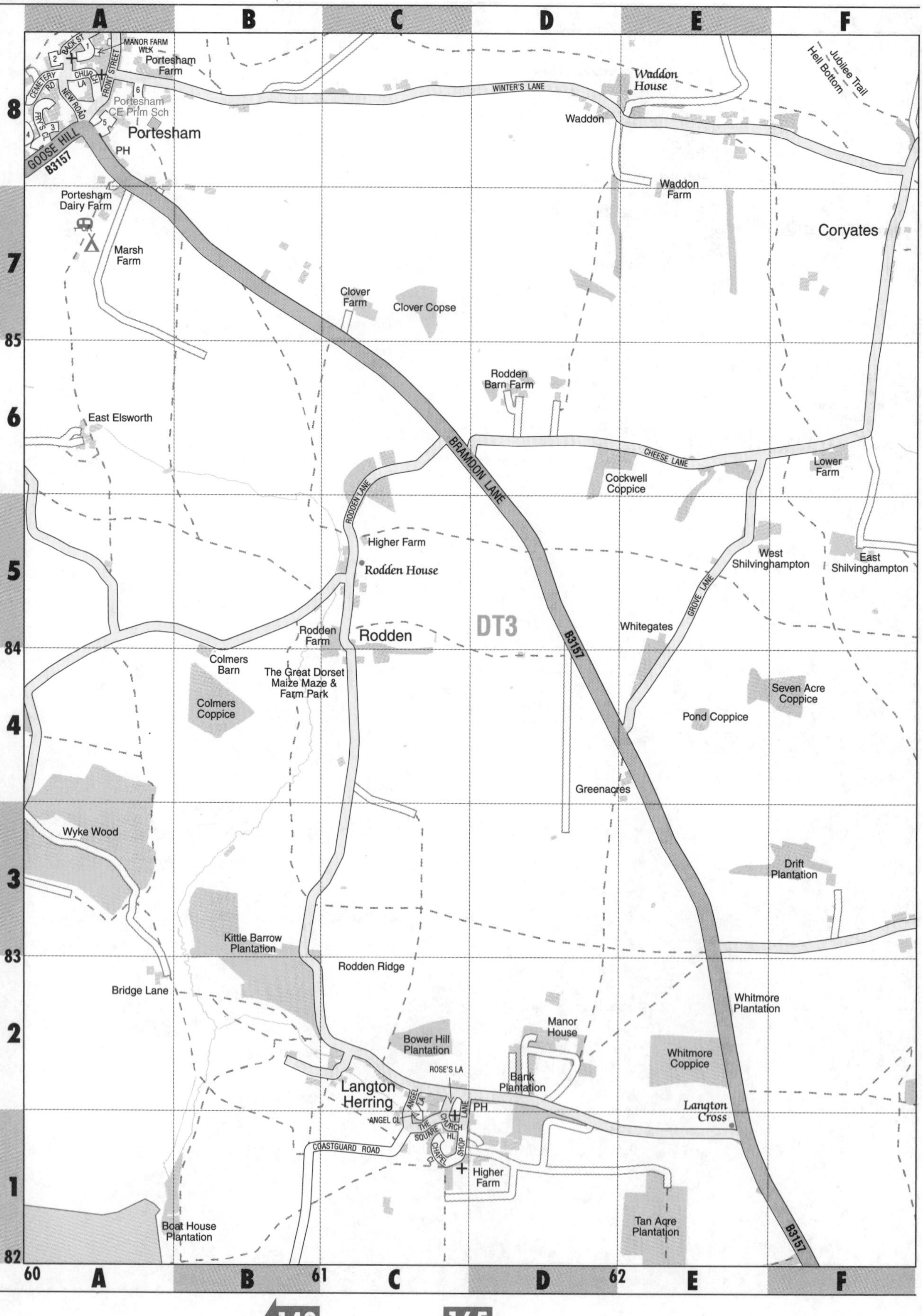

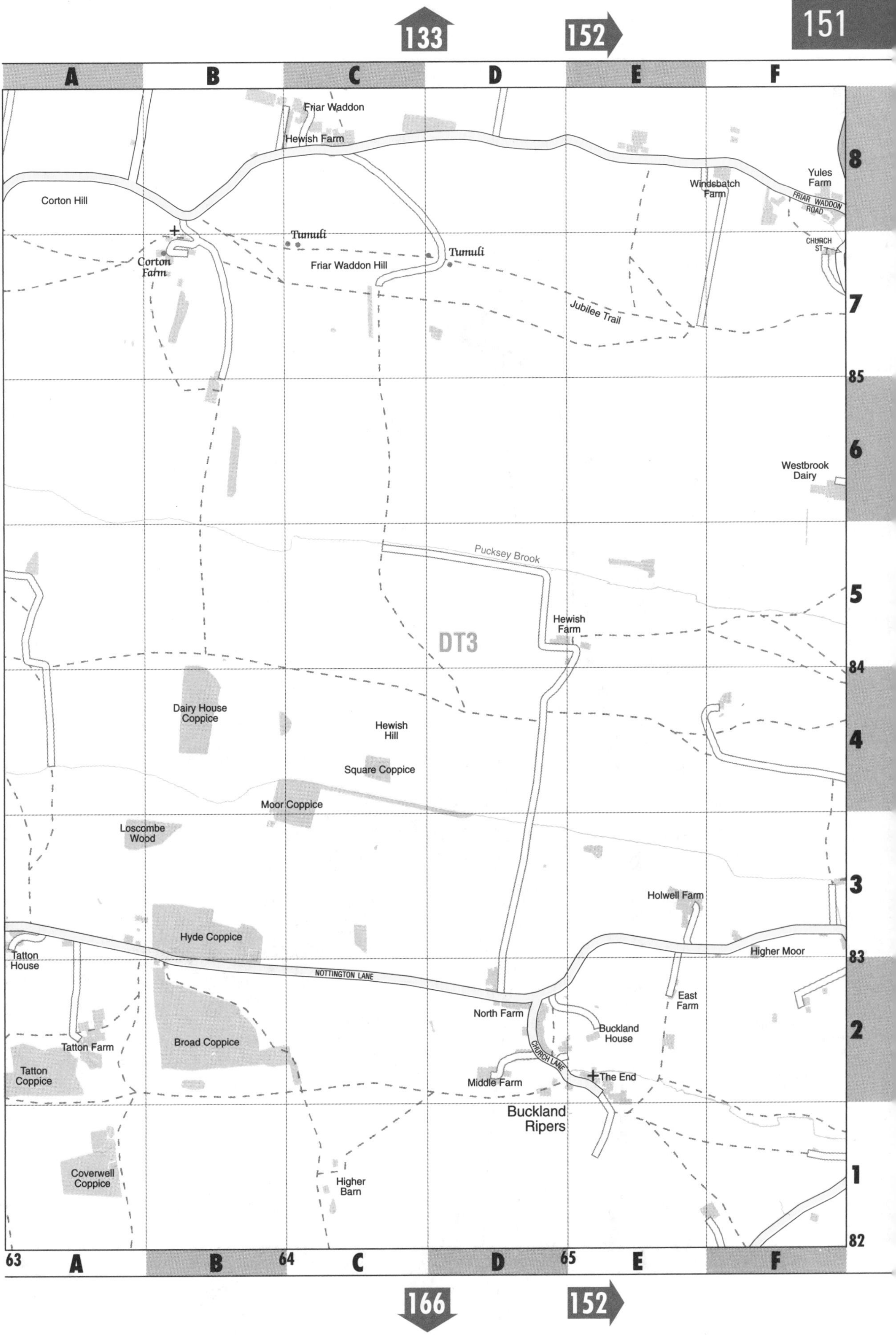

A   B   C   D   E   F

Friar Waddon

Hewish Farm

8

Yules
Farm

Corton Hill

Windsbatch
Farm

FRIAR WADDON ROAD

+

Tumuli

CHURCH
ST

Corton
Farm

Friar Waddon Hill

Tumuli

7

Jubilee Trail

85

Westbrook
Dairy

6

Pucksey Brook

5

DT3

Hewish
Farm

84

Dairy House
Coppice

Hewish
Hill

4

Square Coppice

Moor Coppice

Loscombe
Wood

3

Holwell Farm

Hyde Coppice

Higher Moor

83

Tatton
House

NOTTINGTON LANE

East
Farm

2

North Farm

Buckland
House

Tatton Farm

Broad Coppice

CHURCH LANE

Middle Farm

+ The End

Tatton
Coppice

Buckland
Ripers

Coverwell
Coppice

Higher
Barn

1

82

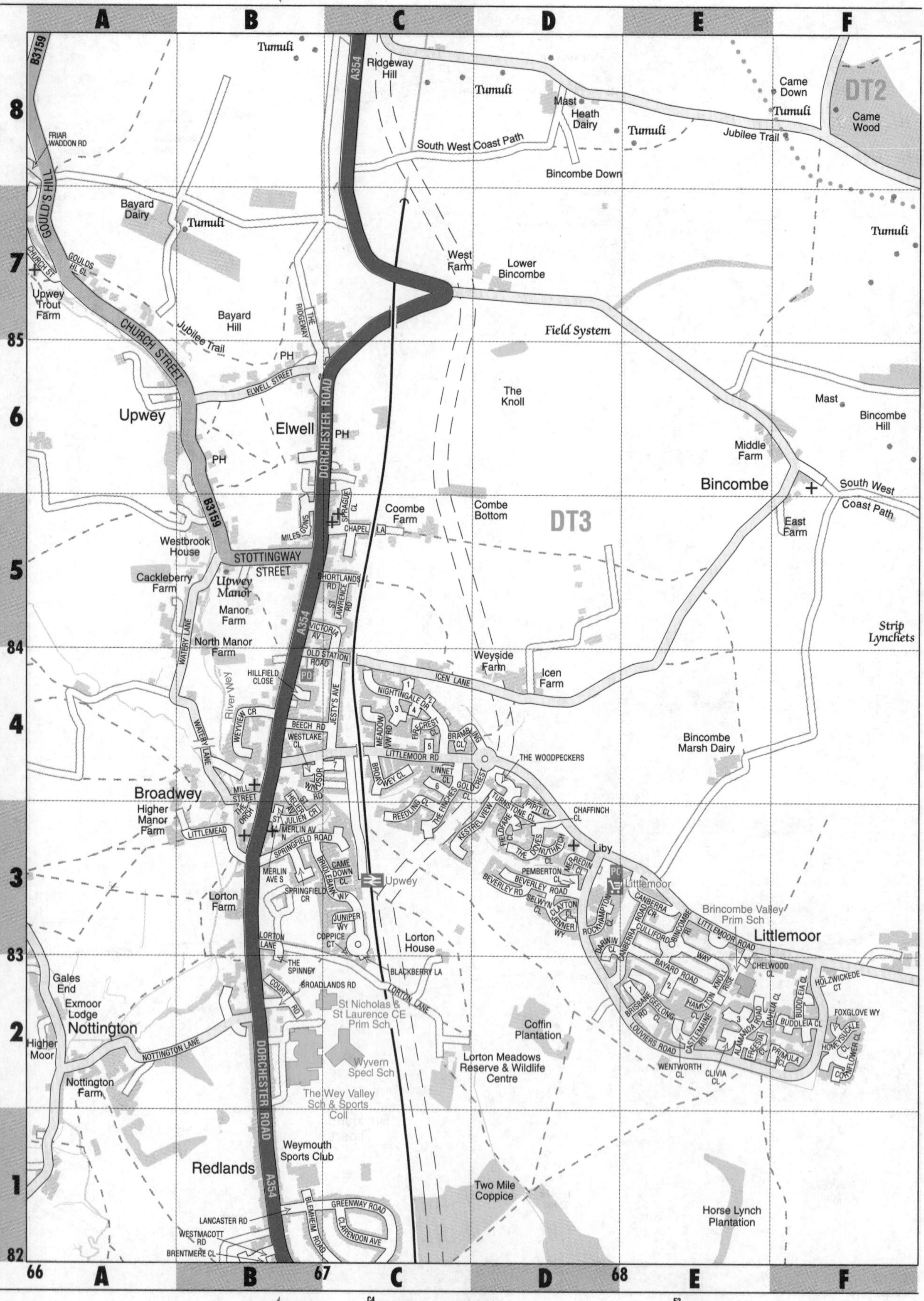

C4
1 REDPOLL CL
2 ROBIN CL
3 STONECHAT CL
4 WHEATEAR CL
5 JORDAN WY
6 SANDERLING CL
7 REGENCY DR

E2
1 KIMBERLEY CL
2 GLADSTONE CL
3 MAGNOLIA CL

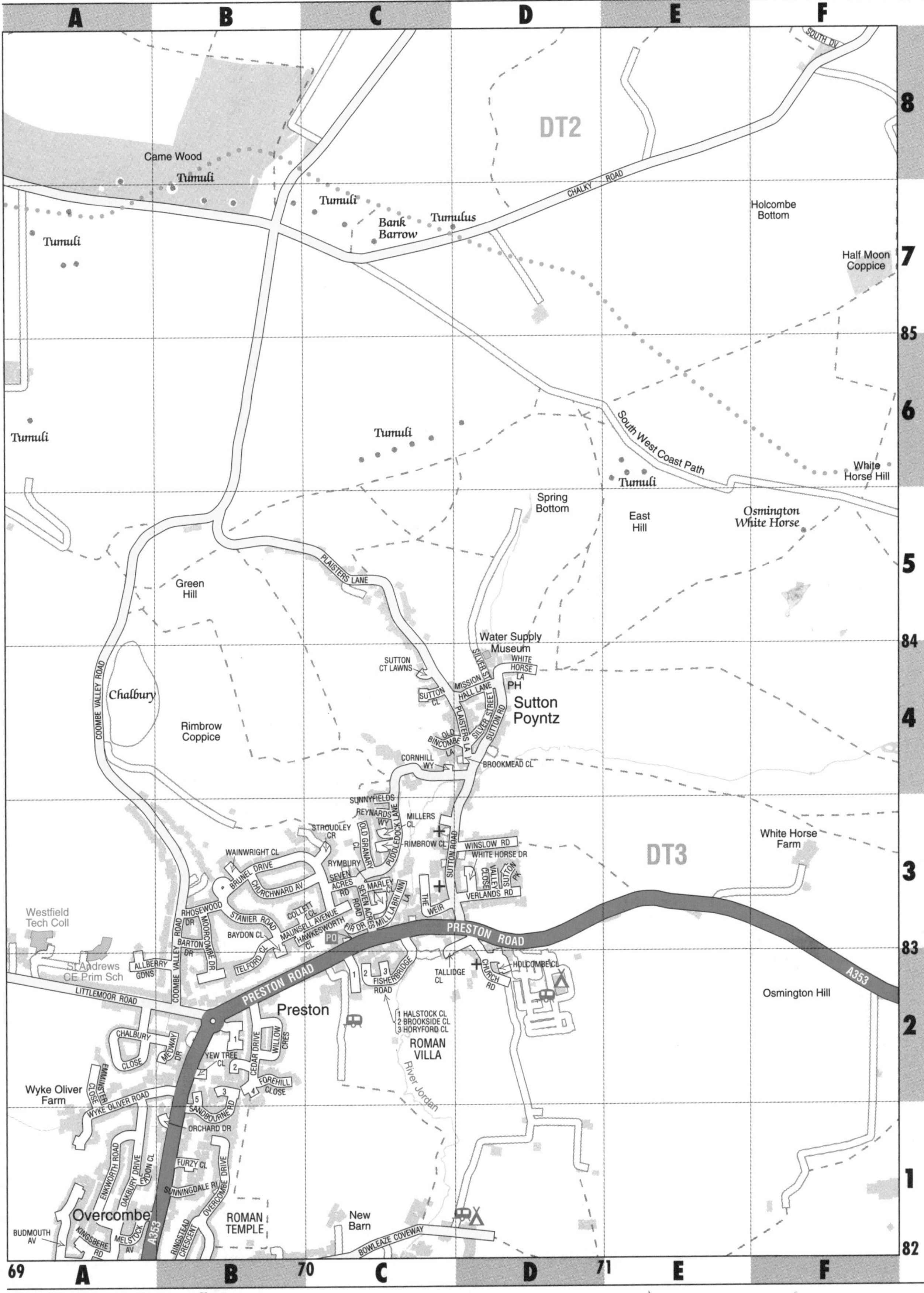

A   B   C   D   E   F

8

DT2

Came Wood

Tumuli

Tumuli

Tumuli   Bank
Barrow   Tumulus

CHALKY ROAD

Holcombe
Bottom

Half Moon
Coppice   7

85

6

South West Coast Path

White
Horse Hill

Tumuli

Tumuli

Spring
Bottom

East
Hill

Osmington
White Horse

Green
Hill

PLAISTERS LANE

5

Water Supply
Museum

84

Chalbury

COOMBE VALLEY ROAD

Rimbrow
Coppice

SUTTON
CT LAWNS

SUTTON
CL

MISSION
HALL LANE

WHITE
HORSE
LA   PH

Sutton
Poyntz   4

OLD
BINCOMBE
LA

PLAISTERS LA

SILVER STREET

SUTTON ROAD

CORNHILL
WY   BROOKMEAD CL

DT3

SUNNYFIELDS

REYNARDS

MILLERS
CL

STROUDLEY
CR

PUDDLEDOCK LANE

RIMBROW CL   WINSLOW RD

White Horse
Farm

WAINWRIGHT CL

OLD GRANARY
CL

SUTTON ROAD   WHITE HORSE DR

Westfield
Tech Coll

BRUNEL DRIVE

CHURCHWARD AV

RYMBURY

SEVEN
ACRES
RD   SEVEN ACRES   MARLEY
CL

MILL LA
BU INN   SUTTON
CL   SUTTON
RD   3

RHOSEWOOD
DR   STANIER ROAD

COLLETT
CL   MAUNSELL AVENUE

HAWKESWORTH

PH DR   THE WEIR   VERLANDS RD

BARTON
DR

MORCOMBE DR

BAYDON CL

TELFORD CL

PRESTON ROAD   A353   83

St Andrews
CE Prim Sch

ALLBERRY
GDNS

PRESTON ROAD

PO

1 2 3
FISHERBRIDGE
ROAD

TALLIDGE
CL   HOLCOMBE CL

CHURCH RD

Osmington Hill

LITTLEMOOR ROAD

COOMBE VALLEY ROAD

Preston

1 HALSTOCK CL
2 BROOKSIDE CL
3 HORYFORD CL   2

CHALBURY
CLOSE

YEW TREE
CL   CEDAR DRIVE   WILLOW
CRES

ROMAN
VILLA

River Jordan

Wyke Oliver
Farm

WYKE OLIVER ROAD

FORESTED CLOSE

FORGEHILL
CLOSE

2

5

SANDBOURNE RD

ORCHARD DR

FURZY CL

SUNNINGDALE RI

OVERCOMBE DRIVE

1

BUDMOUTH
AV

Overcombe   KINGSBERE RD   MELSTOCK AV   RINGSTEAD CRESCENT   A353

ROMAN
TEMPLE

New
Barn

BOWLEAZE COVEWAY   82

69   A   B   70   C   D   71   E   F

B2
1 CHALBURY LODGE
2 HAZEL DR
3 WINGREEN CL
4 MAPLE CL
5 DEANSLEIGH CL

168   154

A B C D E F

8
Glebe Farm
Friarmayne Farm
Conygar
Roman Hill Farm
Nordale Farm
Roman Hill Trading Estate
A352
Brick Hill

7
Warmwell Down Barn
Warmwell Cross Farm
A353

85

6
Poxwell Grove
DT2
POXWELL DROVE

5
Tumuli
Manor Farm
Poxwell
Tumulus

84
Pixon Barn
Poxwell Manor
Coombe Bottom
Strip Lynchets

4
South West Coast Path
Halls Farm
Strip Lynchets
Strip Lynchets
Poxwell Cairn Circle

Netherton Farm
Grove Farmhouse
3
Charity Farm
DT3
Osmington House
Abbeyfeale Farm
Lower Dairy Farm
Poxwell Big Wood
West Farm
CHURCH LA
VILLAGE ST
ROMAN RD
Upton Farm
WEST FARM

83
Osmington
Manor House
CHAPEL LANE
PH
Fir Coppice
Upton

2
Hitts Farm
HILL VW
East Farm
Wally's Lake
A353
GLEBE CL
Brambledown Stables
SHORTLAKE LANE
MILLS ROAD
Toll
Tumuli

1
Osmington Bay Holiday Centre
Osmington Mills
Spring Bottom Hill

Shortlake Farm
South West Coast Path

82
Black Head

72 A 73 B C 73 D 74 E F

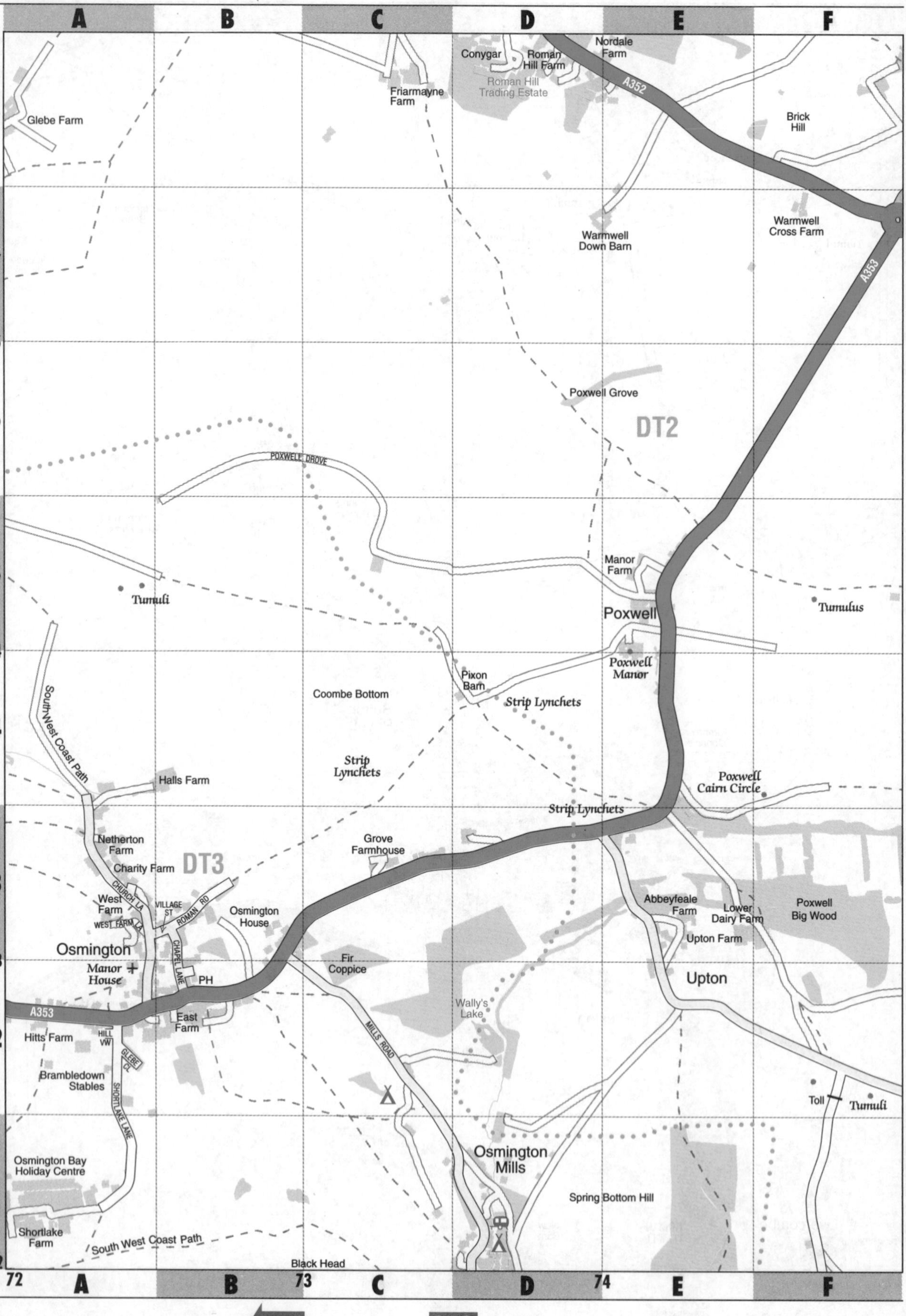

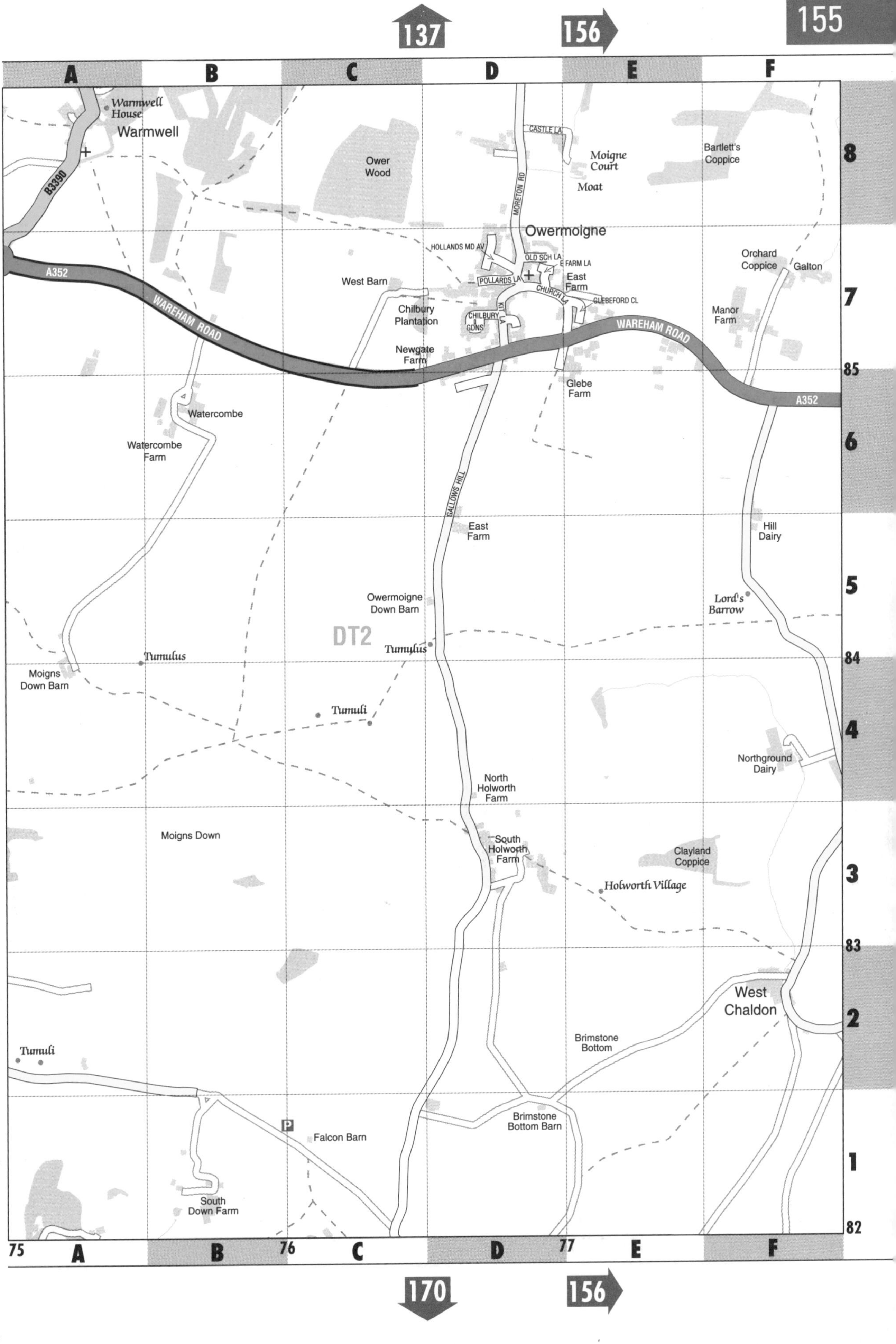
137
156
A
B
C
D
E
F
Warmwell House
Warmwell
B3390
Ower Wood
CASTLE LA
MORETON RD
Moigne Court
Moat
Bartlett's Coppice
8
Owermoigne
HOLLANDS MD AV
OLD SCH LA
E FARM LA
POLLARDS LA
East Farm
CHURCH LA
GLEBEFORD CL
A352
WAREHAM ROAD
West Barn
Chilbury Plantation
CHILBURY GDNS
KIT LA
Orchard Coppice
Galton
Manor Farm
7
Newgate Farm
Glebe Farm
85
A352
Watercombe
Watercombe Farm
6
GALLOWS HILL
East Farm
Hill Dairy
5
Owermoigne Down Barn
Lord's Barrow
DT2
Tumulus
Tumulus
84
Moigns Down Barn
Tumuli
4
Northground Dairy
North Holworth Farm
Moigns Down
South Holworth Farm
Clayland Coppice
3
Holworth Village
83
West Chaldon
2
Brimstone Bottom
Tumuli
Brimstone Bottom Barn
P
Falcon Barn
1
South Down Farm
82
75
76
77
170
156

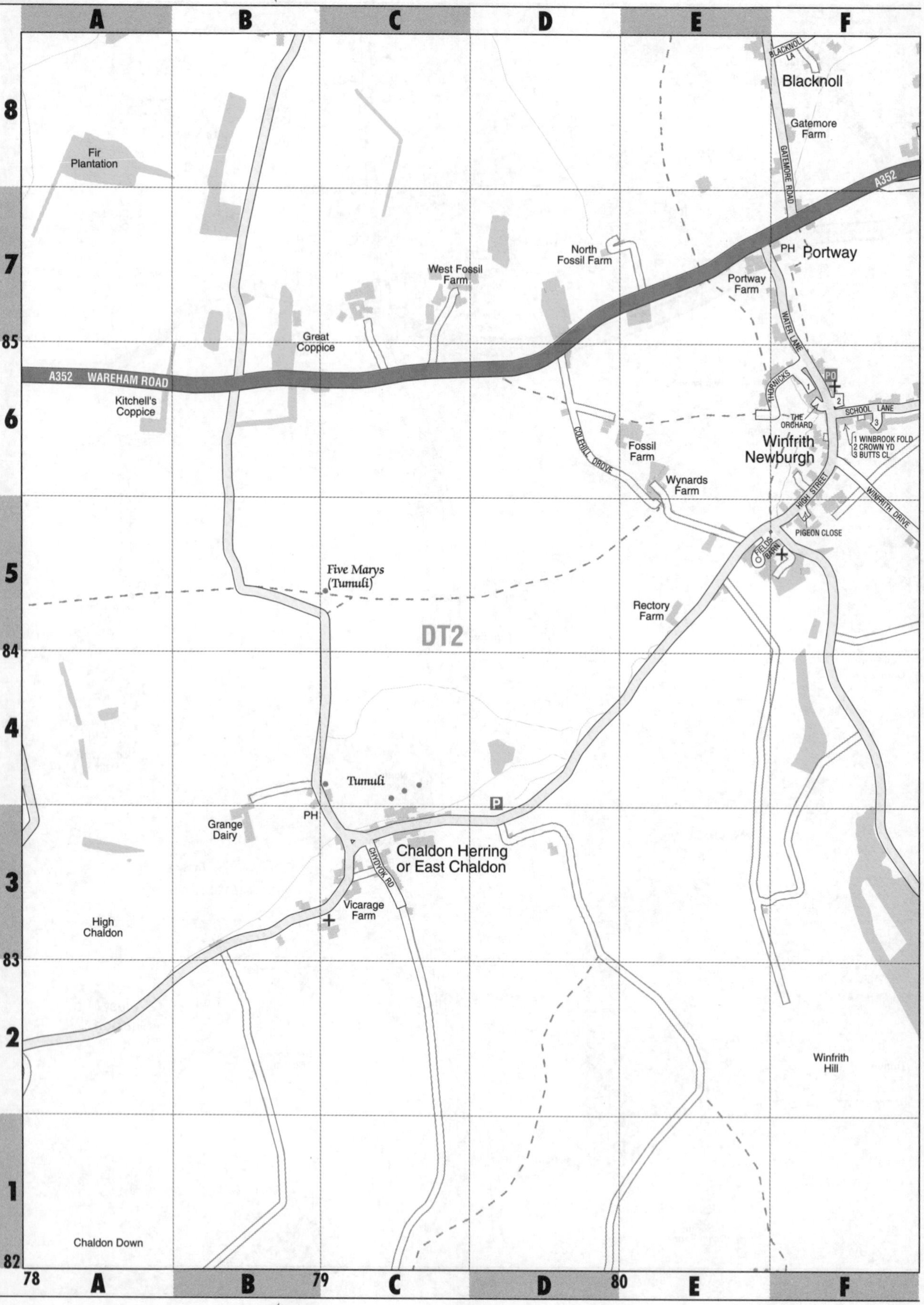

155
138

A B C D E F

8

7

85

6

5

84

4

3

83

2

1

82

78 79 80

Blacknoll
BLACKNOLL LA
Gatemore Farm
A352
PH Portway
Portway Farm
WATER LANE
North Fossil Farm
West Fossil Farm
Great Coppice
THE ORCHARD
Winfrith Newburgh
SCHOOL LANE
1 WINBROOK FOLD
2 CROWN YD
3 BUTTS CL
Fossil Farm
Wynards Farm
HIGH STREET
WINFRITH DRIVE
PIGEON CLOSE
CHFELDS BARN
A352 WAREHAM ROAD
Kitchell's Coppice
COXHILL DRIVE
Fir Plantation
Five Marys (Tumuli)
DT2
Rectory Farm
Tumuli
PH
Grange Dairy
Chaldon Herring or East Chaldon
P
CHYDOCK RD
High Chaldon
Vicarage Farm
Winfrith Hill
Chaldon Down

139
158

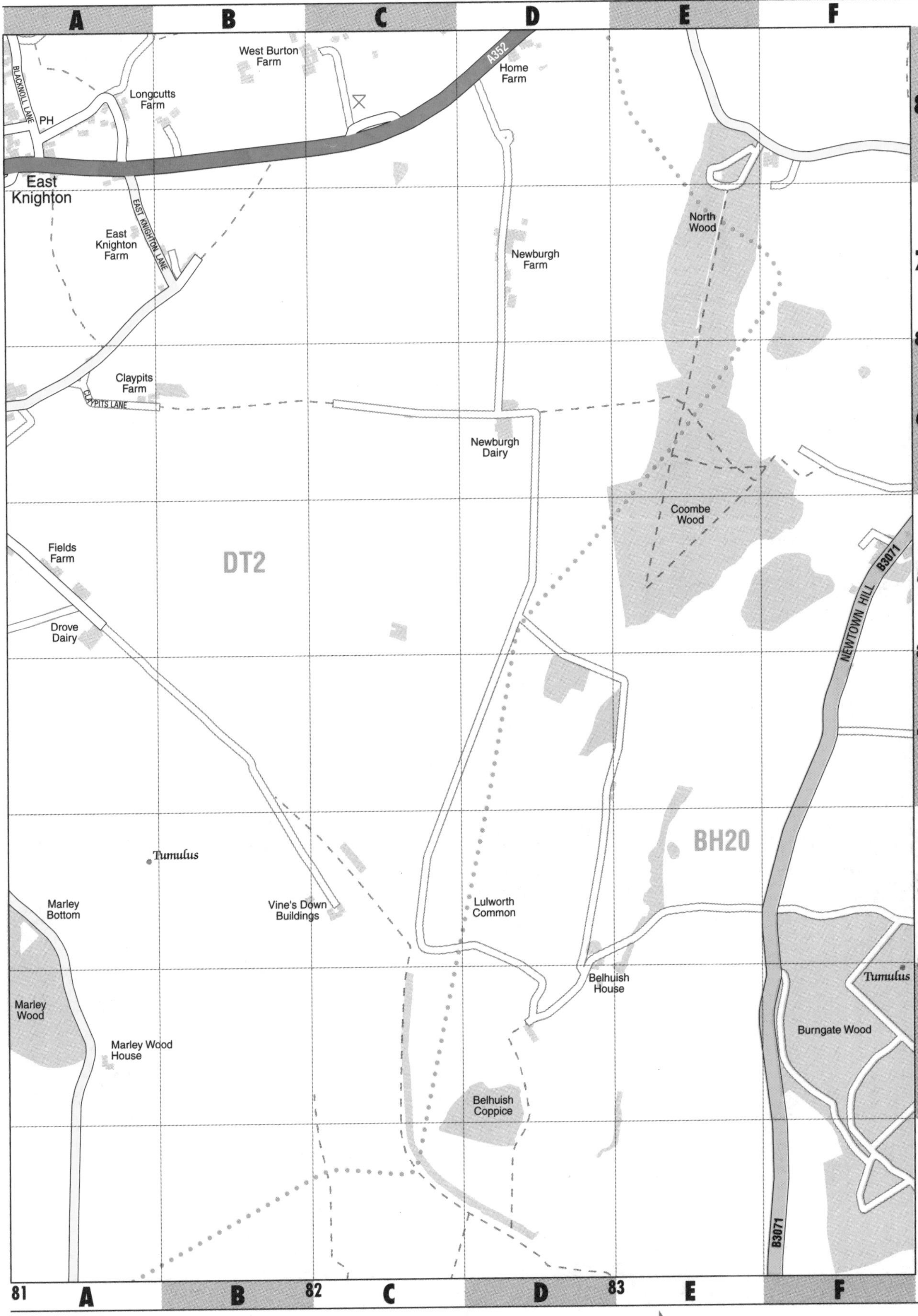
A
B
C
D
E
F
West Burton Farm
A352
Home Farm
BLACKNOLL LANE
PH
Longcutts Farm
East Knighton
EAST KNIGHTON LANE
East Knighton Farm
Newburgh Farm
North Wood
Claypits Farm
CLAYPITS LANE
Newburgh Dairy
Coombe Wood
Fields Farm
DT2
B3071
NEWTOWN HILL
Drove Dairy
BH20
Tumulus
Marley Bottom
Vine's Down Buildings
Lulworth Common
Belhuish House
Tumulus
Marley Wood
Marley Wood House
Burngate Wood
Belhuish Coppice
B3071
8
7
85
6
5
84
4
3
83
2
1
82
81
82
83

172
158

157
140

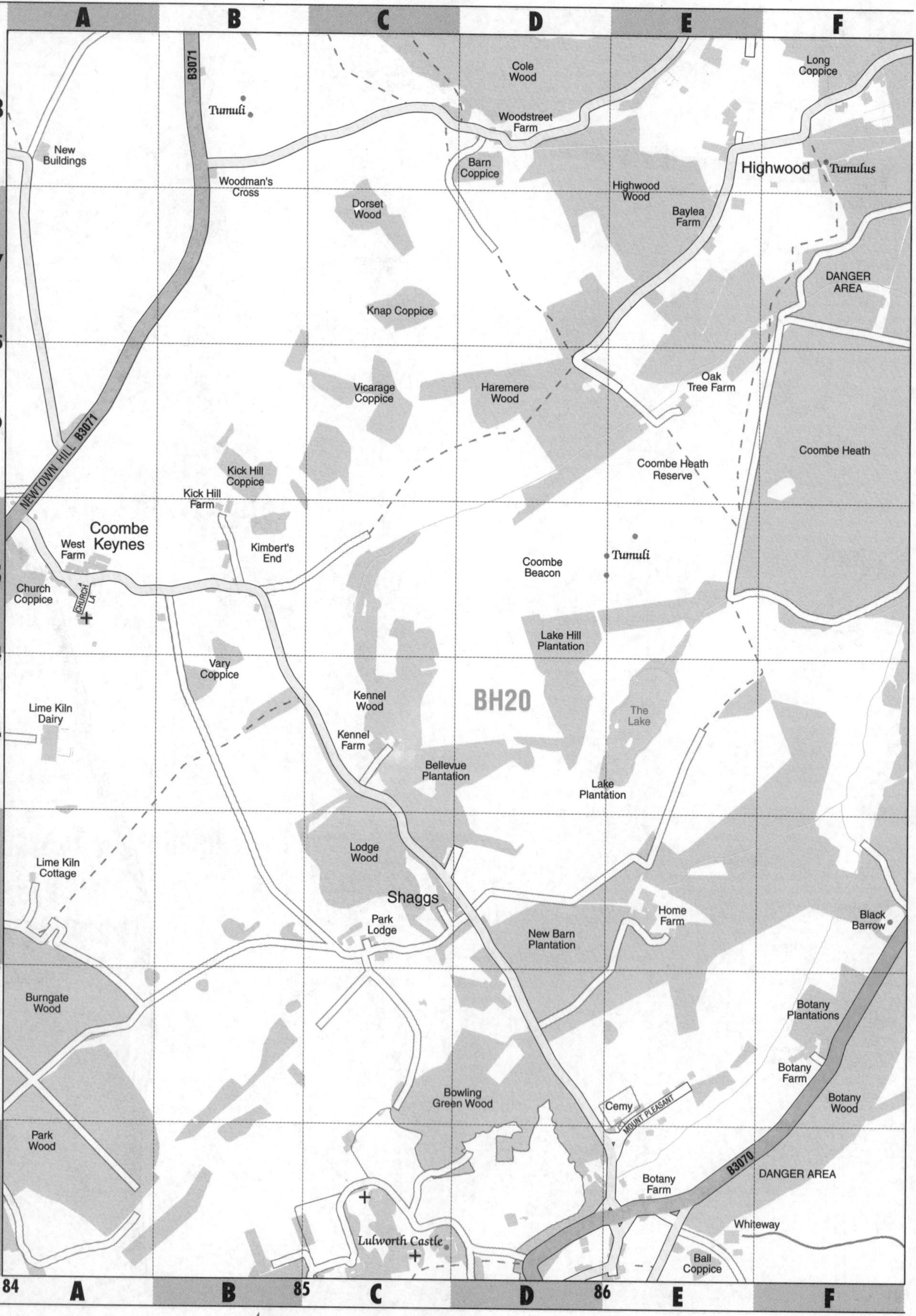

A B C D E F

8

New Buildings

B3071

Tumuli

Cole Wood

Woodstreet Farm

Long Coppice

Highwood

Tumulus

Woodman's Cross

Barn Coppice

Dorset Wood

Highwood Wood

Baylea Farm

7

DANGER AREA

85

Knap Coppice

Vicarage Coppice

Haremere Wood

Oak Tree Farm

6

NEWTOWN HILL B3071

Coombe Heath Reserve

Coombe Heath

Kick Hill Coppice

Kick Hill Farm

Coombe Keynes

West Farm

Kimbert's End

Coombe Beacon

Tumuli

5

Church Coppice

CHURCH LA

84

Vary Coppice

Lake Hill Plantation

Lime Kiln Dairy

Kennel Wood

BH20

The Lake

4

Kennel Farm

Bellevue Plantation

Lake Plantation

Lodge Wood

3

Lime Kiln Cottage

Shaggs

Park Lodge

New Barn Plantation

Home Farm

Black Barrow

83

Burngate Wood

Botany Plantations

2

Botany Farm

Botany Wood

Park Wood

Bowling Green Wood

Cemy

MOUNT PLEASANT

1

Botany Farm

B3070

DANGER AREA

Whiteway

Lulworth Castle

Ball Coppice

82

157
173

141
160

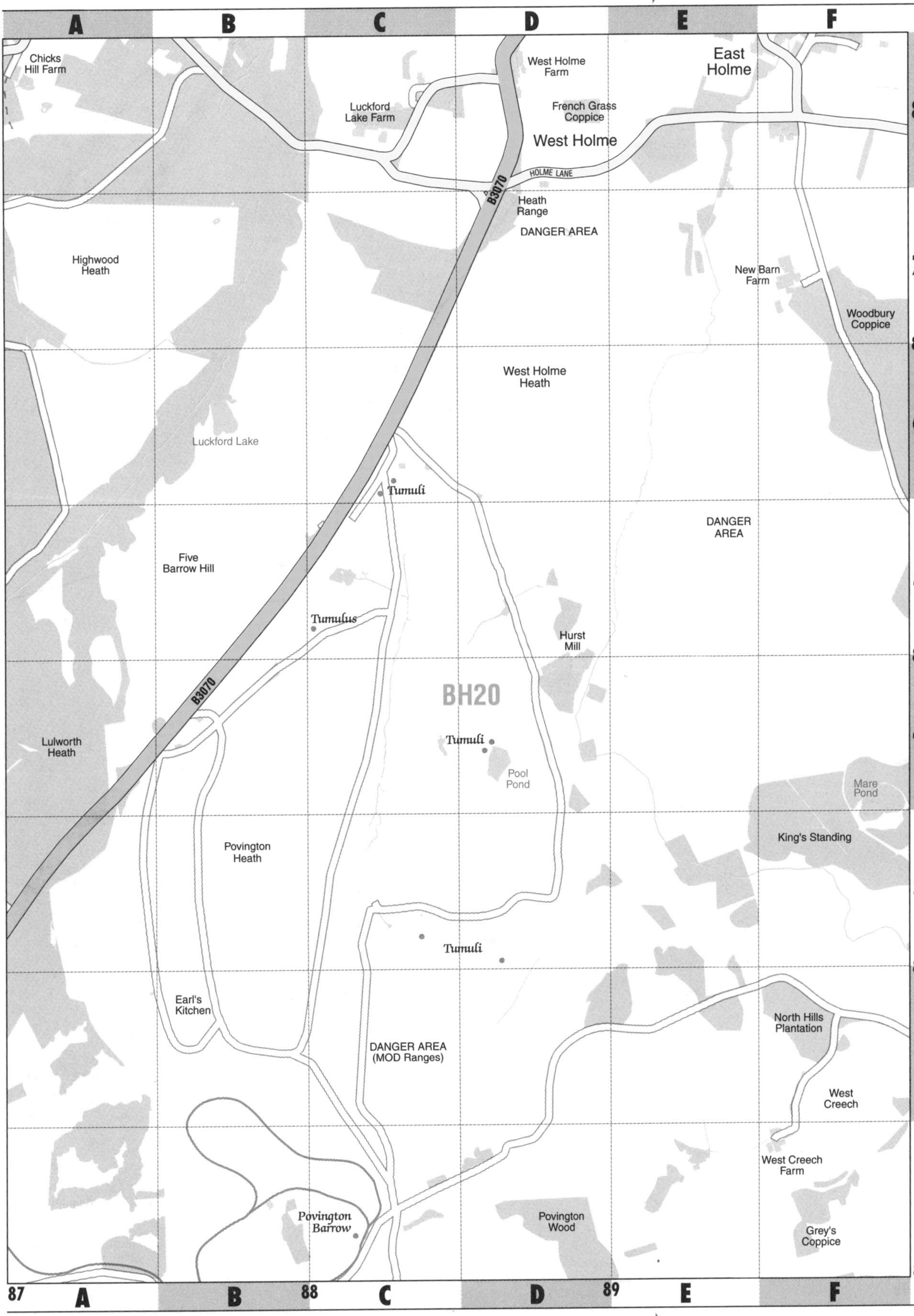
A
B
C
D
E
F
Chicks Hill Farm
West Holme Farm
East Holme
Luckford Lake Farm
French Grass Coppice
West Holme
HOLME LANE
B3070
Heath Range
DANGER AREA
Highwood Heath
New Barn Farm
Woodbury Coppice
West Holme Heath
Luckford Lake
Tumuli
Five Barrow Hill
DANGER AREA
Tumulus
Hurst Mill
BH20
Lulworth Heath
Tumuli
Pool Pond
Mare Pond
King's Standing
Povington Heath
Tumuli
Earl's Kitchen
North Hills Plantation
DANGER AREA (MOD Ranges)
West Creech
West Creech Farm
Povington Barrow
Povington Wood
Grey's Coppice
8
7
85
6
5
84
4
3
83
2
1
82
87
88
89

174
160

159
142

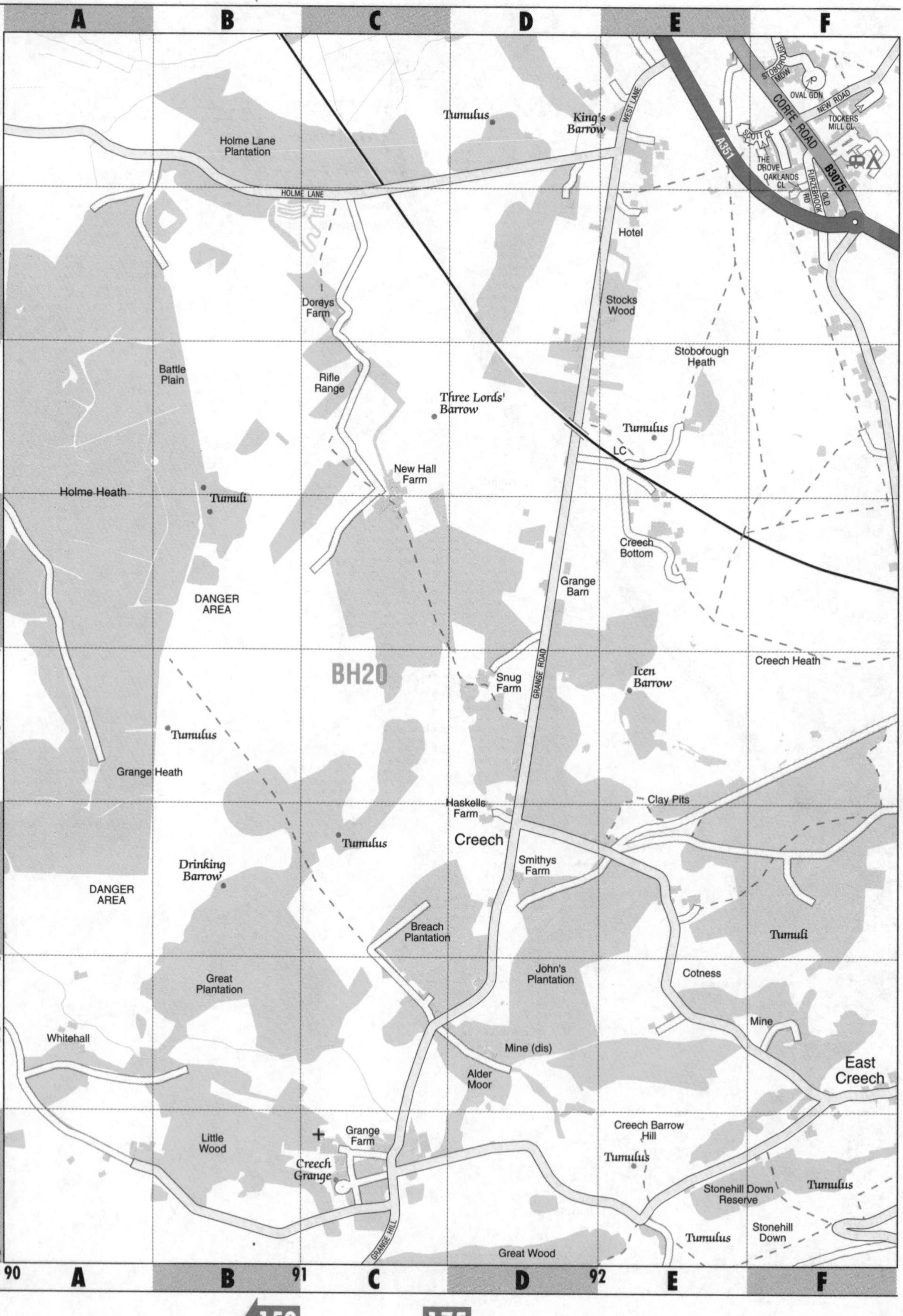

A B C D E F

8

Holme Lane
Plantation

Tumulus

King's
Barrow

WEST LANE

HEPTOON
LMON
STOBORO
LMON
OVAL GDN
CORFE ROAD
NEW ROAD
TUCKERS
MILL CL.
SCOTT CL
THE
DROVE
OAKLANDS
CL.
FURZEBROOK
RD
A351
B3075
OLD

HOLME LANE

7

Hotel

Doreys
Farm

Stocks
Wood

85

Battle
Plain

Rifle
Range

Stoborough
Heath

6

Three Lords'
Barrow

Tumulus

Holme Heath

Tumuli

New Hall
Farm

LC

Creech
Bottom

5

DANGER
AREA

Grange
Barn

Creech Heath

84

BH20

Snug
Farm

Icen
Barrow

GRANGE ROAD

4

Tumulus

Grange Heath

Haskells
Farm

Clay Pits

Tumuli

3

Drinking
Barrow

Tumulus

Creech

Smithys
Farm

DANGER
AREA

Cotness

83

Breach
Plantation

John's
Plantation

Great
Plantation

Mine

2

Whitehall

Mine (dis)

Alder
Moor

East
Creech

Little
Wood

Grange
Farm

Creech Barrow
Hill

Tumulus

1

Creech
Grange

Stonehill Down
Reserve

Tumulus

Stonehill
Down

GRANGE HILL

Tumulus

82

90 A B 91 C D 92 E F

Great Wood

143
162

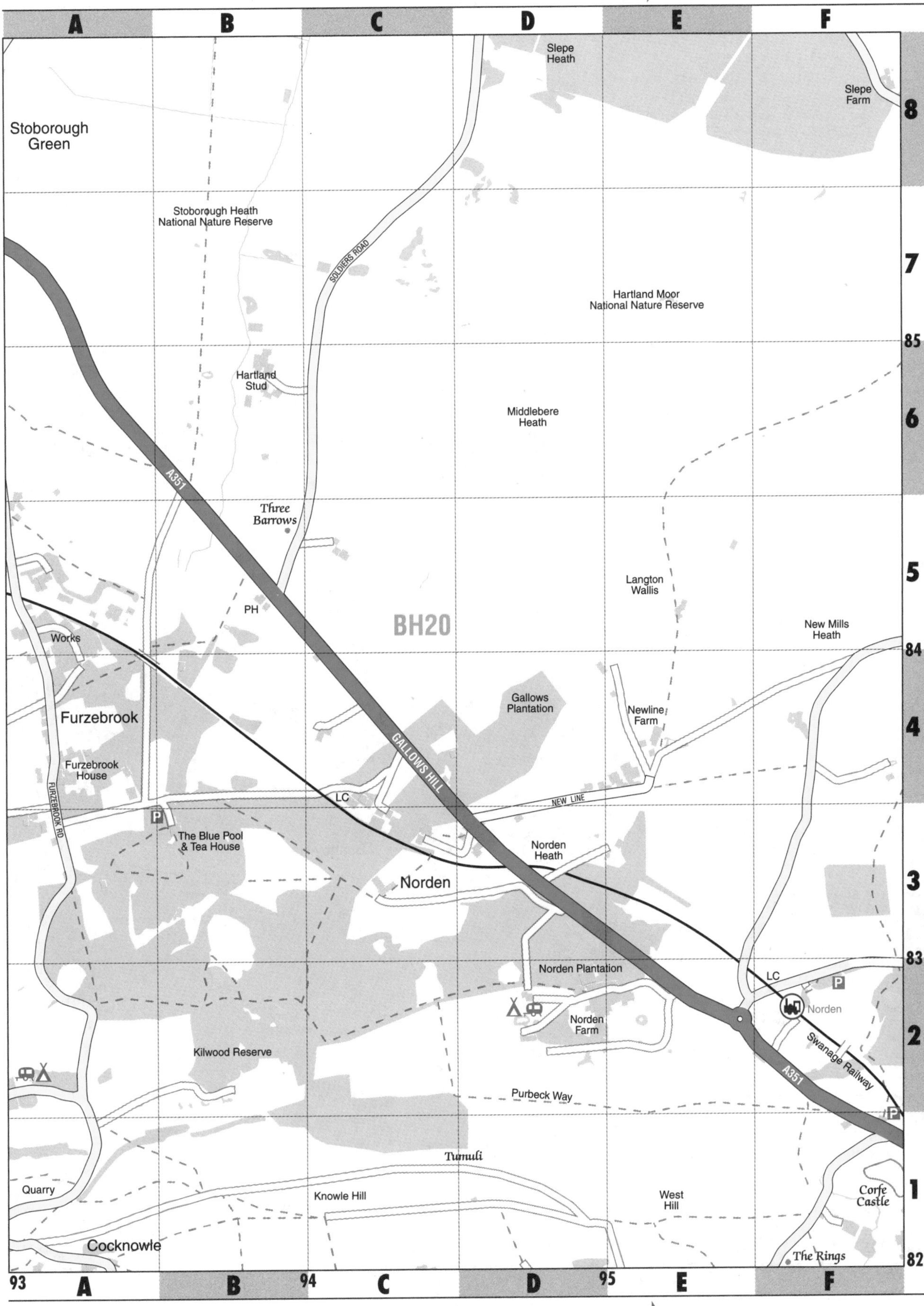
A
B
C
D
E
F
Slepe Heath
Slepe Farm
8
Stoborough Green
Stoborough Heath National Nature Reserve
SOLDIERS ROAD
7
Hartland Moor National Nature Reserve
85
Hartland Stud
Middlebere Heath
6
A351
Three Barrows
5
Langton Wallis
PH
BH20
New Mills Heath
Works
84
Gallows Plantation
Newline Farm
Furzebrook
4
GALLOWS HILL
Furzebrook House
FURZEBROOK RD
LC
NEW LINE
P
The Blue Pool & Tea House
Norden Heath
Norden
3
83
Norden Plantation
LC
P
Norden
Norden Farm
2
Swanage Railway
Kilwood Reserve
A351
Purbeck Way
P
Tumuli
Quarry
Knowle Hill
West Hill
Corfe Castle
1
Cocknowle
The Rings
82
93
A
B
94
C
D
95
E
F

176
162

161
144

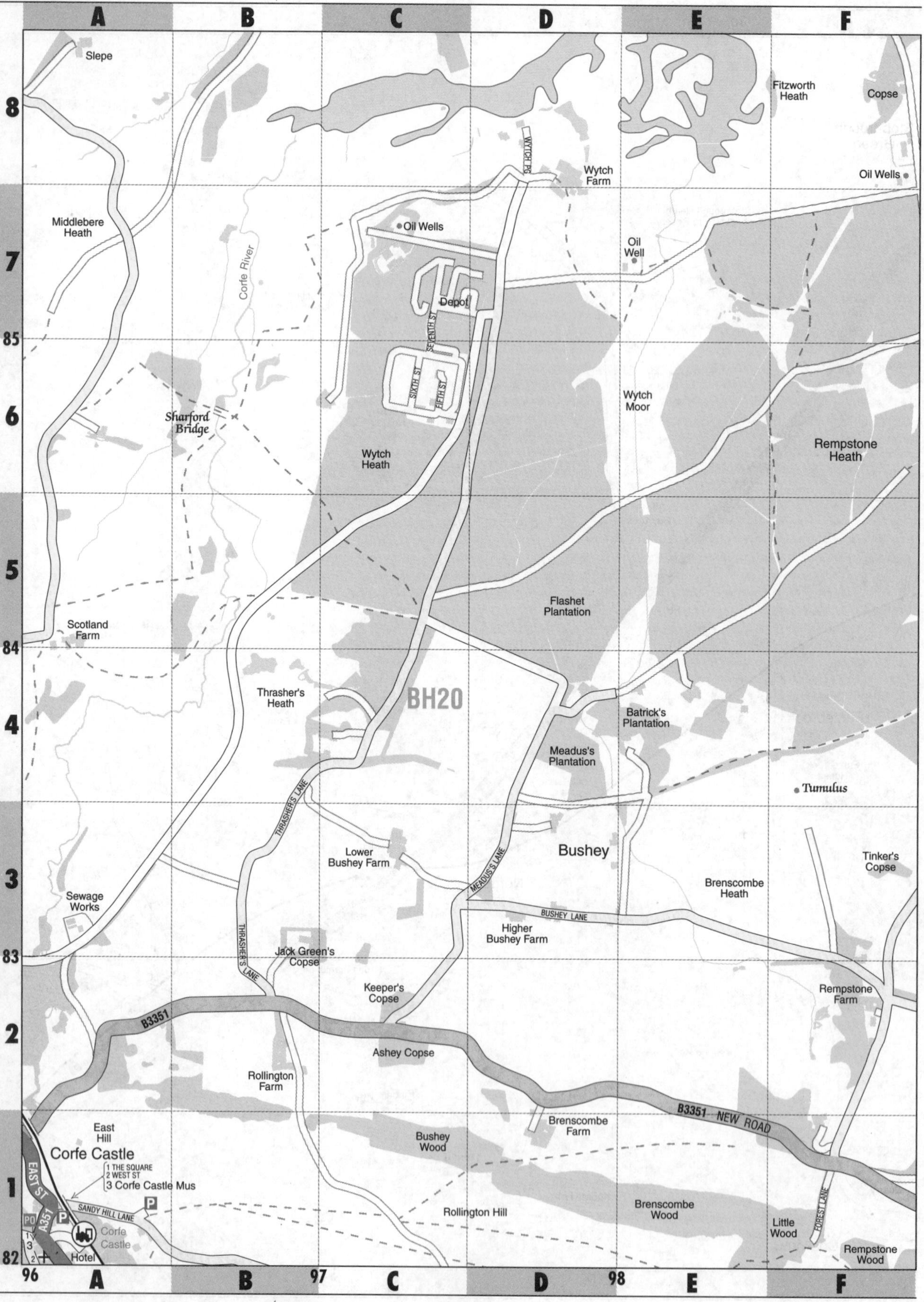

A B C D E F

8
7
85
6
5
84
4
3
83
2
1
82

96 A B 97 C D 98 E F

Slepe

Middlebere
Heath

Corfe River

Fitzworth
Heath

Copse

Wytch Rd.

Wytch
Farm

Oil Wells

Oil Wells

Oil
Well

Depot

SEVENTH ST

SIXTH ST

FIFTH ST

Wytch
Moor

Rempstone
Heath

Sharford
Bridge

Wytch
Heath

Scotland
Farm

Flashet
Plantation

BH20

Thrasher's
Heath

Batrick's
Plantation

Meadus's
Plantation

Tumulus

THRASHER'S LANE

Lower
Bushey Farm

MEADUS'S LANE

Bushey

Brenscombe
Heath

Tinker's
Copse

Sewage
Works

BUSHEY LANE

Higher
Bushey Farm

Rempstone
Farm

Jack Green's
Copse

Keeper's
Copse

B3351

Ashey Copse

B3351 NEW ROAD

Rollington
Farm

Brenscombe
Farm

FOREST LANE

East
Hill

Corfe Castle

1 THE SQUARE
2 WEST ST
3 Corfe Castle Mus

EAST ST

A351

SANDY HILL LANE

Corfe
Castle

Hotel

PO

Bushey
Wood

Rollington Hill

Brenscombe
Wood

Little
Wood

Rempstone
Wood

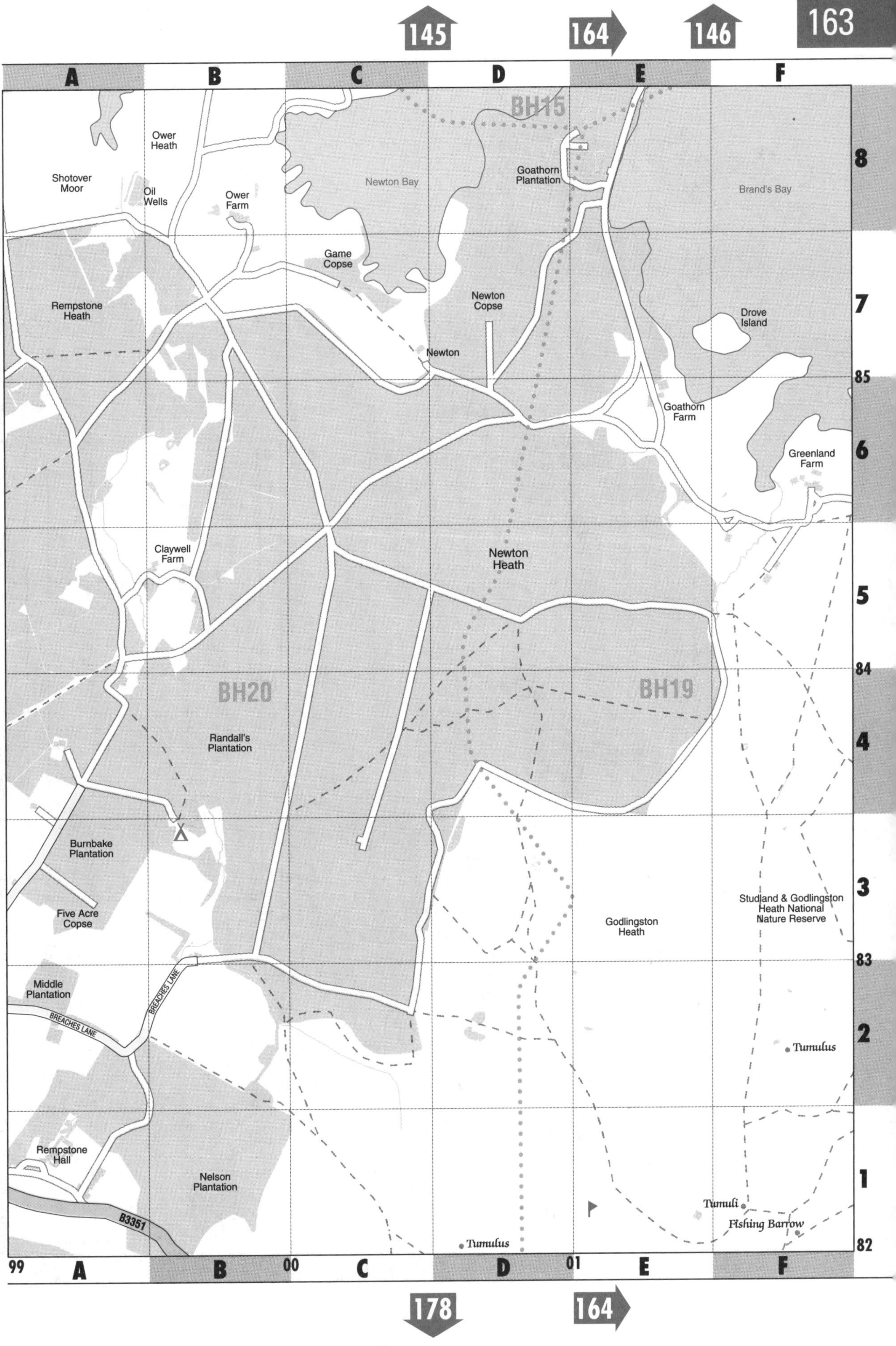

A   B   C   D   E   F

8

7

85

6

5

84

4

3

83

2

1

82

Shotover
Moor

Ower
Heath

Oil
Wells

Ower
Farm

Newton Bay

Goathorn
Plantation

BH15

Brand's Bay

Game
Copse

Newton
Copse

Drove
Island

Rempstone
Heath

Newton

Goathorn
Farm

Greenland
Farm

Claywell
Farm

Newton
Heath

BH20

BH19

Randall's
Plantation

Studland & Godlingston
Heath National
Nature Reserve

Burnbake
Plantation

Godlingston
Heath

Five Acre
Copse

Tumulus

Middle
Plantation

BREACHES LANE

BREACHES LANE

Tumuli
Fishing Barrow

Rempstone
Hall

Nelson
Plantation

B3351

Tumulus

Tumulus

A B C D E F

8

7

85

6

Redhorn
Quay

Studland Heath

Studland & Godlingston
Heath National
Nature Reserve

Little Sea

5

84

Studland Heath

BH19

Sewage
Works

Ferry Road

Visitor
Centre

P

179

Knoll House
Hotel

Studland Beach and
Nature Reserve

B3351

3

Puckstone

Tumuli

Tumulus

Redend
Point

Wadmore
Farm

WADMORE LANE

Ferry Road

83

Agglestone

Hotel

P

2

Black Down

HEATHERSIDE

RECTORY LANE

BEACH ROAD

BEACH ROAD

Cliff End

AGGLESTONE
ROAD

Manor
Farm

MANOR ROAD

P

PH

SCHOOL LANE

CHURCH RD

South West Coast Path

HEATH GREEN ROAD

PO

WATERY LANE

1

West Wood

SWANAGE ROAD

Studland

WATERY LANE

The Warren
Wood

B3351

82

King Barrow

02 A B 03 C D 04 E F

South West Coast Path

05

Old Harry's
Wife

Studland
Wood

Old
Harry

The Foreland or
Handfast Point

BH19

South West Coast Path

The Pinnacles

82

82

05

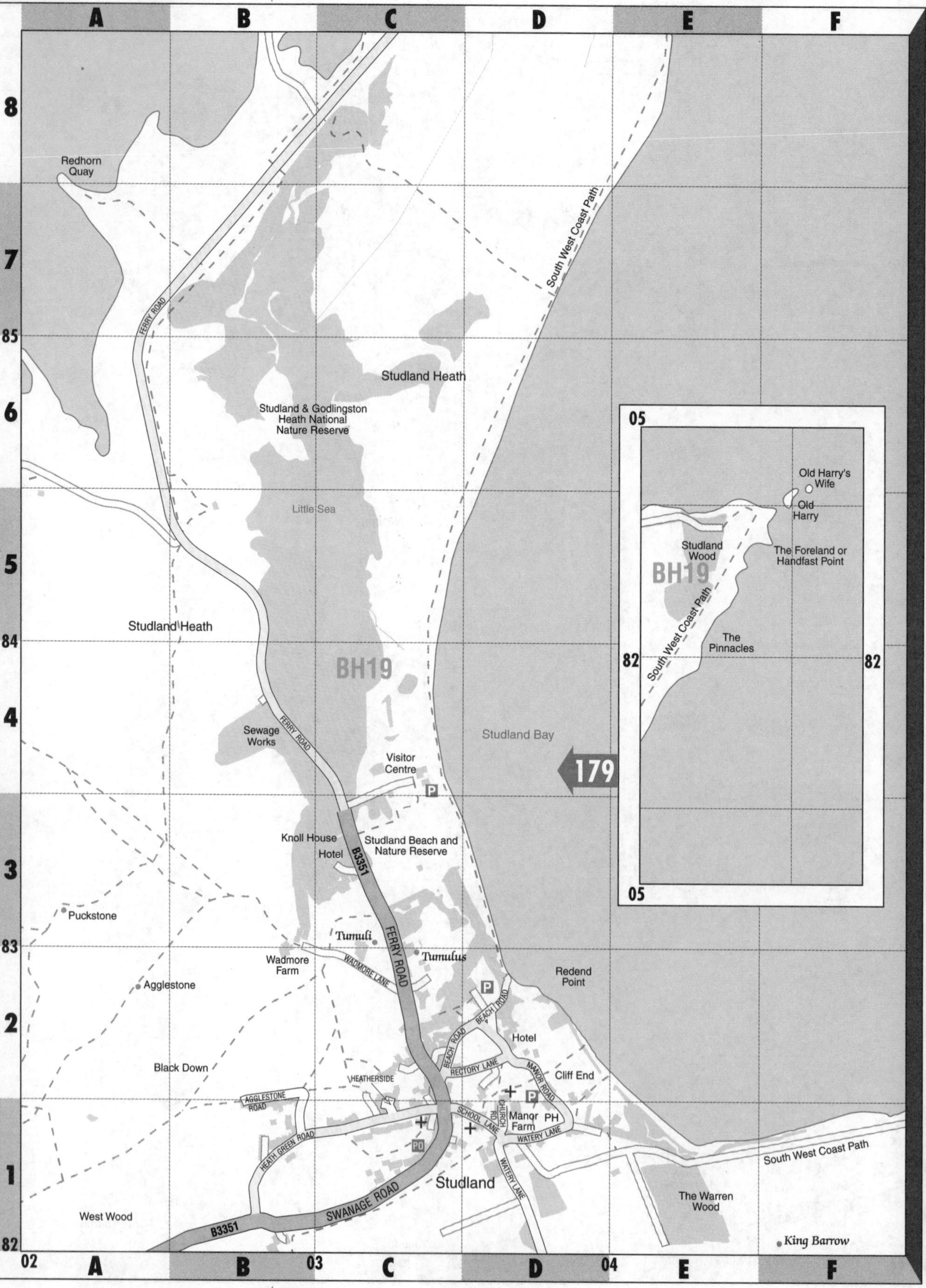

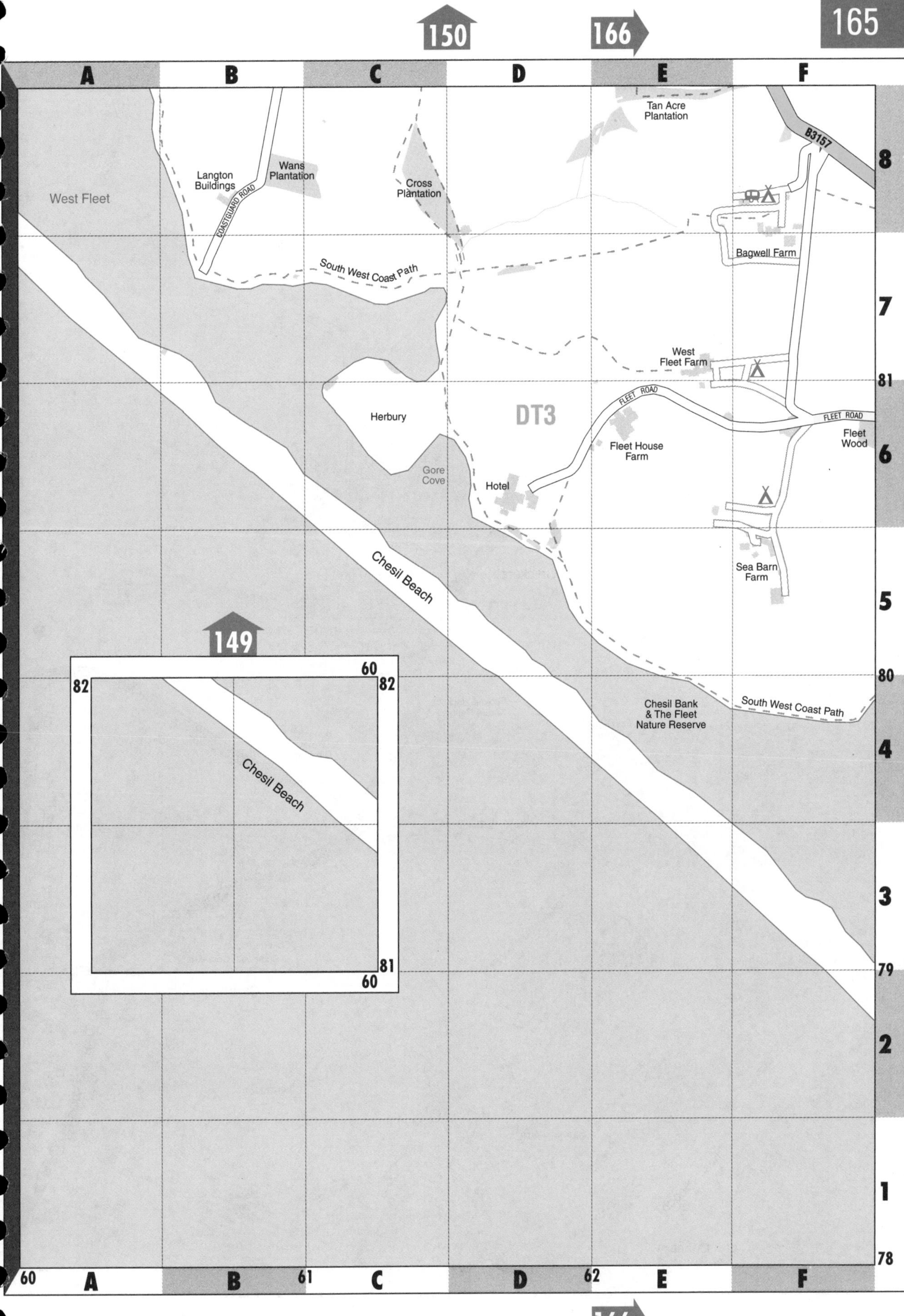

A B C D E F

8

West Fleet

Langton
Buildings

Wans
Plantation

Cross
Plantation

Tan Acre
Plantation

B3157

Bagwell Farm

South West Coast Path

7

81

Herbury

West
Fleet Farm

DT3

FLEET ROAD

FLEET ROAD

Fleet
Wood

6

Gore
Cove

Hotel

Fleet House
Farm

Sea Barn
Farm

5

Chesil Beach

149

80

82   60

82

Chesil Bank
& The Fleet
Nature Reserve

South West Coast Path

4

Chesil Beach

81
60

3

79

2

1

78

60   A   B   61   C   D   62   E   F

165
151

D5
1 CURLEW CL
2 GREBE CL
3 HERON CL

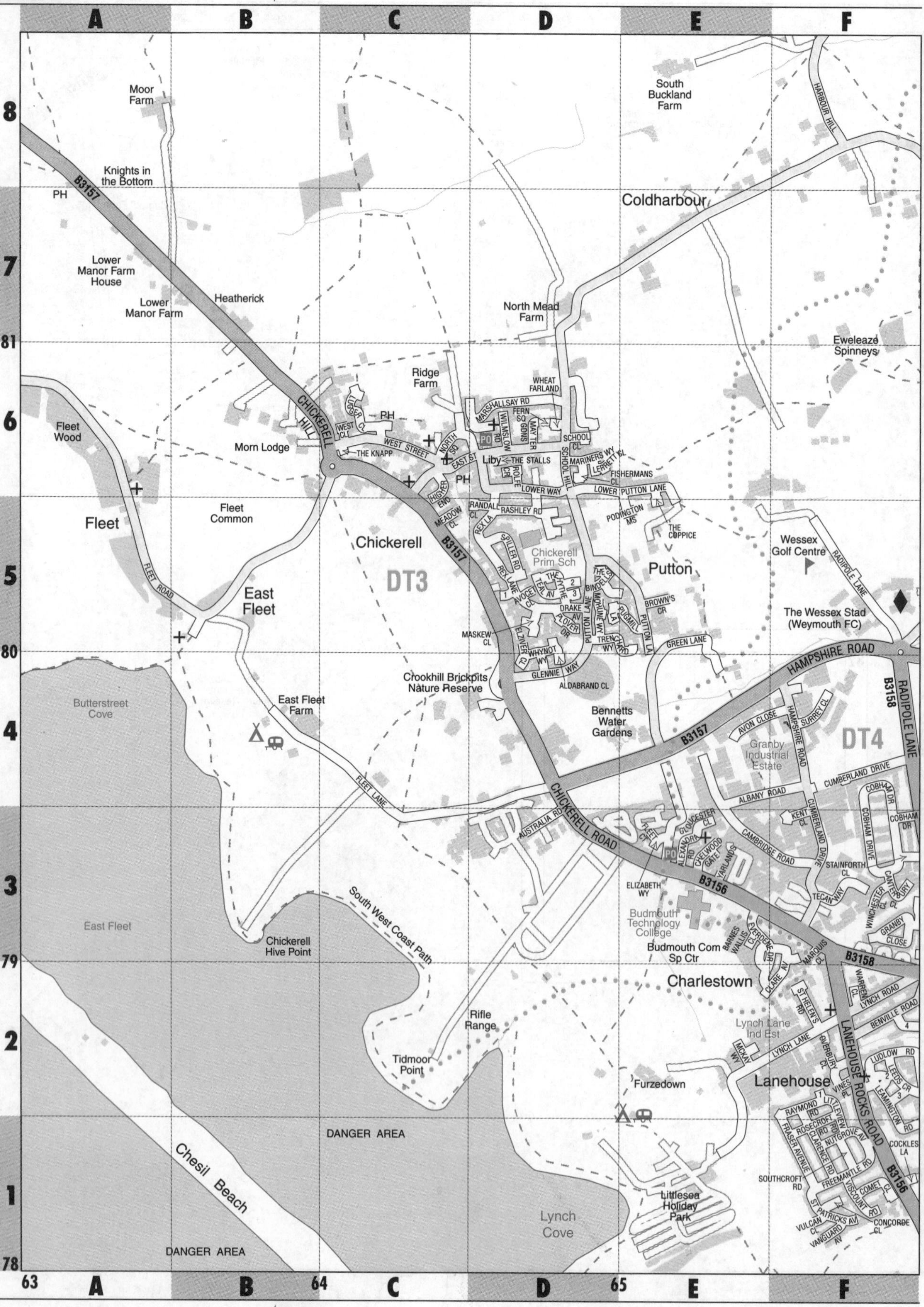

A B C D E F

8

Moor Farm

South Buckland Farm

Knights in the Bottom

B3157

PH

Coldharbour

7

Lower Manor Farm House

Heatherick

North Mead Farm

Lower Manor Farm

81

Eweleaze Spinneys

Ridge Farm

WHEAT FARLAND

MARSHALLSAY RD

FERN SQ GDNS

MAY TER

6

Fleet Wood

CHICKERELL HILL

Morn Lodge

WEST CL

PH

WEST STREET

THE KNAPP

NORTH SQ

EAST ST

Liby

SCHOOL CL

MARINERS WY

LERRETT CL

FISHERMANS CL

THE STALLS

SCHOOL HL

LOWER WAY

LOWER PUTTON LANE

PH

PUTTE END

MEADOW CL

RANDALL CL

RASHLEY RD

PODINGTON MS

THE COPPICE

Wessex Golf Centre

RADIPOLE LANE

Fleet

Fleet Common

Chickerell

DT3

B3157

SPILLER RD

AVOCET CL

REEL RD

RA LA

THE TEAL AV

BINDER CL

2

3

Chickerell Prim Sch

Putton

BROWN'S CR

The Wessex Stad
(Weymouth FC)

5

East Fleet

MASKEW CL

PLOVER CL

DRAKE AV

PUTTON WY

TRENCH WY

PUTTON LA

GREEN LANE

80

Butterstreet Cove

East Fleet Farm

WHYNOT CL

GLENNIE WAY

ALDABRAND CL

Crookhill Brickpits Nature Reserve

Bennetts Water Gardens

B3157

AVON CLOSE

SURREY CL

HAMPSHIRE ROAD

HAMPSHIRE ROAD

B3158

RADIPOLE LANE

DT4

4

FLEET ROAD

FLEET LANE

Granby Industrial Estate

CUMBERLAND DRIVE

COBHAM CL

COBHAM DR

ALBANY ROAD

KENT CL

STAINFORTH CL

CAMBRIDGE ROAD

AUSTRALIA RD

CHICKERELL ROAD

PO

GLOUCESTER

CHELWOOD GATE

CUMBERLAND DRIVE

CHESTER CL

GRANBY CLOSE

CANTER CT

East Fleet

Chickerell Hive Point

South West Coast Path

B3156

ELIZABETH WY

Budmouth Technology College

Budmouth Com Sp Ctr

BARNES WALLIS

MARQUIS CL

CLARE AV

B3158

LYNCH ROAD

ST HELENS CL

BENVILLE ROAD

79

Charlestown

Lynch Lane Ind Est

LUDLOW RD

LEEDS CL

LEMINGTON RD

Rifle Range

LYNCH LANE

MOHUN CL

VINES CL

Lanehouse

LANEHOUSE ROCKS ROAD

LITTLELAW

VISCOUNT RD

2

Tidmoor Point

Furzedown

RAYMOND RD

ROSECROFT RD

NUTGROVE AV

FRASER AVENUE RD

FREEMANTLE RD

VULCAN CL

COMET CL

COCKLES LA

1

Chesil Beach

Lynch Cove

Littlesea Holiday Park

SOUTHCROFT RD

ST PATRICKS AV

VANGUARD AV

VISCOUNT RD

CONCORDE CL

B3156

78

DANGER AREA

DANGER AREA

63 A 64 B C 65 D E F

165
180

F2
1 GORDON CR
2 LINCOLN RD
3 LIVERPOOL RD
4 TOLLERDOWN RD

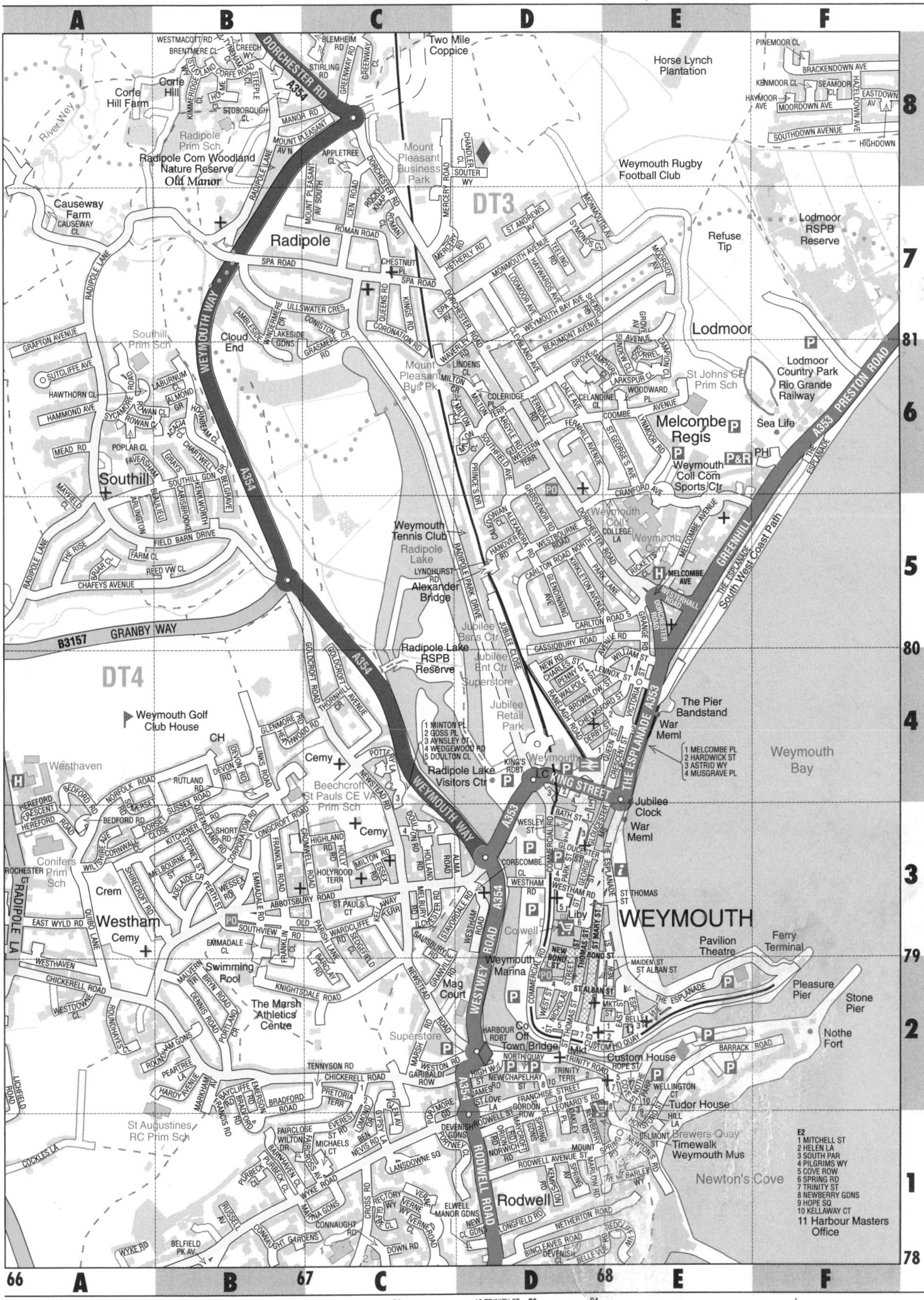

152 168 180 181 168

C1
1 Holy Trinity CE Prim Sch
2 Thornlow Prep Sch

C2
1 ASHTON RD
2 GYPSY LA
3 PRINCE OF WALES RD

D2
1 CHAPELHAY HEIGHTS
2 HARTLEBURY TERR
3 SPRING LA
4 LOWER ST ALBAN ST
5 LOWER ST EDMUND ST
6 ST EDMUND ST
7 ST MARY ST
8 DORSET TERR
9 PROSPECT PL

10 TRINITY CT

D3
1 CLIFTON PL
2 QUEBEC PL
3 TURTON ST
4 WOOPERTON ST
5 CAROLINE PL
6 SCHOOL ST

D4
1 STANLEY ST
2 UPWAY ST
3 JUBILEE CL
4 EDWARD ST
5 ALBERT ST

E2
1 MITCHELL ST
2 HELEN LA
3 SOUTH PAR
4 PILGRIMS WY
5 COVE ROW
6 SPRING RD
7 TRINITY ST
8 NEWBERRY GDNS
9 HOPE SQ
10 KELLAWAY CT
11 Harbour Masters Office

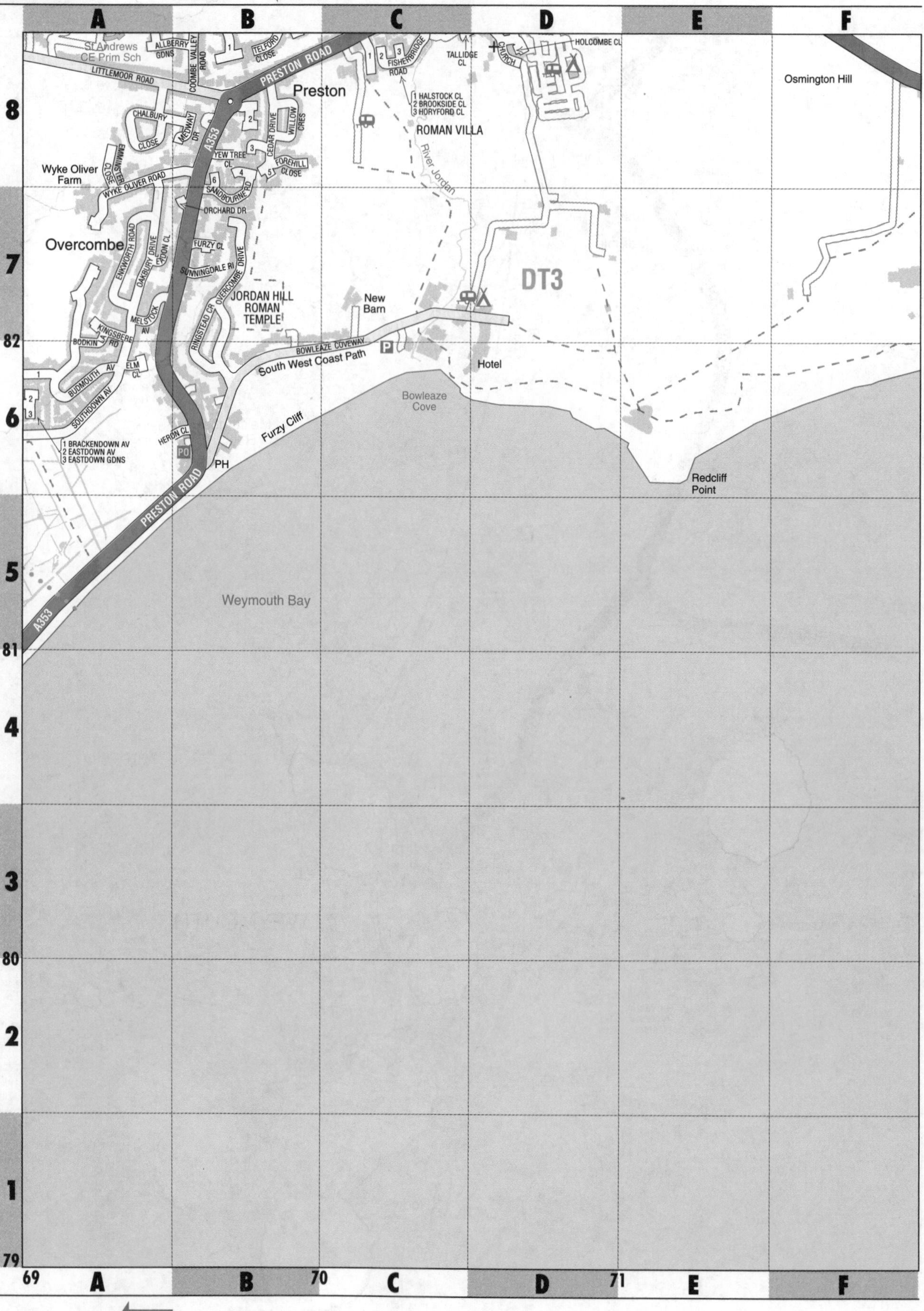

B8
1 MOORCOMBE DR
2 CHALBURY LODGE
3 HAZEL DR
4 WINGREEN CL
5 MAPLE CL
6 DEANSLEIGH CL

St Andrews CE Prim Sch
ALLBERRY GDNS
COOMBE VALLEY ROAD
LITTLEMOOR ROAD
TELFORD CLOSE
PRESTON ROAD
Preston
FISHERS ROAD
TALLIDGE CL
HOLCOMBE CL
CHURCH
Osmington Hill

CHALBURY CLOSE
MOTWAY DR
A353
YEW TREE CL
CEDAR DRIVE
WILLOW CRES
FORGHILL CLOSE
1 HALSTOCK CL
2 BROOKSIDE CL
3 HORYFORD CL
ROMAN VILLA

Wyke Oliver Farm
WYKE OLIVER ROAD
SANDBOURNE RD
ORCHARD DR
River Jordan
DT3

Overcombe
ERNWORTH ROAD
OAKBURY DRIVE
PRESTON CL
FURZY CL
SUNNINGDALE RI
OVERCOMBE DRIVE
JORDAN HILL ROMAN TEMPLE
New Barn

KINGSBERE RD
MELSTOCK AV
RINGSTEAD CR
BOWLEAZE COVEWAY
South West Coast Path
P
Hotel

BODKIN CL
ELM CL
82

BUDMOUTH AV
SOUTHDOWN AV
1
2
3
HERON CL
Furzy Cliff
Bowleaze Cove
Redcliff Point

1 BRACKENDOWN AV
2 EASTDOWN AV
3 EASTDOWN GDNS
PO
PH
PRESTON ROAD

Weymouth Bay

A353

8
7
82
6
5
81
4
3
80
2
81
1
79

69
A
B
70
C
D
71
E
F

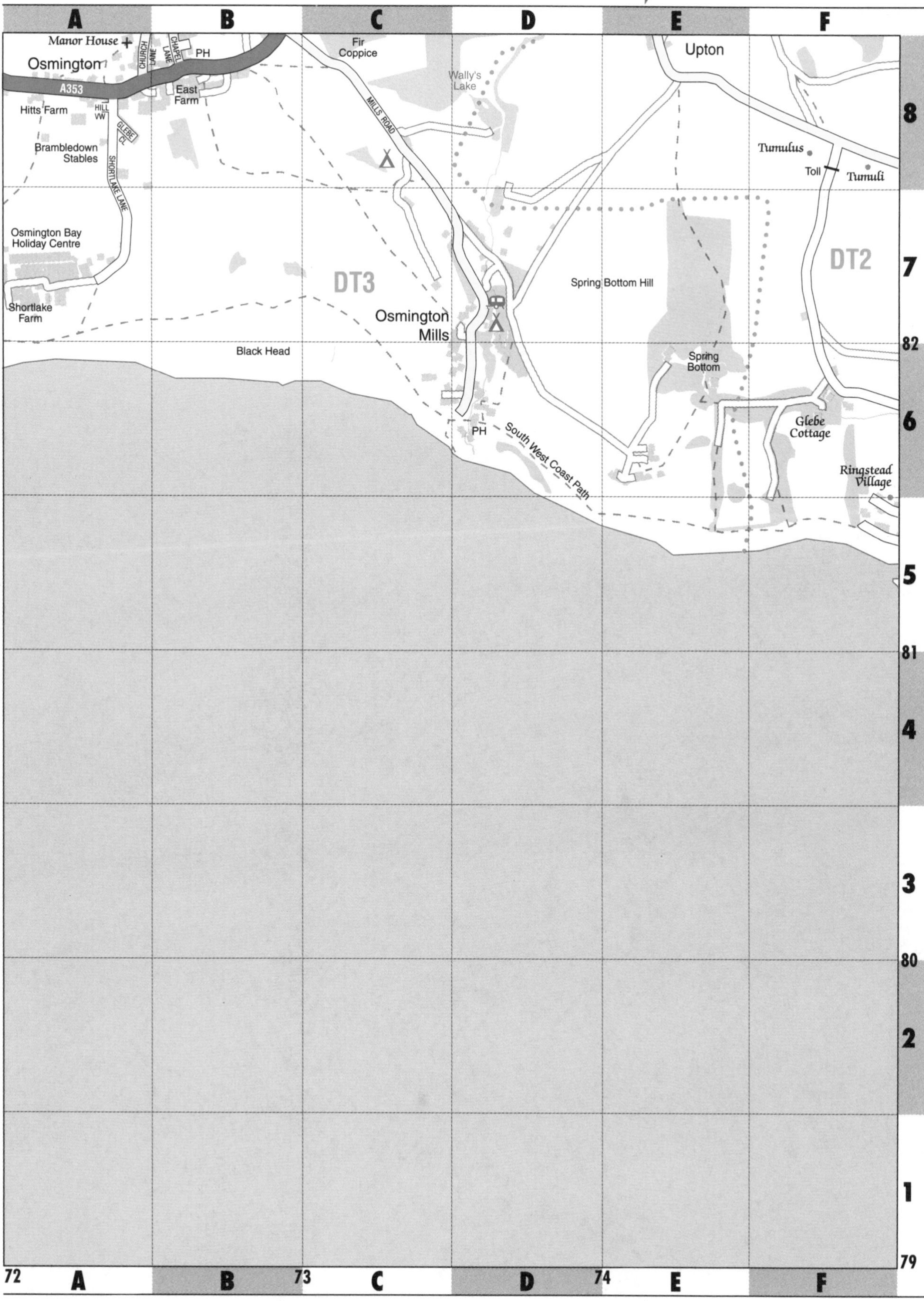
154
170
A
B
C
D
E
F
Manor House
Osmington
CHURCH LANE
CHAPEL LANE
PH
A353
East Farm
Fir Coppice
Wally's Lake
Upton
Hitts Farm
HILL VW
GLEBE CL
Brambledown Stables
SHORTLAKE LANE
MILLS ROAD
Tumulus
Toll
Tumuli
Osmington Bay Holiday Centre
DT3
Spring Bottom Hill
DT2
Shortlake Farm
Osmington Mills
Black Head
Spring Bottom
PH
South West Coast Path
Glebe Cottage
Ringstead Village
8
7
82
6
5
81
4
3
80
2
1
79
72
73
74

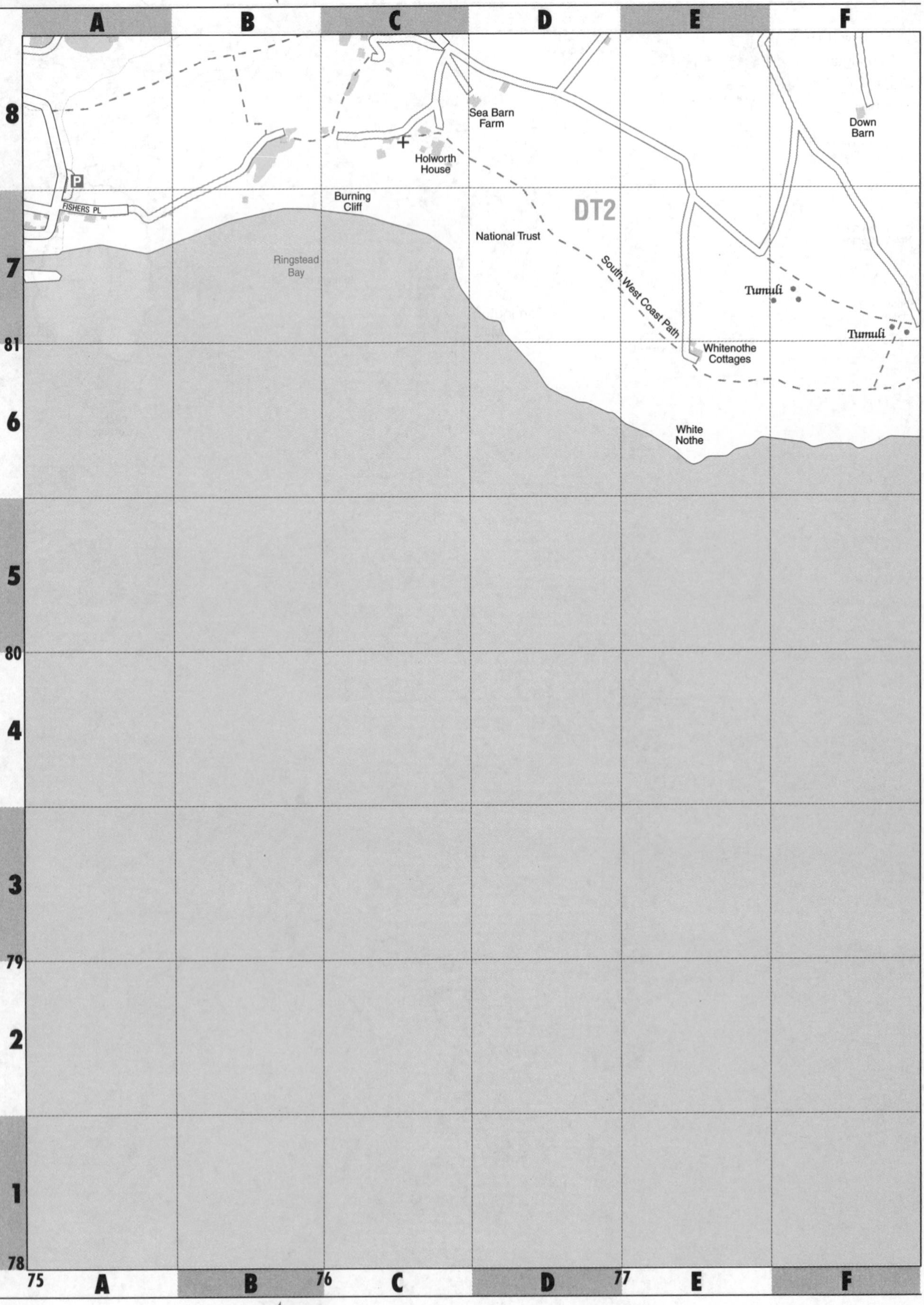

A B C D E F

8

Sea Barn
Farm

Down
Barn

P

FISHERS PL

Holworth
House

Burning
Cliff

DT2

81

7

Ringstead
Bay

National Trust

South West Coast Path

Tumuli

Tumuli

Whitenothe
Cottages

6

White
Nothe

5

80

4

3

79

2

1

78

75 A B 76 C D 77 E F

156
172

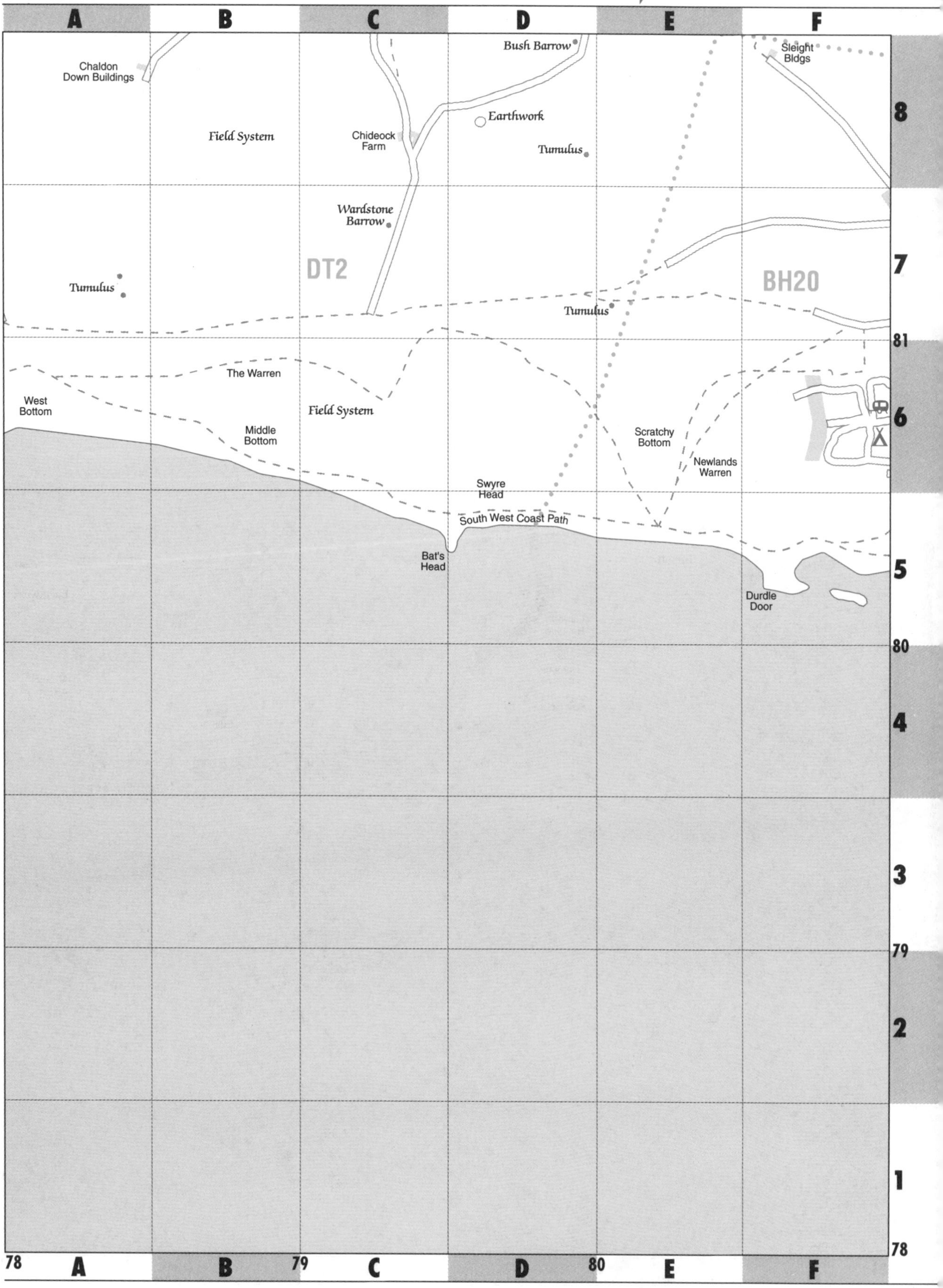
A
B
C
D
E
F
Chaldon Down Buildings
Field System
Chideock Farm
Bush Barrow
Earthwork
Tumulus
Sleight Bldgs
8
Wardstone Barrow
DT2
Tumulus
Tumulus
BH20
7
81
The Warren
West Bottom
Field System
Middle Bottom
Scratchy Bottom
Newlands Warren
6
Swyre Head
South West Coast Path
Bat's Head
Durdle Door
5
80
4
3
79
2
1
78
78
79
80

172

171
157

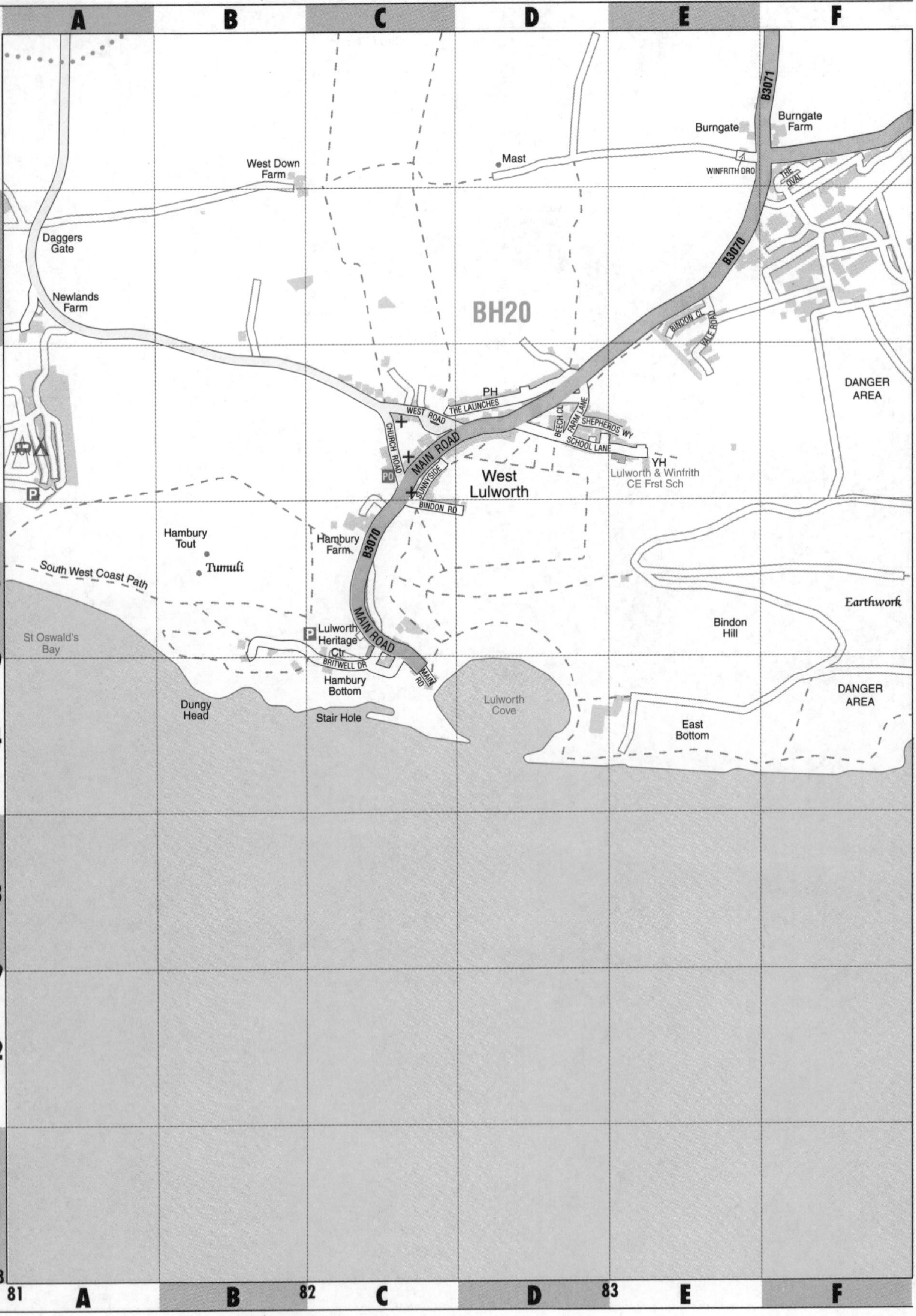
A
B
C
D
E
F
8
7
81
6
5
80
4
3
79
2
1
78
81
82
83
West Down Farm
Mast
Burngate
Burngate Farm
WINFRITH DRO
THE OVAL
B3071
B3070
Daggers Gate
Newlands Farm
BH20
BINDON CL
VALE ROAD
DANGER AREA
PH
THE LAUNCHES
WEST ROAD
CHURCH ROAD
MAIN ROAD
BEECH CL
FARM LANE
SHEPHERDS WY
SCHOOL LANE
YH
Lulworth & Winfrith CE Frst Sch
PO
SUNNYSIDE
West Lulworth
BINDON RD
Hambury Tout
Tumuli
Hambury Farm
South West Coast Path
Earthwork
Bindon Hill
St Oswald's Bay
P
Lulworth Heritage Ctr
BRITWELL DR
MAIN RD
Hambury Bottom
Dungy Head
Stair Hole
Lulworth Cove
DANGER AREA
East Bottom

171

158
174

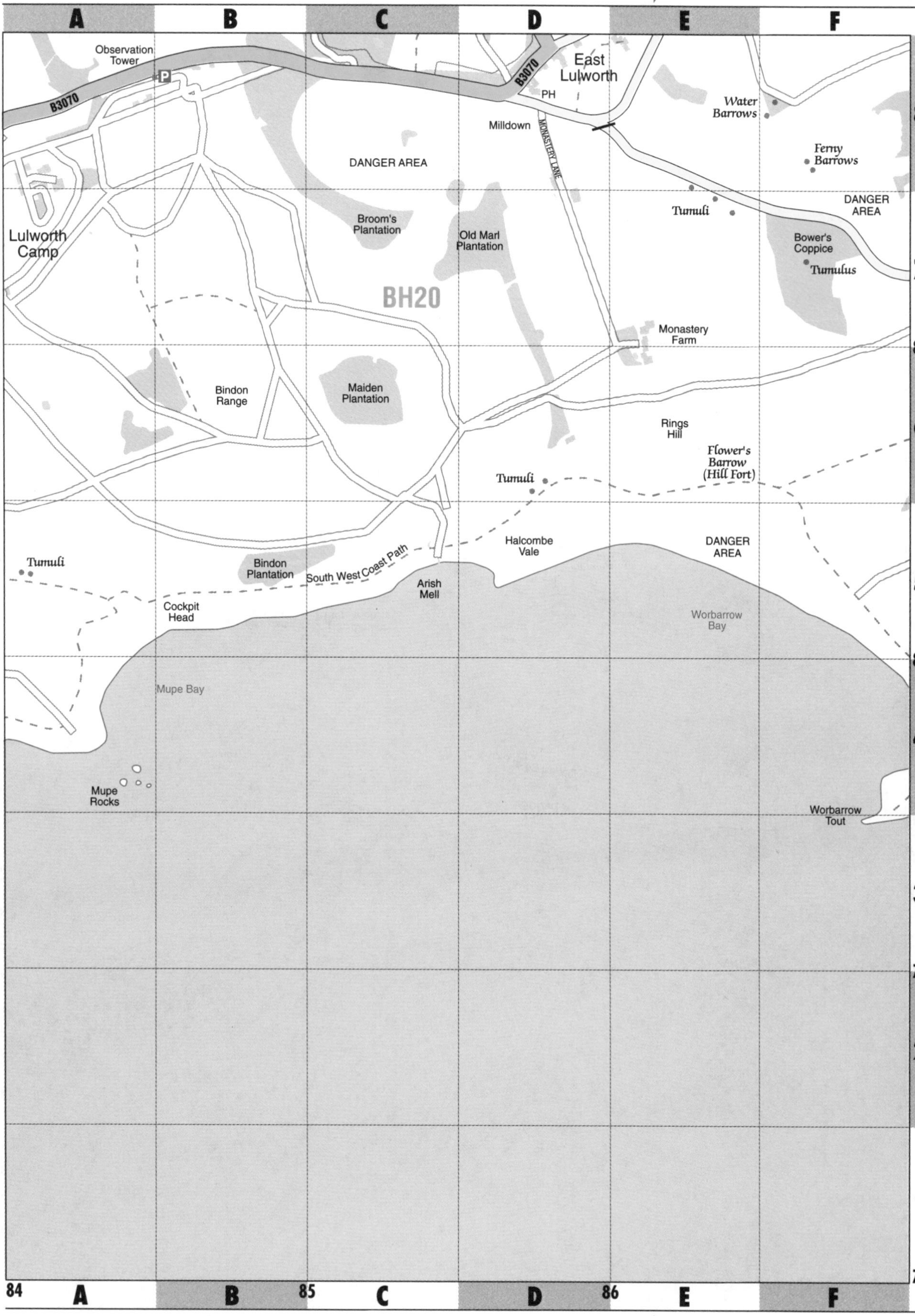
A
B
C
D
E
F
Observation Tower
P
B3070
East Lulworth
PH
Milldown
Water Barrows
Ferny Barrows
DANGER AREA
Lulworth Camp
MONASTERY LANE
Tumuli
DANGER AREA
Broom's Plantation
Old Marl Plantation
Bower's Coppice
Tumulus
BH20
Monastery Farm
Bindon Range
Maiden Plantation
Rings Hill
Flower's Barrow (Hill Fort)
Tumuli
Halcombe Vale
DANGER AREA
Tumuli
Bindon Plantation
South West Coast Path
Arish Mell
Cockpit Head
Worbarrow Bay
Mupe Bay
Mupe Rocks
Worbarrow Tout
8
7
81
6
5
80
4
3
79
2
1
78
84
85
86

174

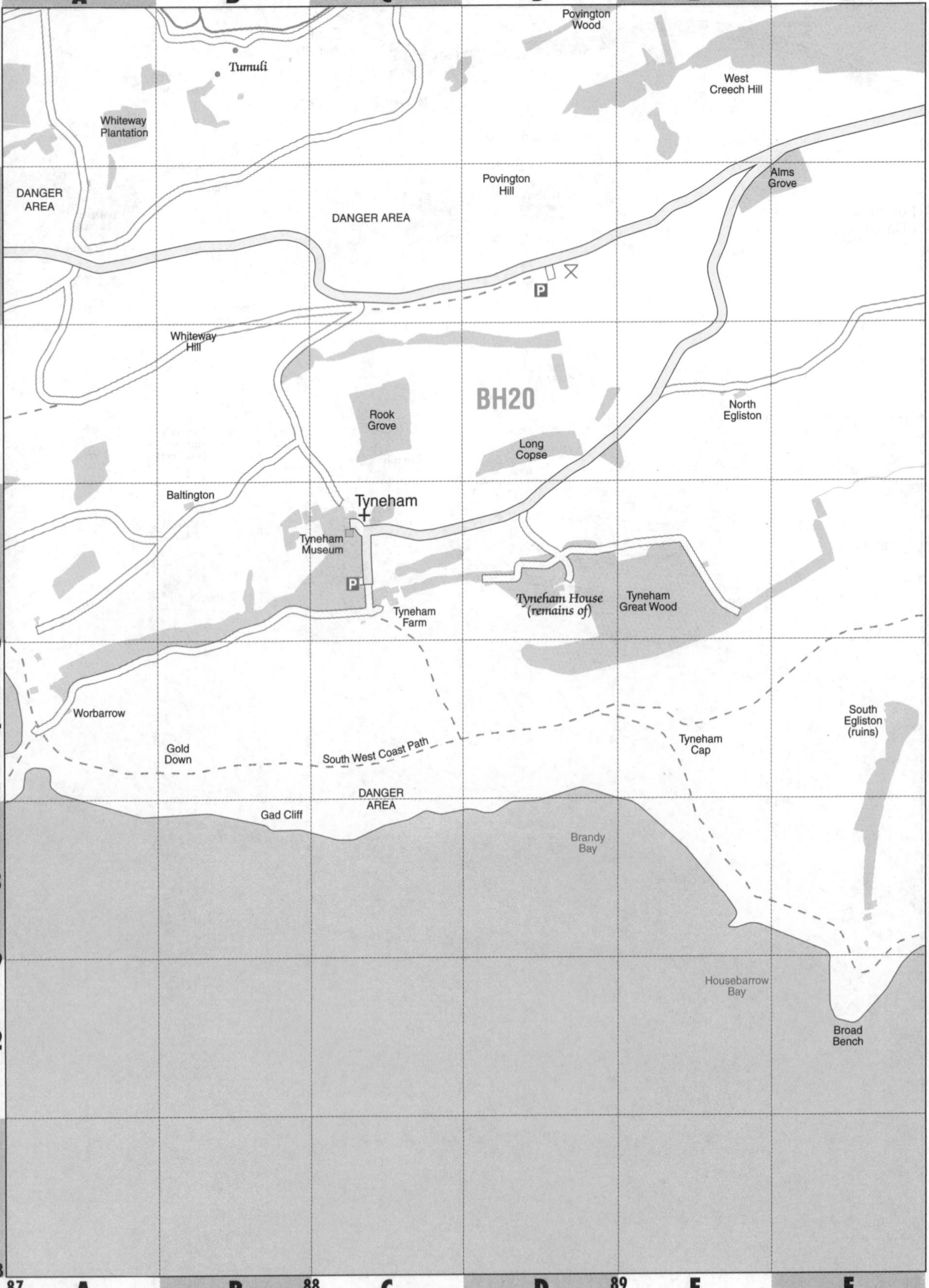

8

Tumuli

Whiteway
Plantation

Povington
Wood

West
Creech Hill

DANGER
AREA

Povington
Hill

Alms
Grove

7

DANGER AREA

81

Whiteway
Hill

BH20

Rook
Grove

North
Egliston

6

Long
Copse

Baltington

Tyneham

Tyneham
Museum

Tyneham House
(remains of)

Tyneham
Great Wood

5

Tyneham
Farm

80

Worbarrow

Gold
Down

South West Coast Path

Tyneham
Cap

South
Egliston
(ruins)

4

DANGER
AREA

Gad Cliff

Brandy
Bay

3

Housebarrow
Bay

79

Broad
Bench

2

1

78

87 A B 88 C D 89 E F

160
176

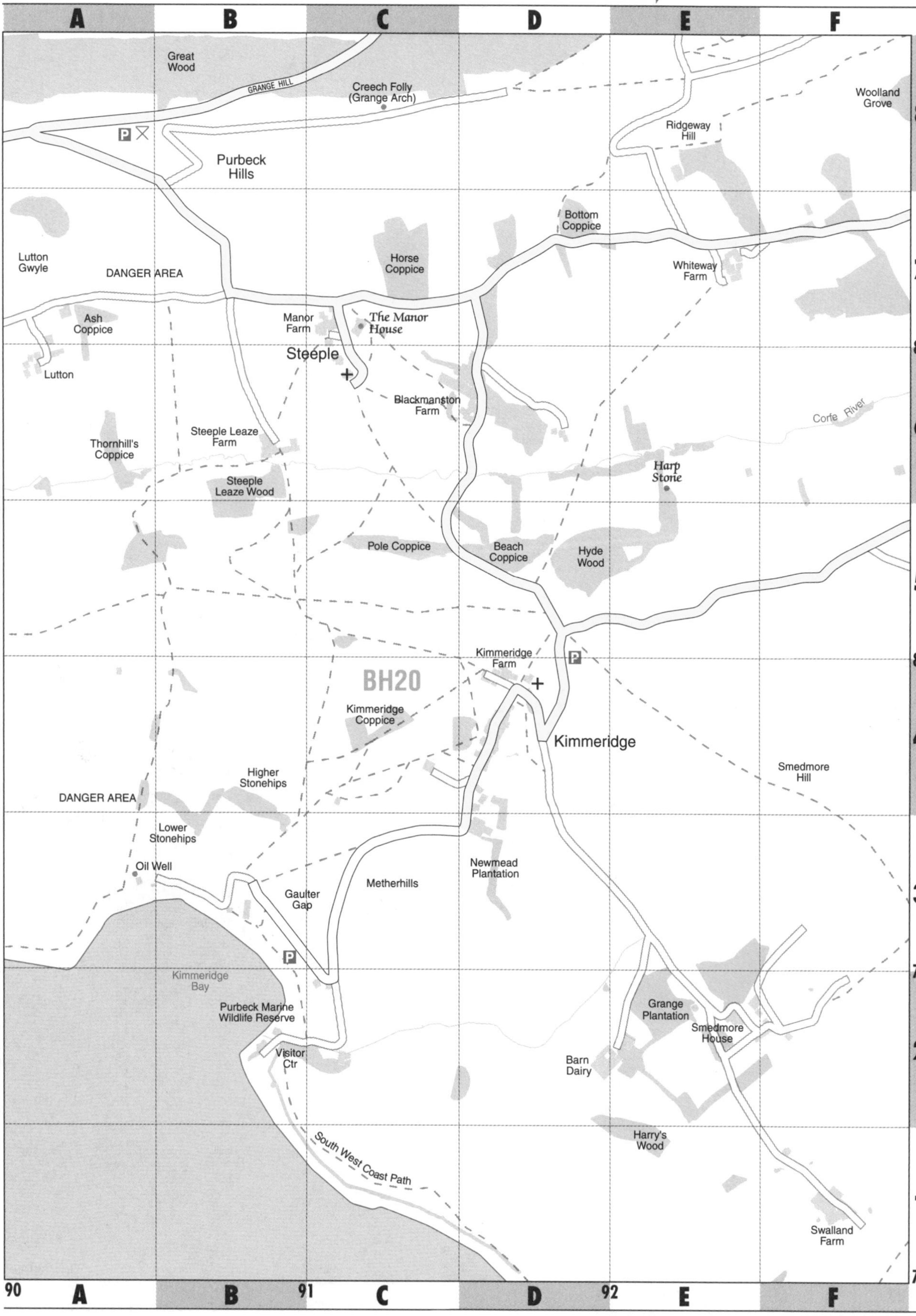
A
B
C
D
E
F
Great Wood
GRANGE HILL
Creech Folly (Grange Arch)
Woolland Grove
Ridgeway Hill
Purbeck Hills
Bottom Coppice
Lutton Gwyle
DANGER AREA
Horse Coppice
Whiteway Farm
Ash Coppice
Manor Farm
The Manor House
Steeple
Lutton
Blackmanston Farm
Corfe River
Thornhill's Coppice
Steeple Leaze Farm
Steeple Leaze Wood
Harp Stone
Pole Coppice
Beach Coppice
Hyde Wood
Kimmeridge Farm
BH20
Kimmeridge Coppice
Kimmeridge
Smedmore Hill
Higher Stonehips
DANGER AREA
Lower Stonehips
Oil Well
Gaulter Gap
Metherhills
Newmead Plantation
Kimmeridge Bay
Purbeck Marine Wildlife Reserve
Visitor Ctr
Grange Plantation
Smedmore House
Barn Dairy
Harry's Wood
South West Coast Path
Swalland Farm
8
7
81
6
5
80
4
3
79
2
1
78
90
91
92

176
182

175
161

A | B | C | D | E | F

8

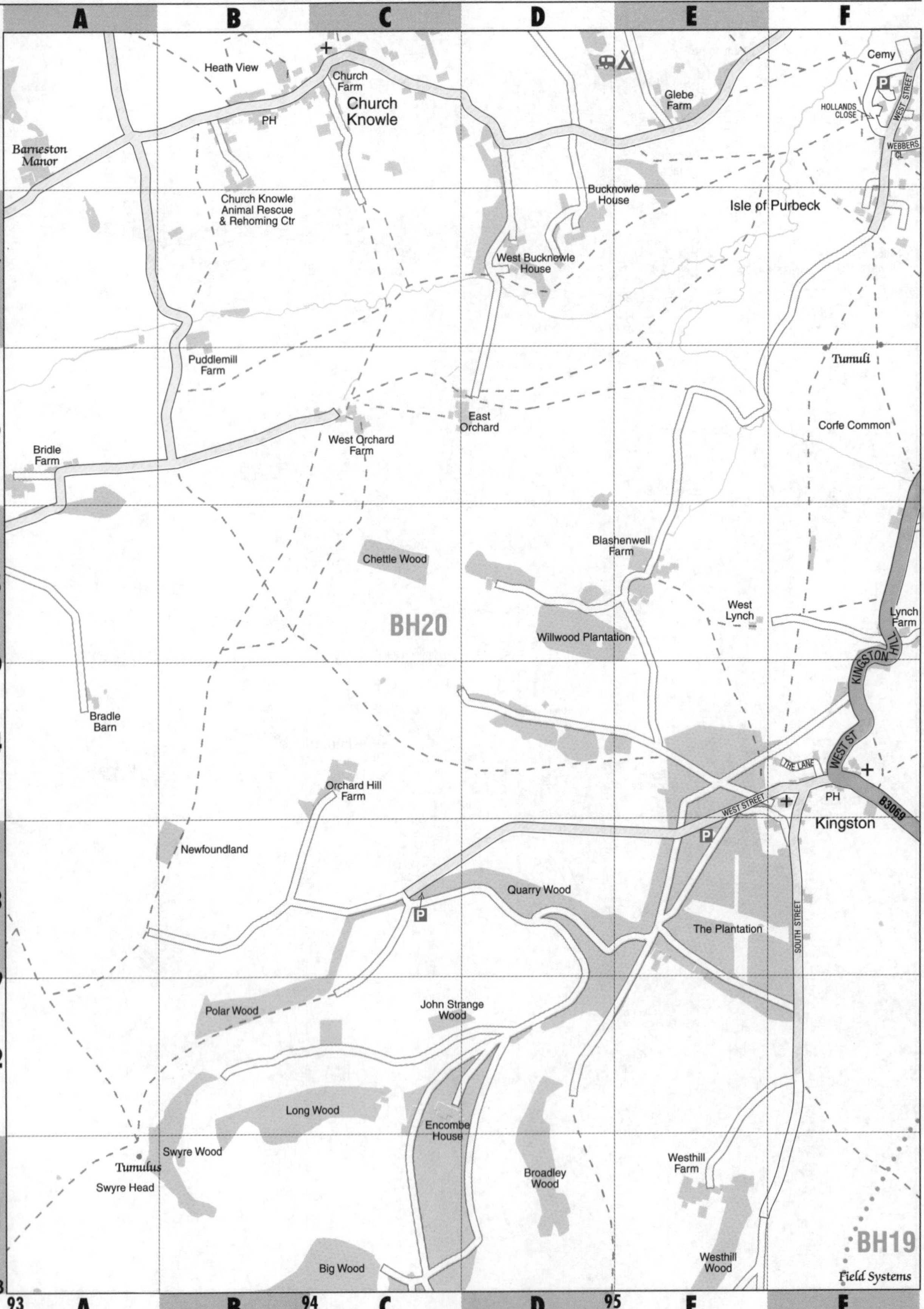

Heath View

Church Farm

Church Knowle

PH

Barneston Manor

Glebe Farm

Bucknowle House

Isle of Purbeck

Cemy

HOLLANDS CLOSE

WEBBERS CL

WEST STREET

7

Church Knowle Animal Rescue & Rehoming Ctr

West Bucknowle House

81

Puddlemill Farm

Tumuli

Corfe Common

6

Bridle Farm

West Orchard Farm

East Orchard

5

Chettle Wood

Blashenwell Farm

West Lynch

Lynch Farm

BH20

Willwood Plantation

KINGSTON TWL

80

Bradle Barn

4

THE LANE

WEST ST

B3069

Orchard Hill Farm

WEST STREET

PH

Kingston

3

Newfoundland

Quarry Wood

P

The Plantation

SOUTH STREET

P

79

Polar Wood

John Strange Wood

2

Long Wood

Encombe House

Broadley Wood

Westhill Farm

1

Swyre Wood

Tumulus

Swyre Head

BH19

Westhill Wood

Field Systems

78

Big Wood

93 | A | B | 94 | C | D | E | 95 | F

175
182

162
178

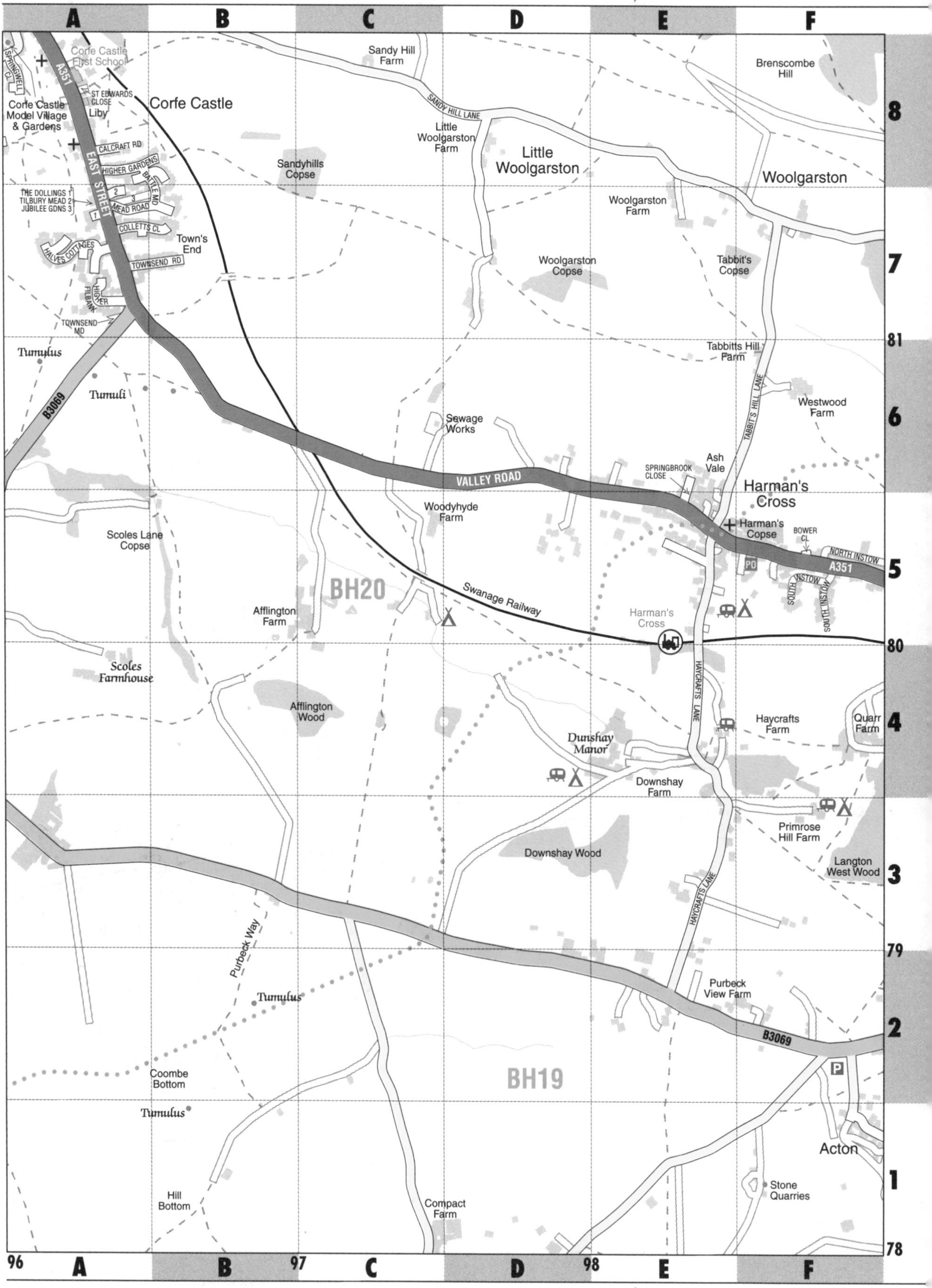
A
B
C
D
E
F
8
7
81
6
5
80
4
3
79
2
1
78
96
97
98
Corfe Castle First School
SPRINGWELL CL
A351
ST EDWARDS CLOSE
Liby
Corfe Castle
Corfe Castle Model Village & Gardens
CALCRAFT RD
EAST STREET
HIGHER GARDENS
BATTLE MD
THE DOLLINGS 1
TILBURY MEAD 2
JUBILEE GDNS 3
MEAD ROAD
COLLETTS CL
HALVES COTTAGES
Town's End
TOWNSEND RD
HIGHER FILBANK
TOWNSEND MD
Tumulus
Tumuli
B3069
Sandy Hill Farm
SANDY HILL LANE
Little Woolgarston Farm
Little Woolgarston
Sandyhills Copse
Brenscombe Hill
Woolgarston
Woolgarston Farm
Woolgarston Copse
Tabbit's Copse
Tabbitts Hill Farm
TABBIT'S HILL LANE
Westwood Farm
Sewage Works
VALLEY ROAD
Ash Vale
SPRINGBROOK CLOSE
Harman's Cross
Harman's Copse
BOWER CL
NORTH INSTOW
SOUTH INSTOW
PO
Woodyhyde Farm
Scoles Lane Copse
BH20
Swanage Railway
Affington Farm
Harman's Cross
Scoles Farmhouse
Afflington Wood
HAYCRAFTS LANE
Haycrafts Farm
Quarr Farm
Dunshay Manor
Downshay Farm
Primrose Hill Farm
Downshay Wood
Langton West Wood
Purbeck Way
Tumulus
Purbeck View Farm
B3069
P
BH19
Coombe Bottom
Tumulus
Acton
Stone Quarries
Hill Bottom
Compact Farm

183
178

177 163

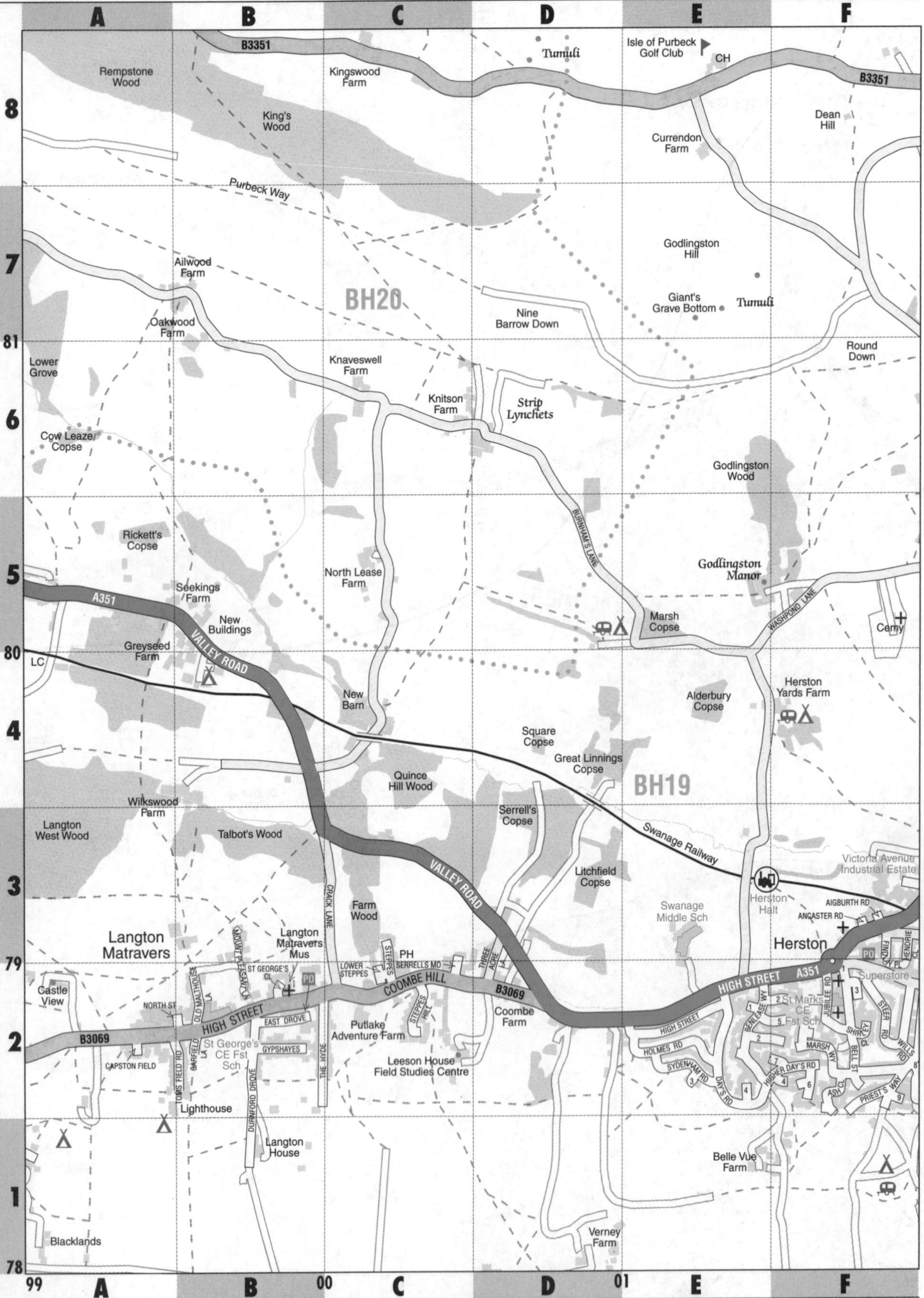

A | B | C | D | E | F

8
Rempstone Wood
B3351
Kingswood Farm
King's Wood
Tumuli
Isle of Purbeck Golf Club
CH
B3351
Dean Hill
Currendon Farm

Purbeck Way

7
Ailwood Farm
BH20
Godlingston Hill
Oakwood Farm
Giant's Grave Bottom
Tumuli

81
Lower Grove
Knaveswell Farm
Nine Barrow Down
Round Down

6
Cow Leaze Copse
Knitson Farm
Strip Lynchets
Godlingston Wood

Rickett's Copse
BURNHAM'S LANE

5
A351
Seekings Farm
North Lease Farm
Godlingston Manor
WASHPOND LANE
Cemy
New Buildings
Marsh Copse

80
LC
Greyseed Farm
VALLEY ROAD
New Barn
Herston Yards Farm
Alderbury Copse

4
Wilkswood Farm
Square Copse
Great Linnings Copse
BH19
Quince Hill Wood
Langton West Wood
Serrell's Copse
Swanage Railway

3
Talbot's Wood
VALLEY ROAD
Litchfield Copse
Swanage Middle Sch
Herston Halt
Victoria Avenue Industrial Estate
AIGBURTH RD
Farm Wood
ANCASTER RD
Langton Matravers Mus
CHICK LANE
STEPPES
PH SERRELLS MD
THREE ACRE LA
Herston
Langton Matravers
St George's C of E
PO
LOWER STEPPES
COOMBE HILL
B3069
HIGH STREET A351
PO
Superstore

79
Castle View
NORTH ST
OLD MALTHOUSE LA
MOUNT PLEASANT LA
EAST DROVE
STEPPES HILL
Coombe Farm
St Marks CE Fst Sch
JUBILEE RD
BALTAGE WY
STEER RD
SHIRLEY RD
HENDRIE PL
WILLIS WY
BELL ST
FINDLAY PL

2
B3069
CAPSTON FIELD
TOMS FIELD RD
BARFIELD LA
GYPSHAYES
St George's CE Fst Sch
Putlake Adventure Farm
Leeson House Field Studies Centre
HIGH STREET
HOLMES RD
SYDENHAM RD
HIGHER DAY'S RD
DAY'S RD
MARSH
PRIEST'S WAY

Lighthouse
DURNFORD DRIVE
THE DROVE

1
Langton House
Belle Vue Farm
Verney Farm

78
Blacklands

99 | A | 00 | B | C | 00 | D | 01 | E | F

177 184

164

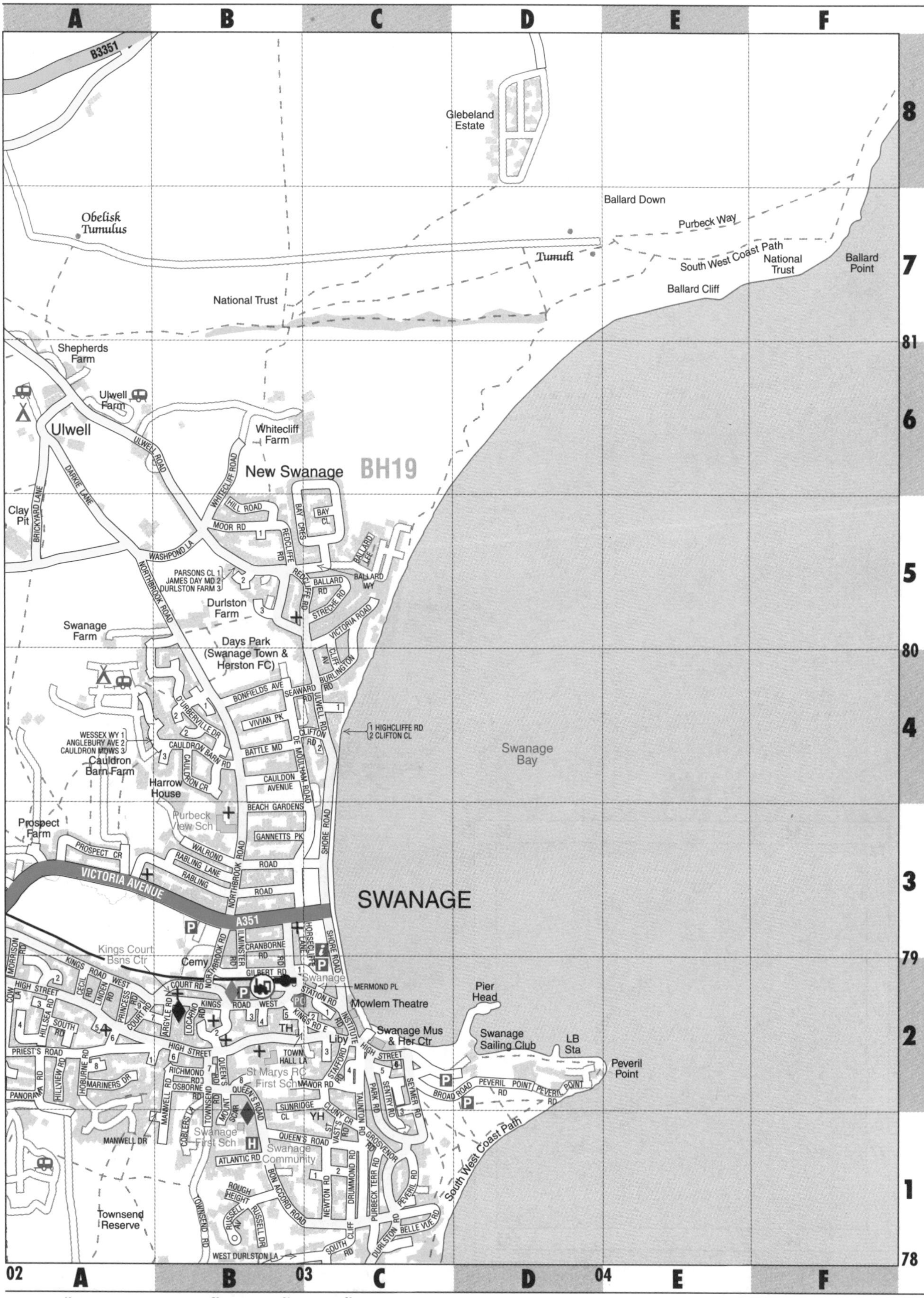

A2
1 COWLEASE
2 NEWTON MANOR CL
3 WEST DR
4 NEWTON RISE
5 HOWARD RD
6 GORDON RD
7 HANBURY RD
8 FOXHILL CL
9 BISHOPS ROW

B2
1 STATION PL
2 CHURCH HL
3 CHURCH CL
4 SPRINGFIELD RD
5 ELDON TERR
6 MANWELL'S LA
7 DUNFORD PL
8 QUEENS MD

C1
1 KNOLLSEA CL
2 SALISBURY RD
3 BELVEDERE RD

C2
1 COMMERCIAL RD
2 CORNWALL RD
3 MOUNT PLEASANT LA
4 EXETER RD
5 MARSHALL ROW
6 BURT'S PL

185

B6
1 BEACHVIEW CL
2 JASMINE WY
3 CUNNINGHAM CL
4 FOSSETT WY
5 WESTHILL CL

C6
1 LANEHOUSE ROCKS RD
2 WYKE RD
3 LYMES CL
4 CHURCHILL CL
5 SWAFFIELD GDNS
6 MARTLEAVES CL

7 WYKE SQ

D7
1 HILLBOURNE RD
2 DOWNCLOSE

D8
1 BELFIELD PK DR
2 BUXTON CL
3 BELFIELD CL
4 CARRINGTON CL

E8
1 CROSS RD
2 CONNAUGHT RD

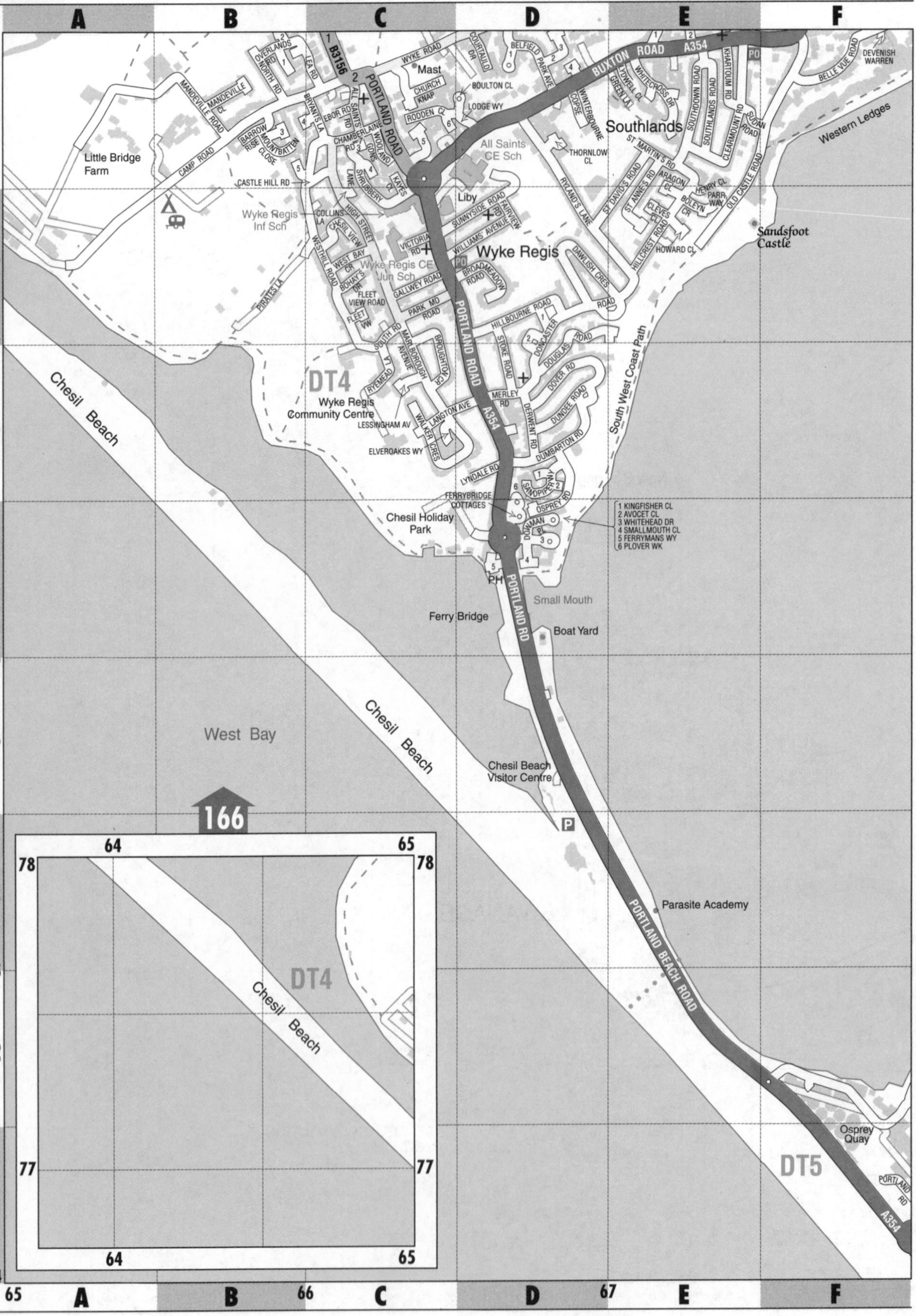

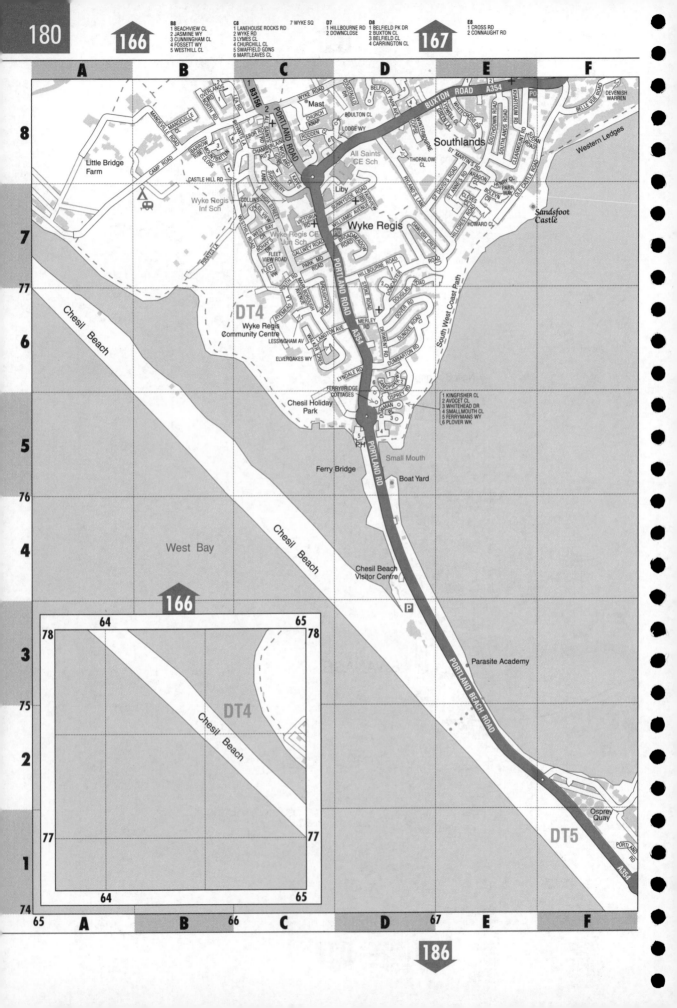

1 KINGFISHER CL
2 AVOCET CL
3 WHITEHEAD DR
4 SMALLMOUTH CL
5 FERRYMANS WY
6 PLOVER WK

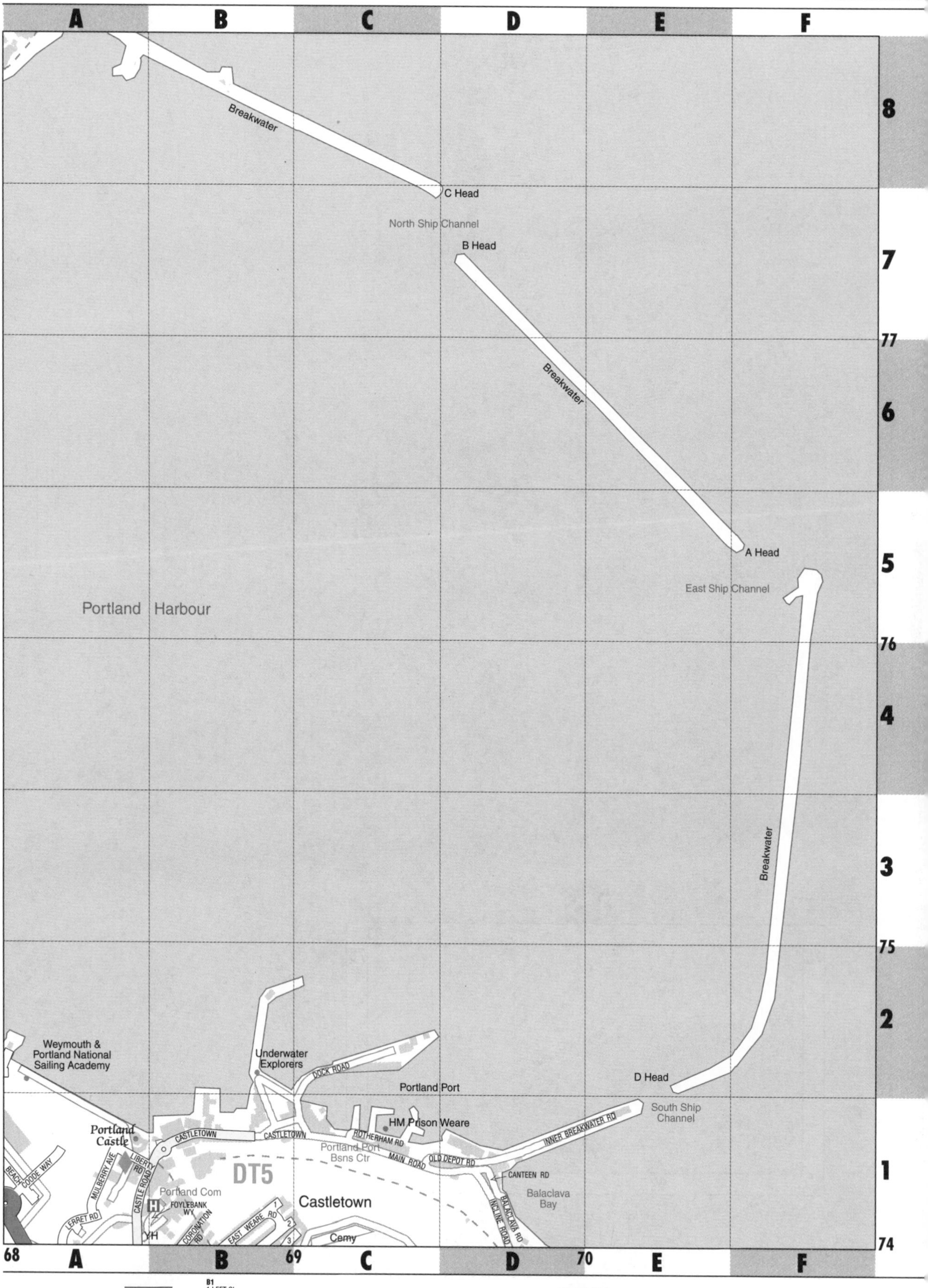

A B C D E F

8

C Head

North Ship Channel

B Head

7

77

Breakwater

6

A Head

5

East Ship Channel

76

Portland Harbour

4

Breakwater

3

75

2

Weymouth &
Portland National
Sailing Academy

Underwater
Explorers

DOCK ROAD

Portland Port

D Head

South Ship
Channel

HM Prison Weare

ROTHERHAM RD

Portland Port
Bsns Ctr

INNER BREAKWATER RD

Portland
Castle

CASTLETOWN

CASTLETOWN

MAIN ROAD

OLD DEPOT RD

MULBERRY AVE

LIBERTY RD

DT5

CANTEEN RD

1

Portland Com

BEACH LODGE WAY

CASTLE ROAD

FOYLEBANK
WY

Castletown

EAST WEARE RD

Balaclava
Bay

FERRET RD

CORONATION RD

Cemy

INCLINE ROAD

BALACLAVA RD

H

YH

74

68   A   B   69   C   D   70   E   F

B1
1 LEET CL
2 BEEL CL
3 AMELIA CL

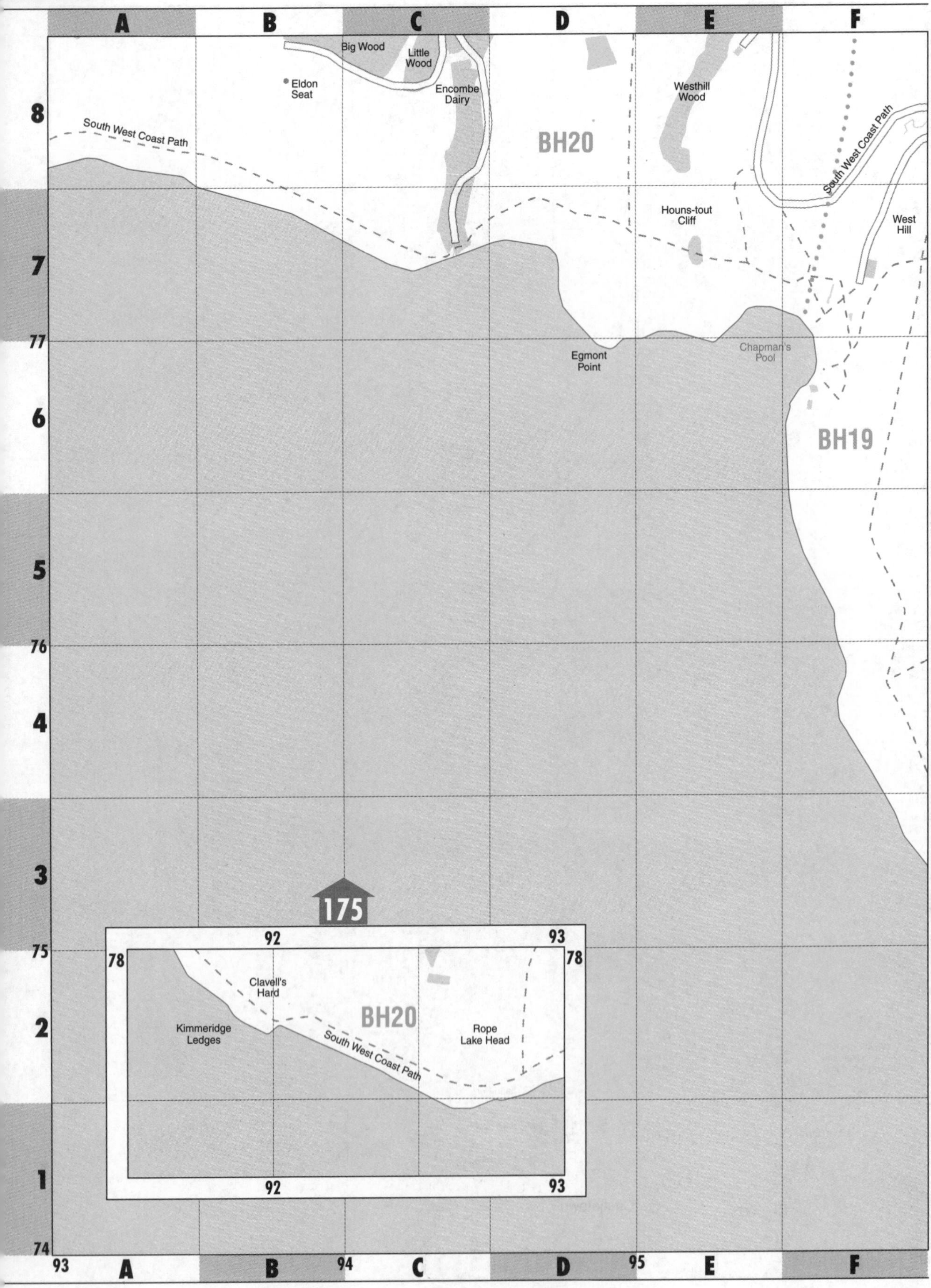

A   B   C   D   E   F

Big Wood

Little
Wood

Eldon
Seat

Encombe
Dairy

Westhill
Wood

BH20

South West Coast Path

8

Houns-tout
Cliff

West
Hill

7

Egmont
Point

Chapman's
Pool

77

6

BH19

5

76

4

3

175

92   93

75   78   78

Clavell's
Hard

Kimmeridge
Ledges

BH20

Rope
Lake Head

2

South West Coast Path

1

92   93

74

93   A   B   94   C   D   95   E   F

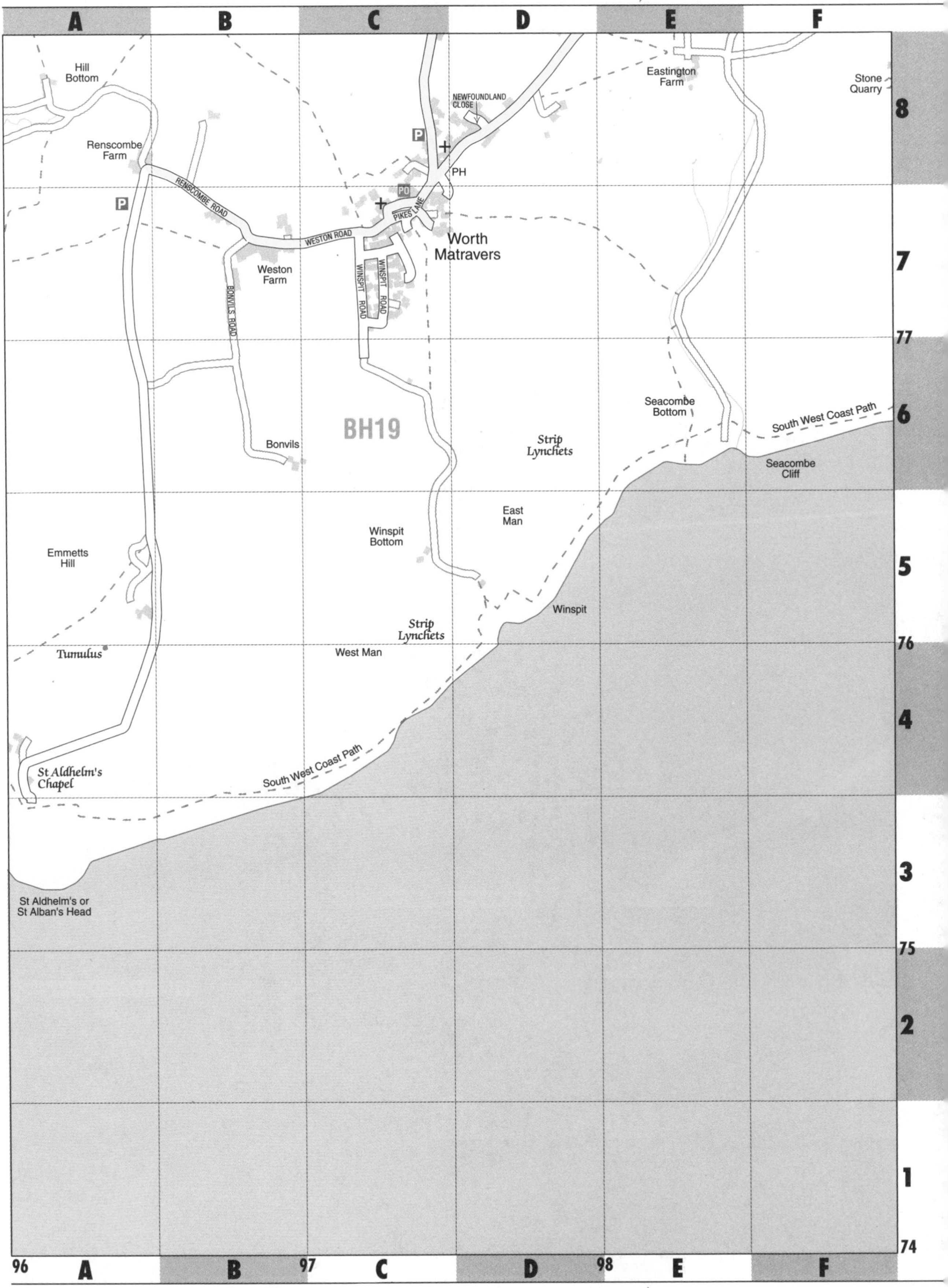

A   B   C   D   E   F

8

Hill Bottom

Stone Quarry

NEWFOUNDLAND CLOSE

Eastington Farm

Renscombe Farm

P

P

PH

PO

PIKES LANE

RENSCOMBE ROAD

WESTON ROAD

7

Worth Matravers

Weston Farm

WINSPIT ROAD

BONVILS ROAD

77

BH19

Bonvils

Seacombe Bottom

South West Coast Path

6

Strip Lynchets

Seacombe Cliff

East Man

Emmetts Hill

Winspit Bottom

5

Winspit

Strip Lynchets

76

Tumulus

West Man

4

South West Coast Path

St Aldhelm's Chapel

3

St Aldhelm's or St Alban's Head

75

2

1

74

183
178

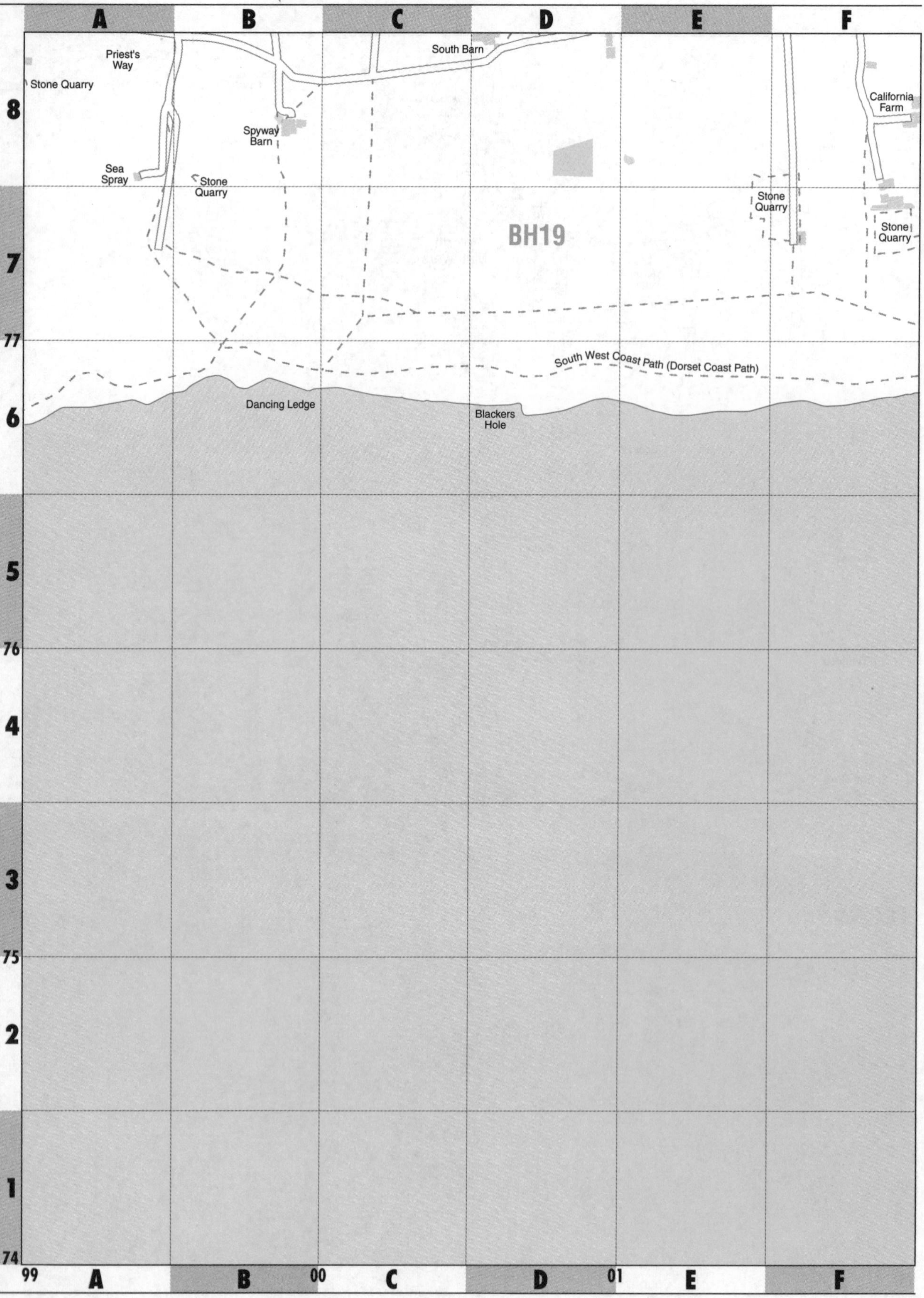

A   B   C   D   E   F

8

Stone Quarry

Priest's Way

South Barn

California Farm

Spyway Barn

Sea Spray

Stone Quarry

BH19

Stone Quarry

Stone Quarry

7

77

South West Coast Path (Dorset Coast Path)

6

Dancing Ledge

Blackers Hole

5

76

4

3

75

2

1

74

99   A   B   00   C   D   01   E   F

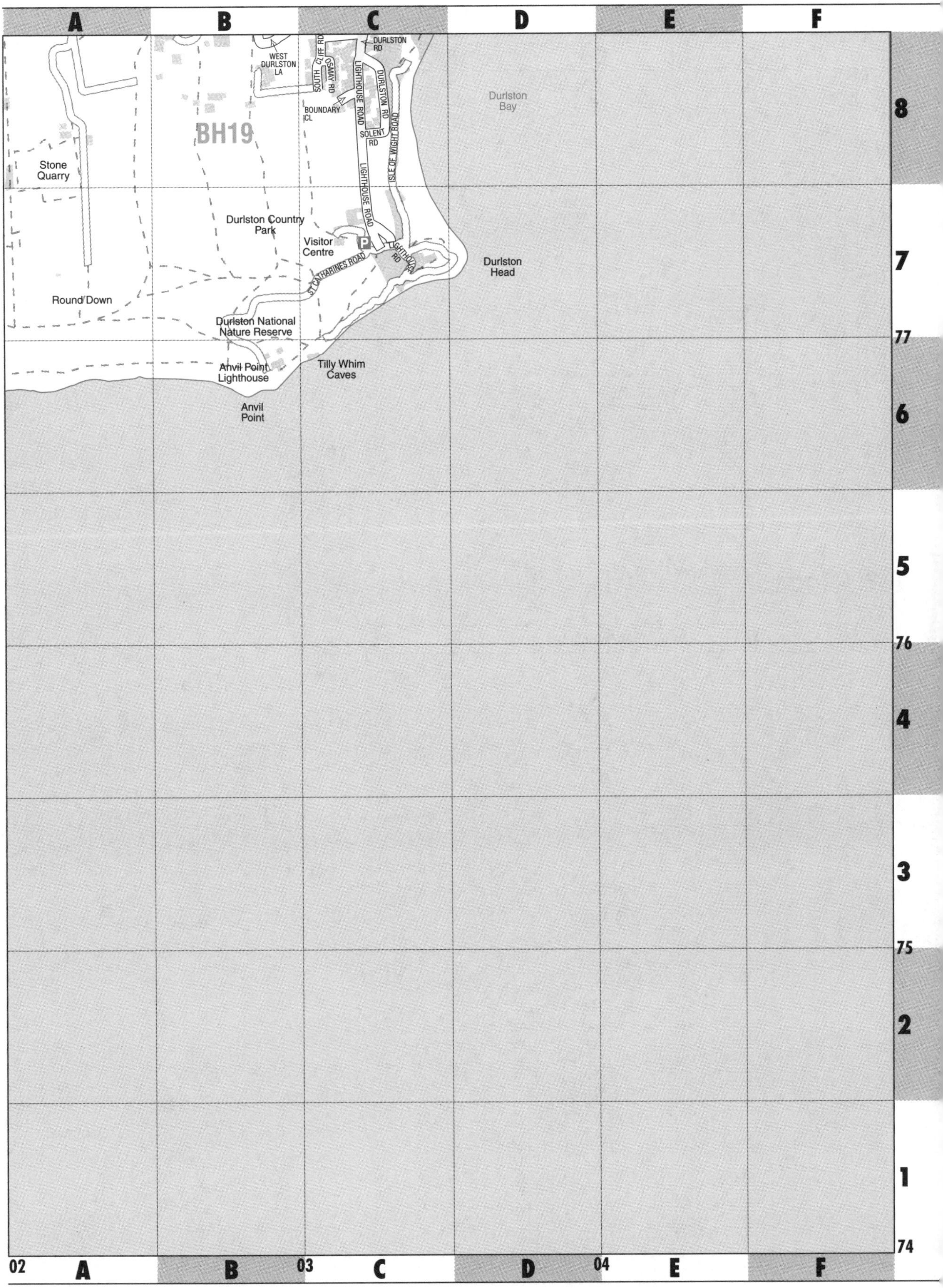
A
B
C
D
E
F
WEST DURLSTON LA
SOUTH CLIFF RD
OSMAY RD
DURLSTON RD
LIGHTHOUSE ROAD
DURLSTON RD
BOUNDARY CL
SOLENT RD
ISLE OF WIGHT ROAD
Durlston Bay
BH19
Stone Quarry
Durlston Country Park
Visitor Centre
LIGHTHOUSE RD
ST CATHARINES ROAD
Durlston Head
Round Down
Durlston National Nature Reserve
Anvil Point Lighthouse
Tilly Whim Caves
Anvil Point
8
7
77
6
5
76
4
3
75
2
1
74
02
03
04

A   B   C   D   E   F

8   12   7   11   73   69   6   10   5   9   72   4   3   71   2   1   70

70   68   E   F   69   70

D   68   E   F   69

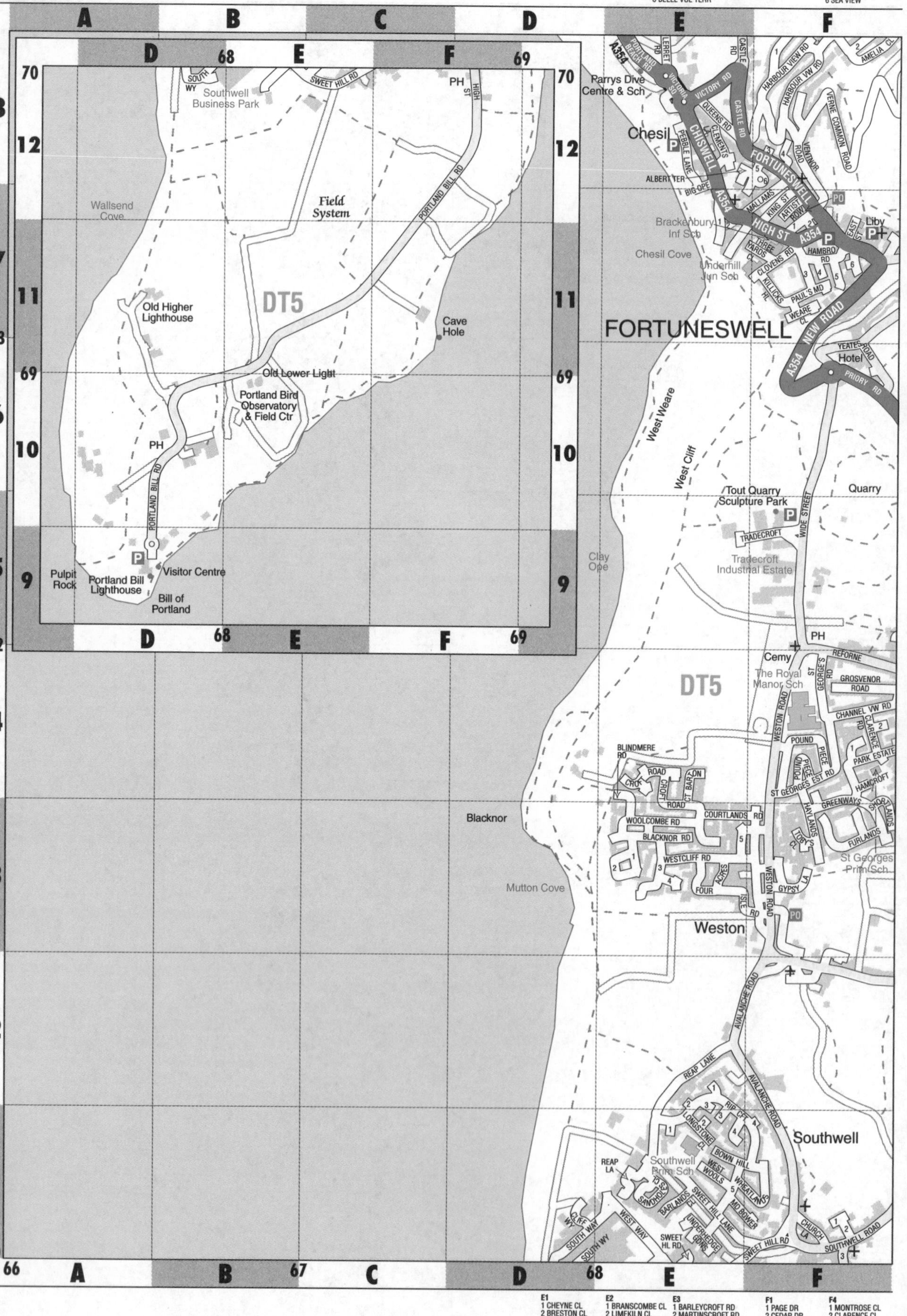

Southwell Business Park
SOUTH WY
SWEET HILL RD
PH
HIGH ST

Wallsend Cove
Field System

DT5

Old Higher Lighthouse

Cave Hole

Old Lower Light

Portland Bird Observatory & Field Ctr

PH

PORTLAND BILL RD

Pulpit Rock
Portland Bill Lighthouse
Visitor Centre
P
Bill of Portland

Clay Ope

Chesil
Parrys Dive Centre & Sch
A354
LERRET
VICTORY RD
QUEENS RD
CASTLE RD
BEACH RD
HARBOUR VIEW RD
HARBOUR VW RD
VERNE COMMON ROAD
AMELIA CL
CLEMENTS LA
CHISWELL
FORTUNESWELL
ALBERT TERR
BIG OPE
A354
MALLAMS
KING ST
ARTISTS ROW
EAST ST
PO
Libry

Brackenbury Inf Sch
HIGH ST
A354
THREE YARDS
CLOVENS RD
HAMBRO RD

Chesil Cove
Underhill Jun Sch
KILLICKS
PAUL'S RD
WEARE RD
NEW ROAD

FORTUNESWELL

YEATES ROAD
Hotel
PRIORY RD
A354

West Weare

West Cliff

Tout Quarry Sculpture Park
P
WIDE STREET
Quarry

TRADECROFT
Tradecroft Industrial Estate

PH
Cemy
REFORNE
The Royal Manor Sch
GEORGE'S RD
GROSVENOR ROAD

DT5

WESTON ROAD
CHANNEL VW RD
CLARENCE RD
PARK ESTATE
POUND PIECE
ST GEORGES EST RD
HAMCROFT
GREENWAYS
FURLANDS

BLINDMERE RD
CROFT
BARTON ROAD
ROAD
HAYLANDS

Blacknor

WOOLCOMBE RD
BLACKNOR RD

COURTLANDS
St Georges Prim Sch

Mutton Cove

WESTCLIFF RD
FOUR ACRES
WESTON ROAD
ISLE RD
GYPSY LA

PO
Weston

REAP LANE
AVALANCHE ROAD

LONGSTONE
RIP CROFT
BOWN HILL
Southwell Prim Sch
WEST WOOLS
WHEATLANDS

Southwell

REAP LA
SANDHOLES
WEST WAY
BARLANDS
SWEET HILL LANE
MD BOWER
UNDERCROFT
CHURCH
SOUTH WY
SWEET HL RD.
SWEET HILL RD
SOUTHWELL ROAD

66   A   B   67   C   D   68   E   F

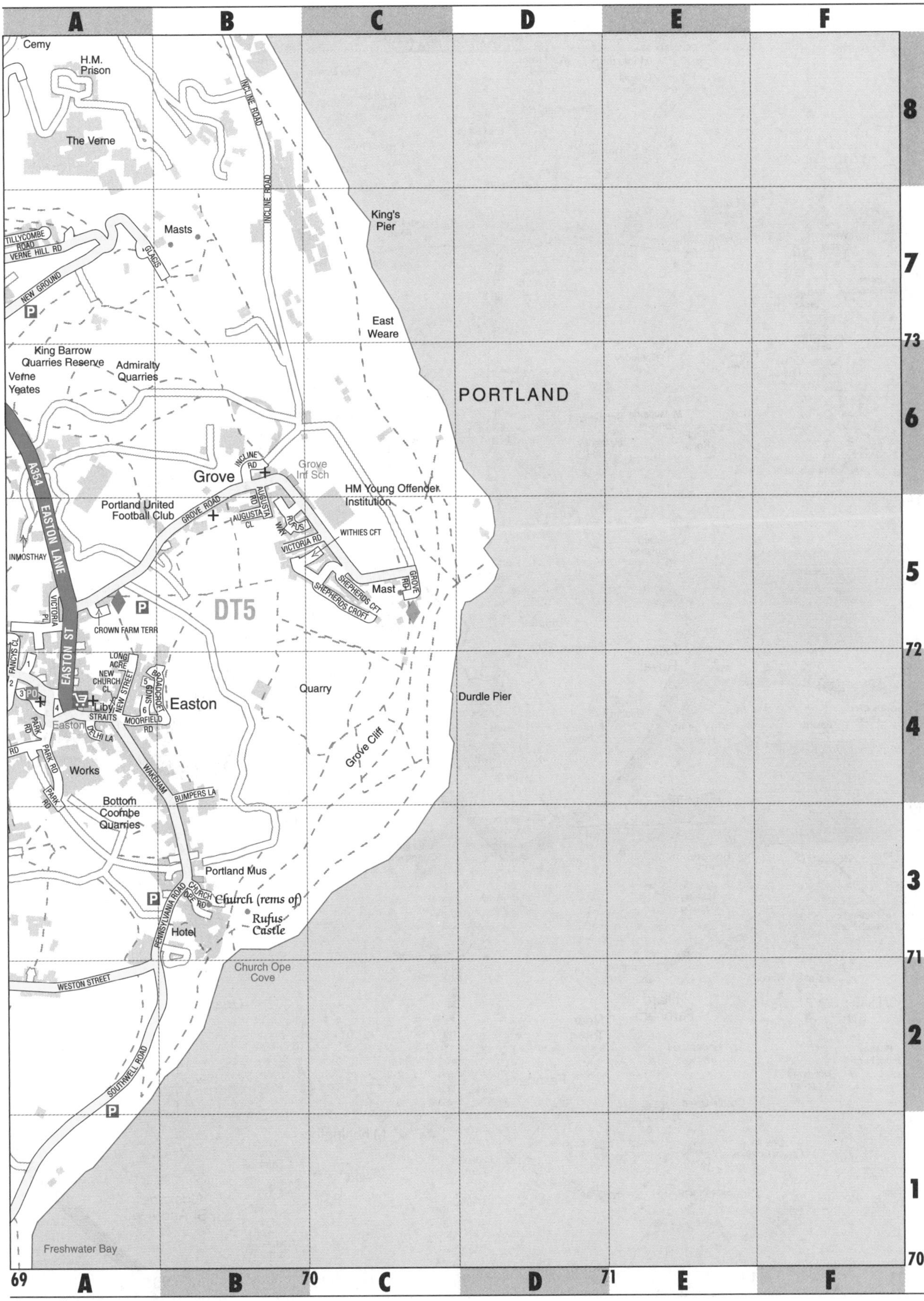

A4
1 REFORNE CL
2 STATION RD
3 LADYMD CL
4 EASTON SQ
5 SILKLAKE MEWS
6 LOVELLS CFT

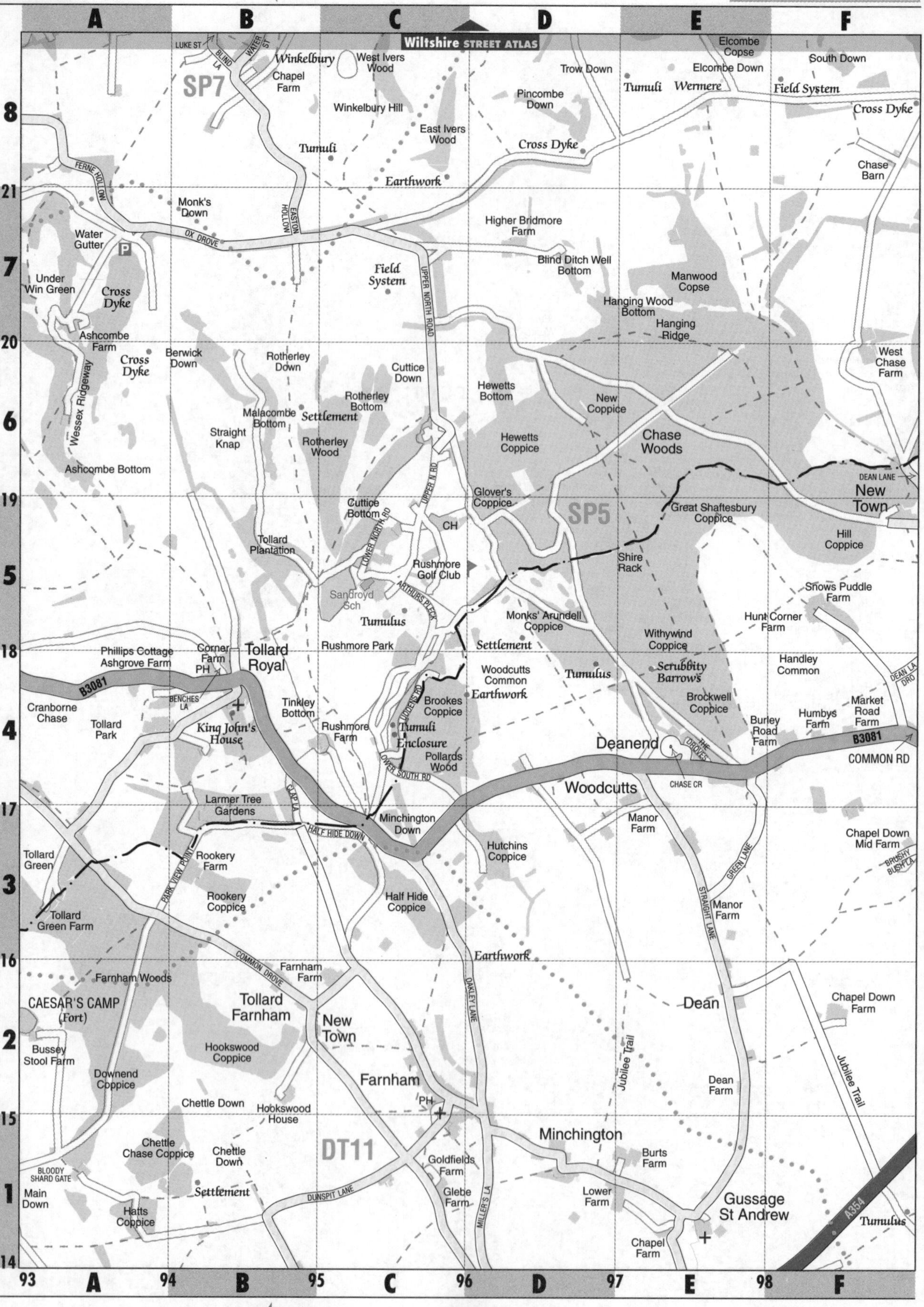

Scale: 1¾ inches to 1 mile

0   ¼   ½ mile
0 250m 500m 750m 1 km

Wiltshire STREET ATLAS

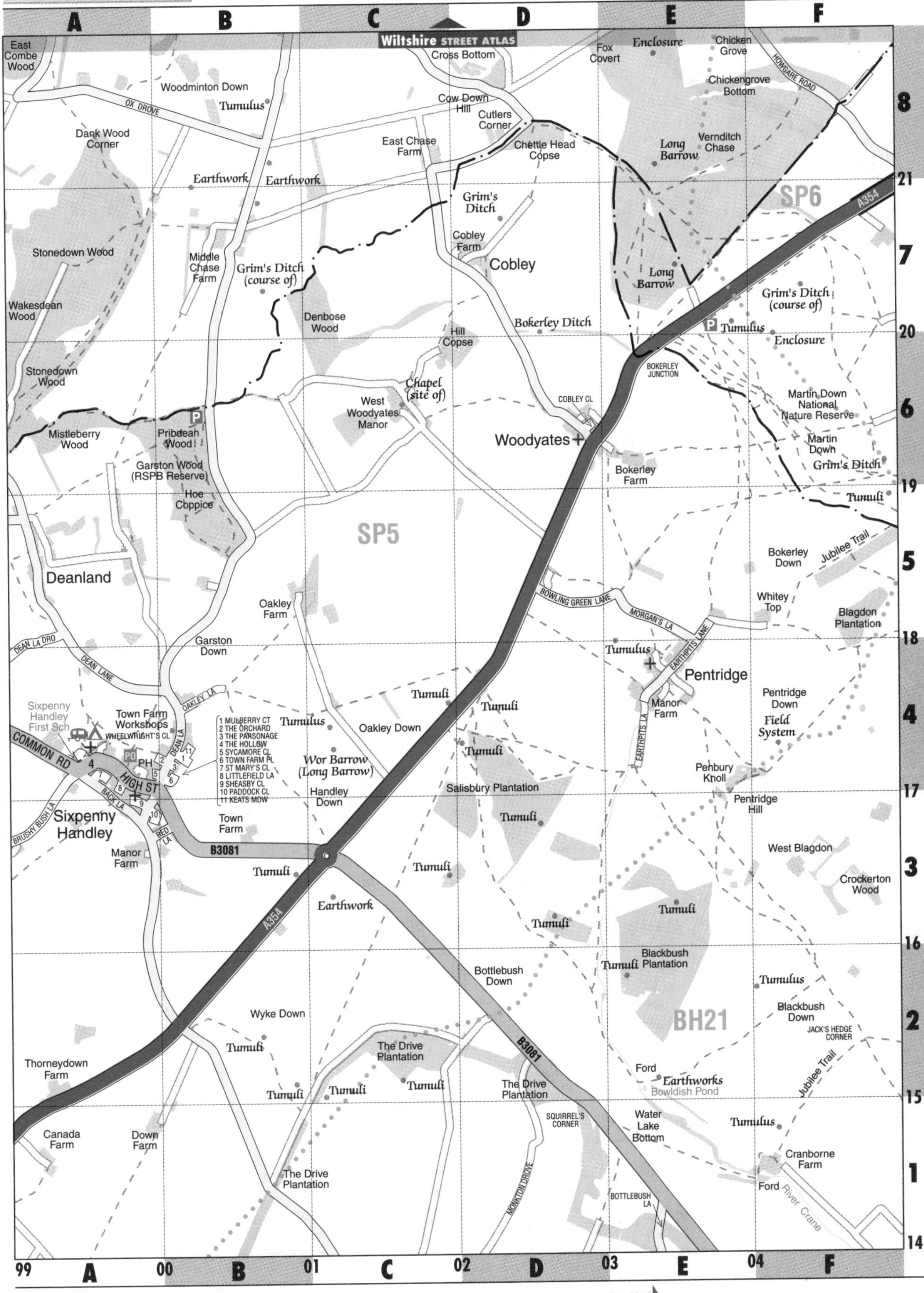

Scale: 1¾ inches to 1 mile

0   ¼   ½ mile
0 250m 500m 750m 1 km

Wiltshire STREET ATLAS

Row A:
East Combe Wood
Woodminton Down
Tumulus
OX DROVE
Dank Wood Corner
Earthwork   Earthwork
Stonedown Wood
Middle Chase Farm
Grim's Ditch (course of)
Denbose Wood
Wakesdean Wood
Stonedown Wood
Mistleberry Wood
Pribdean Wood
Garston Wood (RSPB Reserve)
Hoe Coppice
Deanland
DEAN LA DRO
DEAN LANE
Garston Down
Oakley Farm
Town Farm Workshops
WHEELWRIGHT'S CL
Sixpenny Handley First Sch
COMMON RD
PH
PO
HIGH ST
BACK LA
BRUSHY BUSH LA
Sixpenny Handley
Manor Farm
B3081
Town Farm
Thorneydown Farm
Canada Farm
Down Farm
The Drive Plantation

Centre:
Cross Bottom
Cow Down Hill
Cutlers Corner
East Chase Farm
Grim's Ditch
Cobley Farm
Cobley
Hill Copse
Bokerley Ditch
Chapel (site of)
West Woodyates Manor
SP5
1 MULBERRY CT
2 THE ORCHARD
3 THE PARSONAGE
4 THE HOLLOW
5 SYCAMORE CL
6 TOWN FARM PL
7 ST MARY'S CL
8 LITTLEFIELD LA
9 SHEASBY CL
10 PADDOCK CL
11 KEATS MDW
Oakley Down
Wor Barrow (Long Barrow)
Handley Down
Tumulus
Tumuli
Tumuli
Earthwork
Tumuli
Bottlebush Down
Wyke Down
Tumuli
The Drive Plantation
Tumuli
Tumuli
MONKTON DROVE
The Drive Plantation
Squirrel's Corner

Right:
Fox Covert
Enclosure
Chicken Grove
Chickengrove Bottom
HONEGARE ROAD
Chettle Head Copse
Long Barrow
Verndtich Chase
SP6
A354
Grim's Ditch (course of)
Long Barrow
Tumulus
Enclosure
Bokerley Junction
Martin Down National Nature Reserve
Cobley Cl
Woodyates
Martin Down
Grim's Ditch
Bokerley Farm
Tumuli
Bokerley Down
Jubilee Trail
Whitey Top
Blagdon Plantation
BOWLING GREEN LANE
MORGAN'S LA
EARTHPITS LANE
Tumulus
Pentridge
Pentridge Down
Field System
Manor Farm
Penbury Knoll
Pentridge Hill
West Blagdon
Crockerton Wood
Salisbury Plantation
Tumuli
Tumuli
Blackbush Plantation
Tumuli
BH21
Blackbush Down
Tumulus
Jack's Hedge Corner
Ford
Earthworks
Bowldish Pond
Water Lake Bottom
Tumulus
Cranborne Farm
Ford
BOTTLEBUSH LA
River Crane
Jubilee Trail

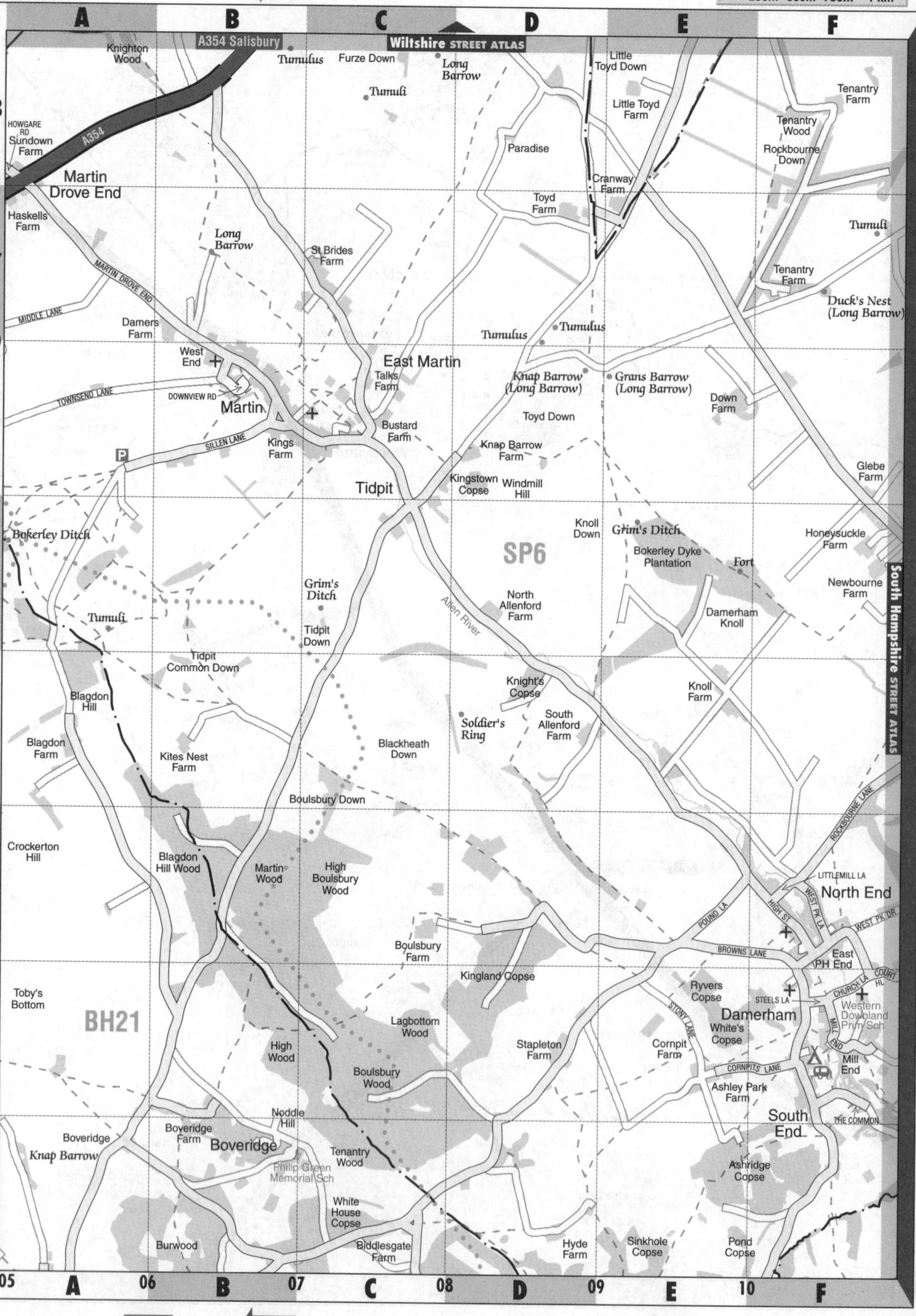

Scale: 1¾ inches to 1 mile
0   ¼   ½ mile
0 250m 500m 750m 1 km

Wiltshire STREET ATLAS

A   B   C   D   E   F

South Hampshire STREET ATLAS

Knighton Wood

A354 Salisbury

Furze Down
Tumulus
Tumuli
Long Barrow
Little Toyd Down
Little Toyd Farm
Tenantry Farm

HOWGARE RD
Sundown Farm
Paradise
Tenantry Wood
Rockbourne Down

A354

Martin Drove End
Toyd Farm
Cranway Farm

Haskells Farm
Tenantry Farm
Tumuli

MARTIN DROVE END
Long Barrow
St Brides Farm
Duck's Nest (Long Barrow)

MIDDLE LANE
Damers Farm
Tumulus
Tumulus

West End
East Martin
Knap Barrow (Long Barrow)
Grans Barrow (Long Barrow)
Down Farm

TOWNSEND LANE
DOWNVIEW RD
Martin
Talks Farm
Toyd Down

Kings Farm
Bustard Farm
Knap Barrow Farm
Glebe Farm

P
SILLEN LANE
Tidpit
Kingstown Copse
Windmill Hill

Bokerley Ditch
Knoll Down
Grim's Ditch
Honeysuckle Farm

SP6
Bokerley Dyke Plantation
Fort
Newbourn Farm

Grim's Ditch
North Allenford Farm
Damerham Knoll

Tumuli
Tidpit Down
Allen River
Knoll Farm

Tidpit Common Down
Knight's Copse
Blagdon Hill
South Allenford Farm

Blagdon Farm
Kites Nest Farm
Blackheath Down
Soldier's Ring

Boulsbury Down
Crockerton Hill
LITTLEMILL LA
North End

Blagdon Hill Wood
Martin Wood
High Boulsbury Wood
ROCKBOURNE LANE

POUND LA
HIGH ST
WEST PK LA
WEST PK DR

BH21
Toby's Bottom
Boulsbury Farm
Kingland Copse
BROWNS LANE
East End
COURT HL
CHURCH LA

Ryvers Copse
STEELS LA
Western Downland Prim Sch

High Wood
Lagbottom Wood
Damerham
White's Copse
MILL END

Boulsbury Wood
Stapleton Farm
Cornpit Farm
CORNPITS LANE
Mill End

Noddle Hill
Ashley Park Farm
South End
THE COMMON

Boveridge Farm
Boveridge
Tenantry Wood
Ashridge Copse

Knap Barrow
Philip Green Memorial Sch
White House Copse

Burwood
Biddlesgate Farm
Hyde Farm
Sinkhole Copse
Pond Copse

8 21 7 20 6 19 5 18 4 17 3 16 2 15 1 14

05 A 06 B 07 C 08 D 09 E 10 F

Scale: 1¾ inches to 1 mile
0 ¼ ½ mile
0 250m 500m 750m 1 km

F5
1 ASHLANDS CL
2 BINCOMBE DR
3 WHITEHALL CT
4 BRICKYARD LA
5 BEECHWOOD DR
6 WINDMILL RISE
7 THE LAURELS
8 BRAMLEY CL
9 CHERRY TREE CT
10 ASPEN WY
11 HAZEL VW
12 MAPLE DR
13 LABURNUM CRES
14 SYCAMORE DR
15 HAWTHORNE CL
16 FOX MDWS
17 OLD MILL LA
18 GIBBS CT
19 BERE CT
20 OAK DR
21 CHESNUT AVE
22 BIRCH WY
23 WILLOW WY
24 JASMINE CL

192

F7
1 SHERLANDS
2 THE PIECE
3 HITCHEN
4 OLD HITCHEN
5 FARR'S ORCHARD
6 GLEBELANDS
7 GREYS RD
8 THE CLOSE
9 MANOR DR
10 SPEKE CL
11 GOUGH CL
12 SHERLANDS GDNS

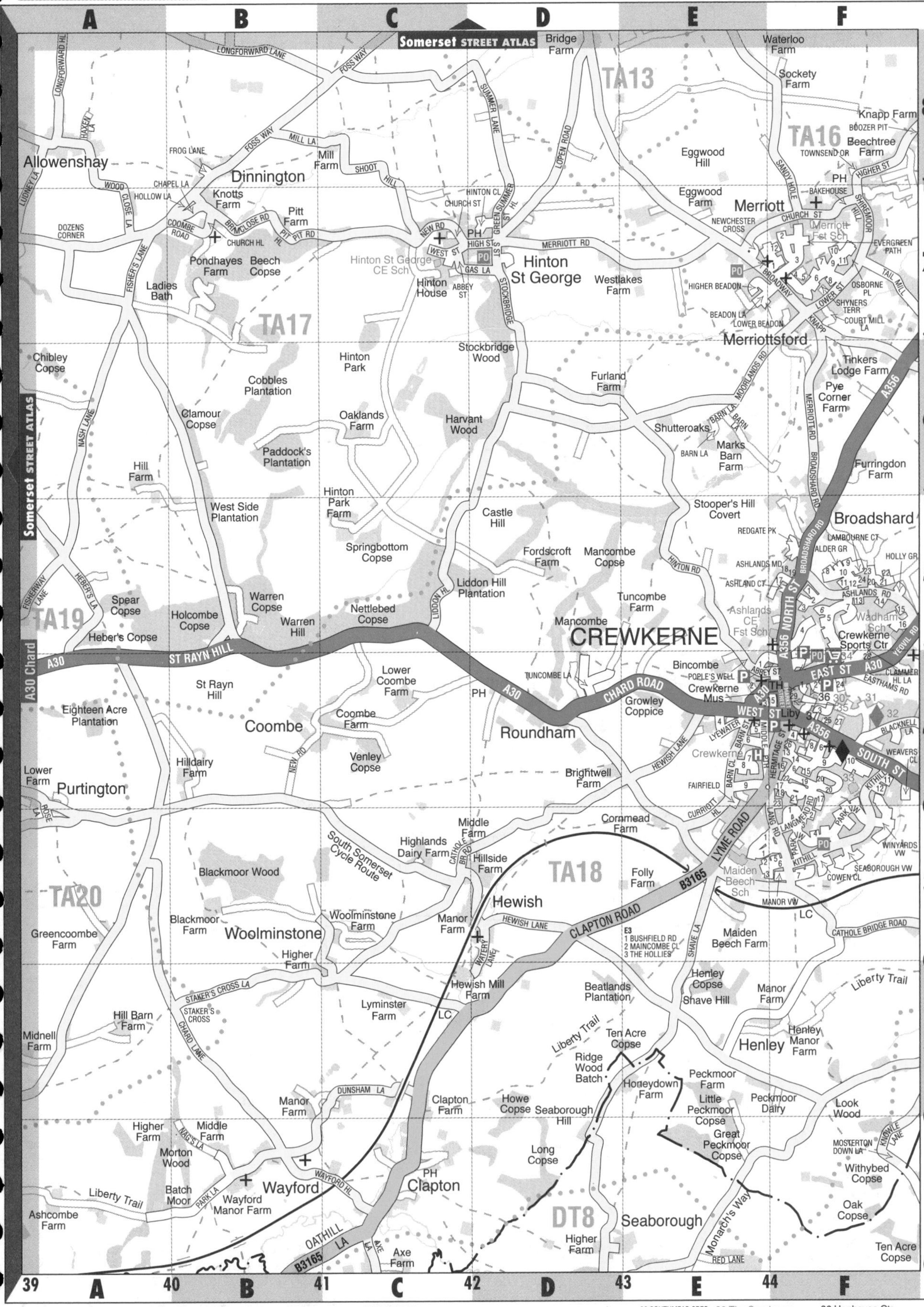

F3
1 LANGMEAD SQ
2 VALLEY RD
3 LANGMEAD PL
4 VALE CL
5 BUCKHILL CL
6 KINGSWOOD RD
7 HENLEY VW

E4
1 ROSE LA
2 CHURCH PATH
3 COURT BARTON
4 BULLS LA
5 BIRD'S CL
6 TOWER HILL RD
7 BARN CRES
8 BARN CL
9 CURRIOTT HILL RD

F4
1 ROSE LA
2 ORCHARD LA
3 HENHAYES LA
4 PULMANS LA
5 OXEN RD
6 FURLAND RD
7 ORCHARD RISE
8 BOWHAYES
9 RHYDDERCH WY
10 THOMSON DR
11 SHUTE LAKE LA
12 CHARLTON CL
13 FOUNDRY SQ
14 IVELWAY
15 FLAXFIELD DR
16 MULBERRY GDNS
17 SEVERALLS PARK AVE
18 CHOWINS RD
19 MEMORIAL AVE

203

192

20 SOUTHMEAD CRES
21 HARPER RD
22 BLAKE RD
23 HARDY CT
24 WYVERN CT
25 BOWDITCH ROW
26 FOUNDRY SQ
27 THE LINEN YARD
28 MOUNT PLEASANT
29 GEORGE LA
30 The Crewkerne Business Park
31 Cropmead Trad Est
32 Blacknell Ind Est
33 St Bartholomew's CE Fst Sch
34 The George Sh Ctr
35 Falkland Square
36 Henhayes Ctr
37 Crewkerne Aqua Ctr

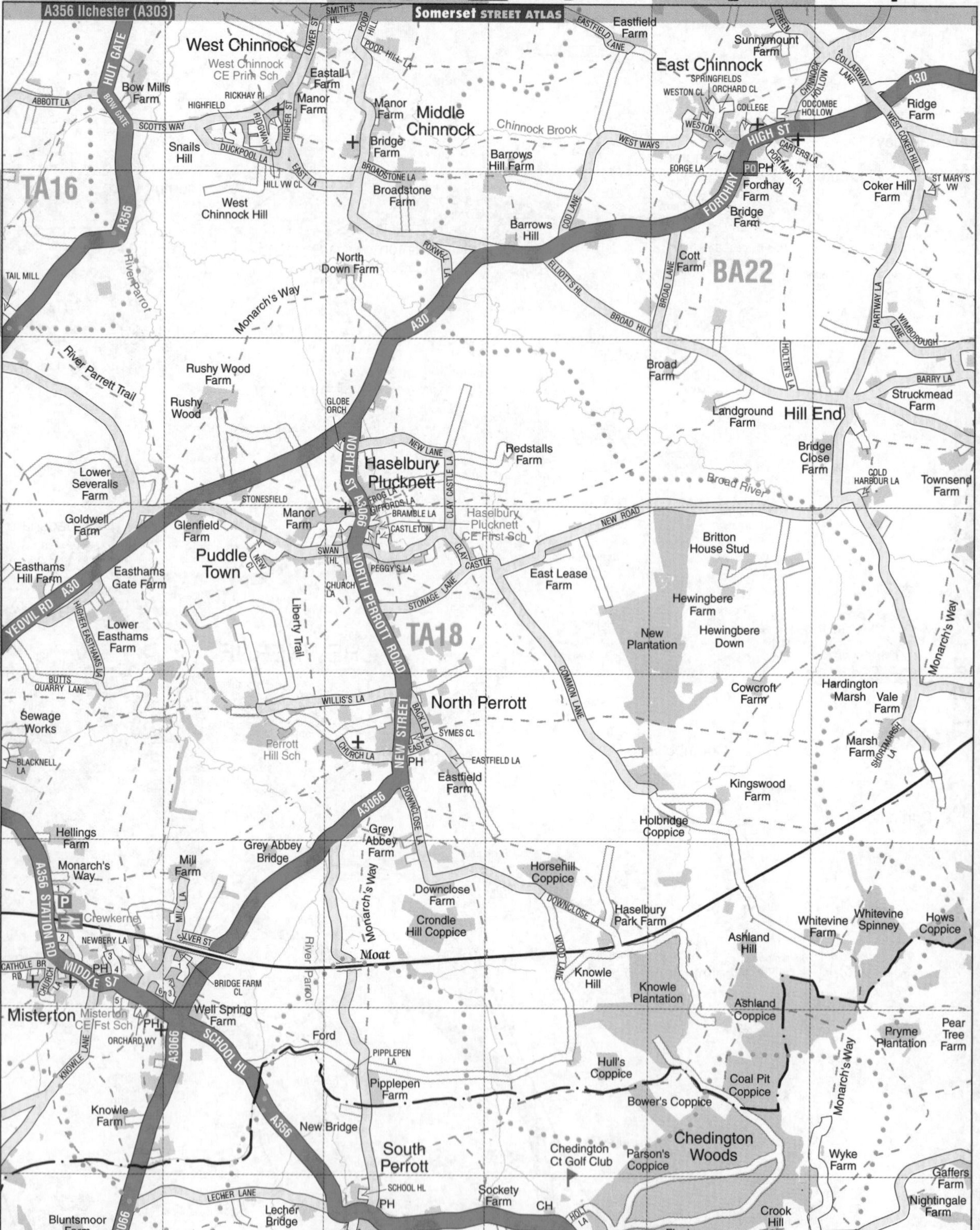

Scale: 1¾ inches to 1 mile

0   ¼   ½ mile
0   250m 500m 750m 1 km

Somerset STREET ATLAS

A356 Ilchester (A303)

A | **B** | **C** | **D** | **E** | **F**

West Chinnock
West Chinnock CE Prim Sch
Eastall Farm
Manor Farm

SMITH'S HL
POOP-HILL LA
LOWER ST
HIGHER ST
RICKHAY RI
HIGHFIELD
RIGWAY LA
DUCKPOOL LA
EAST LA
HILL VW CL

Eastfield Farm
Eastfield Lane
Sunnymount Farm
East Chinnock
SPRINGFIELDS
WESTON CL
ORCHARD CL
COLLEGE
CHINNOCK
COLLABWAY
ODCOMBE HOLLOW
HIGH ST
POP H
FORDHAY
CARTERS LA
DURHAM CT
GREEN
A30
Ridge Farm

8

Bow Mills Farm
HUT GATE
BOW GATE
SCOTTS WAY
ABBOTT LA
A356

TA16

13

Snails Hill
Bridge Farm
Middle Chinnock
Manor Farm
BROADSTONE LA
West Chinnock Hill
Broadstone Farm
Chinnock Brook
WEST WAYS
FORGE LA
COLD LANE
Barrows Hill Farm

WESTON ST
Fordhay Farm
Bridge Farm
Coker Hill Farm
St Mary's VW
WIMBOROUGH LANE
PARTWAY LA

BA22

7

TAIL MILL
River Parrott
North Down Farm
ROXWELL LA
A30
Barrows Hill
ELLIOTT'S HL
BROAD HILL
Cott Farm
BROAD LA
BARRY LA
Struckmead Farm

12

River Parrett Trail
Rushy Wood Farm
Rushy Wood
GLOBE ORCH
Broad Farm
Landground Farm
Hill End
HOLTEN'S LA
Bridge Close Farm
COLD HARBOUR LA
Townsend Farm

6

Lower Severalls Farm
Goldwell Farm
STONESFIELD
Glenfield Farm
Manor Farm
NORTH ST
A3066
Haselbury Plucknett
NEW LANE
FROG LA
GIFFORDS
BRAMBLE LA
CASTLETON
CLAY CASTLE LA
Redstalls Farm
Haselbury Plucknett CE First Sch
NEW ROAD
Broad River
Britton House Stud

11

Easthams Hill Farm
Easthams Gate Farm
A30
HIGHER EASTHAMS LA
Puddle Town
SWAN HL
LEVEN CT
PEGGY'S LA
CHURCH LA
NORTH PERROTT ROAD
STONAGE LANE
CLAY CASTLE
East Lease Farm
Hewingbere Farm
Hewingbere Down

5

Lower Easthams Farm
Liberty Trail
TA18
New Plantation
Cowcroft Farm
Hardington Marsh
Vale Farm
Marsh Farm
SHORTMARSH LA
Monarch's Way

10

BUTTS QUARRY LANE
Sewage Works
WILLIS'S LA
North Perrott
BACK LA
EAST ST
SYMES CL
EASTFIELD LA
Common Lane
Kingswood Farm

4

BLACKNELL LA
Perrott Hill Sch
CHURCH LA
PH
Eastfield Farm
A3066
NEW STREET
DOWNCLOSE LA
Holbridge Coppice

09

Hellings Farm
Monarch's Way
A356
Mill Farm
Grey Abbey Bridge
Grey Abbey Farm
Downclose Farm
Horsehill Coppice
DOWNCLOSE LA
Haselbury Park Farm
WOOD LANE
Ashland Hill
Whitevine Farm
Whitevine Spinney
Hows Coppice

3

STATION RD
P
Crewkerne
NEWBERY LA
SILVER ST
MILL LA
River Parrott
Monarch's Way
Moat
Crondle Hill Coppice
Knowle Hill
Knowle Plantation
Ashland Coppice

CATHOLE BR RD
MIDDLE ST
PH
HORN LA
Misterton CE Fst Sch
PH
ORCHARD WY
A3066
SCHOOL HL
BRIDGE FARM CL
Well Spring Farm
Ford
PIPPLEPEN LA
Pipplepen Farm
Hull's Coppice
Bower's Coppice
Coal Pit Coppice
Monarch's Way
Pryme Plantation
Pear Tree Farm

08

Misterton
KNOWLE LANE
Knowle Farm
New Bridge
South Perrott
Chedington Ct Golf Club
Parson's Coppice
Chedington Woods
Wyke Farm

2

Bluntsmoor Farm
LECHER LANE
Lecher Bridge
SCHOOL HL
PH
Sockety Farm
CH
Flaxley Coppice
Crook Hill
Gaffers Farm
Nightingale Farm

07

Mosterton Down
MOSTERTON DOWN LA
Chapel Court Farm
Mohun Castle
MANOR LA
PARRETT MD
Sockety
DT8
Manor Farm
Holts Farm
HOLT LA
A356
North Hill Plantation
Monarch's Way
Close Plantation
Redland Coppice
DT2

1

Orchard Farm
POCKET LA
WESTON LANE
Winyard's Gap
PH
Twelve Acre Coppice

06

45 | A | 46 | B | 47 | C | 48 | D | 49 | E | 50 | F

A3
1 BRADFORD ROAD
2 BROUGHTONS DRIVE
3 CLARK'S LANE
4 UNITY LANE
5 CLOSE DRIVE
6 THE AVENUE

B3
1 PACKERS' WAY
2 TURNPIKE CLOSE
3 TURNPIKE GREEN

Scale: 1¾ inches to 1 mile

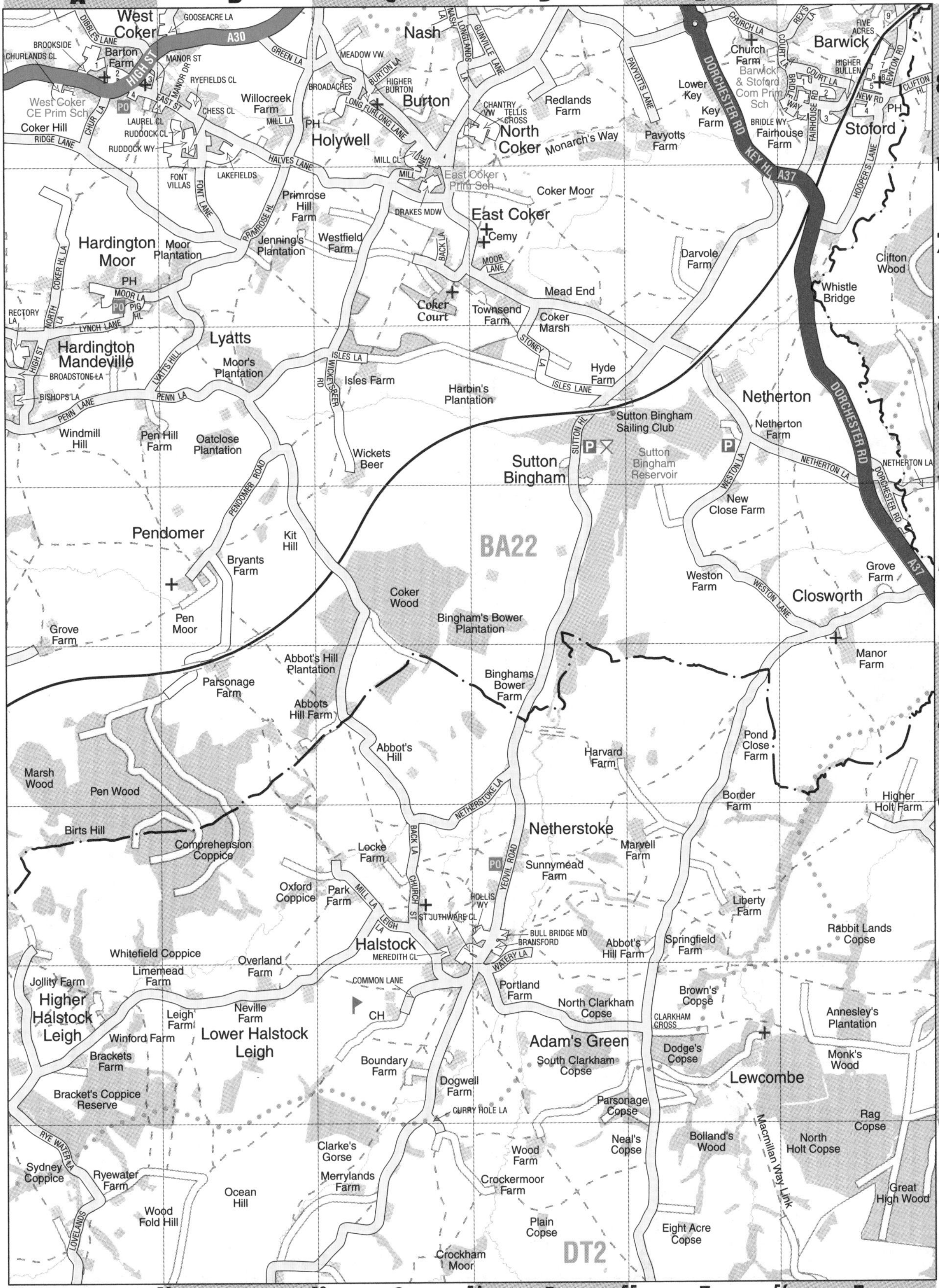
0 ¼ ½ mile
0 250m 500m 750m 1 km
26
A8
1 CEDAR FIELDS
2 CHURCH STREET
3 DENZIL CLOSE
4 ORCHARD CLOSE
F8
1 MOWLEAZE
2 WHITCROSS
3 CLIFTON VIEW
4 SILVER STREET
5 COURT LANE
6 ACRES COURT
7 MEADOW VIEW
8 HAMPTON CLOSE
9 HILLSIDE VIEW
27
194
West Coker
Barton Farm
West Coker CE Prim Sch
Coker Hill
Nash
Burton
Holywell
North Coker
Willocreek Farm
Redlands Farm
Pavyotts Farm
Lower Key
Key Farm
Church Farm
Barwick
Barwick & Stoford Com Prim Sch
Fairhouse Farm
Stoford
East Coker Prim Sch
Coker Moor
East Coker
Cemy
Primrose Hill Farm
Hardington Moor
Moor Plantation
Jenning's Plantation
Westfield Farm
Darvole Farm
Clifton Wood
Whistle Bridge
Mead End
Coker Court
Townsend Farm
Coker Marsh
Lyatts
Hardington Mandeville
Moor's Plantation
Isles Farm
Harbin's Plantation
Hyde Farm
Netherton
Netherton Farm
Windmill Hill
Pen Hill Farm
Oatclose Plantation
Wickets Beer
Sutton Bingham Sailing Club
Sutton Bingham
Sutton Bingham Reservoir
New Close Farm
Pendomer
Kit Hill
BA22
Bryants Farm
Weston Farm
Grove Farm
Closworth
Pen Moor
Coker Wood
Bingham's Bower Plantation
Manor Farm
Abbot's Hill Plantation
Parsonage Farm
Binghams Bower Farm
Abbots Hill Farm
Pond Close Farm
Abbot's Hill
Harvard Farm
Marsh Wood
Pen Wood
Border Farm
Higher Holt Farm
Birts Hill
Netherstoke
Comprehension Coppice
Locke Farm
Marvell Farm
Sunnymead Farm
Oxford Coppice
Park Farm
Liberty Farm
Rabbit Lands Copse
Halstock
Abbot's Hill Farm
Springfield Farm
Whitefield Coppice
Overland Farm
Limemead Farm
Jollity Farm
Portland Farm
North Clarkham Copse
Brown's Copse
Annesley's Plantation
Higher Halstock Leigh
Leigh Farm
Neville Farm
Lower Halstock Leigh
CH
Adam's Green
Dodge's Copse
Winford Farm
Brackets Farm
South Clarkham Copse
Monk's Wood
Lewcombe
Boundary Farm
Bracket's Coppice Reserve
Dogwell Farm
Parsonage Copse
Rag Copse
Clarke's Gorse
Neal's Copse
Bolland's Wood
North Holt Copse
Sydney Coppice
Ryewater Farm
Wood Farm
Merrylands Farm
Crockermoor Farm
Macmillan Way Link
Great High Wood
Ocean Hill
Wood Fold Hill
Plain Copse
Eight Acre Copse
DT2
Crockham Moor
A30
A37
DORCHESTER RD
KEY HL
Monarch's Way
A B C D E F
8 13 7 12 6 11 5 10 4 09 3 08 2 07 1 06
51 52 53 54 55 56

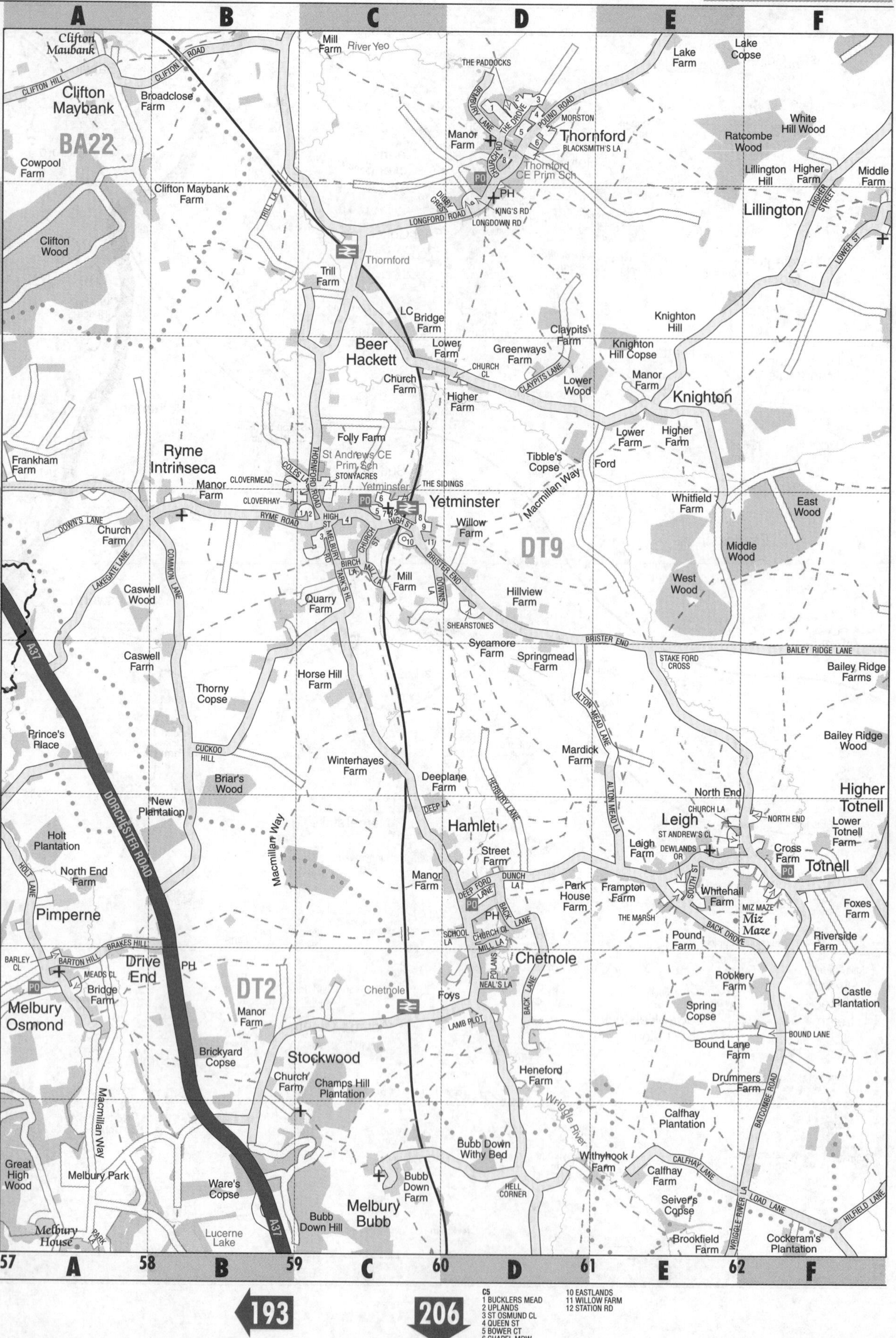

D8
1 GRANGE PARK
2 GIFLE VIEW
3 SARUM
4 EASTFIELD
5 THE WALDRONS
6 BLACKBIRDS
7 BOOT LA
8 GLEBE CL

Scale: 1¾ inches to 1 mile

0   ¼   ½   mile
0 250m 500m 750m 1 km

A B C D E F

8 Clifton
Maubank
Clifton
Maybank
Clifton Road
Broadclose
Farm
BA22

Mill Farm
River Yeo
THE PADDOCKS
Lake
Farm
Lake
Copse

Clifton Hill
Cowpool
Farm

13 Clifton Maybank
Farm
Trill La
Manor
Farm
Thornford
BLACKSMITH'S LA
Thornford
CE Prim Sch
MORSTON
Ratcombe
Wood
White
Hill Wood
Lillington
Hill
Higher
Farm
Middle
Farm

7 Clifton
Wood
Trill
Farm
Thornford
PO
PH
KING'S RD
LONGFORD ROAD
LONGDOWN RD
Lillington
Lower St

12 LC
Bridge
Farm
Beer
Hackett
Lower
Farm
CHURCH CL
Greenways
Farm
Claypits
Farm
Knighton
Hill Copse
Knighton
Hill

6 Frankham
Farm
Church
Farm
Folly Farm
St Andrews CE
Prim Sch
STONYACRES
Higher
Farm
CLAYPITS LANE
Lower
Wood
Manor
Farm
Knighton
Higher
Farm

11 Ryme
Intrinseca
Manor
Farm
CLOVERMEAD
THORNFORD ROAD
COLES LA
CLOVERHAY
Yetminster
THE SIDINGS
Tibble's
Copse
Lower
Farm
Higher
Farm
Ford
Macmillan Way
Whitfield
Farm
East
Wood

DOWN'S LANE
RYME ROAD
HIGH ST
PO
HIGH ST
Willow
Farm
DT9
Middle
Wood

5 Church
Farm
LAKEGATE LANE
COMMON LANE
MELBURY RD
BIRCH
TANK'S HILL
CHURCH LA
Mill
Farm
DOWNS
BRISTER END
Hillview
Farm
West
Wood

Caswell
Wood
Quarry
Farm
SHEARSTONES

10 Caswell
Farm
A37
Horse Hill
Farm
Sycamore
Farm
Springmead
Farm
BRISTER END
STAKE FORD
CROSS
BAILEY RIDGE LANE
Bailey Ridge
Farms

4 Prince's
Place
Thorny
Copse
CUCKOO
HILL
Winterhayes
Farm
Mardick
Farm
ALTON MEAD LANE
Bailey Ridge
Wood

09 New
Plantation
Briar's
Wood
Macmillan Way
DEEP LA
Deeplane
Farm
BERRYLI LANE
Hamlet
ALTON MEAD LA
North End
CHURCH LA
NORTH END
Higher
Totnell

3 Holt
Plantation
North End
Farm
DORCHESTER ROAD
Street
Farm
Manor
Farm
DUNCH
LA
Park
House
Farm
Frampton
Farm
Leigh
St Andrew's CL
DEWLANDS
OR
SOUTH ST
Cross
Farm
PO
Totnell
Lower
Totnell
Farm

Pimperne
HOLT LANE
DEEP FORD
LANE
PO
PH
BACK
LANE
THE MARSH
Whitehall
Farm
MIZ MAZE
Miz
Maze
Foxes
Farm

08 BARLEY
CL
BARTON HILL
BRAKES HILL
PH
SCHOOL LA
MILL LA
CHURCH CL
Chetnole
Pound
Farm
BACK DROVE
Rookery
Farm
Castle
Plantation

Melbury
Osmond
PO
MEADS CL
Bridge
Farm
Drive
End
NEAL'S LA
POLANS
Riverside
Farm

2 DT2
Manor
Farm
Chetnole
Foys
LAMB PILOT
Heneford
Farm
Spring
Copse
BOUND LANE
Bound Lane
Farm
Drummers
Farm

Brickyard
Copse
Church
Farm
Champs Hill
Plantation
Wriggle River
Calfhay
Plantation

07

1 Great
High
Wood
Melbury Park
Macmillan Way
Ware's
Copse
Bubb Down
Withy Bed
Withyhook
Farm
HELL
CORNER
Calfhay
Farm
CALFHAY LANE
Seiver's
Copse
BATCOMBE ROAD
LOAD LANE

Melbury
House
A37
Lucerne Lake
Bubb
Down Hill
Melbury
Bubb
Bubb
Down
Farm
WRIGGLE RIVER LA
HILFIELD LA
Cockeram's
Plantation

06 Brookfield
Farm

57 A 58 B 59 C 60 D 61 E 62 F

C5
1 BUCKLERS MEAD
2 UPLANDS
3 ST OSMUND CL
4 QUEEN ST
5 BOWER CT
6 CHAPEL MDW
7 CHAPEL LA
8 SUSSEX FARM WAY
9 BRIERLEY HAY
10 EASTLANDS
11 WILLOW FARM
12 STATION RD

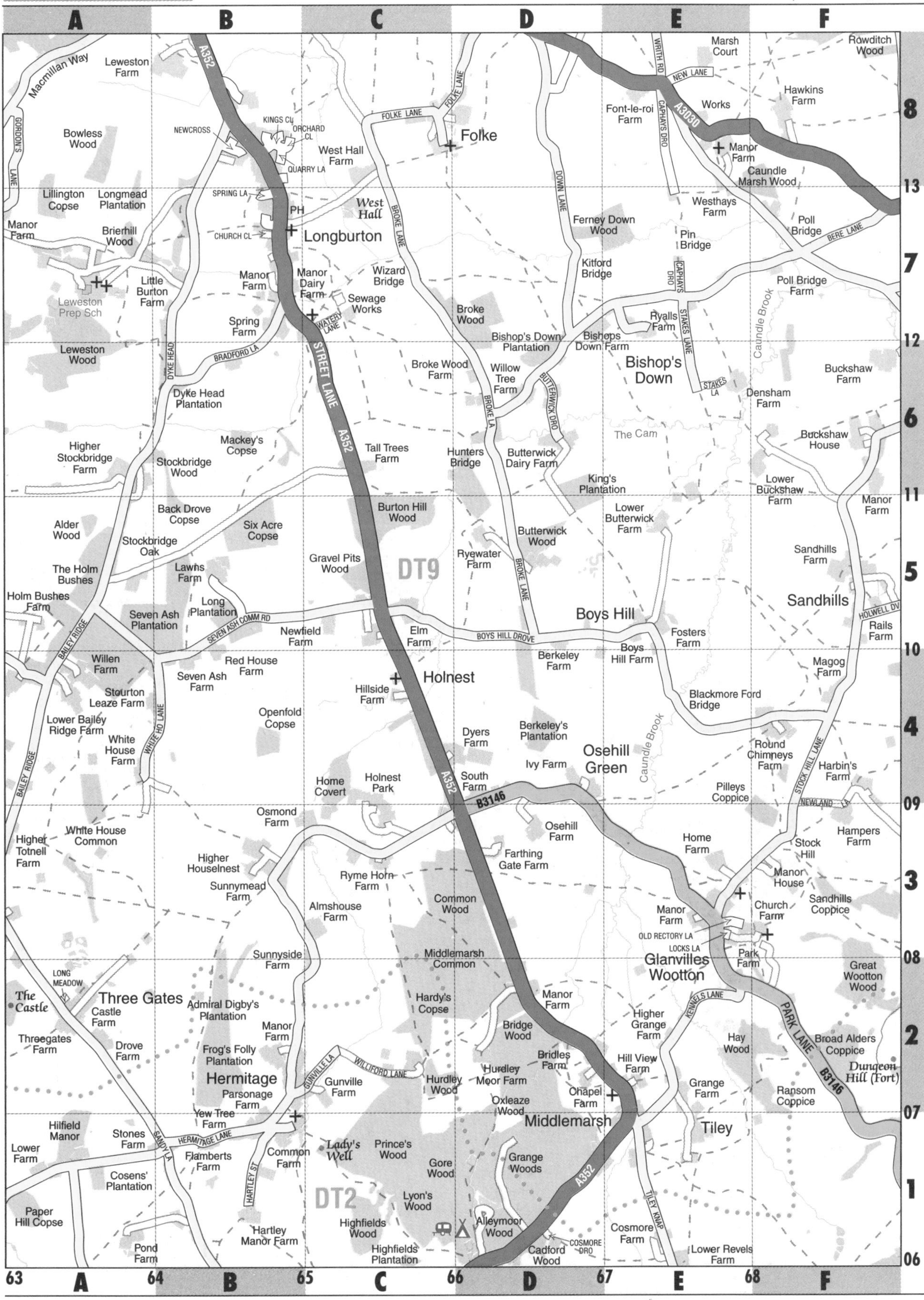

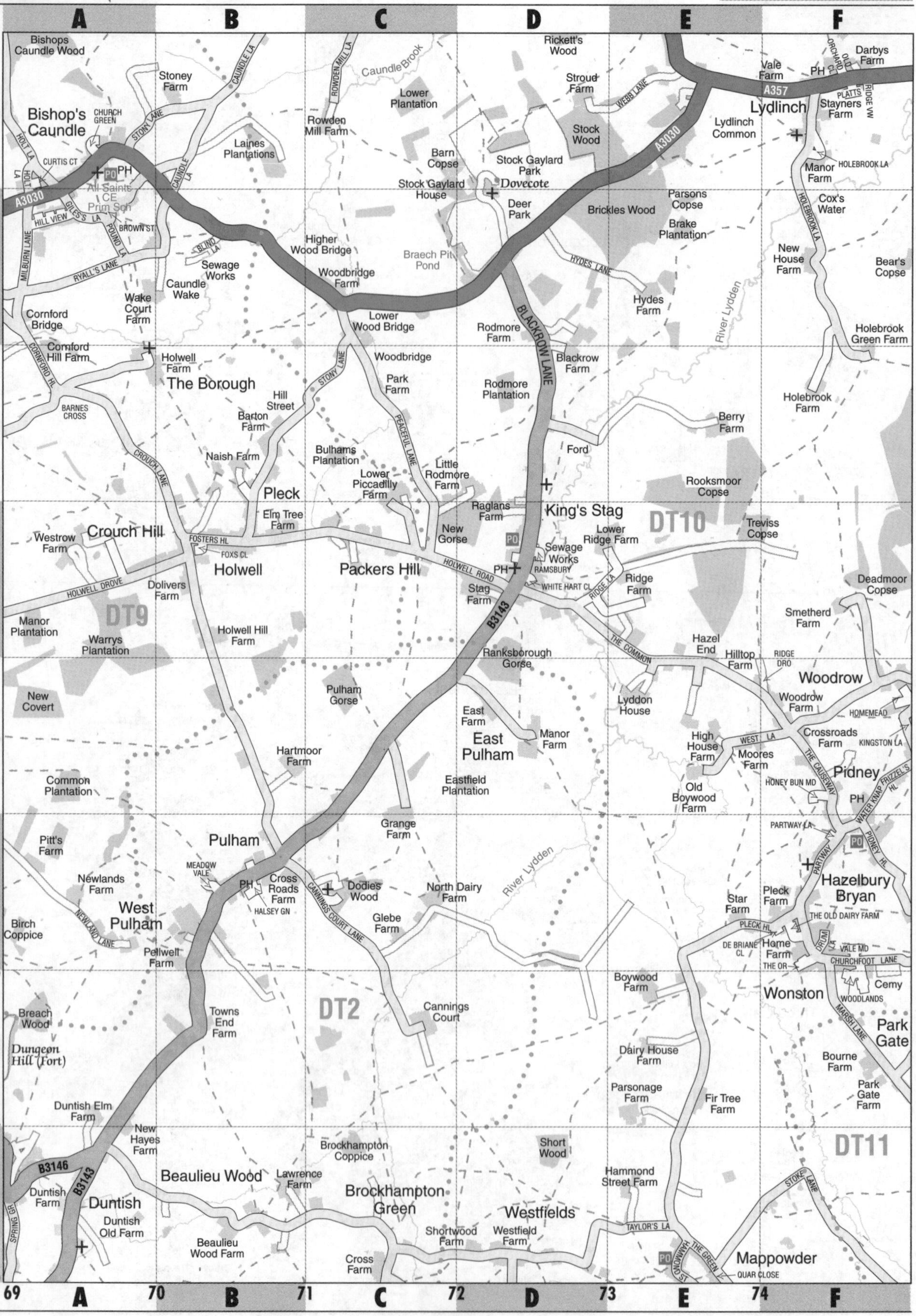

A   B   C   D   E   F

8

Bishops Caundle Wood
Bishop's Caundle
CHURCH GREEN
Stoney Farm
CAUNDLE LA
Rowden Mill Farm
ROWDEN MILL LA
Caundle Brook
Lower Plantation
Rickett's Wood
Stroud Farm
Vale Farm
ORCHARD
Darbys Farm
PH
Lydlinch
A357
Lydlinch Common
Lydlinch Common
Stayners Farm
RIDGE VW
PLATTS
WEBB LANE

13
CURTIS CT
PO PH
A3030
All Saints CE Prim Sch
BRIG'S LA
HILL VIEW
BROWN ST
POUND LA
BLIND LA
Laines Plantations
Rowden Mill Farm
Barn Copse
Stock Gaylard House
Stock Wood
Stock Gaylard Park
Dovecote
Deer Park
Brickles Wood
Parsons Copse
Brake Plantation
A3030
HOLEBROOK LA
Manor Farm
HOLEBROOK LA
Cox's Water
Bear's Copse

7
HOLT LA
MILBURN LANE
RYALL'S LANE
Sewage Works
Caundle Wake
Higher Wood Bridge
Woodbridge Farm
Lower Wood Bridge
Braech Pit Pond
HYDES LANE
Hydes Farm
River Lydden
New House Farm
Holebrook Green Farm

12
Cornford Bridge
CORNFORD HL
Cornford Hill Farm
Holwell Farm
The Borough
STONY LANE
Woodbridge
Park Farm
Rodmore Farm
BLACKROW LANE
Blackrow Farm
Berry Farm
Holebrook Farm

6
BARNES CROSS
CROUCH LANE
Hill Street
Barton Farm
Naish Farm
Bulhams Plantation
PEACEFUL LANE
Lower Piccadilly Farm
Little Rodmore Farm
Rodmore Plantation
Ford
Rooksmoor Copse

11
Westrow Farm
Crouch Hill
FOSTERS HL
FOXS CL
Pleck
Elm Tree Farm
New Gorse
Raglans Farm
King's Stag
PO
Lower Ridge Farm
DT10
Treviss Copse

5
HOLWELL DROVE
Holwell
Dolivers Farm
Packers Hill
HOLWELL ROAD
Stag Farm
Sewage Works
RAMSBURY
WHITE HART CL
PH
RIDGE LA
Ridge Farm
Deadmoor Copse
Smetherd Farm

10
Manor Plantation
DT9
Warrys Plantation
Holwell Hill Farm
B3143
Ranksborough Gorse
THE COMMON
Hazel End
Hilltop Farm
RIDGE DRO
Woodrow
Woodrow Farm
HOMEMEAD

4
New Covert
Pulham Gorse
Hartmoor Farm
East Farm
East Pulham
Manor Farm
Lyddon House
High House Farm
WEST LA
Moores Farm
HONEY BUN MD
THE CAUSEWAY
Crossroads Farm
KINGSTON LA
Pidney
PH
PRITZEL'S
WATER KNAP

09
Common Plantation
Pitt's Farm
Eastfield Plantation
Grange Farm
Old Boywood Farm
PARTWAY LA
PARTWAY LA
PO

3
Newlands Farm
NEWLAND LANE
West Pulham
Pulham
MEADOW VALE
PH
Cross Roads Farm
HALSEY GN
CANNINGS COURT LANE
Dodies Wood
Glebe Farm
North Dairy Farm
River Lydden
Star Farm
Pleck Farm
PLECK HL
Hazelbury Bryan
PARTWAY
THE OLD DAIRY FARM
VALE MD
CHURCHFOOT LANE
Cemy
WOODLANDS

08
Birch Coppice
Pellwell Farm
DE BRIANE CL
Home Farm
THE OR
Wonston
MARSH LANE
Park Gate

2
Breach Wood
Dungeon Hill (Fort)
Towns End Farm
DT2
Cannings Court
Boywood Farm
Dairy House Farm
Parsonage Farm
Fir Tree Farm
Bourne Farm
Park Gate Farm

07
Duntish Elm Farm
New Hayes Farm
Brockhampton Coppice
Short Wood
DT11

1
B3146
SPRING GR
B3143
Duntish Farm
Duntish
Duntish Old Farm
Beaulieu Wood
LAWRENCE Farm
Brockhampton Green
Westfields
Hammond Street Farm
TAYLOR'S LA
THE GREEN
STONE LANE
Mappowder

06
Beaulieu Wood Farm
Shortwood Farm
Cross Farm
Westfield Farm
PO
HAMMOOD ST
QUAR CLOSE

69   A   70   B   71   C   72   D   73   E   74   F

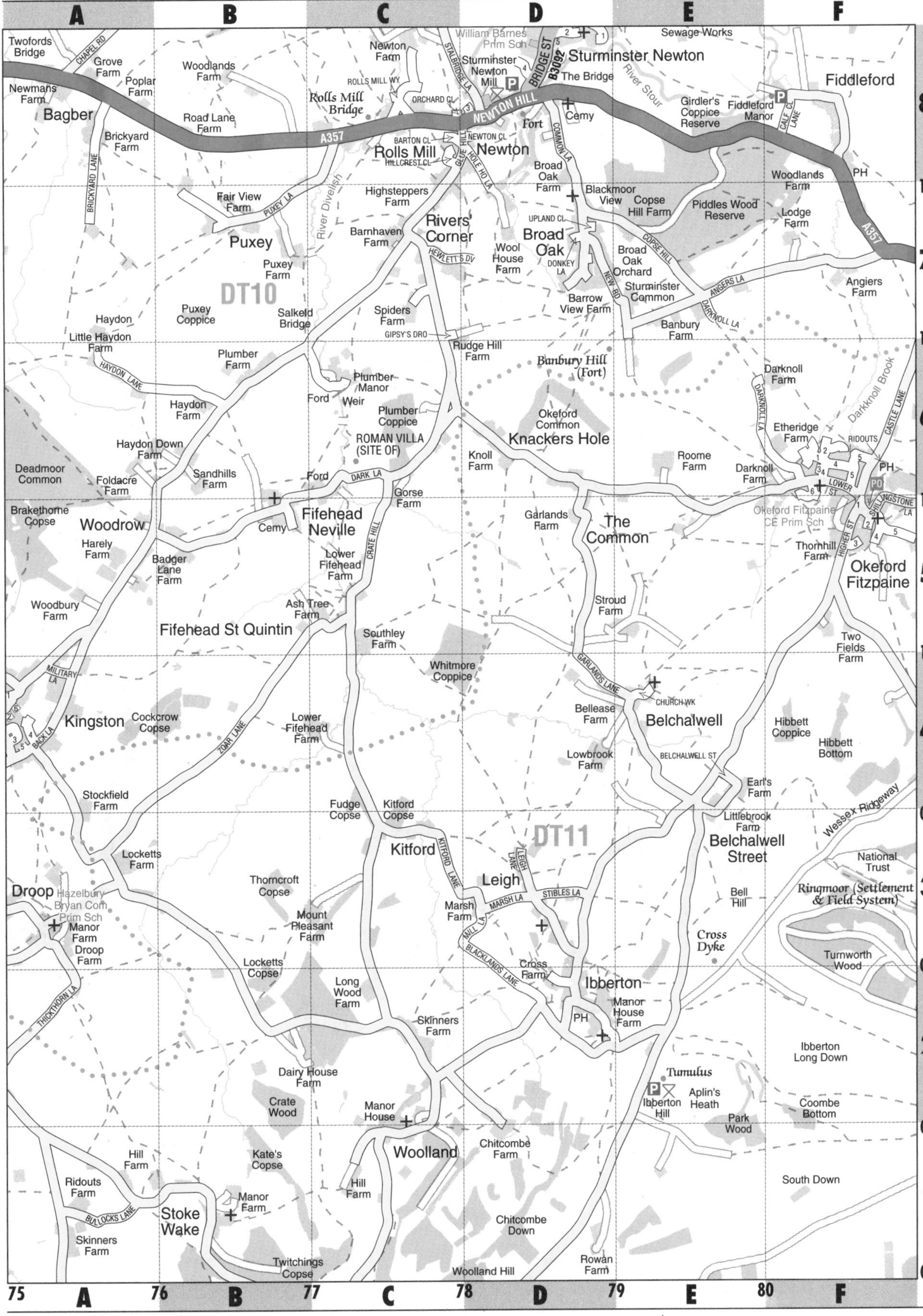
A
B
C
D
E
F
Twofords Bridge
CHAPEL RD
Grove Farm
Newmans Farm
Poplar Farm
Bagber
Woodlands Farm
Road Lane Farm
Brickyard Farm
BRICKYARD LANE
A357
Newton Farm
Rolls Mill Bridge
ROLLS MILL WY
ORCHARD CL
STALBRIDGE LA
Sturminster Newton Mill
William Barnes Prim Sch
Sturminster Newton
BRIDGE ST
B3092
The Bridge
NEWTON HILL
River Stour
Sewage Works
Fort
Cemy
Girdler's Coppice Reserve
Fiddleford Manor
Fiddleford
CALF CL LANE
BARTON CL
NEWTON CL
HILLCREST CL
Rolls Mill
Newton
GLUE HILL
HOLE HO LA
COMMON LA
Broad Oak Farm
Blackmoor View
Copse Hill Farm
Piddles Wood Reserve
Woodlands Farm
PH
Lodge Farm
Fair View Farm
PUXEY LA
River Divelish
Highsteppers Farm
Puxey
Barnhaven Farm
Rivers' Corner
HEWLETT'S DV
UPLAND CL
Broad Oak
Wool House Farm
DONKEY LA
Broad Oak Orchard
COPSE HILL
NEW RD
Sturminster Common
ANGERS LA
Angiers Farm
Puxey Farm
DT10
Salkeld Bridge
Puxey Coppice
Haydon
Little Haydon Farm
Spiders Farm
GIPSY'S DRO
Barrow View Farm
Banbury Farm
DARKNOLL LA
Rudge Hill Farm
Banbury Hill (Fort)
Plumber Farm
HAYDON LANE
Plumber Manor
Weir
Ford
Darknoll Farm
Darknoll Brook
Haydon Farm
Plumber Coppice
Okeford Common
Knackers Hole
Etheridge Farm
CASTLE LANE
RIDOUTS
ROMAN VILLA (SITE OF)
Haydon Down Farm
Knoll Farm
Roome Farm
Darknoll Farm
PH
Deadmoor Common
Foldacre Farm
Sandhills Farm
Ford
DARK LA
LOWER ST
Gorse Farm
SHILLINGSTONE LA
Brakethorne Copse
Woodrow
Cemy
Fifehead Neville
Garlands Farm
The Common
Okeford Fitzpaine CE Prim Sch
HIGHER ST
Harely Farm
Badger Lane Farm
CRATE HILL
Lower Fifehead Farm
Thornhill Farm
Okeford Fitzpaine
Woodbury Farm
Ash Tree Farm
Stroud Farm
Fifehead St Quintin
Southley Farm
Two Fields Farm
MILITARY LA
Whitmore Coppice
GARLANDS LANE
CHURCH WK
Kingston
Cockcrow Copse
Lower Fifehead Farm
Bellease Farm
Belchalwell
Hibbett Coppice
Hibbett Bottom
BACK LA
ZOAR LANE
Lowbrook Farm
BELCHALWELL ST
Stockfield Farm
Earl's Farm
Fudge Copse
Kitford Copse
DT11
Littlebrook Farm
Wessex Ridgeway
Belchalwell Street
National Trust
Locketts Farm
Kitford
KITFORD LANE
LEIGH LANE
Leigh
STIBLES LA
Thorncroft Copse
Bell Hill
Ringmoor (Settlement & Field System)
Droop
Hazelbury Bryan Com Prim Sch
Manor Farm
Droop Farm
Mount Pleasant Farm
Marsh Farm
MARSH LA
MILL LA
Cross Dyke
BLACKLANDS LANE
Cross Farm
Turnworth Wood
Locketts Copse
Ibberton
THICKTHORN LA
Long Wood Farm
Manor House Farm
PH
Skinners Farm
Ibberton Long Down
Tumulus
Dairy House Farm
Aplin's Heath
Ibberton Hill
Crate Wood
Manor House
Park Wood
Coombe Bottom
Hill Farm
Kate's Copse
Woolland
Chitcombe Farm
Ridouts Farm
Hill Farm
South Down
Manor Farm
BULLOCKS LANE
Stoke Wake
Skinners Farm
Chitcombe Down
Twitchings Copse
Woolland Hill
Rowan Farm
8
13
7
12
6
11
5
10
4
09
3
08
2
07
1
06
75
76
77
78
79
80

197
36
37

B5
1 EVERETTS LA
2 HONEYSUCKLE GDNS
3 GUNN LA
4 WESSEX AVE
5 COOMBE RD
6 SCHELIN WY

B6
1 COOKSWELL
2 STATION RD
3 POPLAR HL
4 LANCHARDS
5 CHURCH RD
6 CANDY'S LA

C7
1 APPLE ACRE
2 JACOBS LADDER
3 THE CROSS
4 UPPER ST
5 ST NICHOLAS CT
6 HOMEFIELD
7 KNOTTS CL
8 ALLEN CL
9 CHALWELL
10 GREENWAY
11 MELWAY GDNS
12 THE BUTTS

C8
1 OLIVERS MD
2 MILLBROOK CL
3 MILLBROOK CT
4 NUTMEAD CL
5 PORTMAN DR
6 COMMON DRO

Scale: 1¾ inches to 1 mile
0 ¼ ½ mile
0 250m 500m 750m 1 km

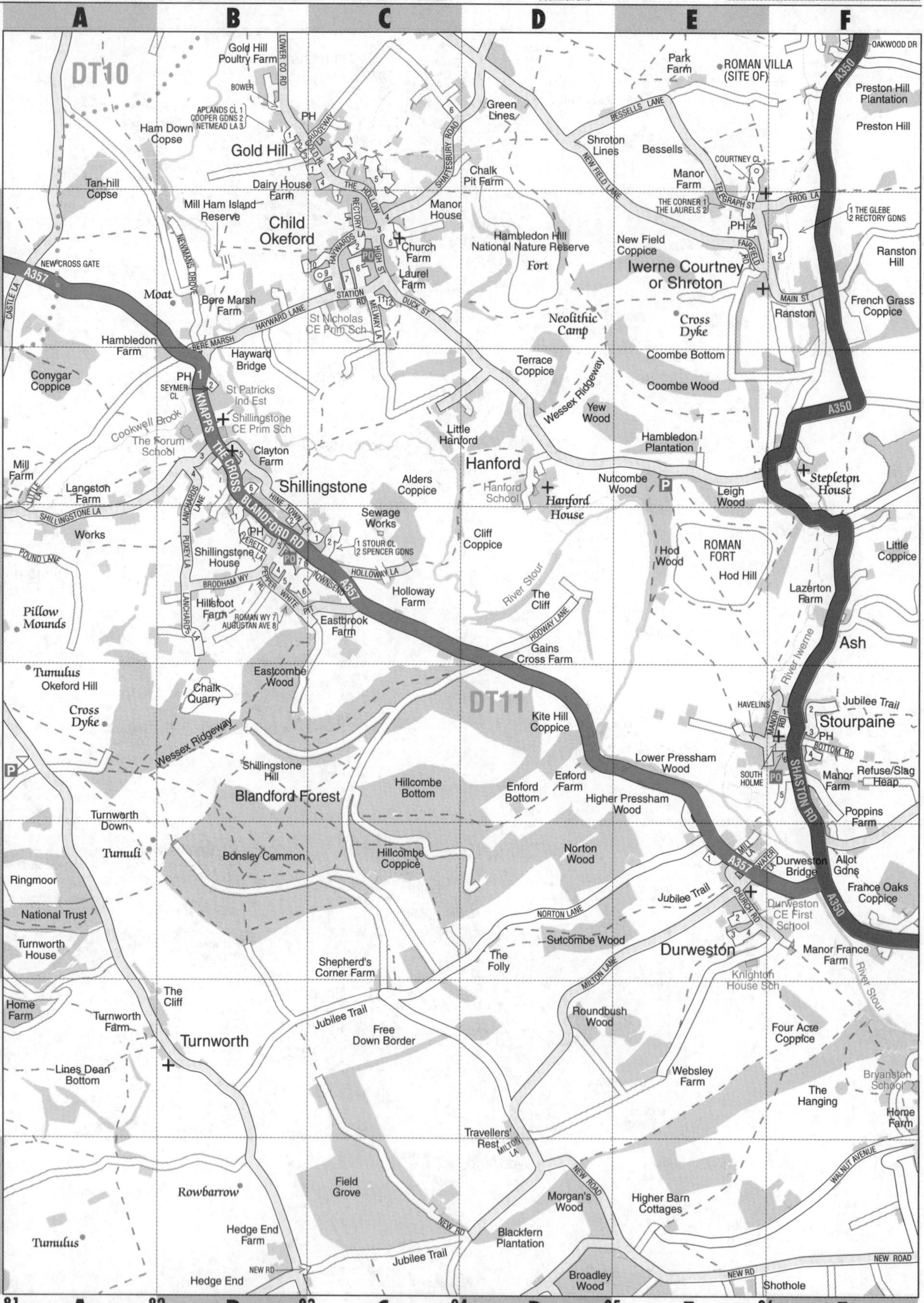

197
210

E3
1 WYNCHARD BANK
2 ST NICHOLAS GDNS
3 THE GLEBE
4 HAYCOMBE

F4
1 COACH RD
2 HOD VW
3 PARK CL
4 ORCHARD CL
5 ROWLANDS RD
6 CHURCH VW

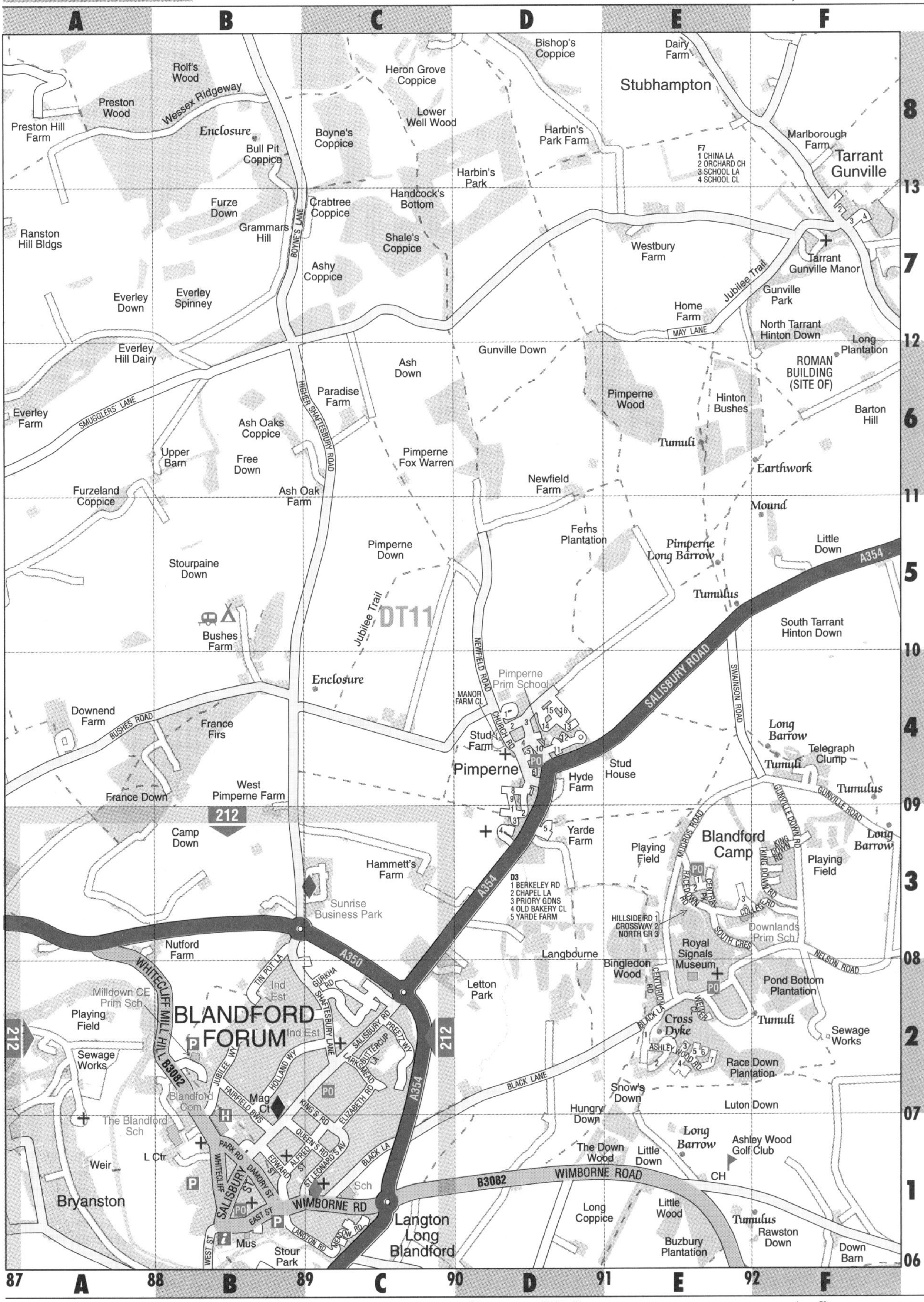

For full street detail of the highlighted area see page 212.

212 211 200

D4
1 ST PETER'S CL
2 ARLECKS LA
3 DOWN RD
4 SCHOOL LA
5 PARR GR
6 HYDE GDNS
7 COLLINGWOOD CL
8 BERKELEY RISE
9 BERKELEY CL
10 ANVIL RD
11 PORTMAN RD
12 THE CLOSE
13 WALTERS DR
14 BOYTE RD
15 MARSH WY
16 FRAMPTON RD

E2
1 SNOWDOWN RD
2 DOWN WOOD RD
3 LUTON DOWN RD
4 CRAWFORD DOWN RD
5 MONKTON DOWN RD
6 RAWSTON DOWN RD
7 KEYNSTON DOWN RD

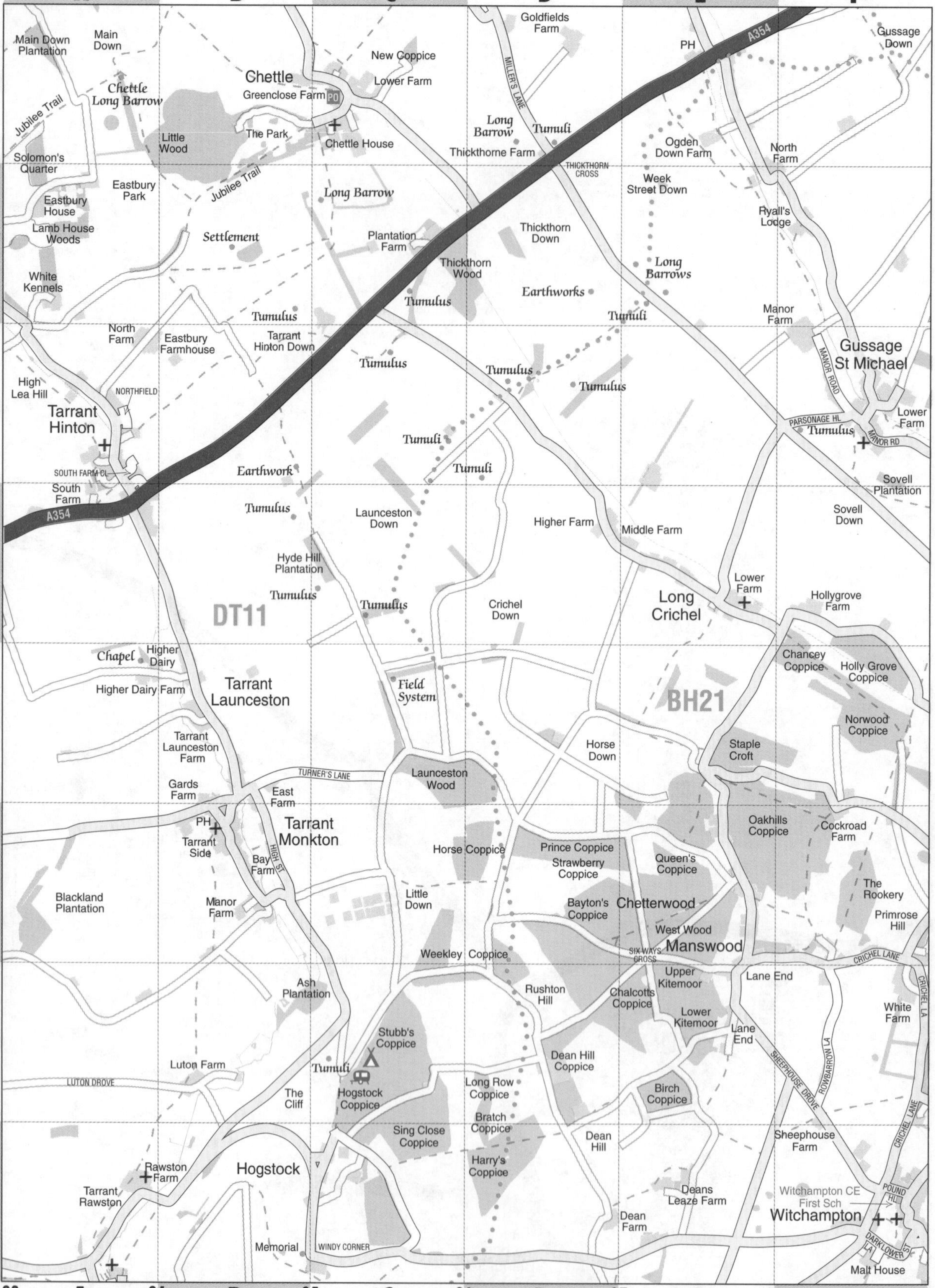
Main Down Plantation
Main Down
Chettle Long Barrow
Jubilee Trail
Chettle
Greenclose Farm
New Coppice
Lower Farm
Goldfields Farm
Millers Lane
PH
A354
Gussage Down
Solomon's Quarter
Little Wood
The Park
Chettle House
Long Barrow
Tumuli
Thickthorn Farm
Ogden Down Farm
North Farm
Thickthorn Cross
Eastbury Park
Eastbury House
Lamb House Woods
Week Street Down
Ryall's Lodge
Settlement
Plantation Farm
Thickthorn Down
Thickthorn Wood
Long Barrows
White Kennels
Tumulus
Earthworks
Manor Farm
Gussage St Michael
Manor Road
North Farm
Eastbury Farmhouse
Tarrant Hinton Down
High Lea Hill
Northfield
Tarrant Hinton
Parsonage Hl
Lower Farm
Manor Rd
South Farm Cl
South Farm
Earthwork
Sovell Plantation
Sovell Down
Launceston Down
Higher Farm
Middle Farm
Hyde Hill Plantation
Crichel Down
Long Crichel
Lower Farm
Hollygrove Farm
DT11
Chapel
Higher Dairy
Higher Dairy Farm
Tarrant Launceston
Field System
Chancey Coppice
Holly Grove Coppice
BH21
Norwood Coppice
Tarrant Launceston Farm
Horse Down
Staple Croft
Turner's Lane
Launceston Wood
Gards Farm
East Farm
Tarrant Monkton
High St
Oakhills Coppice
Cockroad Farm
Tarrant Side
Horse Coppice
Prince Coppice
Strawberry Coppice
Queen's Coppice
Bay Farm
Blackland Plantation
Manor Farm
Little Down
Bayton's Coppice
Chetterwood
The Rookery
Primrose Hill
West Wood
Manswood
Six Ways Cross
Weekley Coppice
Crichel Lane
Ash Plantation
Rushton Hill
Upper Kitemoor
Chalcotts Coppice
Lane End
Lower Kitemoor
White Farm
Stubb's Coppice
Lane End
Sheephouse Drove
Rowbarrow La
Crichel La
Luton Farm
Luton Drove
Dean Hill Coppice
Long Row Coppice
Hogstock Coppice
The Cliff
Birch Coppice
Batch Coppice
Sing Close Coppice
Dean Hill
Sheephouse Farm
Crichel Lane
Rawston Farm
Hogstock
Harry's Coppice
Tarrant Rawston
Deans Leaze Farm
Witchampton CE First Sch
Pound Hl
Witchampton
Dean Farm
Memorial
Windy Corner
Dark La
Lower St
Malt House
A B C D E F
8 13 7 12 6 11 5 10 4 09 3 08 2 07 1 06
93 94 95 96 97 98

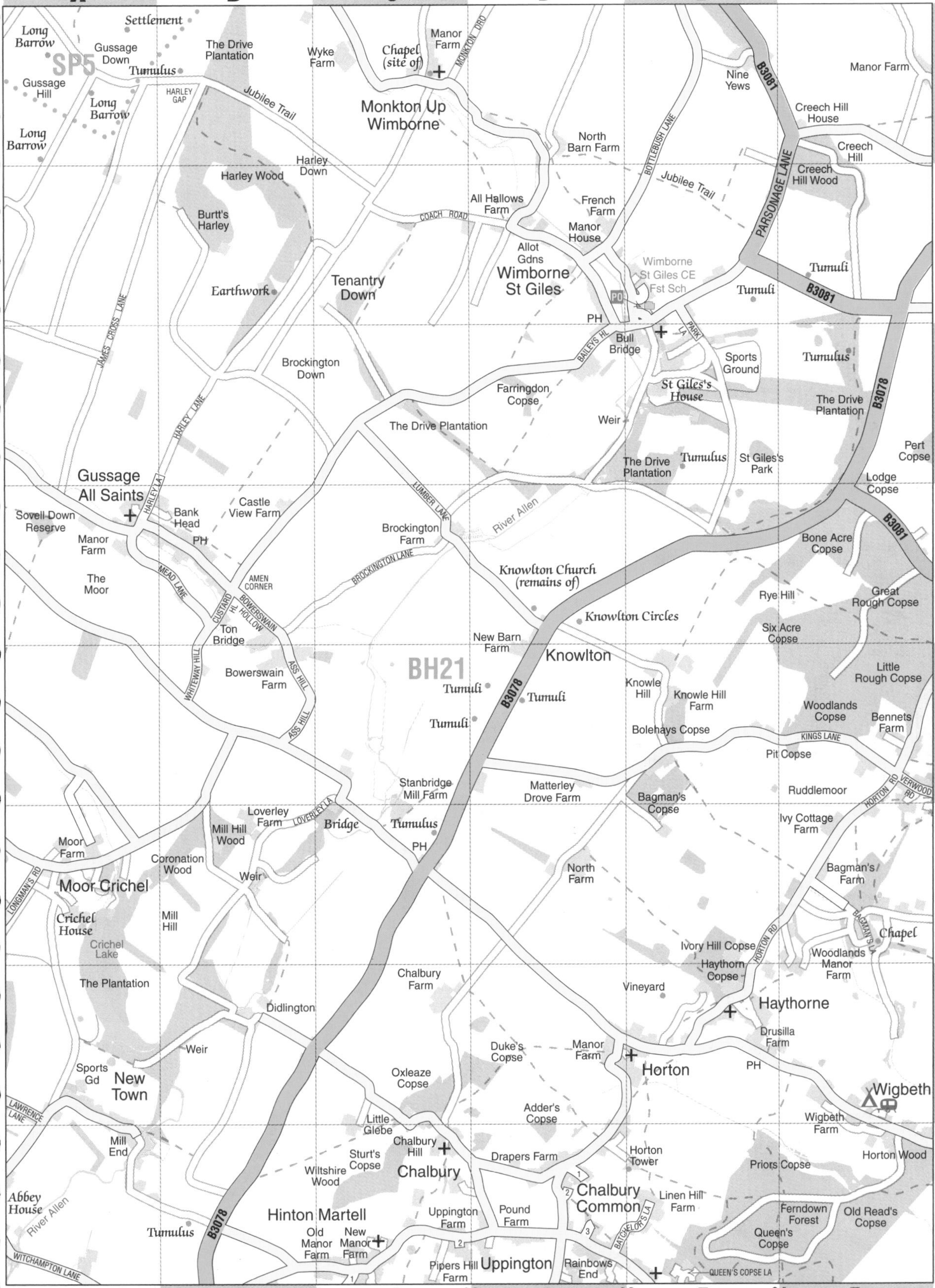

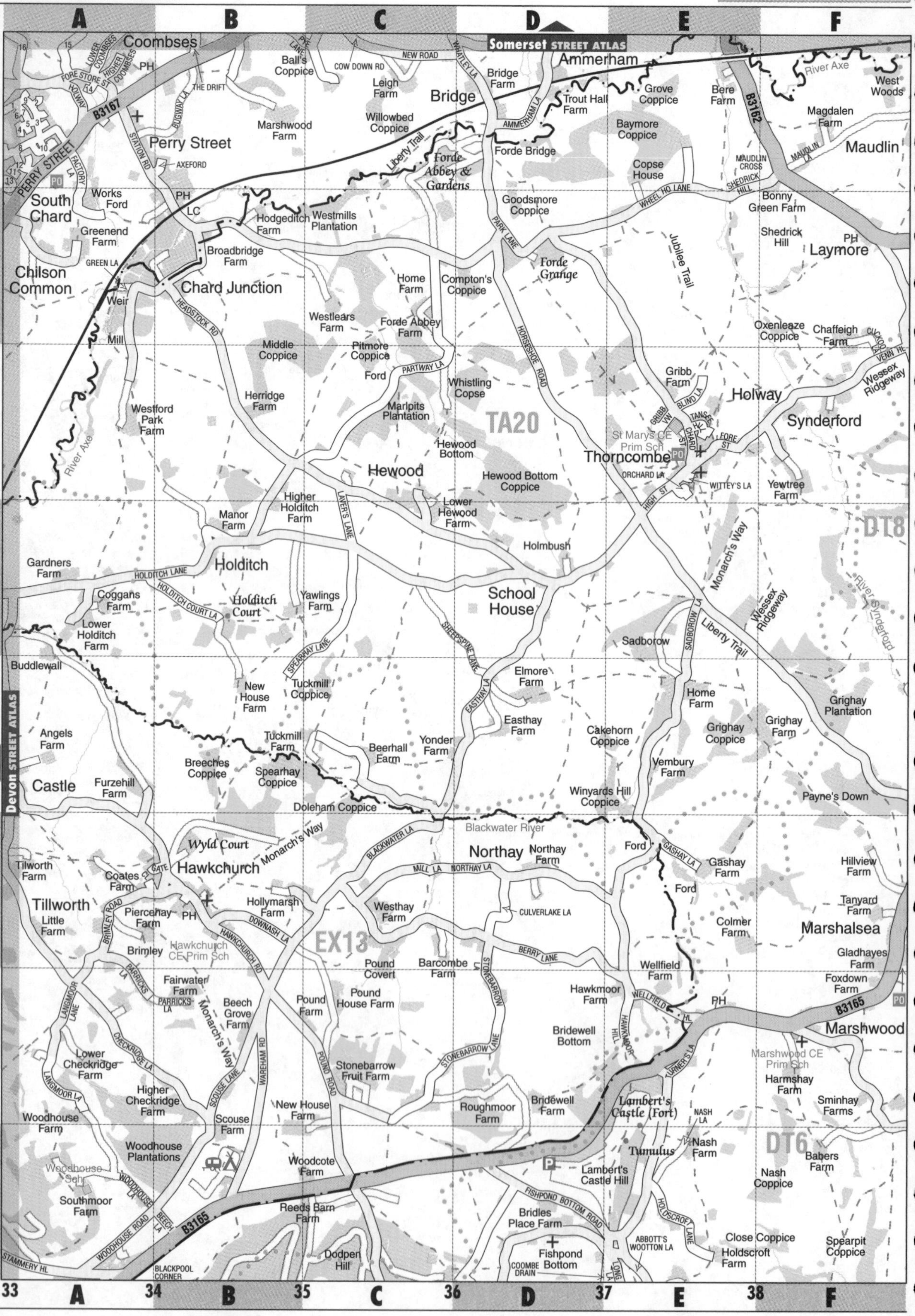

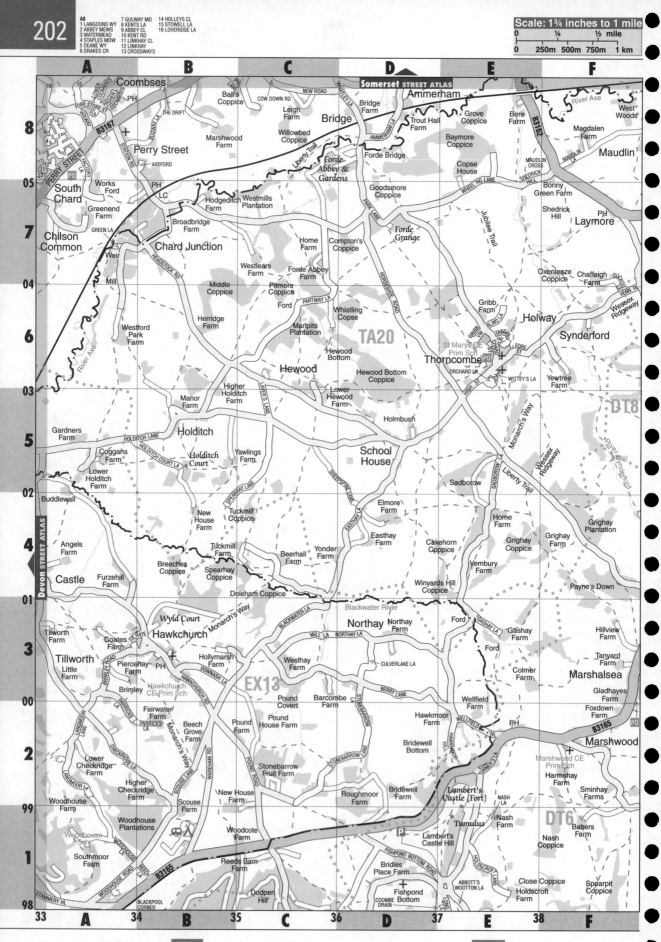

A8
1 LANGDONS WY
2 ABBEY MEWS
3 WATERMEAD
4 STAPLES MDW
5 DEANE WY
6 DRAKES CR
7 GULWAY MD
8 KENTS LA
9 ABBEY CL
10 KENT RD
11 LINKHAY CL
12 LINKHAY
13 CROSSWAYS
14 HOLLEYS CL
15 STOWELL LA
16 LOVERIDGE LA

Somerset STREET ATLAS

Coombses
Ball's Coppice
NEW ROAD
Ammerham
River Axe
West Woods
Bridge
Leigh Farm
COW DOWN RD
WHATLEY LA
Bridge Farm
Trout Hall Farm
Grove Coppice
Bere Farm
Magdalen Farm
Maudlin
Perry Street
Marshwood Farm
Willowbed Coppice
AMMERHAM LA
Forde Bridge
Baymore Coppice
MAUDLIN CROSS
SHEDRICK HILL
Bonny Green Farm
Shedrick Hill
Laymore
THE DRIFT
Axeford
Forde Abbey & Gardens
Goodsmoore Coppice
Copse House
WHEEL HO LANE
Laymore
PH
South Chard
Works Ford
PH
LC
Hodgeditch Farm
Westmills Plantation
PARK LANE
Forde Grange
Jubilee Trail
Oxenleaze Coppice
Chaffeigh Farm
Greenend Farm
Broadbridge Farm
Home Farm
Compton's Coppice
Wessex Ridgeway
Chilson Common
GREEN LA
Chard Junction
Westlears Farm
Forde Abbey Farm
HORSESHOE ROAD
Gribb Farm
GRIBB VW
BLIND LA
TANS LA
Holway
Weir
Mill
HEADSTOCK RD
Middle Coppice
Pitmore Coppice
Ford
Whistling Copse
St Marys CE Prim Sch
FORE ST
Synderford
Westford Park Farm
Herridge Farm
Marlpits Plantation
TA20
Hewood Bottom Coppice
Thorncombe
PO
ORCHARD LA
WITTEY'S LA
Yewtree Farm
DT8
River Axe
Hewood
HIGH ST
Holmbush
Higher Holditch Farm
LAYER'S LANE
Lower Hewood Farm
Monarch's Way
Wessex Ridgeway
River Synderford
Gardners Farm
Manor Farm
Holditch
School House
Liberty Trail
HOLDITCH LANE
Coggans Farm
Holditch Court
Yawlings Farm
SHEEPSPINE LANE
Sadborow
Grighay Plantation
Lower Holditch Farm
HOLDITCH COURT LA
SPEARWAY LANE
Elmore Farm
Home Farm
Grighay Coppice
Grighay Farm
Buddlewall
New House Farm
Tuckmill Coppice
EASTHAY LA
Easthay Farm
Cakehorn Coppice
Vembury Farm
Angels Farm
Tuckmill Farm
Beerhall Farm
Yonder Farm
Payne's Down
Castle
Furzehill Farm
Breeches Coppice
Spearhay Coppice
Winyards Hill Coppice
Devon STREET ATLAS
Doleham Coppice
Blackwater River
Northay
Northay Farm
Ford
GASHAY LA
Gashay Farm
Hillview Farm
Tilworth
Wyld Court
Monarch's Way
Hawkchurch
BLACKWATER LA
MILL LA
NORTHAY LA
Ford
Tanyard Farm
Tillworth
Coates Farm
Hollymarsh Farm
Westhay Farm
CULVERLAKE LA
Colmer Farm
Marshalsea
Little Farm
Piercehay Farm
PH
DOWNASH LA
Hawkchurch CE Prim Sch
EX13
Pound Covert
Barcombe Farm
BERRY LANE
STONEBARROW
Wellfield Farm
WELLFIELD HL
PH
B3165
Gladhayes Farm
Foxdown Farm
PO
Marshwood
Brimley
Fairwater Farm
PARRICKS LA
Beech Grove Farm
Pound Farm
Pound House Farm
Hawkmoor Farm
Bridewell Bottom
Marshwood CE Prim Sch
Harmshay Farm
Lower Checkridge Farm
CHECKRIDGE LA
Higher Checkridge Farm
WAREHAM RD
New House Farm
POUND ROAD
Stonebarrow Fruit Farm
STONEBARROW LANE
Bridewell Farm
Lambert's Castle (Fort)
NASH LA
Sminhay Farms
Woodhouse Farm
LANGMOOR LA
Scouse Farm
SCOUSE LANE
Roughmoor Farm
TURNER'S LA
Tumulus
Nash Farm
DT6
Babers Farm
Woodhouse Sch
Woodhouse Plantations
Woodcote Farm
P
Lambert's Castle Hill
FISHPOND BOTTOM ROAD
HOLSCROFT LANE
Nash Coppice
Southmoor Farm
WOODHOUSE ROAD
BEECH
B3165
Reeds Barn Farm
Bridles Place Farm
Fishpond Bottom
ABBOTT'S WOOTTON LA
Close Coppice
Holscroft Farm
Spearpit Coppice
STAMMERY HL
BLACKPOOL CORNER
Dodpen Hill
COOMBE DRAIN

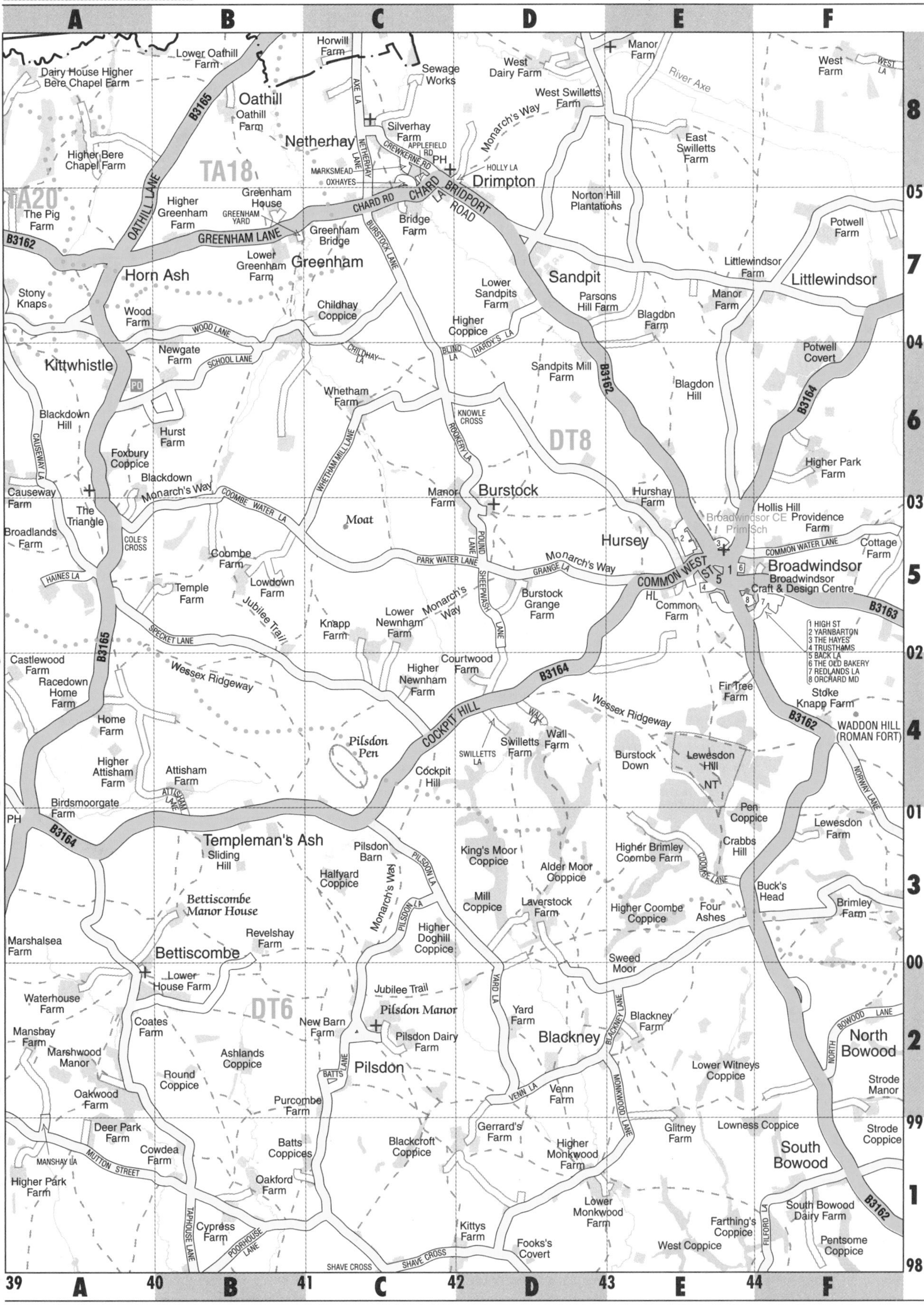

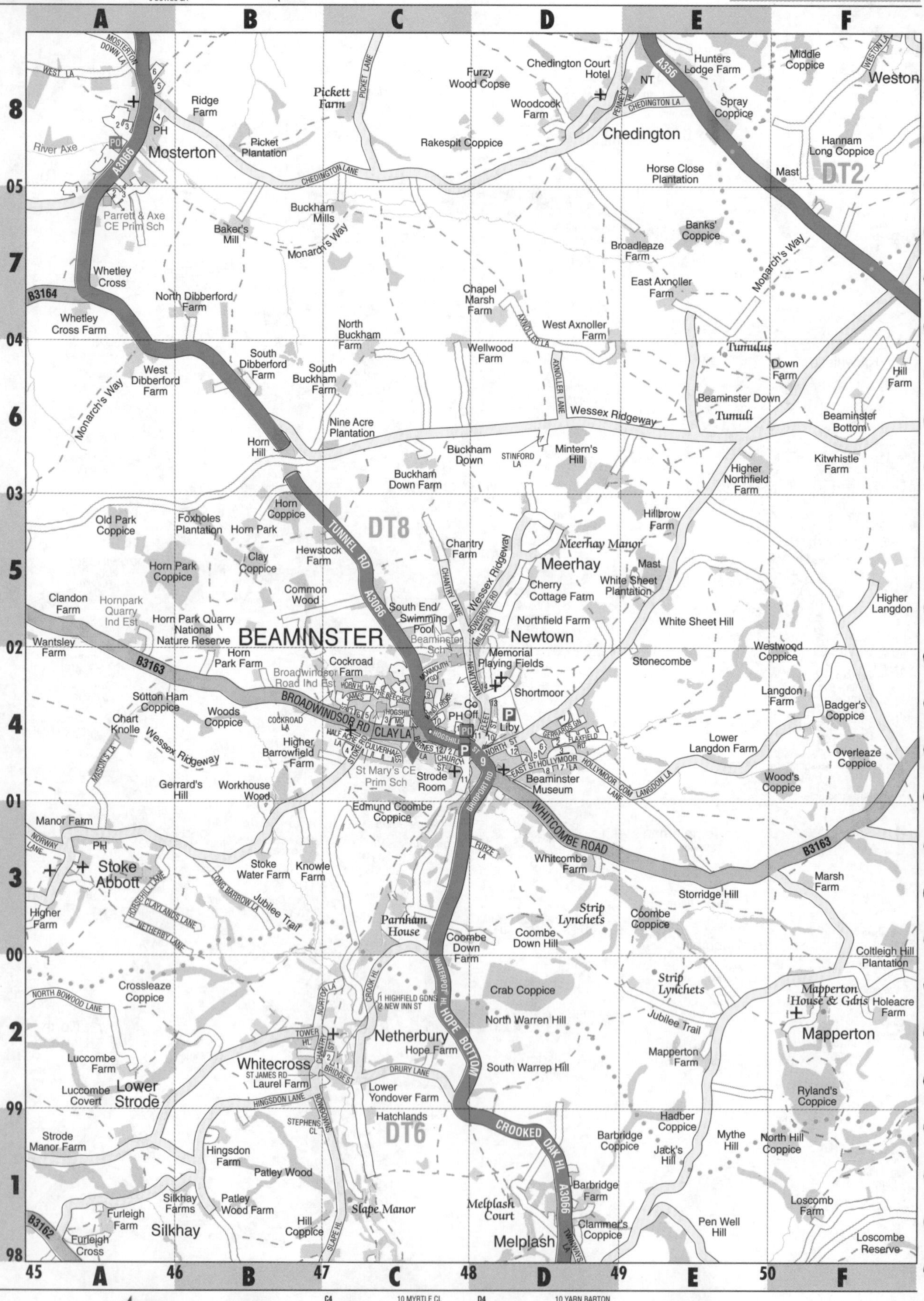

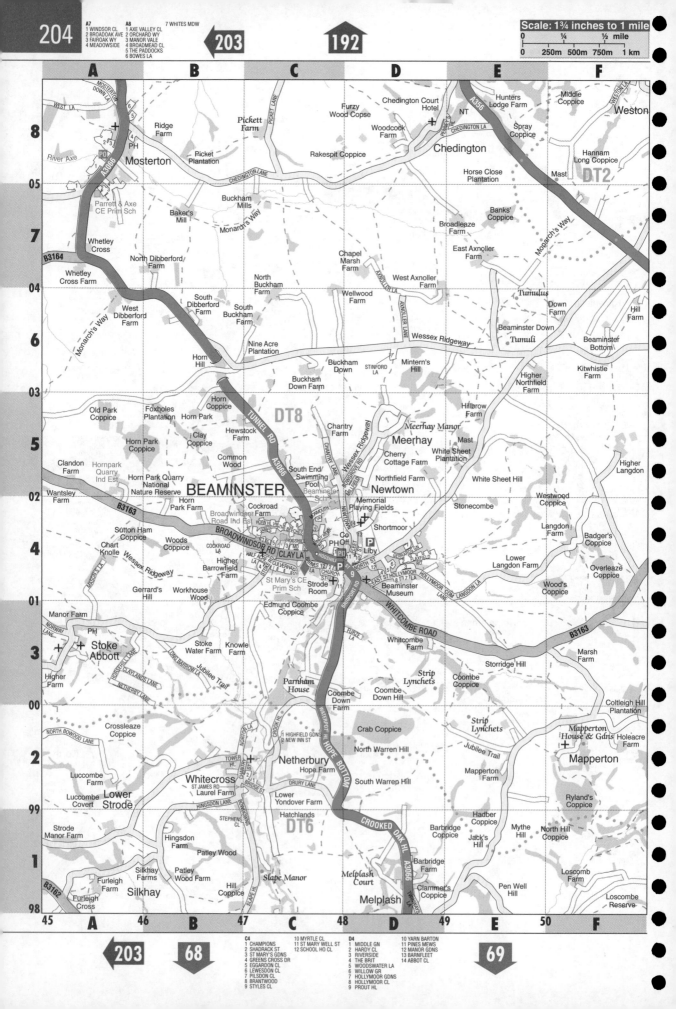

204

A7
1 WINDSOR CL
2 BROADOAK AVE
3 FAIROAK WY
4 MEADOWSIDE

A8
1 AXE VALLEY CL
2 ORCHARD WY
3 MANOR VALE
4 BROADMEAD CL
5 THE PADDOCKS
6 BOWES LA

7 WHITES MDW

203

192

A   B   C   D   E   F

8

05

7

04

6

03

5

02

4

01

3

00

2

99

1

98

45   A   46   B   47   C   48   D   49   E   50   F

C4
1 CHAMPIONS
2 SHADRACK ST
3 ST MARY'S GDNS
4 GREENS CROSS DR
5 EGGARDON CL
6 LEWESDON CL
7 PILSDON CL
8 BRANTWOOD
9 STYLES CL

10 MYRTLE CL
11 ST MARY WELL ST
12 SCHOOL HO CL

D4
1 MIDDLE GN
2 HARDY CL
3 RIVERSIDE
4 THE BRIT
5 WOODSWATER LA
6 WILLOW GR
7 HOLLYMOOR GDNS
8 HOLLYMOOR CL
9 PROUT HL

10 YARN BARTON
11 PINES MEWS
12 MANOR GDNS
13 BARNFLEET
14 ABBOT CL

Map labels

West La • Mosterton Down La • Ridge Farm • Pickett Farm • Picket Plantation • Furzy Wood Copse • Chedington Court Hotel • Woodcock Farm • NT • Hunters Lodge Farm • Middle Coppice • Weston

River Axe • PO • PH • Mosterton • Picket Plantation • Rakespit Coppice • Chedington • Chedington La • Spray Coppice • Hannam Long Coppice • DT2

A3066 • A356 • Mast

Parrett & Axe CE Prim Sch • Baker's Mill • Buckham Mills • Monarch's Way • Horse Close Plantation • Broadleaze Farm • Banks' Coppice

Whetley Cross • Chedington Lane • Chapel Marsh Farm • East Axnoller Farm • Monarch's Way

B3164 • North Dibberford Farm • North Buckham Farm • West Axnoller Farm • Axnoller La • Tumulus • Down Farm • Hill Farm

Whetley Cross Farm • South Dibberford Farm • South Buckham Farm • Axnoller Lane • Wellwood Farm • Wessex Ridgeway • Beaminster Down • Tumuli • Beaminster Bottom

Monarch's Way • West Dibberford Farm • Nine Acre Plantation • Horn Hill • Buckham Down • Stinford La • Mintern's Hill • Higher Northfield Farm • Kitwhistle Farm

Old Park Coppice • Foxholes Plantation • Horn Park • Horn Coppice • DT8 • Chantry Farm • Meerhay Manor • Hillbrow Farm

Horn Park Coppice • Clay Coppice • Hewstock Farm • Tunnel Rd • Chantry La • Meerhay • Cherry Cottage Farm • White Sheet Plantation • Mast • Higher Langdon

Clandon Farm • Hornpark Quarry Ind Est • Common Wood • A3066 • Wessex Ridgeway • South End • Swimming Pool • Northfield Farm • White Sheet Hill • Westwood Coppice

Wantsley Farm • Horn Park Quarry National Nature Reserve • BEAMINSTER • Beaminster Sch • Newtown • Stonecombe • Langdon Farm • Badger's Coppice

B3163 • Horn Park Farm • Cockroad Farm • Broadwindsor Road Ind Est • Memorial Playing Fields • Shortmoor • Lower Langdon Farm • Overleaze Coppice

Sutton Ham Coppice • Woods Coppice • Cockroad La • BROADWINDSOR RD • CLAY LA • Co • PH • PO • Off • Liby • P • East St • Hollymoor • Hollymoor Com • Langdon La • Wood's Coppice

Chart Knolle • Mason's La • Wessex Ridgeway • Higher Barrowfield Farm • Half Acre La • Church St • North St • Beaminster Museum • Flaxfield Rd

Gerrard's Hill • Workhouse Wood • St Mary's CE Prim Sch • Strode Room • Bridport Rd • Whitcombe Road • B3163

Manor Farm • Norway La • PH • Stoke Abbott • Edmund Coombe Coppice • Furze La • Whitcombe Farm • Storridge Hill • Marsh Farm

Higher Farm • Claylands Lane • Stoke Water Farm • Knowle Farm • Jubilee Trail • Parnham House • Coombe Down Farm • Strip Lynchets • Coombe Coppice • Coltleigh Hill Plantation

Long Barrow Trail • Netherby Lane • Crook Hl • Coombe Down Hill • Crab Coppice • Strip Lynchets • Mapperton House & Gdns • Holeacre Farm

North Bowood Lane • Crossleaze Coppice • Norton La • Tower Hl • Chantry St • 1 Highfield Gdns • 2 New Inn St • Netherbury • Hope Farm • North Warren Hill • Jubilee Trail • Mapperton

Luccombe Farm • Whitecross • St James Rd • Laurel Farm • Bridge St • Hope Bottom • Drury Lane • Hope Farm • South Warren Hill • Mapperton Farm • Ryland's Coppice

Luccombe Covert • Lower Strode • Hingsdon Lane • Lower Yondover Farm • Hatchlands • DT6 • Waterpit Hl • Hadber Coppice • Mythe Hill • North Hill Coppice

Strode Manor Farm • Stephens Cl • Hingsdon Farm • Patley Wood • Crooked Oak Hl • A3066 • Barbridge Coppice • Jack's Hill • Barbridge Farm • Loscomb Farm

B3162 • Silkhay Farms • Patley Wood Farm • Hill Coppice • Slape Manor • Slape Hl • Melplash Court • Pen Well Hill • Loscombe Reserve

Furleigh Farm • Furleigh Cross • Silkhay • Melplash • Clammer's Coppice

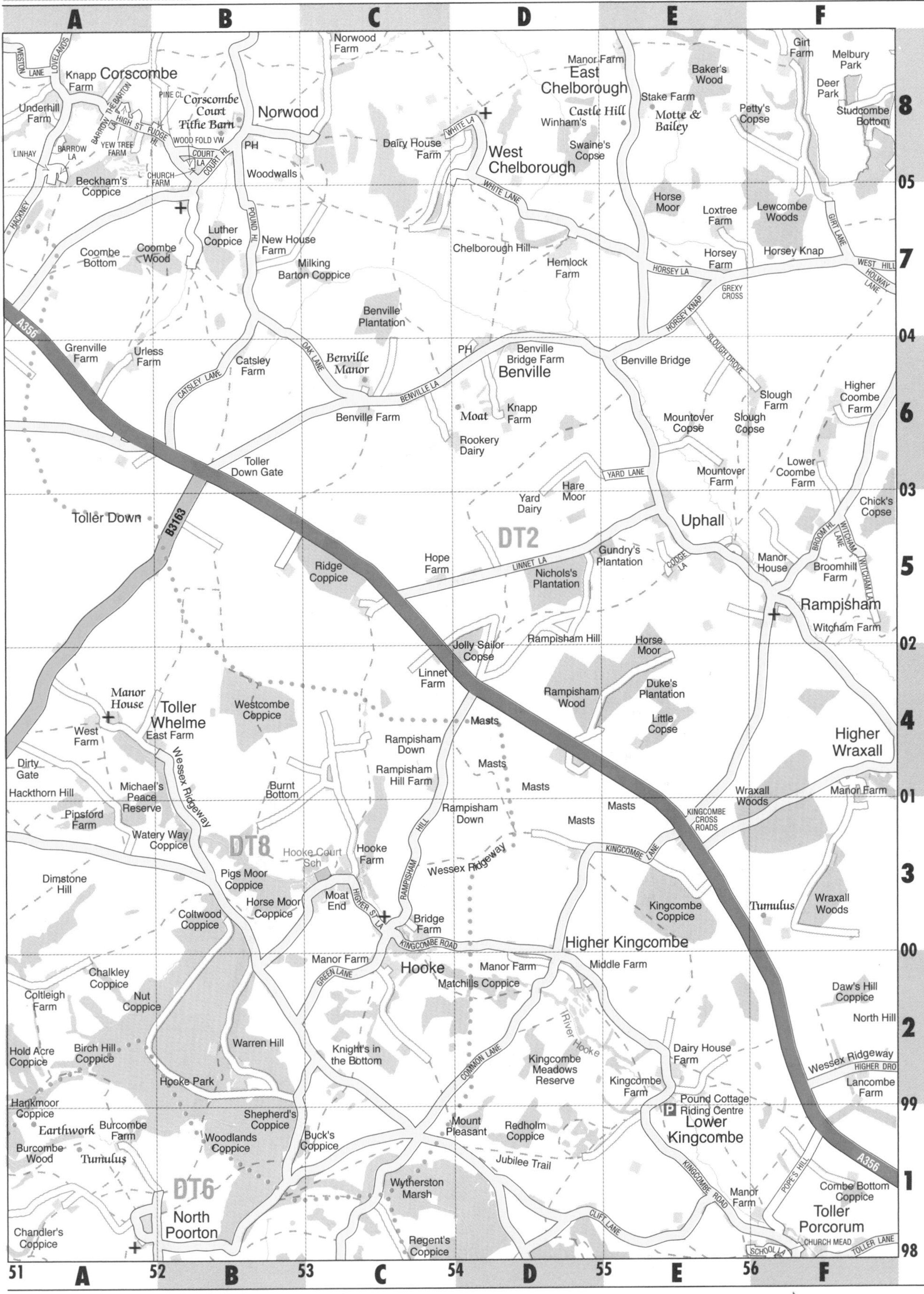

Scale: 1¾ inches to 1 mile
0   ¼   ½ mile
0   250m 500m 750m 1 km

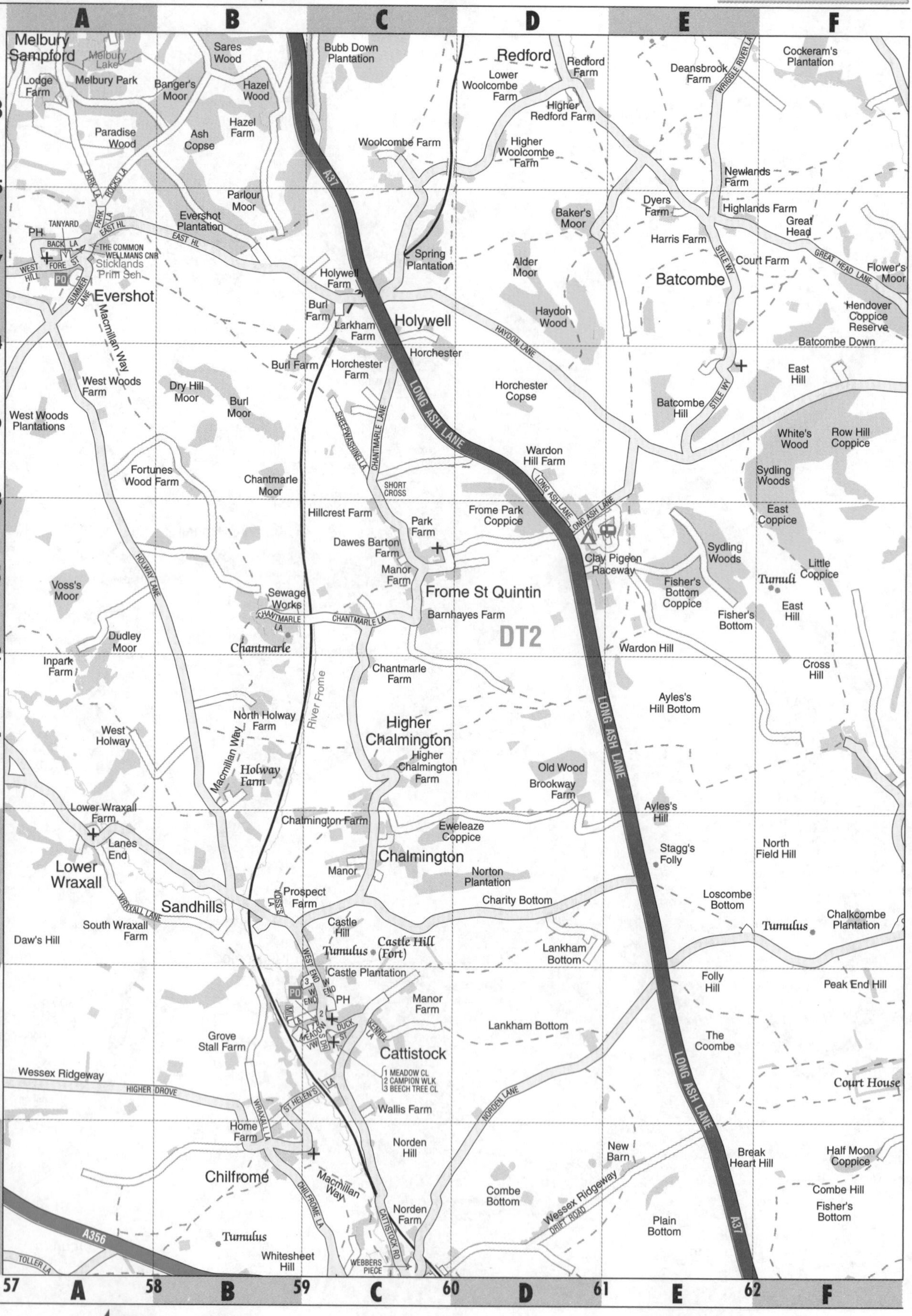

Row 8
Melbury Sampford
Melbury Lake
Melbury Park
Lodge Farm
Banger's Moor
Sares Wood
Hazel Wood
Bubb Down Plantation
Redford
Redford Farm
Lower Woolcombe Farm
Deansbrook Farm
Cockeram's Plantation
Paradise Wood
Ash Copse
Hazel Farm
Woolcombe Farm
Higher Woolcombe Farm
Higher Redford Farm
Newlands Farm

05

Parlour Moor
Evers022hot Plantation
Baker's Moor
Dyers Farm
Highlands Farm
Great Head

7
PH
TANYARD
BACK LA
EAST HL
THE COMMON
WELLMANS CNR
Sticklands Prim Sch
WEST HILL
FORE
PO
SUMMER LANE
Eversho
Holywell Farm
Spring Plantation
Harris Farm
Alder Moor
Court Farm
GREAT HEAD LANE
Flower's Moor
Batcombe
Hendover Coppice Reserve

04
Burl Farm
Larkham Farm
Holywell
Horchester
Haydon Wood
HAYDON LANE
Batcombe Down

Macmillan Way
West Woods Farm
Dry Hill Moor
Burl Farm
Horchester Farm
Burl Moor
Horchester Copse
Horchester Copse
Batcombe Hill
East Hill

6
West Woods Plantations
HOLWAY LANE
CHANTMARLE LANE
SHEEPWASHING LA
Wardon Hill Farm
White's Wood
Row Hill Coppice
Sydling Woods

03
Fortunes Wood Farm
Chantmarle Moor
Hillcrest Farm
Park Farm
Frome Park Coppice
SHORT CROSS
LONG ASH LANE
East Coppice

5
Voss's Moor
Dawes Barton Farm
Manor Farm
Clay Pigeon Raceway
Sydling Woods
Tumuli
Little Coppice
Fisher's Bottom Coppice
East Hill
Dudley Moor
Chantmarle
Frome St Quintin
Barnhayes Farm
Fisher's Bottom

02
Inpark Farm
CHANTMARLE LA
CHANTMARLE LA
Chantmarle Farm
DT2
Wardon Hill
Cross Hill

North Holway Farm
Sewage Works
River Frome
Ayles's Hill Bottom

4
West Holway
Macmillan Way
Higher Chalmington
Higher Chalmington Farm
Old Wood
Brookway Farm
Ayles's Hill

01
Lower Wraxall Farm
Lanes End
Holway Farm
Chalmington Farm
Eweleaze Coppice
Stagg's Folly
North Field Hill

3
Lower Wraxall
WRAXALL LANE
Sandhills
VOSS'S LA
Prospect Farm
Manor
Chalmington
Norton Plantation
Loscombe Bottom
Tumulus
Chalkcombe Plantation
South Wraxall Farm
Castle Hill
Castle Hill (Fort)
Charity Bottom
Daw's Hill
Tumulus

00
WEST END
Castle Plantation
Lankham Bottom
Folly Hill
Peak End Hill

2
PO
W END
PH
DUCK ST
Manor Farm
KENNEL LANE
The Coombe
Grove Stall Farm
MEADOW VW
Lankham Bottom
Wessex Ridgeway
HIGHER DROVE
Cattistock
NORDEN LANE
Court House

99
ST HELEN'S LA
Wallis Farm
1 MEADOW CL
2 CAMPION WLK
3 BEECH TREE CL
Home Farm
Norden Hill
New Barn
Break Heart Hill
Half Moon Coppice

1
WRAXALL LA
Macmillan Way
Chilfrome
DHILFROME LA
CATTISTOCK RD
Norden Farm
Combe Bottom
Wessex Ridgeway
DRIFT ROAD
Combe Hill
Fisher's Bottom
A37
Plain Bottom

98
A356
TOLLER LA
Tumulus
Whitesheet Hill
WEBBERS PIECE

57 A 58 B 59 C 60 D 61 E 62 F

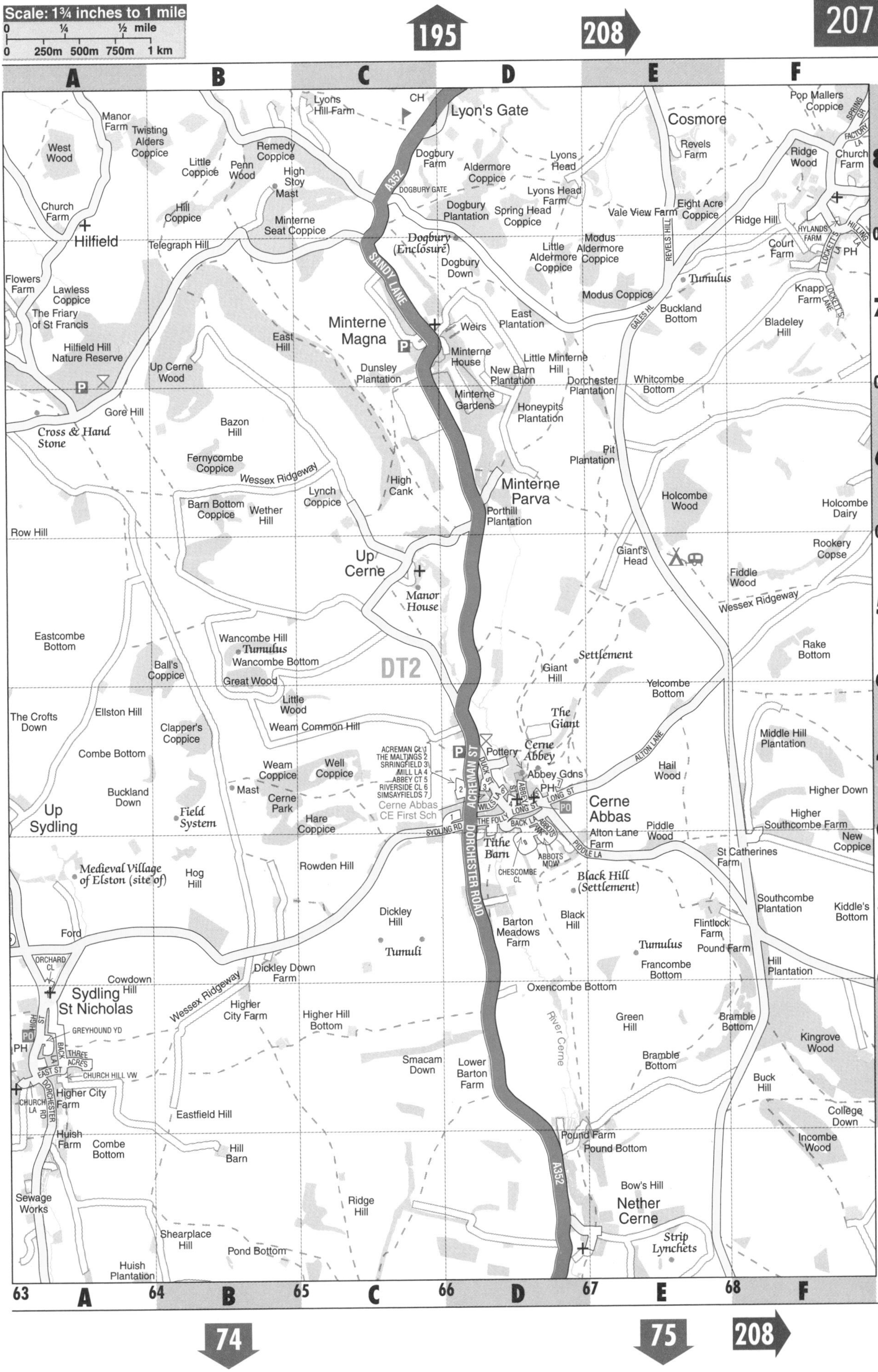

Scale: 1¾ inches to 1 mile
0 ¼ ½ mile
0 250m 500m 750m 1 km
195
208
A B C D E F
Lyons Hill Farm
CH
Lyon's Gate
Cosmore
Pop Mallers Coppice
Manor Farm
Twisting Alders Coppice
West Wood
Little Coppice
Penn Wood
Remedy Coppice
High Stoy Mast
Dogbury Farm
Aldermore Coppice
Lyons Head
Revels Farm
Ridge Wood
Church Farm
Hill Coppice
Minterne Seat Coppice
Dogbury Gate
Dogbury Plantation
Spring Head Coppice
Lyons Head Farm
Vale View Farm
Eight Acre Coppice
Ridge Hill
Church Farm
Hilfield
Telegraph Hill
Dogbury (Enclosure)
Dogbury Down
Little Aldermore Coppice
Modus Aldermore Coppice
Court Farm
PH
Hylands Farm
Flowers Farm
Lawless Coppice
The Friary of St Francis
Sandy Lane
Modus Coppice
Tumulus
Buckland Bottom
Knapp Farm
Minterne Magna
East Hill
Weirs
East Plantation
Bladeley Hill
Hilfield Hill Nature Reserve
Up Cerne Wood
Dunsley Plantation
Minterne House
New Barn Plantation
Little Minterne Hill
Dorchester Plantation
Whitcombe Bottom
Gore Hill
Cross & Hand Stone
Bazon Hill
Minterne Gardens
Honeypits Plantation
Fernycombe Coppice
Wessex Ridgeway
Pit Plantation
Barn Bottom Coppice
Wether Hill
Lynch Coppice
High Cank
Minterne Parva
Holcombe Wood
Holcombe Dairy
Porthill Plantation
Row Hill
Up Cerne
Manor House
Giant's Head
Rookery Copse
Fiddle Wood
Wessex Ridgeway
Eastcombe Bottom
Wancombe Hill
Tumulus
Wancombe Bottom
Ball's Coppice
DT2
Settlement
Rake Bottom
Giant Hill
Great Wood
Yelcombe Bottom
The Crofts Down
Ellston Hill
Little Wood
The Giant
Clapper's Coppice
Weam Common Hill
Middle Hill Plantation
Combe Bottom
Acreman Cl 1
The Maltings 2
Springfield 3
Mill La 4
Abbey Ct 5
Riverside Cl 6
Simsayfields 7
Cerne Abbas CE First Sch
Pottery
Cerne Abbey
Abbey Gdns
Alton Lane
Hail Wood
Weam Coppice
Well Coppice
Mast
Acreman St
Dick's St
Long St
PO
Higher Down
Buckland Down
Cerne Park
Cerne Abbas
Up Sydling
Field System
Hare Coppice
The Folly
Back La
Abbots Wk
Higher Southcombe Farm
Piddle Wood
Alton Lane Farm
New Coppice
Sydling Rd
Tithe Barn
Piddle La
St Catherines Farm
Medieval Village of Elston (site of)
Hog Hill
Rowden Hill
Abbots Mdw
Chescombe Cl
Black Hill (Settlement)
Dorchester Road
Southcombe Plantation
Kiddle's Bottom
Dickley Hill
Barton Meadows Farm
Black Hill
Flintlock Farm
Ford
Tumuli
Tumulus
Pound Farm
Orchard Cl
Francombe Bottom
Hill Plantation
Dickley Down Farm
Cowdown Hill
Oxencombe Bottom
Sydling St Nicholas
Wessex Ridgeway
Higher City Farm
Higher Hill Bottom
Green Hill
Bramble Bottom
Greyhound Yd
River Cerne
Kingrove Wood
High St
PO
PH
Back La
Three Acres
Smacam Down
Lower Barton Farm
Bramble Bottom
East St
Church Hill Vw
Buck Hill
Higher City Farm
Church La
Dorchester Rd
Eastfield Hill
College Down
Huish Farm
Combe Bottom
Hill Barn
Pound Farm
Pound Bottom
Incombe Wood
A352
Bow's Hill
Sewage Works
Ridge Hill
Nether Cerne
Shearplace Hill
Strip Lynchets
Pond Bottom
Huish Plantation
63 64 65 66 67 68
05 04 03 02 01 00 99 98
8 7 6 5 4 3 2 1
74
75
208

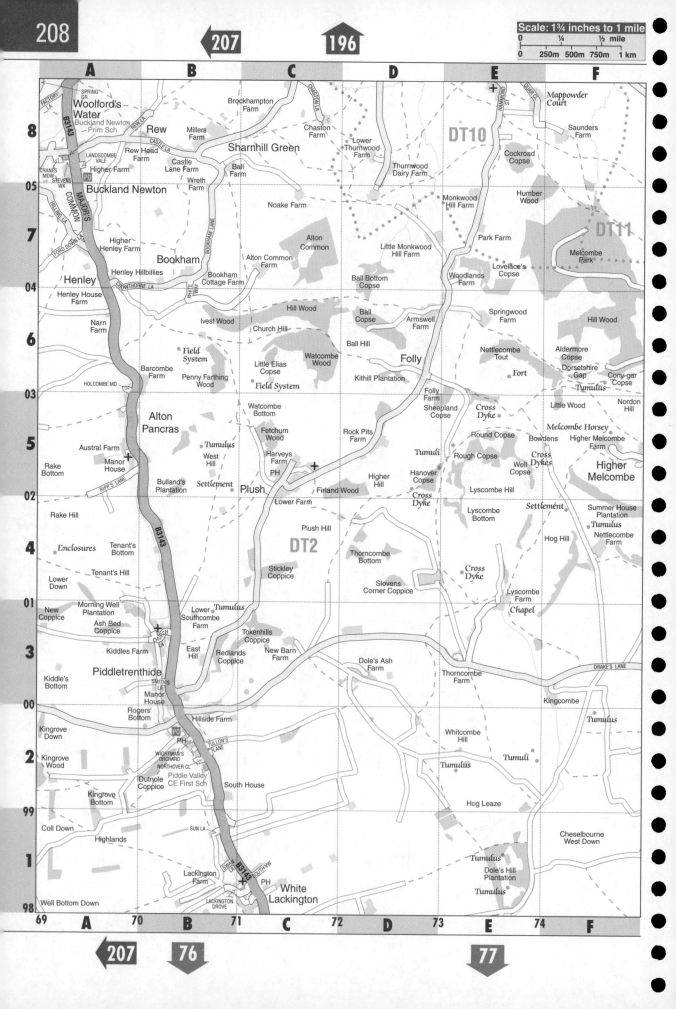

207
196

Scale: 1¾ inches to 1 mile

0   ¼   ½   mile
0   250m 500m 750m 1 km

Map labels (top to bottom, left to right)

FACTORY LA
SPRING GR
Woolford's Water
Buckland Newton Prim Sch
B3143
Brockhampton Farm
CHASTON LA
HAMMOND ST
QUAR CL
Mappowder Court
DT10

Rew
REW LA
Millers Farm
Chaston Farm
Lower Thurnwood Farm
Saunders Farm
Cockroad Copse
+

CASTLE LA
Sharnhill Green
Thurnwood Dairy Farm
Humber Wood

CRANES MDW
LANDSCOMBE VALE
Rew Head Farm
Castle Lane Farm
Ball Farm
Monkwood Hill Farm

STEVENS WK
Higher Farm
Wreth Farm
Noake Farm
Park Farm
DT11

Buckland Newton
HILLING LA
MAJOR'S COMMON

Henley
Higher Henley Farm
Bookham
Alton Common Farm
Alton Common
Little Monkwood Hill Farm
Woodlands Farm
Lovelace's Copse
Melcombe Park

FORD DOWN
CRONTHORNE LA
Henley Hillbillies
BOOKHAM LANE
Bookham Cottage Farm
Ball Bottom Copse

Henley House Farm
WHITE WAY
Hill Wood
Springwood Farm
Hill Wood

Narn Farm
Ivest Wood
Church Hill
Ball Copse
Armswell Farm
Ball Hill
Folly
Nettlecombe Tout
Fort
Aldermore Copse
Dorsetshire Gap
Cony-gar Copse

HOLCOMBE MD
Field System
Watcombe Wood
Kithill Plantation
Tumulus
Little Wood
Nordon Hill

Barcombe Farm
Penny Farthing Wood
Little Elias Copse
Folly Farm
Sheepland Copse
Cross Dyke

Alton Pancras
Field System
Watcombe Bottom
Rock Pits Farm
Round Copse
Melcombe Horsey
Bowdens
Higher Melcombe Farm

Austral Farm
Tumulus
Fetchum Wood
Tumuli
Rough Copse
Well Copse
Cross Dykes

Rake Bottom
Manor House
West Hill
Harveys Farm
PH
Hanover Copse
Higher Hill
Lyscombe Hill
Higher Melcombe

RIPP'S LANE
Bulland's Plantation
Settlement
Plush
Firland Wood
Cross Dyke
Settlement

Rake Hill
Lower Farm
Plush Hill
Lyscombe Bottom
Hog Hill
Summer House Plantation
Tumulus
Nettlecombe Farm

B3143
Enclosures
Tenant's Bottom
DT2
Thorncombe Bottom
Cross Dyke

Lower Down
Tenant's Hill
Stickley Coppice
Slovens Corner Coppice
Lyscombe Farm
Chapel

New Coppice
Morning Well Plantation
Lower Southcombe Farm
Tumulus
Tokenhills Coppice
Dole's Ash Farm

Ash Bed Coppice
CHURCH LA
Kiddles Farm
East Hill
Redlands Coppice
New Barn Farm
DRAKE'S LANE
Kingcombe

Kiddle's Bottom
Piddletrenthide
SMITH'S LA
Manor House
Thorncombe Farm
Tumulus

Rogers' Bottom
Hillside Farm
Whitcombe Hill
Tumuli

Kingrove Down
PO
PH
TULLON'S LANE
Tumulus

Kingrove Wood
WIGHTMAN'S ORCHARD
NORTHOVER CL
Piddle Valley CE First Sch
Dutnole Coppice
South House

Kingrove Bottom
SUN LA
Hog Leaze
Cheselbourne West Down

Coll Down
Highlands
SWAN LA
Tumulus
Dole's Hill Plantation

Well Bottom Down
B3143
SOUTH VW
Lackington Farm
LACKINGTON DROVE
PH
White Lackington
Tumulus

Grid letters: A B C D E F
Grid numbers (left): 8 05 7 04 6 03 5 02 4 01 3 00 2 99 1 98
Grid numbers (bottom): 69 70 71 72 73 74

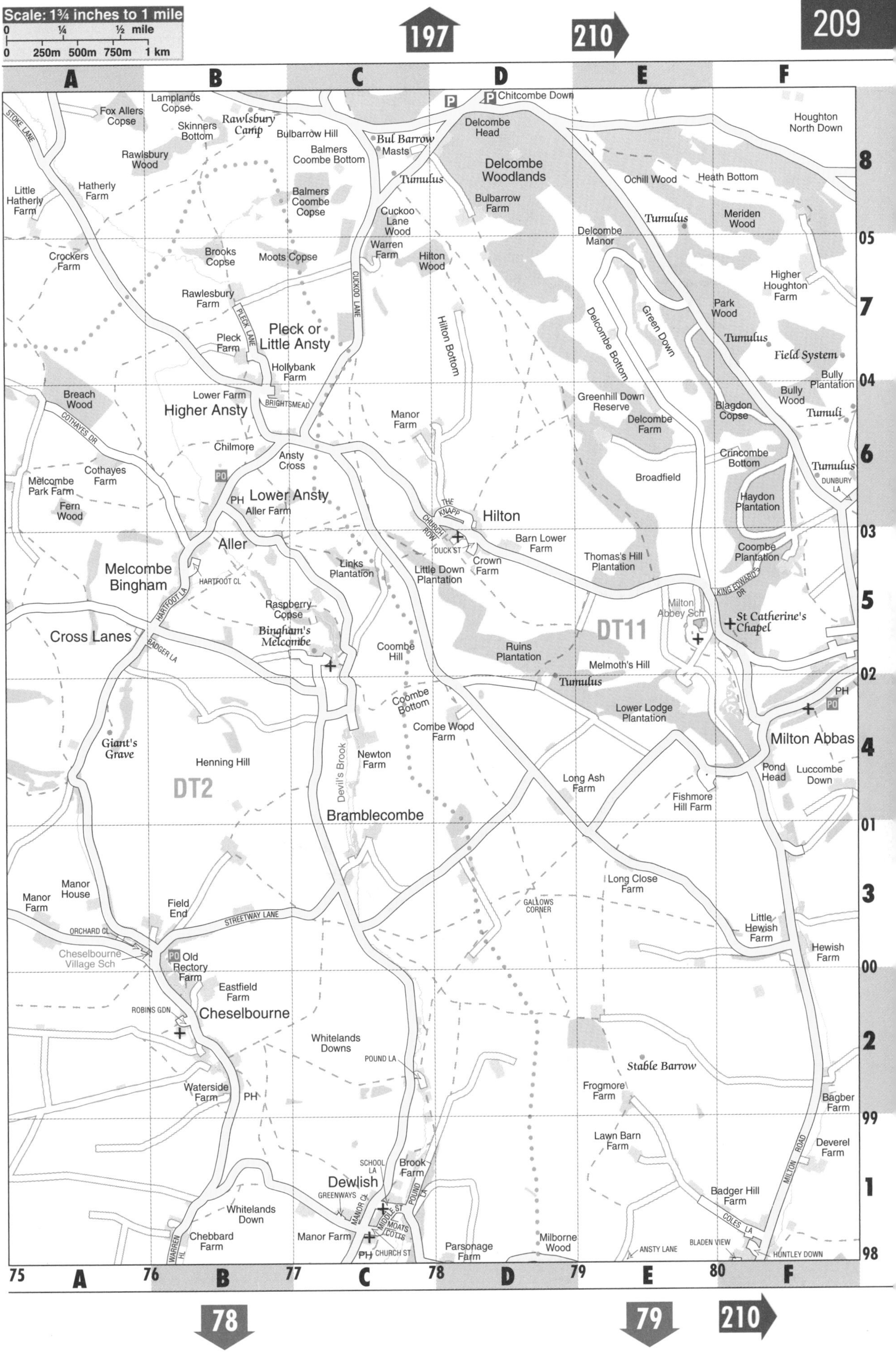
Scale: 1¾ inches to 1 mile
0 ¼ ½ mile
0 250m 500m 750m 1 km
197
210
78
79
210
Fox Allers Copse
Lamplands Copse
Skinners Bottom
Rawlsbury Camp
Bulbarrow Hill
Bul Barrow
Masts
Chitcombe Down
Delcombe Head
Delcombe Woodlands
Houghton North Down
Rawlsbury Wood
Balmers Coombe Bottom
Tumulus
Little Hatherly Farm
Hatherly Farm
Balmers Coombe Copse
Bulbarrow Farm
Ochill Wood
Heath Bottom
Cuckoo Lane Wood
Meriden Wood
Delcombe Manor
Crockers Farm
Brooks Copse
Moots Copse
Warren Farm
Hilton Wood
Higher Houghton Farm
Rawlesbury Farm
Cuckoo Lane
Pleck Lane
Hilton Bottom
Delcombe Bottom
Green Down
Park Wood
Pleck or Little Ansty
Pleck Farm
Field System
Hollybank Farm
Bully Plantation
Bully Wood
Breach Wood
Lower Farm
Higher Ansty
Brightsmead
Greenhill Down Reserve
Blagdon Copse
Tumuli
Manor Farm
Delcombe Farm
Cothayes Dr
Chilmore
Ansty Cross
Crincombe Bottom
Cothayes Farm
Broadfield
Melcombe Park Farm
PO
Lower Ansty
PH
Dunbury La
Haydon Plantation
Fern Wood
Aller Farm
The Knapp
Church Row
Hilton
Aller
Barn Lower Farm
Duck St
Coombe Plantation
Melcombe Bingham
Links Plantation
Crown Farm
Thomas's Hill Plantation
Little Down Plantation
Hartfoot Cl
King Edward's Dr
Hartfoot La
Raspberry Copse
Milton Abbey Sch
St Catherine's Chapel
DT11
Cross Lanes
Bingham's Melcombe
Badger La
Coombe Hill
Ruins Plantation
Melmoth's Hill
Coombe Bottom
Lower Lodge Plantation
Combe Wood Farm
Milton Abbas
Giant's Grave
Newton Farm
Henning Hill
Devil's Brook
Long Ash Farm
Pond Head
Luccombe Down
DT2
Fishmore Hill Farm
Bramblecombe
Manor House
Long Close Farm
Manor Farm
Field End
Streetway Lane
Gallows Corner
Little Hewish Farm
Orchard Cl
Hewish Farm
Cheselbourne Village Sch
Old Rectory Farm
Eastfield Farm
Robins Gdn
Cheselbourne
Whitelands Downs
Stable Barrow
Pound La
Waterside Farm
Frogmore Farm
Bagber Farm
Lawn Barn Farm
School La
Brook Farm
Deverel Farm
Milton Road
Dewlish
Greenways
Badger Hill Farm
Whitelands Down
Manor Cl
Middle St
Pound La
Moats Cotts
Coles La
Chebbard Farm
Manor Farm
Milborne Wood
Parsonage Farm
Warren Hl
Church St
Ansty Lane
Bladen View
Huntley Down
A B C D E F
8 7 6 5 4 3 2 1
05 04 03 02 01 00 99 98
75 76 77 78 79 80

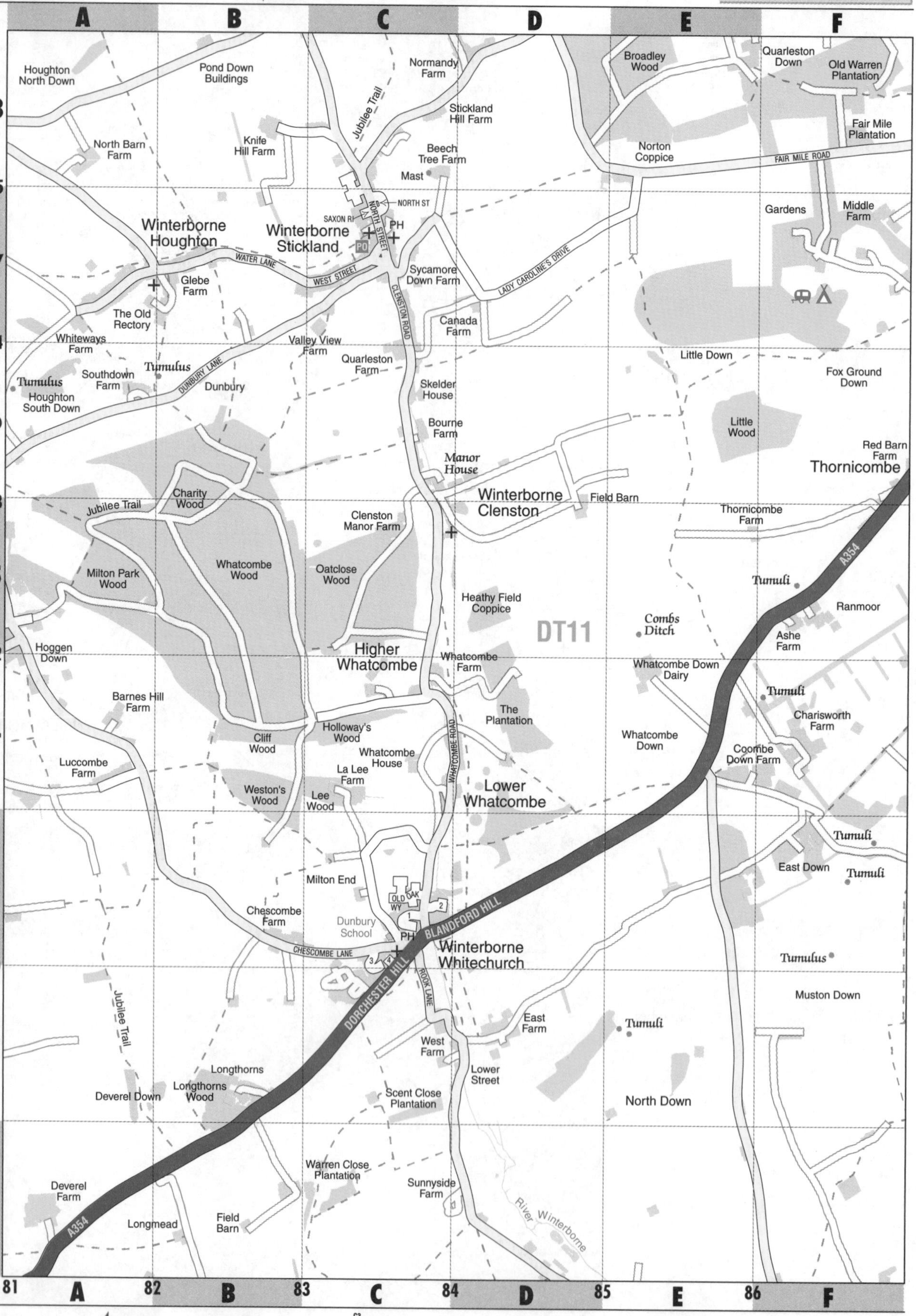

210

209

198

Scale: 1¾ inches to 1 mile
0   ¼   ½   mile
0   250m 500m 750m 1 km

A   B   C   D   E   F

8

Houghton
North Down

Pond Down
Buildings

Normandy
Farm

Broadley
Wood

Quarleston
Down

Old Warren
Plantation

North Barn
Farm

Knife
Hill Farm

Stickland
Hill Farm

Norton
Coppice

Fair Mile
Plantation

05

Beech
Tree Farm

Mast

FAIR MILE ROAD

JUBILEE TRAIL

NORTH STREET

NORTH ST

Winterborne
Houghton

Winterborne
Stickland

SAXON RI

PH

PO

Gardens

Middle
Farm

7

WATER LANE

WEST STREET

Sycamore
Down Farm

LADY CAROLINE'S DRIVE

Glebe
Farm

The Old
Rectory

Valley View
Farm

Canada
Farm

04

Whiteways
Farm

Tumulus

Quarleston
Farm

Little Down

Fox Ground
Down

Tumulus

Southdown
Farm

DUNBURY LANE

Dunbury

Skelder
House

CLENSTON ROAD

Houghton
South Down

Bourne
Farm

Little
Wood

Red Barn
Farm

6

Manor
House

Thornicombe

03

Jubilee Trail

Charity
Wood

Winterborne
Clenston

Field Barn

Thornicombe
Farm

A354

Clenston
Manor Farm

5

Milton Park
Wood

Whatcombe
Wood

Oatclose
Wood

Tumuli

Ranmoor

02

Hoggen
Down

Heathy Field
Coppice

DT11

Combs
Ditch

Ashe
Farm

Higher
Whatcombe

Whatcombe
Farm

Whatcombe Down
Dairy

Tumuli

Barnes Hill
Farm

The
Plantation

Charisworth
Farm

4

Cliff
Wood

Holloway's
Wood

Whatcombe
House

WHATCOMBE ROAD

Whatcombe
Down

Coombe
Down Farm

Luccombe
Farm

La Lee
Farm

Lower
Whatcombe

Weston's
Wood

Lee
Wood

Tumuli

01

East Down

Tumuli

3

Milton End

Chescombe
Farm

OLD OAK WY

2

East
Farm

BLANDFORD HILL

Dunbury
School

PH

Winterborne
Whitechurch

Tumulus

00

CHESCOMBE LANE

3

DORCHESTER HILL

BROOK LANE

Muston Down

2

Jubilee Trail

West
Farm

East
Farm

Tumuli

Longthorns

Scent Close
Plantation

Lower
Street

North Down

99

Longthorns
Wood

Deverel Down

Warren Close
Plantation

Sunnyside
Farm

1

Deverel
Farm

River Winterborne

A354

Longmead

Field
Barn

98

81   A   82   B   83   C   84   D   85   E   86   F

C3
1 FIELD'S CL
2 FOSTERS MDWS
3 ST MARY'S CL
4 SANDERS GN

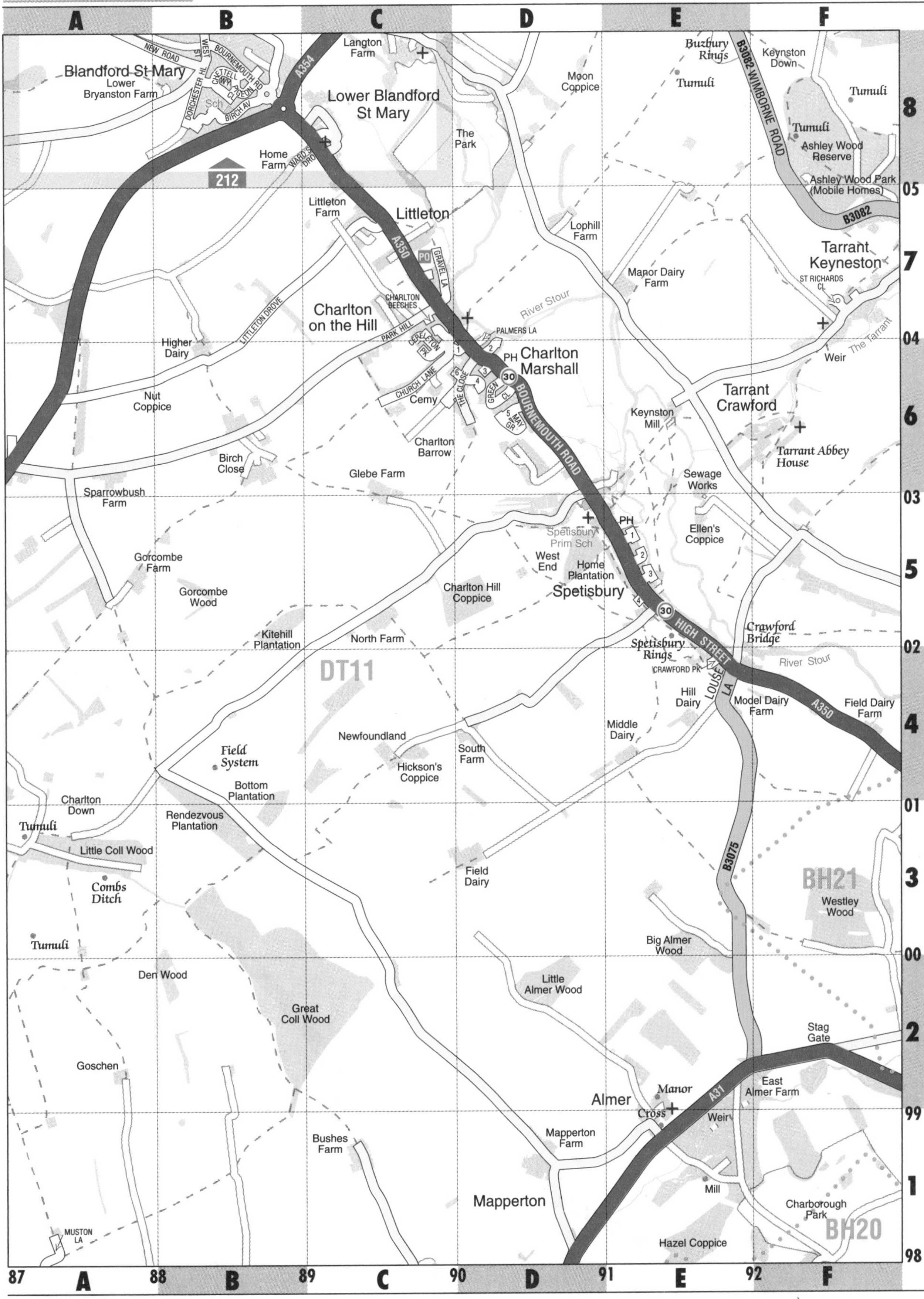

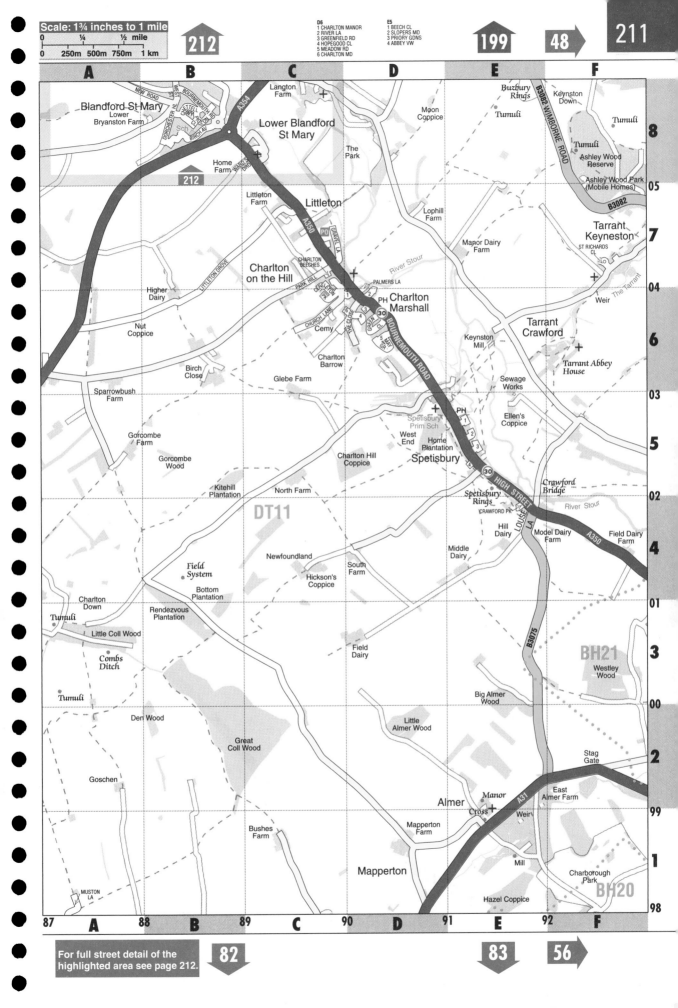

198
199
199

E5
1 HOLMLEA
2 STEVENS CL
3 NEWMAN CL
4 RICHMOND RD

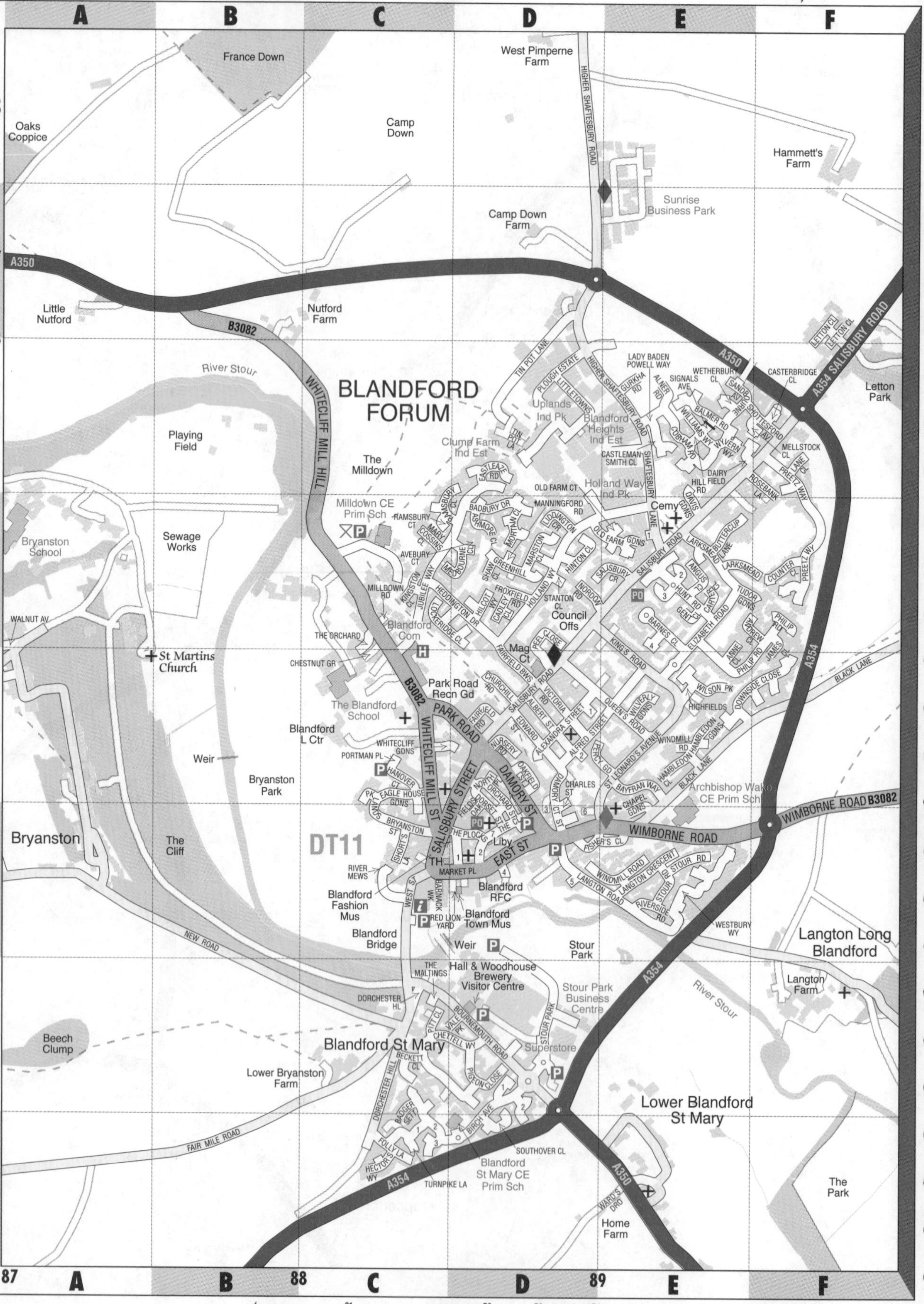

210
211
211

C1
1 UPPER SCHOOL LA
2 LOWER SCHOOL LA
3 BIRCH AVE

D2
1 KNIGHTS CL
2 ROSEFIELDS

D3
1 CHURCH LA
2 SHEEP MKT HL
3 DAMORY CT ST
4 COMMON LA
5 MEADOW VW
6 THE MOUNT
7 THE TABERNACLE

D4
1 BOUNDARY VW
2 FIELD VW RD

Index

Place name May be abbreviated on the map → **Church Rd** [6] Beckenham BR2..........**53** C6

Location number Present when a number indicates the place's position in a crowded area of mapping

Locality, town or village Shown when more than one place has the same name

Postcode district District for the indexed place

Page and grid square Page number and grid reference for the standard mapping

Cities, towns and villages are listed in CAPITAL LETTERS

Public and commercial buildings are highlighted in magenta **Places of interest** are highlighted in blue with a star★

Abbreviations used in the index

Acad	**Academy**	Comm	**Common**	Gd	**Ground**	L	**Leisure**	Prom	**Promenade**
App	**Approach**	Cott	**Cottage**	Gdn	**Garden**	La	**Lane**	Rd	**Road**
Arc	**Arcade**	Cres	**Crescent**	Gn	**Green**	Liby	**Library**	Recn	**Recreation**
Ave	**Avenue**	Cswy	**Causeway**	Gr	**Grove**	Mdw	**Meadow**	Ret	**Retail**
Bglw	**Bungalow**	Ct	**Court**	H	**Hall**	Meml	**Memorial**	Sh	**Shopping**
Bldg	**Building**	Ctr	**Centre**	Ho	**House**	Mkt	**Market**	Sq	**Square**
Bsns, Bus	**Business**	Ctry	**Country**	Hospl	**Hospital**	Mus	**Museum**	St	**Street**
Bvd	**Boulevard**	Cty	**County**	HQ	**Headquarters**	Orch	**Orchard**	Sta	**Station**
Cath	**Cathedral**	Dr	**Drive**	Hts	**Heights**	Pal	**Palace**	Terr	**Terrace**
Cir	**Circus**	Dro	**Drove**	Ind	**Industrial**	Par	**Parade**	TH	**Town Hall**
Cl	**Close**	Ed	**Education**	Inst	**Institute**	Pas	**Passage**	Univ	**University**
Cnr	**Corner**	Emb	**Embankment**	Int	**International**	Pk	**Park**	Wk, Wlk	**Walk**
Coll	**College**	Est	**Estate**	Intc	**Interchange**	Pl	**Place**	Wr	**Water**
Com	**Community**	Ex	**Exhibition**	Junc	**Junction**	Prec	**Precinct**	Yd	**Yard**

Index of towns, villages, streets, hospitals, industrial estates, railway stations, schools, shopping centres, universities and places of interest

A

Aaron Cl BH17 .... 119 F7
Abbey Cl
Sherborne DT9 .... 30 B5
[9] Tatworth TA20 .... 202 A8
Abbey Ct DT2 .... 207 D4
Abbey Gdns★ DT2 .... 207 D4
Abbey Gdns BH21 .... 60 D5
Abbey Mews [2] TA20 .... 202 A8
Abbey Prim Sch SP7 .... 12 D1
Abbey Rd
Sherborne DT9 .... 30 B6
West Moors BH22 .... 62 A8
Yeovil BA21 .... 26 F6
Abbey St
Cerne Abbas DT2 .... 207 D4
Crewkerne TA18 .... 191 E4
Hinton St George TA17 .... 191 C7
Abbey Trading Est BA21 .... 26 E6
Abbey View [4] DT11 .... 211 E5
Abbey Wlk SP7 .... 12 E2
Abbot Cl [14] DT8 .... 204 D4
ABBOTSBURY DT3 .... 149 B8
Abbotsbury Abbey (ruin)★ DT3 .... 149 B7
Abbotsbury Castle (Hill Fort)★ DT3 .... 130 D2
Abbotsbury Children's Farm★ DT3 .... 149 B7
Abbotsbury Hill DT3 .... 130 D1
Abbotsbury La DT2 .... 130 F7
Abbotsbury Rd
Corfe Mullen BH18 .... 86 F5
Weymouth DT4 .... 167 B3
Abbotsbury Subtropical Gdns★ DT3 .... 148 E7
Abbotsbury Swannery★ DT3 .... 149 B5
Abbots Cl BH23 .... 125 F7
Abbots Mdw DT2 .... 207 D3
Abbots Meade BA21, BA20 .... 26 F5
Abbots Quay [4] BH20 .... 142 E3
Abbots Way
Sherborne DT9 .... 29 F5
Yeovil BA21 .... 26 F7
Abbots Wlk DT2 .... 207 D4
Abbott Cl BH9 .... 122 A8
Abbott La TA16 .... 192 A8
Abbott Rd BH9 .... 122 A8
Abbotts Mdw BH16 .... 84 D3
Abbott St BH21 .... 57 F6
Abbotts Way BH22 .... 62 A8
Abbott's Way SP8 .... 5 F3
Abbott's Wootton La
Marshwood DT6 .... 202 E1
Whitechurch Canonicorum DT6 .... 65 D7
Abder Cross DT9 .... 14 F4
Abels La DT9 .... 14 E2
Aberdare Rd BH10 .... 89 E3
Abingdon Dr BH23 .... 126 C8
Abingdon Rd BH17 .... 119 D8
Abinger Rd BH7 .... 123 B6
Abney Rd BH10 .... 89 D3
Acacia Ave BH31 .... 45 E4
Acacia Cl DT4 .... 167 B6
Acacia Dr DT2 .... 75 D2
Acacia Rd SO41 .... 95 F3
Acer Ave [2] DT6 .... 68 F1
Acer Dr BA21 .... 26 E7
Ackerman Rd DT1 .... 108 C1
Acland Rd
Bournemouth BH9 .... 122 B8
[6] Dorchester DT1 .... 108 A2
Aconbury Ave [2] DT1 .... 107 C1
Acorn Ave BH15 .... 119 D2
Acorn Bsns Pk BH12 .... 120 B8
Acorn Cl
Christchurch BH23 .... 123 F8
New Milton BH25 .... 95 C4
St Leonards BH24 .... 54 A3
Acorns The
West Moors BH24 .... 62 B8
Wimborne Minster BH21 .... 60 A4
Acorn Way BH31 .... 45 C6
Acreman Cl DT2 .... 207 D4
Acreman Ct DT9 .... 30 A6
Acreman Pl DT9 .... 30 B5
Acreman St
Cerne Abbas DT2 .... 207 D4
Sherborne DT9 .... 30 B6
Acres Ct [6] BA22 .... 193 F8
Acres Rd BH11 .... 89 B2
ACTON BH19 .... 177 F1
Acton Rd BH10 .... 89 B1
Adamsfield Gdns BH10 .... 89 C2
ADAM'S GREEN BA22 .... 193 D2
Adastral Rd BH17 .... 119 F8
Adastral Sq BH17 .... 119 F8
Ad Astro Fst Sch BH17 .... 87 F1
ADBER DT9 .... 14 F5
Adber Cl BA21 .... 28 A8
Addington Pl BH23 .... 124 D6
Addiscombe Rd BH23 .... 124 A7
Addison Cl SP8 .... 6 A1
Addison Sq BH24 .... 55 D7
Addlewell La BA20 .... 27 D4
Adelaide Cl BH23 .... 123 F8
Adelaide Cres DT4 .... 167 B3
Adelaide La [17] BH1 .... 121 F3
Adeline Rd BH1, BH5 .... 122 E4
Admirals Cl DT9 .... 30 D8
Admirals Way BH20 .... 142 E6
Admirals Wlk [13] BH2 .... 121 D2
Admiralty Rd BH6 .... 123 F3
Adventure Wonderland★ BH23 .... 90 E7
Aerial Pk BH21 .... 60 E6
AFFPUDDLE DT2 .... 111 F7
Aggis Farm Rd BH31 .... 45 A6
Agglestone Rd BH19 .... 164 B1
Aigburth Rd BH19 .... 178 F3
Airetons Cl BH18 .... 87 C3
Airfield Cl DT2 .... 137 D5
Airfield Ind Est BH23 .... 124 F6
Airfield Rd BH23 .... 124 F6
Airfield Way BH23 .... 124 F7
Airspeed Rd BH23 .... 125 B7
Akeman Cl [8] BA21 .... 26 F7
Akeshill Cl BH25 .... 95 B5
Alamanda Rd DT3 .... 152 E2
Alamein Rd BH20 .... 139 F6
Alan Ct [10] BH23 .... 126 B7
Alastair Cl BA21 .... 27 B7
Alastair Dr BA21 .... 27 B7
Albany BH1 .... 122 C3
Albany Cl
Old Milton BH25 .... 94 F1
Sherborne DT9 .... 30 C8
Albany Ct [6] BH2 .... 121 F4
Albany Dr BH21 .... 45 A1
Albany Gdns BH15 .... 118 F2
Albany Ho [17] BH13 .... 121 A4
Albany Pk BH17 .... 119 B8
Albany Rd DT4 .... 166 E4
Albemarle Rd BH3 .... 121 F7
Albert Cl BA21 .... 27 A7
Albert Rd
Bournemouth BH1 .... 121 F3
Dorchester DT1 .... 107 F1
Ferndown BH22 .... 61 D5
New Milton BH25 .... 94 F2
Poole BH12 .... 120 D6
Poole BH21 .... 85 E5
Albert St
Blandford Forum DT11 .... 212 D4
[5] Radipole DT4 .... 167 D4
Albert Terr DT5 .... 186 E8
Albion Cl BH12 .... 120 B7
Albion Rd BH23 .... 91 F1
Albion Way BH31 .... 44 F6
Alby Rd BH12 .... 120 F5
ALCESTER SP7 .... 12 D2
Alcester Rd BH12 .... 120 D6
Aldabrand Cl DT3 .... 166 D4
Aldbury Ct BH25 .... 127 A7
Alderbury Cl [5] BH19 .... 178 F2
Alder Cl
Burton BH23 .... 92 D1
[3] Sandford BH20 .... 116 A1
Sturminster Newton DT10 .... 35 C2
Alder Cres BH12 .... 120 F7
Alder Dr SP6 .... 42 B5
Alder Gr
Crewkerne TA18 .... 191 F5
Yeovil BA20 .... 27 A2
Alder Hills BH12 .... 121 A7
Alder Hills Ind Pk BH12 .... 121 A7
Alder Hills Nature Reserve★ BH12 .... 121 A7
ALDERHOLT SP6 .... 42 B6
Alderholt Sports Club SP6 .... 42 C5
Alder Hts BH12 .... 121 A7
Alderley Rd BH10 .... 89 D4
ALDERNEY 88 C1
Alderney Ave BH12 .... 88 D1
Alderney Hospl BH12 .... 88 C2
Alderney Rdbt BH12 .... 88 D2
Alder Rd
Poole BH12 .... 120 F6
Sturminster Newton DT10 .... 35 C2
Aldis Gdns BH15 .... 118 E2
Aldondale Gdns BA20 .... 27 C3
Aldridge Rd
Bournemouth BH10 .... 89 C5
Ferndown BH22 .... 61 E3
Aldridge Way BH22 .... 61 F3
Alexander Cl
Christchurch BH23 .... 124 E6
New Milton BH25 .... 95 A3
Alexander Gdns [6] BH9 .... 90 A1
Alexandra Ct DT6 .... 100 C5
Alexandra Lodge [8] BH1 .... 122 A3
Alexandra Rd
Bournemouth BH6 .... 123 C5
Bridport DT6 .... 100 C6
Dorchester DT1 .... 107 F1
Poole BH14 .... 120 D5
Radipole DT4 .... 167 D5
Alexandra Rd *continued*
Weymouth DT4 .... 166 E3
Yeovil BA21 .... 27 F6
Alexandra St DT11 .... 212 D4
Alexandra Terr [8] DT1 .... 108 A2
Alexandria Ct BH22 .... 61 E3
Alford Rd BH3 .... 121 D7
Alfred Pl DT1 .... 108 B1
Alfred Rd DT1 .... 108 A1
Alfred St DT11 .... 212 D4
Alice Rd DT1 .... 107 E1
Alington [22] BH4 .... 121 C3
Alington Ave [1] DT1 .... 108 C1
Alington Cl BH14 .... 147 C7
Alington Ho BH14 .... 147 C7
Alington Rd
Bournemouth BH3 .... 122 A6
Dorchester DT1 .... 108 B1
Poole BH14 .... 147 C7
Alington St [4] DT1 .... 108 A2
Alington Terr [6] DT1 .... 108 B2
Alipore Cl BH14 .... 120 D3
Alipore Hts BH14 .... 120 D3
Alisons The BH20 .... 139 E2
Allberry Gdns DT3 .... 168 A8
Allenbourn Mid Sch BH21 .... 59 C5
Allenby Cl BH17 .... 87 B2
Allenby Rd BH17 .... 87 B2
Allen Cl [8] DT11 .... 198 C7
Allen Ct BH21 .... 59 C5
Allen Rd BH21 .... 59 C4
Allens La BH16 .... 117 F5
Allens Rd BH16 .... 117 F6
Allenview Rd BH21 .... 59 C5
ALLER DT2 .... 209 B5
Allingham Rd BA21 .... 27 E7
ALLINGTON DT6 .... 100 B7
Allington Gdns [3] DT6 .... 100 B8
Allington Mead [3] DT6 .... 100 C8
Allington Pk DT6 .... 100 B7
ALLOWENSHAY TA17 .... 191 A8
All Saints CE Prim Sch DT9 .... 196 A7
All Saints CE Sch DT4 .... 180 D8
All Saints' Rd
Dorchester DT1 .... 108 B2
Weymouth DT4 .... 180 C8
Alma Rd
Bournemouth BH9 .... 122 A7
Weymouth DT4 .... 167 C3

EAST END 58 E1
Easter Rd BH9 . . . . 90 A2
East Farm La DT2 . . . . 155 D7
Eastfield 4 DT9 . . . . 194 D8
Eastfield Ct BH24 . . . . 55 E7
Eastfield La
North Perrott TA18 . . . . . . 192 C4
Ringwood BH24 . . . . 55 E7
West Chinnock BA22 . . . . . 192 D8
EAST FLEET DT3 . . . . 166 B5
Easthams Rd TA18 . . . . . . 191 F4
Easthay La TA20 . . . . 202 D4
East Hill
Charminster DT2 . . . . 107 D6
Evershot DT2 . . . . 206 A7
EAST HOLME BH20 . . . . 159 E8
EAST HOLTON BH16 . . . . . . 117 A3
EAST HOWE 89 C3
East Howe La BH10 . . . . . . 89 C4
EAST KNIGHTON DT2 . . . . . 157 A8
East Knighton La DT2 . . . . 157 A7
East La TA18 . . . . 192 B8
Eastlake Ave BH12 . . . . . . 120 C6
Eastland Rd BA21 . . . . 27 E5
Eastlands
New Milton BH25 . . . . 95 B1
10 Yetminster DT9 . . . . 194 C5
Eastleaze Rd DT11 . . . . . . 212 D6
EAST LULWORTH BH20 . . . 173 D8
EAST MARTIN SP6 . . . . 190 C6
EAST MELBURY SP7 . . . . 24 D5
East Mill La DT9 . . . . 30 C6
EAST MORDEN BH20 . . . . . . 83 D4
East Morden Dro BH20 . . . . 83 D6
EASTON DT5 . . . . 187 B4
Easton Hollow SP7 . . . . . . 188 B7
Easton La DT5 . . . . 187 A5
Easton Sh Ctr DT5 . . . . . . 187 A4
Easton Sq 4 DT5 . . . . 187 A4
Easton St DT5 . . . . 187 A4
Eastop La DT10 . . . . 33 B5
EAST ORCHARD SP7 . . . . 36 E8
East Overcliff Dr BH1 . . . 122 C3
EAST PARLEY 90 B8
EAST PULHAM DT2 . . . . 196 D4
East Quay 10 BH15 . . . . . . 119 C1
East Quay Rd BH15 . . . . . . 119 C1
East Rd DT6 . . . . 100 E6
East Rd Bsns Pk DT6 . . . . 100 E6
East St
Beaminster DT8 . . . . 204 D4
Blandford Forum DT11 . . . 212 D3
Bourton SP8 . . . . 1 E1
Bridport DT6 . . . . 100 D6
Chickerell DT3 . . . . 166 C6
Corfe Castle BH20 . . . . 162 A1
Crewkerne TA18 . . . . 191 F4
Fortuneswell DT5 . . . . 186 F7
Milborne Port DT9 . . . . 17 D2
North Perrott TA18 . . . . . . 192 C4
Poole BH15 . . . . 119 C1
Radipole DT4 . . . . 167 E2
Sydling St Nicholas DT2 . . . 207 A2
Wareham BH20 . . . . 142 E3
West Coker BA22 . . . . 193 A8
Wimborne Minster BH21 . . . 59 C4
9 Winterborne Kingston DT11 . . . . 81 E8
EAST STOKE BH20 . . . . 140 F1
East Stoke Fen Reserve* BH20 . . . . 140 E2
EAST STOUR SP8 . . . . 10 E3
EAST STOUR COMMON SP8 . . . . 11 A3
East View Rd BH24 . . . . 55 D7
Eastville BA21 . . . . 27 E5
East Walls BH20 . . . . 142 F3
East Way
Bournemouth BH8 . . . . 90 C1
Poole BH21 . . . . 85 F5
East Weare Rd DT5 . . . . . 181 B1
Eastwell La DT10 . . . . 35 A8
Eastwood Ave BH22 . . . . . . 61 E6
Eastworth Rd BH31 . . . . . . 45 A7
East Wyld Rd DT4 . . . . 167 A3
Eaton Rd BH13 . . . . 121 A2
EBBLAKE BH31 . . . . 45 F4
Ebblake Cl BH31 . . . . 45 E3
Ebblake Ind Est BH31 . . . . . 45 E4
Ebenezer La 6 BH24 . . . . . 55 B7
Ebor Cl BH22 . . . . 61 E2
Ebor Rd
Poole BH12 . . . . 120 D6
Weymouth DT4 . . . . 180 C8
Ebury Ct 7 BH4 . . . . 121 C3
Eccles Rd BH15 . . . . 119 A2
ECCLIFFE SP8 . . . . 10 D7
Eddison Ave DT1 . . . . 108 C1
Eddy Green Rd BH16 . . . . . 84 B2
Eden Ct
9 Bournemouth BH1 . . . . 122 B3
11 Bournemouth, Westbourne BH4 . . . . 121 C2
Eden Gr BH21 . . . . 59 D3
Edenhurst 12 BH4 . . . . 121 C3
Edgarton Rd BH17 . . . . 87 D3
Edgehill Rd
Bournemouth BH9 . . . . 89 F1
Bridport DT6 . . . . 100 B5
Edgemoor Rd BH22 . . . . . . 53 C1
Edifred Rd BH9 . . . . 90 A4
Edith Ct 2 SP8 . . . . 5 E1
EDMONDSHAM BH21 . . . . . . 40 C3
Edmondsham Ho 16 BH2 121 E3
Edmondsham House & Gdns* BH21 . . . . 40 C4
Edmondsham Rd BH31 . . . 45 A7
Edmunds Cl 8 BH25 . . . . . 95 A1
Edward Cl BA22 . . . . 26 D6
Edward Cres BH20 . . . . . . 142 E4
Edward May Ct BH11 . . . . . 89 A4
Edward Rd
Bournemouth BH11 . . . . 89 B3
Christchurch BH23 . . . . . . 124 F8
Dorchester DT1 . . . . 107 F1
Poole BH14 . . . . 120 C5
Edwards Ct BH23 . . . . 126 A8
Edward St
Blandford Forum DT11 . . . 212 D4
4 Radipole DT4 . . . . 167 D4
Edwina Cl BH24 . . . . 47 E1
Edwina Dr BH17 . . . . 87 B2
Egdon Cl
Bere Regis BH20 . . . . 81 B2
Ferndown BH22 . . . . 61 B3
Egdon Ct 5 BH16 . . . . 117 D7
Egdon Dr BH21 . . . . 87 E8
Egdon Glen DT2 . . . . 137 E6
Egdon Rd
Dorchester DT1 . . . . 135 B7
Northport BH20 . . . . 142 D5
Egerton Ct BH8 . . . . 122 D6
Egerton Gdns BH8 . . . . . . 122 D6
Egerton Rd BH8 . . . . 122 D6
Eggardon Cl 5 DT8 . . . . . 204 C4
Eggardon Hill (Fort)* DT6 . . . . 71 A2
Egmont Cl BH24 . . . . 54 E2
Egmont Dr BH24 . . . . 54 F2
Egmont Gdns BH24 . . . . . . 54 E2
Egmont Rd BH16 . . . . 117 D4
Eight Acre Wood Nature Reserve* BH20 . . . . 140 A5
Eight August Rd BH20 . . . 139 E7
Elbury View SP7 . . . . 37 E7
Elderberry La BH23 . . . . . 124 F6
Elder Rd BH20 . . . . 81 A2
Eldon Ave BH25 . . . . 126 E8
Eldon Cl BH25 . . . . 126 E8
Eldon Ct 5 BH14 . . . . 120 A4
Eldon Pl BH4 . . . . 121 B3
Eldon Rd BH9 . . . . 89 E1
Eldons Dro BH16 . . . . 84 C3
Eldon Terr 5 BH19 . . . . . 179 B2
Eldridge Cl 3 DT1 . . . . . . 134 F7
Eleanor Ct BH25 . . . . 94 F1
Eleanor Dr BH11 . . . . 88 D5
Eleanor Gdns BH23 . . . . . 123 E8
Elfin Dr BH22 . . . . 61 C7
Elgar Rd BH10 . . . . 89 D4
Elgin Rd
Bournemouth BH4 . . . . 121 D6
Poole BH14 . . . . 120 C2
Elijah Cl BH15 . . . . 118 E2
Eliot Ho 8 BH25 . . . . 95 A2
Eliotts Dr BA21 . . . . 27 A7
Elise Cl BH7 . . . . 123 B8
Elizabeth Ave
Bridport DT6 . . . . 100 C5
Christchurch BH23 . . . . . . 123 F8
Elizabeth Cl 1 DT7 . . . . . . 96 C6
Elizabeth Ct
1 Bournemouth BH1 . . . . . 122 B3
Ferndown BH22 . . . . 61 D6
8 New Milton BH25 . . . . 95 B2
Elizabeth Gdns BH23 . . . . 125 D7
Elizabeth Pl DT1 . . . . 107 D1
Elizabeth Rd
Blandford Forum DT11 . . . 212 E5
Poole BH15 . . . . 119 D3
3 Upton BH16 . . . . 117 E7
Wimborne Minster BH21 . . . 59 C5
Elizabeth Way DT3 . . . . . . 166 E3
Ellerslie Cl DT2 . . . . 107 E6
Ellesdon DT6 . . . . 97 B8
Ellesfield Dr BH22 . . . . 61 D2
Elles Rd BH20 . . . . 139 D7
ELLINGHAM BH24 . . . . 47 B5
Ellingham Dr BH24 . . . . 46 E4
Ellingham Dro BH24 . . . . . . 47 E5
Ellingham Rd BH25 . . . . . 126 D8
Elliott Rd BH11 . . . . 88 F3
Elliott's Hill BA22 . . . . . . 192 D7
Elm Ave
Christchurch BH23 . . . . 91 E1
Holton Heath BH16 . . . . . . 116 B3
New Milton BH25 . . . . 95 A2
Elm Cl
Motcombe SP7 . . . . 7 B1
Overcombe/Preston DT3 . . 168 A6
Sturminster Newton DT10 . . 35 C1
Elm Ct 5 BH25 . . . . 95 A2
Elmes Rd BH9 . . . . 89 F2
Elmgate Dr BH7 . . . . 123 A7
Elm Gdns BH4 . . . . 121 C5
ELM HILL SP7 . . . . 7 B1
Elmhurst Ave BA21 . . . . 27 D7
Elmhurst Rd
Bournemouth BH11 . . . . 89 A5
Ferndown BH22 . . . . 53 B1
Elmhurst Way BH22 . . . . . . 53 B1
Elm La DT2 . . . . 75 D2
Elmleigh BA21 . . . . 26 E7
Elmore Dr BH24 . . . . 54 A6
Elmrise Cty Prim Sch BH11 . . . . 89 A4
Elms Ave BH14 . . . . 120 A1
Elms Cl BH14 . . . . 120 A1
Elmstead Rd BH13 . . . . . . 147 F8
Elms Way BH6 . . . . 123 E4
Elm Tree Wlk BH22 . . . . . . 89 E8
Elmwood Way BH23 . . . . . 126 A7
Elphinstone Rd BH23 . . . . . 94 B1
Elsdon's La DT6 . . . . 64 B4
Elston Medieval Village of* DT2 . . . . 207 A3
Eltham Cl BH7 . . . . 123 B8
Elvastone St 1 DT1 . . . . . 107 C1
Elveroakes Way DT4 . . . . 180 C6
Elvin Cl SO41 . . . . 95 F3
ELWELL DT3 . . . . 152 B6
Elwell DT6 . . . . 100 E5
Elwell Manor Gdns DT4 . 167 D1
Elwell St DT3 . . . . 152 B6
Elwood Cl BH20 . . . . 142 F8
Elwyn Rd BH1, BH8 . . . . . 122 C5
Elysium Ct BH22 . . . . 61 E3
Elziver Cl DT3 . . . . 166 D5
Embankment Way BH24 . . 55 D6
Emberley Cl BH22 . . . . 62 A6
Emerald Cl BH24 . . . . 54 A6
Emerson Cl 12 BH15 . . . . . 119 C2
Emerson Rd
Poole BH15 . . . . 119 D2
Weymouth DT4 . . . . 167 B2
Emily Cl BH23 . . . . 92 A1
Emily Ct BH14 . . . . 120 E5
Emley La 1 BH21 . . . . 201 C1
Emma Cl BH10 . . . . 89 D6
Emmadale Rd DT4 . . . . 167 B3
Emmanuel CE Mid Sch The BH31 . . . . 45 A4
Emminster Cl DT3 . . . . . . 168 A8
Empool Cl DT2 . . . . 137 D5
Emsbury Rd DT10 . . . . 35 C3
Encombe Cl BH12 . . . . 120 F8
Encombe Rd BH20 . . . . . . 142 D3
Endeavour Ind Pk BH24 . . 55 D6
Endfield Cl BH23 . . . . 91 F1
Endfield Rd
Bournemouth BH9 . . . . 90 A2
Christchurch BH23 . . . . 91 E1
Enfield Ave BH15 . . . . 119 E6
Enfield Cres BH15 . . . . . . 119 E6
Enfield Rd BH15 . . . . 119 E6
Englands Way BH11 . . . . . . 88 D4
English Ct 15 BH2 . . . . 121 D4
Enkworth Rd DT3 . . . . 168 A7
ENMORE GREEN SP7 . . . . . . 12 D3
ENSBURY 89 F6
Ensbury Ave BH10 . . . . 89 D1
Ensbury Cl BH10 . . . . 89 D1
Ensbury Ct BH10 . . . . 89 E2
ENSBURY PARK 89 C2
Ensbury Park Rd BH9 . . . . 89 E2
Enterprise Way BH23 . . . . . 90 C8
Epiphany CE Prim Sch The BH9 . . . . 90 B4
Erica Dr BH21 . . . . 85 F6
Ericksen Rd BH11 . . . . 89 C3
Erinbank Mans BH1 . . . . . 122 C3
Erin Rd BH20 . . . . 139 E7
Ermine St BA21 . . . . 26 F7
Erpingham Rd BH12 . . . . . 121 A5
Esmonde Way BH17 . . . . . 119 F8
Esplanade
Bridport DT6 . . . . 100 B1
Poole BH13 . . . . 147 F7
Portland DT5 . . . . 186 E8
Radipole DT4 . . . . 167 E2
Esplanade The DT4 . . . . . 167 E5
Essex Ave BH23 . . . . 91 F1
Essex Rd DT4 . . . . 167 C3
Etches Cl BH10 . . . . 89 D4
Ethelbert Rd BH21 . . . . 59 D4
Eton Gdns BH4 . . . . 121 C4
Eton Mans 2 BH6 . . . . 123 E3
Ettrick Rd BH13 . . . . 121 A1
Eucalyptus Ave BH24 . . . . . 54 C2
Euston Gr BH24 . . . . 55 C6
Evans Cl
Bournemouth BH11 . . . . 88 F1
St Leonards BH24 . . . . 54 A6
Evelyn Mews 1 BH9 . . . . . 89 F1
Evelyn Rd BH9 . . . . 90 A2
Evening Glade BH22 . . . . . . 61 E4
Eventide Homes BH8 . . . . . . 90 E2
Everdene Cl BH22 . . . . 61 C2
Everdene Dr DT3 . . . . 166 E3
Everdene Rd 2 DT1 . . . . . 135 B8
Everest Rd
Christchurch BH23 . . . . . . 124 E8
Weymouth DT4 . . . . 167 C1
Everetts La 1 DT11 . . . . . 198 B5
Everglades Cl BH22 . . . . . . 61 D7
Evergreen Cl BH21 . . . . 53 A8
Evergreen Path TA16 . . . . 191 F7
Evergreens BH24 . . . . 54 A6
Evering Ave BH12 . . . . 88 D1
Evering Gdns BH12 . . . . 88 C1
Everon Gdns BH25 . . . . 95 B1
EVERSHOT DT2 . . . . 206 A7
Evershot Rd BH8 . . . . 90 E2
Evershot Wlk 19 DT1 . . . . 107 D1
Eversleigh 10 BH2 . . . . 121 D2
Everton Rd 2 BA20 . . . . . . 27 C4
Evesham Ave BA21 . . . . 26 E6
Evesham Cl BH7 . . . . 123 B8
Evesham Ct BH13 . . . . 121 A1
Exbourne Manor BH1 . . . . 122 C3
Exbury Dr BH11 . . . . 88 F5
Excelsior Rd BH14 . . . . . . 120 C3
Exeter Cres BH2 . . . . 121 F3
Exeter Ct 5 BH23 . . . . 126 B7
Exeter La BH2 . . . . 121 F2
Exeter Park Mans BH2 . . 121 F2
Exeter Park Rd BH2 . . . . . 121 F2
Exeter Rd
Bournemouth BH2 . . . . 121 F3
4 Swanage BH19 . . . . 179 C2
Exton Rd BH6 . . . . 123 D7
Eynon Mews BH24 . . . . 55 B6
Eype Down Rd DT6 . . . . . . 99 E5

F

Factory Hill SP8 . . . . 1 F3
Factory La
Buckland Newton DT2 . . . . 207 F8
Tatworth & Forton TA20 . . . 202 A8
Factory Rd BH16 . . . . 117 E6
Fairclose DT4 . . . . 167 B1
Faircourt 8 BH25 . . . . 95 B3
Faircross Ave DT4 . . . . . . 167 C1
Fairey Cl SP8 . . . . 5 F3
Fairey Cres SP8 . . . . 5 F3
Fairfax DT6 . . . . 99 A6
Fairfield
Christchurch BH23 . . . . 124 B7
Crewkerne TA18 . . . . 191 E4
Sherborne DT9 . . . . 30 B7
Fairfield Bglws DT11 . . . . 212 D5
Fairfield Cl
Christchurch BH23 . . . . 124 B7
2 Okeford Fitzpaine DT11 197 F6
Wimborne Minster BH21 . . . 59 F5
Fairfield Hts DT9 . . . . 30 B7
Fairfield Pk DT7 . . . . 96 C6
Fairfield Rd
Barton on Sea BH25 . . . . . 126 E7
Blandford Forum DT11 . . . 212 D4
2 Dorchester DT1 . . . . 107 F1
Iwerne Courtney or Shroton DT11 . . . . 198 E7
Wimborne Minster BH21 . . . 59 D4
Fairhaven Ct 9 BH5 . . . . . 122 E4
Fairhouse Rd BA22 . . . . . 193 F8
Fairies Dr BH22 . . . . 61 F3
Fairlane SP7 . . . . 13 A2
Fairlawn BH22 . . . . 61 D5
Fair Lea BH2 . . . . 121 E2
Fairlie BH24 . . . . 47 E1
Fairlie Pk BH24 . . . . 47 D1
Fairlight La SO41 . . . . 95 D8
Fairmead Rd BA21 . . . . 27 E8
Fairmead Specl Sch BA21 27 E8
FAIRMILE 91 F1
Fairmile Parade BH23 . . . . 91 F1
Fairmile Rd BH23 . . . . 91 F1
Fair Mile Rd DT11 . . . . 210 F8
Fairoak Way 3 DT8 . . . . . 204 A7
Fairthorn Ct 3 BH2 . . . . . 121 F4
Fairview Cres BH18 . . . . . . 87 A5
Fairview Dr BH18 . . . . 87 A5
Fairview Pk BH14 . . . . 120 C3
Fairview Rd
Broadstone BH18 . . . . 87 A5
Weymouth DT4 . . . . 180 D7
Fairway Dr
Christchurch BH23 . . . . 123 F6
Wareham Town BH20 . . . . 142 C6
Fairway Rd BH14 . . . . 147 C8
Fairways BH22 . . . . 61 F6
Fairway The BH25 . . . . 127 B7
Fairway View BA21 . . . . 27 F6
Fairwinds BH13 . . . . 147 B3
Fairwood Rd BH31 . . . . 45 E5
Fairy Bridge Wlk 1 SP8 . . . . 5 F3
Falcon Dr BH23 . . . . 125 A5
Falconer Dr BH15 . . . . 118 E4
Falkland Sq 35 TA18 . . . . . 191 F4
Falkland Sq 2 BH15 . . . . . 119 C2
Fallows The BH25 . . . . 95 B5
Fancy Rd BH12 . . . . 120 B8
Fancys Cl DT5 . . . . 187 A4
Fancy's Row BH16 . . . . 116 B4
Fantley La SP8 . . . . 2 B1
Farcroft Rd BH12 . . . . 120 B5
Far Ends 4 BH14 . . . . 120 B4
Farfrae Cres DT1 . . . . 135 B8
Farm Cl
Radipole DT4 . . . . 167 A5
Ringwood BH24 . . . . 55 C8
Farm Ct BH21 . . . . 60 A4
Farmdene Cl BH23 . . . . 125 D8
Farmer Palmer's Farm Pk* BH16 . . . . 116 B5
Farmers Wlk 1 BH21 . . . . . 59 B6
Farm La
Christchurch BH23 . . . . 125 A5
West Lulworth BH20 . . . . . 172 D6
Farm Lane N BH25 . . . . . . 127 A8
Farm Lane S BH25 . . . . . . 127 A8
Farm Rd
Bradford Abbas DT9 . . . . . . 28 C2
Ferndown BH22 . . . . 52 F2
FARNHAM DT11 . . . . 188 C2
Farnham Rd BH12 . . . . 121 A7
Farriers Cl BH21 . . . . 60 B6
Farringdon Cl 2 DT1 . . . . 134 F7
FARRINGTON DT11 . . . . 37 A3
Farrington 24 BH4 . . . . 121 C2
Farr's Lodge Gdn* BH21 . 58 D4
Farr's Orch 5 TA16 . . . . . . 191 F7
Farthings Ct The 13 BH1 . 122 A3
Farwell Cl BH23 . . . . 92 C3
Farwell Rd BH12 . . . . 88 C2
Faversham
9 Bournemouth BH2 . . . . . 121 D2
Radipole DT4 . . . . 167 A6
Fawcett Rd BH25 . . . . 94 F2
Fawley Gn BH8 . . . . 90 D3
Fawn Gdns BH25 . . . . 94 F4
Fellowsmead DT10 . . . . 20 F2
Felton Cres BH23 . . . . 125 F8
Felton Ct BH14 . . . . 119 F5
Felton Rd BH14 . . . . 119 F5
Fenleigh Cl BH25 . . . . 95 B1
Fennel Rd BA12 . . . . 3 B6
Fennel Way BA22 . . . . 26 C5
Fenton Rd BH6 . . . . 123 C5
Fenway Cl DT1 . . . . 108 D1
Fenwick Ct BH8 . . . . 122 B5
Fern Bank
5 Bournemouth BH2 . . . . 121 F3
Three Legged Cross BH21 . . 53 A7
Fern Barrow BH12 . . . . . . 121 B7
Fern Brook La SP8 . . . . 6 B1
Fern Cl
Alderholt SP6 . . . . 42 C5
Burton BH23 . . . . 92 C2
Ferncroft Gdns BH10 . . . . . 89 D5
Ferncroft Rd BH10 . . . . 89 D5
Ferndale Gdns BA21 . . . . . 27 A6
Ferndale Rd
New Milton BH25 . . . . 95 B4
Radipole DT4 . . . . 167 D6
FERNDOWN 61 B5
Ferndown Fst Sch BH22 . . 61 C5
Ferndown Ind Est BH21 . . 60 F7
Ferndown L Ctr BH22 . . . . 61 B6
Ferndown Mid Sch BH22 . 61 C5
Ferndown Rd DT7 . . . . 96 C5
Ferndown Upper Sch BH22 . . . . 61 B6
Ferne Hollow SP7 . . . . 188 A8
Fernglade BH25 . . . . 95 A3
Fernheath Cl BH11 . . . . 89 A3
Fernheath Rd BH11 . . . . . . 89 A3
Fern Hill SP8 . . . . 11 A3
Fernhill Ave DT4 . . . . 167 D6
Fernhill Cl BH17 . . . . 88 A2
Fernhill Flats 6 BH2 . . . . . 121 F3
Fernhill Gate BH25 . . . . 95 A5
Fernhill La BH25 . . . . 95 A4
Fernhill Rd BH25 . . . . 95 A3
Fernlea BH23 . . . . 124 D6
Fernlea Ave BH22 . . . . 61 D4
Fernlea Cl
Ferndown BH22 . . . . 61 D4
St Leonards BH24 . . . . 54 A4
Fernlea Gdns BH22 . . . . 61 D4
Fern Rd DT2 . . . . 139 B3
Fernside Ave BH14 . . . . . . 119 F4
Fernside Bsns Pk BH22 . . . 61 A7
Fernside Ct BH15 . . . . 119 E4
Fernside Rd
Bournemouth BH9 . . . . 121 E8
Ferndown BH22 . . . . 53 A2
Poole BH15 . . . . 119 E4
Fernway Cl BH21 . . . . 60 B4
Fernwood Cl BH24 . . . . 54 D5
Ferris Ave BH8 . . . . 90 D2
Ferris Cl BH8 . . . . 90 D2
Ferris Pl BH8 . . . . 90 D2
Ferrymans Way DT4 . . . . . 180 D5
Ferry Rd
Bournemouth BH6 . . . . 123 F3
Poole BH19 . . . . 147 A1
Poole, Lower Hamworthy BH15 . . . . 119 B1
Studland BH19 . . . . 164 C3
Ferry Way BH13 . . . . 147 B3
Feversham Ave BH8 . . . . . . 90 E1
FIDDLEFORD DT10 . . . . 197 F8
Fiddleford Manor* DT10 . . . . 197 F8
Field Barn Dr DT4 . . . . 167 B5
Field Cl DT10 . . . . 35 C2
Fieldfare Cl DT3 . . . . 152 D3
Fielding Rd BA21 . . . . 27 E6
Fieldings The SP8 . . . . 10 D3
Field La
Gillingham SP8 . . . . 5 B4
Kington Magna SP8 . . . . 9 D2
Pen Selwood BA9 . . . . 1 B3
Field Pl
Barton on Sea BH25 . . . . . 126 D8
Verwood BH31 . . . . 45 A7
Fields Barn DT2 . . . . 156 E5
Field's Cl 1 DT11 . . . . 210 C3
Fields Oak DT11 . . . . 212 D4
Fields The BA12 . . . . 3 B6
Field View Rd 2 DT11 . . . 212 D4
Fieldway BH24 . . . . 55 D8
Field Way
Christchurch BH23 . . . . 93 D1
Corfe Mullen BH21 . . . . 86 E8
Fifehead Hill SP8 . . . . 20 F7
FIFEHEAD MAGDALEN SP8 . . . . 20 F7
FIFEHEAD NEVILLE DT10 . . . . 197 C5
FIFEHEAD ST QUINTIN DT10 . . . . 197 B5
Fifehead Wood* SP8 . . . . 20 E8
Fifth St BH20 . . . . 162 C6
Filbridge Rise DT10 . . . . . . 35 C2
FILFORD DT6 . . . . 67 E7
Filford La DT6 . . . . 67 E8
Filleul Rd BH20 . . . . 115 F1
Fillybrook Bsns Pk SP8 . . . . 9 B5
Finches The DT3 . . . . 152 C3
Finchfield Ave BH11 . . . . . . 88 F6
Findlay Pl BH19 . . . . 178 F3
Fineshade 7 BH13 . . . . . . 147 F7
Finger La DT9 . . . . 30 B5
Fippenny Hollow 3 DT11 . . . . 197 F5
Fir Ave
Holton Heath BH16 . . . . . . 116 B3
New Milton BH25 . . . . 95 B2
Firbank Rd BH9 . . . . 122 B8
Firch La DT6 . . . . 101 B6
Fir Cl BH22 . . . . 53 A3

Fir Dr DT3 153 C3
Firecrest Cl DT3 152 C4
Firmain Rd BH12 88 D1
Firs Glen Rd
Bournemouth BH9 121 E8
Ferndown BH22 53 A2
Verwood BH31 45 B5
Firshill BH23 125 E8
Firside Rd BH21 85 E4
Firs La BH14 147 B8
First Cliff Wlk 1 DT6 100 B2
Firs The BH1 122 A4
First Marine Ave BH25 126 F7
Firsway BH16 118 C7
Fir Tree Cl
Dorchester DT1 107 D2
St Leonards BH24 53 F2
Firtree Cres SO41 95 F3
Fir Tree Hill SP6 42 C6
Fir Tree La BH23 93 D1
Fir Vale Rd BH1 121 F3
Fisherbridge Rd DT3 168 C8
Fisherman's Ave BH5 123 B4
Fisherman's Bank BH23 124 E5
Fishermans Cl DT3 166 D6
Fishermans Rd BH15 119 C1
Fisherman's Wlk BH5 123 B4
Fishers Cl DT9 14 E2
Fisher's Cl DT11 212 D3
Fisher's La TA17 191 A7
Fishers Pl DT2 170 A7
Fisherway La TA19 191 A5
Fishey La SP7 36 E5
Fishpond Bottom Rd
DT6 202 D1
Fishweir Fields 1 DT6 68 F1
Fishweir La DT6 68 F1
Fitzharris Ave BH9 122 A7
Fitzmaurice Rd BH23 123 E8
Fitzpain Cl BH22 61 D2
Fitzpain Rd BH22 61 D2
Fitzwilliam Cl BH11 88 E5
Fitzworth Ave BH16 117 E4
Five Acres
Charmouth DT6 97 A7
Yeovil BA22 193 F8
Fiveways Sch BA21 27 F6
Flag Farm BH13 147 D7
Flaghead BH13 147 E6
Flaghead Chine Rd BH13 147 E6
Flaghead Rd BH13 147 F7
Flambard Ave BH23 92 A1
Flambard Rd BH14 120 C2
Flanders Cl DT10 21 A2
Flaxfield Dr 15 TA18 191 F4
Flax La DT9 28 F7
Flax Way BA21 26 E6
Flazen Cl BH11 88 D3
FLEET DT3 166 A5
Fleet Ct DT3 166 E3
Fleet Rd DT3 166 A5
Fleetsbridge Bsns Ctr
BH17 119 B7
Fleet's Cnr BH17 119 B7
Fleets Est BH15 119 B6
Fleets La BH15 119 C6
Fleetspoint Bsns Ctr
BH15 119 B5
Fleet St DT8 204 D4
Fleet View DT4 180 C7
Fleetwood Ct BH15 119 C7
Fletcher Cl BH10 89 D3
Fletcher Rd BH10 89 D3
Flood La DT6 100 D4
Floral Farm BH21 60 A2
Florence Rd
Bournemouth BH5 122 F4
Dorchester DT1 134 E8
Poole BH14 120 D4
Floriston Gdns BH25 95 D3
Flower Ct BH21 59 D3
Flowers Dro BH16 84 D4
Flushing Mdw BA21 28 A5
FOLKE DT9 195 D8
Folke La DT9 31 A1
FOLLY DT2 208 D6
Folly Farm La BH24 54 E6
Folly Fields BA21 27 D7
Folly La
Blandford St Mary DT11 212 C1
Gillingham SP8 10 D5
Kington Magna SP8 9 E4
Nether Compton DT9 28 F8
Wareham BH20 142 E4
Wool BH20 140 A2
Folly Mill Gdns DT6 100 D6
Folly Mill La DT6 100 D6
Folly The DT2 207 D4
Font La BA22 193 B7
Fontmell Down Reserve*
SP5 24 D1
FONTMELL MAGNA SP7 37 F7
FONTMELL PARVA DT11 36 D2
Fontmell Rd BH18 87 C3
Font Villas BA22 193 B7
Footners La BH23 92 C2
Foot's Hill SP7 24 B7
Ford Cl BH22 61 F7
Ford Down La DT2 208 A7
Forde Abbey & Gdns*
TA20 202 C8
Forde Pk BA21 26 E7
Fordhay BA22 192 E7
FORDINGBRIDGE SP6 43 B8
Fordingbridge Rd SP6 42 C7
Fordington Gdns 3 DT1 108 B1
Fordington Gn 5 DT1 108 B2
Ford La BH22 62 A7
Forehill Cl DT3 168 B8
Foreland Cl BH23 91 D4
Foreland Rd BH16 117 D4
Fore St
Evershot DT2 206 A7
Thorncombe TA20 202 E6
Forest Cl
Christchurch BH23 93 D1
Verwood BH24 45 F4
Forest Ct BH25 95 B2
Forest Edge BH25 95 C4
Forest Edge Dr BH24 53 F5
Forest Edge Rd BH20 142 F7
Forest Gate Ct BH24 55 B7
Forest Hill BA20 27 A2
Forest Hills Ct 3 BH24 55 F6
Forest Ho 14 BH1 122 A3
Forest La
Corfe Castle BH20 162 F1
Verwood BH31 45 A7
Forestlake Ave BH24 55 F6
Forest Links Rd BH21 52 D1
Forest Oak Dr BH25 95 A5
Fore Store St TA20 202 A8
Forest Pines BH25 95 A4
Forest Rd
Ferndown BH22 53 B3
Poole BH13 121 A2
Forest Rise BH23 93 D2
Forestside Gdns BH24 47 E1
Forestside The BH31 45 F5
Forest View
Beckley BH25 94 D5
Crossways DT2 137 D6
Forest View Cl BH9 90 A2
Forest View Dr BH21 61 A5
Forest View Rd BH9 90 A3
Forest Way
Christchurch BH23 93 D1
Ferndown BH21 61 A5
Forest Wlk BH25 94 D5
Forge End SP8 10 D2
Forge La
East Chinnock BA22 192 E8
Verwood BH31 44 F5
Zeale SP8 1 F3
Forsters La DT6 69 A1
FORSTON DT2 75 B4
Forsyth Gdns BH10 89 C1
Fort Cumberland Cl 2
BH15 117 F2
Fortescue Rd
Bournemouth BH3 122 A6
Poole BH12 120 D6
Forton Cl BH10 89 E4
Fortress Gn 5 DT1 134 E7
FORTUNESWELL DT5 186 F7
Fortuneswell DT5 186 E8
Forty Foot Way DT6 100 B2
Forum Ctr The DT1 108 A2
Forum Gn 1 DT1 134 E7
Forum Sch The DT11 198 B6
Fosse Cl BA21 26 F7
Fosse Gn 7 DT1 134 E7
Fosse Park Rd BA20 27 B4
Fossett Way 4 DT4 180 B8
Fosse Way 1 BA21 26 F7
Foss Orch DT6 99 A6
Foss Way TA17 191 C8
Fosters Hill DT9 196 B5
Fosters Mdws 2 DT11 210 C3
Fosters Spring BH16 84 D2
Foundry Cl DT6 100 A7
Foundry Knapp DT6 100 A7
Foundry La DT6 100 C6
Foundry Sq 13 TA18 191 F4
Fountain Ct BH13 121 B2
Fountain Mead 3 SP7 12 F4
Fountain Rdbt BH23 124 B6
Fountains Cl BA21 26 E7
Fountain Way BH23 124 B6
Fouracre Cl DT6 100 D8
Four Acres DT5 186 E3
Fourgates Rd 1 DT1 107 E1
Fourth Cliff Wlk DT6 100 B2
Four Wells Rd BH21 60 A7
Foxbury BH20 139 C7
Foxbury Rd BH24 54 B1
Fox Cl DT6 69 A1
Foxcote 1 BA20 26 E2
Foxcote Gdns BH25 94 F3
Foxcroft Dr BH21 60 B5
Foxdale BH23 91 D1
Foxdale Ct 17 BH2 121 E3
Foxes Cl BH31 45 B5
Foxglove Cl
Christchurch BH23 125 C8
Gillingham SP8 5 E2
Foxglove Pl BH25 95 D4
Foxgloves 2 BH16 117 D7
Foxglove Way
Bridport DT6 100 D3
Radipole DT3 152 F2
Yeovil BA22 26 C5
Foxhill Cl 8 BH19 179 A2
Foxhills BH31 45 D6
Foxhills Cres BH16 84 D3
Foxhills Dr BH16 84 D3
Foxhills Rd BH16 84 D3
FOXHOLES 120 A6
Foxholes 1 BH6 123 F4
Foxholes Rd
Bournemouth BH6 123 F4
Poole BH15 119 F6
Fox La BH21 60 C5
Fox La Terr DT10 35 B1
Fox Mdws 16 TA18 191 F5
Foxs Cl DT9 196 B5
Foxwell La TA18 192 C7
Foxwood Ave BH23 124 F5
Foylebank Way DT5 181 B1
Foyle Hill SP7 12 C1
Framerville Rd BH20 139 E7
FRAMPTON DT2 73 F3
Frampton Cl BH25 95 C5
Frampton Pl BH24 55 C7
Frampton Rd
Bournemouth BH9 122 A8
16 Pimperne DT11 199 D4
Francesca Ct 5 BH23 124 E7
Francesca Grange 4
BH23 124 E7
Francesca Lo 1 BH23 124 E6
Frances Ct 7 BH23 126 B7
Frances Rd BH1 122 C4
Franchise St DT4 167 D2
Francis Ave BH11 88 D3
Francis Avenue Ind Est
BH11 88 D3
Francis Rd
Poole BH12 120 E5
Weymouth DT4 167 B2
Francis Wlk DT9 30 C7
Frankland Cres BH14 120 E3
Franklin Cl DT4 167 B2
Franklin Rd
Bournemouth BH9 90 A3
New Milton BH25 95 C4
Weymouth DT4 167 B3
Franklyn Cl BH16 117 D7
Frankston Rd BH6 123 C4
Franks Way BH12 120 B7
Frank Wareham Cottage
Homes The BH9 90 A4
Fraser Ave DT4 166 F1
Fraser Ct BH25 94 F3
Fraser Rd BH12 120 F8
Freame Way SP8 5 D1
Freda Rd BH23 123 F6
Frederica Rd BH9 121 E8
Freedom Ave BA21 27 A6
Freemans Cl BH21 60 B6
Freemans La BH21 60 B5
Freemantle Rd DT4 166 F1
Freesia Cl DT3 152 E2
Fremington Ct 6 BH25 95 B3
French Hill La SP7 23 F4
French Mill La SP7 23 F7
French Mill Rise SP7 12 F1
French Rd BH17 87 B1
French's Farm Rd BH16 117 B7
Frensham Cl BH10 89 E3
Freshwater Cl 4 DT5 186 E1
Freshwater Dr BH15 117 F4
Freshwater Rd BH23 125 C6
Friars Ave BA21 26 F6
Friars Cl 2 DT1 135 C8
FRIARS CLIFF 125 D7
Friars Gate BH23 125 C6
Friars Moor DT10 35 C1
Friars Rd BH23 125 B6
Friars Wlk BH25 127 A8
Friar Waddon Rd DT3 151 F8
Friary Hill DT1 108 A2
Friary La DT1 108 A2
Friday's Heron BH21 40 B7
Frinton Ct 2 BH14 120 A4
Fritham Gdns BH8 90 D3
Frizzel's Hill DT10 196 F4
Frobisher Ave BH12 88 F1
Frobisher Cl
Christchurch BH23 124 F6
Ringwood BH24 47 E1
FROGHAM SP6 43 F7
Frogham Hill SP6 43 F6
Frog La
Crewkerne TA18 192 C5
Dinnington TA17 191 B8
Fordingbridge SP6 43 A7
Iwerne Courtney or Shroton
DT11 198 F7
Motcombe SP7 12 C7
Frogmore La DT2 71 E8
Frog Rd SP8 11 B8
Frome Ave BH20 139 F2
Frome La DT2 72 F7
Frome Rd BH20 142 D3
FROME ST QUINTIN DT2 206 D5
Frome Terr DT1 108 A2
Frome Valley CE Fst Sch
DT2 137 D6
Frome Valley Rd DT2 137 C6
Frome View
Bradford Peverell DT2 107 A6
Maiden Newton DT2 73 A8
Front La BH21 56 D5
Front St
East Stour SP8 10 F3
Portesham DT3 132 A1
Froom's La BH20 81 C1
Frost Rd BH11 88 F3
Froud Way BH21 85 E4
Froxfield Rd DT11 212 D5
Fryer Cl BH11 89 B5
Fryers Copse BH21 60 C6
Fryers Rd BH21 53 A8
Frys Cl BH16 84 C4
Fry's Cl DT3 150 A8
Fry's La DT2 75 A7
Fudge Hill DT2 205 A8
Fulbrooks Cl DT6 100 C7
Fulbrooks La DT6 100 C7
Fulcrum Ctr The BH12 88 C2
Fulmar Rd BH23 125 A5
Fulwood Ave BH11 88 E5
Furbers Paddock DT2 106 E8
Furge Gr BA8 19 A4
Furge La BA8 19 A3
Furland Rd 6 TA18 191 F4
Furlands DT5 186 F3
Furlong La DT9 17 B3
Furlong Mews 3 BH24 55 B7
Furlong Sh Ctr BH24 55 B7
Furlongs The DT9 30 B7
Furlong The BH24 55 B7
Furnell Rd BH15 119 D1
FURZEBROOK BH20 161 A4
Furzebrook Cl BH17 87 E3
Furzebrook Rd BH20 161 A4
Furze Croft BH25 95 A2
FURZEHILL BH21 50 E1
Furzehill
Colehill BH21 59 C8
Holt BH21 50 F1
Furze Hill Dr BH14 120 C1
Furze La DT8 204 D3
Furzelands Rd BH21 53 A8
Furze The 2 BA20 26 E2
Furzey Rd BH16 117 D6
Furzy Cl DT3 168 B7

G

Gablehurst BH16 118 C7
Gabriel Gn 1 DT1 135 B8
Gadbridge Ct 14 BH4 121 C2
Gainsborough DT9 17 C2
Gainsborough Ave BH25 95 B5
Gainsborough Ct 4 BH5 123 B5
Gainsborough Dr DT9 29 E5
Gainsborough Hill DT9 30 C4
Gainsborough Ho BH25 127 A6
Gainsborough Rd
Bournemouth BH7 122 F7
St Leonards BH24 54 A5
Gainsborough Way BA21 28 A8
Galahad Cl 4 BA21 26 F7
Gale Cres DT6 100 C5
Gales Hill DT2 207 E7
Gallop's La BH20 83 C2
Gallop Way BH12 121 C7
Galloway Rd BH15 117 F4
Gallows Cnr
Iwerne Courtney or Shroton
DT11 36 F1
Milton Abbas DT11 209 D3
Gallows Dr BH22 61 E1
Gallows Hill
Arne BH20 161 C4
Owermoigne DT2 155 D6
Gallwey Rd DT4 180 C7
Galton Ave BH23 123 F6
GANNETTS DT10 21 C4
Gannetts Pk BH19 179 B3
Garden Cl
Bridport DT6 100 D7
Litton Cheney DT2 103 B2
New Milton BH25 95 A1
Garden Ct BH1 122 D6
Garden Ho 6 BH1 122 B3
Garden La BH24 54 A3
Gardens Cres BH14 147 B8
Gardens Ct 5 BH15 119 E3
Gardenside 1 DT6 97 A7
Gardens Rd BH14 147 B8
Garden Wlk BH22 61 E7
Gardner Ct BH23 123 E8
Gardner Rd
Christchurch BH23 123 E8
Ringwood BH24 55 D6
Garfield Ave
Bournemouth BH1 122 D5
Dorchester DT1 134 E8
Garfield La BH19 178 B2
Garland Cres DT1 135 B8
Garland Rd BH15 119 D4
Garlands La DT11 197 D4
Garrett Rd BA20 26 F3
Garsdale Cl BH11 89 A6
Garston Hill DT3 166 C6
Garston Wood (RSPB
Reserve)* SP5 189 B6
Gartells 1 DT10 197 A4
Garth Cl BH24 53 F4
Garth Rd BH9 90 A1
Gascoigne's La SP7 23 E8
Gascoyne La DT2 107 B6
Gashay La EX13 202 E3
Gas House Hill DT9 30 C5
Gas La TA17 191 C7
GASPER BA12 1 C7
Gasper St BA12 1 C6
Gassons La DT6 66 A4
Gate Cl EX13 202 A3
Gatecombe Cl 6 DT1 135 C8
Gatemore Rd DT2 138 E1
Gateway The BH13 120 F4
GAUNT'S COMMON BH21 51 B8
Gavel The DT10 35 B1
Gaydon Rise BH11 88 E4
Gazelle Rd BA20 26 F3
Geelong Cl DT3 152 E2
Geneva Ave BH6 123 D5
Gent Cl DT11 212 E5
George La 29 TA18 191 F4
George Rdbt The BH15 119 C3
Georges Cl DT6 97 B8
Georges Mews BH21 85 F7
George Smith Way BA22 26 C6
George St
Bridport DT6 100 C2
Sherborne DT9 30 B6
Georgian Cl BH24 55 C8
Georgian Way BH10 89 F4
Georgina Cl BH12 121 C8
Georgina Talbot Ho
BH12 121 B8
Gerald Rd BH3 122 A6
Germaine Cl BH23 125 F8
Gervis Cres BH14 120 A4
Gervis Pl BH1 121 F3
Gervis Rd BH1 122 B3
Giant's Grave* DT2 209 A4
Gibbs Ct 18 TA18 191 F5
Gibbs Gn BH16 84 D2
Gibbs La DT6 66 C1
Gibbs Marsh Trading Est
DT10 20 A4
Gibson Rd BH17 119 E7
GIDDY GREEN BH20 139 E1
Giddy Green La BH20 139 E2
Giddy Green Rd BH20 139 E2
Giddylake BH21 59 D6
Giffords La TA18 192 C5
Gifle View 2 DT9 194 D8
Gigg La SP8 8 E4
Gilbert Cl SP6 42 D6
Gilbert Rd
Bournemouth BH8 122 D6
Swanage BH19 179 B2
Giles Cl DT2 107 A6
Giles's La
Bishop's Caundle DT9 196 A7
Morden BH20 83 D3
Gillam Rd BH10 89 D5
Gillett Rd BH12 121 C7
GILLINGHAM SP8 5 E1
Gillingham Adult Ed Ctr
SP8 5 F2
Gillingham Cl BH9 90 C4
Gillingham L Ctr SP8 6 A2
Gillingham Mus* SP8 5 E1
Gillingham Prim Sch SP8 5 F2
Gillingham Sch SP8 6 A2
Gillingham Sta SP8 5 F1
Gillion Ct 2 BH23 124 E6
Gipsy's Dro DT10 197 C7
Girdlers Coppice Reserve*
DT10 197 E8
Girt La DT2 205 F7
Glacis DT5 187 A7
Gladdis Rd BH11 88 F3
Gladelands Cl BH18 86 E4
Gladelands Pk BH22 61 F7
Gladelands Way BH18 86 E4
Glade The
Christchurch BH23 91 E1
St Leonards BH24 54 A5
Gladiator Gn 3 DT1 134 E7
Gladstone Cl
Bridport DT6 100 E7
Christchurch BH23 124 D6
2 Radipole DT3 152 E2
Gladstone Rd
Bournemouth BH7 122 F5
Poole BH12 120 C5
Gladstone Road E BH7 122 F5
Gladstone Road W BH1 122 E5
Glamis Ave BH10 89 E5
GLANVILLES WOOTTON
DT9 195 E2
Glastonbury Ct BA21 26 F6
Gleadowe Ave BH23 124 A6
Glebe Cl
Abbotsbury DT3 149 C7
Bridport DT6 100 D5
Maiden Newton DT2 72 F8
Overcombe/Preston DT3 169 A8
8 Thornford DT9 194 D8
Weymouth DT4 167 C1
Glebe Ct 4 DT11 37 F1
Glebefields DT2 106 F7
Glebeford Cl DT2 155 E7
Glebe Gdns SP7 12 B8
Glebeland Cl DT2 136 A7
Glebeland La DT6 65 F7
Glebelands 6 TA16 191 F7
Glebe Rd BH16 84 C1
Glebe The
3 Durweston DT11 198 E3
Iwerne Courtney or Shroton
DT11 198 F7
3 Iwerne Minster DT11 37 F1
Glebe Way DT2 136 C3
Glenair Ave BH14 120 A3
Glenair Cres BH14 120 A3
Glenair Rd BH14 120 A3
Glen Ave DT4 167 C2
Glenavon BH25 95 C2
Glenavon Rd BH23 93 F1
Glen Cl BH25 126 D8
Glencoe Rd
Bournemouth BH7 122 F7
Poole BH12 120 D5
Glendale Ave BH22 61 E6
Glendale Cl
Christchurch BH23 91 D3
Wimborne Minster BH21 59 C5
Glendale Ct BH23 91 D3
Glendale Rd BH6 124 A4
Glendinning Ave DT4 167 D5
Glendon Ave BH10 89 C6
Glendrive BH25 126 C8
Gleneagles
Christchurch BH23 123 F6
Poole BH13 121 B2
Gleneagles Ave BH14 120 D2
Gleneagles Cl BH22 61 F6

Hunt Rd *continued*
Poole BH15 119 E4
Hunt's Hill DT10 21 E5
Hunts Mead DT9 29 F4
Huntvale Rd BH9 90 B3
Hurdles The BH23 123 E8
HURN 91 B7
Hurn Cl BH24 54 F6
Hurn Court La
Christchurch BH23 91 D7
Hurn BH23 90 F6
Hurn Ct BH8 91 A4
Hurn La BH24 54 F6
Hurn Rd
Christchurch BH23 91 D3
St Leonards & St Ives BH24 54 F4
Hurn Way BH23 91 D1
Hurricane Cl DT2 137 D6
HURSEY DT8 203 E5
Hursley Cl BH7 123 C8
HURST DT2 111 C1
Hurstbourne Ave BH23 93 E1
Hurst Cl
Barton on Sea BH25 126 D8
Walkford BH23 94 C2
Hurst Ct 4 BH23 126 A7
Hurstdene Rd BH8 90 C2
Hurst Hill BH14 147 C8
Hurst Rd
Moreton DT2 111 C1
Ringwood BH24 47 C1
Hussar Cl BH23 123 F7
Hussey's DT10 20 E1
Hutchins Cl DT1 134 E7
Hut Gate TA18 192 A8
Hyacinth Cl BH17 86 F1
Hybris Bsns Pk DT2 137 D4
HYDE
Bridport DT6 100 F5
Fordingbridge SP6 43 F6
Hyde CE Prim Sch SP6 43 F5
Hyde Ct BA21 26 E6
Hyde Gdns 6 DT11 199 D4
Hyde La SP6 43 E6
Hyde Rd
Bournemouth BH10 89 C5
Gillingham SP8 5 E3
Wool BH20 140 A2
Hydes La DT10 196 D7
Hyde The
New Milton BH25 94 E4
Swanage BH19 178 C2
Hynesbury Rd BH23 125 C6
Hythe Rd BH15 120 A7
Hythe The DT3 166 D5

I

IBBERTON DT11 197 D2
Ibbertson Cl BH8 90 F2
Ibbertson Rd BH8 90 F2
Ibbertson Way BH8 90 F2
Ibbett Rd BH10 89 C3
IBSLEY BH24 47 C7
Ibsley Cl BH8 122 C6
Ibsley Dro BH24 43 D1
Icen La
Bincombe DT3 152 C4
Shipton Gorge DT6 101 E4
Icen Rd DT3 167 C7
Icen Way DT1 108 A2
Iddesleigh Rd BH3 122 A6
IFORD 123 D7
Iford Bridge Home Pk
BH6 123 D7
Iford Gdns BH7 123 C7
Iford La BH6 123 E6
Iford Mdws Nature Reserve*
BH6 123 E7
Ilchester Rd
Weymouth DT4 167 C3
Yeovil BA21 27 B7
Ilford Cl BH6 123 F5
Ilminster Rd BH19 179 B2
Ilsington House* DT2 78 C1
Ilsington Rd DT2 109 F4
Imber Dr BH23 125 F8
Imber Rd SP7 13 A3
Imbrecourt BH13 147 E7
Imperial Ct 4 BH13 147 F7
Incline Rd DT5 187 B6
Ingarth 7 BH6 123 E3
Inglegreen Cl BH25 94 F1
Inglesham Way BH15 118 E4
Inglewood Ave BH8 90 F1
Inglewood Dr BH25 95 B2
Ingram Wlk 1 BH21 59 D4
Ingworth Rd BH12 121 A5
Inmosthay DT5 187 A5
Inner Breakwater Rd
DT5 181 D1
Innovation Cl BH12 120 A8
Insley Cres BH18 86 E5
Institute Rd BH19 179 C2
International Coll Sherborne
Sch The DT9 30 A6
Inveravon BH23 124 F4
Inverclyde Ho BH14 120 B4
Inverclyde Rd BH14 120 C4
Inverleigh Rd BH6 123 C6
Inverness Rd BH13 147 E7
Ipswich Rd BH12 121 B4
Iris Gdns 6 SP8 5 E1
Iris Rd BH9 89 F1
Irvine Way BH23 124 E8
Irving La BH6 123 D5
Irving Rd BH6 123 D5
Isaacs Cl BH12 121 B7
Island View Ave BH23 125 B5
Island View Rd BH25 126 C7
Isle of Wight Rd BH19 185 C8
Isle Rd DT5 186 E3
Isles La BA22 193 D6
Ivamy Pl BH11 88 F2
Ivel Cl DT1 135 B8
Ivel Ct BA21 27 E4
Ivelway 14 TA18 191 F4
Ivor Rd
Poole BH15 119 A1
Poole BH21 85 F4
Ivy Cl
4 Gillingham SP8 5 D2
St Leonards BH24 53 F4
IVY CROSS SP7 13 A4
Ivy La BH24 47 D4
Ivy Mead BA12 3 B5
Ivy Rd BH21 87 D8
Iwerne Cl BH9 90 B4
IWERNE COURTNEY OR
SHROTON DT11 198 E7
IWERNE MINSTER DT11 37 F1

J

Jacey Ho 6 BH1 122 A3
Jacklin Ct BH18 87 B5
Jack Paul Cl BA12 3 A6
Jack's Hedge Cnr BH21 189 F2
Jackson Gdns BH12 120 C6
Jackson Rd BH12 120 C6
Jack the Treacle Eater
(Folly)* BA22 27 E1
Jacmar Ct 4 BH25 95 B2
Jacobean Cl BH23 94 B1
Jacobs Ladder 2 DT11 198 C7
Jacobs Rd BH15 118 E2
Jacqueline Rd BH12 120 C7
James Cl
Blandford Forum DT11 212 F5
Dorchester DT1 134 E8
James Cross La BH21 201 A6
James Day Mead BH19 179 B5
Jameson Rd BH9 89 F1
James Rd
Dorchester DT1 134 E8
Poole BH12 121 A5
James St DT4 167 D2
Janred Ct BH25 126 E7
Jarvis Cl DT10 33 D7
Jarvis Way DT10 33 D8
Jasmine Cl
24 Crewkerne TA18 191 F5
Yeovil BA22 26 D5
Jasmine Way 2 DT4 180 B8
Jaundrells Cl BH25 95 C3
Jay's Ct BH23 126 B8
Jay Wlk SP8 11 B8
Jeanneau Cl 4 SP7 12 F3
Jefferson Ave BH1 122 D6
Jellicoe Cl BH14 119 F5
Jellicoe Dr BH23 124 F6
Jellyfields Nature Reserve*
DT6 100 F6
Jenner Cl BH31 45 A7
Jenner Way DT3 152 D3
Jenni Cl BH11 89 A6
Jennings Rd BH14 120 C2
Jennys La BH16 84 B4
Jephcote Rd BH11 88 F4
Jeremy Cl BH20 140 B2
Jersey Cl BH12 88 D1
Jersey Rd BH12 88 D1
Jesmond Ave BH23 125 F8
Jesop Cl 1 SP8 5 E1
Jessica Ave BH31 44 F7
Jessopp Ave DT6 100 F7
Jessopp Cl BH10 89 F4
Jessopp Ho 6 BH21 59 C5
Jessopp Rd BH21 60 B6
Jesty's Ave DT3 152 C4
Jewell Rd BH8 91 A2
Jimmy Brown Ave BH21 53 A5
Jock's Hill DT2 78 E6
Johnson Rd BH21 61 A8
Johnson's Ctyd DT9 30 C5
Johns Rd BH20 142 D5
Johnstone Rd BH23 124 E6
Johnston Rd BH15 119 D7
Jolliffe Ave BH15 119 D4
Jolliffe Rd BH15 119 D4
Jonson Trading Pk 3
DT1 108 C1
Jopps Cnr BH23 92 C4
Jordan Hill Roman Temple*
DT3 168 B7
Jordan Way 5 DT3 152 C4
Joshua Cl BH15 118 E2
Journeys End DT6 100 B6
Jowitt Dr BH25 94 F2
Joyce Dickson Cl 2
BH24 55 D6
Joys Rd BH21 53 A8
Juan's La SP8 9 D2
Jubilee Bsns Pk DT4 167 D5
Jubilee Cl
Corfe Mullen BH21 86 E7
3 Radipole DT4 167 D4
Ringwood BH24 55 E8
Jubilee Cres BH12 120 D5
Jubilee Cross BH16 85 A4
Jubilee Ent Ctr DT4 167 D4
Jubilee Gdns
Bournemouth BH10 89 D2
Corfe Castle BH20 177 A7
Jubilee Rd
Corfe Mullen BH21 86 E7
Poole BH12 120 D5
Swanage BH19 178 F2
Jubilee Trail DT2 135 C4
Jubilee Way DT11 212 C5
Julia Cl BH23 125 F8
Julian's Rd BH21 59 A4
Julyan Ave BH12 121 A8
Jumpers Ave BH23 123 E8
JUMPERS COMMON 91 E1
Jumpers Rd BH23 123 F8
Junction Rd
Bournemouth BH9 121 F8
Upton BH16 117 F4
Juniper Cl
Ferndown BH22 61 C8
Three Legged Cross BH21 53 A8
Yeovil BA20 27 B3
Juniper Dr BH23 93 C1
Juniper Flats BH23 123 E8
Juniper Gdns 7 SP8 5 E1
Juniper Way DT3 152 C3
Jupiter Way BH21 86 E8
Justin Bsns Pk BH20 142 F5
Justin Gdns BH10 89 E4

K

Kamptee Copse BH25 95 B6
Kangaw Pl 3 BH15 117 F2
Katherine Chance Cl
BH23 92 C3
Katie Cl BH14 120 C4
Katterns Cl BH23 91 E2
Kay Cl BH23 124 E6
Kayes Cl DT4 180 C8
K&B Est BH17 119 B8
Keats Ho 1 BH25 95 A1
Keats Mdw SP5 189 B4
Keeble Cl BH10 89 D6
Keeble Cres BH10 89 D6
Keeble Rd BH10 89 D6
Keepers La BH21 60 F4
Keep Military Mus The*
DT1 107 F2
Keighley Ave BH18 86 F1
Keith Rd BH3 121 D7
Kellaway Ct 10 DT4 167 E2
Kellaway Rd BH17 119 F8
Kellaway Terr DT4 167 C3
Kelly Cl BH17 119 F8
Kelsall Gdns BH25 95 A3
Kemp Rd BH9 121 F8
Kempston Rd DT4 167 D1
Kemp Welch Ct BH12 121 B8
Kendalls La SP8 5 E5
Kenelm Cl DT9 29 F5
Kenilworth DT4 167 B6
Kenilworth Cl BH25 95 B3
Kenilworth Ct
2 Christchurch BH23 124 A7
1 Poole BH13 147 F8
Kenmoor Cl DT3 167 F8
Kenmore Dr BA21 27 D6
Kennard Ct BH25 94 F3
Kennard Rd BH25 94 F3
Kennart Rd BH17 119 B7
Kennel La DT2 206 C2
Kennels La DT9 195 E2
Kenneth Ct 9 BH23 126 B7
Kennington Rd BH17 119 D8
Kennington Sq 5 BH20 142 E4
Ken Rd BH6 123 E4
Kensington Ct 14 BH13 121 B3
Kensington Dr 1 BH2 121 D4
Kensington Wlk 8 DT1 135 C8
Kent Cl DT4 166 F3
Kent Ho 28 BH4 121 C3
Kentisworth Rd DT10 20 F1
Kent La BH24 43 A1
Kent Rd
Poole BH12 120 E6
10 Tatworth TA20 202 A8
Kents La 8 TA20 202 A8
Kenwyn Rd DT6 100 E7
Kenyon Cl BH15 119 E7
Kenyon Rd BH15 119 E7
Keppel Cl BH24 55 D7
Kerley Rd BH2 121 E2
Kernells Ct 2 BH4 121 B4
Kestrel Cl
Ferndown BH22 61 B7
3 Upton BH16 117 D8
Kestrel Ct BH24 55 C8
Kestrel Dr BH23 125 A6
Kestrel View DT3 152 C3
Kestrel Way SP6 42 D5
Keswick Ct BH25 95 B5
Keswick Rd
Bournemouth BH5 122 F4
New Milton BH25 95 B5
Keswick Way BH31 45 A5
Keverstone Ct BH1 122 D3
Keyes Cl
Christchurch BH23 124 F6
Poole BH12 88 F1
Key Hill BA22 193 E8
Keynston Down Rd 7
DT11 199 E2
Keysworth BH20 143 B7
Keysworth Ave BH25 126 F8
Keysworth Dr BH20 143 A8
Keysworth Rd BH16 117 E4
Khartoum Rd DT4 180 E8
Khyber Rd BH12 120 D5
Kiddles BA21 27 E5
Kidmore Cl 2 DT6 97 A7
Killicks Hill DT5 186 F7
Killock 6 BH13 147 F7
Kilmarnock Rd
1 Bournemouth BH1 122 B4
Bournemouth BH9 89 F1
Kilmington Way BH23 125 F8
Kiln Cl BH21 85 E4
Kiln Way BH31 45 E4
Kilwood Reserve* BH20 161 B2
Kimberley Cl
Christchurch BH23 123 F8
1 Radipole DT3 152 E2
Kimberley Rd
Bournemouth BH6 123 C5
Poole BH14 120 B3
Kimber Rd BH11 88 F3
KIMMERIDGE BH20 175 D4
Kimmeridge Ave BH12 120 C8
Kimmeridge Cl DT3 167 B8
Kine Bush La SP8 10 B7
King Alfred's Way SP7 12 F3
King Arthur Dr BA21 26 F7
King Charles Way DT6 100 F7
King Cl BH24 54 B4
Kingcombe Cross Roads
DT2 205 E3
Kingcombe La DT2 205 E3
Kingcombe Meadows
Reserve* DT2 205 D2
Kingcombe Rd DT8 205 C3
Kingcup Cl BH18 86 E2
King Down Dro BH21 49 C3
King Down Rd DT11 199 F3
King Edmund Ct SP8 5 E2
King Edward Ave BH9 90 A2
King Edward Ct BH9 89 F2
King Edward's Dr DT11 209 F5
Kingfisher Ave SP8 11 B8
Kingfisher Cl
Bournemouth BH6 123 E6
Ferndown BH22 53 B2
Weymouth DT4 180 D6
Kingfisher Ct BH8 122 D6
Kingfisher Park Homes 3
BH10 89 F4
Kingfishers 4 BH23 124 A5
Kingfishers The BH31 45 C5
Kingfisher Way
Christchurch BH23 125 A5
Ringwood BH24 47 D1
King George Ave BH9 89 F2
King George Mobile Home
Pk BH25 94 F1
King George Sh Ctr The 34
TA18 191 F4
King George V Rd BH20 139 E7
King John Ave BH11 88 D5
King John Cl BH11 88 D6
King John Rd SP8 6 A1
Kingland Cres 4 BH15 119 C2
Kingland Rd BH15 119 D2
King Richard Dr BH11 88 D5
Kings Arms La BH24 55 B7
Kings Arms Row BH24 55 B7
Kings Ave BH14 120 D2
King's Ave BH23 123 F6
Kingsbere Ave BH10 89 B2
Kingsbere Cres DT1 135 A7
Kingsbere Gdns BH23 126 A8
Kingsbere La SP7 13 A4
Kingsbere Rd
Overcombe/Preston
DT3 168 A7
Poole BH15 119 E5
Kingsbridge Rd BH14 120 C3
Kings Brook 2 SO41 95 F3
KINGSBURY REGIS DT9 17 D3
Kingsbury's La BH24 55 B7
Kings Chase SP8 6 B1
Kings Cl
Ferndown BH22 53 A1
Longburton DT9 195 B8
Poole BH15 119 D5
Kingscourt Cl 2 SP8 6 B1
King's Court Palace* SP8 6 B1
Kingscourt Rd SP8 6 B1
Kings Cres DT9 30 B7
King's Cres BH14 120 E2
Kings Ct Bsns Ctr BH19 179 B2
Kingsfield BH24 55 C7
Kingsgate 10 BH13 121 B3
Kings Grange 11 BH4 121 D2
Kings High Sch BH10 89 C3
Kings Hill 2 SP7 12 E3
Kings La BH21 201 F4
King's La DT6 70 D5
KINGSLAND DT6 68 A7
Kingsland Ct BH13 147 F7
Kingsland Grange BA21 26 E6
Kingsleigh Prim Sch
BH10 89 C3
Kingsley Ave BH6 124 A4
Kingsley Cl BH6 124 A4
Kingsley House 8 BH9 89 F1
Kingsley Paddock DT2 72 F7
Kingsman La SP7 12 E2
Kings Mead DT2 78 B1
Kingsmead Ct 5 BH21 59 B5
Kingsmill Rd BH17 119 E7
King's Mill Rd DT10 34 B6
Kingsnorth Cl DT6 100 E7
King's Park Athletics Ctr
BH7 122 F6
King's Park Dr BH7, BH1 122 E6
Kings Park Hospl BH7 122 F5
King's Park Prim Sch
BH1 122 E5
King's Park Rd BH7 122 E6
King's Pitt 3 DT1 107 C1
Kings Rd
Dorchester DT1 108 B1
New Milton BH25 95 C3
Radipole DT3 167 C7
Sherborne DT9 30 B7
King's Rd
Blandford Forum DT11 212 E5
Bournemouth BH3 122 A7
Thornford DT9 194 D7
Kings Road E BH19 179 B2
Kings Road W BH19 179 A2
King's St BH21 56 D5
KING'S STAG DT10 196 D5
King St
Bridport DT6 100 D6
Fortuneswell DT5 186 F7
Radipole DT4 167 D4
Wimborne Minster BH21 59 B4
Yeovil BA21 27 D6
Kingsthorn Rd DT1 107 C2
KINGSTON
Corfe Castle BH20 176 F3
Ringwood BH24 55 B1
Sturminster Newton DT10 197 A4
Kingston BA20 27 C5
Kingston Barnyard DT11 81 D8
Kingston Cl DT11 212 C5
Kingston Hill BH20 176 F4
Kingston La DT10 196 F4
Kingston Lacy House*
BH21 58 B7
KINGSTON MAURWARD
DT2 108 F2
Kingston Maurward Coll
DT2 108 F3
Kingston Maurward Park &
Gdns* DT2 108 E3
Kingston Rd BH15 119 D4
KINGSTON RUSSELL
DT2 104 C3
Kingston View BA21 27 D6
Kingsway
Ferndown BH22 61 B8
Lyme Regis DT7 96 C6
Kingsway Cl BH23 91 F1
Kingswell Cl BH10 89 D2
Kingswell Gdns BH10 89 B2
Kingswell Gr BH10 89 B2
Kingswell Rd BH10 89 C2
Kings Williams Head DT6 68 F1
Kingswood 15 BH4 121 C2
Kingswood Cl 2 BH19 178 E2
Kingswood Rd 6 TA18 191 F3
KINGTON MAGNA SP8 9 C3
Kinross Rd BH3 121 E6
Kinsbourne Ave BH10 89 D2
KINSON 89 B5
Kinson Ave BH15 120 A7
Kinson Comm Nature
Reserve* BH11 89 B5
Kinson Gr BH10 89 C6
Kinson Park Rd BH10 89 D6
Kinson Pottery Ind Est
BH14 120 A6
Kinson Prim Sch BH11 89 B5
Kinson Rd BH10 89 C3
Kiosks The 8 BH15 119 C1
Kipling Rd BH14 120 B5
Kirby Cl BH15 119 F6
Kirby Way BH6 123 D4
Kirkham Ave BH23 92 C3
Kirkleton Ave DT4 167 D5
Kirkway BH18 87 B4
Kitchener Cres BH17 87 B2
Kitchener Rd DT4 167 B3
Kite's Nest La SP8 1 E2
KITFORD DT11 197 C3
Kitford La DT11 197 C3
KIT HILL SP7 23 A4
Kithill TA18 191 F3
Kit La DT2 155 D7
Kitscroft Rd BH10 89 C5
Kitt Hill DT9 30 A6
Kittiwake Cl BH6 123 D6
Kitton La DT9 29 A8
KITTWHISTLE DT8 203 A6
Kiwi Cl BH15 119 E3
KNACKERS HOLE DT11 197 D6
Knap Barrow (Long
Barrow)* SP6 190 D6
Knapp Cl BH23 124 A8
KNAPP HILL SP7 7 C2
Knapp Mill Ave BH23 124 A8
Knapps DT11 198 B6
Knapp The
Chickerell DT3 166 C6
Fontmell Magna SP7 37 F6
Hilton DT11 209 D6
Shaftesbury SP7 12 D3
Knapwater Wlk 12 DT1 135 B8
KNIGHTON
Bournemouth 88 D8
Yetminster 194 E6
Knighton Heath Cl BH11 88 E4
Knighton Heath Ind Est
BH11 88 E2
Knighton Heath Rd BH11 88 E4
Knighton House Sch
DT11 198 E3
Knighton La
Bournemouth BH21 88 D7
Broadmayne DT2 136 C2
Knighton Pk BH25 126 E8

Overcliffe Mans BH1 122 C3
OVERCOMBE DT3 168 A7
Overcombe BA8 18 D8
Overcombe Cl BH17 87 E2
Overcombe Dr DT3 168 B7
OVER COMPTON DT9 28 E7
Overlands Rd DT4 180 B8
Over Links Dr BH14 120 D2
Overton Cl DT7 96 C7
Ovington Ave BH7 123 C7
Ovington Gdns BH7 123 C7
OWERMOIGNE DT2 155 E7
Owlshotts BH13 147 F7
Owls Rd
Bournemouth BH5 122 E3
Verwood BH31 45 C5
OXBRIDGE DT6 68 F8
Ox Drove SP5 188 B7
Oxencroft 4 SP7 12 F4
Oxen Rd 5 TA18 191 F4
Oxey Cl BH25 95 A1
Oxford Ave BH6 123 B5
Oxford La BH11 89 B6
Oxford Rd
Bournemouth BH8 122 B4
Yeovil BA21 28 B7
Oxhayes DT8 203 C8
Oxley Sports Ctr DT9 30 A6
Ozone Terr DT7 96 B4

P

Paceycombe Way DT1 107 C2
PACKERS HILL DT9 196 C5
Packers' Way 1 TA18 192 B3
Paddington Cl BH11 88 D4
Paddington Gr BH11 88 D3
Paddock Cl
Ferndown BH21 61 A5
Lytchett Matravers BH16 84 D4
Poole BH12 120 B7
Shaftesbury SP7 13 A1
Sixpenny Handley SP5 189 A3
St Leonards BH24 54 B4
Paddock Gr BH31 45 C5
Paddock's Cross DT6 67 B8
Paddock's La DT6 67 B8
Paddocks The
Bournemouth BH10 89 D4
Bridport DT6 100 E4
1 Iwerne Minster DT11 37 F1
Mere BA12 3 A5
5 Mosterton DT8 204 A8
Thornford DT9 194 D8
Paddock The
Dorchester DT2 105 D2
West Moors BH24 62 C8
West Stafford DT2 136 B8
Paddock Wlk DT9 17 C2
Padfield Cl BH6 123 E6
Padget Rd BH24 47 E1
Padstow Pl SP6 43 A8
Pageant Dr DT9 30 B5
Pageants Cl DT6 68 F1
Page Dr 1 DT5 186 F1
Paget Cl BH21 60 A7
Paget Rd BH11 89 A4
Paisley Rd BH6 123 C5
Palace Rd SP8 6 A1
Palfrey Rd BH10 89 D5
PALLINGTON DT2 111 C3
Palma Ct BH23 126 A7
Palmer Pl BH25 95 A4
Palmer Rd BH15 119 C5
Palmers Brewery★ DT6 100 C5
Palmers La DT11 211 D7
Palmers Orch BH16 84 C3
Palmerston Ave BH23 124 D6
Palmerston Cl 1 BH16 117 F7
Palmerston Rd
Bournemouth BH1 122 E5
Poole BH14 120 D4
Upton BH16 117 E7
PAMPHILL 58 E6
Pamphill CE Fst Sch BH21 58 E5
Panorama Rd
Poole BH13 147 B3
Swanage BH19 179 A2
Pans Cnr BH22 61 F3
Parade The
4 Bournemouth BH6 123 E3
New Milton BH25 95 D3
Old Milton BH25 94 F1
Poole BH17 87 B1
Paradise Rd BH21 51 F7
Paradise St 14 BH15 119 B1
Parcroft Gdns BA20 27 B5
Parcroft Jun Sch BA20 27 B5
Pardys Hill BH21 85 E8
Parfields BA20 27 B5
Parham Cl BH25 94 E3
Parham Rd BH10 89 C2
Paris Ct SP8 5 F1
Parish Mews 3 BA21 26 E5
Parish Rd BH15 119 E3
Park Ave BH10 89 C6
Park Cl
Burton BH23 92 C3
New Milton BH25 95 C5
3 Stourpaine DT11 198 F4
Park Ct 12 BH13 121 B3
Park Dr
Holton Heath BH16 116 B3
Verwood BH31 45 A7
Parkelea 3 BH21 56 D4
Parker Rd BH9 121 F7
Parkers Cl BH24 47 E1
Park Est Rd DT5 186 F4
Park Farm Cl DT2 133 E6
PARK GATE DT11 196 F2
Park Gate BH25 95 A2
Park Gate Mews 7 BH2 121 E3
Park Gdns
Christchurch BH23 124 E7
Yeovil BA20 27 C5
Park Gr DT10 33 C8
Park Hill DT11 211 C6
Park Homer Dr BH21 60 A6
Park Homer Rd BH21 59 F6
Park La
Alderholt SP6 42 B6
Bournemouth BH10 89 F4
Evershot DT2 206 A7
Glanvilles Wootton DT9 195 F2
Henstridge BA8 19 B7
Radipole DT4 167 D5
Shapwick DT11 48 C1
Thorncombe TA20 202 D7
Wayford TA18 191 B1
Wimborne Minster BH21 59 C4
Wimborne St Giles BH21 201 E7
Woodlands BH21 44 B6
Park Lake Rd BH15 119 E2
Parkland Cl BH31 45 F4
Parkland Dr BH25 126 F8
Parkland Pl BH25 95 A2
Parklands 11 BH4 121 C3
Park Lands DT11 212 C4
Park Mead Rd DT4 180 C7
Park Pl BH14 119 F4
Park Rd
Blandford Forum DT11 212 C4
Bournemouth BH8 122 A5
Bridport DT6 100 C7
Easton/Weston DT5 187 A4
Henstridge BA8 19 A4
New Milton BH25 95 C5
Old Milton BH25 94 F1
Poole BH15, BH14 119 F3
Stalbridge DT10 33 C8
Swanage BH19 179 C2
Yeovil BA20 27 D5
Park Sch The
Bournemouth BH8 122 D7
Yeovil BA20 27 C5
Parkside
Christchurch BH23 93 D1
Ringwood BH24 55 B6
Parkside Gdns BH10 89 E2
Parkside Ind Est BH24 55 C5
Parkside Rd BH14 120 C4
Park's La DT2 130 D7
Park St
Radipole DT4 167 D3
Yeovil BA20 27 D3
7 Yeovil BA20 27 D4
Parkstone Ave BH14 120 D4
Parkstone Gram Sch
BH17 87 B1
Parkstone Hts BH14 120 A5
Parkstone Rd BH15 119 E3
Parkstone Sta BH14 120 B3
Park The
Barton on Sea BH25 126 C7
Wimborne Minster BH21 60 A1
Yeovil BA20 27 C5
Parkview BH2 121 E4
Park View
Crewkerne TA18 191 F3
New Milton BH25 95 A2
7 Poole BH15 119 E3
Park View Ct BH8 122 C7
Park View Mews BH25 95 A2
Park View Point SP5 188 B3
Park Water La DT8 203 C5
PARKWAY BA22 14 F7
Parkway DT6 97 B7
Park Way BH22 53 A2
Parkway Dr BH8 122 E8
Parkwood La 7 BH5 123 B5
Parkwood Rd
Bournemouth BH5 123 A4
Wimborne Minster BH21 59 C4
Parley Cl BH22 61 F1
Parley Cross BH22 89 E8
Parley Fst Sch BH22 61 D3
PARLEY GREEN 90 C7
Parley Green La BH23 90 B7
Parley La BH23 90 D7
Parley Rd BH9 90 A2
Parmiter Dr BH21 59 E4
Parmiter Rd BH21 59 E4
Parmiter Way BH21 59 E4
Parrett & Axe CE Prim Sch
DT8 204 A7
Parrett Mead DT8 192 C1
Parr Gr 5 DT11 199 D4
Parr Ho 1 BH14 120 A4
Parricks La EX13 202 A3
Parr St BH14 120 A4
Parsonage Barn La BH24 55 C7
Parsonage Ct 9 BH8 122 A5
Parsonage Hill BH21 200 F6
Parsonage La BH21 201 E7
Parsonage Rd
Bournemouth BH1 122 A3
Bridport DT6 100 C8
Parsonage St SP7 37 F6
Parsonage The SP5 189 B4
Parsons Cl BH19 179 B5
Parsons La DT2 102 E6
Parsons Pool 3 SP7 12 E3
Partridge Cl BH23 125 A5
Partridge Dr BH14 120 C1
Partridge Gn BH25 95 B6
Partridge Wlk BH14 120 B1
Partway DT10 196 F3
Partway La
Hardington Mandeville
BA22 192 F7
Hazelbury Bryan DT10 196 F3
Thorncombe TA20 202 C6
Pascoe Cl BH14 120 A4
Pasture Way DT6 100 D5
Patchins Rd BH16 117 D4
Patchins The BH14 147 C8
Patson Hill La DT9 15 C2
Pattinson Cl BA21 27 F6
Paul's Mead DT5 186 F7
Pauls Way DT2 137 D6
Pauncefote Rd BH5 123 A5
Pauntley Rd BH23 124 E5
Pavan Gdns BH10 89 C2
Pavilion The 23 BH4 121 C2
Pavilion The★ BH4 121 F2
Pavilion Theatre★ DT4 167 E3
Pavyotts La BA22 193 E8
Payne Cl BH21 53 A5
Paynes Cl DT2 76 E7
Peace Cl BH23 93 A8
Peaceful La DT10 196 C6
PEACEMARSH SP8 5 E3
Peacemarsh Farm Cl 3
SP8 5 E4
PEAR ASH BA9 1 C4
Pear Ash La BA9 1 C4
Pearce Ave BH14 120 A1
Pearce Gdns BH14 120 A1
Pearce Rd BH16 117 D6
Pearce-Smith Ct BH25 126 F7
Pear Cl BH12 121 B4
Pearl Gdns BH10 89 C4
Pearl Rd BH10 89 C4
Pearson Ave BH14 120 B5
Pearson Gdns BH10 89 D6
Pear Tree Cl
Alderholt SP6 42 B5
Bransgore BH23 93 B8
Peartree La DT4 167 B2
Peascombe Reserve★
DT6 69 E1
Peatons La BH16 84 B4
Pebble La DT5 186 E8
Peckham Ave BH25 95 A2
Peddlars Wlk 4 BH24 55 B7
Peeks Mews BH6 123 F5
Peel Cl
Blandford Forum DT11 212 D5
Poole BH12 120 C5
Peelers Ct DT6 100 D7
Pegasus Ct
Bournemouth BH1 122 A5
8 New Milton BH25 95 A3
Pegasus Lodge BH22 61 D5
Peggy's La TA18 192 C5
Pelham 21 BH13 121 A4
Pelham Cl BH23 124 D6
Pelhams Park L Ctr BH10 89 C6
Pelican Mead BH24 55 E5
Pemberton Cl DT3 152 D3
Pembroke Cl BA21 28 A7
Pembroke Ct 4 BH23 126 B7
Pembroke Rd
Bournemouth BH4 121 B2
Poole BH12 120 D7
Penbugle Yd 14 DT1 107 D1
Pen Craig 2 BH13 121 B3
PENDOMER BA22 193 B5
Pendomer Rd BA22 193 B5
Pendruffle La 12 DT1 107 D1
Penelope Ct 12 BH23 126 B7
Penfield BA21 27 E5
Pengelly Ave BH10 89 E5
Penhale Wlk 17 DT1 107 D1
PEN MILL BA21 28 A6
Pen Mill Hill BA12 1 E3
Pen Mill Inf Sch BA21 27 F6
Pen Mill Trading Est
BA21 28 B6
Penmore Rd DT9 15 C5
PENN DT6 64 C3
Pennant Way BH23 124 F7
Penn Cl BH25 94 E1
Penn Cross DT6 64 D1
Penn Hill BA20 27 D4
Penn Hill Ave BH14 120 D3
Penn Hill Pk BA20 27 D4
Penn Hill View DT2 106 D8
Pennine Ct 8 BH23 124 F8
Pennine Way BH31 45 B5
Pennington Cl BH22 52 F1
Pennington Cres BH22 52 F2
Pennington Ho 6 BH4 121 C2
Pennington Rd BH22 52 F2
Penn La BA22 193 A6
Pennsylvania Rd DT5 187 B3
Penny Hedge BH25 127 B8
Penny Plot DT7 96 A6
Penny's Cnr SO41 95 F4
Penny's Ct BH22 61 D5
Penny's La BH21 40 B7
Penny's Mead BH21 40 B7
Penny St
Radipole DT4 167 D4
Sturminster Newton DT10 35 B1
Penny's Wlk BH22 61 D5
Penny Way BH23 125 C6
Pennywell Gdns BH25 95 D4
Penrith Cl BH31 45 A5
Penrith Rd BH5 123 A4
Penrose Cl BH16 84 C2
Penrose Rd BH22 61 D6
PENSELWOOD BA9 1 B4
Pentons Hill SP6 43 F6
PENTRIDGE SP5 189 E4
Pentridge La DT10 34 D4
Peppercorn Cl BH23 124 E8
Pepper Hill DT11 198 B5
Percivale Rd 6 BA21 26 F7
Percy Gdns DT11 212 D4
Percy Rd
Bournemouth BH5 122 F4
Yeovil BA21 27 F6
Peregrine Rd BH23 125 A5
Pergin Cres BH17 119 B7
Pergin Way BH17 119 B7
Perrott Hill Sch TA18 192 B4
Perryfield Gdns BH7 123 B8
Perry Gdns BH15 119 C1
Perry St TA20 202 A7
PERRY STREET TA20 202 B8
Persley Rd BH10 89 E4
Perth Cl BH23 91 E1
Perth St DT4 167 B3
Peter Grant Way BH22 61 C5
Peters Cl BH16 117 E6
Petersfield Pl BH7 123 B7
Petersfield Rd BH7 123 B7
Petersham La BH21 51 A4
Petersham Rd BH17 119 A8
Peters Rd BH22 61 F3
Peter St 3 BA20 27 D4
Petit Rd BH9 90 A3
Petter's Way BA20 27 D4
Pettitts Cl DT9 28 C2
Pettridge La BA12 3 A5
Pettycrate La DT6 98 F5
Petwyn Cl BH22 62 A6
Peverell Avenue E DT1 107 C2
Peverell Avenue W DT1 107 B2
Peverell Rd BH16 117 D4
Peveril Cl BH24 54 B6
Peveril Point Rd BH19 179 D2
Peveril Rd BH19 179 C1
Pheasant Way SP8 11 B8
Phelipps Rd 2 BH21 85 F6
Philip Green Meml Sch
BH21 190 C1
Philip Rd DT11 212 E4
Phillips Rd DT10 21 A2
Philpot Mus The★ DT7 96 C5
Phippard Way BH15 119 D2
Phyldon Cl BH12 120 B5
Phyldon Rd BH12 120 B6
Piccadilly La DT11 56 C8
Pickard Rd BH22 61 F7
Pickering Cl BH18 87 A2
Picket La DT8 192 C1
Pickett La BA21 27 C7
Picketts Cross DT2 74 A4
Pickford Rd BH9 89 E1
PIDDLEHINTON DT2 76 F7
Piddlehinton Ent Pk DT2 77 A6
Piddle La DT2 207 D3
Piddles Wood Reserve★
DT10 197 E7
PIDDLETRENTHIDE DT2 208 A3
Piddle Valley CE Fst Sch
DT2 208 B2
PIDNEY DT10 196 F4
Pidney Hill DT10 196 F3
Piece Rd DT9 17 C3
Piece The 2 TA16 191 F7
Pierston Fields SP8 5 C6
Pigeon Cl
Blandford Forum DT11 212 D2
Winfrith Newburgh DT2 156 F5
Pig Hill BA22 193 A7
PIG OAK BH21 51 A3
Pig Shoot La BH23 90 F5
Pikes La BH19 183 C7
Pile La DT10 32 F5
PILFORD 60 A8
Pilford Heath Rd BH21 60 B7
Pilford La BH21 51 D2
Pilgrims Pk BH24 55 E8
Pilgrim's Cl BH25 95 C3
Pilgrims Way
Poole BH17 119 A7
4 Radipole DT4 167 E2
Pill Mdw SP8 9 C3
PILLWELL DT10 21 A3
Pilot Hight Rd BH11 89 A4
PILSDON DT6 203 C2
Pilsdon Cl 7 DT8 204 C4
Pilsdon Dr BH17 87 E3
Pilsdon La DT6 203 C3
Pilsdon Pen★ DT6 203 C4
Pilwell DT10 21 A3
Pimperleaze Rd
Mere BA12 3 F1
Warminster BA12 3 E4
Pimpern Cl BH17 87 F2
PIMPERNE
Blandford Forum DT11 199 D4
Yeovil DT2 194 A3
Pimpernel Ct 6 SP8 5 D2
Pimperne Long Barrow★
DT11 199 E5
Pimperne Prim Sch
DT11 199 D4
Pineapple Bsns Pk DT6 68 B6
Pineapple La DT6 68 C6
Pine Ave
Bournemouth BH6 123 C4
Poole BH12 120 F6
Pinebeach Ct BH13 147 G8
Pine Cl
Barton on Sea BH25 126 E8
Ferndown BH22 61 C7
Pinecliffe Ave BH6 123 C4
Pinecliffe Rd BH25 126 C7
Pinecliff Rd BH13 147 G8
Pine Cres
Christchurch BH23 125 E8
Holton Heath BH16 116 B3
Pine Dr
Poole BH13 120 F3
St Leonards BH24 54 B4
Pine End BH22 61 F3
Pine Glen Ave BH22 61 C8
Pine Grange 4 BH1 122 A3
Pine Ho BH25 95 A3
Pineholt Cl BH24 54 C5
Pinehurst Ave BH23 124 F5
PINEHURST PARK BH22 53 A1
Pinehurst Pk BH22 61 F8
Pinehurst Rd BH22 53 A1
Pine Lodge 10 BH13 147 F7
Pine Manor Rd BH24 53 F5
Pine Mans 3 BH1 122 D4
Pinemoor Cl DT3 167 F8
Pine Park Mans 16 BH13 121 A4
Pine Rd
Alderholt SP6 42 B5
Bournemouth BH9 122 A8
East End BH21 58 F1
Pine Ridge DT7 96 C7
Pineside BH9 122 A8
Pines Mews 11 DT8 204 D4
Pinesprings Dr BH18 86 E2
Pine Springs Nature
Reserve★ BH18 86 E2
Pines The BH13 121 A2
Pine Tree Ave BA20 27 B3
Pine Tree Cl BH21 59 D5
Pine Tree Glen BH4 121 C3
Pinetree Wlk BH17 118 F8
Pine Vale Cres BH10 89 F3
Pine View DT6 100 B6
Pine View Cl
Upton BH16 117 E6
Verwood BH31 44 F7
Pine View Gdns BH10 89 F4
Pine View Rd BH31 44 F7
Pine Wlk
Lyme Regis DT7 96 B4
Verwood BH31 45 D5
Pinewood Ave BH10 89 D5
Pinewood Cl
Bournemouth BH10 89 D5
5 Upton BH16 117 C7
Walkford BH23 94 A2
Pinewood Gdns BH22 61 D7
Pinewood Rd
Christchurch BH23 93 F1
Ferndown BH22 61 C7
Hordle SO41 95 F3
Poole BH13 121 B1
St Leonards BH24 54 B4
Upton BH16 117 C7
Pinford La DT9 30 E6
Pink Knoll Hollow DT9 15 E8
Pinnacle The 7 BH1 122 A3
Pipers Ash 2 BH24 55 E8
Pipers Dr BH23 125 A7
Pipit Cl DT3 152 D3
Pippin Cl BH23 91 E2
Pippin Equestrian★ SP8 10 D7
Pipplepen La DT8 192 C2
Pirates La DT4 180 B7
Pitcher Cl 3 DT11 81 E8
Pitchers DT6 68 B6
Pitcote La 15 DT1 107 D1
Pitfield Cnr BA22 15 A6
Pit Hill TA17 191 B7
Pitman's La DT6 66 B1
Pit Rd TA17 191 B7
Pitt Cl DT11 212 C2
Pitthouse La BH23 91 D8
Pitt La DT6 65 E3
Pittmore Rd BH23 92 C2
Pitt's Dro BH21 49 E1
Pitts La
Melbury Abbas SP7 23 F5
Sedgehill & Semley SP7 7 C5
Pitts Orchard DT10 35 B1
Pitts Pl BH25 95 D2
Pitwines Cl BH15 119 D2
Pix Mead Gdns SP7 13 A2
Place Mill★ BH23 124 C5
Placket La BA20 27 A1
Plain The DT2 109 A6
Plaisters La DT3 153 C5
Plantagenet Chase BA20 27 A2
Plantagenet Cres BH11 88 D5
Plantagenet Pk BA20 27 A3
Plantagenet Way 8 SP8 5 D2
Plantation Ct BH17 87 C1
Plantation Dr BH23 94 A2
Plantation Rd
Christchurch BH23 63 B4
Poole BH17 87 C1
Plant Park Rd BH24 54 E2
Plassey Cl DT1 107 E2
Plassey Cres BH10 89 C5
Platts DT10 196 F8
Playfield Cl 2 BA8 19 A4
Playfields Dr BH12 120 E6
Pleasance Way BH25 94 F3
PLECK
Marnhull DT10 34 E8
Sturminster Newton DT9 196 B6
Pleck Hill DT10 196 E3
Pleck La DT2 209 B7

PLECK OR LITTLE ANSTY DT2 . . . 209 C7
Plecy Cl BH22 . . . 61 D2
Plemont Cl BH12 . . . 88 E1
Plocks The DT11 . . . 212 C3
Plot La DT9 . . . 14 F1
Plott La BA8 . . . 19 C5
Plough Est DT11 . . . 212 D6
Plover Cl 2 DT9 . . . 17 C2
Plover Ct BA21 . . . 26 F6
Plover Dr DT3 . . . 166 D5
Plover Rd DT9 . . . 17 C2
Plover Wlk DT4 . . . 180 D6
Plowman Cl DT10 . . . 21 A3
Plucknett Row BA20 . . . 26 E5
Plumbley Mdws 6 DT11 . . 81 E8
Plumbtree Gdns DT6 . . . 100 E5
Plumer Rd BH17 . . . 87 A1
Plum Orch DT9 . . . 28 F7
Plumptree Gdns DT6 . . . 100 E5
PLUSH DT2 . . . 208 C5
Podington Mdws DT3 . . . 166 D5
Point The BH5 . . . 122 E3
POKESDOWN . . . 123 A4
Pokesdown Prim Sch 8 BH5 . . . 123 B5
Pokesdown Sta BH7 . . . 123 A5
Polans DT9 . . . 194 D2
Policemans La BH16 . . . 117 B7
Pollards La DT2 . . . 155 D7
Polly's Cl DT2 . . . 137 D6
Pomona Cl BH22 . . . 61 D6
Pompey's Cnr BH21 . . . 61 A4
Pompey's La BH22 . . . 61 B2
Pond Cl
Henstridge BA8 . . . 19 A4
New Milton BH25 . . . 95 A3
Pond End DT6 . . . 68 D2
Pond Head BH21 . . . 51 C6
Pond Wlk DT10 . . . 33 C8
Ponsonby Rd BH14 . . . 120 D4
Pony Dr BH16 . . . 117 F7
POOLE . . . 119 B3
Poole Commerce Ctr BH12 . . . 120 F5
Poole Gram Sch BH17 . . . 87 D2
Poole High Sch BH15 . . . 119 C4
Poole Hill BH2 . . . 121 D3
Poole Hospl BH15 . . . 119 D3
Poole La BH11 . . . 89 B5
Poole Mus* BH15 . . . 119 B1
Poole Rd
Bournemouth BH4 . . . 121 C3
Lytchett Matravers BH16 . . . 84 F5
Poole BH13 . . . 121 A4
Sturminster Marshall BH21 . 56 D2
Upton BH16 . . . 117 E7
Wimborne Minster BH21 . . . 59 C4
Poole's Ct 4 DT7 . . . 96 C5
Poole Sta BH15 . . . 119 C3
POOLESTOWN DT10 . . . 33 E5
Pool Lane Rdbt BH11 . . . 88 E4
Poop Hill TA18 . . . 192 C8
Poop Hill La TA18 . . . 192 C8
Poorhouse La DT6 . . . 66 C8
Pope's La DT9 . . . 17 D2
Popes Rd BH15 . . . 119 D6
Poplar Cl
Bransgore BH23 . . . 93 C8
Christchurch BH23 . . . 126 B8
3 Poole BH15 . . . 119 B1
Radipole DT4 . . . 167 A6
Wimborne Minster BH21 . . . 59 D5
Poplar Cres BH24 . . . 55 D7
Poplar Dr
Brympton BA21 . . . 26 E7
Dorchester DT2 . . . 75 D2
Poplar Hill 3 DT11 . . . 198 B6
Poplar La BH23 . . . 93 C8
Poplar Rd BH25 . . . 95 D4
Poplar Way BH24 . . . 55 D7
Pople's Well TA18 . . . 191 E4
Poppies The BH20 . . . 139 E1
Poppy Cl
Christchurch BH23 . . . 125 C8
Upton BH16 . . . 117 B7
Yeovil BA22 . . . 26 D5
Poppyfields SP8 . . . 5 F4
Poppy Way DT6 . . . 100 D2
Portadene 1 BH4 . . . 121 D2
Portarlington Cl BH4 . . . 121 D2
Portarlington Ct 44 BH4 . 121 C3
Portarlington Rd BH4 . . . 121 C2
Portchester Ct 3 BH8 . . . 122 B5
Portchester Pl BH8 . . . 122 B5
Portchester Rd BH8 . . . 122 A5
Portchester Sch BH7 . . . 123 A7
Portelet Cl BH12 . . . 88 D2
Porter Rd BH17 . . . 119 B7
Porters La BH21 . . . 60 C6
Portesham CE Prim Sch DT3 . . . 150 A8
Portesham Gdns BH9 . . . 90 B4
Portesham Hill DT3 . . . 132 A1
Portesham Way BH17 . . . 87 E3
Portfield Cl BH23 . . . 124 A7
Portfield Rd BH23 . . . 124 A7
Portfield Sch BH23 . . . 90 B8
Portiere Ho BH11 . . . 89 A4
Port La DT6 . . . 101 D3
Portland Beach Rd DT4 . 180 E3
Portland Bill Lighthouse* DT5 . . . 186 D9
Portland Bird Obsy & Field Ctr* DT5 . . . 186 E10
Portland Castle* DT5 . . . 181 A1
Portland Com Hospl DT5 . . . 181 B1
Portland Cres DT4 . . . 167 B2
Portland Ct DT7 . . . 96 A5
Portland Mus* DT5 . . . 187 B3
Portland Pl BH2 . . . 121 F4
Portland Port DT5 . . . 181 C2
Portland Port Bsns Ctr DT5 . . . 181 C1
Portland Rd
Bournemouth BH9 . . . 122 A8
Weymouth DT4 . . . 180 C7
Portman Cres BH5 . . . 123 B4
Portman Ct BA22 . . . 192 E8
Portman Dr 5 DT11 . . . 198 C8
Portman Pl DT11 . . . 212 C4
Portman Rd
Bournemouth BH7 . . . 122 F5
11 Pimperne DT11 . . . 199 D4
Portman Terr BH5 . . . 123 B4
Portmore Cl BH18 . . . 87 C6
Portmore Gdns DT4 . . . 167 C1
Portnell's La BA12 . . . 1 F4
Portreeve Dr BA21 . . . 27 D6
Port Regis Sch SP7 . . . 12 B5
Portswood Dr 2 BH10 . . . 90 A4
PORTWAY DT2 . . . 156 F7
Portway DT2 . . . 102 C6
Portwey Cl DT4 . . . 167 C1
Possessions Cnr SP5 . . . 25 B3
POST GREEN BH16 . . . 116 F7
Post Green Rd BH16 . . . 116 F7
Post Office Bldgs BH9 . . . 121 F8
Post Office La BH24 . . . 54 C5
Post Office Rd
18 Bournemouth BH1 . . . 121 F3
Gillingham SP8 . . . 5 D6
Potterne Hill Nature Reserve* BH31 . . . 45 C4
Potterne Way
Verwood BH21 . . . 45 D4
Wimborne BH21 . . . 45 C4
Potterne Wood Cl BH31 . . 45 E4
Potters Way BH14 . . . 120 C2
Pottery Junc BH14 . . . 120 E5
Pottery La DT4 . . . 167 C4
Pottery Lines BH20 . . . 142 F7
Pottery Rd BH14 . . . 120 B2
POULNER BH24 . . . 55 F8
Poulner Hill BH24 . . . 55 F8
Poulner Jun & Inf Schs BH24 . . . 47 E2
Poulner Pk BH24 . . . 47 E1
Poundbury Camp* DT1 . 107 E3
Poundbury Cres DT1 . . . 107 E2
Poundbury Rd DT1 . . . 107 E3
Poundbury West Ind Est DT1 . . . 107 E2
Pound Cl
Charminster DT2 . . . 107 D6
Poole BH15 . . . 119 F5
Ringwood BH24 . . . 55 C8
Stalbridge DT10 . . . 33 C8
Yeovil BA21 . . . 26 E5
Pound Cottage Riding Ctr* DT2 . . . 205 E2
Pound Hill
Corscombe DT2 . . . 205 B7
Witchampton BH21 . . . 200 F1
Pound La
Bishop's Caundle DT9 . . . 196 A7
Burstock DT8 . . . 203 D5
1 Christchurch BH23 . . . 124 B6
Damerham SP6 . . . 190 E3
Dewlish DT2 . . . 209 C1
2 Dorchester DT1 . . . 108 B2
Gillingham SP8 . . . 5 D2
5 Okeford Fitzpaine DT11 197 F5
Okeford Fitzpaine DT11 . . . 198 A5
Poole BH15 . . . 119 E5
Shaftesbury SP7 . . . 13 A3
Wareham BH20 . . . 142 E3
Wootton Fitzpaine DT6 . . . 64 B6
Pound Piece
Easton/Weston DT5 . . . 186 F4
Maiden Newton DT2 . . . 72 F8
Pound Rd
Hawkchurch EX13 . . . 202 C2
Lyme Regis DT7 . . . 96 B5
Sherborne DT9 . . . 30 B3
Thornford DT9 . . . 194 D8
Pound St DT7 . . . 96 B5
Pound The BA12 . . . 3 B5
Powell Rd BH14 . . . 120 B3
Powell Theatre* DT9 . . . 30 B6
Powerscourt Rd BH25 . . . 126 E7
POWERSTOCK DT6 . . . 70 B5
Powerstock CE Prim Sch DT6 . . . 70 A5
Powerstock Comm Reserve* DT6 . . . 70 F6
Powis Cl BH25 . . . 95 B3
Powys Cl DT1 . . . 134 E8
Powys Gn DT9 . . . 30 A6
Powys La DT9 . . . 30 B6
POXWELL DT2 . . . 154 E5
Poxwell Cairn Circle* DT2 . . . 154 F4
Poxwell Dro DT2 . . . 154 B4
POYNTINGTON DT9 . . . 16 D4
Prankerds Rd 3 DT9 . . . 17 C2
Preetz Way DT11 . . . 212 F6
PRESTON DT3 . . . 168 B8
Preston CE Prim Sch BA21 . . . 26 E7
Preston Cl 10 BH16 . . . 117 E7
Preston Ct
Northport BH20 . . . 142 E5
Yeovil BA20 . . . 27 B4
Preston Gr BA20 . . . 27 A5
Preston La BH23 . . . 92 D3
PRESTON PLUCKNETT BA20 . . . 26 F4
Preston Rd
Overcombe/Preston DT3 . . . 153 C3
Poole BH15 . . . 119 C6
Weymouth DT3 . . . 167 F6
Yeovil BA22 . . . 26 C5
Preston Sch BA21 . . . 26 F5
Preston Way BH23 . . . 125 D8
Prestwood Cl BH25 . . . 94 F1
Pretoria Terr DT4 . . . 167 C2
Prideaux Dr SP7 . . . 7 B1
Pride Cl DT2 . . . 137 F7
Priest La BH23 . . . 92 B7
Priestlands DT9 . . . 30 B7
Priestlands La DT9 . . . 30 B7
Priestley Rd BH10 . . . 89 B1
Priest's House Mus The* 12 BH21 . . . 59 B5
Priest's Rd BH19 . . . 179 A2
Priest's Way BH19 . . . 178 F2
Prime La DT6 . . . 65 F7
Primrose Cl 3 SP8 . . . 5 D2
Primrose Gdns BH17 . . . 86 F1
Primrose Hill BA22 . . . 193 B7
Primrose La BA21 . . . 14 A1
Primrose Way
Christchurch BH23 . . . 125 C8
Corfe Mullen BH21 . . . 86 E7
Primula Cl DT3 . . . 152 F2
Prince of Wales Rd
Bournemouth BH4 . . . 121 C4
Dorchester DT1 . . . 108 A1
3 Weymouth DT4 . . . 167 C2
Prince of Wales Sch The DT1 . . . 134 D8
Princes Ct 8 BH13 . . . 121 A4
Prince's Ct BH22 . . . 61 D5
Prince's Dr DT4 . . . 167 D6
Prince's Pl BH25 . . . 95 C3
Princes Rd BH22 . . . 61 D5
Princess Ave BH23 . . . 124 B6
Princess Rd
Bournemouth BH4 . . . 121 B4
Bridport DT6 . . . 100 C5
Poole BH13 . . . 121 A4
Swanage BH19 . . . 179 A2
Princes St BA20 . . . 27 D4
Prince's St DT1 . . . 108 A2
Pringles Cl BH22 . . . 61 E5
Pringles Dr BH22 . . . 61 E5
Prior Cl BH7 . . . 122 F5
Priors Cl BH23 . . . 125 C7
Priors Cnr 2 BH21 . . . 201 D1
Priors Rd BH17 . . . 119 A8
Priors Wlk 3 BH21 . . . 59 B5
Priory CE Prim Sch The 6 BH23 . . . 124 B6
Priory Cl BA20 . . . 26 F1
Priory Gdns
3 Pimperne DT11 . . . 199 D3
3 Spetisbury DT11 . . . 211 E5
West Moors BH22 . . . 62 A8
Priory Glade BA21 . . . 26 E6
Priory Ho BH23 . . . 124 C5
Priory Ind Pk BH23 . . . 125 B7
Priory Quay BH23 . . . 124 C5
Priory Rd
Bournemouth BH2 . . . 121 E2
Portland DT5 . . . 186 F6
West Moors BH22 . . . 62 A8
Priory View Ct 4 BH23 . . 124 B6
Priory View Pl 3 BH9 . . . 90 A3
Priory View Rd
Bournemouth BH9 . . . 90 A3
Burton BH23 . . . 92 C2
Privet Rd BH9 . . . 121 F8
Promenade BH23 . . . 125 B5
Prospect Cl 2 SP8 . . . 6 A1
Prospect Cres BH19 . . . 179 A3
Prospect Pl
Mere BA12 . . . 2 F5
9 Weymouth DT4 . . . 167 D2
Prospect Rd
Dorchester DT1 . . . 107 E2
Lytchett Matravers BH16 . . . 84 D3
Prosperous St 1 BH15 . . 119 C1
Prout Hill 9 DT8 . . . 204 D4
Prunus Cl BH22 . . . 61 B7
Prunus Dr BH22 . . . 61 B7
Pryors Wlk BH16 . . . 84 D2
Pud Brook 2 DT9 . . . 17 D1
Puddledock La DT3 . . . 153 C3
PUDDLETOWN DT2 . . . 78 A1
PUDDLE TOWN TA18 . . . 192 B5
Puddletown CE Fst Sch DT2 . . . 78 B1
Puddletown Cres BH17 . . . 87 F2
Puddletown Rd
Arne BH20 . . . 142 A3
Bere Regis BH20 . . . 140 E7
East Stoke BH20 . . . 113 B1
Pugmill La DT3 . . . 166 D5
Pugs Hole Nature Reserve* BH4 . . . 121 C5
PULHAM DT2 . . . 196 B3
Pullman Way BH24 . . . 55 C6
Pulmans La 4 TA18 . . . 191 F4
PUNCKNOWLE DT2 . . . 129 F6
Purbeck Ave BH15 . . . 118 E1
Purbeck Cl
Loders DT6 . . . 101 F8
Purbeck Cl *continued*
Lytchett Matravers BH16 . . . 84 D3
Upton BH16 . . . 117 D7
Weymouth DT4 . . . 167 B1
Purbeck Ct
Bournemouth BH5 . . . 123 B3
3 Christchurch BH23 . . . 124 F8
Purbeck Dr BH31 . . . 45 B5
Purbeck Gdns BH14 . . . 119 F5
Purbeck Hts BH14 . . . 120 B5
Purbeck Marine Wildlife Reserve* BH20 . . . 175 B2
Purbeck Rd
Barton on Sea BH25 . . . 126 D7
Bournemouth BH2 . . . 121 E2
Lytchett Matravers BH16 . . . 84 D4
Purbeck Sch The BH20 . . . 142 C2
Purbeck Sports Ctr & Swimming Pool BH20 . . 142 C2
Purbeck Terr Rd BH19 . . . 179 C1
Purbeck View 9 BH19 . . 178 F2
Purbeck View Pk BH20 . . 142 E4
Purbeck View Sch BH19 . 179 B3
Purchase Rd BH12 . . . 121 C7
Purdy Ho BH11 . . . 89 A4
PUREWELL . . . 124 D7
Purewell BH23 . . . 124 D6
Purewell Cl BH23 . . . 124 E6
Purewell Cross BH23 . . . 124 E6
Purewell Cross Rd BH23 124 D7
Purewell Ct 2 BH23 . . . 124 E7
Purewell Mdws Nature Reserve* BH23 . . . 124 D7
Purewell Rdbt BH23 . . . 124 E6
Purns Mill La SP8 . . . 5 F5
PURSE CAUNDLE DT9 . . . 32 B8
PURTINGTON TA20 . . . 191 A4
Pussex La BH23 . . . 91 A7
Putlake Adventure Farm* BH19 . . . 178 C2
PUTTON DT3 . . . 166 E5
Putton La DT3 . . . 166 D5
Putt's La DT9 . . . 16 B8
PUXEY DT10 . . . 197 B7
Puxey La
Shillingstone DT11 . . . 198 B5
Sturminster Newton DT10 . 197 B7
Pye Cl BH21 . . . 86 E7
Pye Cnr BH21 . . . 59 B4
Pye La
Cranborne BH21 . . . 41 A6
Tatworth & Forton TA20 . . . 202 B8
Wimborne Minster BH21 . . . 59 B4
PYMORE DT6 . . . 68 D1
Pymore La DT6 . . . 68 C3
Pymore Rd DT6 . . . 68 E1

Q

Quadrant Ctr The BH1 . . . 121 F3
Quantock Ct 7 BH23 . . . 124 F8
Quar Cl DT10 . . . 196 E1
Quarr Dr DT9 . . . 30 B8
Quarr Hill
Morden BH20 . . . 83 C1
Wool BH20 . . . 140 B1
Quarr La
Lytchett Matravers BH16 . . . 84 A1
Sherborne DT9 . . . 30 B8
Symondsbury DT6 . . . 99 D8
Quarr Nature Reserve The* DT9 . . . 30 B7
Quarry Chase 4 BH4 . . . 121 C3
Quarry Cl
Shipton Gorge DT6 . . . 101 D4
Stour Provost SP8 . . . 21 D8
Sturminster Newton DT10 . . 35 B2
8 Swanage BH19 . . . 178 F2
Wimborne Minster BH21 . . . 60 B7
Quarry Dr BH21 . . . 60 B7
Quarry Fields Ind Est BA12 . 2 E5
Quarry La
Bothenhampton DT6 . . . 100 E4
Bradford Abbas DT9 . . . 28 C3
Longburton DT9 . . . 195 B8
Melbury Abbas SP7 . . . 24 B5
Quarry Rd BH21 . . . 60 B7
Quarterjack Mews 1 BH21 . . . 59 C4
Quayle Dr BH11 . . . 88 F6
Quay Point 7 BH15 . . . 119 C1
Quay Rd BH23 . . . 124 B6
Quayside DT6 . . . 100 C1
Quay The
Poole BH15 . . . 119 C1
3 Wareham Town BH20 . . 142 E3
Quebec Pl 2 DT4 . . . 167 D3
Queen Anne Dr
Oakley BH21 . . . 87 E8
Wimborne Minster BH21 . . . 60 A1
Queen Eleanor Rd SP8 . . . 6 A1
Queen Elizabeth Ct BH21 . 59 B4
Queen Elizabeth L Ctr BH21 . . . 58 F6
Queen Elizabeth's Sch BH21 . . . 58 F6
Queen Mary Ave BH9 . . . 89 F2
QUEEN OAK SP8 . . . 2 A3
Queen's Ave
Christchurch BH23 . . . 124 B5
Dorchester DT1 . . . 134 E8
Queensbury Mans 9 BH1 . . . 122 A3
Queens Cl BH22 . . . 52 F1
Queen's Copse La BH21 . . 51 C8
Queens Ct
16 Bournemouth BH4 . . . 121 D4
Queens Ct *continued*
Bournemouth, Charminster BH8 . . . 122 B8
New Milton BH25 . . . 95 D3
Queens Dr DT2 . . . 137 F7
Queens Gdns BH2 . . . 121 D4
Queens Gr
New Milton BH25 . . . 95 C4
Pen Selwood BA9 . . . 1 C3
Queensland Rd
Bournemouth BH5 . . . 123 A5
Weymouth DT4 . . . 167 B3
Queensmead
Burton BH23 . . . 92 A1
4 Wimborne Minster BH21 59 C5
Queens Mead 8 BH19 . . . 179 B2
Queen's Park Ave BH8 . . 122 D8
Queen's Park Gdns BH8 . 122 D7
Queen's Park Inf Sch BH8 90 C1
Queen's Park Jun Sch BH8 . . . 90 B1
Queen's Park Rd BH8 . . 122 D7
Queen's Park South Dr BH8 . . . 122 D7
Queen's Park West Dr BH8 . . . 122 D7
Queens Rd
Bradford Abbas DT9 . . . 28 D2
Bridport DT6 . . . 100 C6
Ferndown BH22 . . . 61 D7
Fortuneswell DT5 . . . 186 E8
Mere BA12 . . . 3 B6
Radipole DT3 . . . 167 C7
Queen's Rd
Blandford Forum DT11 . . . 212 E4
Bournemouth BH3 . . . 121 D4
Christchurch BH23 . . . 124 E6
Poole BH14 . . . 120 D4
Poole BH21 . . . 85 F5
Swanage BH19 . . . 179 B1
Queen St
Gillingham SP8 . . . 5 F2
Radipole DT4 . . . 167 E4
4 Yetminster DT9 . . . 194 C5
Queensway
New Milton BH25 . . . 94 E3
Ringwood BH24 . . . 55 D7
Yeovil BA20 . . . 27 C5
Queensway Pl BA20 . . . 27 C4
Queens Wlk
Charmouth DT6 . . . 97 B7
Lyme Regis DT7 . . . 96 B6
Queenswood Ave BH8 . . . 90 E1
Queenswood Dr BH22 . . . 61 D7
Queenwell DT6 . . . 68 E1
Quibo La DT4 . . . 167 A3
Quince La BH21 . . . 59 E6
Quintin Cl BH23 . . . 125 F8
Quomp BH24 . . . 55 C7

R

Rabin Hill DT10 . . . 35 B2
Rabling La BH19 . . . 179 B3
Rabling Rd BH19 . . . 179 B3
Racedown Rd DT11 . . . 199 E3
Rachel Cl BH12 . . . 120 C7
RADIPOLE DT3 . . . 167 B7
Radipole Com Woodland Nature Reserve* DT3 . . 167 B8
Radipole La DT4 . . . 167 A5
Radipole Lake RSPB Reserve* DT4 . . . 167 C4
Radipole Lake Visitor Ctr* DT4 . . . 167 D4
Radipole Park Dr DT4 . . . 167 C5
Radipole Prim Sch DT3 . 167 B8
Radipole Rd BH17 . . . 88 A2
Raglan Gdns BH11 . . . 89 A2
Raglan Terr BA21 . . . 27 A7
Railway Dr BH21 . . . 56 D4
Railway Terr 4 SP8 . . . 6 A1
Railway Triangle Ind Est DT1 . . . 107 E2
Raleigh Cl
Christchurch BH23 . . . 124 F5
New Milton BH25 . . . 94 F3
3 Ringwood BH24 . . . 55 E8
Raleigh Rd
Poole BH12 . . . 88 E1
Stalbridge DT10 . . . 33 E8
Ralph Jessop Ct BH12 . . . 120 D7
Ralph Rd BH21 . . . 86 E7
Ram La DT11 . . . 48 C1
Rampart Wlk 4 DT1 . . . 134 E7
RAMPISHAM DT2 . . . 205 F5
Rampisham Hill DT8 . . . 205 C3
Ramsbury DT10 . . . 196 D5
Ramsbury Cl DT11 . . . 212 D5
Ramsbury Ct DT11 . . . 212 C5
Ramsey Ct BH25 . . . 94 F3
Ram's Hill DT10 . . . 21 F2
Randall Cl DT3 . . . 166 D5
Randalls Hill BH16 . . . 85 B1
Randolph Rd
2 Bournemouth BH1 . . . 122 E4
Poole BH14 . . . 120 C5
Ranelagh Rd
Christchurch BH23 . . . 125 F7
Radipole DT4 . . . 167 D4
Rashley Rd DT3 . . . 166 D5
Raspberry La SP7 . . . 12 D2
Ratcliff's Gdn SP7 . . . 12 D2
Ratleigh La DT9 . . . 29 B6
Ravana Ct 4 BH8 . . . 122 A5
Ravenscourt Rd BH6 . . . 123 C5
Ravensdale Cl BH12 . . . 120 C6

Ravenshall 7 BH2 121 D2
Raven Way BH23 125 A5
Ravine Ct BH13 147 F7
Ravine Gdns 5 BH13 147 F7
Ravine Rd
Bournemouth BH5 123 B4
Poole BH13 147 F8
Rawles Way DT6 100 D7
Rawston Down Rd 6
DT11 199 E2
Rax La DT6 100 D7
Raymond Cl BH31 45 D6
Raymond Rd DT4 166 F2
Rayners Dr BH12 120 D6
Rayscliff 21 BH4 121 C2
Reap La DT5 186 E2
Rebbeck Rd BH7 123 A6
Reckleford BA20 27 D5
Reckleford Com Sch
BA21 27 E5
Recreation Rd BH12 120 E6
Rectory Ave BH21 57 F1
Rectory Cl DT2 136 B1
Rectory Gdns DT11 198 F7
Rectory La
Child Okeford DT11 198 C7
Hardington Mandeville
BA22 193 A7
Puncknowle DT2 129 E6
Studland BH19 164 C2
West Stafford DT2 136 A8
Rectory Rd
Broadmayne DT2 136 B2
Piddlehinton DT2 76 E7
Poole BH15 119 C6
Rectory Way DT4 167 C1
Redan Cl BH23 125 F7
Redbreast Rd BH9 90 A3
Redbreast Road N BH9 90 A3
REDBRIDGE DT2 138 B5
Redbridge La DT2 137 F5
Redbridge Rd DT2 137 F6
Redcliffe Cl BH23 92 C3
Redcliffe Rd BH19 179 B5
Redcliff View DT4 167 E1
Redcotts La BH21 59 B5
Redcotts Rd BH21 59 B5
REDFORD DT2 206 D8
Redgate Pk TA18 191 E5
RED HILL 89 F5
Redhill Ave BH9 89 F3
Redhill Cl BH10 89 E3
Redhill Comm Nature
Reserve* BH9 89 F3
Redhill Cres BH9 89 F3
Redhill Ct 1 BH10 90 A4
Redhill Dr BH10 89 E3
Redhill Park Homes 1
BH10 89 F4
Redhill Rdbt BH10 89 F4
Redhoave Rd BH17 87 E2
Redhole La DT9 16 B2
Redhorn Cl BH16 117 E4
Red Horn Cl BH16 118 C4
Red House Cl SP7 7 B1
Red House Mus & Gdns*
BH23 124 B6
Red La
Corfe Mullen BH21 85 C8
Seaborough DT8 191 E1
Sixpenny Handley SP5 189 A3
Todber DT10 21 D4
Weymouth DT3 149 B7
REDLANDS DT3 152 B1
Redlands
Christchurch BH23 125 A7
Poole BH12 120 F5
Redlands La DT8 203 F5
Red Lion Cl 3 DT10 197 D8
Red Lion Yd DT11 212 C3
Redmans La SP7 24 B6
Redmans View BH31 45 A6
Red Oaks Cl BH22 61 B7
Redpoll Cl 1 DT3 152 C4
Red Post
Bloxworth DT11 82 C7
Poyntington DT9 16 C4
Redsails BH13 147 B3
Redshank Cl BH17 86 F1
Redvers Rd BH23 124 E7
Red Wing Rd DT9 17 C2
Redwood Cl BH24 55 D7
Redwood Dr BH22 61 C8
Redwood Rd
Upton BH16 117 C8
Yeovil BA21 28 A8
Reedling Cl DT3 152 C3
Reed View Cl DT4 167 A5
Reeves Orchard BH21 56 D5
Reforne DT5 186 F4
Reforne Cl 1 DT5 187 A4
Regency Cres BH23 123 F8
Regency Ct 9 SP8 5 D2
Regency Dr 7 DT3 152 C4
Regent Ctr* BH23 124 B6
Regent Dr BH7 122 F8
Regents The 2 BA21 26 E6
Regent Way BH23 124 B6
Reid St BH23 124 A8
Rempstone Rd
Oakley BH21 87 D8
Swanage BH19 179 B2
Rempstone Sh Arc 8
BH20 142 E3
Remus Cl DT1 134 E7
Renault Dr BH18 87 A1
Rendalls Wlk DT6 100 B6
Renfrew Cl DT1 135 C8
Renscombe Rd BH19 183 B8
Restharrow BH1 122 A4
Retreat Rd BH21 59 D4
Reuben Dr BH15 117 F2
Revels Hill DT2 207 E7
REW DT2 208 B8
Rew La DT2 208 A8
Rex La DT3 166 D5
Rex's La BA22 27 F1
Reynard Ct BH15 119 F3
Reynards Way DT3 153 C3
Rhine Rd BH20 139 E6
Rhode La DT7 64 A1
Rhosewood Dr DT3 153 B3
Rhydderch Way 9 TA18 191 F4
Ribble Cl BH18 87 A2
Ribbonwood Hts BH14 120 B4
Ricardo Cres BH23 125 A6
Rice Gdns BH16 117 F4
Rice Terr BH16 118 D4
Richard Cl 2 BH16 117 D8
Richmond Cl DT9 30 A5
Richmond Ct 7 BH25 95 A3
Richmond Gdns BH1 121 F3
Richmond Gn DT9 30 A6
Richmond Hill BH2 121 F3
Richmond Hill Dr BH2 121 F3
Richmond Park Ave BH8 122 C7
Richmond Park Cl BH8 122 D6
Richmond Park Cres
BH8 122 C7
Richmond Park Rd BH8 122 C7
Richmond Rd
4 Blandford Forum
DT11 212 E5
Poole BH14 120 C4
Sherborne DT9 30 A5
Swanage BH19 179 B2
Wimborne Minster BH21 59 D4
Yeovil BA20 27 C4
Richmond Rise BH8 122 D6
Richmond Way BA21 26 E6
Richmond Wood Rd
BH8 122 C7
Ricketts Cl DT4 167 E5
Ricketts La DT10 35 B1
Rickhay Rise TA18 192 B8
RIDGE BH20 143 B1
Ridgeback La DT6 69 E8
Ridge Cl SP8 10 E3
Ridge Dro DT10 196 F4
Ridgefield Gdns BH23 125 D8
Ridge La
Hazelbury Bryan DT10 196 D5
West Coker BA22 193 A8
Ridgemead 5 BA20 26 F2
Ridgemount Gdns BH15 118 E3
Ridge The DT9 16 E5
Ridge View DT10 196 F8
Ridgeway
Bradpole DT6 68 F1
Broadstone BH18 87 B4
Corfe Mullen BH21 86 D8
Ferndown BH22 89 E8
Poole BH21 85 F8
Sherborne DT9 29 F5
Ridge Way
Puddletown DT2 76 F1
Shaftesbury SP7 12 F4
Ridgeway La
Child Okeford DT11 198 C8
Hinton St Mary DT10 35 B4
Ridgeway Rd SP8 5 E3
Ridgeway The DT3 152 B7
Ridgway TA18 192 B8
Ridley Rd BH9 121 F8
Ridout Cl BH10 89 B1
Ridouts DT11 197 F6
Ridwood DT6 99 A6
Rigg La DT9 14 F2
Riggs Gdns BH11 88 F2
Rigler Rd BH15 119 A2
Rimbrow Cl DT3 153 C3
Rimbury Way BH23 124 A8
RIMPTON BA22 15 C8
Rimpton Hill BA22 15 A7
Ring St DT10 33 D8
Ringstead Cres DT3 168 B6
Rings The DT11 79 F8
RINGWOOD BH24 47 D1
Ringwood CE Inf Sch
BH24 55 C7
Ringwood Cty Jun Sch
BH24 55 C6
Ringwood L Ctr BH24 55 C7
Ringwood Rd
Alderholt SP6 42 C5
Bournemouth BH11 88 E4
Bransgore BH23 93 D5
Ferndown BH22 61 C4
Fordingbridge SP6 43 C5
Hyde SP6 43 E4
Poole BH12 120 B7
Sopley BH23 92 A7
St Leonards BH24 53 F2
Three Legged Cross BH21 52 F8
Verwood BH31 45 D6
Walkford BH23 94 B1
West Moors BH22 62 A8
Ringwood Road Ret Pk
BH11 88 E3
Ringwood Sch BH24 55 C7
Ringwood Trad Est BH24 55 C6
Ringwood Waldorf Sch
BH24 54 F6
Rip Croft DT5 186 E2
Ripley Ct BH22 61 F7
Ripon Rd BH9 90 A1
Ripp's La DT2 208 A5
Rise The
Radipole DT4 167 A5
Stratton DT2 106 D8
Ritchie Pl BH22 52 F3
Ritchie Rd
Bournemouth BH11 89 B4
Yeovil BA22 26 C5
River Cl BH21 59 C6
Riverdale La BH23 124 A6
River La 2 DT11 211 D6
Riverland Ct 4 BH23 124 A6
Riverlea Rd BH23 124 A6
Rivermead Gdns BH23 91 E2
River Mews DT11 212 C3
River Pk BH6 123 F6
RIVERS' CORNER DT10 197 C7
Riversdale 8 BH21 59 C4
Riversdale Rd BH6 124 A4
Riversdene DT11 48 A6
Riverside
3 Beaminster DT8 204 D4
4 Bournemouth BH10 89 F4
Ringwood BH24 55 B6
Riverside Ave BH7 91 C1
Riverside Cl DT2 207 D4
Riverside Ct 7 BH4 121 D4
Riverside La BH6 123 F5
Riverside Park Ind Est
BH21 59 D3
Riverside Pk BH23 124 A5
Riverside Rd
Blandford Forum DT11 212 E3
Bournemouth BH6 123 F5
Ferndown BH22 52 F2
Riverslea Mews BH23 124 D6
Rivers Mead DT10 35 C2
Riversmeet Ct BH23 124 D6
Rivers Rd BA21 27 F8
Rivervale DT6 100 D8
River View SP8 5 E2
River Way
Charmouth DT6 97 B7
Christchurch BH23 91 D2
Riviera 11 BH1 122 B3
Riviera Ct
Bournemouth BH2 121 D3
3 Poole BH13 147 F7
RIXON DT10 35 C2
Rixon Cl DT10 35 C1
Rixon Hill DT10 35 C1
R L Stevenson Ave BH4 121 B3
RNLI HQ & Mus* BH15 119 C2
Roberts La BH17 118 F7
Robertson Rd BH20 139 D7
Roberts Pl DT1 107 E1
Roberts Rd
Bournemouth BH7 123 A6
Poole BH17 87 B1
Robin Cl 2 DT3 152 C4
Robin Cres BH25 94 D5
Robin Gdns BH23 124 A8
Robin Gr BH25 94 F2
Robins Ct 7 BH21 59 C4
Robins Garth DT1 108 B1
Robins Gdn DT2 209 A2
Robinson Hts DT10 33 D8
Robins Way BH23 125 B5
Robinswood Dr BH22 61 D7
Robsall Cl BH12 120 E7
Robville Ct 3 BH7 123 B6
Roche Cl BA21 26 E7
Rochester Rd BH11 89 B4
Rockbourne Gdns BH25 126 D8
Rockbourne La SP6 190 F3
ROCKFORD BH24 47 E4
Rockford Cl BH6 123 F3
Rockhampton Cl DT3 152 D3
Rockley Mews BH15 118 E2
Rockley Pk Cvn Est BH15,
BH16 118 B3
Rockley Rd BH15 118 E1
Rocks La DT2 206 A7
Rockway DT6 101 C4
Rocky Knap DT3 167 C7
RODDEN DT3 150 C5
Rodden Cl DT4 180 C8
Rodden La DT3 150 C5
Rodden Row DT3 149 B7
Rodgett Cres BH20 142 F8
RODGROVE BA9 8 E6
Rod Hill La DT2 78 B1
Rodney Cl BH12 121 A8
Rodney Ct
Christchurch BH23 125 A6
6 Poole BH15 119 C1
Rodney Dr BH23 124 F6
Rodway BH21 59 C4
RODWELL DT4 167 D1
Rodwell Ave DT4 167 D1
Rodwell Cl BH10 89 C6
Rodwell Rd DT4 167 D1
Rodwell St DT4 167 D1
Roe Ave BA22 26 C5
Roebuck Cl BH25 95 B3
Roe La BA22 15 B8
Roeshot Cres BH23 93 E1
Roeshot Hill BH23 93 C2
Roi-mar Home Pk BH8 90 D4
Roke Rd BH20 80 F4
Rolfe Cres DT3 166 D6
Rolls Bridge La SP8 5 E2
Rolls Bridge Way SP8 5 D2
Rolls Dr BH6 124 B3
ROLLS MILL DT10 197 C8
Rolls Mill Way DT10 197 C8
Roman Cl DT3 167 C7
Roman Hill Trading Est
DT2 154 D6
Roman Hts BH21 86 E8
Roman Rd
Corfe Mullen BH18 86 E5
Dorchester DT1 134 F8
Lyme Regis DT7 96 A6
Osmington DT3 154 A1
Radipole DT3 167 C7
Roman Way
Blandford Forum DT11 198 B5
Pamphill BH21 57 E5
ROMFORD BH31 44 E7
Romney Cl BH10 89 E3
Romney Ct 51 BH4 121 C3
Romney Rd BH10 89 E4
Romsey Rd BA21 28 A7
Romulus Cl DT1 134 E7
Rookery Cl SP8 11 B8
Rookery La
Burstock DT8 203 C6
Uplyme DT7 64 A2
Rookery The DT2 130 F8
Rook Hill Rd BH23 125 B6
Rook La DT11 210 C2
Rook St BA12 3 A4
ROOK STREET BA12 3 A4
Roosevelt Cres BH11 89 B6
Ropers La BH16 117 F7
Roper's La BH20 142 E4
Rope Walks DT6 100 C6
Roping Rd BA21 27 C6
Ropley Rd BH7 123 C7
Rosamond Ave DT6 101 D4
Rosamund Ave BH21 59 E1
Roscrea Cl BH6 124 B4
Roscrea Dr BH6 124 B4
Rosebank La DT11 212 F6
Roseberry Gdns 3 SP8 5 F3
Rosebery Ave BA21 27 F6
Rosebery Cl BH31 45 E5
Rosebery Rd BH5 123 A5
Rosebud Ave 1 BH9 90 A2
Rosecrae Cl BH25 94 F4
Rose Cres BH15 119 F6
Rosecroft Rd DT4 166 F1
Rose Ct
3 Gillingham SP8 6 A1
Poole BH15 119 E3
Rosedale Cl 3 BH23 124 E6
Rose Farm Cl BH22 61 B3
Rosefields 2 DT11 212 D2
Rose Gdns BH9 90 A3
Rose Gdn The BH23 91 D1
Rose La
1 Crewkerne TA18 191 E4
Winsham TA20 191 A4
Roselyn Cres DT9 31 B1
Rosemary Ct 8 BH23 126 B7
Rosemary Gdns BH12 120 B7
Rosemary La DT3 149 B7
Rosemary Rd BH12 120 C7
Rosemary St DT9 17 C2
Rosemount Rd BH4 121 B2
Rose's La DT3 150 C2
Rosewood Gdns BH25 94 F4
Roslin Gdns BH3 121 D7
Roslin Rd BH3 121 E7
Roslin Road S BH3 121 E7
Ross Cl BH20 139 F6
Ross Gdns BH11 88 C5
Ross Glades BH3 121 E6
Rossiters Quay BH23 124 C6
Rossley Cl BH23 93 E2
ROSSMORE 120 E7
Rossmore Com Coll
BH12 120 D8
Rossmore L Ctr BH12 120 D8
Rossmore Par BH12 120 B8
Rossmore Rd BH12 120 D7
Ross Rd BH24 47 E1
Rotary Cl BH21 59 F7
Rothbury Pk BH25 95 B2
Rotherfield Rd
Bournemouth BH5 123 B3
Walkford BH23 94 A1
Rotherham Rd DT5 181 C1
Rothesay Dr BH23 125 E7
Rothesay Rd
Bournemouth BH4 121 C5
Dorchester DT1 135 A8
Rotterdam Dr BH23 124 D7
Rough Down La DT6 65 B2
Rough Height BH19 179 B1
Roumelia La BH1, BH5 122 E4
ROUNDHAM TA18 191 D4
Roundham Gdns
Bridport DT6 100 D3
Weymouth DT4 167 A2
Roundhaye Gdns BH11 88 F6
Roundhaye Rd BH11 88 F6
Roundhayes Cl DT4 167 A2
Roundways BH11 88 F3
Rowan Cl
Christchurch BH23 125 D8
Radipole DT4 167 A6
Sandford BH20 143 A8
St Leonards & St Ives BH24 53 F4
Rowan Dr
Broadstone BH17 86 E1
Christchurch BH23 125 D8
Verwood BH31 45 D4
Rowan Way BA20 27 A3
Rowbarrow Cl BH17 87 E2
Rowbarrow Hill DT9 14 F4
Rowbarrow La BH21 200 F2
Rowden Mill La DT10 32 E1
Rowe Gdns 6 BH12 120 F7
Rowena Rd BH6 123 F5
Rowland Ave BH15 119 E6
ROWLANDS 59 C5
Rowlands Hill BH21 59 D6
Rowlands Rd 5 DT11 198 F4
Rowls La BA9 4 B3
Rownhams Rd BH8 90 D3
Row The DT10 35 A1
Roxborough 47 BH4 121 C3
Royal Arc 5 BH1 122 E4
Royal Bournemouth Hospl
The BH7 91 B1
Royal Cl BA21 27 E6
Royal Manor Sch The
DT5 186 F4
Royal Oak Rd BH10 89 C5
Royal Signals Mus*
DT11 199 E3
Royal Victoria Mews
BH4 121 D3
Royster Cl BH17 87 C1
Royston Dr BH21 59 D5
Royston Pl BH25 127 B8
Rozelle Rd BH14 120 C4
Rozel Manor BH13 121 B2
Ruben Dr BH15 118 D2
Rubens Cl BH25 95 B3
Ruddock Cl BA22 193 B8
Ruddock Way BA22 193 A8
Rue La DT9 31 F4
Rufford Gdns BH6 123 E5
Rufus Castle* DT5 187 B3
Rufus Way DT5 187 B5
Rugby Rd BH17 87 A1
Ruins La DT6 99 A6
Rundlestone Ct 9 DT1 107 B2
Runnymede Ave BH11 88 E6
Runnymede Rd BA21 27 F8
Runton Rd BH12 120 F5
Runway The BH23 125 B7
Rural La DT2 73 F3
Ruscombe La DT6 69 E6
Rushall La BH21 85 C5
Rushcombe Fst Sch BH21 85 F6
Rushcombe Way 3 BH21 85 F6
Rushetts Cl 4 DT5 186 F1
Rushford Warren BH23 124 F5
Rushmere Rd BH6 123 D7
RUSHTON BH20 141 B2
Rushton Cres BH3 121 F6
Ruskin Ave BH9 90 B3
Russell Ave
Swanage BH19 179 B1
Weymouth DT4 167 B1
Russell Cotes Art Gall &
Mus* BH1 122 A2
Russell Cotes Rd BH1 122 A2
Russell Ct 2 BH25 95 A3
Russell Dr
Christchurch BH23 124 D6
Swanage BH19 179 B1
Russell Gdns
St Leonards BH24 54 D5
Upton BH16 117 E4
Russel Pl DT9 17 C3
Russel Rd BH10 89 C6
Russet Cl BH22 61 D6
Russet Gdns DT6 100 F8
Russet Way BA20 26 F2
Rutland Manor 10 BH13 121 A4
Rutland Rd
Bournemouth BH9 122 B8
Christchurch BH23 91 F1
Weymouth DT4 167 B4
RYALL DT6 66 D2
Ryall Rd
Poole BH17 87 D1
Whitechurch Canonicorum
DT6 66 D2
Ryall's La DT9 196 A7
Ryan Cl
Ferndown BH22 61 C7
Northport BH20 142 E5
Ryan Gdns
Bournemouth BH11 89 B6
Ferndown BH22 61 C7
Rydal Cl BH23 91 D4
Rydal Ho 2 BH4 121 C2
Rydal Mews BH21 59 D5
Ryecroft Ave BH11 88 E5
Ryefields Cl BA22 193 B8
Rye Gdns BA20 26 F2
Rye Hill BH20 81 B1
Rye Hill Cl BH20 81 B1
Ryemead La DT4 180 C6
Rye Wr La BA22 193 A1
Ryland's La DT4 180 D8
Rymbury DT3 153 C3
RYME INTRINSECA DT9 194 B6
Ryme Rd DT9 194 B5

S

Sackmore Gn DT10 20 F3
Sackmore La DT10 20 F3
Sackville St DT11 81 E8
Sadborow La TA20 202 E5
Saddle Cl BH21 60 C6
Safety Dr BH17 119 A7
Saffron Ct BH11 88 D3
Saffron Dr BH23 125 B8
Saffron Way BH11 88 D3
St Alban's Ave BH8 122 C7
St Alban's Cres BH8 122 B8

Townsend Way DT6 68 F2
Townsville Rd BH9 90 B2
Tozer Cl BH11 88 F2
Tracey Ct 8 BH23 126 A7
Tradecroft DT5 186 E5
Tradecroft Ind Est DT5 186 F5
Trafalgar Ct BH23 124 F5
Trafalgar Rd BH9 121 F7
Treebys Cl BH23 92 D1
Tree Hamlets BH16 117 E5
Treeside BH23 93 C2
Treetops 9 BH13 147 F7
Trefoil Way BH23 125 C8
Tregonwell Ct 18 BH2 121 E3
Tregonwell Rd BH2 121 E2
Trellech Ct 1 BA22 26 E6
Treloen Ct 3 BH8 122 A5
Trenchard Mdw BH16 84 D3
Trenchard Way DT3 166 D5
Trendle St DT9 30 B5
TRENT DT9 14 E2
Trent Cl
Tolpuddle DT2 79 D1
Yeovil BA21 28 A8
Trent Dr BH20 142 D5
Trentham Ave BH7 123 B8
Trentham Cl BH7 123 B8
Trent Path La DT9 29 E7
Trent Sq SP8 6 B1
Trent Way BH22 62 A6
Tresco Spinney BA21 26 E6
Tresillian Cl BH23 94 B2
Tresillian Way BH23 94 B2
Treves Rd DT1 134 E8
Trevone 5 BH25 95 B3
Triangle The
Bournemouth BH2 121 E3
6 Upton BH16 117 D7
TRICKETT'S CROSS 61 F7
Tricketts La BH22 61 F6
Trigon Rd BH15 119 D7
Trill La DT9 194 B7
Trinidad Cres BH12 120 C8
Trinidad Ho BH12 120 C8
Trinity 2 BH1 122 A3
Trinity CE Fst Sch BH31 45 B8
Trinity Ct 10 DT4 167 D2
Trinity Ind Est BH21 59 E3
Trinity La BH20 142 E3
Trinity Rd
Bournemouth BH1 122 A4
Weymouth DT4 167 D2
Trinity St
Dorchester DT1 108 A2
7 Weymouth DT4 167 E2
Trinity Terr DT4 167 D2
Trinity Way DT6 68 F1
Tristram Cl 7 BA21 26 F7
Troak Cl BH23 124 E8
Troon Rd BH18 87 A5
Trotters La BH21 60 B6
Troublefield Reserve★ BH23 91 A8
Truman Rd BH11 89 B6
Truscott Ave BH9 122 A7
Trusthams DT8 203 E5
Trustin Cl 6 DT6 100 C8
Trystworthy 3 BH2 121 E3
Tuckers La BH15 118 F1
Tuckers Mill Cl BH20 160 F8
Tucks Cl BH23 93 A8
TUCKTON 123 F5
Tuckton Cl BH6 123 D4
Tuckton Gdns BH6 123 E5
Tuckton Rd BH6 123 F5
Tuckton Rdbt BH6 123 F5
Tudor Arc Sh Ctr DT1 108 A2
Tudor Cl SP6 42 C5
Tudor Ct
Bournemouth BH1 122 A5
10 Gillingham SP8 5 D2
Poole BH15 119 E6
Tudor Gdns DT11 212 E5
Tudor Rd BH18 87 B4
Tullon's La DT2 208 B2
Tulse Hill BA12 1 F3
Tuncombe La TA18 191 D4
Tunnel Rd DT8 204 C5
Turbary Cl BH12 120 D8
Turbary Comm Nature Reserve★ BH11 88 F2
Turbary Ct
Bournemouth BH12 89 A1
Ferndown BH22 61 F6
2 Upton BH16 117 E8
Turbary Hts BH11 88 F1
Turbary Park Ave BH11 89 A2
Turbary Rd
Ferndown BH22 61 F6
Poole BH12 120 D8
Turbary Ret Pk BH11 88 E3
Turberville Rd BH20 81 B2
Turbetts Cl BH16 84 C4
Turf Croft Ct BH23 94 B2
Turk's La BH14 120 A1
TURLIN MOOR BH16 117 D4
Turlin Moor Com Sch BH16 117 E4
Turlin Moor Nature Reserve★ BH15 117 D4
Turlin Rd BH16 117 E4
TURMER BH24 46 F8
Turnberry Cl BH23 123 F6
Turner's Barn La BA20 27 B2
Turners La SP8 5 E2
Turner's La
Marshwood DT6 202 E2
Tarrant Monkton DT11 200 B4
TURNERS PUDDLE DT2 112 D8
Turnpike Cl 2 TA18 192 B3
Turnpike Gn 3 TA18 192 B3
Turnpike La DT11 212 C1
Turnstone Cl DT3 152 D4
TURNWORTH DT11 198 B2
Turnworth Cl BH18 87 C3
Turton St 3 DT4 167 D3
Tutankhamun Exhibition The★ 9 DT1 108 A2
Tut Hill DT9 31 E1
Tweedale Rd BH9 90 C3
Twemlow Ave BH14 119 F3
Twin Oak Pk BH23 92 D6
Twin Oaks Cl BH18 87 A3
Twinways La DT6 69 B8
Two Droves DT2 109 F8
Two Elms BA22 14 C8
Two Riversmeet L Ctr BH23 124 C6
Two Tower La BA20, BA22 27 D2
TWYFORD SP7 23 D2
Twyford Cl BH8 90 D2
Twyford Ho BH22 61 F6
Twyford Way BH17 88 A2
Twynham Ave BH23 124 A7
Twynham Rd BH6 123 F4
Twynham Sch BH23 124 A6
Tyberton St DT1 107 C1
Tynedale Cl BH9 90 B4
TYNEHAM BH20 174 C5
Tyneham Ave BH12 120 C8
Tyneham Cl
Radipole DT3 167 B8
Sandford BH20 143 A8
Tyneham Mus★ BH20 174 C5
Tynham Ct BH23 124 C6
Tyrrell Gdns BH8 91 A2
Tytherley Gn BH8 90 D2

U

Ubsdell Cl BH25 95 A3
Uddens Dr
Ferndown Town BH21 51 F1
Wimborne Minster BH21 60 D7
Uddens Rd SP5 188 C4
Uddens Trad Est BH21 60 E6
Ullswater Cres DT3 167 B7
Ullswater Rd BH21 59 C2
ULWELL BH19 179 A6
Ulwell Rd BH19 179 C4
Umbers Hill SP7 12 D2
Undercliff Dr BH1 122 C2
Undercliff Rd BH5 122 E3
Underdown Hollow DT9 28 C3
Underhedge Gdns DT5 186 E1
Underhill
Mere BA12 2 F5
Pen Selwood BA9 1 B2
Underhill Jun Sch DT5 186 E7
Underwater Explorers DT5 181 B2
Underwood Cl BH17 87 B1
Union St 2 BA20 27 D4
Unity La 4 TA18 192 A3
University Rdbt BH10 121 C8
UP CERNE DT2 207 C5
UPHALL DT2 205 E5
Upland Cl DT10 197 D7
Uplands
Bothenhampton DT6 101 A6
2 Yetminster DT9 194 C5
Uplands Ave BH25 127 A8
Uplands Cl BH22 62 A8
Uplands Gdns BH8 90 C2
Uplands Ind Pk DT11 212 D6
Uplands Rd
Bournemouth BH8 90 C2
Ferndown BH22 53 C1
Uplands Sch BH14 120 C3
UPLODERS DT6 101 F8
Uplyme Cl BH17 88 A2
Uplyme Rd DT7 96 A6
UP MUDFORD BA21 14 A2
Upper Fairfield Rd 3 DT1 107 F1
Upper Golf Links Rd BH18 87 B5
Upper Gordon Rd BH23 94 A1
Upper Hinton Rd BH1 121 F3
Upper North Rd SP5 188 C5
Upper Norwich Rd 6 BH2 121 E3
UPPER PARKSTONE 120 B5
Upper Rd BH12 120 C6
Upper School La 1 DT11 212 C1
Upper St 4 DT11 198 C7
Upper Terrace Rd BH2 121 E3
Upper Water St BA12 3 B5
Upper Westhill Rd DT7 96 A5
UPPINGTON BH21 201 D1
Uppington Cl 2 BH21 201 C1
Uppleby Rd BH12 120 C6
UP SYDLING DT2 207 A4
UPTON
Poole BH16 117 F7
Preston DT2 169 E8
Upton Cl BH16 117 D7
Upton Cross Mobile Home Pk 2 BH16 117 E7
Upton Ct BH16 117 E7
Upton Ctry Pk★ BH17 118 F6
Upton Heath Est BH16 117 F7
Upton Heath Nature Reserve★ BH17 117 F8
Upton Heath Reserve★ BH21 85 F2
Upton Ind Est BH16 117 F6
Upton Inf Sch BH16 117 C7
Upton Jun Sch BH16 117 C7
Upton Rd BH17 118 F7
Upton Way BH18 86 F3
Upway St 2 DT4 167 D4
UPWEY DT3 152 A6
Upwey Ave BH15 118 E3
Upwey Sta DT3 152 C3
Utrecht Ct BH23 124 D7

V

Vaggs La SO41 95 E6
Vale Cl
4 Crewkerne TA18 191 F3
Poole BH14 120 E4
Vale Lodge BH1 122 D5
Vale Mans 4 BH1 122 D4
Vale Mead DT10 196 F3
Valencia Cl BH23 91 D4
Vale Pk DT11 212 D2
Vale Rd
Bournemouth BH1 122 D4
Poole BH14 120 E4
Stalbridge DT10 33 D8
West Lulworth BH20 172 E6
Yeovil BA21 28 A6
Vale St BA8 19 A4
Valette Rd BH9 90 A3
Vale View BA8 19 A5
Vale View Pk SO41 95 F7
Valiant Way BH23 125 B7
Valley Cl
Christchurch BH23 91 E3
Overcombe/Preston DT3 153 D3
Yeovil BA21 27 D6
Valley of Stones National Nature Reserve★ DT2 131 F4
Valley Rd
Bournemouth BH8 90 F3
Bridport DT6 100 D4
2 Crewkerne TA18 191 F3
Langton Matravers BH19 178 C3
Worth Matravers BH20 177 D6
Valley View
Bridport DT6 100 F6
Poole BH12 121 B7
Vallis Cl BH15 119 D1
Vanguard Ave DT4 166 F1
Vanguard Rd
Bournemouth BH8 90 E1
6 Poole BH15 119 C2
Vantage Way BH12 88 B2
Veals La DT10 35 A5
Vearse Cl DT6 100 B5
Vecta Cl BH23 125 C6
Vectis Rd BH25 126 D7
Velvet Lawn Rd BH25 94 F4
Venator Pl BH21 59 C6
Venn Hill TA20 202 F6
Venning Ave BH11 88 E5
Venn La
Chideock DT6 66 F2
Stoke Abbott DT6 203 D2
Venn The SP7 12 F3
Ventnor Rd DT5 186 F8
Ventry Cl BH13 120 F4
Ventura Ctr The BH16 118 D6
Ventura Pl BH16 117 F6
Verity Cres BH17 88 A1
Verlands Rd DT3 153 D3
Vermin La BH20, DT11 83 B7
Vernalls Cl BH10 89 D6
Vernalls Ct BH25 95 C5
Vernalls Gdns BH10 89 D5
Vernalls Rd DT9 30 B7
Verne Cl DT4 167 C1
Verne Common Rd DT5 186 F8
Verne Hill Rd DT5 187 A7
Verne Rd
Verwood BH31 45 C5
Weymouth DT4 167 C1
Verne Way DT4 167 C1
Verney Cl BH11 89 B3
Verney Rd BH11 89 A3
Verno La BH23 93 C2
Verona Ave BH6 123 D5
Verriott's La DT6 66 C1
Verulam Pl 8 BH1 121 F3
Verulam Rd BH14 119 F4
VERWOOD BH31 45 B6
Verwood CE Fst Sch BH31 45 A5
Verwood Cres BH6 124 B4
Verwood Heathland Her Str★ BH31 45 B7
Verwood Ind Est BH31 45 D6
Verwood L Ctr BH31 45 B6
Verwood Rd
St Leonards & St Ives BH24 46 C2
Three Legged Cross BH21 45 B1
Verwood BH21 53 A8
Woodlands BH21 44 C7
Verwood Sp Club BH31 45 D6
Vespasian Way DT1 134 E7
Vetch Cl BH23 125 C8
Vian Ct BH25 94 F3
Vicarage Cl 2 BH20 140 A1
Vicarage Cotts BH8 90 F3
Vicarage Ct 4 DT6 100 C8
Vicarage La DT2 107 E6
Vicarage Rd
Bournemouth BH9 89 F1
Poole BH15 119 C6
Verwood BH31 45 B6
Vicarage Way BH23 92 D2
Vickers Cl BH8 91 B2
Vickery Way BH23 124 D8
Victoria Ave
Bournemouth BH9 89 E1
Radipole DT3 152 B5
Swanage BH19 179 A3
Victoria Ave Ind Est BH19 178 F3
Victoria Cl
Poole BH21 85 F4
Wool BH20 139 D6
Yeovil BA21 27 F6
Victoria Cres BH12 120 D6
Victoria Ed Ctr BH13 120 F4
Victoria Gdns
Ferndown BH22 61 D6
Ringwood BH24 55 C6
Victoria Gr DT6 100 D7
Victoria Hospl BH21 59 A5
Victoria Park Pl 4 BH9 89 F1
Victoria Park Rd BH9 89 E1
Victoria Pl
Bournemouth BH1, BH8 122 C5
Easton/Weston DT5 187 A5
Wimborne Minster BH21 59 B5
Victoria Rd
Blandford Forum DT11 212 D4
Bournemouth BH1 122 C5
Christchurch BH23 124 E5
Dorchester DT1 107 F1
Easton/Weston DT5 187 B5
Ferndown BH22 61 D6
Gillingham SP8 6 A1
Poole BH12 120 C6
Swanage BH19 179 C5
Weymouth DT4 180 C7
Wimborne Minster BH21 59 B5
Yeovil BA21 27 F6
Victoria Sq DT5 186 E8
Victoria St
Radipole DT4 167 E4
Shaftesbury SP7 12 E3
Victoria Terr DT9 17 B2
Victor Jackson Ave DT1 107 C1
Victory Cl BH21 53 D6
Victory Rd DT5 186 E8
View Rd DT7 96 B5
Viewside Cl BH21 85 E5
Viking Cl BH6 124 A4
Viking Way
Bournemouth BH6 124 A4
Christchurch BH23 125 A5
Village Rd DT6 68 F1
Village St DT3 154 B3
Villas The BH25 94 E5
Villette Cl BH23 92 A1
Vince Cl BH11 89 B5
Vincent Cl 2 BH25 95 A2
Vincent Pl BA20 27 D5
Vincent Rd 1 BH25 95 A2
Vincents Cl DT9 31 A1
Vine Cl BH7 123 A7
Vine Farm Cl BH12 121 C8
Vine Farm Rd BH12 121 B8
Vine Hill BH21 58 E5
Vineries Cl BH21 59 F6
Vineries The BH21 59 F6
Vinery The BH25 95 B2
Vines Pl DT4 166 F2
Vineyard Cl BH16 84 C3
Vinney Cross DT6 102 A6
Vinneys Cl BH23 92 C2
Violet Farm Cl BH21 86 D8
Violet La BH25 95 A4
Virginia Cl
1 Henstridge BA8 19 A4
Poole BH12 120 C7
Verwood BH31 45 E4
Viscount Cl BH11 88 D5
Viscount Ct BH11 88 D5
Viscount Dr BH23 125 B7
Viscount Rd DT4 166 F1
Viscount Wlk BH11 88 D5
Vista Marina BH13 147 D6
Vivian Pk BH19 179 B4
Vixen Wlk BH25 95 B5
Voss's La DT2 206 B3
Vulcan Cl DT4 166 F1
Vulcan Way BH23 125 B7

W

Waddock Dro DT2 111 E3
Waddon Hill (Roman Fort)★ DT8 203 F4
Waddon Way DT6 69 D2
Wadham Sch TA18 191 F5
Wadmore La BH19 164 C2
Wagtail Dr BH25 94 F2
Wain Rd BH20 139 D7
Wainwright Cl DT3 153 B3
Wakefield Ave BH10 89 E5
Wakeham DT5 187 A4
Wakely Gdns BH11 89 A5
Wakely Rd BH11 89 B5
Walcheren Pl BH15 117 E3
Walcott Ave BH23 91 F1
WALDITCH DT6 101 A6
Walditch Gdns BH17 87 E2
Walditch Rd DT6 100 F6
Waldren Cl BH15 119 E2
Waldrons The 5 DT9 194 D8
Walford Cl BH21 59 C6
Walford Gdns BH21 59 B6
Walford Mill Craft Ctr★ BH21 59 B6
Walker Cres DT4 180 C6
WALKFORD 94 C1
Walkford La BH25 94 D3
Walkford Rd BH23 94 C2
Walkford Way BH23 94 B1
Walking Field La BH15 119 D2
Walkwood Ave BH7 123 B8
Wallace Ct BH18 87 A3
Wallace Rd BH18 87 A3
Walliscott Rd BH11 89 A1
WALLISDOWN 89 A2
Wallisdown Rd BH10 121 C8
Wallisdown Rdbt BH12 89 A1
Wallis Rd BH10 89 B1
Wall La DT8 203 D4
Wallsend Cl 3 DT5 186 E2
Walls View Rd BH20 142 D5
Walnut Ave DT11 198 F1
Walnut Cl BH25 94 F3
Walnut Orch 3 DT3 150 A8
Walnut Rd
Dorchester DT2 139 C2
Mere BA12 3 B4
Walnut Tree Field Nature Reserve★ DT11 56 D5
Walpole Rd BH1 122 E5
Walpole St DT4 167 D4
Walrond Rd BH19 179 B3
Walsford Rd BH4 121 C5
Walsingham Dene BH7 122 F8
Walters Dr 13 DT11 199 D4
Waltham Rd BH7 123 B6
WALTON ELM DT10 34 F8
Walton Elm Hill DT10 35 A8
Walton Rd
Bournemouth BH10 89 C2
Poole BH15 120 A6
Wanchard La DT2 107 C7
Wanderwell DT6 100 D3
Wanderwell Farm La DT6 100 D4
Wanstead Cl BH24 47 D1
Warbler Cl BH16 117 D8
Warburton Rd BH17 119 E8
Wardcliffe Rd DT4 167 C3
Ward's Dro DT11 212 E1
WAREHAM BH20 142 E5
Wareham Com Hospl BH20 142 D4
Wareham Ct
Bournemouth BH7 123 B6
Hamworthy BH15 118 E2
Wareham Mid Sch BH20 142 D3
Wareham Rd
Hawkchurch EX13 202 B2
Lytchett Matravers BH16 84 D3
Lytchett Minster & Upton BH16 116 B6
Owermoigne DT2 155 E7
Poole BH21 85 F5
Wareham St Martin BH16 116 D4
Warmwell DT2 155 B7
Wareham Sta BH20 142 D5
Wareham Town Mus★ BH20 142 E3
Ware La DT7 96 A4
Wares Cl 5 DT11 81 E8
Warland Way BH21 86 E7
WARMWELL DT2 137 A1
Warmwell Cl
Bournemouth BH9 90 B4
Poole BH17 87 F2
Warmwell Leisure Resort DT2 137 C4
Warmwell Rd DT2 137 D5
Warne Hill DT6 100 F7
Warnford Rd BH7 123 B7
WARREN BH20 113 D3
Warren Ave BH23 124 F5
Warren Cl
St Leonards BH24 54 F5
Weymouth DT4 166 F2
Warren Dr BH24 54 F5
Warren Edge Cl BH6 123 F3
Warren Edge Ct BH6 123 F3
Warren Edge Rd BH6 123 F3
Warren Hill DT2 78 C7
Warren La BH24 54 F5
Warren Rd
Bere Regis BH20 113 C4
Bournemouth BH4 121 B2
Poole BH14 120 D4
Puddletown DT2 78 B5
Warren Way BH16 116 D2
Warren Wlk BH22 61 B7
Warrior Ave BA22 26 C6
Warrior Rd BA22 26 D6
Warwick Ave BH25 95 B3
Warwick Pl 1 BH7 123 A5
Warwick Rd
Bournemouth BH7 123 A5
Poole BH14 120 C3
Washington Ave BH1 122 D6
Washpond La BH19 178 F5
Watcombe Rd BH6 123 D5
Watercombe Hts BA20 26 F2
Watercombe La BA20 26 E3
Watercombe Pk BA20 26 F3
WATERDITCH 93 B5
Waterditch Rd BH23 93 A4
Waterford Cl BH14 120 A2
Waterford Gdns BH23 126 A7
Waterford Lodge BH23 125 B6
Waterford Pl BH23 126 B7

Waterford Rd
Christchurch BH23 126 B7
New Milton BH25 95 C3
Waterfront The★ BH4 121 F2
Watergardens BH8 122 A5
Watergates La DT2 136 C3
Water Knap DT10 196 F3
Water La
Bournemouth BH6 123 D7
Durweston DT11 198 E3
Swyre DT6 129 C8
Winfrith Newburgh DT2 156 F7
Winterborne Stickland DT11 210 B7
Water Lane Farm BH10 89 E6
WATERLOO 87 B1
Waterloo Ho BH17 87 B1
Waterloo La
Silton SP8 5 B7
Stourton Caundle DT10 33 A3
Waterloo Rd
Bournemouth BH9 121 F7
Corfe Mullen BH21 85 E5
Poole BH17 119 C8
Waterloo Way 3 BH24 55 C6
Watermead
5 Christchurch BH23 124 A5
3 Tatworth TA20 202 A8
Water Meadow La BH20 139 E2
Watermill Rd BH23 124 A8
Waterpot Hill DT6 204 C2
Waters Edge BH13 147 D6
Watership Dr BH24 55 F5
Waterside BH23 124 F4
Waterside Cl BH24 47 D1
Watersmeet Ct BH23 124 B5
Water St
Berwick St John SP7 188 B8
Cranborne BH21 40 B7
Mere BA12 3 B5
Waterston Cl BH17 87 D1
Waterston La DT2 77 D3
Water Supply Mus★ DT3 153 D4
Water Tower Rd BH18 87 C4
Watery La
Christchurch BH23 125 A8
Donhead St Mary SP7 24 F8
Halstock BA22 193 D2
Iwerne Minster DT11 37 F1
Lytchett Minster & Upton BH16 117 B7
Radipole DT3 152 B4
Sherborne DT9 195 C7
Studland BH19 164 D1
Tincleton DT2 110 D3
West Crewkerne TA18 191 D2
Watford La DT6 68 E2
Watkin Rd 6 BH5 122 F4
Watling St 3 BA21 26 F7
WATTON DT6 100 B4
Watton Cl BH8 91 A2
Watton Cross DT6 100 B5
Watton Gdns DT6 100 E8
Watton La DT6 100 B5
Watton Pk DT6 100 C5
Wattons La BH24 63 C7
Watton View DT6 100 B7
Wavell Ave BH17 87 A1
Wavell Rd BH11 89 B4
Wavendon Ave BH25 126 E8
Wavering La SP8 5 C2
Waverley 14 BH4 121 C3
Waverley Cres BH15 119 D6
Waverley Ho 9 BH25 95 B2
Waverley Rd
New Milton BH25 95 B2
Radipole DT3 167 C6
Wayclose La
Buckhorn Weston SP8 9 B8
Cucklington SP8 4 B2
WAYFORD TA18 191 B1
Wayford Hill TA18 191 B1
Wayground Rd BH21 58 E1
Wayman Rd BH21 86 E6
Wayne Rd BH12 120 B6
Wayside Rd
Bournemouth BH6 123 E4
St Leonards BH24 54 A1
WAYTOWN DT6 68 E8
Waytown Cl BH17 87 D1
Weare Cl DT5 186 F7
Weatherbury Rd SP8 5 E3
Weatherbury Way DT1 135 A7
Weatherby Castle (Obelisk & Hill Fort))★ DT11 79 F5
Weavers Cl
Crewkerne TA18 191 F4
Ferndown BH22 53 A1
Webbers Cl BH20 176 F8
Webbers Piece DT2 206 C1
Webb La DT10 196 E8
Webbs Cl BH24 53 F6
Webb's Way BH11 88 F1
Webster Rd BH9 90 A3
Wedgewood Rd DT4 167 C3
Wedgwood Dr BH14 120 A2
Weiner Cl DT11 199 E2
Weir End Rd DT1 107 C2
Weir The DT3 153 C3
Weir View DT2 107 C6
Welbeck Rd BA21 28 A7
Weldon Ave BH11 88 E5
Welland Ct 10 DT1 107 D1
Welland Rd
Wimborne Minster BH21 59 D4
Yeovil BA21 27 F7
WELL BOTTOM SP5 39 D6
Wellbridge Cl DT1 135 A7
Well Cl BH25 94 F2
Wellesley Ave BH23 125 C7
Wellfield Hill EX13 202 E2
Wellfields Dr DT6 100 F8
Wellington Ave BH23 125 C7
Wellington Ct
7 Bournemouth, Dean Park BH8 122 A5
Bournemouth, Westbourne BH2 121 D3
New Milton BH25 95 A3
Wellingtonia Gdns SO41 95 F4
Wellington Rd
Bournemouth BH8 122 A5
Poole BH14 120 C3
Well La
Poole BH15 119 C4
Powerstock DT6 70 B4
Shaftesbury SP7 12 D3
Wellmans Cnr DT2 206 A7
Wellow Gdns BH15 119 F6
Well Plot DT6 101 D8
Wellstead Rd BH20 142 D6
Wendover Cl BH25 94 F1
Wendy Cres BH22 61 F3
Wenlock Ct 9 BH23 124 F8
Wentwood Gdns BH25 95 D2
Wentworth BH14 147 C7
Wentworth Ave BH5 123 B4
Wentworth Cl
Bournemouth BH5 123 B3
Radipole DT3 152 E2
Wentworth Dr
Broadstone BH18 87 B5
Christchurch BH23 123 F6
Wentworth Grange BH22 61 D7
Wentworth Rd BA21 28 A7
Wentworths Yd BH21 59 E4
Wescott Way BH11 88 E4
Wesley Cl
8 Bournemouth BH8 122 C5
Charmouth DT6 97 B8
Wesley Grange 48 BH4 121 C3
Wesley Ho BH22 61 F6
Wesley Rd
Poole BH12 120 C5
Wimborne Minster BH21 59 E5
Wesley St DT4 167 D3
Wessex Ave
New Milton BH25 95 A2
4 Shillingstone DT11 198 B5
Wessex Cl BH23 125 C7
Wessex Ct BA8 19 A4
Wessex Dr DT9 28 D1
Wessex Est BH24 55 D8
Wessex Gate BH8 122 C6
Wessex Gate Ret Pk BH15 119 B6
Wessex Oval BH20 142 C5
Wessex Rd
Dorchester DT1 107 D2
Poole BH14 120 A3
Ringwood BH24 55 D8
Stalbridge DT10 33 E8
Weymouth DT4 167 B3
Yeovil BA21 27 A8
Wessex Ridgeway DT11 39 C5
Wessex Stadium The (Weymouth FC) DT4 166 F5
Wessex Trade Ctr BH12 120 A7
Wessex Way
Bournemouth, Springbourne BH8 122 C5
Bournemouth, Westbourne BH2, BH4 121 D3
Dorchester DT1 107 D2
Gillingham SP8 5 E3
Swanage BH19 179 B4
West Allington DT6 100 B7
West Ave BH21 53 A8
WEST BAY DT6 100 C2
West Bay Cres DT4 180 C7
West Bay Rd DT6 100 D2
WEST BEXINGTON DT2 129 E2
West Bexington Reserve★ DT2 129 D2
West Borough BH21 59 B5
WESTBOURNE 121 C3
Westbourne Acad BH4 121 B3
Westbourne Cl
Bournemouth BH4 121 C3
Yeovil BA20 27 A5
Westbourne Gate 15 BH4 121 C3
Westbourne Gr BA20 27 A5
Westbourne Park Rd BH4 121 B2
Westbourne Rd DT4 167 D5
WEST BOURTON SP8 4 C7
West Bourton Rd SP8 1 D1
Westbridge Pk DT9 29 F4
West Brook BA21 26 F6
Westbrook Cl BH10 89 D2
Westbrook Rd SP8 10 A8
Westbury
Bradford Abbas DT9 28 D2
Sherborne DT9 30 B4
Westbury Cl
Barton on Sea BH25 127 B8
Bransgore BH23 93 A7
Christchurch BH23 93 D1
Westbury Ct 1 BH14 120 B4
Westbury Rd BH24 55 D7
Westbury Way DT11 212 E3
Westby Rd BH5 122 F4
WEST CHALDON DT2 155 F2
WEST CHELBOROUGH DT2 205 D8
WEST CHINNOCK TA18 192 B8
West Chinnock CE Prim Sch TA18 192 B8
West Cl
Chickerell DT3 166 C6
Verwood BH31 44 F6
WEST CLIFF 121 C1
West Cliff 9 BH2 121 F4
West Cliff Cotts BH2 121 E2
West Cliff Ct 40 BH4 121 C3
West Cliff Gdns BH2 121 E2
Westcliff Ho 8 BH4 121 C2
West Cliff Mews BH2 121 E2
Westcliff Palms 18 BH4 121 C2
Westcliff Rd
Charmouth DT6 96 F7
Easton/Weston DT5 186 E3
West Cliff Rd
Bournemouth BH4 121 C2
Bridport DT6 100 B2
West Close Ho BH6 124 A4
WEST COKER BA22 193 A8
West Coker CE Prim Sch BA22 193 A8
West Coker Hill BA22 192 F8
West Coker Rd
East Coker BA20 26 E1
Yeovil BA20 27 A2
WEST COMPTON DT2 71 E1
Westcott St 1 DT1 107 B2
Westcroft Par 7 BH25 95 B2
Westcroft Pk BH18 87 C4
Westdowne Cl DT4 167 A2
Westdown Rd BH11 89 A5
West Dr
3 Swanage BH19 179 A2
West Moors BH24 62 B8
West Durlston La BH19 179 B1
WEST END DT9 29 E5
West End DT2 206 C2
Westerhall Rd DT4 167 E5
Westerham 7 BH13 121 B3
Westerham Rd BH4 121 B3
Westerleigh 12 BH4 121 C2
Western Ave
Barton on Sea BH25 126 D8
Bournemouth BH10 89 D4
Poole BH13 120 F2
Yeovil BA21 26 D7
Western Cl BH10 89 D5
Western Downland Prim Sch SP6 190 F2
Westerngate 13 BH13 121 B3
Western Rd
Poole BH13 121 A2
Poole, Canford Cliffs BH13 147 F8
Western St DT9 28 D7
West Farm La DT3 154 A3
Westfield
2 Portesham DT3 150 A8
Sherborne DT9 29 F4
10 Wimborne Minster BH21 59 B5
Westfield Ave BA21 27 A6
Westfield Cl BH21 59 B5
Westfield Com Sch BA21 27 A6
Westfield Cres BA21 27 B6
Westfield Est BA12 1 F4
Westfield Gr BA21 27 B7
Westfield Inf Com Sch BA21 27 A6
Westfield Pl BA21 27 A7
Westfield Rd
Bournemouth BH6 123 E4
Yeovil BA21 27 B6
WESTFIELDS DT10 196 D1
Westfield Tech Coll DT3 153 A3
West Gables Cl DT6 100 B7
Westgate Pk BH4 121 B3
WESTHAM DT4 167 A3
Westham Cl BH17 87 E3
Westham Rd DT4 167 D3
Westhaven DT4 167 A2
Westhaven Hospl DT4 167 A4
Westheath Rd BH18 87 B4
West Hendford BA20 27 C4
West Hill
Charminster DT2 107 D6
Evershot DT2 206 A7
Milborne Port DT9 17 D2
Westhill Cl 5 DT4 180 B8
West Hill Pl 8 BH2 121 E3
Westhill Rd DT4 180 C7
West Hill Rd
Bournemouth BH2 121 E2
Lyme Regis DT7 96 B5
WEST HOLME BH20 159 D8
WEST HOWE 88 E4
West Howe Cl BH11 89 A4
West Howe Ind Est BH11 88 E3
WEST HURN 90 F6
WEST KNIGHTON DT2 136 C3
West La
Arne BH20 142 E1
Christchurch BH23 93 A8
Hazelbury Bryan DT10 196 E4
Melbury Abbas SP7 24 B6
Mosterton DT8 204 A8
North Wootton DT9 31 A3
Westlake Cl DT3 152 B4
Westland Rd BA20 27 B4
Westlands Ct BH23 93 A8
Westlands Dr BH13 147 F8
Westleaze DT2 107 E5
Westleaze Cl DT2 107 E5
WEST LULWORTH BH20 172 D6
Westmacott Rd DT3 152 B1
West Mans 3 BH4 121 C3
West Mead DT6 100 B7
WEST MELBURY SP7 24 A5
West Mill Cres BH20 142 D5
West Mill La
Castleton DT9 30 A3
Stalbridge DT10 20 A3
West Mills Rd DT1 107 F2
WEST MILTON DT6 69 E6
Westminster BA22 26 D6
Westminster Cl 2 SP7 12 F4
Westminster Ct BH25 126 F7
Westminster Meml Hospl SP7 12 E2
Westminster Rd
Northport BH20 142 C5
Poole BH13 121 B1
Westminster Road E BH13 121 B1
Westminster Road Ind Est BH20 142 C5
Westminster St 10 BA20 27 D4
WEST MOORS BH22 53 B2
West Moors Mid Sch BH22 53 B1
West Moors Rd
Ferndown BH22 61 D7
Three Legged Cross BH21 53 A7
West Moors BH22 52 F4
WEST MORDEN BH20 83 B4
Westmoreland Ct SO41 95 F3
WESTON
Beaminster DT2 204 F8
Fortuneswell DT5 186 E3
Weston Cl BA22 192 E8
Weston Dr BH1 122 B3
Weston Hill SP8 9 B6
Weston La
Closworth BA22 193 E5
Corscombe DT2 205 A8
Weston Rd
Colehill BH21 59 F7
Easton/Weston DT5 186 F4
Weymouth DT4 167 C2
Worth Matravers BH19 183 C7
Weston St
East Chinnock BA22 192 E8
Easton/Weston DT5 187 A2
Gillingham SP8 9 A6
WEST ORCHARD SP7 36 D6
West Overcliff Dr BH4 121 D1
Westover Hill DT6 64 F2
Westover La BH24 54 F6
Westover Rd
Bournemouth BH1 121 F3
4 Dorchester DT1 107 F1
Westover Retail Pk BH9 90 A4
West Park Dr SP6 190 F3
West Park La SP6 190 F3
WEST PARLEY 61 E1
West Pk BA20 27 B5
Westport Rd BH20 142 D3
WEST PULHAM DT9 196 A3
West Quay Rd BH15 119 B2
Westray Hall BH4 121 C1
West Rd
Bournemouth BH5 123 B4
Bransgore BH23 93 A8
Symondsbury DT6 100 A7
West Lulworth BH20 172 C6
Westridge 6 DT9 30 A5
West Row BH21 59 B4
West Row Mews BH21 59 B4
WEST SOUTHBOURNE 123 D5
West St
Abbas & Templecombe BA8 18 C8
Abbotsbury DT3 149 A7
Bere Regis BH20 81 A3
Blandford Forum DT11 212 C3
Bridport DT6 100 C6
Broadwindsor DT8 203 E5
Chickerell DT3 166 C6
Corfe Castle BH20 162 A1
Crewkerne TA18 191 E4
Fontmell Magna SP7 37 E6
Hinton St George TA17 191 C7
Kington Magna SP8 9 C2
Poole BH15 119 B2
Radipole DT4 167 D2
Ringwood BH24 55 A7
Shapwick DT11 56 B8
Wareham BH20 142 E3
Wimborne Minster BH21 59 B5
Winterborne Kingston DT11 81 D8
Winterborne Stickland DT11 210 C7
Yeovil BA20 27 B4
WEST STAFFORD DT2 136 B8
West Station Terr BH4 121 D3
WEST STOUR SP8 10 A2
West Street Ct 8 BH21 59 B5
West Undercliff Prom
Bournemouth BH2 121 D1
Poole BH13 147 F7
West View SP7 37 E7
West View Rd
Christchurch BH23 124 E6
Poole BH15 119 C4
Westville BA21 27 E5
West Walks Rd DT1 107 F2
West Walls BH20 142 D3
West Way
Bournemouth BH9 90 B2
Broadstone BH18 86 F3
Easton/Weston DT5 186 E1
Winterbourne Abbas DT2 105 D2
West Way Cl BH9 90 B1
West Ways BA22 192 D8
Westwey Rd DT4 167 D2
West Wlk DT6 100 B2
Westwood Ave BH22 61 D6
Westwoods & Glendene Pk BH25 94 D6
West Wools DT5 186 E1
Wetherby Cl DT11 212 E6
Wetherby Cl
Broadstone BH18 87 A2
Milborne St Andrew DT11 79 F7
Wet La BA12 3 D2
Weyman's Ave BH10 89 C6
Weymans Dr BH10 89 C6
WEYMOUTH DT4 167 E3
Weymouth Ave DT1 134 F8
Weymouth Bay Ave DT3 167 D7
Weymouth Coll DT4 167 E5
Weymouth Coll Com Sports Ctr DT4 167 E6
Weymouth Com Hospl DT4 167 E5
Weymouth Marina★ DT4 167 D2
Weymouth Mus★ DT4 167 E1
Weymouth & Portland National Sailing Acad★ DT6 181 A2
Weymouth & Portland Swimming Pool DT4 167 B2
Weymouth Rd
Dorchester DT1 134 F7
Poole BH14 120 C5
Weymouth Road DT2 133 E6
Weymouth Sports Club DT3 152 B1
Weymouth Sta DT4 167 D4
Weymouth Way DT4 167 B6
Wey Valley Sch & Sports Coll The DT3 152 C2
Weyview Cres DT3 152 B4
Wharf Cl BH12 120 E6
Wharfdale Rd
Bournemouth BH4 121 D4
Poole BH12 120 E6
Wharncliffe Ct BH23 125 F7
Wharncliffe Gdns BH23 126 A7
Wharncliffe Rd
Bournemouth BH5 122 D4
Christchurch BH23 126 A7
Whatcombe Rd DT11 210 D4
Whately Rd SO41 127 F5
Whatleigh Cl BH15 119 C1
Whatley La TA20 202 C8
Wheat Cl 4 DT10 197 A4
Wheatear Cl 4 DT3 152 C4
Wheat Farland DT3 166 D6
Wheathill Cl 1 DT9 17 D2
Wheathill La DT9 17 E3
Wheathill Way DT9 17 D2
Wheatlands DT5 186 E1
Wheaton Grange 4 BH4 121 D4
Wheaton Rd BH7 123 A5
Wheatplot Park Homes 2 BH10 89 F4
Wheelers La BH11 88 D6
Wheel House La TA20 202 E7
Wheelwright's Cl SP5 189 A4
Whetham Mill La DT8 203 C6
Whetland's La DT6 69 D1
Whimbrel Ct BH23 125 A6
Whincroft Cl BH22 61 E7
Whincroft Dr BH22 61 E6
Whitby Ave BH18 87 A2
Whitby Cl BH23 91 D4
Whitby Cres BH18 87 A2
WHITCHURCH BA8 19 A6
Whitchurch Ave BH18 87 C3
WHITCHURCH CANONICORUM DT6 66 A4
Whitchurch La BA8 19 A6
Whitcliff Mill Hill DT11 212 C6
WHITCOMBE DT2 135 F5
Whitcombe Rd DT8 204 D3
Whitcross 2 BA22 193 F8
Whitebeam Cl DT2 75 D2
Whitebeam Way BH31 45 D5
White Cl
3 Bridport DT6 68 F1
Poole BH15 120 A7
Whitecliff Cres BH14 120 A2
Whitecliff Gdns DT11 212 C4
Whitecliff Mill St DT11 212 C4
Whitecliff Rd
Poole BH14 119 F2
Swanage BH19 179 B5
WHITECROSS DT6 204 B2
WHITE CROSS BA12 1 E5
Whitecross Cl BH17 87 E3
Whitecross Dr DT4 180 E8
White Farm Cl BH10 121 D8
WHITEFIELD BH20 83 A2
Whitefield Dr SP8 10 D3
Whitefield Rd
New Milton BH25 95 A2
Poole BH14 120 A2
Whitehall BH23 124 B6
Whitehall Ct 3 TA18 191 F5
White Hart Cl DT10 196 D5
Whitehart Fields 1 BH24 55 E8
White Hart La SP7 12 E2
Whitehayes Cl BH23 92 D2
Whitehayes Rd BH23 92 C1
Whitehead Dr DT4 180 D5

PHILIP'S MAPS

the Gold Standard for drivers

◆ **Philip's street atlases cover all of England, Wales, Northern Ireland and much of Scotland**

- ◆ Every named street is shown, including alleys, lanes and walkways
- ◆ Thousands of additional features marked: stations, public buildings, car parks, places of interest
- ◆ Route-planning maps to get you close to your destination
- ◆ Postcodes on the maps and in the index
- ◆ Widely used by the emergency services, transport companies and local authorities

For national mapping, choose **Philip's Navigator Britain** the most detailed road atlas available of England, Wales and Scotland. Hailed by Auto Express as 'the ultimate road atlas', Navigator shows every road and lane in Britain.

Street atlases currently available

England

Bedfordshire and Luton	Surrey
Berkshire	East Sussex
Birmingham and West Midlands	West Sussex
Bristol and Bath	Tyne and Wear
Buckinghamshire and Milton Keynes	Warwickshire and Coventry
Cambridgeshire and Peterborough	Wiltshire and Swindon
Cheshire	Worcestershire
Cornwall	East Yorkshire Northern Lincolnshire
Cumbria	North Yorkshire
Derbyshire	South Yorkshire
Devon	West Yorkshire
Dorset	
County Durham and Teesside	**Wales**
Essex	Anglesey, Conwy and Gwynedd
North Essex	Cardiff, Swansea and The Valleys
South Essex	Carmarthenshire, Pembrokeshire and Swansea
Gloucestershire and Bristol	
Hampshire	Ceredigion and South Gwynedd
North Hampshire	
South Hampshire	Denbighshire, Flintshire, Wrexham
Herefordshire Monmouthshire	Herefordshire Monmouthshire
Hertfordshire	Powys
Isle of Wight	
Kent	**Scotland**
East Kent	Aberdeenshire
West Kent	Ayrshire
Lancashire	Dumfries and Galloway
Leicestershire and Rutland	Edinburgh and East Central Scotland
Lincolnshire	Fife and Tayside
Liverpool and Merseyside	Glasgow and West Central Scotland
London	Inverness and Moray
Greater Manchester	Lanarkshire
Norfolk	Scottish Borders
Northamptonshire	
Northumberland	**Northern Ireland**
Nottinghamshire	County Antrim and County Londonderry
Oxfordshire	County Armagh and County Down
Shropshire	
Somerset	Belfast
Staffordshire	County Tyrone and County Fermanagh
Suffolk	

Philip's maps and atlases are available from bookshops, motorway services and petrol stations.

For further details visit
www.philips-maps.co.uk